The Social Psychology of Motivation

The Social Psychology of Motivation

Edited by Jason Plaks

OXFORD
UNIVERSITY PRESS

OXFORD
UNIVERSITY PRESS

8 Sampson Mews, Suite 204, Don Mills, Ontario M3C 0H5
www.oupcanada.com

Oxford University Press is a department of the University of Oxford.
It furthers the University's objective of excellence in research, scholarship,
and education by publishing worldwide in

Oxford   New York

Auckland Cape Town Dar es Salaam Hong Kong Karachi Kuala Lumpur
Madrid Melbourne Mexico City Nairobi New Delhi Shanghai Taipei Toronto

With offices in

Argentina Austria Brazil Chile Czech Republic France Greece Guatemala Hungary Italy
Japan Poland Portugal Singapore South Korea Switzerland Thailand Turkey Ukraine Vietnam

Oxford is a trade mark of Oxford University Press in the UK and in certain other countries

Published in Canada by Oxford University Press

Copyright © 2011 Oxford University Press Canada

The moral rights of the author have been asserted

Database right Oxford University Press (maker)

First Published 2011

Library and Archives Canada Cataloguing in Publication

Plaks, Jason
The social psychology of motivation / Jason Plaks.

Includes bibliographical references and index.
ISBN 978-0-19-543185-8

1. Motivation (Psychology)—Textbooks.   2. Motivation (Psychology)—
Social aspects—Textbooks.   I. Title.

HM1201.P53 2010   153.8   C2010-903392-2

Cover image: Fancy Photography/Veer

Oxford University Press is committed to our environment.
This book is printed on Forest Stewardship Council certified paper,
harvested from a responsibly managed forest.

Printed and bound in Canada.

1 2 3 4 – 14 13 12 11

Mixed Sources
Product group from well-managed
forests and other controlled sources
www.fsc.org   Cert no. SW-COC-000952
© 1996 Forest Stewardship Council

FSC

Contents

Introduction

For decades, motivation was the 'poor stepsister' of psychological research. Compared with such topics as perception, neurophysiology, or animal behaviour, motivation was considered by many to be overly 'soft', difficult to measure, or requiring too many mentalistic assumptions. This began to change about 25 years ago. Although there had been some researchers who continued to investigate motivation all along, the 1980s saw a full-fledged renaissance of research on the motivation–cognition interface. For the first time, edited volumes began to have such titles as *Motivation and Cognition* and *The Ontario Symposium on Motivation,* and journals began to have such names as *Motivation and Emotion.* Social psychologists were at the forefront of this change. Important theories such as Higgins's self-discrepancy theory, Dweck's goal theory, Kruglanski's lay epistemics theory, Baumeister and Leary's need to belong theory, and Deci and Ryan's self-determination theory began explicitly to address the multifaceted relationships between wanting and thinking.

By 2000, most of the major theories in social psychology either explicitly or implicitly rested on motivational assumptions. Moreover, the impact of social psychological theories of motivation had begun to reach well beyond the boundaries of the discipline to such diverse fields as management, economics, education, and political science.

Given the paradigm shift that has occurred, it is surprising that there are not more texts intended to train the next generation of students in the emerging principles of motivation. As research on motivation flourishes, the teaching of motivation needs to catch up. This book, which has grown from a course that I have taught for the past nine years, represents an attempt to fill that void. In presenting a compendium of seminal articles—both classic and contemporary—in the social psychology of motivation, this book is intended to contribute to the much needed standardization of curricula on the psychology of motivation.

A Distinctly Social Psychological Approach

This book focuses on the social-cognitive level of analysis. What does a social-cognitive approach provide beyond the insights furnished by, for example, a more behaviour-oriented way of understanding motivation? Perhaps the best way to answer this question is to refer to the 1959 paper by Robert White included in this volume (Unit 2). White contended that much of the behaviour that is characteristic of everyday experience cannot be accounted for by animal models alone. Such models are excellent for helping us understand how organisms (including humans) cope with various forms of stress or emergency (e.g., hunger, sexual deprivation), but these models are considerably weaker when it comes to *non-emergency* behaviour. As such, they have a hard time accounting for such fundamental human experiences as curiosity, novelty seeking, and risk taking. To address this gap, White found himself going against the prevailing behaviourist zeitgeist by proposing such highly mentalistic, social-cognitive constructs as 'mastery' and 'effectance'.

Indeed, the social-psychological level of analysis frequently hypothesizes the existence of latent constructs that can only be measured indirectly. For example, you cannot 'see' high-level versus low-level action identification (Vallacher & Wegner, 1987, Unit 6 in this volume). You can, however, measure its systematic effects on behaviour. This book argues that, with a social-psychological approach, any losses incurred by going beyond the directly measurable are offset by enormous gains in explanatory and predictive power. Only by invoking latent social-psychological constructs can one begin to explain why some people respond to success by lowering their level of aspiration while others raise it (see Lewin, 1936; Grant & Dweck, 2003, Unit 4 in this volume), why some people go out of their way to identify with stigmatized minority groups (Pickett et al. 2002, Unit 1 in this volume), or why people become more patriotic after thinking about their death (Pyszczynski, Greenberg, & Solomon, 2003). The social-psychological level of analysis, in other words, provides the raw material for making predictions about how people will behave in the kinds of consequential life situations we care about most.

While a social-psychological approach provides a broader context for understanding human actions, it also furnishes added specificity. For example, while most economic theories assume that humans are driven by 'self-interest', social-psychological theories begin to unpack that vague term by identifying and operationalizing different *varieties* of self-interest. In so doing, several social-psychological theories portray the mind as a battleground in which multiple motives of self-interest engage in a pitched battle for control over the individual's action (e.g., Brewer, 1991; Swann, 1990).

Other theories helpfully point out that the same goal may be mentally represented in different ways (e.g., Higgins, 1997; Dweck & Leggett, 1988; Vallacher & Wegner, 1987; Carver & Scheier, 1987). This point is important: A recurring theme of many of the readings in this book is that *how we mentally represent our goal is a critical predictor of our behaviour*. Of all the areas of psychology, social psychology has had the most to say about the role of mental representation in behaviour.

Historical Roots

Although the social-psychological study of motivation has proliferated in recent decades, many of the themes have considerably older origins. While writings about issues we would now classify as 'motivation' date back to antiquity, one of the most cogent Enlightenment-era statements was produced by the English philosopher Jeremy Bentham. In his 1815 monograph *Springs of Action,* Bentham presented a useful catalogue of 'pleasures and pains'. Some of these may be categorized as more biologically rooted, for example pleasures and pains 'of the senses', 'of the palate', and 'of the sexual appetite'. Others, however, have a considerably more social-psychological feel, for example those relating to 'moral and popular sanction', 'curiosity,' and 'amity'. Bentham further noted that people are rarely driven by only one goal; at any given moment, multiple—even opposing—motives may operate simultaneously. Moreover, he alluded to a concept that later came to be referred to as 'substitutability'; if one means to a goal is blocked, the individual will often substitute another means for achieving the goal. We see this principle at work in numerous social-psychological theories. For example, research on self-affirmation by Steele and colleagues (e.g., Steele, Spencer, & Lynch, 1993) has shown that a blow to one's self-esteem in one area may be compensated for by a sense of validation in another completely unrelated area. (For related ideas, see also Heine, Proulx & Vohs, 2006.)

From psychological theory and research in the first half of the twentieth century, several important influences stand out. Foremost perhaps is Sigmund Freud. Although much of his theory of behaviour has fallen out of favour in scientific psychology, several key principles have enjoyed something of a renaissance. True, today's researchers have different ways of operationalizing the unconscious and consider a wider range of motivations than just psychosexual ones, but the general notion that much of human behaviour is governed by unconscious motives operating in the background is virtually taken for granted by many of today's researchers. Moreover, several prominent theories have used the advanced tools of social cognition to directly address issues related to such classically Freudian concepts as the suppression—and expression—of unwanted thoughts (e.g., Wegner, 1987; Liberman & Forster, 2000) and the anxiety engendered by thoughts about one's death (e.g., Pyszczynski et al., 1990).

A second important influence is the work of Clark Hull, whose drive theory has many echoes in contemporary research. Based on careful observation of rats and other animals, Hull (1943, 1951) argued several fundamental points. First, a good deal of behaviour originates from a deficit of some sort (e.g., hunger, wakefulness) that the organism seeks to remedy. A drive, according to Hull, was a reflection of the animal's energy or vigour in attempting to remedy the deficit. Second, Hull suggested that separate drives feed into one non-specific pool and this aggregation of drives is what ultimately propels the organism into action. This idea has been revisited in several contemporary theories, including Baumeister et al.'s theory of self-regulation (Unit 8 in this volume). Third, behaviour is not reducible to drives; it is also a function of the animal's learning history (i.e., how it has been trained to respond to different stimuli) and the power of the incentive (i.e., how appealing different stimuli are, independent of one's state of deprivation). These findings were summarized in Hull's famous equation

$$B = D \times H \times I$$
(Behaviour = Drive × Habit × Incentive)

Although several of Hull's assertions have been contested over the years, each of his postulates continues to find empirical backing in contemporary research (even if today's researchers are not always quick to recognize his influence!).

Another important forefather of motivational research was Neal Miller. Miller applied many of Hull's concepts to draw elegant mathematical models of how an organism navigates the conflict between two competing motivations. In Miller's case, these two motivations were the *approach* of pleasure and the *avoidance* of pain. Miller noted from data with animals and humans that the strength of the drive to approach a desired stimulus increases as one draws nearer to it, and the strength of the drive to avoid an undesired stimulus also increases as one draws nearer to it. However, these two drives do not act in identical ways; the strength of the avoidance tendency increases more rapidly with proximity to the stimulus than does the strength of the approach tendency. In other words, at short distances, fear is stronger than desire, but at longer distances, desire is stronger than fear. This may begin to explain why people tend to focus only on the positive aspects of events in the distant future but tend to focus on the negative aspects of events in the near future (e.g., Eyal, Liberman, Trope, & Walther, 2004). The readings in Unit 3 (Reward and Punishment) and Unit 4 (Success and Failure) bear the stamp of Miller's influence.

At this point you may be thinking to yourself, 'This is all well and good, but what *is* motivation?' Obviously, different theoretical perspectives suggest different definitions. Rather than presuming to provide a definitive one here, I'd like to suggest a cluster of concepts that, taken together, identify many of the key characteristics. These include *need fulfillment*, *discrepancy reduction*, or more generally, *wanting* (Higgins & Kruglanski, 2000).

At a more specific level, several theories have highlighted a distinction between non-directional and directional aspects of motivation (e.g., Kunda, 1990; Kruglanski & Webster, 1996), or one characterized by 'force' and one by 'direction' (Young, 1961). In other words, directional motivation refers to 'the what', or the *object* of someone's goal, and non-directional motivation refers to 'the how much', or the *vigour* with which the goal is pursued. To use an automotive analogy, directional motivation refers to the action of the steering wheel, whereas non-directional motivation refers to the action of the gas pedal.

Motivation Affects Cognition and Cognition Affects Motivation

An important theme of this book is that motivation affects more than overt, observable behaviour—it also affects unobservable cognitive processes (e.g., attention, recognition, judgment) in systematic and measurable ways. This is why I have labelled Unit 5 'Motivation's Effect on Cognition'. For prime examples of this concept, see the Kunda (1990) and Higgins (1996) articles in Unit 5. As I note in the introduction to that Unit, however, the notion that motivation biases our cognition has not gone uncontested, resulting in the establishment of firmer criteria for what counts as motivated cognition.

A second important point is that the arrow goes both ways—cognition also affects motivation. How we mentally represent our action or our goal is a good predictor of what precise behaviour we will pursue and how hard we will try. Good examples of this can be seen in the Grant and Dweck (Unit 4) and Vallacher and Wegner (Unit 6) articles. For this reason, I have labelled Unit 6 'Cognition's Effect on Motivation'. Finally, many motivational variables have cognitive properties. For example, particular goals may be subtly activated, or *primed*, just like any other cognitive concept. For good examples, see the Kruglanski (Unit 2) and Higgins (Unit 5) articles.

More generally, most of the articles in this book either implicitly or explicitly highlight the inseparability of cognition and motivation. In Carver and Scheier's goal feedback theory of emotion (Unit 7), for example, cognitive, motivational, and emotional components all have critical roles in creating a circular feedback system. Similar interplay occurs in Weiner's theory of emotion (Unit 7), Higgins's regulatory focus theory (Unit 5), Festinger's cognitive dissonance theory (Unit 3), and Mischel et al.'s theory of self-regulation (Unit 8).

Organization of the Book

I have organized the book into nine units, each with two to three articles. The first four units are dedicated to isolating and describing four social-psychological needs that may be characterized as 'basic': *belongingness* (articles 1 and 2), *certainty*

(articles 3 and 4), *control* (articles 6 and 7), and *self-worth* (articles, 5, 8, 9, and 10). The remainder of the book focuses on general properties and mechanisms of motivation—how motivation interfaces with cognition, how contextual influences affect motivation, and how pre-existing individual differences in motivational variables affect basic processes. In other words, the first half of the book may be considered 'the what' of the social psychology of motivation, and the latter half the 'the how'.

The aim of this book is to provide enough material for an advanced undergraduate or graduate course in the social psychology of motivation. Such a course is most likely to be offered in psychology departments, but may also be offered in business schools, education schools, physical education departments, and clinical/professional psychology programs. Moreover, the audience of the book need not be limited to university students. Professionals and practitioners in such fields as education, personnel, psychotherapy, addiction, physical education, law, and public health may benefit from the insights into human motivation provided by these articles.

The list of readings contains a mix of empirical journal articles and theoretical reviews, with 'classic' works from social psychology's early history mixed with contemporary articles representing the state-of-the-art research in the field. One of the pleasures of any 'best of' list is to have healthy debates about perceived errors of commission and omission. Indeed, the present list should not be taken as the canon of the 20 most important articles in motivation. Instead, to be included in this book, articles had to be major articles in the field, while at the same time meeting a range of other criteria: (a) not too technical; (b) written in an engaging style; and (c) not too long (note that most of the articles have been abridged slightly to highlight the most important elements).

The final list of articles is the product of years of 'pilot-testing' in my advanced seminar in motivation, taught first at the University of Washington and then at the University of Toronto. In recognition that this book makes no claim of representing the 'definitive' canon, I have included a Further Readings section at the end of each Unit, in which I describe a number of related articles that could easily have been included in this book and were excluded only for technical, rather than substantive, reasons.

Over the years, I have come to appreciate the importance of several articles that may not be especially familiar even to experienced researchers in the field. These include Lewin's elegant description of the psychology of level of aspiration, dating back to 1936 (Unit 4) and White's 1959 paper on 'Motivation Reconsidered' (Unit 2). It is remarkable to look back at some of these earlier texts from today's vantage point and recognize their prescience and sophistication.

I have written prefaces for each article explaining its historical and conceptual importance. I have also written prefaces for each Unit describing the theme of the unit and explaining its status as an organizing principle for the study of motivation. Following each article are a series of two to four thought-provoking questions meant to help stimulate classroom discussions. Among the purposes of these questions is to draw links among articles in an attempt to encourage students to think about general, overarching *principles* of motivation (as opposed to discrete, isolated phenomena). An additional theme integrated throughout the book is to draw connections between earlier work and contemporary studies. Readers are encouraged to consider classic ideas that remain to be tested using contemporary methodologies and technologies.

Finally, I would be remiss if I did not acknowledge the enormous debt this project owes to several sources. First, Bernard Weiner's formidable book *Human Motivation* (1980, Spinger-Verlag) has been an invaluable resource, especially regarding historical theories of motivation. Higgins and Kruglanski's book *Motivational Science* (2000, Psychology Press) represents an important earlier compilation that shared many of the goals of the present book. I am also thankful to the hundreds of undergraduate and graduate students who have 'pilot-tested' both the readings and the original text over the years and provided helpful feedback. Finally, Kathryn West and Nancy Reilly at Oxford University Press have been remarkably flexible, patient, and helpful throughout the editorial process.

Unit One

Social Needs

Early humans were physically unimpressive. They did, however, possess large and complex brains that proved useful for solving the many fearsome challenges that threatened survival. One solution was to band together in groups. By engaging in coordinated, co-operative action, our prehistoric ancestors could gather food and construct shelters more efficiently than could an equal number of individuals working alone. Indeed, those who did *not* join groups missed these advantages and were likely 'selected out' of history. Thus, even though adaptive challenges have changed dramatically in recent centuries, human beings remain deeply motivated to create and maintain social bonds.

So goes the evolutionary story that forms the background to much of the contemporary research on human social behaviour. To that end, several theorists have claimed—with considerable empirical backing—that the need to belong is a fundamental human motivation. The authors in this Unit argue that the motivation to form and maintain social relationships is intensely powerful and is a need that is analogous in important ways to physiological needs such as those for food, water, and shelter.

Baumeister and Leary (1995) cite evidence from a diverse range of literature suggesting that when people maintain at least a minimum number of meaningful relationships they experience benefits to their psychological and physical well-being, but when they fail to maintain that level of social connectedness, a host of problems result, including some that might seem counterintuitive at first glance. Their theoretical article—which also provides something of a metatheoretical how-to guide for constructing a theory of motivation—is one of the most-cited articles in the field and has spawned a large number of studies in the intervening years that have tested its specific predictions (e.g., MacDonald & Leary, 2005; Stinson et al., 2008).

In 1991, Marilynn Brewer proposed optimal distinctiveness theory (ODT). This theory places the need to belong in a broader psychological context by pointing out that it is possible to have *too much* social connectedness. According to ODT, rather than relentlessly striving to strengthen ties with one's group at all costs, people instead balance this need with the need to feel special and unique—that is, to avoid being 'just another face in the crowd'. When people have accomplished this, they have attained optimal distinctiveness. To test this idea, Brewer and her colleagues devised ingenious ways to make their laboratory participants feel either too common or too distinctive. They found that when participants felt too common they took steps to assert their distinctiveness, and when participants felt too distinctive they took steps to assert their commonness. The article presented in this Unit, by Pickett, Silver, and Brewer (2002), represents a good example of these complementary processes at work.

According to Brewer and her colleagues, ODT provides a useful account for several vexing phenomena. For example, why do members of low-status groups often enthusiastically display their group membership, rather than disavowing it? Why do people sometimes sacrifice their own self-interest for the sake of their group? Can you use the principles of optimal distinctiveness theory to explain these phenomena?

Need to belong theory and optimal distinctiveness theory are not the only perspectives that explain social motivation. Beginning in the early 1990s, Pyczszynski, Solomon, Greenberg, and colleagues proposed an influential theory of motivation called terror management theory (TMT). In contrast to the need to belong theory, TMT argued that people do not necessarily want to belong to a group for its own sake, but rather as a means to an end. What is that end? According to these theorists, what people really desire to achieve is symbolic immortality. Drawing from intellectual traditions both inside and outside of mainstream experimental psychology (including existential philosophy and psychoanalytic theory), these researchers proposed that many motivational phenomena (including but not restricted to the need to belong) are merely elaborate defences against the dread associated with knowing that one's life is finite.

How could one possibly provide evidence for this claim? In numerous studies, these researchers have forced participants to think about their death and found that doing so leads to a general tendency toward defensiveness and closed-mindedness. Most relevant to the present Unit, mortality salience has been shown to produce a strong tendency to affirm and strengthen one's ties to favoured social groups (e.g., family, nation, race, etc.). For example, TMT theorists did not find it at all surprising that Americans displayed a dramatic rise in adherence to symbols of authority and patriotism immediately after the 9/11 attacks. TMT is enormously ambitious in its scope as it purports to account for many of social psychology's long-cherished theories. As such, many of its claims have been the source of considerable controversy. For examples of the application of TMT to belongingness-related phenomena, see the following sources:

Greenberg, J., Pyszczynski, T., & Solomon, S. (1990). Anxiety concerning social exclusion: Innate response or one consequence of the need for terror management? *Journal of Social and Clinical Psychology, 9,* 202–213.

Mikulincer, M., Florian, V., & Hirschberger, G. (2003). The existential function of close relationships—introducing death into the science of love. *Personality and Social Psychology Review, 7,* 20–40.

The following is a good source for a reconciliation of the TMT perspective and the need to belong perspective:

Wisman, A. & Koole, S.L. (2003). Hiding in the crowd: Can mortality salience promote affiliation with others who oppose one's worldview? *Journal of Personality and Social Psychology, 84,* 511–526.

1. The Need to Belong: Desire for Interpersonal Attachments as a Fundamental Human Motivation

Roy F. Baumeister, Case Western Reserve University
Mark R. Leary, Wake Forest University

□ ■ □

Editor's Introduction

Like other sciences, social psychology has been marked in recent decades by a proliferation of ever more specialized theories that account for an ever smaller range of human behaviour. As such, whenever a broader theoretical framework arrives on the scene—one that helps to consolidate and synthesize a wide range of seemingly unrelated phenomena—it is most welcome.

In this article, Roy Baumeister and Mark Leary argue that people possess a powerful need to belong. They further propose that this starting assumption provides an explanatory thread that connects a broad swath of interpersonal and intergroup phenomena. In so doing, they contrast the need to belong hypothesis with psychoanalytic theory and attachment theory; whereas the latter two focus primarily on the bonds between child and mother, the need to belong hypothesis states that *all* social bonds serve a crucial psychological function.

Baumeister and Leary also spell out a list of criteria that must be met for a new theory of social motivation to have any credibility. These include generality (it must account for a broad range of behaviour), satiation (it must account for when and why people *stop* pursuing certain goals), and substitution (it must account for the fact that, if one means to goal satisfaction is thwarted, another means may take its place). Keep these criteria in mind as you read and evaluate other theories throughout this book. Do you think that the need to belong theory as stated in this article meets all the criteria that Baumeister and Leary set out?

□ ■ □

The purpose of this review is to develop and evaluate the hypothesis that a need to belong is a fundamental human motivation and to propose that the need to belong can provide a point of departure for understanding and integrating a great deal of the existing literature regarding human interpersonal behaviour. More precisely, the belongingness hypothesis is that human beings have a pervasive drive to form and maintain at least a minimum quantity of lasting, positive, and significant interpersonal relationships. Satisfying this drive involves two criteria: First, there is a need for frequent, affectively pleasant interactions with a few other people, and second, these interactions must take place in the context of a temporally stable and enduring framework of affective concern for each other's welfare. Interactions with a constantly changing sequence of partners will be less satisfactory than repeated interactions with the same person(s), and relatedness without frequent contact will also be unsatisfactory. A lack of belongingness should constitute severe deprivation and cause a variety of ill effects. Furthermore, a great deal of human behaviour, emotion, and thought is caused by this fundamental interpersonal motive.

The hypothesis that people are motivated to form and maintain interpersonal bonds is not new, of course. John Donne (1572–1631) has been widely quoted for the line 'No [person] is an island'. In psychology, the need for interpersonal contact was asserted in several ways by Freud (e.g., 1930), although he tended to see the motive as derived from the sex drive and from the filial bond. Maslow (1968) ranked 'love and belonging-ness needs' in the middle of his motivational hier-archy; that is, belongingness needs do not emerge until food, hunger, safety, and other basic needs are satisfied, but they take precedence over esteem and self-actualization. Bowlby's (e.g., 1969, 1973) attachment theory also posited the need to form and maintain relationships. His early thinking followed the Freudian pattern of deriving attach-ment needs from the relationship to one's mother; he regarded the adult's need for attachment as an effort to recapture the intimate contact that the individual had, as an infant, with his or her mother.[1] Horney (1945), Sullivan (1953), Fromm (1955, 1956), de Rivera (1984), Hogan (1983), Epstein (1992), Ryan (1991), Guisinger and Blatt (1994), and others have made similar suggestions. The existence of a need to belong is thus a famil-iar point of theory and speculation, although not all theorists have anticipated our particular for-mulation of this need as the combination of fre-quent interaction plus persistent caring. Moreover, most theorists have neglected to provide system-atic empirical evaluation of this hypothesis. For example, Maslow's (1968) influential assertion of a belongingness need was accompanied by neither original data nor review of previous findings.

Thus, despite frequent speculative assertions that people need to belong, the belongingness hypothesis needs to be critically evaluated in light of empirical evidence. A main goal of the pres-ent article is to assemble a large body of empirical findings pertinent to the belongingness hypothesis to evaluate how well the hypothesis fits the data.

Another goal of this article is to demonstrate the broad applicability of the need to belong for under-standing human motivation and behaviour. Even though many psychological theorists have noted human affiliative tendencies in one form or another, the field as a whole has neglected the broad appli-cability of this need to a wide range of behaviours.

Thus, for example, the motive literature has been dominated by research on the respective needs for power, achievement, intimacy, approval, and, to a lesser extent, affiliation. But the need for power may well be driven by the need to belong, as we suggest later. Likewise, people prefer achievements that are validated, recognized, and valued by other people over solitary achievements, so there may be a substantial interpersonal component behind the need for achievement. And the needs for approval and intimacy are undoubtedly linked to the fact that approval is a prerequisite for forming and maintaining social bonds, and intimacy is a defin-ing characteristic of close relationships. The need to belong could thus be linked to all of them.

Furthermore, even a quick glance at research on social behaviour from the perspective of the belongingness hypothesis raises the possibility that much of what human beings do is done in the service of belongingness. Thus, the belong-ingness hypothesis might have considerable value for personality and social psychology and even for psychology as a whole. As a broad integrative hypothesis, it might help rectify what some observ-ers have criticized as fragmentation and atomiza-tion in the conceptual underpinnings of the field (see Vallacher & Nowak, 1994; West, Newsom, & Fenaughty, 1992).

. . .

Conceptual Background

Fundamental Motivations: Metatheory

Before proceeding with our examination of the need to belong, we must consider briefly the metatheoretical requirements of our hypothesis. That is, what criteria must be satisfied to conclude that the need to belong, or any other drive, is a fundamental human motivation? We suggest the following: A fundamental motivation should (a) produce effects readily under all but adverse con-ditions, (b) have affective consequences, (c) direct cognitive processing, (d) lead to ill effects (such as on health or adjustment) when thwarted, (e) elicit goal-oriented behaviour designed to satisfy it (subject to motivational patterns such as object substitutability and satiation), (f) be universal in the sense of applying to all people, (g) not be derivative of other motives, (h) affect a broad variety of behaviours, and (i) have implications that go beyond immediate psychological functioning. We consider each of these criteria in turn.

The first criterion is that a fundamental motivation should operate in a wide variety of settings: Any motive that requires highly specific or supportive circumstances to produce effects cannot properly be called fundamental. Certain circumstances may retard or prevent its operation, but in general the more widely it can produce effects, the stronger its claim to being a fundamental motivation.

The second and third criteria refer to emotional and cognitive patterns. Cognitive and emotional responses reflect subjective importance and concern, and a motivation that fails to guide emotion and cognition (at least sometimes) can hardly be considered an important one. In addition, most motivational and drive systems involve hedonic consequences that alert the individual to undesired state changes that motivate behaviour to restore the desired state and whose removal serves as negative reinforcement for goal attainment.

The fourth criterion is that failure to satisfy a fundamental motivation should produce ill effects that go beyond temporary affective distress. A motivation can be considered to be fundamental only if health, adjustment, or well-being requires that it be satisfied. Also, motivations can be sorted into wants and needs, the difference being in the scope of ill effects that follow from non-satisfaction: Unsatisfied needs should lead to pathology (medical, psychological, or behavioural), unlike unsatisfied wants. Thus, if belongingness is a need rather than simply a want, then people who lack belongingness should exhibit pathological consequences beyond mere temporary distress.

Substitution and satiation are two familiar hallmarks of motivation. If the need to belong is a fundamental need, then belonging to one group should satisfy it and hence obviate or reduce the need to belong to another group. People may be driven to form social bonds until they have a certain number, whereafter the drive to form attachments would presumably subside. Furthermore, attachment partners should be to some degree interchangeable. Of course, this does not mean that a 20-year spouse or friend can simply be replaced with a new acquaintance. In the long run, however, a new spouse or friend should do as well as the previous one.

The sixth and seventh criteria involve universality and non-derivativeness. Any motivation that is limited to certain human beings or certain circumstances, or any motivation that is derived from another motive, cannot be regarded as fundamental. Universality can be indicated by transcending cultural boundaries. Establishing that a motive is not derivative is not easy, although path-analytic models can suggest derivative patterns. Satisfying the first criterion may also help satisfy the seventh, because if the motivation operates in a broad variety of situations without requiring particular, favourable circumstances, then it may be presumed to be fundamental. Meanwhile, if the evidence contradicts evolutionary patterns or fails to indicate physiological mechanisms, then the hypothesis of universality or innateness would lose credibility.

The eighth criterion is the ability to affect a wide and diverse assortment of behaviours. The more behaviours that appear to be influenced by a particular motive, the stronger its case for being one of the fundamental motives. Lastly, we suggest that a fundamental motive should have implications that go beyond psychological functioning. If a motivation is truly fundamental, it should influence a broad range of human activity, and hence it should be capable of offering viable and consistent interpretations of patterns observed in historical, economic, or sociological studies.

Falsification is only one relevant approach to evaluating a broad hypothesis about belongingness being a fundamental motivation. The belongingness hypothesis could indeed be falsified if it were shown, for example, that many people can live happy, healthy lives in social isolation or that many people show no cognitive or emotional responses to looming significant changes in their belongingness status. In addition to such criteria, however, hypotheses about fundamental motivations must be evaluated in terms of their capacity to interpret and explain a wide range of phenomena. Part of the value of such a theory is its capacity to provide an integrative framework, and this value is a direct function of the quantity and importance of the behaviour patterns that it can explain in a consistent, intelligible fashion. We therefore pay close attention to the potential range of implications of the belongingness hypothesis, in addition to examining how many falsification tests the hypothesis has managed to survive.

The Need to Belong Theory

In view of the metatheoretical requirements listed in the previous section, we propose that a need to belong, that is, a need to form and maintain at least a minimum quantity of interpersonal relationships, is innately prepared (and hence nearly universal) among human beings. Thus, unlike the Freudian (1930) view that regarded sexuality and aggression as the major driving psychological forces, and unlike the most ambitious behaviourist views that considered each newborn a tabula rasa, our view depicts the human being as naturally driven toward establishing and sustaining belongingness. The need to belong should therefore be found to some degree in all humans in all cultures, although naturally one would expect there to be individual differences in strength and intensity, as well as cultural and individual variations in how people express and satisfy the need. But it should prove difficult or impossible for culture to eradicate the need to belong (except perhaps for an occasional, seriously warped individual).

The innate quality presumably has an evolutionary basis. It seems clear that a desire to form and maintain social bonds would have both survival and reproductive benefits (see Ainsworth, 1989; Axelrod & Hamilton, 1981; Barash, 1977; Bowlby, 1969; D.M. Buss, 1990, 1991; Hogan, Jones, & Cheek, 1985; Moreland, 1987). Groups can share food, provide mates, and help care for offspring (including orphans). Some survival tasks, such as hunting large animals or maintaining defensive vigilance against predatory enemies, are best accomplished by group co-operation. Children who desired to stay together with adults (and who would resist being left alone) would be more likely to survive until their reproductive years than other children because they would be more likely to receive care and food as well as protection. Cues that connote possible harm, such as illness, danger, nightfall, and disaster, seem to increase the need to be with others (see also Rofe, 1984), which again underscores the protective value of group membership. Adults who formed attachments would be more likely to reproduce than those who failed to form them, and long-term relationships would increase the chances that the offspring would reach maturity and reproduce in turn (see also Shaver, Hazan, & Bradshaw, 1988).[2]

Competition for limited resources could also provide a powerful stimulus to forming interpersonal connections. There are several potential, although debatable, advantages to forming a group under conditions of scarcity. For example, groups may share resources and thus prevent any individual from starving (although sharing deprives other group members of some of their resources), and groups may appropriate resources from nonmembers (although there is the problem of how to distribute them in the group). What appears less debatable is the severe competitive disadvantage of the lone individual confronting a group when both want the same resource. When other people are in groups, it is vital to belong to a group oneself, particularly a group of familiar, co-operative people who care about one's welfare. Thus, an inclination to form and sustain social bonds would have important benefits of defending oneself and protecting one's resources against external threats.

The likely result of this evolutionary selection would be a set of internal mechanisms that guide individual human beings into social groups and lasting relationships. These mechanisms would presumably include a tendency to orient toward other members of the species, a tendency to experience affective distress when deprived of social contact or relationships, and a tendency to feel pleasure or positive affect from social contact and relatedness. These affective mechanisms would stimulate learning by making positive social contact reinforcing and social deprivation punishing.

Our version of the belongingness hypothesis does not regard the need as derived from a particular relationship or focused on a particular individual. In this it differs from the early Freudian version of Bowlby's work, in which the relationship to the mother was regarded as the cause of the desire for attachment. Thus, Bowlby suggested that adult attachments to work organizations, religious groups, or others are derived from the child's tie to the mother and revolve around personal attachment to the group leader or supervisor (Bowlby, 1969, p. 207). In contrast, we propose that the need to belong can, in principle, be directed toward any other human being, and the loss of relationship with one person can to some extent be replaced by any other. The main obstacle to such substitution is that formation of new relationships takes time, such as in the gradual accumulation of intimacy and shared experience (see Sternberg, 1986, on the time course of intimacy). Social contact with a long-term intimate would therefore provide some satisfactions, including a sense of belonging that would not be available in interactions with strangers or new acquaintances.

The belongingness hypothesis can be distinguished from a hypothesized need for mere social contact in terms of whether interactions with strangers or with people one dislikes or hates would satisfy the need. It can be distinguished from a hypothesized need for positive, pleasant social contact in terms of whether nonhostile interactions with strangers would satisfy

it. The need to belong entails that relationships are desired, so interactions with strangers would mainly be appealing as possible first steps toward long-term contacts (including practising social skills or learning about one's capacity to attract partners), and interactions with disliked people would not satisfy it.

Additional differences between the belongingness hypothesis and attachment theory could be suggested, although it may be a matter of interpretation whether these are merely differences of emphasis or fundamental theoretical differences. In our understanding, the (very real) strengths of attachment theory are twofold. First, attachment theory has emphasized the task of elaborating individual differences in attachment style (e.g., Hazan & Shaver, 1994a, 1994b; Shaver et al., 1988), whereas we focus on the commonality of the overarching need to belong. Second, attachment theory has emphasized certain emotional needs and satisfactions implicit in certain kinds of relationships, whereas we regard it as at least plausible that the need to belong could be satisfied in other ways. For example, one might imagine a young person without any family or intimate relationships who is nonetheless satisfied by being heavily involved in an ideologically radical political movement. There are undoubtedly strong emotional mechanisms associated with belongingness, as we show later, but these could be understood as mediating mechanisms rather than as essential properties.

As a fundamental motivation, the need to belong should stimulate goal-directed activity designed to satisfy it. People should show tendencies to seek out interpersonal contacts and cultivate possible relationships, at least until they have reached a minimum level of social contact and relatedness. Meanwhile, social bonds should form easily, readily, and without requiring highly particular or conducive settings. (Indeed, if social attachments form through shared unpleasant experiences, contrary to what simple association models might predict, this would be especially compelling support for the belongingness hypothesis.) Cognitive activity should reflect a pervasive concern with forming and maintaining relationships. Emotional reactions should follow directly from outcomes that pertain to the need to belong. More precisely, positive affect should follow from forming and solidifying social bonds, and negative affect should ensue when relationships are broken, threatened, or refused.

If belongingness is indeed a fundamental need, then aversive reactions to a loss of belongingness should go beyond negative affect to include some types of pathology. People who are socially deprived should exhibit a variety of ill effects, such as signs of maladjustment or stress, behavioural or psychological pathology, and possibly health problems. They should also show an increase in goal-directed activity aimed at forming relationships.

In addition, the belongingness hypothesis entails that people should strive to achieve a certain minimum quantity and quality of social contacts but that once this level is surpassed, the motivation should diminish. The need is presumably for a certain minimum number of bonds and quantity of interaction. The formation of further social attachments beyond that minimal level should be subject to diminishing returns; that is, people should experience less satisfaction on formation of such extra relationships, as well as less distress on terminating them. Satiation patterns should be evident, such that people who are well enmeshed in social relationships would be less inclined to seek and form additional bonds than would people who are socially deprived. Relationships should substitute for each other, to some extent, as would be indicated by effective replacement of lost relationship partners and by a capacity for social relatedness in one sphere to overcome potential ill effects of social deprivation in another sphere (e.g., if strong family ties compensate for aloneness at work).

We propose that the need to belong has two main features. First, people need frequent personal contacts or interactions with the other person. Ideally, these interactions would be affectively positive or pleasant, but it is mainly important that the majority be free from conflict and negative affect.

Second, people need to perceive that there is an interpersonal bond or relationship marked by stability, affective concern, and continuation into the foreseeable future. This aspect provides a relational context to one's interactions with the other person, and so the perception of the bond is essential for satisfying the need to belong. When compared with essentially identical interactions with other people with whom one is not connected, a strictly behavioural record might reveal nothing special or rewarding about these interactions. Yet an interaction with a person in the context of an ongoing relationship is subjectively different from, and often more rewarding than, an interaction with a stranger or casual acquaintance. To satisfy the need to belong, the person must believe that the other cares about his or her welfare and likes (or loves) him or her.

Ideally this concern would be mutual, so that the person has reciprocal feelings about the other. M.S. Clark and her colleagues (e.g., Clark, 1984; Clark & Mills, 1979; Clark, Mills, & Corcoran, 1989; Clark, Mills, & Powell, 1986) have shown that a framework of mutual concern produces a relationship qualitatively different from one based on self-interested social exchange. Still, it is plausible that mutuality is merely desirable rather than essential. The decisive aspect may be the perception that one is the recipient of the other's lasting concern.

Viewed in this way, the need to belong is something other than a need for mere affiliation. Frequent contacts with non-supportive, indifferent others can go only so far in promoting one's general well-being and would do little to satisfy the need to belong. Conversely, relationships characterized by strong feelings of attachment, intimacy, or commitment but lacking regular contact will also fail to satisfy the need. Simply knowing that a bond exists may be emotionally reassuring, yet it would not provide full belongingness if one does not interact with the other person. Thus, we view the need to belong as something more than either a need for affiliation or a need for intimate attachment.

The notion that people need relationships characterized by both regular contact and an ongoing bond has been anticipated to some degree by Weiss (1973; see also Shaver & Buhrmester, 1983), who suggested that feelings of loneliness can be precipitated either by an insufficient amount of social contact (social loneliness) or by a lack of meaningful, intimate relatedness (emotional loneliness). Weiss's distinction has been criticized on conceptual and empirical grounds (e.g., Paloutzian & Janigian, 1987; Perlman, 1987), and efforts to operationalize and test the distinction have met with mixed results (DiTommaso & Spinner, 1993; Saklofske & Yackulic, 1989; Vaux, 1988). In our view, the difficulty with this distinction arises from the assumption that people have a need for mere social contact and a separate need for intimate relationships. Rather, the need is for regular social contact with those to whom one feels connected. From an evolutionary perspective, relationships characterized by both of these features would have greater survival and reproductive value than would relationships characterized by only one. Accordingly, the need to belong should be marked by both aspects.

Review of Empirical Findings

We searched the empirical literature of social and personality psychology for findings relevant to the belongingness hypothesis. The following sections summarize the evidence we found pertaining to the series of predictions about belongingness.

Forming Social Bonds

A first prediction of the belongingness hypothesis is that social bonds should form relatively easily, without requiring specially conducive circumstances. Such evidence not only would attest to the presence and power of the need to belong but would suggest that the need is not a derivative

of other needs (insofar as it is not limited to circumstances that meet other requirements or follow from other events).

There is abundant evidence that social bonds form easily. Indeed, people in every society on earth belong to small primary groups that involve face-to-face, personal interactions (Mann, 1980). The anthropologist Coon (1946) asserted that natural groups are characteristic of all human beings. Societies differ in the type, number, and permanence of the groups that people join, but people of all cultures quite naturally form groups.

The classic Robbers Cave study conducted by Sherif, Harvey, White, Hood, and Sherif (1961/1988) showed that when previously unacquainted boys were randomly assigned to newly created groups, strong loyalty and group identification ties ensued rapidly. In fact, later in that study, the two strongly opposed groups were recombined into a single group with co-operative goals, and emotional and behavioural patterns quickly accommodated to the new group (although the prior antagonistic identifications did hamper the process).

The tendency for laboratory or experimentally created groups to quickly become cohesive has also been noted in the *minimal intergroup* situation (Brewer, 1979). Tajfel and his colleagues (Billig & Tajfel, 1973; Tajfel, 1970; Tajfel & Billig, 1974; Tajfel, Flament, Billig, & Bundy, 1971) showed that assigning participants to categories on a seemingly arbitrary basis was sufficient to cause them to allocate greater rewards to ingroup members than to outgroup members. Indeed, the original goal of Tajfel et al. (1971) was not to study group formation but to understand the causes of ingroup favouritism. To do this, they sought to set up an experimental group that would be so trivial that no favouritism would be found, intending then to add other variables progressively so as to determine at what point favouritism would start. To their surprise, however, ingroup favouritism appeared at once, even in the minimal and supposedly trivial situation (see also Turner, 1985).

This preferential treatment of ingroup members does not appear to be due to inferred self-interest or to issues of novelty and uncertainty about the task (Brewer & Silver, 1978; Tajfel, 1970; Tajfel & Billig, 1974). Inferred similarity of self to ingroup members was a viable explanation for many of the early findings, but Locksley, Ortiz, and Hepburn (1980) ruled this out by demonstrating that people show ingroup favouritism even when they have been assigned to groups by a random lottery. Thus, patterns of ingroup favouritism, such as sharing rewards and categorizing others relative to the group, appeared quite readily, even in the absence of experiences designed to bond people to the group emotionally or materially.

Several other studies suggest how little it takes (other than frequent contact) to create social attachments. Bowlby (1969) noted that infants form attachments to caregivers very early in life, long before babies are able to calculate benefits or even speak. Festinger, Schachter, and Back (1950) found that mere proximity was a potent factor in relationship formation; people seemed to develop social bonds with each other simply because they lived near each other. Nahemow and Lawton (1975) replicated those findings and also showed that pairs of best friends who differed by age or race were particularly likely to have lived very close together, suggesting that extreme proximity may overcome tendencies to bond with similar others. Wilder and Thompson (1980) showed that people seem to form favourable views toward whomever they spend time with, even if these others are members of a previously disliked or stereotyped outgroup. In their study, intergroup biases decreased as contact with members of the outgroups increased (and as ingroup contact decreased).

We noted that the formation of social attachments under adverse circumstances would be especially compelling evidence because it avoids the alternative explanations based on classical conditioning (i.e., that positive associations breed attraction). Latané, Eckman, and Joy (1966) found that participants who experienced electric shock together tended to like each other more than control participants who did not experience shock, although the effect was significant only among first-borns. Kenrick and Johnson (1979) found that participants rated each other more positively in the presence of aversive than non-aversive noise. Elder and Clipp (1988) compared the persistence of attachments among military veterans and found that the greatest persistence occurred among groups that had undergone heavy combat resulting in the deaths of some friends and comrades. Although it would be rash to suggest that all shared negative experiences increase attraction, it does appear that positive bonding will occur even under adverse circumstances.

The development of interpersonal attraction under fearful circumstances has been explained in terms of both misattribution (i.e., people may misinterpret their anxious arousal as attraction to another person) and reinforcement theory (i.e., when the presence of some other person reduces one's distress, a positive emotional response becomes associated with that person; Kenrick & Cialdini, 1977). The misattribution explanation is largely irrelevant to the belongingness hypothesis, but the reinforcement explanation is germane. Specifically, although others may reduce one's distress through various routes (such as distraction, humour, or reassurance), evidence suggests strongly that the mere presence of other people can be comforting (Schachter, 1959). Such effects may well be conditioned through years of experience with supportive others, but they also may indicate that threatening events stimulate the need to belong.

The fact that people sometimes form attachments with former rivals or opponents is itself a meaningful indicator of a general inclination to form bonds. Cognitive consistency pressures and affective memories would militate against forming positive social bonds with people who have been rivals or opponents. Yet, as we have already noted, the Robbers Cave study (Sherif et al., 1961 /1988) showed that people could join and work together with others who had been bitterly opposed very recently, and Wilder and Thompson (1980) showed that social contact could overcome established intergroup prejudices and stereotypes. Orbell, van de Kragt, and Dawes (1988) likewise showed that impulses toward forming positive attachments could overcome oppositional patterns. In their study using the prisoner's dilemma game, having a discussion period led to decreased competition and increased co-operation, as a result of either the formation of a group identity that joined the potential rivals together or explicit agreements to co-operate. Thus, belongingness motivations appear to be able to overcome some antagonistic, competitive, or divisive tendencies.

Similar shifts have been suggested by M.S. Clark (1984, 1986; Clark, Mills, & Powell, 1986; Clark, Ouellette, Powell, & Milberg, 1987), who showed that people move toward a communal orientation when there is a chance to form a relationship. When participants were confronted with a person who seemingly would not be amenable to relationship formation (i.e., because she was already married), they interacted with her on the basis of norms of equitable exchange and individuality; when they believed she would be a possible relationship partner, however, they interacted with her on a communal basis (i.e., mutuality and sharing, without respect to individual equity concerns).

Critical Assessment

The remarkable ease with which social bonds form has been shown with experimental methods and confirmed by other methods. The main limitation would be that people do not always form relationships with all available or proximal others, which could mean that satiation processes limit the number of relationships people seek and which also indicates that other factors and processes affect the formation of relationships. Some patterns (e.g., ingroup favouritism in minimal groups) have been well replicated with careful efforts to rule out alternative explanations.

Conclusion

In brief, people seem widely and strongly inclined to form social relationships quite easily in the absence of any special set of eliciting circumstances or ulterior motives. Friendships and group allegiances seem to arise spontaneously and readily, without needing evidence of material advantage or inferred similarity. Not only do relationships emerge quite naturally, but people invest a great deal of time and effort in fostering supportive relationships with others. External threat seems to increase the tendency to form strong bonds.

Not Breaking Bonds

The belongingness hypothesis predicts that people should generally be at least as reluctant to break social bonds as they are eager to form them in the first place. A variety of patterns supports the view that people try to preserve relationships and avoid ending them. In fact, Hazan and Shaver (1994a, p. 14) recently concluded that the tendency for human beings to respond with distress and protest to the end of a relationship is nearly universal, even across different cultures and across the age span.

Some relationships are limited in time by external factors, and so these are logically the first place to look for evidence that people show distress and resistance to breaking bonds. Encounter groups and training groups, for example, are often convened with the explicit understanding that the meetings will stop at a certain point in the future. Even so, it is a familiar observation in the empirical literature (e.g., Egan, 1970; Lacoursiere, 1980; Lieberman, Yalom, & Miles, 1973) that the members of such groups resist the notion that the group will dissolve. Even though the group's purpose may have been fulfilled, the participants want to hold on to the social bonds and relationships they have formed with each other. They promise individually and sometimes collectively to stay in touch with each other, they plan for reunions, and they take other steps to ensure a continuity of future contacts. In actuality, only a small minority of these envisioned reunions or contacts takes place, and so the widespread exercise of making them can be regarded as a symptom of resistance to the threatened dissolution (Lacoursiere, 1980, p. 216).

Other relationships are limited in time by external transitions such as graduating from college, moving to a different city, or getting a new job. As such transitions approach, people commonly get together formally and informally and promise to remain in contact, to share meals or other social occasions together, to write and call each other, and to continue the relationship in other ways. They also cry or show other signs of distress over the impending separation (Bridges, 1980). These patterns seem to occur even if the dissolving relationship (e.g., with neighbours) had no important practical or instrumental function and there is no realistic likelihood of further contact.

More generally, many social institutions and behaviour patterns seem to serve a need to preserve at least the appearance of social attachment in the absence of actual, continued interaction. Reunions constitute an occasion for people to see former acquaintances. The massive exchange of greeting cards during the Christmas holiday season includes many cases in which the card is the sole contact that two people have had during the entire year, but people still resist dropping each other's name from the mailing list because to do so signifies a final dissolution of the social bond. In fact, most people will send Christmas cards to perfect strangers from whom they receive cards (Kunz & Woolcott, 1976). People seem not to want to risk damaging a relationship even if they do not know the identity of the other person!

Likewise, social rituals involving greetings and farewells serve to assure others of the continuation of one's relationships with them. Many greetings, particularly those directed at family members and close friends, seem designed to indicate that one's relationship has remained intact since the last contact, and farewells often include some hint that the relationship will be maintained until the people see one another again (Goffman, 1971). The

importance of such rituals in the maintenance of belongingness is reflected in the distress people sometimes experience when they feel that another's greeting is inadequately warm or that the other's farewell expresses insufficient concern about the impending separation.

In many cases, people seem reluctant to dissolve even bad or destructive relationships. The apparent unwillingness of many women to leave abusive, battering spouses or boyfriends (Roy, 1977; Strube, 1988) has prompted several generations of speculative explanations, ranging from masochistic or self-destructive liking for abuse to calculations of economic self-interest that supposedly override considerations of physical harm. The belongingness hypothesis offers yet one more potential perspective: The unwillingness to leave an abusive intimate partner is another manifestation of the strength of the need to belong and of the resulting reluctance to break social bonds. The fact that people resist breaking off an attachment that causes pain attests to how deeply rooted and powerful the need to belong is.

Moreover, when people do decide to break off an intimate relationship, they typically experience considerable distress over the dissolution (which we cover in more detail in the later section on emotion). This is ironic: Although goal attainment is usually marked by positive affect such as satisfaction and joy, attaining the goal of getting a divorce is generally accompanied by negative affect. To be sure, in some cases the distress over divorce is accompanied by an admixture of positive affect, but the negative affect nonetheless indicates the resistance to breaking the bond.

It is also relevant and noteworthy that the social bond often continues despite the divorce. In her study on divorce, Vaughan (1986) concluded that 'in most cases [marital] relationships don't end. They change, but they don't end' (p. 282). Weiss (1979) also found that some form of (often ambivalent) attachment persists after divorce. The persistence of intimate relationships past the occasion of mutually agreed and formally institutionalized dissolution may be yet another indication of people's reluctance to break social bonds.

Critical Assessment

Because ethical and practical constraints prevent laboratory experimentation on the ending of significant relationships, the evidence in this section was drawn from observational studies and other methods, and so the hypothesis of resistance to relationship dissolution is not as conclusively supported as might be desired. Alternative explanations exist for some of the findings. For example, the persistence of relatedness after divorce is partly due to ongoing practical concerns, such as joint responsibility for child care; although Vaughan (1986) was emphatic in asserting that such pragmatic concerns fall far short of explaining the extent of continuing attachments, she was vague about the evidence to back up her assertion. Also, as we noted, the tendency for battered women to return to their abusive partners has been explained in many ways, and the hypothesized reluctance to break off a relationship is only one of them.

On the positive side, however, the persistence of such bonds has been observed by a variety of researchers. The fact that these researchers are from different disciplines suggests that these conclusions do not stem from a single methodological or theoretical bias. More systematic research on possible boundary and limiting conditions of the resistance to dissolve bonds would be desirable.

Conclusion

Despite some methodological weaknesses and ambiguities, the weight of the evidence does favour the conclusion that people strongly and generally resist the dissolution of relationships and social bonds. Moreover, this resistance appears to go well beyond rational considerations of practical or material advantage.

Cognition

Intelligent thought is generally recognized as the most important adaptive trait among human beings, and so it seems reasonable to assume that issues of fundamental concern and importance are likely to be the focus of cognitive activity. The belongingness hypothesis therefore would predict that people will devote considerable cognitive processing to interpersonal interactions and relationships.

Basic patterns of thought appear to reflect a fundamental concern with social relationships. Sedikides, Olsen, and Reis (1993) showed that relationships are natural categories; that is, people spontaneously classify incoming information in terms of social relationships. Participants stored information about relationship partners together, and they did this more for strong, close relationships (marriage) than for weak or distant ones (e.g., acquaintanceship). Pryor and Ostrom (1981) showed that people use the individual person as a cognitive unit of analysis for familiar people more than for unfamiliar people. These researchers began by questioning the basic assumption that the person is the fundamental unit of social perception. That is, information is not necessarily or inherently processed and stored in memory on a person-by-person basis, but it is, in fact, processed and stored on such a basis when it pertains to significant others. Ostrom, Carpenter, Sedikides, and Li (1993) provided evidence that information about outgroup members tends to be stored and organized on the basis of attribute categories (such as traits, preferences, and duties), whereas ingroup information is processed on the basis of person categories. Thus, social bonds create a pattern in cognitive processing that gives priority to organizing information on the basis of the person with whom one has some sort of connection.

Several studies have pursued the notion that people process information about close relationship partners differently from the way they process information about strangers or distant acquaintances. For example, research has shown that, when a group of people take turns reading words aloud, they each have high recall for the words they personally speak but have poor recall for the words preceding and following their performance. Brenner (1976) found that this next-in-line effect occurs not only for one's own performance but also for words spoken by one's dating partner (and the words immediately preceding and following).

In a series of studies, Aron, Aron, Tudor, and Nelson (1991) showed that close relationship partners, unlike strangers, have cognitive effects similar to those of the self. Thus, when people form an image of themselves or their mothers interacting with some object, they have more difficulty recalling that object than if they imagined a famous but personally unacquainted person interacting with that same object. In another study, participants had more difficulty in making me–not me judgments about traits on which they differed from their spouse than in making judgments about traits on which they resembled the spouse. These results suggest that cognitive processes tend to blur the boundaries between relationship partners and the self, in the form of 'including [the] other in the self' (p. 241). In short, these studies confirm that information about relationship partners is singled out for special processing, and they raise the possibility that the need to belong leads to a cognitive merging of self with particular other people. Such patterns of subsuming the individual in the interpersonal unit indicate the importance of these relationships.

Many of the special biases that people exhibit for processing information in ways that favour and flatter themselves are extended to partners in close relationships. Fincham, Beach, and Baucom (1987) showed that self-serving biases that take credit for success and refuse blame for failure operate just as strongly—or even more strongly—when people interpret their spouses' outcomes as when they interpret their own outcomes. That is, events are interpreted in a way that is maximally flattering to the spouse, just as they are interpreted in ways that enhance and protect the self. (These patterns are extended only to partners in good, strong, happy relationships, however; high marital distress is correlated with a breakdown in these partner-serving attributions.)

Likewise, the 'illusion of unique invulnerability' (Perloff & Fetzer, 1986) turns out not to be as unique as first thought. Although people are more extremely and unrealistically optimistic about themselves than about some vague target such as the average person, they are equally optimistic about their closest friends and family members. That is, they think that bad things are not as likely to happen either to themselves or to their close friends as to strangers or to a hypothetical average person.[3] Along the same lines, Brown (1986) showed that people (particularly those with high self-esteem) tend to extend self-serving biases to their friends. Specifically, people rate both self and a same-sex friends more favourably than they rate people in general.

Group memberships also appear to exert important influences on cognitive patterns. People expect more favourable and fewer objectionable actions by their ingroup than by outgroup members, and these expectations bias information processing and memory, leading people to forget the bad things (relative to good things) that their fellow ingroup members do (Howard & Rothbart, 1980). People also make group-serving or 'sociocentric' attributions for the performance of the groups to which they belong. Members of a successful group may make group-serving attributions that put the entire group in a good light, whereas, after failure, group members may join together in absolving one another of responsibility (Forsyth & Schlenker, 1977; Leary & Forsyth, 1987; Zander, 1971).

Linville and Jones (1980) showed that people tend to process information about outgroup members in extreme, black-and-white, simplistic, polarized ways, whereas similar information about members of their own group is processed in a more complex fashion. Thus, the mere existence of a social bond leads to more complex (and sometimes more biased) information processing.

· · ·

Conclusion

Concern with belongingness appears to be a powerful factor shaping human thought. People interpret situations and events with regard to their implications for relationships, and they think more thoroughly about relationship (and interaction) partners than about other people. Moreover, the special patterns of processing information about the self are sometimes used for information about relationship partners as well. Thus, both actual and potential bonds exert substantial effects on how people think.

Emotion

The main emotional implication of the belongingness hypothesis is that real, potential, or imagined changes in one's belongingness status will produce emotional responses, with positive affect linked to increases in belongingness and negative affect linked to decreases in it. Also, stable or chronic conditions of high belongingness should produce a general abundance of positive affect, whereas chronic deprivation should produce a tendency toward abundant negative affect.

Positive Affect

In general, the formation of social bonds is associated with positive emotions. Perhaps the prototype of relationship formation is the experience of falling in love, which is typically marked by periods of intense bliss and joy, at least if the love is mutual (e.g., Steinberg, 1986). When love arises without belongingness, as in unrequited love, the result is typically distress and disappointment (Baumeister & Wotman, 1992). Belongingness is thus crucial if love is to produce bliss.

Likewise, occasions such as new employment, childbirth, fraternity or sorority pledging, and religious conversion, all of which are based on the entry into new relationships and the formation of new social bonds, are typically marked by positive emotions and celebrated as joyous. Childbirth is especially significant in this regard because the

data show that parenthood reduces happiness and increases stress, strain, and marital dissatisfaction (e.g., Anderson, Russell, & Schumm, 1983; Campbell, Converse, & Rodgers, 1976; Glenn & McLanahan, 1982; for reviews, see Baumeister, 1991; Bernard, 1982; Campbell, 1981; Spanier & Lewis, 1980), yet people nonetheless retain a positive image of it, celebrate it, and feel positive about it, both in advance and in retrospect. It is plausible that the formation of the new social bond is directly responsible for the joy and positive feelings, whereas the negative aspects and feelings associated with parenthood arise indirectly from the hassles, conflicts, and stresses that accompany the social bond.

If the formation of bonds is one occasion for joy, a second occasion comes when the bond is formalized into a more recognizably permanent status. A wedding, for example, does not create a new relationship, at least in modern Western cultures, because the bride and groom typically have known each other intimately for some time. The wedding does, however, signify an increase in commitment to maintaining the relationship permanently, and the joyful celebration of the wedding can be regarded as an affective consequence of solidifying the social bond. It is noteworthy that many traditional wedding vows include an actuarially implausible pledge that the marriage will never end ('till death do us part'). In essence, such vows are an institutionalized mechanism for committing people to meet their spouse's belongingness needs.

Although we have emphasized the view of affect as a result of attachment, positive affect may in turn help solidify social attachment. Probably the most influential view of this sort was developed by Shaver et al. (1988), who portrayed romantic love as a kind of glue designed by nature to solidify the attachment between two adults whose interaction is likely to lead to parenting. In their view, love elaborates on sexual attraction in a way that will hold the couple together when their sexual intercourse leads to reproduction. Along the same lines, various studies have found that positive affective experiences increase attraction and solidify social bonds (Clark & Watson, 1988; Gouaux, 1971; May & Hamilton, 1980; Veitch & Griffitt, 1976). Moreland (1987) concluded that the development of shared emotions is one of the principal causes of the formation of small groups.

More generally, happiness in life is strongly correlated with having some close personal relationships. Research suggests that it does not seem to make a great deal of difference what sort of relationship one has, but the absence of close social bonds is strongly linked to unhappiness, depression, and other woes (e.g., Argyle, 1987; Freedman, 1978; Myers, 1992). People with high levels of intimacy motivation tend to enjoy higher levels of happiness and subjective well-being (McAdams & Bryant, 1987), which is likely a result of their tendency to form and maintain a rich network of friendships and other social bonds (McAdams, 1985). Having some intimate bond appears to be important and perhaps even necessary for happiness. Social isolation is practically incompatible with high levels of happiness.

Negative Affect

Threats to social attachments, especially the dissolution of social bonds, are a primary source of negative affect. People feel anxious at the prospect of losing important relationships, feel depressed or grief stricken when their connections with certain other people are severed, and feel lonely when they lack important relationships (Leary, 1990; Leary & Downs, 1995; Tambor & Leary, 1993).

Anxiety is often regarded as the extreme or prototype of negative affect, and it is clearly linked to damaged, lost, or threatened social bonds. In fact, social exclusion may well be the most common and important cause of anxiety (Baumeister & Tice, 1990). Horney (1945) identified the source of 'basic anxiety' as the feeling of 'being isolated and helpless in a potentially hostile world' (p. 41); of course, that formula mixes two different sources, insofar as isolation is a function of

the belongingness need, whereas helplessness is a frustration of control (which is probably another fundamental motivation). Anxiety and general distress seem to be a natural consequence of being separated from important others. Children as young as one year old show extreme distress—separation anxiety—on being separated from their mothers (Bowlby, 1973), and adults show similar reactions when they must leave loved ones for an extended period of time. Furthermore, people's memories of past rejections are tainted with anxiety (Tambor & Leary, 1993), and even just imagining social rejection increases physiological arousal (Craighead, Kimball, & Rehak, 1979).

Consistent with the social exclusion theory of anxiety, Barden, Garber, Leiman, Ford, and Masters (1985) found that anxiety ensues if people are excluded from social groups, but experiences of social inclusion appear to counteract the effects of exclusion and remove the anxiety. Mathes, Adams, and Davies (1985) predicted that a threat to self-esteem would mediate the link between jealousy and anxiety, but their results did not support their hypothesis. Instead, they found that the loss of relationship led directly to anxiety.

Like anxiety, depression may be precipitated by a variety of events, but failing to feel accepted or included is certainly one of them. Both general depression and social depression (i.e., dysphoria about the nature of one's social relationships) are inversely related to the degree to which one feels included and accepted by others (Tambor & Leary, 1993). Hoyle and Crawford (1994) found that both depression and anxiety were significantly correlated (negatively) with students' sense of belonging to their university.

Jealousy is another negative affective state that is a common response to threats to one's relationships. Pines and Aronson (1983) reported that, in a series of surveys, some experience of jealousy was essentially universal, in the sense that everyone experiences it sooner or later. Moreover, more than half of their respondents described themselves as being 'a jealous person' and correctly estimated that slightly more than half of the other partici-pants would respond in that same way; however, they also said that the true incidence of jealous people was even higher, because some jealous people deny their jealousy. Pines and Aronson emphasized that 'feeling excluded' is a major cause of jealousy.

Regarding jealousy, perhaps the most relevant finding for our purposes was that of Reiss (1986), who concluded that jealousy is cross-culturally universal. Reiss carefully investigated the extrava-gant claims made by some observers and anthro-pologists that, in certain cultures, people are able to exchange sexual partners and intimate partners without any possessiveness or jealousy, and in every case the claim turned out to be unwarranted. Cultures may indeed vary as to which particular actions or signs of affection are regarded as justify-ing jealous reactions, and they may differ in how people express their jealousy, but sexual jealousy is found in all cultures.

Loneliness reflects 'an individual's subjective perception of deficiencies in his or her social rela-tionships' (Russell, Cutrona, Rose, & Yurko, 1984, p. 1313). In other words, people feel lonely when their belongingness needs are being insufficiently met. Moreover, it appears that belongingness, rather than mere social contact, is the crucial fac-tor. Mere social contact does not, by itself, buffer people against loneliness. Lonely and non-lonely people do not differ markedly in the amount of time they spend with other people. However, lonely people spend less time with friends and family—those who are most likely to fulfill their needs to belong—than non-lonely people (Jones, 1981). Furthermore, loneliness is much more strongly related to one's sense of social isolation than to objective indexes of one's social network, such as one's sheer number of friends (Williams & Solano, 1983). In one study, the correlation between self-reported loneliness and the degree to which people felt included and accepted by others was found to be −0.71 (Spivey, 1990). Generally, loneliness seems to be a matter more of a lack of intimate connections than of a lack of social con-tact (Reis, 1990; Wheeler, Reis, & Nezlek, 1983).

Yet another highly aversive emotional state is guilt. Despite a long tradition of analyzing guilt in terms of self-evaluation according to abstract moral standards, recent work has increasingly empha-sized the interpersonal structure of guilt (Baumeis-ter, Stillwell, & Heatherton, 1994; Cunningham, Steinberg, & Grev, 1980; Jones & Kugler, 1992; Jones, Kugler, & Adams, 1995; Miceli, 1992; Tang-ney, 1992). Empirical studies of how people induce guilt in others have found that such inductions are almost entirely confined to close interpersonal relationships and that a major reason for inducing guilt is to cause one's partner to exert himself or herself more to maintain the interpersonal rela-tionship (e.g., by spending more time with or pay-ing more attention to oneself; Baumeister, Stillwell, & Heatherton, 1995; Vangelisti, Daly, & Rudnick, 1991). Many episodes of guilt can thus be under-stood as responses to disturbances or threats to interpersonal attachments.

. . .

Conclusion

Many of the strongest emotions people experience, both positive and negative, are linked to belong-ingness. Evidence suggests a general conclusion that being accepted, included, or welcomed leads to a variety of positive emotions (e.g., happiness, elation, contentment, and calm), whereas being rejected, excluded, or ignored leads to potent nega-tive feelings (e.g., anxiety, depression, grief, jeal-ousy, and loneliness).

Although the evidence was not equally abun-dant or equally strong for all emotions, the con-sistency across multiple emotions was impressive. It seems quite safe to conclude that both positive and negative emotional reactions are pervasively linked to relationship status. The existence of an interpersonal bond changes the way one responds emotionally to the performances and actions of a relationship partner and indeed intensifies many emotional reactions. Moreover, actual or possible changes in belongingness status constitute an important cause of emotions. The evidence is sufficiently broad and consistent to suggest that one of the basic functions of emotion is to regulate behaviour so as to form and maintain social bonds.

Consequences of Deprivation

The general argument is that deprivation of belongingness should lead to a variety of affiliative behaviours and cause various undesirable effects, including decrements in health, happiness, and adjustment. We have already documented (in the preceding section) that loss of social bonds causes emotional distress, which is sufficient to show that belongingness is something people want. To regard it as a need, however, it is necessary to show effects that go beyond mere frustration and emotional distress.

Considerable research shows that people who do not have adequate supportive relationships experience greater stress than those who do. In part, this is because having other people available for support and assistance can enhance coping and provide a buffer against stress. However, evidence suggests that simply being part of a supportive social network reduces stress, even if other people do not provide explicit emotional or practical assistance (Cohen & Wills, 1985). Although this finding has been interpreted in terms of the stress-reducing effects of social support, an equally plausible explanation is that the deprivation of the need to belong is inherently stressful.

Direct evidence that deprivation of belongingness is maladaptive was provided by DeLongis, Folkman, and Lazarus (1988). They found that happily married couples were less likely to experience psychological and somatic health problems, both on and after stressful days, than other participants. Medical research has suggested that these beneficial effects extend beyond mere health complaints. Lynch (1979) summarized the evidence from many studies by stating that 'U.S. mortality rates for all causes of death . . . are consistently higher for divorced, single, and widowed

individuals' than for married individuals (p. 38). Lynch's own data showed the greater incidence of fatal heart attacks among unattached individuals than among married people, but he noted that similar effects can be found for tuberculosis, cancer, and many other illnesses, as well as overall patterns. Of course, there are multiple possible explanations for such an effect that might have nothing to do with belongingness, but efforts to control for these variables have often found a persistent, independent, robust effect of social relations. Goodwin, Hunt, Key, and Samet (1987) found that married participants survived cancer better than single ones even after the timing of diagnosis, likelihood of receiving treatment, and cigarette smoking had been controlled, and they cited other evidence that the effect remains after family income has been controlled.

Indeed, being deprived of belongingness may have direct effects on the immune system. Kiecolt-Glaser, Garner, et al. (1984) found that loneliness was associated with a decrease in immunocompetence, specifically in natural killer cell activity, and this effect was independent of changes in perceived distress. Kiecolt-Glaser, Ricker, et al. (1984) replicated this effect and also found elevated urinary cortisol levels among lonely participants. Kiecolt-Glaser et al. (1987) found poorer immune function on several measures among women suffering from marital disruption, including divorce, separation, and unhappy marriage.

The effects of belongingness on mental illness parallel those on physical illness. Rejected children have a higher incidence of psychopathology than other children (Bhatti, Derezotes, Kim, & Specht, 1989; Hamachek, 1992). Children who grow up without receiving adequate attention from caregivers show emotional and behavioural pathologies, as demonstrated experimentally by Harlow, Harlow, and Suomi (1971) with animals and as corroborated by observations of human children by Bowlby (1969, 1973; see also Rutter, 1979).[4]

Marital status also has strong correlations with mental illness. Bloom, White, and Asher (1979) reviewed the literature and concluded that, in all studies, mental hospital admission rates are highest among divorced and separated people, intermediate among never-married people, and lowest among married people. In fact, as measured by admissions to mental hospitals,[5] mental illness is at least three and possibly up to 22 times higher among divorced people than among married people.

Even problems that might at first seem unrelated to social interaction and relationships are sometimes found to have social deprivation or failed belongingness as an underlying cause. Problems with attachment have been identified as a major factor in eating disorders. Sours (1974), for example, noted that patients with eating disorders tended to have been (as children) overly sensitive to separation from their mothers. Armstrong and Roth (1989) found that women with eating disorders had significantly more intense and severe separation and attachment difficulties than a normal comparison group.

Combat-related stress is also moderated by belongingness. Veterans who perceive that they have a high degree of social support are significantly less likely to experience post-traumatic stress disorder than those who have lower perceived support (Hobfall & London, 1986; Solomon, Waysman, & Mikulincer, 1990). In fact, the authors of one study concluded that loneliness 'is the most direct antecedent of psychopathology and social dysfunction' in combat stress reactions (Solomon et al., 1990, p. 468).

. . .

The benefits of social support appear to be well established. Thus, for example, Cohen, Sherrod, and Clark (1986) showed that the availability of social support—which can be restated as the existence of social bonds—buffers people against the ill effects of stress. Cutrona (1989) showed that social support reduced depression during pregnancy and postpartum depression among adolescent girls. Responding to methodological criticisms that had attacked social support research as merely self-report bias, Cutrona's study included ratings

of each girl's support network by an adult informant who knew the girls well, and these external informants' ratings predicted health outcomes (in some cases, even better than the girls' own ratings of their support). Thus, the benefits of belongingness in coping with major life stress appear to go beyond mere self-report bias.

Older adults who have a close, intimate friend (i.e., a 'confidant') maintain higher morale in the face of life stresses such as retirement and spousal death than individuals who lack such a relationship. For example, Lowenthal and Haven (1968) found that widows who have a confidant have been found to be only slightly more depressed than married women, whereas those without a confidant have been found to be much more dysphoric. These researchers also found that the majority of older adults who recently lost a confidant were depressed, but the majority who currently had a confidant were satisfied.

Rook (1987b) distinguished between social support and companionship. Social support was in this case rather narrowly interpreted in terms of direct help, whereas companionship meant the expressive aspects of social interaction. Both were found to be important and beneficial, but companionship may be the more important of the two, especially for psychological well-being, social satisfaction, and coping with minor stress. These data are particularly important for the relevance of social support research to the belongingness hypothesis because one could conceivably argue that belongingness per se is irrelevant and that the practical, material help that people derive from their social networks is solely responsible for the benefits of social support. Rook's data suggested, on the contrary, that the practical help is secondary (except in extreme circumstances in which major assistance is needed), whereas belongingness is highly beneficial by itself.

Perhaps most generally, general well-being and happiness in life depend on having some close social ties. Social isolation is strongly related to various patterns of unhappiness (for reviews, see

Argyle, 1987; Baumeister, 1991; Freedman, 1978; Myers, 1992). Indeed, Baumeister (1991) noted that it is about the only objective factor that shows a substantial correlation with subjective well-being. Happiness also appears to be fairly stable across time and circumstance (e.g., Costa, McCrae, & Zonderman, 1987), leading many to conclude that it is linked to personality factors. The broad trait of extraversion appears to be strongly related to happiness and positive affectivity (see Costa & McCrae, 1980, 1984), and extraversion encompasses several factors, such as sociability, gregariousness, warmth, and social involvement, that seem likely to enhance the tendency to form and maintain social ties. Moreover, belongingness appears to be sufficient to overcome the relative deficit in happiness that introverts suffer. Hotard, McFatter, McWhirter, and Stegall (1989) found that introverts who have a good network of social relationships are just as happy as extraverts. Thus, introverts' deficit in happiness may be a result of their experiencing less belongingness.

Further support for the importance of belongingness to psychological well-being is provided by the fact that the psychotherapeutic process is facilitated by close personal bonds. Numerous therapeutic orientations stress the importance of the relationship between the therapist and the client. Rogers (1959), for example, urged psychotherapists to display a willingness to accept and support the client regardless of his or her behaviour or contribution to the relationship. Such 'unconditional positive regard' is perhaps the ultimate way to fulfill another person's belongingness needs. From the standpoint of the belongingness hypothesis, however, the essential ingredient in client-centred therapy is not unconditional positive regard (i.e., appraisal) but unconditional social acceptance (i.e., belongingness).[6]

Furthermore, some have suggested that one goal of psychotherapy should be enhance clients' ability to elicit social support in their everyday lives (Brehm, 1987). To the extent that people who have strong connections with others are happier,

healthier, and better able to cope with the stresses of everyday life, most clients would presumably benefit from enhancing their belongingness.

The psychotherapeutic usefulness of belonging can also be seen in the effectiveness of group therapy. As Lewin (1951) flatly stated, 'It is easier to change individuals formed into a group than to change them separately' (p. 228). In part, the effectiveness of group therapy seems to depend on engendering a sense of belongingness, as some authors have asserted (Larkin, 1972; Yalom, 1985). Forsyth (1991), in his review of research on group therapy, observed that therapeutic groups provide the member 'with a sense of belonging, protection from harm, and acceptance' (p. 675).

People differ, of course, in the degree to which they believe that their belongingness needs are being met irrespective of the extensiveness of their social networks or the strength of social support they receive. Lakey and Cassady (1990) provided data suggesting that perceived social support operates much like a cognitive schema. People have relatively stable, organized beliefs about the extent and quality of their interpersonal relationships. These belief systems lead to biased interpretation of social interactions, as well as to a biased recall of past interpersonal events. As a result, some people have a predisposition to perceive others as unsupportive, leading them to experience belongingness deprivation even when others are in fact being supportive.

Critical Assessment

The diversity of methodologies and the multiplicity of disciplines that have furnished the evidence reviewed in this section make it highly implausible to suggest that all such evidence can be explained away as the result of confounds or artifacts. At worst, some of the findings have alternate explanations. Not all studies have maintained careful distinctions between the pragmatic benefits of certain relationships and the direct benefits of belongingness. The fact that happily married people commit fewer crimes than other adults, for example, might be partly (or even wholly) due to the material benefits of being married. Even so, researchers who have maintained such distinctions (such as several of the social support researchers) have found pragmatic benefits to be a secondary factor. Belongingness thus has important and direct benefits.

A more serious limitation is that several of the findings are correlational. The higher rates of mental and physical illness among loners could reflect a tendency for people to reject deviants as potential relationship partners. By the same token, the higher levels of life satisfaction found among happily married people could be partly due to a tendency for chronically unhappy people to be rejected as marriage partners. Still, those studies that have provided evidence about the direction of causality have consistently identified belongingness as the causal factor.

Conclusion

Deprivation of stable, good relationships has been linked to a large array of aversive and pathological consequences. People who lack belongingness suffer higher levels of mental and physical illness and are relatively highly prone to a broad range of behavioural problems, ranging from traffic accidents to criminality to suicide. Some of these findings may be subject to alternative explanations, and for some the direction of causality has not been established; however, the weight of evidence suggests that lack of belongingness is a primary cause of multiple and diverse problems. It therefore seems appropriate to regard belongingness as a need rather than simply a want.

. . .

Innateness, Universality, and Evolutionary Perspectives

We proposed that a fundamental need would presumably be innate, which would entail that it is found in all human beings and is not derivative of other motives. This will, of course, be quite difficult to verify, because empirical criteria for testing such a hypothesis are not widely recognized. One

approach, however, would be to examine how well the empirical evidence conforms to evolutionary arguments. If evolution has instilled the motivation, then it is presumably universal among human beings and will be present in each person without needing to be derived from other motives.

Barchas (1986) has asserted that 'over the course of evolution, the small group became the basic survival strategy developed by the human species' (p. 212). He went on to suggest that the brain and small groups evolved and adapted together, with multiple interrelationships. The evidence reviewed by Barchas remains preliminary, but it does seem that any link between brain structures and small-group formation would strengthen the case for an innate motivation.

Although the psychobiological systems involved in social attachment are not yet well understood, early evidence implicates the brain opioid system. According to Panksepp, Siviy, and Normansell (1985), both the tendency to form social bonds and the emotional effects of social loss (e.g., sadness or grief) are mediated by opioids. The formation and validation of relationships apparently stimulate opioid production, whereas the dissolution of relationships impedes it. As Panksepp et al. put it, 'social affect and social bonding are in some fundamental neurochemical sense opioid addictions' (p. 25). Thus, in their view, the tendency to seek social connections with others is based not only on the secondary reinforcements that other people provide but on psychophysiological mechanisms as well.

Multiple evolutionary reasons could be suggested for the readiness to form groups easily. Groups can share labour, resources, and information; diffuse risk; and co-operate to overcome stress or threat (Hogan et al., 1985). Defence against rival groups would also be a significant factor: If other people form into groups, lone individuals would be at a competitive disadvantage in many situations, and so evolution may have selected for people who would form groups defensively. Hence, the evolutionary argument would fit any evidence that group formation or cohesion patterns are increased by external threat.

It has long been noted that external threats increase group cohesion, and some writers have treated this as axiomatic. Stein (1976) reviewed these views in light of the evidence and found that a broad variety of methods have yielded generally consistent findings; that is, external threats do increase cohesion most of the time. There are some circumstances in which groups disintegrate under threat, especially if the threat pertains only to some members of the group or if group members must compete against each other to survive the threat (e.g., if there are too few lifeboats). Staw, Sandelands, and Dutton (1981) also found evidence that group cohesion is sometimes weakened in the aftermath of a threat, especially if the group has failed to defeat the threat and the group members blame each other. Apart from these circumscribed exceptions, however, it is safe to conclude that external threats do generally increase group cohesion.

A remarkable demonstration of the power of external threat to forge lasting bonds was provided by Elder and Clipp's (1988) study of World War II veterans' groups. In Elder and Clipp's results, the effects of maximum threat were discernible 40 years later. That is, four decades after the war, the most enduring and strongest ties were found among veterans who had experienced heavy combat together and had suffered the deaths of some close comrades. Units that had experienced combat without fatalities were less close 40 years later, but they retained stronger ties than the units that had not been in combat together. In other words, the sharing of military experience provided some lasting bonds, these bonds were intensified by shared experience of combat, and they were especially strong if it had been heavy combat that had killed some members of the group. It seems clear that there would be survival benefits to a pattern in which the death of a group member strengthened the ties among the survivors, especially in the face of external danger.

The group formation effects in the Robbers Cave study (described earlier; Sherif et al., 1961/1988) accelerated rapidly after the mutual discovery of the existence of the two rival groups; that is, the implicit threat posed by the opposing group seemed to motivate each boy to cling to his own group more strongly. Similar processes have been observed in terrorist groups, which mainly become cohesive in the face of external threat and danger. During periods when the conflict with outsiders lapses, terrorist groups experience internal dissent and conflict and may fall apart (see McCauley & Segal, 1987).

Compelling evidence in favour of emphasizing the competitive disadvantage motive for affiliating was provided by Hoyle, Pinkley, and Insko (1989). These researchers noted the irony that encounters between individuals are generally pleasant and supportive, whereas encounters between groups are frequently unpleasant and confrontational, and their first study confirmed these general expectations and stereotypes empirically. In their second study, they sought to determine the decisive factor by comparing interactions between persons, between groups, and between one person and one group. To their surprise, they found that participants' expectations about the interaction were determined mainly by the other party rather than by participants' own belongingness status. When participants expected to interact with a group, they expected an abrasive interaction; when they expected to interact with an individual, they anticipated a pleasant, agreeable interaction. Identical effects were found regardless of whether the participant expected to be alone or to be part of a group. Thus, apparently, the presence of an outgroup causes people to anticipate conflict and problematic interactions. Such an expectation could well elicit a motivation to form a group to protect oneself.

A similar conclusion was suggested by Lauderdale, Smith-Cunnien, Parker, and Inverarity (1984). Following Schachter's (1951) studies on group rejection of deviants, they found that increasing an external threat led to increased rejection. The implication was that groups become increasingly oriented toward solidarity when confronted with an external threat.

Apart from threat, the possibility of gaining resources also seems to trigger group cohesion, even when it is functionally irrelevant. Rabbie and Horwitz (1969) assigned participants randomly to two groups. The random assignment alone yielded no effects of group cohesion on their measures of ingroup preference, but they did find significant effects after a manipulation in which one group was given a prize (a transistor radio) based on a coin flip. The rewarded group and the deprived group both showed increased ingroup preference. The prize was logically irrelevant to subsequent group activities and preferences. The implication is apparently that the combination of limited resources and multiple groups triggers an ingroup preference response that has no apparent practical or rational basis, which is consistent with the view that it is a deeply rooted and possibly innate tendency rather than a strategic or rational choice.

Critical Assessment
The evidence linking external threat to increased group cohesion is convincing but does not prove an evolutionary hypothesis of innateness or universality. The evidence for brain mechanisms is likewise supportive but inadequate to prove innateness. The evidence in this section is perhaps best described by stating that the evolutionary hypothesis nicely survived several tests that could have contradicted it.

Conclusion
Several patterns seem consistent with evolutionary reasoning. It remains plausible (but unproven) that the need to belong is part of the human biological inheritance. If so, the case for universality and non-derivativeness would be strong. At present, it seems fair to accept these hypotheses as tentative working assumptions while waiting for further evidence.

Apparent Counterexamples
Although the evidence presented thus far has been largely supportive of the belongingness hypothesis, one might object that our literature search has been structured in ways that predisposed it toward just such favourable indications. It is therefore desirable to examine behavioural patterns that would seemingly constitute boundary conditions or counterexamples to the need to belong. This section briefly considers several.

Refusal to Help or Co-operate
People generally show a significant willingness to help others, but often there may be self-interested motives lurking behind the apparent altruism (e.g., Cialdini, Darby, & Vincent, 1973; Manucia, Baumann, & Cialdini, 1984). To be sure, in many cases people appear to put self-interest ahead of the welfare of others, leading them to disdain opportunities for helping others or co-operating. Entering into the long-running debate about the possibility and reality of truly altruistic behaviour is beyond the scope of this article; our goal is merely to ask whether such cases do indeed contradict the belongingness hypothesis. In particular, it is necessary to ask whether these non-helpful, non-co-operative behaviour patterns are reduced or eliminated by belongingness.

One of social psychology's best-known findings concerns the unhelpfulness of multiple bystanders at an emergency site. As Darley and Latané's (1968) study and many subsequent investigations (see Latané & Nida, 1981) showed, people tend not to come to the aid of an emergency victim when many other people are also present. Among the reasons for the bystander effect are the sense that it is not one's own responsibility to help and the fear that helping may bring negative consequences to the self. Various findings suggest, however, that belongingness can overcome the non-responsiveness of bystanders. The bystander effect is apparently robust among strangers (e.g., Darley & Latané, 1968), but in cohesive groups, the opposite pattern is found, namely that larger groups produce more helping (Rutkowski, Gruder, & Romer, 1983). Even the mere anticipation of future interaction among group members is enough to eliminate the bystander effect, making group members quite willing and likely to come to each other's aid (Gottlieb & Carver, 1980).

Social loafing is another pattern in which people put self-interest ahead of co-operative concern for others (e.g., Latané, Williams, & Harkins, 1979). In social loafing, people reduce their efforts when submerged in the group, thereby gaining benefits of the group success without having to exert themselves maximally. Group membership can foster a sense of duty or obligation that can effectively override tendencies to engage in social loafing, however. Harkins and Petty (1982) showed that if people believe that they can make a unique contribution to the group, they do not engage in social loafing, even if individual contributions to the group will not be identified (and thus even if they will not receive credit for their contribution; see also Hardy & Grace, 1991).

The prisoner's dilemma game has been widely used to examine how people choose between a self-interested, individualistic (competitive) response and a co-operative response that can potentially maximize everyone's collective outcomes at the cost or risk of individual vulnerability to loss. Once again, the presence or apparent possibility of social attachments seems to shift people away from the self-oriented mode toward a more co-operative, collectively beneficial mode of response. The expectation of future interaction increases helpful co-operation in the prisoner's dilemma game, although this effect appears to obtain mainly among high self-monitors (Danheiser & Graziano, 1982). The opportunity to meet and talk with strangers appears to be sufficient to alter responses to a subsequent prisoner's dilemma game in favour of increased co-operation and decreased exploitation–defensiveness (Orbell et al., 1988).

Lastly, the commons dilemma (in which people deplete renewable resources for short-term individual gain) is another pattern in which people typically seek personal advantage at the expense of long-range collective welfare. The commons dilemma also can be reduced or overcome by belongingness, however. Kramer and Brewer (1984) showed that when belongingness is stimulated by making the group identity salient, people are more likely to restrain their self-interested tendencies and instead co-operate with others for the greater good of the group.

More generally, helping appears to be increased by the existence of social bonds. Schoenrade, Batson, Brandt, and Loud (1986) found that the existence of a social relationship increases the motivation for helping. In the absence of a relationship, people help only for egoistic reasons (i.e., self-interest); when a relationship exists, however, people will help for relatively selfless, altruistic reasons (see also Toi & Batson, 1982). Even among strangers, familiarity leads to increased helping, as does a sense of interpersonal dependency (Pearce, 1980). The fact that belongingness can overcome self-interested patterns is shown by evidence that people prefer reciprocity in social exchange to the extent that even over-benefited individuals sometimes feel uncomfortable and distressed even though material self-interest is maximally served under conditions of being over-benefited (Rook, 1987a). The concern with equity and with aiding others is further indicated by the occasionally negative responses of would-be helpers to having their helpful efforts spurned by the intended recipients (e.g., Rosen, Mickler, & Collins, 1987).

Throughout this article, we have suggested that the need to belong may be biologically prepared. Evidence with animal species is therefore relevant here. Masserman, Wechkin, and Terris (1964) taught rhesus monkeys to pull a chain for food and then, in one condition, added the contingency that pulling the chain would cause a shock to be delivered to another monkey. Most monkeys refrained from pulling the chain under those conditions, even to the extent of starving themselves for several days rather than cause another monkey to be shocked. These patterns were particularly strong when the two animals had previously been cage-mates and thus may be presumed to have formed some sort of bond; when the animals were strangers to each other, less than a third showed this form of altruistic, self-sacrificing behaviour.

Non-Reciprocation of Love

Although mutual love provides strong satisfactions and hedonic benefits, there are many cases in which people do not reciprocate another's affection and romantic interest. Such refusals to form a social bond might be taken as evidence against the belongingness hypothesis.

On closer examination, however, inspection of patterns of unrequited love does not provide a serious challenge to the belongingness hypothesis, for several reasons. First, most people do want to form a close romantic relationship, and their refusals are typically based on either already having such a relationship with another partner (consistent with the satiation hypothesis) or perceiving the aspiring partner as unsuitable for some reason, such as unattractiveness or incompatibility. Moreover, in many cases, rejectors experience considerable distress such as guilt and empathic pain when rejecting another's offer of love. This distress is consistent with the view that rejecting social attachment goes against some deeply rooted aspect of human nature, even when the person is quite certain that he or she does not want this particular attachment (Baumeister & Wotman, 1992; Baumeister et al., 1993).

Shyness

Shy behaviour patterns may seem antisocial insofar as the shy person sometimes avoids social encounters, withdraws from ongoing interactions, and acts in other ways that reduce the chances of forming relationships (Leary, 1983). In fact, however, shy people are strongly motivated to form relationships, and shyness may reflect an interpersonal strategy that partially protects the individual against rejection.

When people do not believe that they will be regarded in ways that will result in social acceptance, they may avoid absolute rejection by disaffiliating. Although reticence and withdrawal are unlikely to make particularly good impressions or to bring hearty acceptance from others, they reduce the risk of saying or doing something that others might regard negatively. When one fears rejection, the best tactic may seem to be to participate as little as possible, thereby giving others few reasons to reject one (Shepperd & Arkin, 1990).

At the same time that they pull back, however, shy people engage in behaviours that have been characterized as 'innocuously sociable' (Leary, 1983). They smile more (even though they feel anxious rather than happy), nod their heads more in agreement, ask more questions, and use more verbal reinforcers when others are speaking. These behaviours may reflect last-resort tactics to maintain a minimum degree of interpersonal connection in otherwise difficult or threatening encounters (Leary, Knight, & Johnson, 1987).

General Discussion

We have considered a broad assortment of evidence pertaining to the hypothesis that the desire for interpersonal attachments—the need to belong—is a fundamental human motivation. Most of the metatheoretical requirements we outlined for evaluating such a hypothesis appear to be satisfied, although some issues remain. We begin by reviewing the major conclusions.

Again and again, we found evidence of a basic desire to form social attachments. People form social bonds readily, even under seemingly adverse conditions. People who have anything in common, who share common (even unpleasant) experiences, or who simply are exposed to each other frequently tend to form friendships or other attachments. Moreover, people resist losing attachments and breaking social bonds, even if there is no material or pragmatic reason to maintain the bond and even if maintaining it would be difficult.

Abundant evidence also attests that the need to belong shapes emotion and cognition. Forming or solidifying social attachments generally produces positive emotion, whereas real, imagined, or even potential threats to social bonds generate a variety of unpleasant emotional states. In short, change in belongingness is a strong and pervasive cause of emotion in ways that support the hypothesis of a need to belong. It is also evident that people think a great deal about belongingness. They devote a disproportionate amount of cognitive processing to actual or possible relationship partners and interaction partners, and they reserve particular, more extensive, and more favourable patterns of information processing for people with whom they share social bonds.

Deficits in belongingness apparently lead to a variety of ill effects, consistent with the view that belongingness is a need (as opposed to merely a want). Both psychological and physical health problems are more common among people who lack social attachments. Behavioural pathologies, ranging from eating disorders to suicide, are more common among people who are unattached. Although most of these findings are correlational and many alternative explanations can be suggested, recent efforts have begun controlling for these other factors, and the pure, primary effects of belongingness appear to remain strong. It appears, then, that belongingness is not only pleasant but also apparently very beneficial to the individual in multiple ways.

We proposed two aspects of the need to belong, and both appear to be important. That is, people seem to need frequent, affectively pleasant or positive interactions with the same individuals, and they need these interactions to occur in a framework of long-term, stable caring and concern. People who can satisfy one component but not the other tend to be less satisfied and less well off than people who can satisfy both, but they do seem to derive some benefits from satisfying the one component (as opposed to satisfying neither). More and better evidence is needed on this point, however; most evidence pertains to people who have the bond and lack interactions, rather than

the reverse. Also, it is unclear whether the interactions must be pleasant or can be satisfactory if they are merely neutral. The evidence suggests merely that aversive or conflictual interactions fail to satisfy the need. Some evidence suggests that a framework of mutual, reciprocal concern is best, but the effects and importance of mutuality need further investigation.

The need to belong also appears to conform to motivational patterns of satiation and substitution. People need a few close relationships, and forming additional bonds beyond those few has less and less impact. Having two as opposed to no close relationships may make a world of difference to the person's health and happiness; having eight as opposed to six may have very little consequence. When a social bond is broken, people appear to recover best if they form a new one, although each individual life tends to involve some particularly special relationships (such as filial or marital bonds) that are not easily replaced. People without intimate partners engage in a variety of activities to find partners, but people who have partners already are much less active at seeking additional relationships, consistent with the satiation hypothesis.

We reviewed evidence that the need to belong affects a broad variety of behaviours; indeed, the range is sufficiently broad as to render less plausible any notion that the need to belong is a product of certain other factors or motives. We also noted that evidence about belongingness seems to implicate some brain mechanisms and to conform to patterns that evolutionary theory would suggest, both of which seem consistent with the argument that the need is innate in humans. Still, the non-derivative hypothesis is probably the least well supported aspect of our theory, not because of any clear evidence deriving the need to belong from other motives, but simply, perhaps, because it is relatively difficult to collect compelling data to show that a motive is not derivative. The issue of which motives derive from which others appears to be an important challenge for future motivation research.

We also considered several counterexamples that at least superficially suggested tendencies to reject social attachment. On close inspection, these patterns did not stand up as counterexamples, and indeed there was generally strong evidence of a positive need to belong that increased the subjective difficulty of rejecting or avoiding attachment.

We conclude, then, that the present state of the empirical evidence is sufficient to confirm the belongingness hypothesis. The need to belong can be considered a fundamental human motivation.

. . .

Concluding Remarks

At present, it seems fair to conclude that human beings are fundamentally and pervasively motivated by a need to belong, that is, by a strong desire to form and maintain enduring interpersonal attachments. People seek frequent, affectively positive interactions within the context of long-term, caring relationships. As a speculative point of theory or impressionistic observation, the need to belong is not a new idea; indeed, we noted a variety of previous psychological theorists who have proposed it in one form or another. What is new, however, is the existence of a large body of empirical evidence with which to evaluate that hypothesis.

If psychology has erred with regard to the need to belong, in our view, the error has not been to deny the existence of such a motive so much as to underappreciate it. This review has shown multiple links between the need to belong and cognitive processes, emotional patterns, behavioural responses, and health and well-being. The desire for interpersonal attachment may well be one of the most far-reaching and integrative constructs currently available to understand human nature.

Notes

1. His later thinking may, however, have moved beyond this view to regard attachment needs as having a separate, even innate, basis rather than being derived from the contact with one's mother; in this later view, he treated the relationship to one's mother as simply an influential prototype of attachment.

2. A possible sex difference could be suggested in the mode of expressing this need, however, in that men may be more oriented toward forming relationships, whereas women may be more oriented toward maintaining them. Men can reproduce many times by forming many brief relationships, whereas women can reproduce only about once per year, and so their most effective reproductive strategy would be to enable each child to receive maximal care and attention (Buss, 1991).

3. Perloff and Fetzer (1986) favoured an interpretation for their results in terms of the vagueness of the comparison target over the motivational explanation that people want to regard their closest relationship partners as equally vulnerable (equal to themselves). This discrimination between the two hypotheses rested on the 'one of your friends' conditions in their second study: They found that the 'closest friend' was seen as being highly invulnerable, whereas when participants chose one of their other friends, this person was seen as more vulnerable. Their findings suggested that participants in that condition selected a friend who seemed most likely to have the problem asked about, so it is difficult to evaluate the motivational hypothesis. Thus, the interpretation emphasized here is consistent with all of Perloff and Fetzer's findings, as they acknowledged, even though their own interpretations tended to favour explanation in terms of vague versus specific targets.

4. Several studies have shown that physically unattractive people have a higher incidence of psychopathology than attractive people (e.g., Barocas & Vance, 1974; Cash, 1985; Farina, Burns, Austad, Bugglin, & Fischer, 1986; O'Grady, 1989). One reason may be that they lack belongingness, because society tends to reject unattractive individuals (Berscheid & Walster, 1974).

5. Admittedly, hospital admissions is an imprecise measure. One might object that married people can stay out of institutions because they have someone at home to take care of them. On the other hand, many people are admitted to such institutions at the behest of family members, and so one could argue that the true difference is even larger. Given the size and consistency of the effect, it seems reasonable to conclude that marital status is related to mental illness, although further and methodologically better evidence is needed.

6. The two overlap in many ways, of course. Cutrona (1986) has noted that esteem support is an important element of social support, particularly for helping people avoid depressive reactions to stressful events.

Discussion Questions

1. How do the authors operationalize the need to belong? What criteria must be met for the motivation for belongingness to be satisfied?
2. Why does the case for the need to belong need to be made?
3. Is belonging to a political/ideological movement really substitutable for interpersonal relationships, as Baumeister and Leary claim? Might the psychological benefit of joining a movement be as much about lending meaning to one's life as it is about belongingness?
4. Contrast the experience of satisfying one's belongingness needs with satisfying the need for distinctiveness proposed by Brewer's optimal distinctiveness theory (see the Pickett, Silver, & Brewer article that follows).
5. In recent years, people have increasingly taken to forming social bonds via virtual communities using tools such as Facebook and Twitter. Can the need to belong be satisfied entirely online? What are the differences, if any, between virtual and face-to-face social connection?

2. The Impact of Assimilation and Differentiation Needs on Perceived Group Importance and Judgments of Ingroup Size

Cynthia L. Pickett, University of Illinois at Urbana-Champaign
Michael D. Silver, Ohio State University
Marilynn B. Brewer, Ohio State University

□ ■ □

Editor's Introduction

Think back to your high school days. Did you ever notice that within each clique of non-conformists all members tended to dress the same, listen to the same music, and speak in the same slang? Perhaps you were in such a group of highly conforming nonconformists? This phenomenon cuts to the heart of a fundamental tension that humans must continually navigate: the motivation to be a part of a group versus the motivation to be a distinctive individual. This delicate balance between commonness and uniqueness informs a host of everyday choices ranging from of what clothes to wear to what words to use in conversation. Optimal distinctiveness theory, as proposed by Marilynn Brewer and colleagues (1991, 1993) articulates this tension and generates specific predictions about an individual's relationship with his or her group as well as intergroup relations. In this article, Pickett, Silver, and Brewer provide an elegant demonstration of how experiencing a deficit on either dimension (commonness or uniqueness) leads to motivated distortions of thought aimed at rectifying the problem and restoring the state of 'optimal distinctiveness'.

Optimal distinctiveness theory speaks to a prior influential theory, social identity theory (SIT; Abrams & Hogg, 1990; Tajfel, 1978). Proponents of SIT argue that a crucial part of one's self-concept is derived from one's group membership. This *social* aspect of one's identity is distinct from one's personal identity, which is derived from one's

idiosyncratic personality traits and relationships with other individuals. According to SIT, people experience higher self-esteem if they perceive that a group to which they belong is highly regarded. As such, people display motivated cognition aimed toward enhancing their group's standing. Interestingly, studies have shown that these effects apply even when the group is arbitrarily defined in the lab by experimenters, in what is known as the 'minimal groups' paradigm. For example, in one set of studies, participants guessed how many jelly beans were in a jar. The experimenters then randomly assigned participants to be told that they were in the group of underestimaters versus overestimaters. Even based on such trivial group distinctions, participants showed clear favouritism toward their own group and antipathy toward the other group.

While the Baumeister and Leary article in this Unit demonstrates the psychological necessity of group membership, Brewer and her colleagues have argued that there is such a thing as too much connection with one's group. Studies have shown that people 'fix' both too much commonness and too much uniqueness in a variety of creative ways. For example, Gardner, Pickett, and Brewer (2000) showed that people who had been rejected in an experimenter-engineered online chat room subsequently displayed better memory for explicitly social events. Similarly, Pickett, Bonner, and Coleman (2002) showed that some people who feel too distanced from their group will strategically increase their use of stereotypes about their own group to describe themselves (self-stereotyping).

In so doing, these researchers demonstrate some of the motivated biases in cognition that we will cover in more detail in Unit 5.

□ ■ □

According to optimal distinctiveness theory (ODT; Brewer, 1991), two fundamental motivations behind social identification exist—the need for assimilation and the need for differentiation. Social identities are selected and activated to the extent that they can satisfy these needs. Brewer (1991, 1993a, 1993b; Brewer & Pickett, 1999) points out that the need for assimilation and the need for differentiation work in opposition to each other. Thus, at high levels of group inclusiveness (i.e., groups that contain a large number of members), there will be very little arousal of the need for assimilation but high arousal of the need for differentiation. At very low levels of group inclusiveness, there will be very little arousal of the need for differentiation but high arousal of the need for assimilation. Movement toward extreme deindividuation of the self (which should be more likely for a member of a highly inclusive group) should activate the drive for differentiation, and movement toward extreme individuation should activate the need for assimilation.

According to Baumeister and Leary (1995), a fundamental human motivation should 'elicit goal-oriented behaviour designed to satisfy it' (p. 498). Integral to ODT (Brewer, 1991) is the idea that one way that humans go about satisfying their assimilation and differentiation needs is by identifying with social groups. Individuals seek social assimilation and group inclusion to alleviate or ward off the isolation or stigmatization that may result from being highly individuated. When we adopt a particular social identity, our sense of self is extended beyond the individual level. Self-categorization theorists have conceived of social identities as involving 'a shift towards the perception of self as an interchangeable exemplar of some social category and away from the perception of self as a unique person' (Turner, Hogg, Oakes, Reicher, & Wetherell, 1987, p. 50). Because social identification involves this type of depersonalization, where one's sense of self is defined by group memberships, social identities can provide individuals with a sense of connection with others. For this reason, group memberships are hypothesized to play an important role in the satisfaction of the need for assimilation.

At the same time, social identities are important for the satisfaction of the need for differentiation. When individuals define themselves in terms of their category memberships, they establish a ready basis for distinguishing themselves from others. A psychologist who categorizes himself or herself as a social psychologist can meet his or her need for differentiation via intergroup comparisons; for example, distinguishing social psychologists from cognitive and clinical psychologists. This example suggests that the need for differentiation can be satisfied in two ways: (a) making intragroup distinctions, that is, dividing an overly inclusive category into more exclusive subgroups and categorizing oneself in terms of a smaller subgroup, and (b) making intergroup comparisons between one's ingroup and an outgroup. Given the importance of intergroup comparisons for individuals' sense of distinctiveness, social identities are as essential for the satisfaction of differentiation needs as they are for the satisfaction of assimilation needs.

However, according to ODT (Brewer, 1991), certain asymmetries can be expected to arise as a function of whether the need for assimilation or the need for differentiation is more highly aroused. When a situation activates a person's need for differentiation, social groups that are particularly conducive to distinctive intergroup comparisons should be perceived as being more important to that person's self-definition than social groups or identities that allow for less intergroup distinctiveness. One factor in determining the distinctiveness of a group is how inclusive or exclusive the group is. In general, larger, more inclusive groups (e.g., Caucasians) are less distinctive than smaller, more exclusive groups (e.g., African Americans). For this reason, differentiation need arousal should lead to stronger preferences for exclusive social identities than inclusive social identities. This line of reasoning also applies to the need for assimilation. Satisfaction of the need for social assimilation is directly related to the level of inclusiveness of a social group. When one's need for assimilation is particularly strong, then the optimal level of category inclusiveness necessary to satisfy this need should be greater than if the need for assimilation were not as strongly activated. When individuals feel a strong assimilation need, they should prefer their more inclusive ingroup identities (e.g., nationality) to their highly exclusive ingroup identities.

Because of the relationship between the strength of activation of the needs for assimilation and differentiation and the level of category inclusiveness needed to satisfy these needs, the importance attached to a particular social group identity should vary as a function of the relative strength of assimilation and differentiation needs and the level of inclusiveness of the social group. It should be noted, however, that although level of inclusiveness is hypothesized to be an important determinant of how well a group can satisfy the needs for assimilation and differentiation, other features of the group also can influence need satisfaction. For example, intragroup similarity, clarity of group boundaries, and intergroup similarity can all affect how distinctive a group is, which will in turn influence the group's ability to satisfy optimal distinctiveness needs. As noted by others (e.g., Vignoles, Chryssochoou, & Breakwell, 2000), distinctiveness is not a unitary construct, and multiple sources of distinctiveness may exist. The current research focuses primarily on inclusiveness as one

aspect of group distinctiveness with the hypothesis that arousal of assimilation and differentiation needs will lead to differences in preferences for groups that vary in inclusiveness.

Relevant Prior Research

Previous research has examined how arousal of assimilation and differentiation needs influence individuals' judgments about the groups to which they belong. For example, in one of the few studies that manipulated both assimilation and differentiation needs, Simon and colleagues (1997) found that under conditions of mortality salience, participants who were told that they were socially deviant overestimated social consensus for their attitudes, whereas participants who were told that they had conformist tendencies underestimated social consensus for their attitudes. Hornsey and Hogg (1999) examined how perceptions of superordinate group inclusiveness were related to participants' evaluations of their subgroup identities. These researchers found that the more inclusive participants perceived the superordinate category to be, the more subgroup bias they demonstrated. This was particularly the case among those participants who felt that the superordinate category lacked distinctiveness. Similarly, Abrams (1994) found that members of minority political parties, which are more inclusive and distinctive, garnered greater commitment among supporters than majority parties. Finally, Brewer, Manzi, and Shaw (1993) found evidence that depersonalization (exciting the need for differentiation) resulted in greater ingroup positivity when the ingroup was a minority group.

In our own research, we have demonstrated that heightened assimilation and differentiation needs can lead to increased self-stereotyping (Brewer & Pickett, 1999; Pickett, Bonner, & Coleman, 2002) and heightened perceptions of ingroup homogeneity (Pickett & Brewer, 2001). In these studies, participants either experienced a threat to intragroup inclusion or a threat to the distinctiveness of the ingroup (similar in form to the manipulations employed in Study 2 of the present article). In response to these threats, participants perceived themselves more stereotypically as evidenced by higher ratings of the perceived self-descriptiveness of stereotype-relevant traits but not stereotype-irrelevant traits (Pickett et al., 2002). Participants also responded to these threats by increasing their perceptions of ingroup and outgroup homogeneity and perceiving the group as a whole more stereotypically. These changes in perceived homogeneity and self-stereotyping have the effect of enhancing participants' perceptual identity with other ingroup members (thus satisfying assimilation needs) and creating greater perceptual contrast between the ingroup and the outgroup (thus serving differentiation needs).

In summary, the research reviewed above demonstrates that individuals do exhibit particular responses as a result of heightened needs for assimilation or differentiation. Arousal of the need for assimilation appears to lead to responses that either increase the number of similar others (Simon et al., 1997) or enhance intragroup similarity and coherence (Pickett & Brewer, 2001; Pickett et al., 2002). Both types of responses can help individuals achieve a sense of intragroup belonging and inclusion. The research reviewed also indicates that differentiation need arousal leads to responses that decrease the number of similar others (Simon et al., 1997) or enhance intergroup distinctiveness (via intragroup similarity and enhanced stereotypical perceptions of the ingroup and outgroup). These responses can help individuals achieve a sense of distinctiveness at the group level, thereby satisfying the need for differentiation.

However, what is missing from this body of work are studies that directly address one of the primary tenets of ODT—that preferences for relatively inclusive or exclusive social identities are influenced by the level of activation of assimilation and differentiation needs. The research by Simon and colleagues (1997) demonstrated that individuals overestimate or underestimate social consensus

under conditions of assimilation and differentiation need arousal, respectively. However, these results were obtained only when participants' mortality was made salient, and the overestimation and underestimation of consensus was general in nature (in reference to 'other people in the general population'), not in reference to a particular social identity. Thus, the research by Simon and colleagues (1997) does not directly bear on the question of whether arousal of optimal distinctiveness needs affects individuals' preferences for inclusive versus exclusive social identities. Similarly, other research using the optimal distinctiveness framework has demonstrated that certain responses (e.g., bias, identification, discrimination) are more likely when a group is distinctive or is a minority group (see Abrams, 1994; Hornsey & Hogg, 1999; Leonardelli & Brewer, 2001). However, in this research, the needs for assimilation and differentiation were not experimentally manipulated; thus, it is impossible to conclude that need arousal caused participants to exhibit greater bias, discrimination, and so forth. The two studies described in this article were designed to fill this gap in the literature and provide evidence for the predicted preferences for inclusive versus exclusive social identities as a function of assimilation and differentiation need arousal.

These two studies are based, in part, on a pilot study conducted by Silver (1997). In this pilot study, participants were randomly assigned to receive one of three types of feedback regarding a personality test that they had taken at the beginning of the school term. In the differentiation need condition, participants were told that they were chosen to be part of the study because their personality test indicated that they fell into a very common personality category. In the assimilation need condition, participants were told that they were selected for the study because they fell into a very rare personality category. In the no need arousal condition, participants were simply told that they were asked to participate in order for the experimenter to get a representative sample of the various personality types in the population. After receiving this feedback, participants then were asked to indicate their level of identification with one very inclusive identity ('people your own age') and one relatively exclusive identity (chosen idiosyncratically for each participant). Results of this study revealed a significant interaction between need state and group inclusiveness, which indicated that participants who received differentiation need feedback exhibited significantly greater identification with their exclusive ingroup identity than did assimilation need and no need arousal participants. The results of this pilot study are informative because they suggest that need arousal may indeed be an important determinant of the types of group identities that individuals find most important and satisfying at a particular time.

The purpose of the two studies reported here was to replicate and extend the findings of this initial study using different methods of inducing need arousal and a variety of dependent measures. The primary prediction for Study 1 was that arousal of assimilation and differentiation needs would alter the perceived importance of ingroup identities that vary in their level of inclusiveness. More specifically, inclusive identities should be perceived as more important when assimilation needs have been aroused and less important when differentiation needs have been aroused. Similarly, exclusive identities should be perceived as more important when differentiation need has been aroused and less important when assimilation need has been aroused. In Study 2, we sought to provide further support for the role of group inclusiveness in the satisfaction of assimilation and differentiation needs by examining group members' reactions to the size of a single ingroup under conditions of assimilation and differentiation need arousal. We predicted that group members' desire to restrict ingroup membership and their perceptions of ingroup size and ingroup inclusiveness would vary as a function of which need was experimentally induced.

Study 1

Method

Participants

The study included 148 University of Illinois undergraduate students (78 women, 70 men) who participated in return for course credit in their introductory psychology course.

Procedure

Participants were told that they were participating in a study on 'Memory and Judgment' and that they would be asked to describe two specific events from their past and then complete a series of ratings. The recall exercise (described below) was used as our manipulation of assimilation and differentiation needs. After completing the recall exercise, participants were presented with two questionnaires. In the first questionnaire, participants were asked to rate 10 groups (of which they were members) in terms of how important they perceived the group to be to them on a scale from 1 = *not at all important* to 9 = *very important*. These groups were presented in the same randomly ordered list for all participants.

The groups that participants rated were selected to correspond to Lickel and colleagues' (2000) typology of intimacy groups, task groups, social categories, and weak social relationships (see Table 2.1 for the list of groups). As indicated in Lickel and colleagues (2000) research, intimacy groups and task groups tend to be characterized by high levels of interaction and perceived importance and small size. In contrast, social categories and weak social relationships (e.g., 'people in your neighbourhood') are characterized by relatively low levels of interaction and perceived importance and are rated as being relatively large in size (see Lickel et al., 2000, Tables 3 and 7). For the purposes of the present study, we were most interested in participants' ratings of the social categories because those groups most closely map onto what are usually considered to be group-based social identities;

Table 2.1 Groups Rated in Study 1 by Group Type

Exclusive Groups		Inclusive Groups	
Intimacy Groups	Task Groups	Social Categories	Weak Social Relationships
Family	People you work with	Nationality	Other Psych 100 students
Friends	People you play sports with	Ethnicity	Other people in this experiment with you
		Religious affiliation	People in your academic major

for example, nationality and ethnicity. However, participants' importance ratings of the other three group types also are informative. For example, because weak social relationships are groups that are defined by a relative lack of ingroup boundaries (i.e., very high permeability), these groups should be especially unappealing to participants whose need for differentiation has been aroused.

In the second questionnaire, participants were asked to rate these 10 groups again in terms of how group-like or entitative they perceived the groups to be using a 9-point scale, which ranged from 1 = *not at all a group* to 9 = *very much a group*.[1] The entitativity rating measure was used as a check to ensure that the perceived groupness of the rated groups corresponded to expectations based on the taxonomy and did not differ across need state conditions. After completing these ratings, participants completed a brief demographic questionnaire and were then debriefed, thanked, and dismissed.

Need State Manipulations

According to ODT, extreme individuation should result in heightened assimilation need, whereas extreme deindividuation should lead to heightened differentiation need. To manipulate these needs experimentally, participants were asked to recall two instances from their past where they felt either extremely individuated or extremely deindividuated, or neither. The specific instructions were as follows for the need for assimilation condition:

Please take a moment and think of times when you felt very different from people. In other

words, think of times and situations where you did not feel that you fit in with other people around you and that you 'stuck out'. Please write a brief description of two memories of such times.

In the need for differentiation condition, the instructions were as follows:

Please take a moment and think of times when you felt overly similar to other people. In other words, think of times and situations where you felt that you were so much like other people around you that you did not have your own identity. Please write a brief description of two memories of such times.

Finally, in the no need arousal condition, the instructions were as follows:

Please take a moment and think of times when you felt that you were similar to some people around you but different from others. In other words, think of times and situations where you knew that there were some people around that were very much like yourself but that there were other people around that were different from you. Please write a brief description of two memories of such times.

Because optimal distinctiveness is achieved through a balance between assimilation and differentiation, we predicted that these instructions would lead participants to think of situations where they experienced equilibrium between these two needs, thus leading to no need arousal.

Similar to autobiographical recall techniques used to induce various mood states (e.g., Baker & Guttfreund, 1993), it was assumed that having participants recall instances where they felt too similar or too different would put participants in a mental state that mirrors the original experience.

Results

Entitativity Check

Participants' entitativity ratings of each group were combined into four indexes: intimacy groups ($\alpha = 0.30$), task groups ($\alpha = 0.43$), social categories ($\alpha = 0.73$), and weak social relationships ($\alpha = 0.63$). The analysis design for participants' ratings was a 3 (need state: need for assimilation, need for differentiation, no need arousal) × 4 (group type) mixed-model factorial with repeated measures on the last factor. Results of this ANOVA revealed the expected main effect of group type, $F(3, 393) = 244.06$, $p < .001$. The intimacy groups were seen as being most entitative ($M = 8.45$, $SD = 0.88$), followed by social categories ($M = 6.50$, $SD = 1.77$), task groups ($M = 6.08$, $SD = 1.54$), and weak social relationships ($M = 3.57$, $SD = 1.98$). Of importance, no need state main effect or interactions with need state emerged on participants' entitativity ratings of the four types of groups, all $Fs < 1$, indicating that participants' perceptions of group entitativity were not significantly affected by the need state manipulations.

Perceived Group Importance

Participants' importance ratings of each group were combined into four indexes: intimacy groups ($\alpha = 0.16$), task groups ($\alpha = 0.35$), social categories ($\alpha = 0.70$), and weak social relationships ($\alpha = 0.61$).[2] A 3 (need state: need for assimilation, need for differentiation, no need arousal) × 4 (group type) mixed-model ANOVA with repeated measures on the last factor was performed on participants' perceived importance ratings. This analysis revealed

a significant main effect of group type, $F(3, 390) = 310.96$, $p < .001$. Participants perceived their intimacy groups to be most important to them ($M = 8.65$, $SD = 0.53$), followed by the task groups ($M = 6.02$, $SD = 1.48$), social categories ($M = 5.84$, $SD = 2.04$), and weak social relationships ($M = 3.47$, $SD = 1.39$).

This analysis also revealed a main effect of need state, $F(2, 130) = 3.28$, $p < .05$, which was moderated by the critical interaction between need state and group type, $F(6, 390) = 2.40$, $p < .03$, (see Figure 2.1). In line with predictions, participants in the need for differentiation condition perceived their broad social category memberships as being less important to them ($M = 5.33$, $SD = 2.19$) than did no need arousal participants ($M = 5.84$, $SD = 1.94$) and participants in the need for assimilation condition ($M = 6.33$, $SD = 1.89$). Follow-up comparisons revealed that the importance ratings for need for differentiation participants differed significantly from those of need for assimilation participants, $t(130) = 2.36$, $p < .02$. A similar pattern was found for the weak social relationships category. Need for differentiation participants perceived these group memberships to be less important ($M = 3.07$, $SD = 1.27$) than did need for assimilation participants ($M = 3.71$, $SD = 1.41$) and no need arousal participants ($M = 3.62$, $SD = 1.44$). The need for assimilation condition and the need for differentiation condition differed significantly from each other, $t(130) = 2.22$, $p < .03$. In addition, the need for differentiation condition also differed marginally from the no need arousal condition, $t(130) = 1.87$, $p = .06$.

Differences between the need state conditions did not emerge on participants' ratings of their intimacy groups. In fact, a clear ceiling effect emerged where all participants, regardless of need state, perceived these groups to be extremely important ($Ms = 8.68$ [$SD = 0.57$], 8.63 [$SD = 0.59$], and 8.64 [$SD = 0.40$] in the assimilation, differentiation, and no need arousal conditions, respectively). Because intimacy groups are not social identities in the sense that identities are often conceptualized

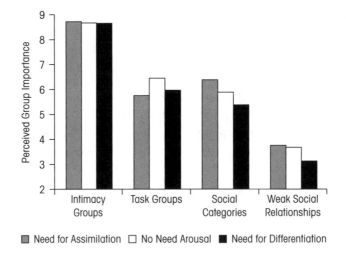

Figure 2.1   Mean group importance ratings as a function of group type and need state condition, Study 1.

Note: Higher numbers indicate greater perceived ingroup importance.

(Tajfel & Turner, 1986), in retrospect, it seems quite logical that need arousal would not have a large impact on the perceived importance of these groups. In general, a person's friends and family are highly important regardless of the person's needs for assimilation or differentiation.

In this study, it was of interest to examine the effects of need arousal on participants' importance ratings of the task groups because these tend to be smaller, more distinctive groups. A somewhat surprising finding was that participants in the assimilation and differentiation conditions did not differ in their importance ratings of the task groups (Ms = 5.72 [SD = 1.43] and 5.93 [SD = 1.56], respectively), $t < 1$. However, the two need arousal conditions did tend to rate these groups as less important to them than did no need arousal participants (M = 6.42, SD = 1.40), $t(130) = 2.25$, $p < .05$ and $t(130) = 1.55$, ns, for pair-wise comparisons between the no need arousal condition and the assimilation and differentiation need conditions, respectively. Because task groups tend to be relatively small and interactive (Lickel et al., 2000), one might expect differentiation need participants

to perceive these groups to be more important than assimilation need participants. However, the design of this study required that we describe the task groups in very generic terms (e.g., 'people you work with'). In other research (Lickel et al., 2000), the task groups were specifically identified, for example, 'a jury', 'members of a student campus committee'. It is likely that the generic descriptions of the task groups in this study affected the perceived properties of the groups (e.g., permeability, similarity) and hence their attractiveness to assimilation and differentiation need participants. In our prior research (Silver, 1997), arousing the need for differentiation did increase identification with more exclusive ingroups when these groups were more specifically defined.

Discussion

Study 1 focused on a variety of group types to demonstrate that assimilation and differentiation needs would affect the perceived importance of groups that vary in level of inclusiveness. The significant Need State × Group Size interaction and the pattern of means for the inclusive groups indicated that whereas assimilation need arousal led to greater perceived importance of inclusive groups, differentiation need arousal led to less perceived importance of these groups. Significant differences between the need arousal conditions were not found for the intimacy and task groups. Overall, this first study provides some initial support for ODT's predictions. According to the optimal distinctiveness model (Brewer, 1991), heightened assimilation need will motivate a search for more inclusive social identities, whereas heightened differentiation need will reduce the value of inclusive social identities and motivate a search for more exclusive or distinctive social identities. In accordance with ODT predictions, participants in this study who were exposed to the differentiation-need manipulation perceived their broad, inclusive identities—groups that provide little basis for distinctiveness—as less important than did participants who had been assigned to the assimilation-need condition.

The results of Study 1 also shed some light on the issues raised by Sherman, Hamilton, and Lewis (1999) regarding the relationship between entitativity and the social identity value of group memberships. According to Sherman and colleagues (1999), groups may vary in certain properties (e.g., size) and these properties can have implications for both the perceived entitativity of the group and the social identity value of the group. The results of Study 1 are in line with other work (i.e., Lickel et al., 2000), which indicates that groups that vary in entitativity also vary in their perceived importance to group members (i.e., their social identity value). However, the current research extends this finding by demonstrating that the specific needs of perceivers and the properties of the group can interact to lead to systematic variations in the value derived from particular social identities (see also Brewer & Harasty, 1996).

In a second study, we sought to provide further evidence for ODT predictions. We decided to take a different tack and investigate whether assimilation and differentiation needs would motivate

individuals to change their current ingroup to be more inclusive or exclusive. In other words, when the situation is constrained and other potential ingroup memberships are not made salient to participants (as they were in Study 1), we predicted that individuals would exhibit more creative responses to heightened assimilation and differentiation needs. More specifically, we predicted that arousal of differentiation need would lead to greater agreement with the perception that the ingroup is too large and a greater desire to restrict ingroup membership. In addition, we predicted that differentiation need arousal would result in distortions in perceived group size such that individuals would underestimate the size of the group and perceive the ingroup as being too inclusive. Thus, in lieu of seeking a more distinct group with which to identify, group members may make the ingroup more distinctive by mentally shrinking the group. By contrast, heightened assimilation need is predicted to result in the opposite pattern of effects, that is, the tendency to overestimate the size of the ingroup and a lesser tendency to perceive the ingroup as being overly inclusive.

Study 2

Procedurally, there were two major changes between Study 1 and Study 2. First, in Study 2, we employed a different method of arousing assimilation and differentiation needs. Rather than have participants recall past instances where they experienced a lack of distinctiveness or inclusion, participants in Study 2 received false feedback on a personality test designed to create these feelings in the lab (described below). This procedure has the benefit of allowing the experimenter to hold information constant across need state conditions and is also likely to lead to less within-condition variability. Although the manipulation of need state is different in Study 2, it is important to point out that the underlying mechanism for arousal of assimilation and differentiation needs is the same.

Having participants recall past instances where they felt very different from others is conceptually parallel to telling participants that the results of a personality test indicate that they are very different from others. In both cases, participants should experience a lack of inclusion and a heightened need for assimilation.

Similarly, having participants recall a time when they felt that they lacked distinctiveness should be parallel to reducing distinctiveness by blurring intergroup boundaries and effectively creating an overly inclusive ingroup. According to ODT, individuals should respond to membership in an overly inclusive group (where distinctiveness is lacking) by engaging in actions that would restore group distinctiveness, thereby satisfying the need for differentiation. As noted earlier, individuals can do this through both intragroup and intergroup strategies. In Study 2, the ingroup for participants was 'Ohio State students' and the distinctiveness of this group was threatened by telling participants that the ingroup overlaps greatly with an outgroup (other US college students) in terms of their scores on a personality test. In response to this information, individuals should be motivated to achieve greater distinctiveness. Theoretically, this may involve an intergroup strategy, that is, distinguishing Ohio State students as a subgroup of the broader category (i.e., other US college students), and perceiving the ingroup as being relatively small and distinctive in relation to other outgroups. On the other hand, it is also possible that individuals may engage in an intragroup strategy and make within-group distinctions among different types of Ohio State students (e.g., honours students, arts and humanities majors). However, given the intergroup context that was established by the manipulations (Ohio State University [OSU] students vs other US college students), and given that all of our participants were highly identified as OSU students, we predicted that participants' primary motive would be to restore the distinctiveness of the original ingroup (OSU students) and that they would approach this through intergroup differentiation.

Method

Participants

Prior to the experimental sessions, a mass-testing session was conducted at the beginning of the school term. One of the questionnaires completed during this session was a measure of identification with the group 'Ohio State students'. Levels of identification were assessed using a 9-point rating scale where higher numbers reflect greater group identification. Because the needs for assimilation and differentiation were to be manipulated in the context of a single ingroup for all participants, a minimum level of ingroup identification with that group was assumed to be necessary before participants would exhibit compensatory responses to identity threat (Branscombe, Ellemers, Spears, & Doosje, 1999; Doosje & Ellemers, 1997). Therefore, only those participants who scored above the scale midpoint of five were included in the analyses reported below. The final sample included a total of 76 Ohio State University undergraduate students (42 women, 33 men, one unknown). Participants received course credit in their introductory psychology course in return for their participation.

Procedure

After arriving at the experimental sessions, participants were informed that they would be filling out a series of questionnaires about themselves and their perceptions of Ohio State students as a group and that they would be receiving feedback on one particular questionnaire—the Self-Attributes Questionnaire (SAQ).[3] (Participants were led to believe that they would be engaging in a discussion with another student in the session and that their results on the SAQ were needed to facilitate this discussion.) The needs for assimilation and differentiation were manipulated through false feedback (described below) provided to participants regarding their scores on the SAQ. Participants randomly received feedback designed to arouse either the need for assimilation or need for differentiation or feedback designed to result in no need arousal. After reading their feedback, participants then completed the dependent measures, a series of manipulation check items, and were then debriefed, thanked, and dismissed.[4]

Need State Manipulations

After participants completed the SAQ, the experimenter gathered participants' questionnaires and pretended to enter and score each of them. After several minutes, the experimenter then provided each participant with a brief form that provided general information regarding the performance of OSU students on the SAQ (compared to other US college students) and participants' own (bogus) score. This information is described below and summarized in Table 2.2.

No need arousal condition.   For no need arousal participants, the score that they received on the SAQ was only 1 point away from the ingroup mean. Participants in the no need arousal condition also were told on their form:

Studies of past and current OSU students have consistently demonstrated that one of the areas

in which OSU students and other US college students differ is in their scores on the self-attributes questionnaire.

Below this verbal information, a pictorial representation of the SAQ scores of OSU and other US college students was provided. Two identical normal curves (one labelled 'Ohio State Students' and the other labelled 'US College Students') were displayed. In the no need arousal condition, these curves contained very little overlap (approximately 20 per cent) in line with the idea that OSU students are distinct from other college students. In addition, the difference between the ingroup and outgroup means was 30 points.

The feedback given to participants in the no need arousal condition was designed such that participants' need for assimilation would be met through the knowledge that their SAQ score is similar to that of other OSU students. Furthermore, participants' need for differentiation also would be satisfied through the confirmation that OSU students are distinct and different from other US college students.

Need for assimilation condition.   The feedback form given to participants in the need for assimilation condition was identical to the feedback form in the no need arousal condition with the exception of one piece of information. Instead of receiving a score that was only 1 point away from the ingroup mean, participants in the need for assimilation condition were given a score that was 12 points away from the ingroup mean. This information was designed to make participants feel quite different from other ingroup members, thus threatening their secure status as an ingroup member and heightening their need for assimilation.

Need for differentiation condition.   In the need for differentiation condition, participants were again given a score that was only 1 point away from the ingroup mean (similar to no need arousal participants). However, unlike the no need arousal

Table 2.2 Summary of SAQ Feedback Provided to Participants in Study 2

	Self-Ingroup Distance	Ingroup–Outgroup Distance
Order 1		
Need for assimilation	−12	+30
No need arousal	−1	+30
Need for differentiation	−1	**+3**
Order 2		
Need for assimilation	**+12**	−30
No need arousal	−1	−30
Need for differentiation	−1	**−3**

Note: The boldfaced numbers represent the critical information given in each need arousal condition to arouse either the need for assimilation or the need for differentiation.

condition, participants in the need for differentiation condition were told:

> Studies of past and current OSU students have consistently demonstrated that one of the areas in which OSU students and other (non-OSU) US college students *do not* differ is in their scores on the self-attributes questionnaire.

In this condition, the ingroup and outgroup means differed by only 3 points. In addition, the overlap of the ingroup and outgroup curves was approximately 80 per cent, thus threatening the distinctiveness of the ingroup in relation to the outgroup and heightening participants' need for differentiation.

Counterbalancing. The direction of relative ingroup and outgroup distance and self-ingroup distance was counterbalanced across the conditions (see Table 2.2). Thus, for half of the participants the ingroup was 30 points (or 3 points in the differentiation need condition) above the outgroup mean and for the other half the ingroup was 30 (or three) points below the outgroup mean. In addition, half of the need for assimilation participants were given a score that placed them 12 points above the ingroup mean and the other half were given a score that placed them 12 points below the ingroup mean. Because these position differences did not interact with need arousal on any of the dependent measures, we have collapsed across this factor in all of the reported analyses.

Dependent Measures

There were three primary dependent measures: estimates of ingroup size, perceptions of ingroup inclusiveness, and a measure of participants' desire to restrict ingroup membership. These measures were presented in the order listed above and were contained on a single sheet of paper.

Estimated ingroup size. The first of the dependent measures that participants completed was a one-item question designed to assess how numerous participants perceived the ingroup to be. Participants were asked to answer the following question: 'If you had to guess, how many undergraduates would you guess are enrolled at Ohio State?' A blank line was provided below the question for participants to write in their answer.

Perceptions of ingroup inclusiveness. Immediately below participants' estimate was a single-item question designed to measure how overly inclusive or overly exclusive participants perceived the ingroup to be: 'How do you feel about the number of undergraduate students that attend Ohio State?' A 5-point response scale was provided anchored by 1 = *not enough* and 5 = *too many.* The midpoint of the scale (3) was labelled *just right.*

Desire to restrict ingroup membership. A measure was included to test whether arousal of assimilation and differentiation needs would result in a greater desire to restrict group membership. Research on the ingroup overexclusion effect (Leyens & Yzerbyt, 1992; Yzerbyt, Leyens, & Bellour, 1995; Yzerbyt, Castano, Leyens, & Paladino, 2000) suggests that individuals are especially cautious about determining whether a person should be classified as an ingroup member (as opposed to an outgroup member) because of their desire to protect the integrity of the ingroup.

In the current study, we were interested in whether differences in ingroup restrictiveness would be found as a function of assimilation and differentiation need arousal. In other words, would participants be willing to endorse actions that would result in larger or smaller ingroup size? Participants were asked to express their agreement with the following two statements: 'The admissions office should make it more difficult for people to get into Ohio State' and 'The admissions office should make it easier for people to get into Ohio State'. A 7-point response scale anchored by 1 = *disagree strongly* and 7 = *agree strongly* was provided.

Manipulation Check and Suspicion Probes

On a separate sheet, participants completed a set of manipulation check and suspicion-probe items. Participants were asked to recall their own SAQ score and the average ingroup and outgroup SAQ score. Participants also were asked to indicate whether their personal score was the same as, below, or above the ingroup average and whether the ingroup SAQ average was 'about the same' or 'very different' from the outgroup SAQ average. Finally, two questions were asked to probe participants for suspicion regarding the experimental manipulations.

Results

Manipulation Check and Suspicion Probes

All participants correctly recalled their own score and the ingroup score and outgroup score within 3 points of the actual score. In addition, all participants correctly answered the two questions regarding how their score compared to the average score of other OSU students and how OSU students scored in comparison to other non-OSU college students. The difference between the SAQ score that participants listed for themselves and the score listed for the ingroup was used as a check on perceived intragroup distance. The difference between the reported ingroup and outgroup SAQ score was used as a check on perceived ingroup–outgroup distance. One-way ANOVAs with need state condition entered as the between-participants factor were conducted on the absolute value of these difference scores. Results indicated that need for assimilation participants perceived significantly greater self-ingroup distance (M_{diff} = 11.70) than did participants in the need for differentiation (M_{diff} = 0.96) and no need arousal conditions (M_{diff} = 1.04), $F(2, 73)$ = 545.12, $p < .001$. In addition, participants in the need for differentiation condition perceived significantly less ingroup–outgroup distance (M_{diff} = 3.22) than did participants in the need for assimilation (M_{diff} = 27.78) and no need arousal conditions (M_{diff} = 30.46), $F(2, 73)$ = 367.21, $p < .001$.

Finally, none of the participants expressed suspicion regarding the SAQ feedback, and they were not able to guess the true hypotheses of the study.

Dependent Measures

Initial one-way ANOVAs were conducted on each of the dependent measures to examine the effects of need arousal. Of additional theoretical interest were the relationships between the dependent variables within each of the need arousal conditions (e.g., the correlation between ingroup size and the desire to restrict ingroup membership). Thus, sets of correlational analyses were conducted to further test optimal distinctiveness predictions.

Estimated ingroup size. Participants' estimates of the number of undergraduates enrolled at OSU were analyzed using a one-way ANOVA with need state entered as the between-participants factor. This analysis revealed the predicted need state main effect, $F(2, 73)$ = 6.41, $p < .01$ (see Figure 2.2). Participants in the need for assimilation condition perceived the ingroup to be much larger (M = 48,925, SD = 34,001) than did participants in the no need arousal condition (M = 33,942, SD = 14,421), $t(73)$ = 2.31, $p < .05$, and participants in the need for differentiation condition (M = 25,417, SD = 15,810), $t(93)$ = 3.51, $p < .001$. The difference between the need for differentiation condition and the no need arousal condition did not reach significance, $t(93)$ = 1.26, ns.

The actual number of OSU undergraduates enrolled at the time this study was conducted was 35,647.[5] Paired t tests indicated that compared to the actual number of students enrolled, participants in the no need arousal condition were quite accurate in their estimates of ingroup size, $t(73) < 1$, ns. However, participants in the need for assimilation condition tended to significantly overestimate ingroup size, $t(73)$ = 2.18, $p < .02$, and need for differentiation participants tended to underestimate ingroup size, although this effect failed to reach statistical significance, $t(73)$ = 1.62, $p < .11$. The average overestimation on the part

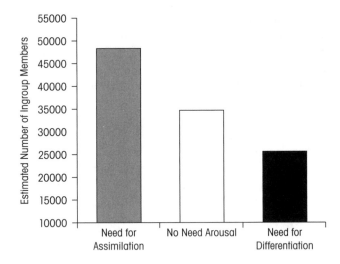

Figure 2.2 **Estimated number of Ohio State students (ingroup members as a function of need state condition, Study 2.**

of assimilation-motive participants was approximately 13,000 students, and the average underestimation by differentiation-motive participants was approximately 10,000 students.

Perceptions of ingroup inclusiveness.   The scale used to measure ingroup inclusiveness ranged from 1 to 5, such that a score below the scale midpoint of 3 would indicate that the respondent believed that there were not enough OSU students and a score above 3 would indicate that there were too many OSU students. Given that Ohio State University is a very large university, only 2 of the 76 participants in the study provided a score below 3 on this measure. Thus, the appropriate interpretation of this dependent variable is that it captures varying degrees of perceived ingroup overinclusiveness, that is, variations in the perception that there are too many ingroup members. Results of a one-way ANOVA with need state condition as the between-participants factor revealed only a directional main effect of need state, $F(2, 73) = 2.73$, $p < .12$. However, this effect was driven by a significant difference between need for assimilation and need for

differentiation participants. Need for differentiation participants felt to a greater degree that there were 'too many' ingroup members ($M = 3.57$, $SD = 0.66$) than did need for assimilation participants ($M = 3.19$, $SD = 0.56$), and this difference was statistically significant, $t(73) = 2.10$, $p < .04$ (see Figure 2.3). The mean for participants in the no need arousal condition ($M = 3.35$, $SD = 0.69$) fell between the means of the two need arousal conditions but did not differ significantly from either condition, $ts < 1.20$, *ns.*

Desire to restrict ingroup membership.   Participants' responses to the question asking whether they would like to make it easier for students to gain admission to OSU was reverse-scored so that higher numbers on the item reflect a greater desire to restrict ingroup membership.[6] This item was then averaged with the item asking whether participants would like to make it more difficult for students to gain admission to form a single index of ingroup restrictiveness ($\alpha = 0.75$). Although results of a one-way ANOVA on this index failed to reveal a significant main effect of need arousal,

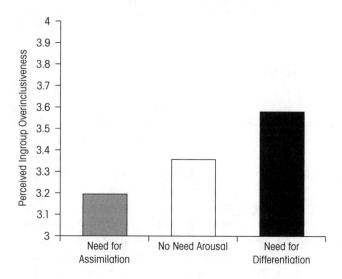

Figure 2.3 **Perceived ingroup (over-)inclusiveness by need state condition, Study 2.**

$F(2, 73) = 1.63$, *ns*, the means from this analysis were generally in the predicted directions (*Ms* = 4.63 [*SD* = 1.47], 4.58 [*SD* = 1.44], 5.20 [*SD* = 0.91] in the need for assimilation, no need arousal, and need for differentiation conditions, respectively). Participants in the need for differentiation condition exhibited the highest scores on the restrictiveness measure, which differed marginally, $t(73) = 1.64$, $p = .10$, from the no need arousal condition but did not differ significantly from the assimilation need condition, $t(73) = 1.52$, $p = .13$. Results of a contrast comparing the differentiation need condition to the two other conditions was marginally significant, $F(1, 73) = 3.25$, $p < .08$. These analyses indicate limited support for the hypothesis that differentiation need would result in a greater desire to restrict ingroup membership.

Correlational Analyses

Participants first provided estimates of ingroup size and then answered questions designed to assess perceptions of ingroup inclusiveness and the desire to restrict ingroup membership (the two-item index). According to ODT, the direction of

the association between these dependent measures should vary as a function of participants' need state. To examine these associations, correlations were computed between the three dependent measures (estimated ingroup size, perceived ingroup inclusiveness, and the desire to restrict ingroup membership). The correlations were conducted separately within each need state condition.

Estimated ingroup size and desire to restrict ingroup membership.   For participants in the need for differentiation condition, estimates of ingroup size should be positively related to the desire to restrict ingroup membership. The larger they believe the ingroup to be, the more they should want to restrict its size. By contrast, for assimilation need participants, the larger they perceive the ingroup to be, the less they should want to restrict its size. Results of the correlational analysis support these predictions. The association between estimated ingroup size and restrictiveness was positive for differentiation need participants, $r = 0.39$, $p = .06$. This association was considerably weaker for participants in the no need arousal condition, $r = 0.10$, ns, and in the opposite direction for assimilation need participants, $r = -0.38$, $p < .05$. The difference between the correlations for the assimilation and differentiation need conditions was statistically significant, $Z = 2.68$, $p < .05$.

Perceived inclusiveness and desire to restrict ingroup membership. For participants in the need for differentiation condition, greater perceived inclusiveness of the ingroup (that there are 'too many' ingroup members) should be positively related to the desire to restrict ingroup membership. The more inclusive they believe the ingroup to be, the more they should want to restrict its size. By contrast, for assimilation need participants, the more inclusive they perceive the ingroup to be, the less they should want to restrict its size. For participants in the need for differentiation condition, perceived ingroup inclusiveness was strongly correlated with the desire to restrict ingroup membership, $r = 0.52$, $p = .01$. Of importance, however, this effect was weaker for participants in the no need arousal condition, $r = 0.13$, ns, and in the opposite direction for participants in the assimilation need condition, $r = -0.24$, ns. The difference between the correlations for the assimilation and differentiation need conditions was statistically significant, $Z = 2.51$, $p < .05$. Thus, among differentiation need participants, the perception that there were too many ingroup members made them more willing to endorse actions that would restrict the size of the group, whereas this relationship was in the opposite direction for assimilation need participants.

Estimated ingroup size and perceived inclusiveness. The relationship between estimated ingroup size and perceived ingroup inclusiveness was similar across the three need state conditions (see Table 2.3). Within each condition, higher estimates of ingroup size were associated with a greater perception that the ingroup contained too many ingroup members. Of importance, however, the means associated with the different values on the perceived inclusiveness measure differed widely across the three conditions. In the need for differentiation condition, participants felt that there were too many ingroup members (scale values of 4–5) when their estimates were only at an average of 28,181 students. By contrast, in the no need arousal condition, the average estimate of ingroup members for those respondents who responded at the highest end of the perceived inclusiveness scale was 42,500. Finally, in the need for assimilation condition, participants at the high end of the perceived inclusiveness scale estimated the size of the ingroup to be at an average of 74,800 students! Thus, although the direction of the relation between estimates of ingroup size and perceived inclusiveness was similar across conditions, participants' thresholds for how many students counts as 'too many' was much higher for assimilation need participants and much lower for differentiation need participants.

Table 2.3 Intercorrelations between dependent measures by need state condition, Study 2

Measure	Estimated Ingroup Size			Desire to Restrict Ingroup			Perceived Ingroup Inclusiveness		
	NFA	NNA	NFD	NFA	NNA	NFD	NFA	NNA	NFD
Estimated ingroup size	—	—	—	−0.38*	0.10	0.39†	0.63**	0.38†	0.16
Desire to restrict ingroup				—	—	—	−0.24	0.13	0.52**
Perceived ingroup inclusiveness							—	—	—

Note: NFA = need for assimilation condition, NNA = no need arousal condition, NFD = need for differentiation condition.
†$p \leq 0.07$. *$p \leq 0.05$. **$p \leq 0.01$.

Optimal Distinctiveness

An important feature of the perceived inclusiveness scale is that it was anchored by 1 = *not enough* and 5 = *too many* and the midpoint of the scale (3) was labelled *just right*. According to ODT, optimal identities are those identities that are at a level of inclusiveness that fits individuals' current need state. In the need for assimilation condition, those participants who perceived the ingroup as being 'just right' also believed that the ingroup contained an average of 44,286 students. For participants in the no need arousal condition, this value was 31,324. Finally, in the differentiation need condition, the average group size provided by participants who felt that the ingroup was 'just right' was 22,883. The difference between the estimates of need for assimilation participants and need for differentiation participants who thought the ingroup size was 'just right' was approximately 20,000 students and represents a significant difference, $t(1, 47) = 3.98$, $p < .001$. One of the basic tenets of ODT is that 'the optimal level of category distinctiveness or inclusiveness is a function of the relative strength (steepness) of the opposing drives for assimilation and differentiation' (Brewer, 1991, p. 478). The above analysis suggests that need arousal did indeed alter participants' judgments of where the point of optimal distinctiveness lies.

Discussion

The goal of Study 2 was to provide further support for the relationship between group inclusiveness and the satisfaction of assimilation and differentiation needs. In Study 1, we demonstrated that participants' perceptions of the perceived importance of their inclusive ingroup identities varied depending on need arousal. Under conditions of heightened assimilation need, individuals should prefer relatively inclusive group identities, and under conditions of heightened differentiation need, individuals should prefer relatively exclusive group identities. It was assumed that these preferences were driven by the relative inclusiveness of these groups as predicted by ODT. In Study 2, we wanted

to test this assumption more directly by focusing on group members' reactions to the size of a single ingroup (OSU students) under conditions of assimilation and differentiation need arousal. As predicted, experimentally arousing individuals' need for differentiation (through threats to intergroup distinctiveness) resulted in a greater perception that the group contained too many ingroup members and a bias toward underestimating the size of the ingroup. By contrast, arousal of assimilation need resulted in less perceived group (over-) inclusiveness and a significant overestimation of ingroup size. The results from the correlational analyses were especially informative. The relationships between perceived ingroup size/ingroup inclusiveness and participants' desire to restrict ingroup membership were in opposite directions for assimilation and differentiation need participants. These results are exactly what would be predicted from the optimal distinctiveness model.

General Discussion

The two studies reported here were designed to test one of the fundamental assumptions of ODT—that the satisfaction of social identity needs is a joint function of the level of arousal of the needs for assimilation or differentiation and the level of inclusiveness of the ingroup. This was tested in two different ways. In Study 1, we demonstrated that the perceived importance of specific ingroups—particularly of highly inclusive ingroups—varied depending on the arousal of the need for differentiation relative to the need for assimilation. In Study 2, arousing needs for assimilation or differentiation by altering the perceived inclusiveness or distinctiveness of a particular ingroup led participants to seek changes in group composition in the direction of a more optimal level of inclusiveness. Overall, the research presented here lends support to the idea that individuals draw on and see as important some ingroup identities more than others because of pressures to satisfy their needs for assimilation and differentiation.

What the results of the two experiments presented here demonstrate is that group identification may change not only as features of the group or the intergroup context change but also as individuals' needs for assimilation and differentiation change. As stated in self-categorization theory (Turner et al., 1987; Turner, Oakes, Haslam, & McGarty, 1994), social identification is fluid and context-sensitive. Although self-categorization theorists (Turner et al., 1987) have focused on the social cognitive processes related to group identification, they also recognize the importance of social motivations in determining the final outcome of those processes within a given context. ODT points to the importance of the motivations for assimilation and differentiation as partial determinants of the level of importance assigned to a given identity at a particular time or in a particular context.

Notes

1. The authors thank Brian Lickel for providing the wording for this questionnaire.

2. The development of the intimacy and task group indexes was based on previous research (Lickel et al., 2000) where the types of groups included in these indexes were found to cluster together. For this reason, it was surprising that the reliabilities of the group importance indexes for the intimacy groups and task groups were so low. Because of the low reliabilities, the advisability of collapsing the importance ratings into these indexes is called into question. To address this issue, a 3 (need state) × 2 (type of group: friends vs family) ANOVA was performed for just the intimacy groups to determine whether the effects of need state significantly differ across the two group types. A similar ANOVA was performed for just the two task groups ('people you work with' and 'people you play sports with'). Results of these ANOVAs revealed non-significant Need State × Type of Group interactions, $Fs < 1$, indicating that participants in the various need state conditions did not exhibit significant differences in perceived importance ratings between the types of groups that comprised the intimacy group and task group indexes. For this reason and because there are theoretical reasons to maintain the indexes (doing so allows for greater comparability with other research on entitativity), we chose to maintain the original index structure.

3. The Self-Attributes Questionnaire (SAQ) (Pelham & Swann, 1989) was chosen as the bogus personality measure because the SAQ measures a wide variety of self-domains (e.g., luck, leadership ability, common sense, emotional stability). It was expected that use of such a global measure (averaging across many specific domains) would lead participants to assume that their score on the SAQ reflects how generally similar or different they are from other students.

4. Participants in this study also completed a measure designed to assess levels of self-stereotyping. Because the hypotheses being tested by that measure were unrelated to the hypotheses being tested in the current article, the results have been reported elsewhere (in Pickett, Bonner, & Coleman, 2002).

5. This figure refers to the number of undergraduate students enrolled at the Ohio State University, Columbus, campus in the fall of 1998. (Source: The Office of University Communications, Ohio State University.) Study 2 was conducted during the spring of 1998.

6. Only nine out of the 76 participants were above the scale midpoint on the item asking if participants felt that the admissions committee should make it easier for students to get into Ohio State University. Thus, similar to the perceived overinclusiveness measure, this measure captures variability in the desire to restrict ingroup membership and should not be interpreted as a measure of variability in participants' desire to expand ingroup membership.

Discussion Questions

1. Much research in the social sciences has assumed that people are primarily motivated by self-interest. How does ODT account for people who will sacrifice their individual goals for the sake of their group?
2. Many multi-ethnic individuals have one parent from a high status group (e.g., whites) and one parent from a lower status group (e.g., blacks). Many of these individuals identify more strongly with the lower status group (e.g., self-identify as black). Why would anyone voluntarily do that? How might ODT account for this?
3. Baumeister and Leary (1995) make the argument that having a strong need to belong is a product of our evolutionary history and has adaptive benefits. If that's the case, why do people ever strive for distinctiveness?

Unit One Further Reading

A considerable amount of research published since the Baumeister and Leary article's 1995 debut has focused on the devastating consequences of failing to satisfy one's belongingness needs. Williams and colleagues, for example, have shown that even trivial forms of rejection (e.g., not having a ball passed to you during an online game of catch) can produce surprisingly powerful feelings of sadness, isolation, and loss of control:

Williams, K.D., Cheung, C.K., & Choi, W. (2000). Cyberostracism: Effects of being ignored over the Internet. *Journal of Personality and Social Psychology, 79*, 748–62.

The need to belong has further been demonstrated by MacDonald and Leary (2005) and Eisenberg, Lieberman, and Williams (2003), who made a strong case that the analogy between physical pain and social pain is more than metaphorical; each share a good deal of psychological and even neurological overlap:

MacDonald, G. & Leary, M.R. (2005). Why does social exclusion hurt? The relationship between social and physical pain. *Psychological Bulletin, 131*, 202–23.
Eisenberg, N.I., Lieberman, M.D., & Williams, K.D. (2003). Does rejection hurt? An fMRI study on social exclusion. *Science, 302*, 290–92.

Indeed, Stinson and colleagues (2008) found that poor-quality social bonds reduced self-esteem over time, which in turn translated into more physical health problems:

Stinson, D.A., Logel, C., Zanna, M.P., Holmes, J.G., Camerson, J.J., Wood, J.V., & Spencer, S.J. (2008). The cost of lower self-esteem: Testing a self- and social-bonds model of health. *Journal of Personality and Social Psychology, 94*, 412–28.

For further implications of people's efforts to navigate the tension between feeling too unique and too ordinary, see

Pickett, C.L., Bonner, B.L., & Coleman, J.M. (2002). Motivated self-stereotyping: Heightened assimilation and differentiation needs result in increased levels of positive and negative self-stereotyping. *Journal of Personality and Social Psychology, 82*, 543–62.
Gardner, W.L., Pickett, C.L., & Brewer, M.B. (2000). Social exclusion and selective memory: How the need to belong influences memory for social events. *Personality and Social Psychology Bulletin, 26*, 486–96.

Unit Two

Epistemic Needs

One of the central motivations for human beings is the need to reduce uncertainty. This powerful motivation underlies much of the intricate reasoning that people perform when analyzing both their own behaviour and the behaviour of others (Heider, 1958; Kelley, 1971). At the same time, however, novelty and unpredictability can be exciting. We can all think of times when we intentionally went out of our way to embrace strange, new situations and experiences that were, by definition, high in uncertainty (e.g., travelling in a foreign country). How do people reconcile the tug of these two opposing forces? The articles in this section delve into the motivations to pursue certainty and novelty, examining why some situations lead people to perform elaborate mental gymnastics to maintain a sense of certainty, while others lead people to favour a more expansive, flexible, and open-minded approach that relishes at least a certain amount of uncertainty.

Historically, a number of constructs have dealt with the psychology of avoiding versus embracing uncertainty. Psychoanalytically influenced theorists such as Frenkel-Brunswik (1949), Eysenck (1954), and Rokeach (1960) focused on the motivational bases for uncertainty reduction, coining such terms as 'intolerance of ambiguity', 'perceptual-cognitive rigidity', and 'closed-mindedness'. According to such approaches, some people are more averse to uncertainty than others for reasons stemming from the particular way they were raised by their parents. More recent researchers have reframed such constructs in the language of social cognition, though typically still with an emphasis on individual differences. For example, Sorrentino and colleagues (e.g., Sorrentino & White, 1986) distinguished between those who were 'certainty oriented' versus 'uncertainty oriented' and identified a range of basic cognitive and motivational tasks on which these people differ. Weary and colleagues have demonstrated that being in a state of high 'causal uncertainty' causes people to think more deeply and systematically about the behaviour of other people (e.g., Weary et al., 2001; Weary & Edwards, 1994). In related work, McGregor and colleagues (e.g., McGregor & Marigold, 2003) have begun to catalogue some of the ways in which threats to self-certainty can lead to extreme behaviour. Finally, Swann and colleagues have noted that the desire for self-certainty is so strong that it can lead people, at least in some cases, to prefer unflattering information about themselves over flattering information. That is, people sometimes prefer self-verification over self-enhancement.

Starting in the 1980s, Arie Kruglanski and colleagues defined and operationalized the 'need for closure' and the 'need to avoid closure'. In so doing, these researchers made the explicit analogy between everyday social cognition and scientific hypothesis testing. Like scientists, laypersons may at times be more methodical, systematic, and open-minded when testing their assumptions. At other times, however, they may test their assumptions in a comparatively biased and closed-minded manner. When the latter is the case, people tend to (in Kruglanski's words) 'seize' on desired information and 'freeze' their thought so that no new, potentially contaminating evidence is permitted to enter. The 1996 article included as the second reading in this Unit represents a definitive review of the motivational antecedents, mechanisms, and social psychological consequences of variation in the need for closure. As you read the article, notice how these epistemic concerns exert a systematic influence on a wide spectrum of every-day thought behaviour, including stereotyping and group decision making.

Much of the research in this area owes a considerable debt to the personality psychol-ogist Robert White. In the 1959 article included in this Unit, White proposed a dramatic departure from prevailing perspectives on motivation. White's contribution was to point out that both humans and non-humans display a proclivity for exploration that did not appear to serve any basic need like food, sex, or shelter. The data documenting this tendency posed a challenge to the prevailing behaviourist and psychodynamic perspectives, which tended to focus on an organism's behaviour in 'emergency' situations. To address this apparent curiosity motive, White felt compelled to propose a novel, latent motivational construct—*effectance*, or the desire to effect and observe change on one's environment. He described how the construct of effectance may shed light on how people establish their sense of competence. In other words, when an infant repeatedly drops her spoon onto the floor, as exasperating as it may be for the parents, this act serves an important purpose: The child is learning basic cause-and-effect relationships that help her to infer rules about a highly complex and confusing world. Look for further influence from White's ideas in later units.

3. Motivation Reconsidered: The Concept of Competence

Robert W. White, Harvard University

□ ■ □

Editor's Introduction

What are the primary goals that people pursue? Food, mating, and shelter come to mind. Indeed, much of the early history of motivational psychology—whether from a behaviourist or psychodynamic perspective—focused on how organisms respond when faced with some sort of deprivation or irregularity in one or more of these basic needs. By the late 1950s, however, Robert White noticed an array of findings suggesting that it was inappropriate to reduce human motivation to just these basic needs. If so, why would a rat run through an electrified grid merely for the experience of a new maze (with no bodily type of reinforcement provided)? Something more was needed, namely, a new theory of motivation that began to explain the pedestrian behaviour we spend most of our time doing, that is, in *non-emergency* situations.

According to White, that additional 'something' is our desire for mastery of the environment, an idea enshrined in his twin concepts of competence and effectance. When all of our basic needs have been met, we still *do* things, and much of that behaviour is in the service of exploring and gaining information about the world. When an infant repeatedly drops his spoon onto the floor, what looks like a game is actually, according to White, 'serious business'. It is an attempt to test hypotheses about the properties of objects and about cause and effect. This process is itself pleasurable as the child experiences, in the words of Groos (1901), 'joy in being a cause'. On the one hand, there is a clear evolutionary function to learning the rules of how the world works as a means to ensuring our survival. On the other hand, White suggests that in many respects this information-seeking motive

has evolved so that it has become an end unto itself. People (and perhaps even rats) simply want to learn for learning's sake.

The echoes of White's ideas have reverberated in a range of subsequent lines of inquiry in social psychology. Researchers such as Thane Pittman, Gifford Weary, and Ian McGregor have, in their own fashion, suggested that the motivation to feel as if the world is a knowable, predictable, and controllable place is something people are powerfully motivated to pursue. When that sense of prediction and control has been disturbed (by, for example, experiencing a situation of high uncertainty), people appear to respond by paying extra attention to their environment and systematically and methodically observing their surroundings with the aim of reasserting that sense that 'I am a good predictor of what will happen next.' Indeed, people will sometimes even prefer to receive bad news about themselves if it solidifies this sense of prediction confidence (e.g., Plaks & Stecher, 2007).

Bandura's (1977) well-known social cognitive theory of self-efficacy likewise demonstrates the central role of that feeling of competence. Bandura and colleagues have noted that in many areas of life it is difficult to measure with any objectivity just how competent you are. Thus, when deciding whether or not to do a task, people must rely on a difficult-to-verify belief about their likelihood of succeeding. In dozens of studies, Bandura and colleagues have demonstrated that people with high self-efficacy outperform people with low self-efficacy in any number of domains, including education, health, sports, and relationships. Simply believing that you are competent often precipitates a kind of self-fulfilling prophecy, while believing that one is not competent can cause a downward spiral into incompetence.

Other researchers have documented the link between effectance and attachment (Elliot & Reis, 2003). Attachment theory posits that in early childhood people development one of several distinct styles of relating to other people, some of which are 'secure' and predictors of social success, and some of which are 'insecure' and predictors of social problems (Bowlby, 1969; 1988). Elliot and Reis (2003) argued that, at its core, a secure attachment style reflects that sense of serene competence that allows people to view a difficult situation as a *challenge* rather than a *threat* and gives people the confidence to explore and grow.

□ ■ □

When parallel trends can be observed in realms as far apart as animal behaviour and psychoanalytic ego psychology, there is reason to suppose that we are witnessing a significant evolution of ideas. In these two realms, as in psychology as a whole, there is evidence of deepening discontent with theories of motivation based upon drives. Despite great differences in the language and concepts used to express this discontent, the theme is everywhere the same: Something important is left out when we make drives the operating forces in animal and human behaviour.

The chief theories against which the discontent is directed are those of Hull and of Freud. In their respective realms, drive-reduction theory and psychoanalytic instinct theory, which are basically very much alike, have acquired a considerable air of orthodoxy. Both views have an appealing simplicity, and both have been argued long enough so that their main outlines are generally known. In decided contrast is the position of those who are not satisfied with drives and instincts. They are numerous, and they have developed many pointed criticisms, but what they have to say has not thus far lent itself to a clear and inclusive conceptualization. Apparently there is an enduring difficulty in making these contributions fall into shape.

In this paper I shall attempt a conceptualization which gathers up some of the important things left out by drive theory. To give the concept a name, I have chosen the word *competence*, which is intended in a broad biological sense rather than in its narrow everyday meaning. As used here, competence will refer to an organism's capacity to interact effectively with its environment. In organisms capable of but little learning, this capacity might be considered an innate attribute, but in the mammals and especially man, with their highly plastic nervous systems, fitness to interact with the environment is slowly attained through prolonged feats of learning. In view of the directedness and persistence of the behaviour that leads to these feats of learning, I consider it necessary to treat competence as having a motivational aspect, and my central argument will be that the motivation needed to attain competence cannot be wholly derived from sources of energy currently conceptualized as drives or instincts. We need a different kind of motivational idea to account fully for the fact that man and the higher mammals develop a competence in dealing with the environment which they certainly do not have at birth and certainly do not arrive at simply through maturation. Such an idea, I believe, is essential for any biologically sound view of human nature.

. . .

The Trend in Animal Psychology

One of the most obvious features of animal behaviour is the tendency to explore the environment. Cats are reputedly killed by curiosity, dogs characteristically make a thorough search of their surroundings, and monkeys and chimpanzees have always impressed observers as being ceaseless investigators. Even Pavlov, whose theory of behaviour was one of Spartan simplicity, could not do without an investigatory or orientating reflex. Early workers with the obstruction method, such as Dashiell (1925) and Nissen (1930), reported that rats would cross an electrified grid simply for the privilege of exploring new territory. Some theorists reasoned that activity of this kind was always in the service of hunger, thirst, sex, or some other organic need, but this view was at least shaken by the latent learning experiments, which showed that animals learned about their surroundings even when their major needs had been purposely sated. Shortly before 1950 there was a wave of renewed interest not only in exploratory behaviour, but also in the possibility that activity and manipulation might have to be assigned the status of independent motives.

Exploratory Behaviour

In 1953 Butler reported an experiment in which monkeys learned a discrimination problem when the only reward was the opening of a window which permitted them to look out upon the normal comings and goings of the entrance room to the laboratory. The discriminations thus formed proved to be resistant to extinction. In a later study, Butler and Harlow (1957) showed that monkeys could build up a series of four different discriminations solely for the sake of inspecting the entrance room. Butler concluded that 'monkeys—and presumably all primates—have a strong motive toward visual exploration of their environment and that learning may be established on the basis of this motive just as it may be established on the basis of any motive that regularly and reliably elicits responses.' Montgomery, in 1954, reported a study with rats in which the animals, their major organic needs satiated, learned to avoid the short arm of a Y maze and to take the path which led them into additional maze territory suitable for exploration. Similar findings have been described by Myers and Miller (1954), whose rats learned to press a bar for the sake of poking their heads into a new compartment and sniffing around. Zimbardo

and Miller (1958) enlarged upon this study by varying the amount of novelty in the two compartments. In their report 'the hypothesis advanced is that opportunity to explore a "novel" environment or to effect a stimulus change in the environment is the reinforcing agent.'

These experiments make a strong case for an independent exploratory motive. The nature of this motive can be more fully discerned in situations in which the animals are allowed a varied repertory of behaviour. In 1950 Berlyne published a searching paper on curiosity, a theme which he further developed in subsequent years (1955, 1957, 1958). The rats in his experiments were confronted with an unfamiliar space and later with various novel objects placed in it. Approaching, sniffing, and examining were readily elicited by each novelty, were fairly rapidly extinguished, but were restored nearly to original strength when a fresh novelty was added. Exploration on the part of chimpanzees has been studied by Welker (1956), who put various pairs of objects before the animals and observed the course of their interest. The objects were often first approached in a gingerly manner, with signs of uneasiness, then examined and handled quite fully, then discarded. Introducing a new pair of objects promptly reproduced the whole sequence, just as it did with the rats in Berlyne's experiments. Welker used pairs of objects to find out whether or not the chimpanzees would have common preferences. Bigness and brightness evoked more interest, and greater time was spent upon objects which could be moved, changed, or made to emit sounds and light.

Recent reviews by Butler (1958) and Cofer (1959) show that a great deal of similar work is going on in animal laboratories, generally with similar results.

Exploration as a Drive

The designers of these experiments have favoured the idea that exploration should be listed as an independent primary drive. In all cases the experimental plan calls for the elimination of other primary drives by satiation. It is recognized, however, that a confirmed advocate of orthodoxy might bring up two objections to the proposed enlargement of the list of primary drives. He might claim that exploratory behaviour could be explained as a consequence of secondary reinforcement, or he might contend that it is reinforced by reduction of anxiety.

The first argument meets an immediate difficulty in Butler's finding that discriminations learned on the basis of visual exploration are resistant to extinction. When reinforcement of primary drive never takes place in the experimental situation, it is to be expected that secondary reinforcement will not prevent extinction (Miller, 1951). But even in those cases where extinction is rapid, as it was with Berlyne's rats and Welker's chimpanzees, serious problems are raised by the quick recovery of exploratory behaviour when a novel stimulus is introduced (Berlyne, 1950). In order to sustain the idea that secondary reinforcement accounts for this fact, we should have to suppose that primary rewards have often been connected with the exploration of novelties. It would have to be assumed, for instance, that the securing of food by young animals occurred with considerable frequency in connection with the investigation of novel objects. This image may seem to fit mature animals who search the environment for their food, but it certainly cannot apply to young mammals before they are weaned. Here the learning process can do virtually nothing to reinforce an interest in novelties. Gratification comes from following the same old cues to the same old consummatory responses, and the animal whose attention strays to some novel variation of the breast will only find himself frustrated. One can say that the whole mammalian pattern of infancy works in the opposite direction. The mother is more active than the young in providing gratifications, and the babies must be pursued and retrieved if they stray from the scene of her ministry. However one looks at it, the hypothesis of secondary reinforcement seems to me to demand improbable assumptions about the relationship in the lives of young animals between exploration and primary need gratification.

The hypothesis that exploratory behaviour is related to fear and receives its reinforcement from the reduction of anxiety is at first glance considerably more plausible. It seems justified by the observation that Welker's chimpanzees showed uneasiness on first contact with novel objects, and it fits the behaviour of rats in a new maze, as reported by Whiting and Mowrer (1943), where initial terror gave place to an exploration so feverish that the food reward was not eaten. Montgomery and Monkman (1955) have undertaken to challenge this hypothesis by a direct experimental attack. They showed that fear induced in rats before entering a novel situation did not increase exploratory behaviour, and that fear induced within the novel situation decreased exploration to an extent correlated with the intensity of the fear. They find it more reasonable to suppose that fear and exploration are conflicting forms of behaviour, and this view can also be defended on purely logical grounds. Fear shows itself in either freezing or avoidance, whereas exploration is clearly an instance of approach. There is hardly a more perfect example of conflict between incompatible responses than that of an animal hesitating between investigation and flight. It is clear that exploration can sometimes serve to reduce anxiety, but the proposition that it comes into existence only for this purpose cannot be so easily accepted.

What assumptions have to be made to support the thesis that exploration is motivated by anxiety reduction? It has to be assumed that certain characteristic stimuli arouse anxiety and that exploration of these stimuli is then found to reduce the anxiety. If the characteristics in question are those of novelty and unfamiliarity, we must heed Berlyne's reminder that for the infant all experience is novel and unfamiliar. Berlyne (1950) proposes that the exploratory reaction 'may be one that *all* stimuli originally evoke, but which disappears (becomes habituated) as the organism becomes familiar with them.' But if all stimuli at first arouse anxious tension, we would have to deduce that all responses would consist of avoidance in the interest of reducing that tension. Approaching a stimulus and taking steps to increase its impact could not occur. An exploratory tendency must be there in the first place before it can achieve the function of reducing anxiety. As Woodworth (1958) expresses it, 'if there were no exploratory drive to balance and overbalance the fear drive, an animal would be helpless in a novel situation.' I find it hard to believe that creatures so liberally endowed with fear could ever achieve a working mastery of the environment if they were impelled toward it only by the pressure of organic needs.

Both hypotheses thus far examined—secondary reinforcement and anxiety reduction—require us to make improbable assumptions. There remains the possibility that exploration should simply be added to the list of primary drives and otherwise treated in orthodox fashion. Myers and Miller (1954) suggest that this is the appropriate course, provided the new drive shows the same functional properties as those already known: 'If an exploratory tendency can produce learning like other drives such as hunger, and also show a similar pattern of satiation and recovery, these functional parallels to already known drives would help to justify its classification in the same category.' Logically the problem can be dealt with in this way, but we must consider very carefully what happens to the category of drive if we admit this new applicant to membership.

Using hunger as the chief model, the orthodox conception of drive involves the following characteristics: (a) there is a tissue need or deficit external to the nervous system that acts upon that system as a strong persisting stimulus; (b) this promotes activity which is terminated by a consummatory response with consequent reduction of need; (c) the reduction of need brings about the learning which gradually shapes behaviour into an economical pursuit of suitable goal objects. In this scheme the tension of an aroused drive is interpreted as unpleasant, at least in the sense that the

animal acts in such a way as to lower the drive and becomes quiescent when it is lowered. There are probably no living champions of so simple an orthodoxy, yet the scheme remains pervasive, and it is therefore worthwhile to observe that the proposed exploratory drive hardly fits it at all.

In the first place, the exploratory drive appears to bear no relation whatever to a tissue need or deficit external to the nervous system. It is, of course, clearly related to certain characteristics of stimulation from the external environment, a source of motivation which Harlow (1953) would like to see restored to a serious place in contemporary psychology; but it certainly cannot be correlated with a visceral need comparable to hunger, thirst, or sex. Considering the pattern of satiation and recovery shown by Welker's chimpanzees, Woodworth (1958) remarks that 'what becomes satiated is not the exploratory tendency in general, but the exploring of a particular place or object.' It is possible, as Hebb (1955) has pointed out, that the so-called 'reticular activation system' in the brain stem creates a kind of general drive state, and this mechanism might indeed be flexibly responsive to changes in sensory stimulation. This interesting suggestion, however, is still a far cry from viscerogenic drives; it commits us instead to the novel idea of a neurogenic motive, one in which the state of the nervous system and the patterns of external stimulation conspire to produce motivated behaviour. There is even a good deal of trouble in supposing that the adequate stimuli for exploration are either strong or persistent. Novelty certainly cannot be equated with strength or persistence, and animals seem readily able to disregard the stimuli to exploration when they are weary.

In the second place, exploratory behaviour cannot be regarded as leading to any kind of consummatory response. It is usual for the animal's investigation to subside gradually. If the animal at some point turns away and leaves the once novel object we may say that its curiosity is 'satisfied', but we do not mean by this that the equivalent of a consummatory response has just taken place. The sequence suggests rather that curiosity wears out and slowly falls to a level where it no longer guides behaviour, at least until a fresh novelty comes into view.

Finally, in the case of exploratory behaviour there is real difficulty in identifying reinforcement with need reduction. Montgomery (1954), describing the learning of the Y maze, points out that the short arm, essentially a dead end, would tend to reduce the exploratory drive, whereas the long arm, itself a complex maze, would increase it— but the long arm is chosen. If the long arm functions as a reinforcing agent, 'the mechanism underlying this reinforcement is an *increase*, rather than a decrease, in the strength of the exploratory drive.' In this experiment, as in their natural habitat, animals do not wait to have novelty thrust upon them, nor do they avoid situations in which novelty may be found. Such behaviour can be most readily conceptualized by admitting that under certain circumstances reinforcement can be correlated with an increase in arousal or excitement rather than a decrease. A drive which has no consummatory climax seems almost to require this formulation. It is distinctly implausible to connect reinforcement with the waning of an agreeable interest in the environment or with a general progress from zestful alertness to boredom.

If we admit exploration to the category of drive we are thus committing ourselves to believe that drives need have no extraneural sources in tissue deficits or visceral tensions, that they are not necessarily activated by strong or persistent stimuli, that they do not require consummatory responses, and that drive increase can sometimes be a mechanism of reinforcement.

Activity and Manipulation

Exploration is not the only motive proposed by critics of drive orthodoxy, and novelty is not the only characteristic of the environment which appears to incite motivated behaviour. Some workers have suggested a need for activity, which can be strengthened by depriving animals of their normal opportunities for movement. Kagan and Berkun (1954) used running in an activity wheel as the reward for learning and found it 'an adequate reinforcement for the instrumental response of bar pressing.' Hill (1956) showed that rats will run in an activity wheel to an extent that is correlated with their previous degree of confinement. It is certain that the activity wheel offers no novelty to the animals in these experiments. Nevertheless, they seem to want to run, and they continue to run for such long times that no part of the behaviour can readily be singled out as a consummatory response. Perhaps an unpleasant internal state created by inactivity is gradually worked off, but this is certainly accomplished by a tremendous increase of kinesthetic stimulation and muscular output which would seem to imply increased excitation in the system as a whole.

Harlow and his associates (Harlow, 1953; Harlow, Harlow, & Meyer, 1950) maintain that there is also a manipulative drive. It is aroused by certain patterns of external stimulation and reduced by actively changing the external pattern. The experiments were done with rhesus monkeys, and they involve the solving of a mechanical problem which, however, leads to no further consequences or rewards. The task might be, for instance, to raise a hasp which is kept in place by both a hook and a pin; all that can be accomplished is to raise the hasp, which opens nothing and leads to no fresh discoveries. When the hasp problem is simply installed in the living cages, the monkeys return to it and solve it as many as seven or eight times over several days. It seems unlikely that novelty can be postulated as the essential characteristic of the stimulus which evokes this repeated behaviour. The simplest interpretation is rather that value lies for the animal in the opportunity, as Zimbardo and Miller (1958) express it, 'to effect a stimulus change in the environment.' This formulation suggests something like the propensities toward mastery or power that have often been mentioned in discussions of human motivation.

The addition of activity and manipulation to the list of primary drives can only make more serious the difficulties for the orthodox model that resulted from admitting exploration. But recent research with animals has put the orthodox model on the defensive even on its home grounds. It has become increasingly clear that hunger, thirst, and sex cannot be made to fit the simple pattern that seemed so helpful 40 years ago.

Changing Conceptions of Drive

In a brief historical statement, Morgan (1957) has pointed out that the conception of drive as a noxious stimulus began to lose its popularity among research workers shortly after 1940. 'On the whole', he says, 'the stimulus concept of drive owed more to wishful thinking than to experimental fact.' When technical advances in biochemistry and brain physiology made it possible to bring in an array of new facts, there was a rapid shift toward the view that 'drives arise largely through the internal environment acting on the central nervous system.' One of the most influential discoveries was that animals have as many as a dozen specific hungers for particular kinds of food, instead of the single hunger demanded by Cannon's model of the hunger drive. If an animal's diet becomes deficient in some important element such as salt, sugar, or the vitamin-B complex, foods containing the missing element will be eagerly sought while other foods are passed by, a selectivity that obviously cannot be laid to contractions of the stomach. Similarly, a negative food preference can be produced by loading either the stomach or the blood stream with some single element of the normal diet. The early work of Beach (1942) on sexual behaviour brought out similar complications in what had for a time been taken as a relatively simple drive. Hormone levels appeared to be considerably more important than peripheral stimulation in the arousal and maintenance of the sex drive. Further work led Beach (1951) to conclude that sexual behaviour is 'governed by a complex combination of processes.' He points out that the patterns of control differ tremendously from one species to another and that within a single species the mechanisms may be quite different for males and females. Like hunger, the sex drive turns out to be no simple thing.

New methods of destroying and of stimulating brain centres in animals have had an equally disastrous effect on the orthodox drive model. The nervous system, and especially the hypothalamus, appears to be deeply implicated in the motivational process. Experimental findings on hypothalamic lesions in animals encourage Stellar (1954) to believe that there are different centres 'responsible for the control of different kinds of basic motivation,' and that in each case 'there is one main excitatory centre and one inhibitory centre which operates to depress the activity of the excitatory centre.' As research findings accumulate, this picture may seem to be too cleanly drawn. Concerning sexual behaviour, for example, Rosvold (1959) concludes a recent review by rejecting the idea of a single centre in the cerebrum; rather, the sex drive 'probably has a wide neural representation with a complex interaction between old and new brain structures and between neural and humoral agents.' Nevertheless, Miller's (1958) careful work seems to leave little doubt that motivated behaviour in every way similar to normal hunger and normal pain-fear can be elicited by electrical stimulation of quite restricted areas of the hypothalamus. It is clear that we cannot regress to a model of drives that represents the energy as coming from outside the nervous system. Whatever the effects of peripheral stimulation may be, drives also involve neural centres and neural patterns as well as internal biochemical conditions.

What sort of model becomes necessary to entertain these newly discovered facts? In 1938 Lashley expressed the view that motivation should not be equated with disturbance of organic equilibrium but rather with 'a partial excitation of a very specific sensorimotor mechanism irradiating to affect other systems of reaction'. Beach (1942) postulated that there must be in the nervous system 'a condition analogous to Sherrington's central excitatory state.'

. . .

And as a final blow to the orthodox hypothesis comes the finding by Olds and Milner (1954) that positive reinforcement can be brought about by direct electrical stimulation of certain areas of the brain. . . .

Twenty years of research have thus pretty much destroyed the orthodox drive model. It is no longer appropriate to consider that drives originate solely in tissue deficits external to the nervous system, that consummatory acts are a universal feature and goal of motivated behaviour, or that the alleviation of tissue deficits is the necessary condition for instrumental learning. Instead we have a complex picture in which humoral factors and neural centres occupy a prominent position; in which, moreover, the concept of neurogenic motives without consummatory ends appears to be entirely legitimate. Do these changes remove the obstacles to placing exploration, activity, and manipulation in the category of drives?

Perhaps this is no more than a question of words, but I should prefer at this point to call it a problem in conceptual strategy. I shall propose that these three new 'drives' have much in common and that it is useful to bring them under the single heading of competence. Even with the loosening and broadening of the concept of drive, they are still in important respects different from hunger, thirst, and sex. In hunger and thirst, tissue deficits, humoral factors, and consummatory responses retain an important position. The mature sex drive depends heavily on hormonal levels and is sharply oriented toward consummation. Tendencies like exploration do not share these characteristics, whatever else they have in common with the better known drives. It is in order to emphasize their intrinsic peculiarities, to get them considered in their own right without a cloud of surplus meanings, that I prefer in this essay to speak of the urge that makes for competence simply as motivation rather than as drive.

Related Developments in General Psychology

If a systematic survey were in order, it would be easy to show a parallel drift of opinion in other parts of the psychological realm. Among theorists of personality, for example, something like drive orthodoxy is to be found in the work of Dollard and Miller (1950), who have translated the main concepts of Freud's psychoanalysis, including processes such as repression and displacement, into the language of reinforcement theory. With them we might put Mowrer (1950), whose searching analysis of fear as an acquired drive has led him to postulate anxiety reduction as the master motive behind the development of the ego. Discontent with drive orthodoxy has long been expressed by Allport (1937, 1946), who not only argues for a functional autonomy of motives from their infantile roots in primary drives but also seriously questions the law of effect, the very cornerstone of reinforcement theory. Little comfort for the orthodox can be found in Murray's (1938) detailed taxonomy of needs, especially when it comes to needs such as achievement and construction, which can be tied to primary drives only by conceptual acrobatics. Murray and Kluckhohn (1953), moreover, have made a case for pleasure in activity for its own sake, reviving the *Funktionslust* proposed many years ago by Karl Buhler (1924) and recently developed in some detail by French (1952). They also argue for intrinsic mental needs: 'The infant's mind is not acting most of the time as the instrument of some urgent animal drive, but is preoccupied with *gratifying itself.*' Murphy (1947) takes the view that all tissues can become seats of tension and thus participants in drive; in addition to visceral drives, he postulates two independent forms—activity drives and sensory drives. Then there are workers such as Goldstein (1939) who approach the whole problem with a holistic philosophy which precludes the dictatorship of any isolated or partial drives. Goldstein (1940) assumes one master tendency, that toward self-actualization, of which the so-called visceral drives are but partial and not really isolated expressions, and which can find expression also in an urge toward perfection— toward completing what is incomplete, whether it be an outside task or the mastery of some function such as walking. It has been shown by the Ansbachers (1956) that Adler, never a friend of instinct orthodoxy, in his later years reached an idea very similar to the urge toward perfection. Maslow (1954, 1955), too, belongs with the heterodox. He insists that we should take account of growth motivation as well as the deficiency motivation implied in the visceral drives, and he offers the valuable idea of a hierarchy of motives, according to which the satisfaction of 'lower' needs makes it possible for 'higher' needs to emerge and become regnant in behaviour.

Mention of these names must suffice here to show that the trends observed in animal psychology and psychoanalytic ego psychology are pervasive in contemporary psychological thought. Doubtless the same controversies and problems could be pointed out in child development, in cognitive psychology, and in other fields. But in order to advance to my main theme, I shall select only certain developments which bear directly on the concept of competence.

Needs for Excitement and Novelty

Human experience provides plentiful evidence of the importance of reducing excessive levels of tension. Men under wartime stress, men under pressure of pain and extreme deprivation, men with excessive workloads or too much exposure to confusing social interactions, all act as if their nervous systems craved that utterly unstimulated condition which Freud once sketched as the epitome of neural bliss. But if these same men be granted their Nirvana they soon become miserable and begin to look around for a little excitement. Human experience testifies that boredom is a bad state of affairs about which something must be done. Hebb (1949) has been particularly insistent in reminding us that many of our activities, such as

reading detective stories, skin-diving, or driving cars at high speeds, give clear evidence of a need to raise the level of stimulation and excitement. Men and animals alike seem at times bent on increasing the impact of the environment and even on creating mild degrees of frustration and fear.

. . .

The concept of optimal stimulation has been developed by Leuba (1955), who sees it as helpful in resolving some of the problems of learning theory. Believing that most theorizing about motivation has been based upon 'powerful biological or neurotic drives', Leuba bids us look at the much more common learning situations of nursery, playground, and school, where 'actions which increase stimulation and produce excitement are strongly reinforced, sometimes to the dismay of parents and teachers.' He proposes that there is an optimal level of stimulation, subject to variation at different times, and that learning is associated with movement toward this optimal level, downward when stimulation is too high and upward when it is too low. . . .

In recent papers Young (1949, 1955) has argued for a hedonic theory of motivation, one in which affective processes 'constitute a form of primary motivation.' According to Young's theory, 'an organism behaves so as to maximize positive affective arousal (delight, enjoyment) and to minimize negative arousal (distress).' McClelland (1953) has offered a version of hedonic theory which is of particular value in understanding the significance of novelty. Affective arousal occurs when a stimulus pattern produces a discrepancy from the existing adaptation level. Small discrepancies produce pleasant affect and a tendency to approach; large ones produce unpleasantness and a tendency toward avoidance. The child at play, like the young chimpanzee and the exploring rat, needs frequent novelty in the stimulus field in order to keep up his interest—in order to maintain pleasant discrepancies from whatever adaptation level he has reached. Hebb's (1949) theory of the neurological correlates of learning also deals with novelty, though in a somewhat different way. He equates sustained interest with a state of neural affairs in which 'phase sequences' are relatively complex and are growing, in the sense of establishing new internal relations. Such a state follows most readily from a stimulus field characterized by difference-in-sameness; that is, containing much that is familiar along with certain features that are novel. If the field is entirely familiar, phase sequences run off quickly, are short-circuited, and thus fail to produce sustained interest. Hebb's theory, which has the engaging quality of being able to explain why we enjoy reading a detective story once but not right over again, expresses in a neurological hypothesis the familiar fact that well-learned, habituated processes do not in themselves greatly interest us. Interest seems to require elements of unfamiliarity: of something still to be found out and of learning still to be done.

It seems to me that these contributions, though differing as to details, speak with unanimity on their central theme and would force us, if nothing else did, to reconsider seriously the whole problem of motivation. Boredom, the unpleasantness of monotony, the attraction of novelty, the tendency to vary behaviour rather than repeating it rigidly, and the seeking of stimulation and mild excitement stand as inescapable facts of human experience and clearly have their parallels in animal behaviour. We may seek rest and minimal stimulation at the end of the day, but that is not what we are looking for the next morning. Even when its primary needs are satisfied and its homeostatic chores are done, and organism is alive, active, and up to something.

Dealing with the Environment

If we consider things only from the viewpoint of affect, excitement, and novelty, we are apt to overlook another important aspect of behaviour, its effect upon the environment. Moving in this direction, Diamond (1939) invites us to consider the motivational properties of the sensorineural system, the apparatus whereby higher animals

'maintain their relations to the environment.' He conceives of this system as demanding stimulation and as acting in such a manner as to 'force the environment to stimulate it.' Even if one thinks only of the infant's exploring eyes and hands, it is clear that the main direction of behaviour is by no means always that of reducing the impact of stimulation. When the eyes follow a moving object, or when the hand grasps an object which it has touched, the result is to preserve the stimulus and to increase its effect. In more elaborate explorations the consequence of a series of actions may be to vary the manner in which a stimulus acts upon the sense organs. It is apparent that the exploring, manipulating child produces by his actions precisely what Hebb's theory demands as a basis for continuing interest: He produces differences-in-sameness in the stimulus field.

. . .

Being interested in the environment implies having some kind of satisfactory interaction with it. Several workers call attention to the possibility that satisfaction might lie in having an effect upon the environment, in dealing with it, and changing it in various ways. Groos (1901), in his classical analysis of play, attached great importance to the child's 'joy in being a cause', as shown in making a clatter, 'hustling things about', and playing in puddles where large and dramatic effects can be produced. 'We demand a knowledge of effects', he wrote, 'and to be ourselves the producers of effects.' Piaget (1952) remarks upon the child's special interest in objects that are affected by his own movements. This aspect of behaviour occupies a central place in the work of Skinner (1953), who describes it as 'operant' and who thus 'emphasizes the fact that the behaviour *operates* upon the environment to generate consequences.' These consequences are fed back through the sense organs and may serve to reinforce behaviour even when no organic needs are involved. A rat will show an increased tendency to press a bar when this act produces a click or a buzz. A baby will continue to investigate when his efforts produce rattling or tinkling sounds or sparkling reflections from a shiny object. The young chimpanzees in Welker's experiment spent the longest time over objects which could be lighted or made to emit sounds. Skinner finds it 'difficult, if not impossible, to trace these reinforcing effects to a history of conditioning.' 'We may plausibly argue', he continues, 'that a capacity to be reinforced by any feedback from the environment would be biologically advantageous, since it would prepare the organism to manipulate the environment successfully before a given state of deprivation developed.'

Woodworth's Behaviour-Primacy Theory

The most far-reaching attempt to give these aspects of behaviour a systematic place in the theory of motivation is contained in Woodworth's recent book, *Dynamics of Behaviour* (1958). Woodworth takes his start from the idea that a great deal of human behaviour appears to be directed toward producing effects upon the environment without immediate service to any aroused organic need. 'Its incentives and rewards are in the field of behaviour and not in the field of homeostasis.' This is illustrated by exploratory behaviour, which is directed outward toward the environment. . . .

More complex play, such as building with blocks, illustrates the same outgoing tendency and reveals more plainly the element of finding out what one can and cannot do with objects. Even social play falls into the pattern. Playmates do not chiefly supply affection or satisfy organic needs; rather, they 'afford the opportunity to do something interesting in the environment.'

Woodworth draws a contrast between *need-primacy* theories of motivation and the *behaviour-primacy* theory. The latter holds that 'all behaviour is directed primarily toward dealing with the environment.' It is to be noted that 'dealing with the environment' means a good deal more than receiving stimuli and making responses. Stimuli must be taken as indicators of objects in space, and responses must be adapted to produce effects upon these objects. Even the so-called 'mental'

capacities, such as memory and ideational thinking, become in time high-level methods of dealing with the environment. Woodworth leaves no doubt as to what he considers basic in motivation. 'We are making the claim that this direction of receptive and motor activity toward the environment is the fundamental tendency of animal and human behaviour and that it is the all-pervasive primary motivation of behaviour.' Organic drives have to break into this constantly flowing stream of activity and turn it in a special direction. But the goals of drives cannot be achieved without effective action upon one's surroundings. The ever-present, ever-primary feature of motivation is the tendency to deal with the environment.

. . .

Bearing in mind these examples, as well as the dealings with environment pointed out by other workers, we must now attempt to describe more fully the possible nature of the motivational aspect of competence. It needs its own name, and in view of the foregoing analysis I propose that this name be *effectance*.

Effectance

The new freedom produced by two decades of research on animal drives is of great help in this undertaking. We are no longer obliged to look for a source of energy external to the nervous system, for a consummatory climax, or for a fixed connection between reinforcement and tension reduction. Effectance motivation cannot, of course, be conceived as having a source in tissues external to the nervous system. It is in no sense a deficit motive. We must assume it to be neurogenic, its 'energies' being simply those of the living cells that make up the nervous system. External stimuli play an important part, but in terms of 'energy' this part is secondary, as one can see most clearly when environmental stimulation is actively sought. Putting it picturesquely, we might say that the effectance urge represents what the neuromuscular system wants to do when it is otherwise unoccupied or is gently stimulated by the environment. Obviously there are no consummatory acts; satisfaction would appear to lie in the arousal and maintaining of activity rather than in its slow decline toward bored passivity. The motive need not be conceived as intense and powerful in the sense that hunger, pain, or fear can be powerful when aroused to high pitch. There are plenty of instances in which children refuse to leave their absorbed play in order to eat or to visit the toilet. Strongly aroused drives, pain, and anxiety, however, can be conceived as overriding the effectance urge and capturing the energies of the neuromuscular system. But effectance motivation is persistent in the sense that it regularly occupies the spare waking time between episodes of homeostatic crisis.

In speculating upon this subject we must bear in mind the continuous nature of behaviour. This is easier said than done; habitually we break things down in order to understand them, and such units as the reflex arc, the stimulus-response sequence, and the single transaction with the environment seem like inevitable steps toward clarity. Yet, when we apply such an analysis to playful exploration we lose the most essential aspect of the behaviour. It is constantly circling from stimulus to perception to action to effect to stimulus to perception, and so on around; or, more properly, these processes are all in continuous action and continuous change. Dealing with the environment means carrying on a continuing transaction which gradually changes one's relation to the environment. Because there is no consummatory climax, satisfaction has to be seen as lying in a considerable series of transactions, in a trend of behaviour rather than a goal that is achieved. It is difficult to make the word 'satisfaction' have this connotation, and we shall do well to replace it by 'feeling of efficacy' when attempting to indicate the subjective and affective side of effectance.

It is useful to recall the findings about novelty: the singular effectiveness of novelty in engaging interest and for a time supporting persistent behaviour. We also need to consider the selective

continuance of transactions in which the animal or child has a more or less pronounced effect upon the environment—in which something happens as a consequence of his activity. Interest is not aroused and sustained when the stimulus field is so familiar that it gives rise at most to reflex acts or automatized habits. It is not sustained when actions produce no effects or changes in the stimulus field. Our conception must therefore be that effectance motivation is aroused by stimulus conditions which offer, as Hebb (1949) puts it, difference-in-sameness. This leads to variability and novelty of response, and interest is best sustained when the resulting action affects the stimulus so as to produce further difference-in-sameness. Interest wanes when action begins to have less effect; effectance motivation subsides when a situation has been explored to the point that it no longer presents new possibilities.

We have to conceive further that the arousal of playful and exploratory interest means the appearance of organization involving both the cognitive and active aspects of behaviour. Change in the stimulus field is not an end in itself, so to speak; it happens when one is passively moved about, and it may happen as a consequence of random movements without becoming focalized and instigating exploration. Similarly, action that has effects is not an end in itself, for if one unintentionally kicks away a branch while walking, or knocks something off a table, these effects by no means necessarily become involved in playful investigation.

. . .

Some objection may be felt to my introducing the word *competence* in connection with behaviour that is so often playful. Certainly the playing child is doing things for fun, not because of a desire to improve his competence in dealing with the stern hard world. In order to forestall misunderstanding, it should be pointed out that the usage here is parallel to what we do when we connect sex with its biological goal of reproduction. The sex drive aims for pleasure and gratification, and reproduction is a consequence that is presumably unforeseen by animals and by man at primitive levels of understanding. Effectance motivation similarly aims for the feeling of efficacy, not for the vitally important learnings that come as its consequence. If we consider the part played by competence motivation in adult human life we can observe the same parallel. Sex may now be completely and purposefully divorced from reproduction but nevertheless pursued for the pleasure it can yield. Similarly, effectance motivation may lead to continuing exploratory interests or active adventures when in fact there is no longer any gain in actual competence or any need for it in terms of survival. In both cases the motive is capable of yielding surplus satisfaction well beyond what is necessary to get the biological work done.

In infants and young children it seems to me sensible to conceive of effectance motivation as undifferentiated. Later in life it becomes profitable to distinguish various motives such as cognizance, construction, mastery, and achievement. It is my view that all such motives have a root in effectance motivation. They are differentiated from it through life experiences which emphasize one or another aspect of the cycle of transaction with environment. Of course, the motives of later childhood and of adult life are no longer simple and can almost never be referred to a single root. They can acquire loadings of anxiety, defence, and compensation, they can become fused with unconscious fantasies of a sexual, aggressive, or omnipotent character, and they can gain force because of their service in producing realistic results in the way of income and career. It is not my intention to cast effectance in the star part in adult motivation. The acquisition of motives is a complicated affair in which simple and sovereign theories grow daily more obsolete. Yet, it may be that the satisfaction of effectance contributes significantly to those feelings of interest which often sustain us so well in day-to-day actions, particularly when the things we are doing have continuing elements of novelty.

The Biological Significance of Competence

The conviction was expressed at the beginning of this paper that some such concept as competence, interpreted motivationally, was essential for any biologically sound view of human nature. This necessity emerges when we consider the nature of living systems, particularly when we take a longitudinal view. What an organism does at a given moment does not always give the right clue as to what it does over a period of time. Discussing this problem, Angyal (1941) has proposed that we should look for the general pattern followed by the total organismic process over the course of time. Obviously this makes it necessary to take account of growth. Angyal defines life as 'a process of self-expansion'; the living system 'expands at the expense of its surroundings', assimilating parts of the environment and transforming them into functioning parts of itself. Organisms differ from other things in nature in that they are 'self-governing entities' which are to some extent 'autonomous'. Internal processes govern them as well as external 'heteronomous' forces. In the course of life there is a relative increase in the preponderance of internal over external forces. The living system expands, assimilates more of the environment, transforms its surroundings so as to bring them under greater control. 'We may say', Angyal writes, 'that the general dynamic trend of the organism is toward an increase of autonomy. . . . The human being has a characteristic tendency toward self-determination, that is, a tendency to resist external influences and to subordinate the heteronomous forces of the physical and social environment to its own sphere of influence.' The trend toward increased autonomy is characteristic so long as growth of any kind is going on, though in the end the living system is bound to succumb to the pressure of heteronomous forces.

Of all living creatures, it is man who takes the longest strides toward autonomy. This is not because of any unusual tendency toward bodily expansion at the expense of the environment. It is rather that man, with his mobile hands and abundantly developed brain, attains an extremely high level of competence in his transactions with his surroundings. The building of houses, roads, and bridges, the making of tools and instruments, the domestication of plants and animals, all qualify as planful changes made in the environment so that it comes more or less under control and serves our purposes rather than intruding upon them. We meet the fluctuations of outdoor temperature, for example, not only with our bodily homeostatic mechanisms, which alone would be painfully unequal to the task, but also with clothing, buildings, controlled fires, and such complicated devices as self-regulating central heating and air conditioning. Man as a species has developed a tremendous power of bringing the environment into his service, and each individual member of the species must attain what is really quite an impressive level of competence if he is to take part in the life around him.

We are so accustomed to these human accomplishments that it is hard to realize how long an apprenticeship they require. At the outset the human infant is a slow learner in comparison with other animal forms. Hebb (1949) speaks of 'the astonishing inefficiency of man's first learning, as far as immediate results are concerned', an inefficiency which he attributes to the large size of the association areas in the brain and the long time needed to bring them under sensory control. The human lack of precocity in learning shows itself even in comparison with one of the next of kin: As Hebb points out, 'the human baby takes six months, the chimpanzee four months, before making a clear distinction between friend and enemy.' Later in life the slow start will pay dividends. Once the fundamental perceptual elements, simple associations, and conceptual sequences have been established, later learning can proceed with ever increasing swiftness and complexity. In Hebb's words, 'learning at maturity concerns patterns and events whose parts at least are familiar and which already have a number of other associations.'

This general principle of cumulative learning, starting from slowly acquired rudiments and proceeding thence with increasing efficiency, can be illustrated by such processes as manipulation and locomotion, which may culminate in the acrobat devising new stunts or the dancer working out a new ballet. It is especially vivid in the case of language, where the early mastery of words and pronunciation seems such a far cry from spontaneous adult speech. A strong argument has been made by Hebb (1949) that the learning of visual forms proceeds over a similar course from slowly learned elements to rapidly combined patterns. Circles and squares, for example, cannot be discriminated at a glance without a slow apprenticeship involving eye movements, successive fixations, and recognition of angles. Hebb proposes that the recognition of visual patterns without eye movement 'is possible only as the result of an intensive and prolonged visual training that goes on from the moment of birth, during every moment that the eyes are open, with an increase in skill evident over a period of 12 to 16 years at least.'

On the motor side there is likewise a lot to be cumulatively learned. The playing, investigating child slowly finds out the relationships between what he does and what he experiences. He finds out, for instance, how hard he must push what in order to produce what effect. Here the S-R formula is particularly misleading. It would come nearer the truth to say that the child is busy learning R-S connections—the effects that are likely to follow upon his own behaviour. But even in this reversed form the notion of bonds or connections would still misrepresent the situation, for it is only a rare specimen of behaviour that can properly be conceived as determined by fixed neural channels and a fixed motor response. As Hebb has pointed out, discussing the phenomenon of 'motor equivalence' named by Lashley (1942), a rat which has been trained to press a lever will press it with the left forepaw, the right forepaw, by climbing upon it, or by biting it; a monkey will open the lid of a food box with either hand, with a foot, or even with a stick; and we might add that a good baseball player can catch a fly ball while running in almost any direction and while in almost any posture, including leaping in the air and plunging forward to the ground. All of these feats are possible because of a history of learnings in which the main lesson has been the effects of actions upon the stimulus fields that represent the environment. What has been learned is not a fixed connection but a flexible relationship between stimulus fields and the effects that can be produced in them by various kinds of action.

One additional example, drawn this time from Piaget (1952), is particularly worth mentioning because of its importance in theories of development. Piaget points out that a great deal of mental development depends upon the idea that the world is made up of objects having substance and permanence. Without such an 'object concept' it would be impossible to build up the ideas of space and causality and to arrive at the fundamental distinction between self and external world. Observation shows that the object concept, 'far from being innate or ready-made in experience, is constructed little by little'. Up to seven and eight months the Piaget children searched for vanished objects only in the sense of trying to continue the actions, such as sucking or grasping, in which the objects had played a part. When an object was really out of sight or touch, even if only because it was covered by a cloth, the infants undertook no further exploration. Only gradually, after some study of the displacement of objects by moving, swinging, and dropping them, does the child begin to make an active search for a vanished object, and only still more gradually does he learn, at 12 months or more, to make allowance for the object's sequential displacements and thus to seek it where it has gone rather than where it was last in sight. Thus, it is only through cumulative learning that the child arrives at the idea of permanent substantial objects.

The infant's play is indeed serious business. If he did not while away his time pulling strings, shaking rattles, examining wooden parrots, dropping pieces of bread and celluloid swans, when would he learn to discriminate visual patterns, to catch and throw, and to build up his concept of the object? When would he acquire the many other foundation stones necessary for cumulative learning? The more closely we analyze the behaviour of the human infant, the more clearly do we realize that infancy is not simply a time when the nervous system matures and the muscles grow stronger. It is a time of active and continuous learning, during which the basis is laid for all those processes, cognitive and motor, whereby the child becomes able to establish effective transactions with his environment and move toward a greater degree of autonomy. Helpless as he may seem until he begins to toddle, he has by that time already made substantial gains in the achievement of competence.

Under primitive conditions survival must depend quite heavily upon achieved competence. We should expect to find things so arranged as to favour and maximize this achievement. Particularly in the case of man, where so little is provided innately and so much has to be learned through experience, we should expect to find highly advantageous arrangements for securing a steady cumulative learning about the properties of the environment and the extent of possible transactions. Under these circumstances we might expect to find a very powerful drive operating to ensure progress toward competence, just as the vital goals of nutrition and reproduction are secured by powerful drives, and it might therefore seem paradoxical that the interests of competence should be so much entrusted to times of play and leisurely exploration. There is good reason to suppose, however, that a strong drive would be precisely the wrong arrangement to secure a flexible, knowledgeable power of transaction with the environment. Strong drives cause us to learn certain lessons well, but they do not create maximum familiarity with our surroundings.

This point was demonstrated half a century ago in some experiments by Yerkes and Dodson (1908). They showed that maximum motivation did not lead to the most rapid solving of problems, especially if the problems were complex. For each problem there was an optimum level of motivation, neither the highest nor the lowest, and the optimum was lower for more complex tasks. The same problem has been discussed more recently by Tolman (1948) in his paper on cognitive maps. A cognitive map can be narrow or broad, depending upon the range of cues picked up in the course of learning. Tolman suggests that one of the conditions which tends to narrow the range of cues is a high level of motivation. In everyday terms, a man hurrying to an important business conference is likely to perceive only the cues that help him to get there faster, whereas a man taking a stroll after lunch is likely to pick up a substantial amount of casual information about his environment. The latent learning experiments with animals, and experiments such as those of Johnson (1953) in which drive level has been systematically varied in a situation permitting incidental learning, give strong support to this general idea. In a recent contribution, Bruner, Matter, and Papanek (1955) make a strong case for the concept of breadth of learning and provide additional evidence that it is favoured by moderate and hampered by strong motivation. The latter 'has the effect of speeding up learning at the cost of narrowing it.' Attention is concentrated upon the task at hand and little that is extraneous to this task is learned for future use.

These facts enable us to see the biological appropriateness of an arrangement which uses periods of less intense motivation for the development of competence. This is not to say that the narrower but efficient learnings that go with the reduction of strong drives make no contribution to general effectiveness. They are certainly an important element in capacity to deal with the environment, but a much greater effectiveness results from having this capacity fed also from learnings that take place in quieter times. It is then that the infant can attend to matters of lesser urgency, exploring the properties of things he does not fear and does not need to eat, learning to gauge the force of his

string-pulling when the only penalty for failure is silence on the part of the attached rattles, and generally accumulating for himself a broad knowledge and a broad skill in dealing with his surroundings.

The concept of competence can be most easily discussed by choosing, as we have done, examples of interaction with the inanimate environment. It applies equally well, however, to transactions with animals and with other human beings, where the child has the same problem of finding out what effects he can have upon the environment and what effects it can have upon him. The earliest interactions with members of the family may involve needs so strong that they obscure the part played by effectance motivation, but perhaps the example of the well-fed baby diligently exploring the several features of his mother's face will serve as a reminder that here, too, there are less urgent moments when learning for its own sake can be given free rein.

In this closing section I have brought together several ideas which bear on the evolutionary significance of competence and of its motivation. I have sought in this way to deepen the biological roots of the concept and thus help it to attain the stature in the theory of behaviour which has not been reached by similar concepts in the past. To me it seems that the most important proving ground for this concept is the effect it may have on our understanding of the development of personality. Does it assist our grasp of early object relations, the reality principle, and the first steps in the development of the ego? Can it be of service in distinguishing the kinds of defence available at different ages and in providing clues to the replacement of primitive defences by successful adaptive manoeuvres? Can it help fill the yawning gap known as the latency period, a time when the mastery of school subjects and other accomplishments claim so large a share of time and energy? Does it bear upon the self and the vicissitudes of self-esteem, and can it enlighten the origins of psychological disorder? Can it make adult motives and interests more intelligible and enable us to rescue the concept of sublimation from the difficulties which even its best friends have recognized? I believe it can be shown that existing explanations of development are not satisfactory and that the addition of the concept of competence cuts certain knots in personality theory. But this is not the subject of the present communication, where the concept is offered much more on the strength of its logical and biological probability.

Summary

The main theme of this paper is introduced by showing that there is widespread discontent with theories of motivation built upon primary drives. Signs of this discontent are found in realms as far apart as animal psychology and psychoanalytic ego psychology. In the former, the commonly recognized primary drives have proved to be inadequate in explaining exploratory behaviour, manipulation, and general activity. In the latter, the theory of basic instincts has shown serious shortcomings when it is stretched to account for the development of the effective ego. Workers with animals have attempted to meet their problem by invoking secondary reinforcement and anxiety reduction, or by adding exploration and manipulation to the roster of primary drives. In parallel fashion, psychoanalytic workers have relied upon the concept of neutralization of instinctual energies, have seen anxiety reduction as the central motive in ego development, or have hypothesized new instincts such as mastery. It is argued here that these several explanations are not satisfactory and that a better conceptualization is possible, indeed that it has already been all but made.

In trying to form this conceptualization, it is first pointed out that many of the earlier tenets of primary drive theory have been discredited by recent experimental work. There is no longer any compelling reason to identify either pleasure or reinforcement with drive reduction, or to think of motivation as requiring a source of energy external to the nervous system. This opens the way for considering in their own right those aspects of animal and human behaviour in which stimulation and contact with the environment seem to be sought and welcomed, in which raised tension and even mild excitement seem to be cherished, and in which novelty and variety seem to be enjoyed for their own sake. Several reports are cited that bear upon interest in the environment and the rewarding effects of environmental feedback. The latest contribution is that of Woodworth (1958), who makes dealing with the environment the most fundamental element in motivation.

The survey indicates a certain unanimity as to the kinds of behaviour that cannot be successfully conceptualized in terms of primary drives. This behaviour includes visual exploration, grasping, crawling and walking, attention and perception, language and thinking, exploring novel objects and places, manipulating the surroundings, and producing effective changes in the environment. The thesis is then proposed that all of these behaviours have a common biological significance: They all form part of the process whereby the animal or child learns to interact effectively with his environment. The word *competence* is chosen as suitable to indicate this common property. Further, it is maintained that competence cannot be fully acquired simply through behaviour instigated by drives. It receives substantial contributions from activities which, though playful and exploratory in character, at the same time show direction, selectivity, and persistence in interacting with the environment. Such activities in the ultimate service of competence must therefore be conceived to be motivated in their own right. It is proposed to designate this motivation by the term effectance, and to characterize the experience produced as a *feeling of efficacy*.

In spite of its sober biological purpose, effectance motivation shows itself most unambiguously in the playful and investigatory behaviour of young animals and children. Specimens of such behaviour, drawn from Piaget (1952), are analyzed in order to demonstrate their constantly transactional nature. Typically they involve continuous chains of events which include stimulation, cognition, action, effect on the environment, new stimulation, etc. They are carried on with considerable persistence and with selective emphasis on parts of the environment which provide changing and interesting feedback in connection with effort expended. Their significance is destroyed if we try to break into the circle arbitrarily and declare that one part of it, such as cognition alone or active effort alone, is the real point, the goal, or the special seat of satisfaction. Effectance motivation must be conceived to involve satisfaction—a feeling of efficacy—in transactions in which behaviour has an exploratory, varying, experimental character and produces changes in the stimulus field. Having this character, the behaviour leads the organism to find out how the environment can be changed and what consequences flow from these changes.

In higher animals and especially in man, where so little is innately provided and so much has to be learned about dealing with the environment, effectance motivation independent of primary drives can be seen as an arrangement having high adaptive value. Considering the slow rate of learning in infancy and the vast amount that has to be learned before there can be an effective level of interaction with surroundings, young animals and children would simply not learn enough unless they worked pretty steadily at the task between episodes of homeostatic crisis. The association of interest with this 'work', making it play and fun, is thus somewhat comparable to the association of sexual pleasure with the biological goal of reproduction. Effectance motivation need not be conceived as strong in the sense that sex, hunger, and fear are strong when violently aroused. It is moderate but persistent, and in this, too, we can discern a feature that is favourable for adaptation. Strong motivation reinforces learning in a narrow sphere, whereas moderate motivation is more conducive to an exploratory and experimental attitude which leads to competent interactions in general, without reference to an immediate pressing need. Man's huge cortical association areas might have been a suicidal piece of specialization if they had come without a steady, persistent inclination toward interacting with the environment.

Discussion Questions

1.   Why do people enjoy and actively seek out experiences that are plainly terrifying (e.g., roller coasters, skydiving)? Every fibre of their being is screaming that this activity is a bad idea and yet people (some more than others) are irresistibly drawn to it. How might White's theory begin to explain this phenomenon?

2.   Consider Brewer's optimal distinctiveness theory (from Unit 1). How might White's ideas of difference-in-sameness relate to the processes and phenomena Brewer describes?

4. Motivated Closing of the Mind: 'Seizing' and 'Freezing'

Arie W. Kruglanski, University of Maryland College Park
Donna M. Webster, University of Florida

Editor's Introduction

Thinking can be hard work. Often—perhaps more often than we care to admit—we opt for the easy way out when solving a problem by going with the first solution that pops into our mind. At other times, however, we might be 'paralyzed with indecision'—methodically ruminating about the pros and cons of the different options. (I'm sure you know someone who always seems to take an eternity when deciding what to order at a restaurant!) When are we more versus less likely to adopt either approach?

While other theorists have noted that thinking is itself a motivated act (see Ziva Kunda's 1990 article in Unit 5), few have developed the distinction between the need for specific closure and the need for non-specific closure as comprehensively and systematically as Arie Kruglanski and his colleagues have. In brief, Kruglanski's theory notes that people are not only driven by directional motivation, or the motivation to seek *specific* conclusions (e.g., 'I am a wonderful person'); they also are guided by non-directional motivation, or the motivation to do more or less *thinking in general* (regardless of what that thinking is about). The emphasis in the present article is on the need for non-specific closure. Kruglanski and Webster systematically spell out (a) numerous ways in which a high need for closure or a high need to avoid closure may be manipulated in the laboratory, and (b) numerous consequences of being in a state of high need for closure versus a high need to avoid closure. For example, people with a high need for closure are comparatively more likely to rely on underlying personality dispositions (rather than situational

pressures) to explain another person's behaviour, more likely to judge people based on first impressions, and more likely to use stereotypes.

Importantly, Kruglanski and colleagues have found that not only is need for closure a variable that can be manipulated in the laboratory, it is also an individual difference variable. That is, some people chronically go through life with a high need for closure (those people who are more apt to make snap judgments) while others go through life with a need to avoid closure (those people who can't decide what to order from the menu). These individual differences can be measured using Kruglanski et al.'s need for closure questionnaire.

According to Kruglanski's model, under a high need for closure, as people gain information about a person or object, a coherent belief emerges at a certain point. Kruglanski's term for this is belief crystallization. Prior to belief crystallization, those with a high need for closure are frantically casting about for a belief to latch on to in a process called seizing. Once belief crystallization has occurred, a high need for closure induces a tendency to lock into that belief and adopt a more closed-minded approach to any additional information. This process is known as freezing. As you read about seizing and freezing, think about how these concepts relate to other motivational concepts covered in this book, including Gollwitzer's concepts of implementational versus deliberative mindsets (Unit 6).

What causes the need to avoid closure? As Kruglanski notes, certain pressures may cause us to delay forming a judgment as long as possible while we continue to gather more and more information.

One such pressure is fear of invalidity (roughly, the fear of being publically proven wrong). Tetlock and colleagues have referred to a similar construct that they call accountability. Accountability refers to 'the implicit or explicit expectation that one may be called on to justify one's beliefs, feelings, and actions to others' (Lerner & Tetlock, 1999, p. 255). The term accountability has become a widely used catchword in many fields of endeavour including politics, education, and management and is viewed by many as a significant check against many decision-making errors. Implicit in people's understanding of accountability is the belief that it induces more rigorous, objective, or even-handed thought. Indeed, early studies found that accountability had a de-biasing effect on primacy effects in impression formation (Tetlock, 1983) and the fundamental attribution error (Tetlock, 1985). But subsequent research painted a more complicated picture; some studies found that accountability can amplify stereotypic thought (e.g., Bodenhausen, Kramer, & Susser, 1994; Lambert et al., 2003). It appears, then, that simply making people afraid of being publically wrong is insufficient; they must also have available the means to make the right decision.

□ ■ □

The construction of new knowledge is a pervasive human pursuit for both individuals and collectives. From relatively simple activities such as crossing a busy road to highly complex endeavours such as launching a space shuttle, new knowledge is indispensable for secure decisions and reasoned actions. The knowledge-construction process is often involved and intricate. It draws on background notions activated from memory and local information from the immediate context. It entails the extensive testing of hypotheses and the piecing of isolated cognitive bits into coherent wholes. It integrates inchoate sensations with articulate thoughts, detects meaningful signals in seas of ambient noise, and more.

Two aspects of knowledge construction are of present interest: its motivated nature and its social character. That knowledge construction has a motivational base should come as no particular surprise. The host of effortful activities it comprises pose considerable demands on resource allocation; hence, it may well require motivation to get under way. Specifically, individuals may desire knowledge on some topics and not others, and they may delimit their constructive endeavours to those particular domains. But what kind of a motivational variable is the 'desire for knowledge'? At least two answers readily suggest themselves: Knowledge could be desired because it conveys welcome news in regard to a given concern or because it conveys any definite news (whether welcome or unwelcome) in instances in which such information is required for some purpose. For instance, a mother may desire to know that her child did well on the Scholastic Aptitude Test (SAT) so that she may send her or him to a selective college, whereas the college admissions officer may desire to simply know how well or poorly the child did so that he or she may make the appropriate admission decision. The former type of desire has been referred to as the need for a specific closure, and the latter has been referred to as the need for a non-specific closure. The need for a specific closure implies the desirability of a particular answer to a question (e.g., that one's child did well on the SAT), whereas the need for a non-specific closure implies the desirability of any answer as long as it is definite (Kruglanski, 1989, 1990a, 1990b). Various needs for specific closure have received considerable emphasis in the social cognition literature (e.g., for reviews, see Kruglanski, 1996; Kunda, 1990). The need for non-specific closure has attracted much less attention. A major purpose of this article is to redress this imbalance by focusing on the latter type of desire.

In addition to its motivated nature, the knowledge-construction process is suffused with social significance. First, various social entities (other persons, groups, or social categories) are often the objects of knowledge-construction endeavours. In other words, constructive efforts are frequently meant to yield socially relevant knowledge. Furthermore, other people may often supply the informational means whereby constructive ends are attained. They may provide social comparison information (Festinger, 1954) or feedback pertinent to self-verification or self-enhancement motives (Swann, 1990). They may supply consensus information in instances in which consensus is desired, confirm one's favourite hypotheses, or bear witness to one's efficacy and control. Of course, people might impede rather than facilitate the attainment of desired knowledge and be occasionally the bearers of 'bad news'. Even then, however, they remain motivationally relevant to one's epistemic purposes as potential sources of pertinent information. An important objective of the present article is, therefore, to flesh out the social psychological significance of knowledge-construction processes, particularly as these processes relate to the need for (non-specific) closure.

In what follows, we present theory and research elucidating the nature of this need, its antecedent conditions, and its consequences. Essentially, we hope to demonstrate that the need for closure exerts a broad range of effects on the knowledge-construction process and hence, indirectly, on a wide range of related social psychological phenomena at the intrapersonal, interpersonal, and group levels of analysis.

The Need for Closure

The need for cognitive closure refers to individuals' desire for a firm answer to a question and an aversion toward ambiguity. As used here, the term *need* is meant to denote a motivated tendency or proclivity rather than a tissue deficit (for a similar usage, see Cacioppo & Petty, 1982). We assume that the need for cognitive closure is akin to a person's goal (Pervin, 1989). As such, it may prompt activities aimed at the attainment of closure, bias the individual's choices and preferences toward closure-bound pursuits, and induce negative affect when closure is threatened or undermined and positive affect when it is facilitated or attained.

A Motivational Continuum in Regard to Closure

We assume that the motivation toward closure varies along a continuum anchored at one end with a strong need for closure and at the other end with a strong need to avoid closure. Closure, in other words, may not be desired universally. Although in some circumstances people may strive to attain it, in other situations they may actively avoid it or exhibit little preference for it over ambiguity. Individuals at the need for closure end of the continuum may display considerable cognitive impatience or impulsivity: They may 'leap' to judgment on the basis of inconclusive evidence and exhibit rigidity of thought and reluctance to entertain views different from their own. At the opposite end of the continuum, denoting a high need to avoid closure, people may savour uncertainty and be reluctant to commit to a definite opinion. In those circumstances, individuals may suspend judgment and be quick to engender alternatives to any emergent view.

Effects of the motivation for closure are assumed to be monotonic along the continuum. By this assumption, the motivational effects should be directionally similar for any pair of points on the continuum: A higher (vs lower) degree of the need for closure should effect a higher or lower degree of some phenomenon, irrespective of the points' specific locations. Thus, comparing low and high need for closure conditions should yield effects directionally similar to those involved in comparing high and low need to avoid closure conditions. Evidence reviewed in subsequent sections consistently supports this assumption.

Antecedents of the Motivation Toward Closure

What conditions may induce a given motivation toward closure? According to the present analysis, these may be conditions that highlight the perceived benefits or desirability of closure or of the absence of closure (see also Kruglanski, 1996). For instance, a potential benefit of closure may be the ability to act or decide in time for meeting an important deadline. Thus, the need for closure should be heightened under time pressure. An alternative benefit of closure is removal of the necessity for further information processing; if so, need for closure should be heightened under conditions that render processing difficult, laborious, or aversive. Some such conditions (e.g., environmental noise) may reside in the exogenous context of processing, whereas others (e.g., tedium and dullness of a cognitive task) may relate to endogenous aspects of processing (Kruglanski, 1975). Yet other conditions may stem from the perceiver's organismic state. For instance, people may find processing particularly arduous when in a state of fatigue. Accordingly, need for closure should be heightened under noise, when the task is unpleasant or dull, or when the individual is fatigued. It should also be heightened when closure is valued by significant others, because possessing closure may promise to earn their esteem and appreciation. Finally, it should be heightened, simply, when judgment on some topic is required (as compared with cases in which the individual feels free to remain opinionless).

The need for closure may be lowered and the need to avoid closure heightened by conditions that highlight the costs of closure and the benefits of openness. In some situations, closure costs may be made salient by 'fear of invalidity', or a gnawing concern about a costly judgmental mistake (e.g., when the perceiver is 'outcome dependent' on the target; cf. Fiske & Neuberg, 1990). Under these conditions, people may desire to suspend judgment or avoid premature closure. This may seem to imply that validity concerns are necessarily at odds with those of closure. Obviously, however, no one would consciously adopt a closure she or he judged invalid. In fact, the very notion of subjective knowledge connotes the joint sense of closure and validity. To know, for example, that Washington, DC is the capital of the United States is at once to have closure on the topic and to believe it to be true. This logic notwithstanding, psychological concerns for closure and validity may arise fairly independently of each other; more important, they may pull information processing in diametrically opposed directions.

When closure concerns loom large, for example, individuals may perform closure-promoting activities without sacrificing their sense of validity. They may generate fewer competing hypotheses or suppress attention to information inconsistent with their hypotheses. Both processes may promote a sense of valid closure uncontested by alternative interpretations or inconsistent evidence. By contrast, when validity concerns are salient, people may engage in a thorough and extensive information search and generate multiple alternative interpretations to account for known facts. To wit, they may process information in exactly the opposite manner to that observed under a heightened need for closure. In fact, when validity represents the overriding concern, individuals may be motivated to postpone closure and, in extreme cases, to avoid it altogether. This is not inevitable, however: If a particular closure appears valid beyond the shadow of a doubt (e.g., because of the impeccable credibility of its source), the fear of invalidity may increase the tendency to embrace it rather than prompting its avoidance or postponement. Thus, closure avoidance should be conceptually distinguished from the fear of invalidity. Although closure avoidance may be often induced by such fear, this may not hold invariably.

The need to avoid (or postpone) closure may arise for alternative reasons, such as when the judgmental task is intrinsically enjoyable and interesting (relative to possible alternative pursuits) and closure threatens to terminate this pleasant activity. Finally, as noted earlier, individuals may exhibit stable personal differences in the degree to which they value closure. Such differences may spring from various sources, such as cultural norms (Hofstede, 1980) or personal socialization histories that place a premium on confidence and 'know-how'. Accordingly, we have recently developed a measure of individual differences in need for closure and established its reliability and validity (Webster & Kruglanski, 1994).

A major upshot of the foregoing analysis is that the need for closure may be operationally denned in a broad variety of ways. If our theory is correct, such diverse operationalizations should prove functionally equivalent in regard to theoretically relevant phenomena. Specific evidence for such an equivalence is examined subsequently.

Consequences of the Need for Closure: The Urgency and Permanence Tendencies

The motivation toward cognitive closure may affect the way individuals process information en route to the formation, alteration, or dissolution of knowledge. Because such processes are typically embedded in social-interaction contexts, they may significantly affect the way a person thinks about, feels about, acts toward, and even talks about others.

What form might such effects assume? We posit two general tendencies that need for closure may instill: the *urgency tendency* and the *permanence tendency*. The urgency tendency refers to the inclination to 'seize' on closure quickly. People under a heightened need for closure may perceive that they desire closure immediately. Any further postponement of closure is experienced as bothersome, and the individual's overriding sense is that he or she simply cannot wait.

The permanence tendency refers to the desire to perpetuate closure, giving rise to the dual inclination (a) to preserve, or 'freeze' on, past knowledge, and (b) to safeguard future knowledge. Individuals under a heightened need for closure may thus desire an enduring closure and, in extreme cases, abhor losing closure ever again. The urgency and permanence notions both rest on the assumption that people under a heightened need for closure experience its absence as aversive. They may, therefore, wish to terminate this unpleasant state quickly (the urgency tendency) and keep it from recurring (the permanence tendency).

The abstract tendencies toward urgency and permanence may translate into a variety of concrete social psychological phenomena. Specifically, people under a heightened need for closure may seize on information appearing early in a sequence and freeze on it, becoming impervious to subsequent data. Such seizing and freezing trends may affect information processing and, indirectly, the multiple social psychological phenomena information processing may mediate.

Extent of Information Processing

Because of the tendency to seize on early information and immediately freeze, people under a heightened need for closure may process less information before committing to a judgment and generate fewer competing hypotheses to account for the available data. Paradoxically, they may feel more assured of those judgments, even though they are less grounded in thorough exploration. Specifically, the less competing hypotheses a person might entertain, the more confidence he or she may have in those hypotheses (Kelley, 1971) simply because fewer alternatives to a given judgment may appear plausible, enhancing the individual's confidence in those that are.

Cue Utilization

A straightforward implication of our seizing and freezing postulate is that people under a heightened need for closure should base their judgments predominantly on early or pre-existing cues rather than on later information. As a concrete implication, people under a high (vs low) need for closure should often exhibit stronger primacy effects in impression formation (Asch, 1946). Furthermore, individuals under a heightened need for closure should rely more on stereotypes than on case specific or individuating information simply because stereotypes represent pre-existing knowledge structures, ready to be used momentarily, whereas individuating information may require extensive further processing. The tendency, based on need for closure, to overutilize early cues implies a disposition to keep one's estimates close to initial anchors rather than correct them in light of subsequent evidence (Tversky & Kahneman, 1974). A similar tendency induced by a heightened need for closure may augment the assimilation of judgments to semantic primes (Higgins, Rholes, & Jones, 1977). The rationale for these predictions is straightforward: Anchors as well as primes define initial bases for a judgment and should be seized and frozen on under a heightened need for closure.

The Quest for Epistemic Permanence: Consensus and Consistency Strivings

Once a person under a heightened need for closure has managed to formulate a belief and freeze on it, he or she may tend to preserve it for future reference. This is what our permanence notion implies. Such a tendency may manifest itself in a preference for consensual opinions that are unlikely to be challenged and potentially undermined by significant others. As a corollary, people high in need for closure should prefer to associate with similar-minded others, feel positively disposed toward group members who facilitate consensus, and feel negatively disposed toward dissenters or opinion deviates who jeopardize consensus.

Beyond the consensus bias, permanence strivings might induce a bias toward consistency, expressed as a preference for general knowledge applicable across situations over situationally

restricted knowledge. Among other things, such a preference may manifest itself in the way people use language in social contexts. Specifically, they may exhibit, under a heightened need for closure, an increased tendency to use trait terms or abstract category labels in describing others, simply because these terms and labels connote transsituational stability (e.g., to say someone is intelligent or friendly means she or he would behave intelligently or in a friendly manner across numerous specific instances).

Separating Seizing from Freezing: The Point of Belief Crystallization

According to the present theory, a demarcation point separating seizing phenomena from those of freezing is the juncture during which a belief crystallizes and turns from hesitant conjecture to a subjectively firm 'fact'. Before that point, it should be possible to observe pure seizing, manifest, for example, in quickened pace and enhanced volume of the informational search under a heightened need for closure. As an additional implication, seizing should dispose people to be relatively open to persuasion attempts because such attempts promise to furnish the coveted closure. Subsequent to crystallization, by contrast, it should be possible to witness freezing manifest as a reluctance to continue information processing or a resistance to persuasive arguments aimed at undermining one's current closure and effecting cognitive change. The notion that the pre-decision action phase is characterized by cognitive openness (the deliberation mindset) and that the post-decision phase is characterized by narrow restrictiveness (the implementation mindset) was stressed also by Gollwitzer (1990).

In summary, our theory (a) views the need for closure as a desire for confident knowledge, (b) suggests that motivation toward closure varies along a continuum from a strong need for closure to a strong need to avoid closure, (c) views the need for closure both as an individual-differences variable and as a situationally inducible state prompted by the perceived benefits or costs of lacking closure, and (d) implies that need for closure may affect how an individual thinks, feels, acts toward, and speaks about socially significant others. The empirical evidence for the present theory is reviewed in subsequent sections of this article. First, however, we consider its conceptual predecessors and examine its relation to those earlier notions. We ultimately argue that, commonalities with alternative formulations notwithstanding, the need for closure construct is unique and fundamentally different from previous relevant notions in its essence, antecedent conditions, and consequences.

Historical Precursors of the Need for Closure Concept

Variability in individuals' tendency toward closed-mindedness or open-mindedness has been addressed in several prior discussions in the personality and social psychology literature. Freud (1923) linked openness to new experiences to the trait of basic trust rooted in successful passage through the oral period. By contrast, closed-mindedness was assumed to reflect a basic distrust rooted in an oral fixation. In its extreme form, such distrust was presumed to foster a paranoid delusional system totally closed off from reality and hence impervious to any informational or logical challenges to its integrity. Frenkel-Brunswik (1949) and Eysenck (1954) used the term *intolerance of ambiguity* to refer to perceptual-cognitive rigidity and emotional ambivalence (Adorno, Frenkel-Brunswik, Levinson, & Sanford, 1950); Rokeach (1960) investigated the phenomenon of closed-mindedness, referring to the impact of belief systems on attitudes toward new information. Kagan (1972) posited that uncertainty resolution is a primary determinant of behaviour, and Sorrentino carried out substantial research on 'certainty' and 'uncertainty' orientations, respectively referring to the degree to which a person 'likes

to stick to familiar events and traditional beliefs' (Sorrentino & Short, 1986, p. 400) or 'attempts to integrate new events or beliefs into already existing belief systems' (Sorrentino & Short, 1986, p. 399).

Need for closure shares some commonality with those earlier notions, but it is also unique in major respects. The primary commonality resides in the fact that those notions too refer to individuals' prejudiced disposition and their tendency to eschew new ideas or experiences. Unlike the need for closure construct, however, the earlier concepts were mostly psychodynamic, referred to personality typologies, were linked to particular contents of beliefs, were often conceived of as cognitive rather than motivational, and often emphasized the deleterious consequences of avoidance of uncertainty or the quest for certainty.

. . .

Empirical Relations of Need for Closure with Related Constructs

The foregoing discussion suggests that although need for closure may share a degree of commonality with alternative constructs relevant to closed-mindedness and open-mindedness, it differs from those alternative concepts in important respects. Empirically, this should result in low to moderate correlations between the need for closure and related concepts. Extant evidence is consistent with this supposition. In psychometric work on the Need for Closure Scale, Webster and Kruglanski (1994) reported correlations of 0.26 between need for closure and the F scale assessing authoritarianism (Sanford, Adorno, Frenkel-Brunswik, & Levinson, 1950), 0.29 between need for closure and intolerance of ambiguity (Frenkel-Brunswik, 1949), and 0.28 between need for closure and dogmatism (Rokeach, 1960).

Intelligence and Need for Closure

Because individuals high in need for closure often limit their information-processing activities, this may suggest a negative relationship between intelligence and need for closure. On the other hand, need for closure may sometimes promote extensive information processing in instances in which closure is lacking. Theoretically, then, the relationship between need for closure and intelligence is not readily apparent. Empirically, this relation is non-significant ($r = -0.17$).

Further Connections and Distinctions: Need for Cognition, Central-Systematic Processing, and Peripheral-Heuristic Processing

The need for cognition refers to the extent to which one 'engages in and enjoys thinking' (Cacioppo & Petty, 1982, p. 1). In other words, for people high in this need, the activity of thinking as such is the desired end. By contrast, for those high in need for closure, the desired end is cognitive closure. Although having closure obviates the necessity to think further about an issue, one may refrain from thinking without necessarily attaining closure. Thus, although some negative relation between the need for cognition and the need for closure should be expected, it should not be very strong. The empirical correlation between the two constructs is, in fact, low and negative ($r = -0.28$; Webster & Kruglanski, 1994).

Need for cognition is one among several variables assumed to effect a processing shift from the reliance on peripheral cues to a thorough consideration of central informational contents (Petty & Cacioppo, 1986). A somewhat similar distinction has been drawn between the processing of information heuristically and systematically (Chaiken, Liberman, & Eagly, 1989). The question, therefore, is how need for closure theory relates to the peripheral-heuristic versus central-systematic distinctions. The answer is that although our theory shares some common ground with those alternative conceptions, it differs in important respects. The commonality resides in the fact that need for closure theory also posits conditions under which people process information briefly and superficially and others wherein they do so thoroughly and methodically. Unlike the

alternative formulations, however, need for closure theory does not postulate two qualitatively different modes of information processing. Rather, it regards the difference between brief and thorough processing as a matter of extent. Furthermore, whereas both the peripheral-central and the heuristic-systematic models may view some of the information-processing costs (produced, for example, by ambient noise, fatigue, or time pressure) as depleting the individual's cognitive capacity, the present analysis stresses their motivating potential in arousing the need for closure. A detailed consideration of the capacity versus motivation issue is undertaken at a later juncture.

Openness to Experience

Finally, the present distinction between closed-mindedness and open-mindedness is shared by the openness factor of the big five (McCrae & Costa, 1985). The specific areas to which one might be open or closed include fantasy, aesthetics, feelings, actions, ideas, and values (Costa & McCrae, 1992; McCrae, 1993–4). As in the present conception, then, the closed and open dimension is seen as relevant to a broad range of domains rather than being restricted to specific contents. Also, both conceptions highlight the possibility of motivated openness, in counterdistinction to alternative notions stressing the ubiquitous quest for certainty. Again, however, openness to experience is essentially an individual-differences dimension to which situational considerations seem rather foreign. Furthermore, the openness to experience construct depicts a general psychological syndrome (manifest, for example, in artistic creativity, susceptibility to hypnosis, rich fantasy lives, and unconventional attitudes) rather than the effects of a specific motivation. The motivational part of the syndrome includes need for change, sensation seeking, and intellectual understanding, which are rather different from need for closure per se. For instance, according to our conception, a person under a need for closure can exhibit openness to information (i.e., seizing) in the pre-crystallization phase of judgment formation. Such a possibility does not seem relevant to the openness construct.

In summary, then, the present need for closure theory seems both conceptually and empirically distinct from relevant alternative formulations. It appears to be more general than historical treatments of open-mindedness and closed-mindedness and less committed to specific antecedents (e.g., of psychosexual origins), cognitive contents (e.g., assumptions about authority), or approach-avoidance trends (e.g., toward certainty and away from uncertainty). It also constitutes a distinctly motivational theory that highlights the effects of its key variable on the extent of processing rather than on shifts from one qualitative processing mode to another. Those unique properties of the need for closure construct yield a variety of predictions not readily derivable from previous formulations. We turn now to the empirical evidence for those predictions.

Empirical Evidence

Seizing and Freezing Effects

Earlier we posited two general tendencies that need for closure may instigate: the urgency tendency of seizing on judgmentally relevant cues and the permanence tendency of freezing on judgments the cues imply. Operating jointly, the seizing and freezing sequence may produce a broad range of judgmental effects observable under a heightened need for closure.

Extent of Information Processing

At a minimum, the seizing and freezing mechanism implies a reduced extent of information processing under a heightened need for closure. The speeded-up reliance on early cues implied by seizing and the truncation of further exploration due to freezing suggest that individuals under a high (vs low) need for closure should consider less evidence before forming a judgment. In an experiment relevant to this proposition, Mayseless and Kruglanski (1987, Study 2) had participants

perform a tachistoscopic recognition task of identifying barely visible digits on a screen. As a means of arousing the need for closure, participants were told that forming unambiguous, clear-cut opinions is positively correlated with high mental concentration and intelligence. This manipulation was designed to enhance the perceived value (or benefit) of closure and, hence, to increase the need for closure. Note that stating that unambiguous or clear-cut opinions are valuable does not, in itself, demand briefer information processing. To the contrary, it seems more reasonable to assume that the arrival at clarity and the dispelling of ambiguity would require, if anything, more rather than less extensive processing. The present seizing and freezing notion implies the opposite, of course.

As a means of inducing the need to avoid closure, participants were given accuracy instructions and promised extra experimental credit for correctly identifying nine of ten digits. A neutral control condition was also included in which no motivational induction took place. Participants were allowed to operate the tachistoscope an unlimited number of times. As predicted, their extent of informational search (number of times they operated the tachistoscope) was lowest in the need for closure condition, intermediate in the control condition, and highest in the need to avoid closure condition.

Hypothesis Generation

In addition to a reduced extent of processing 'external' stimulus information, the seizing and freezing notions imply that, under heightened need for closure, there will be a parallel reduction in 'internal' hypothesis generation. Presumably, those two processes are intimately linked: Examination of external information may suggest new, internally formed hypotheses, the testing of which may require, in turn, further processing of external information. Need for closure effects on hypothesis generation were specifically addressed in another experiment conducted by Mayseless and Kruglanski (1987, Study 3). Participants were shown enlarged photographs of parts of common objects (e.g., a comb, a toothbrush, and a nail). These photos were taken from unusual angles, masking the objects' actual nature. On each trial, participants were urged to list the maximal number of hypotheses concerning an object's identity and ultimately chose the identity most likely to be correct. As in the study mentioned earlier (Mayseless & Kruglanski, 1987, Study 2), need for closure was induced by informing participants that clear-cut opinions relate to mental concentration and intelligence. Again, this, in and of itself, should not artificially 'demand' a curtailment of hypothesis generation. Rather, an emphasis on clarity and intelligence may demand increased hypothesis generation, contrary to the present prediction. To induce the need to avoid closure, the instructions noted a correlation between the desirable mental qualities and correct visual recognition. As in the previous study, a neutral control condition devoid of a motivational induction was included. The results showed, as predicted, that participants in the need to avoid closure condition generated the largest number of hypotheses, followed by participants in the control condition; participants in the need for closure condition produced the fewest hypotheses.

Subjective Confidence

An interesting corollary to the notion that individuals under a high (vs low) need for closure generate fewer hypotheses is that they will be quicker to attain high judgmental confidence. This implication follows from Kelley's (1971) discounting principle, whereby reduction in the number of alternative hypotheses should boost an individual's confidence in each hypothesis. Relevant to this prediction, in the tachistoscopic recognition study conducted by Mayseless and Kruglanski (1987, Study 2), participants' confidence in their initial hypotheses and the magnitude of confidence shifts (upward or downward) occasioned by each successive stimulus presentation were significantly lower in the need to avoid closure condition than in the

need for closure condition, with the control condition falling in the middle.

Elevated confidence of participants under heightened need for closure has been replicated in several studies using widely divergent methods, such as ambient noise (Kruglanski & Webster, 1991; Kruglanski, Webster, & Klem, 1993), dullness of the task (Webster, 1993), and time pressure (Kruglanski & Webster, 1991), of inducing this motivation. Identical results were obtained when need for closure was assessed via our individual differences measure (Webster & Kruglanski, 1994) rather than manipulated situationally.

Elevated confidence under a heightened need for closure is striking against the backdrop of reduced information processing under those very circumstances. This finding is incongruous with the common presumption that attainment of secure views requires more rather than less extensive processing, and it defines an 'unfounded confidence' paradox under a heightened need for closure.

Seeking Diagnostic or Prototypical Information

Restriction of hypothesis generation under a heightened need for closure (Mayseless & Kruglanski, 1987, Study 3) should, finally, affect not only the amount of information sought by hypothesis-testing participants but also the type of information sought. Specifically, under high need for closure, participants may seek prototypical information about a category, whereas, under high need to avoid closure, they might instead seek diagnostic information (Trope & Bassok, 1983) capable of discriminating among different categories. Consider an interviewer testing the focal hypothesis that an interviewee is a painter. Under a high need for closure, this individual may refrain from generating specific competing alternatives to this hypothesis and search for information capable of demarcating it from the diffuse non-painter hypothesis. Such information may pertain to features prototypical of painters (e.g., 'bohemian' lifestyle or artistic ability). The case may be very different, however, if the individual's need to avoid closure was aroused. This might motivate her or him to be sensitive to possible specific alternatives to the hypothesis, such as that the interviewee is an architect. If so, the interviewer might specifically seek information diagnostic in regard to the painter–architect pair: Artistic ability is presumably shared by painters and architects alike and hence is non-diagnostic, whereas bohemian lifestyle is diagnostic because it may principally characterize painters but not architects. In research designed to investigate these possibilities (Kruglanski & Mayseless, 1988), we asked participants to evaluate whether a target belonged to a given professional category, subtly hinting at a competing alternative possibility. As expected, individuals under a high need for closure, manipulated through implied time pressure, sought more prototypical information than diagnostic information, whereas those under need to avoid closure, manipulated through instilled fear of invalidity, sought more diagnostic information capable of differentiating between the competing alternatives.

Early-Cue Utilization

Perhaps the broadest implication of the seizing and freezing mechanism is that under a high (vs low) need for closure, individuals tend to base their final judgments on early cues. Because of the urgency tendency, such cues should be quickly utilized to form an initial judgment (seizing), and, because of the permanence tendency, such a judgment should tend to stay fixed (freezing) rather than be altered in light of subsequent evidence. This fundamental process may underlie a diverse array of phenomena that, at first glance, might appear unrelated.

Impressional Primacy Effects

An obvious such phenomenon is the impressional 'primacy effect' (Asch, 1946; Luchins, 1957), that is, the tendency to base impressions of a social target more on information presented early versus late in a sequence. If primacy effects are an instance of the seizing and freezing process, they should be appropriately magnified under high need for closure and attenuated under high need to avoid closure. This prediction has received support in several studies differing in the ways in which needs for closure or closure avoidance were operationalized. Specifically, need for closure has been variously operationalized in terms of scores on the Need for Closure Scale (Webster & Kruglanski, 1994), time pressure (Freund, Kruglanski, & Schpitzajzen, 1985; Heaton & Kruglanski, 1991; Kruglanski & Freund, 1983), instructions to form an overall evaluative judgment of the target (vs separately evaluating each of his or her characteristics; Freund et al., 1985), and degree of mental fatigue (Webster, Richter, & Kruglanski, 1995). Need to avoid closure has been operationalized in terms of evaluation apprehension (Freund et al., 1985; Kruglanski & Freund, 1983) or potential costs to the evaluation target (in the case of a participant's mistake; Freund et al., 1985). As predicted, in all of these studies, the magnitude of primacy effects varied positively with need for closure and negatively with need to avoid closure.

Note, however, that in the research described thus far, it was relatively easy for participants to downplay the late appearing evidence if motivated to do so. It is quite possible that if the late evidence is particularly compelling and participants high in need for closure are pressured to seriously consider it, they may change their mind more abruptly and completely than those low in need for closure, manifesting a recency effect. In dynamic systems terms (Vallacher & Nowak, 1997), need for closure could serve as a 'control parameter', effecting quick gravitation to 'attractors' representing conclusions implied by the early and late appearing evidence.

Anchoring Effects

A different instance of early-cue utilization may underlie the 'anchoring' effect discovered by Tversky and Kahneman (1974). Consider a probability-estimation task (cf. Bar-Hillel, 1973) in which participants assess the probability of compound conjunctive or disjunctive events. Participants typically use the probability of the simple constituent events as an anchor and then adjust. When the adjustment is insufficient, they should therefore overestimate the probability of conjunctive events (calculation of which involves the multiplication of fractions) and underestimate the probability of disjunctive events (calculation of which involves the addition of fractions). If anchoring represents a special case of cue utilization, it should be appropriately affected by the need for closure. Consistent with this notion, participants' tendency to overestimate the likelihood of conjunctive events and underestimate that of disjunctive events increased under need for closure manipulated via time pressure and decreased under need to avoid closure manipulated by evaluation apprehension (Kruglanski & Freund, 1983, Study 2).

The Correspondence Bias

The correspondence bias in person perception (Jones, 1979) is among the most persistently studied phenomena in social cognition (see discussion by Trope & Higgins, 1993). It is, therefore, of considerable interest that it too may represent a special case of early-cue utilization and be appropriately influenced by the need for closure. The correspondence bias refers to a perceiver tendency to over-ascribe actors' behaviour to personal inclinations, even in the presence of situational pressures that in and of themselves should be capable of eliciting the behaviour. In an original demonstration of this phenomenon, Jones and Harris (1967) presented participants with essays allegedly written by a person given either a free choice or no choice in the matter of doing so. In both cases, that is, even when the writer was denied choice, participants assumed that his or her attitude was largely congruent with the essay content.

Different theorists (Gilbert, Pelham, & Krull, 1988; Jones, 1979; Quattrone, 1982) have implied that the underlying mechanism for the correspondence bias could involve the anchoring and insufficient adjustment process discussed earlier.

Thus, when participants come to judge the writer's attitude, the most salient evidence is the very behaviour that took place. Often, the earliest hypothesis this suggests is that the behaviour faithfully mirrored the writer's attitude. This attitude-correspondence hypothesis may pop to mind spontaneously or 'automatically' and serve as an initial anchor to be subsequently adjusted via a 'controlled' cognitive process during which further relevant evidence (e.g., concerning pertinent situational constraints) is considered.

Such controlled adjustment, however, may require substantial cognitive effort. For instance, Gilbert et al. (1988) found that when perceivers were cognitively busy, the correspondence bias was enhanced. This may mean that the increased effort required by the adjustment process was more than the participants were willing to put out, which suggests that motivational considerations may indeed enter into the correspondence bias. Research by Tetlock (e.g., 1985) supports this possibility. He found that such bias was markedly reduced when participants were made to feel accountable for their judgments. Presumably, manipulation of accountability motivated participants to process information in a more discriminating manner, affording a more adequate adjustment of the initial bias.

The preceding findings are consistent with the notion that, as with the primacy or anchoring effect, the correspondence bias represents an overutilization of early cues. If so, the correspondence bias too should be appropriately affected by the need for closure. In a recent set of studies, Webster (1993) tested this proposition, manipulating the need for closure via task attractiveness. Her underlying assumption was that when an activity is attractive or intrinsically motivated (e.g., Deci & Ryan, 1985; Higgins & Trope, 1990; Kruglanski, 1975), this should induce the motivation to extensively explore it (Berlyne, 1960) and, hence, to avoid premature closure. By contrast, when an activity is extrinsically motivated, the motivation may be to reach closure quickly so as to reach the exogenous reward without delay.

An attitude-attribution task was used in which a target made a speech critical of student-exchange programs under free-choice or no-choice conditions. As a means of portraying this task as unattractive, the task participants expected to perform subsequently (the watching of comedy videos) promised to be particularly attractive. This was assumed to render relatively unappealing or subjectively costly the current, duller task and hence to elevate the need for closure.

As a means of portraying the same task as attractive, the subsequent task promised to be particularly unattractive (watching a video of a statistics lecture). This was assumed to render the current task subjectively appealing and hence to lower the need for closure. Finally, in a third, control condition, the subsequent task was portrayed as largely similar to the current one (also involving attitude attributions), lending it intermediate appeal. Manipulation checks confirmed that the experimental manipulations produced the corresponding differences in need for cognitive closure. Most important, the correspondence bias in the no-choice condition was affected by the need for closure in the predicted manner: Substantial correspondence bias was already present in the control condition (replicating prior research), and such bias was significantly enhanced in the unattractive task condition and completely eliminated in the attractive task condition.

The same pattern of results was obtained in Webster's second study, in which need for closure was assessed via the Need for Closure Scale (Webster & Kruglanski, 1994). Finally, when the initial cues implied a situational rather than a personal attribution, the results of the previous two studies were completely reversed. The tendency to overascribe the essay to the writer's attitude was reduced under a high need for closure (manipulated via task attractiveness) and enhanced under a low need for closure, both as compared with the control condition. This last finding is particularly significant because it demonstrates that need for closure effects are content free and depend on the order in which cues are received rather than on their specific substance (e.g., implying a personal or a situational attribution).

Stereotypic Judgments

From a social psychological perspective, some particularly interesting sources of early cues are previously formed stereotypes, prejudices, or attitudes readily accessible in memory. Such pre-existing knowledge structures may pre-empt the use of case-specific (or individuating) information in the forming of social judgments. The present seizing and freezing mechanism suggests that such pre-emption should be particularly likely under a heightened need for closure, simply because extensive processing of case-specific information may substantially postpone closure. In an early demonstration of those effects, Kruglanski and Freund (1983, Study 3) found that ethnic stereotypes of Ashkenazi and Sephardi Jews influenced grade assignments for a literary composition more in conditions likely to elevate the graders' need for closure (time pressure, lack of accountability, or both) than in conditions likely to reduce it (accountability and no time pressure). Time pressure also increased the degree to which pre-existing prejudice against women in management versus individuating information about specific applicants' qualifications tended to affect discrimination toward female versus male candidates (Jamieson & Zanna, 1989).

Construct Accessibility Effects

A key assumption in predicting more pronounced judgmental influence of stereotypes under a high (vs low) need for closure is that such stereotypes are highly accessible in memory. Such accessible guides to judgment should be seized and frozen on under a heightened need for closure. A direct test of this assumption was recently carried out by Ford and Kruglanski (1995), who used a priming paradigm developed by Higgins et al. (1977). In the context of an allegedly unrelated memory experiment, participants were primed by either the negatively valenced adjective *reckless* or the positively valenced adjective *adventurous*. They were subsequently presented a passage about Donald that was ambiguous with respect to the adventurous–reckless pair. Participants' task was to characterize Donald using a single word. In this situation, participants high in dispositional need for closure (Webster & Kruglanski, 1994) exhibited stronger assimilation of judgment to prime than participants low in this need. That is, participants high (vs low) in need for closure tended more to characterize Donald in terms suggesting recklessness in the negative prime condition and adventurousness in the positive prime condition. An independently executed study by Thompson, Roman, Moscovitz, Chaiken, and Bargh (1994), using a different method of priming (the scrambled sentence technique) and of assessing need for closure (Neuberg & Newsom's 1993 Personal Need for Structure Scale), yielded the same results. Participants high in need for structure-closure exhibited greater assimilation of their judgments to primed constructs than participants low in this need. Finally, both Ford and Kruglanski (1995) and Thompson et al. (1994) succeeded in significantly reducing the assimilation-to-prime effect under accuracy instructions (i.e., in conditions likely to reduce participants' need for closure).

. . .

Interactive Effects of Need for Closure and Initial Confidence on Social Information Seeking

One way in which the pre-crystallization and post-crystallization periods may be differentiated from each other is in terms of judgmental confidence: Before crystallization, individuals' confidence in a judgment should be relatively low, whereas after crystallization, it should be higher by comparison. Furthermore, seizing may be distinguished from freezing by the intensity and extent of the informational search. During the seizing phase, the individual may search for information rather

energetically and voluminously. By contrast, during the freezing phase, she or he may be reluctant to consider new information and, if at all, do so sparingly and hesitantly.

Those notions were tested in two experiments by Kruglanski, Peri, and Zakai (1991). Participants were presented with five series of drawings. All series contained either two or four standard drawings on a given topic (a man, woman, or tree), each drawn by a different person, and a criterion drawing on a different topic (invariably a house) drawn by one of the individuals who had prepared the standard drawings. Participants' task was to identify, for each series, the particular standard drawing of the person responsible for the criterion drawing. The time allotted was three minutes. Participants stated their interim judgment after one minute and, during the remaining two minutes, were allowed to engage in an information search concerning alleged other participants' responses. This was accomplished by having participants turn over some (or all) of the standard drawings, which bore on their backs the percentages of previous participants choosing them as the correct answers.

Initial confidence was manipulated via the number of choice alternatives presented to participants. In the high confidence condition, participants chose from among two standard drawings; in the low confidence condition, they chose from among four drawings. Appropriate checks verified that this confidence manipulation had the intended effect.

The two studies differed in how they manipulated the need for closure. Our pilot research suggested that the novel experimental task was somewhat confusing to participants, introducing a relatively high base level of the need for closure. Rather than attempting to further elevate it via experimental manipulations, we therefore decided to lower it instead in some conditions. In one study, we did so by providing participants with clear criteria for assessing the drawings' similarity (the drawing's size and location on the page, its linear quality, its degree of elaboration, and the presence-absence of a depth dimension). In the second study, we did so via a fear of invalidity induction whereby mistaken judgments were to be punished by a loss of points.

Two aspects of the information search were of interest: (a) the alacrity with which participants commenced it and (b) its overall extent, that is, the number of drawings participants turned over. If low confidence typifies the pre-crystallization phase and high confidence typifies the post-crystallization phase, and if, moreover, the need for closure produces seizing in the former phase and freezing in the latter, need for closure should exert opposite effects on the dependent variables at the two confidence levels. In the low confidence condition, high versus low need for closure should induce seizing manifest in a relatively hurried commencement of the informational search and its relatively ample extent. By contrast, in the high confidence condition, high versus low need for closure should induce freezing manifest via relatively retarded commencement and sparse extent of the informational search. As Table 4.1 indicates, that is exactly what happened. Thus, initial confidence may constitute a boundary condition separating the urgency tendency underlying seizing from the permanence tendency underlying freezing.

Motivated Reactions to Persuasion in the Presence or Absence of Prior Information

The dramatically disparate effects of need for closure on information processing in the pre-crystallization versus post-crystallization phases should have intriguing implications for the persuasion process: In the pre-crystallization phase, heightened need for closure may enhance individuals' tendency to accept persuasion, whereas in the post-crystallization phase, it may enhance their tendency to resist persuasion. Specifically, the discrepancy under a heightened need for closure between actual and desired states before crystallization should induce the tendency to urgently remove it. A persuasive communication offers a means of doing so; hence, it should be quickly accepted. By contrast, in the post-crystallization phase, an absence of discrepancy between the desire for closure and its possession should induce the tendency to maintain this pleasing state in relative permanence. This should induce a resistance to persuasion because it requires at least a temporary unfreezing of one's mind.

These notions were examined in the research by Kruglanski et al. (1993, Studies 2 and 3) referred to earlier. Dyads were formed consisting of a naive participant and a confederate. The experiment was

Table 4.1   Mean Numbers of Drawings Turned Over and Latency of Turning Over the First Drawing

	Confidence level			
	High		Low	
Need for closure	Mean no. of drawings turned over	Latency of turning over first drawing	Mean no. of drawings turned over	Latency of turning over first drawing
	Experiment 1			
High	2.62	65.11	3.60	39.79
Low	3.94	37.01	3.00	47.84
	Experiment 2			
High	2.60	60.39	3.52	33.67
Low	4.37	19.47	2.82	49.01

Note: From 'Interactive Effects of Need for Closure and Initial Confidence on Social Information Seeking,' by A.W. Kruglanski, N. Peri, and D. Zakai, 1991, Social Cognition, 9, pp. 136 and 137. Copyright 1991 Guilford Publications, Inc. Adapted with permission.

portrayed as a psychological investigation of legal juries. A participant and a confederate were presented with the essentials of a legal case (a civil suit against an airline company by a lumber company). For half of the participants, the materials included a 'legal analysis' affording the formation of a definite opinion favouring the defendant or the plaintiff. The remaining participants received no such analysis, and hence they lacked an informational base for a confident opinion.

The presence or absence of an opinion base was crossed orthogonally with need for closure, manipulated via environmental noise produced by a rackety computer printer. Participants read the case materials, recorded their opinion (or hunch) concerning the appropriate verdict, and confronted a confederate who argued for the opposite verdict. The results supported our theoretical analysis. In the absence of the legal analysis assumed to prevent the development of a confident opinion (representing the pre-crystallization phase), participants evinced greater persuadability under noise than under no noise. Specifically, they tended more to change their pre-discussion verdicts and spent less time arguing with the confederate in the noisy versus the quiet condition. Precisely the opposite happened when participants were given the legal analysis affording a crystallized opinion. In this condition, participants under noise (vs no noise) evinced less persuadability. They shifted less in their verdicts and spent more time arguing with the confederate.

This experiment was conceptually replicated with scores on the Need for Closure Scale as a way of operationalizing need for closure. The same data pattern was reproduced: Participants high (vs low) in need for closure, as assessed by our scale, were more readily persuaded in instances in which absence of prior information presumably prevented them from crystallizing an opinion and were less readily persuaded in instances in which prior information made such crystallization possible.

The 'Fight Rather than Switch' Paradox

Note that, in both of our studies, freezing on a prior opinion under a heightened need for closure led to considerable arguing with a different-minded person. Such a tendency to 'fight rather than switch' under a heightened need for closure could be paradoxical and potentially dysfunctional from the individual's own perspective. For instance, an individual who craves closure so as not to expend energy on laborious information processing (e.g., under noise) ends up expending considerable energy, in fact, on heated argument. Apparently, then, even though the goal of closure may have originally evolved on the basis of rational (energy saving) considerations, once in place it may acquire functional autonomy from those incipient considerations and prompt activities that may, ironically, defeat them.

General Discussion

Theoretical Convergence

If knowledge construction constitutes a pervasive cognitive activity typically occurring in social contexts, an epistemic motivation of key relevance to such activity should have significant consequences for diverse aspects and domains of social cognition. We have outlined a conceptual framework in which the need for (non-specific) cognitive closure is identified as one such epistemic motivation and reviewed empirical evidence converging on a broad range of social–cognitive phenomena affected by that need.

We have defined need for closure as a desire for definite knowledge on some issue and the eschewal of confusion and ambiguity. It is assumed to represent a relatively stable dimension of individual differences as well as a situationally inducible state influenced by perceived benefits of closure (or costs of lacking it). Finally, need for closure is presumed to exert its effects via two general tendencies: the urgency tendency, reflecting the inclination to attain closure as quickly as possible, and the permanence tendency, reflecting the tendency to maintain it for as long as possible.

Jointly, the urgency and permanence tendencies may produce the inclinations to seize and then freeze on early judgmental cues. A seizing and freezing sequence under heightened need for closure may (a) reduce the extent of information processing and hypothesis generation (Mayseless & Kruglanski, 1987); (b) elevate judgmental confidence (e.g., Kruglanski & Webster, 1991; Kruglanski et al., 1993; Mayseless & Kruglanski, 1987; Webster & Kruglanski, 1994); (c) focus the information search on prototypical rather than diagnostic evidence (Kruglanski & Mayseless, 1988); (d) effect the use of early cues giving rise to impressional primacy, anchoring effects, or stereotypic judgments (Freund et al., 1985; Heaton & Kruglanski, 1991; Jamieson & Zanna, 1989; Kruglanski & Freund, 1983; Webster & Kruglanski, 1994); (e) induce the tendency to exhibit correspondence or overattribution biases (Webster, 1993); and (f) increase the tendency to assimilate judgments to primed constructs (Ford & Kruglanski, 1995; Thompson et al., 1994).

Beyond the promotion of epistemic freezing, the permanence tendency under a heightened need for closure may effect a preference for consensual knowledge unlikely to be challenged by significant others and a preference for consistent knowledge generalizable across specific situations. The greater predilection for consensus under high (vs low) need for closure has been shown to be manifest in (a) an increased preference for a persuadable partner by participants who are high (vs low) in need for closure and who have a prior opinion base, (b) an increased preference for a persuasive partner by participants who are high (vs low) in need for closure and who do not have a prior opinion base (Kruglanski, Webster, & Klem, 1993), (c) rejection of opinion deviates, and (d) countenance accorded to salient conformists (Kruglanski & Webster, 1991).

The greater predilection for transsituational consistency in knowledge exhibited by participants under high (vs low) need for closure has been shown to be manifest in the tendency to (a) ascribe failures to global (vs specific) self-characteristics (Mikulincer et al., 1991), (b) communicate social knowledge using abstract trait labels (Boudreau et al., 1992), and (c) use abstract linguistic descriptions (Webster, Kruglanski, & Pattison, 1995) in reference to positive in-group behaviours and negative out-group behaviours, consistent with the linguistic intergroup bias (Maass & Arcuri, 1992). Also as predicted, these differences in abstraction were largely absent in reference to positive outgroup and negative ingroup behaviours. In accordance with the theory, the quest for ingroup consensus due to the permanence tendency may inspire stronger ingroup favouritism and protectionism under a heightened need for closure. This may instill the inclination to concretize (and hence situationally restrict) negative ingroup behaviours and positive outgroup behaviours, contrary to the general preference for abstraction associated with permanence strivings under a heightened need for closure.

A significant boundary condition separating the effects of seizing from those of freezing has been hypothesized to reside at the point of belief crystallization. Before that juncture, need for closure is assumed to augment seizing; subsequent to that juncture, it is assumed to enhance freezing. Consistent with these notions, participants under a high (vs low) need for closure have been shown to exhibit shorter latencies of information seeking and more ample information seeking when their initial confidence in a hypothesis is low (assumed to represent a pre-crystallization seizing) and longer latencies and sparser information seeking when their initial confidence is high (assumed to represent post-crystallization freezing; Kruglanski et al., 1991). Similarly, participants under a high need for closure have been shown to be more accepting of persuasion in conditions preventing the formation of a confident opinion (representing pre-crystallization seizing) and more resistant to persuasion in conditions affording the formation of an opinion (representing post-crystallization freezing; Kruglanski et al., 1993).

Methodological Convergence

If, as the present theory maintains, need for closure is generally aroused by the perceived benefits of closure or costs of lacking closure, the same effects should obtain across a broad variety of conditions, the only common element of which relates to such benefits or costs. The data reviewed earlier provide ample support for this supposition. Specifically, similar, theoretically predicted effects emerged under such seemingly disparate conditions as those created by time pressure, ambient noise, mental fatigue, a request (vs no request) for judgment, and exposure to a dull activity. All such conditions may render closure beneficial, and hence they should all induce the motivation to attain it.

Furthermore, many of these effects were replicated by means of an individual-differences measure of need for closure (Webster & Kruglanski, 1994), consistent with the notion that need for closure is both situationally malleable and represents a stable personality trait. Finally, whenever they were used, manipulations designed to lower the need for closure or arouse the need to avoid closure (specifically, accountability, evaluation apprehension, or accuracy instructions) had the exact opposite effects to instructions designed to elevate the need for closure (e.g., time pressure and noise). This supports the monotonicity assumption mentioned earlier, whereby motivational effects are directionally similar across different loci on the need for closure continuum. These results also support the very conception of a continuum as such in that manipulations assumed to heighten the need for closure (noise, mental fatigue, time pressure, and boredom) consistently produced the opposite effects to those assumed to heighten the need to avoid closure (evaluation apprehension, accuracy, and accountability instructions). In summary, then, the multiple operationalism adopted in the research reviewed here

supports the theoretical assumptions concerning the nature of the need for closure and its instigating conditions.

Need for Closure as a Scientific Construct: Its Reality Status, Evidential Support, and Heuristic Value

Any introduction of a novel scientific construct demands a careful critical scrutiny: Is it sufficiently distinct from previous notions? Is it 'real'? Is evidence for it open to plausible alternative interpretations? What advantages does it offer anyway? Does it afford new insights (i.e., does it have a heuristic value?)? Does it point to previously neglected commonalities (i.e., does it have an integrative value?)? The distinctiveness issue has been confronted at an earlier juncture; we have concluded that, as a concept, need for closure contains several unique features that set it apart from previous formulations. It is distinctly motivational, content free, and, by and large, more general than its predecessors. The issues of reality, alternative interpretations, and heuristic and integrative values are considered next.

Is It Real?

The need for closure variable admittedly constitutes a 'hypothetical construct' knowable only indirectly via its effects. To state that a concept is hypothetical does not mean, however, that it is unreal. As Kurt Lewin (1947) remarked in reference to the 'group' notion, a scientific construct is real if its effects are real. Moreover, hypothetical constructs are the rule in science rather than the exception: *Schema, associative network, dissonance,* and *electron,* among others, are examples of hypothetical constructs whose utility may not be doubted. Commenting on this issue (in the heyday of positivism in psychology), MacCorquodale and Meehl (1948, p. 105) noted that if one objected to constructs 'on the ground that they refer to unobservables or are "hypothetical" . . . a large and useful amount of modern science would have to be abandoned.'

Alternative Interpretations: The Issue of Overinclusiveness

A different question altogether is whether the real (i.e., empirically observed) effects obtained in the research described here are ascribable to the need for closure or readily explicable by competing alternative interpretations. In this connection, the very breadth of the need for closure construct raises the spectre of overinclusiveness. Because, by assumption, need for closure is arousable by a wide range of seemingly unrelated conditions (representing the heterogeneous benefits of closure or costs of lacking it), one may wonder whether it does not constitute, in fact, a post hoc explanation invoked to account for any degradation of cognitive performance. A quick reflection suggests that this is not the case. Thus, it is easy to think of conditions that reduce the extent of information processing (e.g., lack of expertise), affect the magnitude of primacy effects (e.g., manipulating attention to early vs late appearing information; Anderson, 1965), or affect the recall of stimulus information before the forming of an impression (Anderson & Hubert, 1963) yet seem largely unrelated to the need for closure construct. Broad though it may be, this construct is apparently not that all encompassing.

Superfluity

A question may be raised as to whether the putative effects of the need for closure may not be explicable, alternatively, by the various situational demands used to operationalize it. Such a state of affairs would render the construct redundant and superfluous. For instance, if it seems 'intuitively obvious' that time pressure and fatigue augment the use of simplistic cues, little would be gained by additionally invoking the need for closure in this context. A moment's reflection, however, suggests that need for closure theory has definite advantages over the mere assertion of an empirical relation between situational demands and cue-utilization phenomena. Even if that relation, as such, was intuitively obvious, its underlying mechanisms might not be. Two alternative hypotheses,

involving, respectively, cognitive capacity and motivation, immediately spring to mind in this connection. The first hypothesis states that situational demands may deplete individuals' cognitive resources and impel them to resort to simple cues. The second hypothesis suggests that demands may render the processing of information costly, motivating individuals to simplify the activity and hence save energy and effort. The present theory highlights the latter possibility in particular, and the relationship between that possibility and the depletion of capacity alternative is addressed next.

Motivation versus Capacity Depletion

To understand how situational demands introduced in our experiments may have affected participants' relative[1] cognitive capacity and information-processing motivation, one must consider possible ways in which these constructs interrelate. We assume that, as far as formation of judgments is concerned, relative capacity and motivation are multiplicatively interrelated. That is, at least some degrees of capacity and motivation are required for judgmental activity to occur. Setting either at zero will undermine it, and no amount of increment in the remaining one may compensate for the deficit. Above the zero level, however, the two variables may exhibit a compensatory relation. Reduction in capacity may be offset by an increment in motivation, and vice versa. According to this model, our situational-demand manipulations did not exhaust capacity completely (or set it to zero level). Specifically, our accountability and accuracy instructions clearly and consistently attenuated the effects of such situational demands as time pressure, mental fatigue, and noise (e.g., Kruglanski & Freund, 1983; Webster, Richter, & Kruglanski, 1995). It appears, then, that when sufficiently motivated, participants are perfectly capable of overcoming the effects of various situational constraints on information processing, at least at the magnitudes at which these constraints are typically manipulated in social psychology experiments.

Note that the multiplicative relation between capacity and motivation allows for two separate possibilities: one in which the two are independent of each other and one in which they are causally related. According to the independence assumption, capacity reduction as such (e.g., resulting from organismic energy depletion or situational demands) has no motivational consequences whatsoever, even though it may be compensated for by motivational increments. This is analogous to the case in which deflation of bicycle tires may be compensated for by enhanced pedalling effort even though it does not cause it.

According to the causality assumption, on the other hand, depletion of relative cognitive capacity does induce a motivation to expend less effort on the requisite judgment. This motivation translates into the need for cognitive closure (Kruglanski, 1996), that is, the desire for confidence and clarity, obviating the need for further processing. Our analysis assumes, in fact, that the various effects of our situational-demand manipulations, for example, were due not to capacity reduction as such but to a motivational state it may have engendered. What evidence is there for this contention?

Note that the various situational demands introduced in the present research had a variety of motivational consequences. Specifically, they systematically affected our research participants' preferences and affective reactions to social stimuli. As mentioned already, in research by Kruglanski et al. (1993), participants with firm opinions on a topic, when placed in a noisy environment, expressed a stronger preference for non-persuasive, non-dominant discussion partners unlikely to challenge their pre-existing closure. However, participants lacking a firm opinion expressed a greater preference under noise (vs. no noise) for persuasive and self-assured partners presumably capable of supplying quick closure.

Heightened need for closure should lead to a more negative evaluation of opinion deviates whose dissenting views threaten to undermine closure. Indeed, in research conducted by Kruglanski and Webster (1991), group members under time pressure (vs no pressure) or environmental noise (vs no noise) tended more to reject the opinion deviates and extol the conformists (or 'opinion leaders') whose actions were seen to facilitate consensus.

Note that, as such, the capacity-restriction concept seems incapable of explaining such patterns of interpersonal preferences or evaluations. The notion of cognitive capacity is devoid of specific implications in regard to affective, evaluative, or preferential reactions. On the other hand, a motivational state readily implies preferences and affective expressions (or evaluations) contingent on whether a given state of affairs is perceived to advance the motivational end or undermine it. Thus, the clear motivational effects of situational demands are inconsistent with the independence assumption whereby those demands exert purely cognitive effects (albeit capable of compensation by motivational increments).

Similarly inconsistent with the independence assumption is the pervasive finding that individuals exposed to situational demands exhibit higher judgmental confidence than their non-exposed counterparts. The independence assumption seems to require just the contrary, specifically that a reduction of capacity without an independent compensatory increase in motivation should effect a decline rather than a rise in confidence. Yet one finds, time and time again, that research participants' confidence is at its highest, in fact, when their relative cognitive capacity is reduced (e.g., by noise or fatigue) without introduction of a compensatory motivation (e.g., Kruglanski et al., 1993; Webster, 1993; Webster, Kruglanski, & Pattison, 1995).

Admittedly, situational demands may impair cognitive capacity and induce a motivational state without the two being necessarily related. Thus, it is possible, in principle, that the observed cognitive or judgmental effects of our various manipulations stemmed from capacity restrictions rather than constituting the indirect derivatives of the induced motivation. Some evidence against this possibility was obtained in recent studies (Kruglanski et al., 1993; Webster, 1993) in which the effects of specific situational demands (e.g., noise) were rendered non-significant once the motivation for closure was statistically controlled (Baron & Kenny, 1986), suggesting that those effects were in fact mediated by (rather than independent of) the need for closure. These findings speak most directly in support of the cause–effect model of the capacity–motivation relation and against the independence alternative.

Finally, recall that most effects of the situational demands were replicated by means of our individual-differences measure of the need for closure. Most of the items in that scale (26 of 42) have clear motivational flavour (e.g., terms such as 'I like', 'enjoy', 'hate', 'dislike', or 'prefer'). It is highly unlikely that scores on this measure are readily susceptible to an alternative interpretation in terms of capacity restrictions. Thus, all things considered, it appears that the need for closure theory offers the most comprehensive and parsimonious account of the entire set of present data, including the effects of situational demands and information-processing constraints manipulated in some of our studies.

Heuristic Value

The foregoing discussion suggests that even for relatively straightforward effects such as those of situational demands on the use of simple cues, need for closure theory yields valuable, novel insights. In addition, however, this theory affords the identification of phenomena that, far from appearing obvious or straightforward, may seem complex, surprising, or even paradoxical. For instance, it suggests that the same conditions that increase openness to persuasion in some circumstances may decrease it in other circumstances (Kruglanski et al., 1993), that the same conditions that augment the search for information in some contexts retard it in different contexts (Kruglanski et al., 1991), and that the same situational stresses that foster disapproval and rejection of a deviate may elicit approbation and acceptance of a conformist (Kruglanski & Webster, 1991). Moreover, need for closure theory implies complex linkages between situational demands, for example, and level of linguistic abstraction (Webster, Kruglanski, & Pattison, 1995) rather unanticipated by known

alternative perspectives. Also, it identifies intriguing paradoxes like those of unfounded confidence (higher confidence level despite more restricted information processing) and energy-consuming 'fighting rather than switching', despite conditions favouring energy conservation. It is highly unlikely that these phenomena would be accessed through extant alternative formulations, attesting to the considerable heuristic value of the present analysis.

Integrative Value

The present theory and research highlight the considerable integrative advantages for social psychology of focusing on the fundamental epistemic process whereby judgments or opinions are formed (Kruglanski, 1980, 1989, 1990a). Numerous social psychological phenomena appear to be mediated by such a process in which the need for cognitive closure plays a pivotal part. Indeed, the work reviewed here attests to the relevance of need for closure to such diverse phenomena as primacy effects in impression formation, correspondence biases in causal attribution, stereotyping, groups' reactions to deviates, and the use of language in intergroup contexts.

The need for closure should be just as relevant to numerous other phenomena, unexamined as yet from the present perspective. To mention a few prominent examples, need for closure should enhance the bothersomeness of cognitive inconsistency (that undermines cognitive closure) and hence elevate the magnitude of cognitive dissonance (Festinger, 1957) or balance strivings (Heider, 1958; for a discussion, see Kruglanski & Klar, 1987). Similarly, need for closure should augment the tendency of beliefs to persevere (Ross, Lepper, & Hubbard, 1975), increase the confirmation bias in hypothesis testing (Klayman & Ha, 1987), and enhance the false consensus effect (Ross, Greene, & House, 1977) and the tendency toward self-verification (Swann & Read, 1981). These apparent links among previously unconnected phenomena offer a synthesis of a fragmented social psychological domain (cf. Vallacher & Nowak, 1997) under the aegis of a unified epistemic paradigm.

In conclusion, the theory and research described here suggest that need for cognitive closure represents a useful construct of wide applicability to social psychology. Because of the ubiquitous circumstances of its arousal and its widely ramifying consequences, its continued study promises considerable new insights of both theoretical and real-world significance.

Note

1. The notion of relative cognitive capacity intends to capture the functional commonality shared by situational demand manipulations (time pressure and noise) and momentary decreases in the perceiver's mental powers (e.g., resulting from fatigue or alcoholic intoxication). Both types of manipulation represent a reduction of cognitive capacity in relation to task requirements: Situational demands induce it by increasing task requirements, and mental power decreases, by lowering the perceiver's capabilities.

Discussion Questions

1. The authors describe something of a paradox: Typically, early 'seizing' leads to *more* certainty, rather than less. Logically speaking, this should not be the case because the individual has blocked the flow of potentially useful information. How do you think this increase in certainty occurs?
2. Compare Kruglanski's concepts of a high need for closure versus high need to avoid closure and Gollwitzer's concepts of implementational versus deliberative mindsets (Unit 6). What differences, if any, do you see?
3. How does Kruglanski's model explain the occurrence of the 'illusion of objectivity' in self-enhancement?

Unit Two Further Reading

For more on constructs related to uncertainty, see:

McGregor, I., & Marigold, D.C. (2003). Defensive zeal and the uncertain self: What makes you so sure? *Journal of Personality and Social Psychology, 85,* 838–52.

Weary, G. & Edwards, J.A. (1994). Individual differences in causal uncertainty. *Journal of Personality and Social Psychology, 67,* 308–18.

Sorrentino, R.M., Short, J.C., & Raynor, J.O. (1984). Uncertainty orientation: Implications for affective and cognitive views of achievement behavior. *Journal of Personality and Social Psychology, 46,* 189–206.

For more on related epistemic motivation constructs, such as accountability, personal need for structure, and need for cognition, see:

Tetlock, P.E., & Kim, J.I. (1987). Accountability and judgment processes in a personality prediction task. *Journal of Personality and Social Psychology, 52,* 700–709.

Neuberg, S.L. & Newson, J. (1993). Individual differences in chronic motivation to simplify: Personal need for structure and social-cognitive processing. *Journal of Personality and Social Psychology, 65,* 113–31.

Cacioppo, J.T., & Petty, R.E. (1982) The need for cognition. *Journal of Personality and Social Psychology, 42,* 116–31.

For an insightful recent article that ties together White's concepts of competence and effectance with Bowlby's concept of attachment, see:

Elliot, A.J., & Reis, H.T. (2003). Attachment and exploration in adulthood. *Journal of Personality and Social Psychology, 85,* 317–31.

Unit Three

Reward and Punishment

Intuitively, most people believe that offering a reward to someone for doing a task will improve that person's interest in the task and lead to better performance. However, decades of social psychological research has documented that, in fact, the effect of reward (and punishment) on performance is not at all straightforward; these sorts of inducements sometimes help, but often hurt. The readings in this Unit begin to isolate variables that predict *when* an external inducement is beneficial versus harmful. In so doing, these readings revolve around a central question: In what ways does doing an activity 'for its own sake' (*intrinsic motivation*) differ from doing it as a 'means to an end' (*extrinsic motivation*)?

Lepper, Greene, and Nisbett's highly influential 1973 article (included as the first article in this Unit) was among the first to document the phenomenon that doing a task for the sake of a reward can undermine rather than boost enjoyment of the task (see also Deci, 1971; Kruglanski, Friedman, & Zeevi, 1971). Decades of subsequent research in social and educational psychology has documented the deleterious effect that rewards can have on actual performance, at least under certain conditions (e.g., Harackiewicz & Elliott, 1993). According to the Lepper et al. approach, the undermining effect of rewards is a by-product of people's basic reasoning processes. Typically, we are provided with a reward to coax us to do something we find distasteful. Over time, we come to associate rewards with activities we normally would not like to do. Thus, when offered a reward in advance of an activity, we assume that *if* a reward is being offered *then* the activity must be unpleasant. As you can imagine, Lepper et al.'s findings on the 'overjustification effect' have had an enormous impact in fields such as education and organizational behaviour. Their results also raise critical follow-up questions that you should consider as you read their article: When might an anticipated reward be a good thing? Should corporations stop giving their employees bonuses altogether?

In a series of articles, Deci and Ryan have proposed what they view as a critical refinement to traditional views of intrinsic/extrinsic motivation. According to their theory, the primary predictor of whether a reward or punishment will help or hurt performance is whether the inducement makes the actor feel 'autonomous' or 'controlled'. A feeling of autonomy is associated with the sense that 'I am acting from my own free will'. A feeling of being controlled is associated with the sense that 'I do not have final say in how—or even whether—I will perform this task'. According to Deci and Ryan, this autonomous versus controlled variable is independent of intrinsic versus extrinsic motivation; that is, both extrinsic and intrinsic inducements may feel either autonomous or controlled. In the influential 1987 article included as the second article in this Unit, the authors spell out the antecedents and consequences of the sense of autonomy versus control. In so doing, they highlight a range of intra- and interpersonal factors that may encourage or discourage that vaunted sense of autonomy. As you read their article, keep in mind the following questions: Are the dimensions of intrinsic/extrinsic and autonomy/controlledness really so separate? When might individuals prefer to be controlled?

Sometimes the logical deductions that people make about reward and punishment put them into a quandary. Imagine, for example, that you were given a $100 reward to do something you normally would hate to do (e.g., making a public speech arguing a position that you do not endorse). Imagine that your friend was given $5 to give the same speech. Which one of you, if anyone, do you think would become more convinced by his or her own speech? Most people would say it would be the person who received the bigger reward—that is, you. In fact, decades of research has documented the opposite effect: individuals who get the *smaller* reward exhibit the most change in their behaviour from pre-reward to post-reward. Why is that?

This question cuts to the heart of what is perhaps the most beloved and at the same time most controversial theory in social psychology: Leon Festinger's cognitive dissonance theory. In a landmark 1957 book, Festinger argued that people have a fundamental need to maintain logical consistency not only between their thoughts, but also between their thoughts and behaviour. So strong and basic is this need, Festinger argued, that one might fruitfully make the analogy between the desire for consistency and motivations like hunger and thirst. When people inevitably encounter situations of 'dissonance', they feel an acute sense of anxious unpleasantness that they immediately strive to eliminate. This can lead to elaborate mental gymnastics, such as changing their attitude on a topic so that it becomes consistent with their behaviour (Festinger & Carlsmith, 1959).

Let us return to the issue of rewards. According to Festinger, the institution of a large reward provides sufficient justification for doing something one would normally avoid doing. However, the institution of a small reward provides insufficient justification. When faced with insufficient justification, people are put into a state of cognitive dissonance. More often than not, they resolve this conflict by changing their opinion so that the previously disliked object or task becomes less disliked, or even liked. In the 1961 article included as the last article in this Unit, Festinger articulately describes how the individual's *interpretation* of the reward, rather than the reward's magnitude per se, is what truly predicts behaviour. Moreover, Festinger describes data suggesting that cognitive dissonance reduction even occurs in rats!

As noted in Kunda's (1990) article in Unit 5, Festinger's theory has been subjected to spirited reinterpretations over the years, including those arguing for a non-motivational account (e.g., Bem, 1967). Debates regarding the mechanics and boundary conditions of cognitive dissonance continue to this day, more than 50 years after the theory's debut. Yet its core tenets have stood the test of time and have exerted a significant influence not only on social psychology, but also on other fields such as economics and political science.

5. Undermining Children's Intrinsic Interest with Extrinsic Reward: A Test of the 'Overjustification' Hypothesis

Mark R. Lepper and David Greene, Stanford University
Richard E. Nisbett, University of Michigan

□ ■ □

Editor's Introduction

'How can you 'ave your pudding if you don't eat your meat?!!!' shrieks an unnamed teacher's voice in the background of Pink Floyd's 'Another Brick in the Wall (Part II)' from *The Wall*. Indeed, one of the painful lessons of childhood is coming to grips with this 'if-then' contingency: 'Only if I eat my (bad-tasting) dinner will I get my (good-tasting) dessert' or, more generally, 'Only if I do something undesirable will I get my desirable reward'. Over time, it is understandable that children would come to associate rewards with undesired activities. After all, never once did your parents say to you, 'Only if you eat your ice cream will you get your chocolate cake'.

The insight of the present article by Lepper, Greene, and Nisbett (as well as their contemporaries Deci, 1971, and Kruglanski, Friedman, & Zeevi, 1971) was that this association becomes so strong for most people that it works in both directions: The mere presentation of a reward *must* mean that the task itself is undesirable. Thus, all things being equal, the presentation of a reward can reduce intrinsic interest and enjoyment of a task.

How is this possible? How can this perception be so easily manipulated? Don't we have a firm grasp on how enjoyable or interesting different tasks are? According to Bem (1965, 1967), the answer is no. For many of the activities we are asked to perform in everyday life, we just do them without a clear opinion about how much we like them. Then, if we happen to be asked afterwards how much we like the task, we think back to our own behaviour and infer backwards what our opinion of the task must be. ('If I did that task

willingly then I must have wanted to do it.') In other words, people assume that there will generally be agreement between their desires and their actions. In this respect, the present work draws on Festinger's cognitive dissonance theory: People curb their perceptions and behaviour so that it stays consistent with their beliefs and opinions. It is, in fact, no accident that Lepper et al. refer to their phenomenon as the 'overjustification' effect. Just as in Festinger and Carlsmith (1959), where being rewarded with one dollar was considered by participants to be 'insufficient justification' to perform a boring task, in the present case being given a wonderful reward (a 'Good Player Award') to do an exciting task (playing with markers) constitutes too much justification for doing the task. They are opposite sides of the same coin.

In their analysis of the overjustification effect, Lepper et al. adopt an explicitly attributional approach. This fact is usually underemphasized in most accounts you will see in textbooks about the overjustification effect and intrinsic motivation. But to these authors, the overjustification effect is really just an example of the attributional phenomenon known as the discounting principle (Kelley, 1967). Discounting means that when there are multiple plausible causes for a person's actions, this reduces one's confidence that any one cause was *the* cause. For example, if I fail an exam but I was sick all night before the exam, it is not clear if I failed because of my illness or because I have low aptitude. Similarly, in the case of overjustification, if I played a lot with the markers and was told beforehand that I was receiving an award for doing so, it suddenly becomes unclear to me why I am playing with the markers. Is it because I like the markers or because I am doing it for the award? Thus, my interest in the markers wanes.

More generally, if I am doing something I enjoy but I am receiving a reward or punishment for doing so, I may very well be doing the task out of *extrinsic motivation* (i.e., I am doing the task only as a means to an end). But if I am doing something I enjoy without any external reward or punishment for doing so, I can infer that I am *intrinsically* motivated (i.e., I am doing the task as an end unto itself). Generally, doing a task from a position of

intrinsic motivation leads to greater engagement, more attention, and ultimately better performance than doing a task from a position of extrinsic motivation.

As you might expect, these initial studies in the 1970s spawned an enormous literature in social, educational, and organizational psychology on the effects of rewards (and punishments) on human performance. Clearly, the overjustification effect has major implications for educators trying to get the most out of their students. This research literature has proliferated to this day, complete with its share of debates and controversies.

The process by which man seeks to understand his environment—to discern the causes of events which surround him and explain the behaviour of others toward him—has been of central concern to social psychology for many years (e.g., Brunswik, 1934; Heider, 1958; Michotte, 1946); but only in the past few years have psychologists concerned themselves with the process by which man explains and understands his own actions and their causes (Bem, 1965, 1967, 1972; Jones & Davis, 1965; Jones, Kanouse, Kelley, Nisbett, Valins, & Weiner, 1972; Kelley, 1967). Recently, theoretical analyses of the process of self-perception or self-attribution by Bem (1965, 1967) and by Kelley (1967) have suggested that processes of self-perception have a common ground with those of other-perception.

When an individual observes another person engaging in some activity, he infers that the other is intrinsically motivated to engage in that activity to the extent that he does not perceive salient, unambiguous, and sufficient extrinsic contingencies to which to attribute the other's behaviour. Self-perception theory proposes that a person engages in similar processes of inference about his own behaviour and its meaning. To the extent that the external reinforcement contingencies controlling his behaviour are salient, unambiguous, and

sufficient to explain it, the person attributes his behaviour to these controlling circumstances. But if external contingencies are not perceived, or if they are unclear, invisible, and psychologically insufficient to account for his actions, the person attributes his behaviour to his own dispositions, interests, and desires.

Originally, self-perception theory was proposed as an alternative explanation of the large dissonance literature on 'insufficient justification' (cf. Aronson, 1966), where subjects are induced to engage in unpleasant or attitudinally inconsistent behaviour under conditions of either clearly sufficient or psychologically inadequate external justification. Typically, these studies have demonstrated that subjects given little extrinsic justification for the behaviour they have been induced to perform come to believe that their actions were intrinsically motivated. In a self-perception analysis, this outcome is simply the result of a self-directed inference process. In the low-justification conditions, the subject infers from his behaviour and the lack of apparent external pressure that he must have wished to act as he did; while in the high justification conditions, the subject infers that his behaviour was determined by the external pressures in the situation.

Besides its application to many classic dissonance paradigms, self-perception theory has a number of heuristic implications, one of the most intriguing of which could be termed the 'over-justification' hypothesis—the proposition that a person's intrinsic interest in an activity may be undermined by inducing him to engage in that activity as an explicit means to some extrinsic goal. If the external justification provided to induce a person to engage in an activity is unnecessarily high and psychologically 'oversufficient', the person might come to infer that his actions were basically motivated by the external contingencies of the situation, rather than by any intrinsic interest in the activity itself. In short, a person induced to undertake an inherently desirable activity as a means to some ulterior end should cease to see the activity as an end in itself.

While the existence of such an overjustification effect has been postulated by a number of authors (DeCharms, 1968; Deci, 1971; Kruglanski, Friedman, & Zeevi, 1971; Lepper, 1973; Nisbett & Valins, 1971), this proposition has received virtually no experimental examination. Nisbett and Valins (1971) reviewed several studies which, on reinterpretation, provided evidence consistent with this proposition, but the first study to intentionally pursue a directly related hypothesis was that of Deci (1971).

Specifically, Deci hypothesized that rewarding subjects with money and 'closely related tangible rewards' for engaging in an intrinsically interesting task would decrease their subsequent interest in that task in the absence of such external rewards. To test this proposition, Deci asked college subjects to solve a number of inherently interesting puzzles during three experimental sessions. Following an initial baseline session for all subjects, one group of subjects was paid for solving a second series of puzzles, while a second group was not paid. In a third session neither group was paid. During a break in each session, subjects were left alone for a few minutes to do whatever they wished, including continuing work on the puzzles. During this time, the subjects' behaviour was observed and recorded from behind a one-way mirror. Subjects who had been paid during the second session tended to show a greater decrease in intrinsic interest from the first to the third session than subjects who had not been paid. This result was consistent with the overjustification hypothesis, but unfortunately this finding was of only marginal statistical significance and depended as much on differences between the groups during the baseline session as during the final sessions.

Deci (1971) couched his hypothesis in terms of monetary or other material rewards. As an implication of self-perception theory, however, the overjustification hypothesis is formulated in terms of the perception of oneself as having undertaken an activity *in order to obtain some extrinsic goal*. The nature of the extrinsic goal should be of little consequence. Thus, an overjustification effect is predicted for any situation which results in an extrinsic attribution where previously intrinsic interest was the only salient attribution. Contracting explicitly to engage in an activity for a reward should undermine interest in the activity, even when the reward is insubstantial or merely symbolic. Conversely, receipt of an unforeseen, unexpected reward *after* engaging in an activity should have little or no detrimental effect, even when the reward is a highly prized material one.

This analysis suggests two features necessary for an unequivocal test of the overjustification hypothesis: (a) a subject population intrinsically motivated to engage in a target activity, and (b) a comparison of two experimental treatments—one in which subjects are asked to engage in this activity as a means to some extrinsic goal and one in which subjects are asked to engage in the activity for its own sake but subsequently receive the same extrinsic reward. Subjects who expect a reward should show less subsequent intrinsic interest in the target activity than subjects who do not. An appropriate test of this hypothesis requires a dependent measure taken some time after the experimental sessions and in a situation as different as possible from that in which the rewards were administered. Thus, in this study the rewards were delivered in an experimental room, while the dependent measure of intrinsic interest was obtained in a naturalistic field setting.

The present experiment was conducted with children in an educational setting in order to test the overjustification hypothesis in a context where its practical implications may be greatest. The notion of overjustification immediately raises issues relevant to two widespread 'contractual' techniques—one old and one new—of controlling the behaviour of schoolchildren. The long-established practice of giving grades, gold stars, and similar awards to children is, in the present terms, a contractual one likely to induce the cognition, 'I am doing this [arithmetic, drawing, reading] *in order to . . .*' The newly developed 'token economies', in which children are offered redeemable tokens for desirable behaviour, seem quite likely to produce the same cognition. The overjustification hypothesis implies that such contractual techniques may backfire for at least those children initially interested in the activities presented in such a context. Demonstrating an overjustification effect in an educational setting, therefore, would suggest the need for greater attention to the possible side effects and long-term consequences of powerful systems of extrinsic rewards.

Method

Overview

Preschool children showing initial intrinsic interest in a drawing activity during baseline observations in their classrooms were selected as subjects for the experiment. These subjects were blocked by degree of initial interest in the activity and assigned randomly to one of three treatment conditions: In the expected-award condition, subjects agreed to engage in the drawing activity in order to obtain an extrinsic reward—a certificate with a gold seal and ribbon. In the unexpected-award condition, subjects engaged in the same activity and received the same reward, but had no knowledge of the reward until after they had finished the

activity. In the no-award control condition, subjects neither expected nor received the reward, but otherwise duplicated the experience of the subjects in the other two conditions. These experimental sessions were conducted individually in a room apart from the subjects' classrooms. The target-drawing activity was again introduced into the children's classrooms one to two weeks after the experimental sessions. Measures of subsequent intrinsic interest were obtained unobtrusively by covert observation of the classrooms from behind a one-way mirror.

Subject Population

Subjects were selected from the student population at the Bing Nursery School, located on the Stanford University campus. These children, ranging in age from 40 to 64 months, were of predominantly white, middle-class backgrounds and of average or above-average intelligence. Three black children who would otherwise have been included in the experiment were arbitrarily excluded from the subject pool in order to increase the precision with which the population could be defined.

Observational Setting

The nursery school's facilities included three classrooms in which independent programs were run simultaneously. In each classroom, three different classes, each consisting of about 35 children and four to five teachers, met for either two or three half-days per week. The present study was conducted with four of these classes in the two classrooms equipped with one-way mirrors and sound equipment for observational purposes.

The program in these classrooms was such that, with the exception of a single 15-minute 'juice' break, children were free throughout the day to choose among a variety of activities. Some activities (such as building blocks, easels, housekeeping equipment, and outdoor activities) were available to them continuously; others (such as collage materials, 'play dough', and drawing materials) were made available periodically by their teachers.

Typically, at the beginning of each class session, children took note of the 'periodic' activities, which had been set out for the day on each of three tables located near the centre of the classroom.

For the purposes of the present study, the arrangement provided an opportunity to introduce a novel 'target' activity into the ongoing nursery school program on a periodic basis. Moreover, the activity could easily be integrated into the normal classroom routine without the experimenters having to be present. It was thus possible to obtain an unobtrusive measure of the children's intrinsic interest in the target activity in a situation in which the activity was not associated with the experimenters or any extrinsic reward.

Experimental Activity

The experimental activity was chosen to meet three criteria: (a) sufficient similarity to other typical periodic activities so as not to appear out of place, (b) sufficient attractiveness to ensure that most children would express at least some initial interest, and (c) amenability of the activity to some objective definition of interest. These criteria were met handily by the opportunity to draw freely with multicoloured felt-tipped drawing pens ('magic markers') not normally available in the children's classrooms.

Measurement of Intrinsic Interest

Baseline data on initial interest were collected during the first hour of three consecutive class days. On days when data were to be collected, a few minutes before the class began, the teachers placed a set of magic markers and a sheaf of fine white artist's drawing paper on a hexagonal table located directly in front of the observational mirror. After the first hour of class, these materials were replaced with some other table activity. Thus the target activity was available to a child from the time he arrived until the end of the first hour of class and was presented by the teachers as simply another activity with which the children might choose to play.

During this hour, two observers were stationed behind the one-way mirror, each equipped with a Rustrak eight-track continuous event recorder. The first six channels on both recorders were numbered to correspond to the six positions around the hexagonal target table. One observer was responsible for recording children's actions at Positions 1 through 4; the other was responsible for Positions 4 through 6 and Position 1. The data recorded on Channels 1 and 4 were used to test agreement between observers. For each observer, two additional channels (Channels 7 and 8 of each recorder) were available for recording behaviour not clearly tied to one of the six positions at the table. Hence, the two observers were equipped to record data on up to 10 children at a time.

A child was defined as 'interested' in the target activity whenever he either sat down in one of the six chairs at the target table or put his hand on a marker; he was considered no longer interested when he was neither sitting at the table nor in possession of a marker. In practice, typically, the first discrimination which had to be made by the observer was when the child should be considered 'sitting'. It was decided to regard the target table as a system with six regular inputs, such that whenever a child was effectively occupying one of these inputs to the practical exclusion of another child, he or she was considered to be sitting. This criterion was felt to be a more valid indication of interest than a 'fanny-touching-seat' criterion and was only slightly more difficult to discriminate reliably. When a child reached for a marker before sitting down or got up from his seat to draw on the floor or somewhere else, his behaviour was recorded by one of the observers on Channel 7 or 8.

The measurement procedure was highly reliable. A product-moment correlation of the records of the two observers for the 47 children who appeared on either Channel 1 or 4 proved close to unity ($r = 0.99$). To further ensure that this method of measurement would be as sensitive and accurate as possible, three slight modifications of standard classroom procedure were introduced. First, since the mere presence of an adult at any of the activity tables was highly correlated with the presence of several children, teachers and other adults were asked to defer all requests from children to sit at the table until the experimental activity had been removed. Second, highly similar materials (e.g., crayons, scissors, other paper, etc.) were made inaccessible to the children while the target materials were available in order to avoid forcing observers to make unnecessarily difficult judgments. Third, teachers recorded not only absences but also times of arrival for any children who arrived late on days of data collection. These data allowed the calculation for each child of a more precise index of interest, namely, the percentage of time that he chose to play with the experimental activity out of the total time that he was present while the materials were available.

At least some play was recorded during baseline periods for 102 of the 139 children who appeared in their respective rooms at any time during the three hours of measurement. All children whose total playing time exceeded four minutes of play with the target activity were blocked by class and sex within class and ranked in order of total playing time. Each of the eight class–sex blocks was divided into as many groups of three as possible, with extra children discarded from the bottom of the rankings. This procedure yielded a potential subject population of 24 boys and 45 girls. Within groups of three, a table of random permutations was used to assign subjects to treatment conditions.

Experimental Procedure

Following the third hour of baseline observations in each class, the experimental materials were removed from the classroom until they were needed again for post-experimental observations. Experimental sessions began within two weeks after the baseline period and were completed for each class on three consecutive school days.

Two persons conducted each experimental session: The first experimenter brought the child to and from his classroom and administered the experimental manipulation; the second experimenter stayed with the child while he was in the experimental room and administered the reward. Two (male) experimenters each played the role of the first experimenter for subjects from two of the four classes, and four (two male and two female) assistants each played the role of the second experimenter for subjects from one of the classes.

Potential subjects were approached by the first experimenter in their classrooms, engaged in play and/or conversation, and then asked if they would like to come to the 'surprise room' with him. Twelve of 45 girls and two of 24 boys refused to come to the experimental room on three separate occasions and hence were lost from the experiment. Thus, 55 subjects actually participated in the experiment (19 each in the expected- and unexpected-award conditions, 17 in the no-award control group).

Each subject was brought individually to the experimental room by the first experimenter. The subject was seated at a child-sized table containing a set of magic markers and a sheaf of paper. At this point, the first experimenter had in his possession a sample 'Good Player Award', the extrinsic reward employed in this study. These Good Player Awards—coloured 3 × 5 inch cards with the words 'Good Player Award' and spaces for the child's name and school engraved on the front next to a large gold star and a red ribbon—have proved effective rewards in previous studies (e.g., Harter & Zigler, 1972).

Presenting the drawing materials to the subject, the first experimenter said, 'Do you remember these magic markers that you played with back in your room? Well, there's a man [lady] who's come to the nursery school for a few days to see what kinds of pictures boys and girls like to draw with magic markers.' For subjects in the unexpected-award and the no-award groups, the first experimenter continued, 'Would you like to draw some pictures for him?'

For subjects in the expected-award condition, the first experimenter produced the sample Good

Player Award and continued instead, 'And he's brought along a few of these Good Player Awards to give to boys and girls who will help him out by drawing some pictures for him. See? It's got a big gold star and a bright red ribbon, and there's a place here for your name and your school. Would you like to win one of these Good Player Awards?' Each subject indicated assent to the first experimenter's final question, typically with considerable enthusiasm. For all subjects the first experimenter concluded, 'Good. He should be right outside. I'll go get him.'

The first experimenter introduced the second experimenter to the subject and then excused himself, leaving the second experimenter alone with the subject. The second experimenter sat down across the table from the subject, started a stopwatch, and asked the subject, 'What would you like to draw first?' Most of the time the subject began to draw a picture immediately; when he did not, a little coaxing was always sufficient to get him started. During the session, the second experimenter was friendly but not overly responsive to the subject. Generally, he attempted to show interest in, rather than explicit approval of, the subject's performance.

Each subject was allowed six minutes to draw pictures. If the second experimenter felt that an interruption after precisely six minutes was inopportune, up to 30 seconds more was provided. This procedure was designed to control against confounding of the classroom measure by satiation effects. The drawings made by each child were kept to allow an examination of the child's performance, during experimental sessions, along both quantitative and qualitative dimensions. Ratings of these drawings on a number of descriptive indexes were made by judges blind to the subject's condition.

The second experimenter was completely blind to the subject's condition for the first five minutes of the session. At the end of five minutes, the second experimenter casually looked inside a manila folder, which had been left on the table by the first experimenter to determine whether the subject was to receive an award or not. After this point, the second experimenter knew only whether the subject was in one of the two award conditions as opposed to the no-award control condition.

One minute later, the second experimenter looked conspicuously at his stopwatch and said, 'Well, it looks like our time is up. Thank you very much for helping me out by drawing these pictures for me. You really did a good job.' For subjects who were to receive an award, the second experimenter continued as follows:

In fact, you have been such a big help to me that I have something very special to give you. [The second experimenter rose, got a Good Player Award and a black pen, and returned to the table.] I'm going to give you one of my Good Player Awards, with your name and school on it. [The second experimenter showed the award to the subject and wrote the subject's name and school on the award with a flourish.] Now turn around and let me show you our special Honour Roll board where you can put your award so that everyone will know what a good player you are! [The second experimenter stood as he spoke, walked to the corner of the room, and pulled back a standing slat screen to expose a bulletin board. This board was decorated with the title 'Honour Roll' and contained a standard display of several Good Player Awards. The second experimenter escorted the subject to the bulletin board and placed a push pin through the top of his award.] You can put your Good Player Award anywhere you want on the Honour Roll board. That looks very nice.

Then, for all subjects, the second experimenter said, 'Now, let's see if we can find [the first experimenter] to take you back to your room.' As the second experimenter opened the door, the first experimenter entered and returned the subject to his classroom.

Postexperimental Observations

The observational setting and data collection procedure were the same as during the baseline periods. Observers were blind to the conditions of the subjects. Data collection began 7 to 14 days after the last subject had been run in a given class and was completed over no more than four consecutive school days for each class. In three of the classes, one of the first three class meetings had to be skipped for reasons ranging from the unanticipated arrival of a goat in the classroom to equipment failure. Four subjects were lost during these sessions: Three were never in class during the three observational sessions; a fourth was present for only 10 out of a possible 180 minutes and was discarded, although inclusion of his data would not have affected the significance or pattern of the data reported. The final sample, then, consisted of 51 children—19 males and 32 females. There were 18 subjects in both the expected-award and the unexpected-award conditions and 15 subjects in the no-award condition.

Results

The overjustification hypothesis led to the anticipation that subjects in the expected-award condition would show less subsequent intrinsic interest in the target activity than subjects in the unexpected-award and no-award conditions. The data relevant to this proposition—the mean proportion of time that children chose to play with the target activity in the post-experimental sessions—are presented in Table 5.1.

It may be seen that, as predicted, children in the expected-award condition spent less time playing with the drawing materials than children in the other conditions. Preliminary analysis of the data by sex of child revealed no significant sex difference and no interaction of sex of child with experimental condition. The data were therefore collapsed across this dimension for purposes of analysis. Since the variances of the treatment groups were significantly different (F_{max} = 5.39,

Table 5.1 Mean Percentage of Free-Choice Time That Subjects Chose to Play with the Target Activity, by Treatments

Experimental condition	n	%
Expected award	18	8.59
No award	15	16.73
Unexpected award	18	18.09

df = 3/17, $p < .01$) and the standard deviations of the groups were proportional to the means, a log transformation $|Y = \ln (Y + 1)|$ was performed on the data to produce homogenous treatment variances (Winer, 1962, p. 221). These transformed data were submitted to a one-way unweighted-means analysis of variance, which is presented in Table 5.2. This analysis yielded a significant effect of experimental treatments on subsequent intrinsic interest in the experimental materials (F = 3.25, df = 2/48, $p < .05$). To clarify the precise nature of this effect, a contrast was performed to test the specific prediction of the study. This contrast proved highly significant (F = 6.19, df = 1/48, $p < .025$), accounting for most of the systematic variance and indicating that subjects in the expected-award condition chose to spend a smaller proportion of their time playing with the target materials than subjects in either the unexpected-award (t = 2.32, $p < .025$) or the no-award (t = 2.05, $p < .025$) conditions.[1]

In addition, although blocking subjects on initial interest in the target activity of course

Table 5.2 Analysis of Variance on Transformed Proportions of Time Spent with Target Activity

Source	df	MS	F
Between	2	3.96	3.25*
Contrast	1	7.55	6.19**
Residual	1	0.37	<1
Within	48	1.22	

*$p < 0.05$
**$p < 0.025$

eliminated any between-groups differences in this variable, it is of some interest to compare post-experimental interest with original interest within each treatment condition. Subjects in both the unexpected-award and no-award conditions showed very slight and non-significant (both $ts < 1$) increases in interest from pre-experimental to post-experimental measurement sessions. Subjects in the expected-award condition, however, manifested a significant decrease in interest in the target materials from baseline to post-experimental sessions ($t = 2.61, p < .02$).

Some readers may find it surprising that receipt of the award did not increase the interest of children in the unexpected-award group. It should be recalled, however, that subjects were selected on the basis of their relatively great initial interest in the drawing activity. There would be little reason to expect that the award would have had much effect on the behaviour of children for whom the drawing activity was already highly salient and pleasurable. On the other hand, the range of initial interest was fairly large, and it might be expected that the award would have had some effect among those children in the present sample with relatively little interest. This was apparently the case. Each experimental group was divided into two groups on the basis of initial interest in the drawing activity. Of the resulting six groups, only the children in the unexpected-award group who were below the median in degree of initial interest showed a substantial increase in interest following the experimental manipulation ($t = 2.35, p < .05$). Children above the median in initial interest in the unexpected-award group showed a trivial decrease in interest, and children in the control (no-award) group, whether above or below the median, showed a trivial increase in interest.

It would be of some theoretical interest to know whether the expected-award treatment had a different effect on children high in initial interest than on children low in initial interest. Unfortunately, the data do not allow a clear answer to this question. Both the high group and the low group

declined in interest in the drawing activity. The high group declined more than the low group, but this could have occurred either because the manipulation was more effective for the high group or simply because there was a 'floor effect' for the group already relatively low in interest. It would be interesting to repeat the present experiment in a context avoiding such an artificial restriction of movement.

Finally, it is important to note that the award manipulation also had an immediate effect on children's performance during the experimental sessions. The pictures drawn by the children for the experimenter were rated on overall quality by three blind judges on a scale from 1 (very poor) to 5 (very good). Although the three conditions did not differ in the number of pictures drawn (2.61 for the expected-award, 2.44 for the unexpected-award, and 2.33 for the no-award children), the quality of pictures drawn in the expected-award condition was lower than in the other groups. The average quality ratings for the expected-award group (2.18) differed significantly from both the unexpected-award (2.85) and no-award (2.69) groups ($t = 3.01, p < .01$, and $t = 2.08, p < .05$, respectively). Thus, the detrimental effects of the expected-award manipulation were apparent during the experimental sessions, as well as later in the classroom setting.

Discussion

The present results indicate that it is possible to produce an overjustification effect. In the expected-award condition, children showed decreased interest in the drawing activity after having undertaken it in order to obtain a goal that was extrinsic to the pleasures and satisfaction of drawing in its own right. In the unexpected-award condition, on the other hand, children receiving the same extrinsic reward showed undiminished or increased interest in the activity. This detrimental effect of the expected-award procedure was manifest both in quality of performance during the experimental sessions and in subsequent unobtrusive measures of intrinsic interest in the classroom setting.

As an empirical proposition, the present findings have important practical implications for situations in which extrinsic incentives are used to enhance or maintain children's interest in activities of some initial interest to the child. Such situations, we would suggest, occur frequently in traditional classrooms where systems of extrinsic rewards—whether grades, gold stars, or the awarding of special privileges—are applied as a matter of course to an entire class of children.

Many of the activities we ask children to attempt in school, in fact, are of intrinsic interest to at least some of the children; one effect of presenting these activities within a system of extrinsic incentives, the present study suggests, is to undermine the intrinsic interest in these activities of at least those children who had some interest to begin with. The quite limited manipulation employed in this study, involving a symbolic reward not unlike those routinely employed in the classroom, was sufficient to produce significant differences in the children's subsequent behaviour in a natural preschool classroom. This is consistent with the complaint, from Dewey (1900) and Whitehead (1929) up to the time of Holt (1964) and Silberman (1970), that a central problem with our educational system is its inability to preserve the intrinsic interest in learning and exploration that the child seems to possess when he first enters school. Instead, these authors have suggested, the schooling process seems almost to undermine children's spontaneous interest in the process of learning itself.

At the same time, because the implications of this point of view for social control and socialization are potentially so great, it is important to point immediately to the hazards of overgeneralization from the present experiment. Certainly there is nothing in the present line of reasoning or the present data to suggest that contracting to engage in an activity for an extrinsic reward will always, or even usually, result in a decrement in intrinsic interest in the activity. The present experiment was carefully designed to allow a demonstration of the overjustification effect. The target activity was deliberately chosen to be highly attractive, and subjects were all children who actually manifested some intrinsic interest in the activity. Extrinsic incentives were superfluous. Under such circumstances, there is every reason to believe that it should be relatively easy to manipulate loss of interest and difficult to increase it above its already fairly high level.

The present experiment does not speak to situations which depart very greatly from the present situation. There is considerable evidence from studies of token-economy programs (Fargo, Behrns, & Nolen, 1970; O'Leary & Drabman, 1971) supporting the proposition that extrinsic incentives may often be used effectively to increase interest in certain broad classes of activities. On the present line of reasoning, this proposition should be particularly true when (a) the level of initial intrinsic interest in the activity is very low and some extrinsic device is essential for producing involvement with the activity; or (b) the activity is one whose attractiveness becomes apparent only through engaging in it for a long time or only after some minimal level of mastery has been attained. In fact, such conditions characterize the prototypical token-economy program in that tangible extrinsic rewards are *necessary* to elicit the desired behaviour. Hence, it would be a mistaken overgeneralization from the present study to proscribe broadly the use of token-economy programs to modify children's behaviour.

It has already been recommended by some thoughtful proponents of token economies that their use be limited to circumstances in which less powerful techniques have been tried and found inadequate (O'Leary, Poulos, & Devine, 1972)—in other words, only when they are necessary. It has also been stressed that in any case, the successful implementation of powerful reinforcement systems demands considerable sensitivity as well as ingenuity on the part of the practitioner (Bandura, 1969). The present study provides empirical evidence of an undesirable consequence of the unnecessary use of extrinsic rewards, supporting the case for the exercise of discretion in their application (O'Leary & Drabman, 1971).

Note

1. All p values reported in this article are based on two-tailed tests of significance.

Discussion Questions

1.   In the present study, the authors not only compare a 'reward' condition to a 'no-reward' condition, but also include an 'unexpected reward' condition. What is the purpose of giving some of the participants a surprise reward?
2.   Are rewards always bad? When might they be helpful? When might they be necessary? When might giving a reward lead to better performance than not giving a reward?

6. The Support of Autonomy and the Control of Behaviour

Edward L. Deci and Richard M. Ryan, University of Rochester

□ ■ □

Editor's Introduction

Do you believe that you have free will? This question is, of course, one of the oldest and thorniest questions in the history of human scholarship. Versions of the debate have been played out over the last several decades via the various trends in psychological thought (e.g., behaviourism vs. some forms of cognitivism). In this article, social psychologists Edward Deci and Richard Ryan and their colleagues made a significant contribution to this debate by noting that individuals' *subjective* perception that their action is autonomous versus controlled goes a long way toward predicting motivation and performance. To summarize, feeling that one's actions are controlled, whether by another person or simply the exigencies of the situation, leads to decreased motivation and poorer performance compared to feeling that one's actions are autonomous, or originating from the self.

Like Lepper, Greene, and Nisbett's article on intrinsic motivation included in this Unit, Deci and Ryan are also concerned with optimizing human performance by fostering a sense of focused, self-directed engagement, or 'zest' for the task at hand. As such, the Deci and Ryan program of research has broad implications for fields ranging from education, organizational management, sports, to psychotherapy. The Deci and Ryan conceptualization of autonomous versus controlled behaviour differs, however, from the intrinsic versus extrinsic distinction in a number of key ways.

According to Deci and Ryan, there are two aspects of reward: its informational aspect (i.e., its ability to answer the question 'How am I doing?') and its controlling aspect (i.e., its ability to shape behaviour based on the desire for the reward).

As such, rewards may not necessarily undermine performance. To truly hamper performance, the reward must be experienced as controlling, as a 'bribe' that sends the message that 'I wouldn't spontaneously do this task were it not for this reward'. Rewards that are subjectively interpreted in a more informational manner, as a helpful milestone in an individual's performance trajectory over time, tend to *not* hurt performance, but may even help it. Indeed, Deci (1975) found that making informational aspects of rewards more salient increased participants' intrinsic interest in the task at hand.

In this article, Deci and Ryan systematically describe a range of situational variables and person variables that promote or undermine one's sense of autonomy. Situational variables include the presence/absence of rewards, deadlines, threats, and surveillance. Surprisingly, even positive feedback provided by another person (typically an authority figure) can be construed as controlling (and therefore motivationally unhelpful). Person variables include a high versus low competitive personality, an external versus internal locus of control, and high versus low public self-consciousness. In each of these cases, the former tends to yield a higher sense of being controlled and, thus, poorer overall performance on many tasks.

One of the more intriguing findings is that children in autonomy-supporting classrooms tend to display higher self-esteem than those in more controlling classrooms (Deci, Nezlek, & Sheinman, 1981; Ryan & Grolnick, 1986). Why might this be the case? People may reason as follows: 'I like myself better when I have the sense that most of my behaviour originates from *me* (as opposed to being forced upon me) because, after all, if I am just doing what I am told, I have no basis for judging my true self.'

In subsequent research, these authors and their collaborators have expanded on the ideas in the present article to develop self-determination theory (SDT; e.g., Ryan & Deci, 2000). According to this theory, autonomy is only one of three central motivational needs. The other two are competence and relatedness. (Note that competence and relatedness are addressed in Unit 2 and Unit 1 of the present volume, respectively.) Thus, SDT brings together three pillars of motivation under one umbrella.

□ ■ □

For several decades American psychology was dominated by associationist theories. Assuming that behaviour is controlled by peripheral mechanisms, these theories held that the initiation of behaviour is a function of stimulus inputs such as external contingencies of reinforcement (Skinner, 1953) or internal drive stimulations (Hull, 1943) and that the regulation of behaviour is a function of associative bonds between inputs and behaviours that develop through reinforcement processes. With that general perspective, the central processing of information was not part of the explanatory system, so concepts such as intention were considered irrelevant to the determination of behaviour.

During the 1950s and 1960s, associationist theories gave way to cognitive theories in which the processing of information was assumed to play an important role in the determination of behaviour. On the basis of this assumption, the initiation of behaviour was theorized to be a function of expectations about behaviour-outcome contingencies and of the psychological value of outcomes (e.g., Atkinson, 1964; Tolman, 1959; Vroom, 1964), and the regulation of behaviour was seen as a process of comparing one's current state to a standard (i.e., the desired outcome) and then acting to reduce the discrepancy (e.g., Kanfer, 1975; Miller, Galanter, & Pribram, 1960). Thus, the cognitive perspective shifted the focus of analysis from the effects of past consequences of behaviour to expectations about future consequences of behaviour. The concept of intentionality (Lewin, 1951) became important because behaviour, whether implicitly

or explicitly, was understood in terms of people's intentions to act in a way that would yield certain outcomes.

Within the concept of intentionality, however, a further distinction can usefully be made. Some intentional behaviours, we suggest, are initiated and regulated through choice as an expression of oneself, whereas other intentional behaviours are pressured and coerced by intrapsychic and environmental forces and thus do not represent true choice (Deci & Ryan, 1985b). The former behaviours are characterized by autonomous initiation and regulation and are referred to as *self-determined;* the latter behaviours are characterized by heteronomous initiation and regulation and are referred to as *controlled.*[1]

We shall argue that the distinction between self-determined and controlled behaviours has ramifications for the quality of action and experience and is relevant to the study of both social contexts and personality.

Intentionality and Autonomy

An intention is generally understood as a determination to engage in a particular behaviour (Atkinson, 1964). In the cognitive theories of motivation and action (e.g., Heider, 1960; Lewin, 1951; Tolman, 1959), which have their roots in Gestalt psychology, having an intention implies personal causation and is equivalent to being motivated to act. Intentions are said to derive from one's desire to achieve positively valent outcomes or avoid negatively valent ones.

Using an intentional perspective, psychologists working in a neo-operant reinforcement tradition have emphasized that people's beliefs about whether certain behaviours are reliably related to desired outcomes are of central import. An abundance of research has shown, for example, that when a situation is structured so that outcomes are independent of behaviours (Seligman, 1975) or when people have a generalized belief that behaviours and outcomes are independent (Rotter, 1966), non-intentionality and maladaptation are likely to result. However, believing that behaviours are reliably related to outcomes is not enough to ensure a high level of motivation and adaptation. People must also believe that they are sufficiently competent to execute the requisite behaviours (e.g., Bandura, 1977). Indeed, the expectation of incompetence, like the expectation of behaviour outcome independence, has been shown to result in low motivation and maladaptation (Abramson, Seligman, & Teasdale, 1978). In sum, the cognitive perspective maintains that when people believe that desired outcomes will follow reliably from certain behaviours and that they are competent to execute those behaviours, they will display intentionality and experience personal causation (Heider, 1958).

Our organismic approach diverges from the cognitive approach by distinguishing between those intentional behaviours that are initiated and regulated autonomously and those that are controlled by intrapersonal or interpersonal forces. Whereas the cognitive approach equates the concepts of intention and choice (Lewin, 1951), the organismic approach reserves the concept of choice for those intentional behaviours that are autonomously initiated and regulated, and it uses the concept of control for those intentional behaviours that are not autonomous. Thus, although having perceived control over outcomes (i.e., perceiving behaviour–outcome dependence and competence) promotes intentionality, it does not ensure that the intentional behaviour will be initiated and regulated autonomously.

The concept of autonomy is a theoretical rather than empirical one, though it has clear empirical consequences. Autonomy connotes an inner endorsement of one's actions, the sense that they emanate from oneself and are one's own. Autonomous action is thus chosen, but we use the term *choice* not as a cognitive concept, referring to decisions among behavioural options (e.g., Brehm & Brehm, 1981), but rather as an organismic concept anchored in the sense of a fuller, more integrated functioning. The more autonomous the behaviour, the more it is endorsed by the whole self and is experienced as action for which one is responsible.

Let us clarify this point through some examples. First, consider the behaviour of an anorexic person abstaining from food. Clearly, there is intentionality, yet the person would not appropriately be described as acting autonomously (or through choice), for the experience is one of compulsion (Strauss & Ryan, 1987). In a similar vein, the behaviour of someone who is desperately seeking approval or avoiding guilt is intentional, but it is not autonomous. The person is compelled to engage in the behaviour and would not experience a sense of choice. Finally, a person who follows a therapist's suggestion not out of an integrated understanding but rather out of deference to the therapist's authority is behaving intentionally, but until the action is self-initiated and grasped as one's own solution it would not be characterized as autonomous.

When autonomous, people experience themselves as initiators of their own behaviour: They select desired outcomes and choose how to achieve them. Regulation through choice is characterized by flexibility and the absence of pressure. By contrast, being controlled is characterized by greater rigidity and the experience of having to do what one is doing. There is intention, but lacking is a true sense of choice. When controlled, people are, in the words of deCharms (1968), 'pawns' to desired outcomes, even though they intend to achieve those outcomes.

Initiation and Regulation of Behaviour

When someone engages in a behaviour, there are generally aspects of the context that play a role in the initiation and regulation of that behaviour. We have argued (Deci & Ryan, 1985b) that these contextual factors do not, in a straightforward sense, determine the behaviour. Instead, the person gives psychological meaning (what we call functional significance) to those contextual factors, and that meaning is the critical element in determination of the behaviour.

Of central concern to the issue of autonomy and control in human behaviour is whether people construe contexts as supporting their autonomy (i.e., encouraging them to make their own choices) or controlling their behaviour (i.e., pressuring them toward particular outcomes). Thus, this review will consider varied social–contextual factors that have a functional significance of being either *autonomy supportive* or *controlling*,[2] and it will relate each type of functional significance to the quality of people's experience and behaviour. However, dispositional or person factors are also relevant to the study of autonomy and control. There are evident individual differences in the functional significance people give to contextual factors. Furthermore, individual difference measures of autonomy and control orientations have been used to predict people's experience and behaviour directly, without reference to contextual factors. The current review is intended to give substance to the theoretical concepts of autonomy and control by examining research on both contextual and person factors that are relevant to that distinction. In addition, it will compare this organismic perspective to other perspectives within empirical psychology.

Contextual Factors

There are two broad sets of studies, generally considered to be in the province of social psychology, that focus on the autonomy-supportive versus controlling distinction. The first set explored specific environmental events—things like task-contingent rewards, positive feedback, or imposed deadlines—that tend to promote either self-determined or controlled behaviours and the qualities associated with each. The second set of studies focused on interpersonal or social contexts, showing not only that general contexts can have either an autonomy-supportive or a controlling functional significance, but also that this varied functional significance has predictable effects on people's experience, attitudes, and behaviour within those settings.

When the autonomy-supportive versus controlling distinction was initially made (e.g., Deci & Ryan, 1980; Deci, Schwartz, Sheinman, & Ryan, 1981), it was hypothesized that autonomy-supportive events and contexts would maintain or enhance intrinsic motivation and that controlling events and contexts would undermine intrinsic motivation. Because intrinsic motivation has been so widely explored as the dependent variable in studies of autonomy-supportive versus controlling events and contexts, the effect of an event or context on intrinsic motivation can be used as one criterion for classifying whether that event or context tends to be experienced as autonomy supportive or controlling. Thus, within the reviews of research on external events and on interpersonal contexts, we will first present studies that used intrinsic motivation as a dependent variable, so as to specify the average functional significance of particular events or contexts. Then, within each of the two reviews, we will move on to studies that have explored the relation of those factors to other variables so as to explicate empirically the concomitants and consequences of self-determined versus controlled behaviour.

External Events: Autonomy Supportive or Controlling

The term *event* refers to a specifiable occurrence or condition relevant to the initiation and regulation of behaviour. The offer of a reward, for example, is an event, as is an instance of competence feedback, a demand, a deadline, and an opportunity for choice. The most frequently studied events have been rewards, though many others have also been explored. In this section, studies of the effects of various events on intrinsic motivation will be reviewed so as to allow each event to be classified as tending to be either autonomy supportive or controlling.

Rewards

Dozens of studies have explored the effects of rewards on intrinsic motivation. These have included monetary payments (Deci, 1971), good player awards (Lepper, Greene, & Nisbett, 1973), food (Ross, 1975), and prizes (Harackiewicz, 1979). In general, rewards have been found to undermine intrinsic motivation. When people received rewards for working on an interesting activity, they tended to display less interest in and willingness to work on that activity after termination of the rewards than did people who had worked on the activity without receiving a reward. This phenomenon, labelled the *undermining effect* (Deci & Ryan, 1980), has been most reliably obtained when rewards were expected (Lepper et al., 1973), salient (Ross, 1975), and contingent on task engagement (Ryan, Mims, & Koestner, 1983).

Ryan et al. (1983) pointed out that when rewards are differently structured, they have discernibly different effects. The authors provided a taxonomy of reward structures and related it to reward effects. Their review indicated that task-non-contingent rewards—those that are given independent of task engagement—were least likely to undermine intrinsic motivation because the reward is not given for doing the activity and thus is not salient as a control. Task-contingent rewards—those made contingent on doing the activity—have been consistently and reliably shown to undermine intrinsic motivation, presumably because their controlling function is salient. The effects of performance-contingent rewards—those given for attaining a specified level of good performance—are more complicated. Because they inherently provide positive competence feedback, the appropriate comparison condition is one that conveys the same feedback without a reward. When such comparisons have been made, performance-contingent rewards have generally been found to undermine intrinsic motivation, although they have sometimes been shown to maintain or enhance intrinsic motivation when the controlling aspect is minimized and competence cues are emphasized (Harackiewicz, Manderlink, & Sansone, 1984).

To summarize, many studies have shown that rewards, on average, undermine people's intrinsic motivation. It appears, therefore, that rewards tend to be experienced as controlling, which of course makes sense, as rewards are typically used to induce or pressure people to do things they would not freely do. When people behave in the presence of reward contingencies, the rewards tend to have a functional significance of control, thus representing an external event that restricts self-determination, although under certain circumstances they can be used to support self-determination.

Threats and Deadlines

Using a modified avoidance conditioning paradigm, Deci and Cascio (1972) found that subjects who solved interesting puzzles to avoid an unpleasant noise demonstrated less subsequent intrinsic motivation for the activity than did subjects who solved the puzzles without the threat of noise. Amabile, DeJong, and Lepper (1976) found that the imposition of a deadline for the completion of an interesting activity also decreased subjects' intrinsic motivation for that activity. It appears, therefore, that these events, like rewards, tend to be experienced as controlling and thus to diminish people's self-determination.

Evaluation and Surveillance

Other experiments have indicated that the mere presence of a surveillant or evaluator, even without rewards or aversive consequences, can be detrimental to intrinsic motivation and thus, we suggest, to self-determination more generally. Lepper and Greene (1975), for example, found that surveillance by a video camera undermined the intrinsic motivation of children, and Plant and Ryan (1985) found the same result for college students. Pittman, Davey, Alafat, Wetherill, and Kramer (1980) reported that in-person surveillance also undermined intrinsic motivation.

Harackiewicz et al. (1984) found that subjects who were told that their activity would be evaluated displayed less subsequent intrinsic motivation than did subjects who were not told this, even though the evaluations were positive. Smith (1974) found the same results for intrinsic motivation to learn. Similarly, Benware and Deci (1984) and Maehr and Stallings (1972) have found that learning in order to be tested or externally evaluated has detrimental effects on intrinsic motivation for learning.

The effects of evaluation and surveillance are not surprising, as both are integral to social control. These events tend to limit self-determination and thus reduce intrinsic motivation even when they are not accompanied by explicit rewards or punishments.

Choice

Autonomy-supportive events are defined as those that encourage the process of choice and the experience of autonomy. The one type of event that both fits the definition and has been shown, on average, to enhance intrinsic motivation is the opportunity to choose what to do.

Zuckerman, Porac, Lathin, Smith, and Deci (1978) found that when college student subjects were given a choice about which puzzles to work on and about how much time to allot to each, they were more intrinsically motivated during a subsequent period than were no-choice subjects in a yoked comparison group. The provision of choice enhanced their intrinsic motivation. Swann and Pittman (1977) reported similar results in an experiment with children.

Positive Feedback

The event of positive competence feedback has been widely studied as it relates to intrinsic motivation.[3] Several studies have found that it increased intrinsic motivation (Blanck, Reis, & Jackson, 1984; Boggiano & Ruble, 1979; Vallerand & Reid, 1984), although this has occurred only under certain circumstances (Fisher, 1978; Ryan, 1982) or for certain kinds of people (Boggiano & Barrett, 1985; Deci, Cascio, & Krusell, 1975; Kast, 1983). Taken together, the studies indicate that positive competence feedback neither supports autonomy nor controls behaviour per se. It can enhance intrinsic motivation by affirming competence (e.g., Harackiewicz, Manderlink, & Sansone, 1992) because intrinsic motivation is based in the need for competence as well as the need for self-determination, although it will do so only when the sense of competence is accompanied by the experience of self-determination (Fisher, 1978; Ryan, 1982).[4] But it can also undermine intrinsic motivation by being experienced as a form of interpersonal control (Ryan et al., 1983).

. . .

Effects and Correlates of Autonomy-Supportive versus Controlling Events

The studies just reported used intrinsic motivation as the primary dependent variable and were used to help classify events as tending to be either autonomy supportive or controlling. It is interesting to note that more of the events manipulated in these experiments were experienced as controlling than as autonomy promoting. This makes sense, however, because autonomy must emanate from oneself and can therefore only be facilitated by contextual events, whereas control is something that can be done to people by contextual events and is therefore more easily evidenced. We shall now address additional effects of these autonomy-supportive versus controlling events to begin explicating the qualities of self-determined versus controlled behaviours.

Interest–Enjoyment

Along with the free-choice measure of intrinsic motivation, self-reports of interest are often obtained. Ryan et al. (1983) reported a correlation of 0.42 between the behavioural measure of intrinsic motivation and self-reports of interest, and Harackiewicz (1979) reported a correlation of 0.44 between intrinsic motivation and expressed enjoyment. Although research has not always found these strong correlations (see Ryan & Deci, 1986), self-reports of interest–enjoyment do appear to be related to intrinsic motivation. Furthermore, numerous studies that have not used the free-choice, behavioural measure have found that post-experimental interest–enjoyment is higher following autonomy-supportive events than following controlling events (e.g., Enzle & Ross, 1978).

Creativity

Amabile (1979) reported that subjects who were told that their work would be evaluated produced artistic collages that were rated as less creative than those produced by subjects who did not expect evaluations. Similar effects were found for surveillance (see Amabile, 1983). Furthermore, when children competed for a reward, they produced less creative collages than those produced in a non-competitive condition (Amabile, 1982), and when children contracted for rewards they were also less creative (Amabile, Hennessey, & Grossman, 1986). Additionally, Kruglanski, Friedman, and Zeevi (1971) found that when subjects who wrote stories were rewarded with the opportunity to engage in an interesting activity in the future, their stories were judged to be less creative than the stories of subjects who were not rewarded. In sum, events that are typically controlling appear to affect creativity negatively, whereas events that are more autonomy supportive seem to promote creativity.

Cognitive Activity

Results similar to those for creativity have been reported for cognitive flexibility. McGraw and McCullers (1979) found that monetarily rewarded subjects had a more difficult time breaking set when doing Luchins-type (1942) water-jar problems than did non-rewarded subjects. Benware and Deci (1984) reported that evaluative tests impaired college students' conceptual learning in addition to undermining their intrinsic motivation. Grolnick and Ryan (1987) found impairments in conceptual learning of fifth-grade subjects who learned material under a controlling-evaluative condition rather than an autonomy-supportive one. It appears that when cognitive activity is controlled, it is more rigid and less conceptual, perhaps with a more narrow focus, than when it is self-determined.

Emotional Tone

Garbarino (1975) studied fifth- and sixth-grade girls who were rewarded with movie tickets for teaching younger girls how to do a sorting task. He reported that the rewarded tutors were more critical and demanding than were non-rewarded tutors. In a complementary study, children induced to interact with another child in order to play with a nice game had less positive impressions of that other child than did children who had not been focused on the incentive (Boggiano, Klinger, & Main, 1985). Controlling events, it seems, tend to induce a negative emotional tone and a less favourable view of others in that situation.

Maintenance of Behaviour Change

Rewards have also been studied as they relate to the persistence of behaviour change following the termination of treatment conditions. A study by Dienstbier and Leak (1976) of a weight-loss program, for example, indicated that although rewards facilitated weight loss, their termination led to much of the lost weight being regained.

When behaviour is controlled by events such as rewards, the behaviour tends to persist only so long as the controlling events are present. In terms of effective behaviour change in therapeutic settings, the implication is that behaviour change brought about through salient external controls is less likely to persist following the termination of treatment

than is change that is brought about more autonomously. Behaviour and personality change will be
maintained and transferred, we have argued, when
the change is experienced as autonomous or self-
determined (Deci & Ryan, 1985b).

To summarize, behaviour undertaken when the
functional significance of events is autonomy supportive has been related to greater interest, more
creativity, more cognitive flexibility, better conceptual learning, a more positive emotional tone,
and more persistent behaviour change than has
behaviour undertaken when the functional significance of events is controlling. Thus far, research
has related these motivationally relevant dependent variables primarily to the events of rewards
and evaluation.

Interpersonal Contexts: Autonomy-Supportive versus Controlling

In the preceding discussion we described research
on specific events relevant to the initiation and
regulation of behaviour. Numerous other studies have focused on interpersonal contexts rather
than specific events. For example, in interpersonal
situations the general ambience can tend either
to support autonomy or to control behaviour. We
now turn to that research on interpersonal contexts. We begin, of course, with studies in which
intrinsic motivation was the dependent measure,
because those are the ones that we use to establish
the usefulness of the distinction.

Studies of autonomy-supportive versus controlling contexts have been of two types. Some are
correlational field studies in which the functional
significance of the context is measured and related
to motivationally relevant variables of people in
those contexts. The others are laboratory experiments in which events such as rewards or feedback
are administered within experimentally created
autonomy-supportive versus controlling contexts.

General Contexts

In one field study (Deci, Nezlek, & Sheinman,
1981), teachers and children in fourth- through

sixth-grade classrooms were subjects. The
researchers used a psychometric instrument to
measure individual teachers' orientations toward
supporting children's autonomy versus controlling
children's behaviour. They reasoned that teachers oriented toward supporting autonomy would
tend to create a classroom context that promoted
self-determination, whereas those oriented toward
control would tend to create a controlling context
for the children. The researchers then assessed
the intrinsic motivation of children in the classrooms by using Matter's (1981) measure and found
a strong positive correlation between teachers'
autonomy support and children's intrinsic motivation. In another study, Deci, Schwartz, Sheinman,
and Ryan (1981) analyzed changes in children's
intrinsic motivation from the second day of school
to the end of the second month. They found that
children of autonomy-supportive teachers became
more intrinsically motivated relative to children of
control-oriented teachers.

Events and Interpersonal Contexts

Earlier, we saw that some events tend to be experienced as supporting self-determination and others tend to be experienced as controlling, and now
we have seen that contexts can also be characterized as tending either to support autonomy or to
control. A few studies have explored the effects of
the same event in different experimentally created
contexts.

In one study, Ryan et al. (1983) explored contextual influences on the effects of performance-
contingent rewards: those rewards that people
receive for attaining a specified level of good performance. Previous research had shown that these
rewards generally undermined the intrinsic motivation of their recipients relative to that of subjects who received no rewards but got the same
performance feedback that was inherent in the
performance-contingent rewards. This means, in
essence, that the reward itself tends to be controlling unless its evaluative component is removed
(Harackiewicz et al., 1984). Furthermore, the

positive feedback that is conveyed by the reward can enhance intrinsic motivation by affirming one's competence.

Ryan et al. argued that the effect of a performance-contingent reward could be significantly affected by the way it is conveyed, in other words, by the interpersonal context within which it is received. Two groups of college student subjects received performance-contingent rewards. Those in one group were told that they would receive a reward if they 'performed well', and those in the other group were told that they would receive a reward if they 'performed well, as you *should*'. Following each of three puzzles, subjects received positive feedback that was in line with the initial induction. For example, half were told, 'You have done well', and the other half were told, 'You have done well, just as you should'. Then, at the end of the performance period, subjects were given the reward either 'for doing well' or 'for doing well and performing up to standards'. It was expected, of course, that words like *should* and *standards* would serve to create a controlling context and lead the subjects to experience the rewards as controlling. Results revealed a significant difference between the intrinsic motivation of the two groups of subjects. Those who received rewards in an autonomy-supportive context were more intrinsically motivated than were those who received rewards in a controlling context. In other words, the interpersonal context within which the event (i.e., the reward) was administered affected the functional significance of the event.

The Ryan et al. (1983) results are consistent with others reported by Harackiewicz (1979), who also found significant differences between the intrinsic motivation of two groups of high school subjects receiving performance-contingent rewards. She had made one administration of the rewards less controlling by allowing subjects to self-monitor their performance against a table of norms, and these subjects were more intrinsically motivated than others who were not allowed to self-monitor.

In another study, Ryan (1982) argued that positive competence feedback, which is not inherently either autonomy-supportive or controlling, will be differentially interpreted as autonomy promoting or controlling depending on the nature of the interpersonal context within which it is embedded. College student subjects received positive feedback, which either was made controlling through the use of additional words such as *should* (e.g., 'Excellent, you did just as you should') or was non-controlling. Again, results revealed that the subsequent intrinsic motivation of subjects who received positive feedback in an autonomy-supportive context was significantly greater than that of subjects who received it in a controlling context.

Finally, Koestner, Ryan, Bernieri, and Holt (1984) argued that it is even possible to constrain behaviour in a way that will tend to be experienced as non-controlling. In a field experiment with first- and second-grade children, limits were set regarding the children's being neat while painting a picture. Limits seem to be controlling by nature, yet they may be perceived as less controlling if they are set in a way that minimizes the use of control-related locution and acknowledges the probable conflict between what the limits require and what the person would want to do. The importance of the last point is that this acknowledgement conveys an appreciation of the perspective of the actor, thus decreasing his or her experience of being controlled. As expected, Koestner et al. found that children who received non-controlling limits maintained their intrinsic motivation for painting (it did not differ from a no-limits comparison group), whereas those who received controlling limits showed significantly less intrinsic motivation.

. . .

Health

Langer and Rodin (1976) reported a study of the institutionalized aged in which an ambience that promoted self-determination—what we call an autonomy-supportive interpersonal context—was created for some of the residents. The intervention included a meeting devoted to discussing the residents' taking greater responsibility for themselves (vs. telling them that they would be well cared for by the staff), the opportunity to make choices about when they would attend a movie (vs. being assigned a time), and being given the gift of a plant that they were responsible to care for (vs. being given a plant that the staff would take care of for them).

Results of this study indicated that those elderly residents in the context that emphasized self-determination improved on both questionnaire and behavioural measures of well-being relative to those who lived in a context that did not. In an 18-month follow-up study, Rodin and Langer (1977) reported that there were still significant differences in well-being such that those residents whose self-determination had been supported were healthier than the other residents.

The Langer and Rodin study is often discussed as a study of control over outcomes; however, it went beyond merely providing control. The intervention not only gave residents control; it encouraged them to take initiative, to be more autonomous and self-determining. This can be contrasted with a study by Schulz (1976) in which elderly residents were given control over the hours they would be visited by volunteers in a visitation program. That intervention did not, however, encourage autonomous initiation and self-determination. The results did indicate short-term positive health effects for having control over outcomes, but a follow-up study (Schulz & Hanusa, 1978) showed that after the visitation program was terminated, the subjects who had had control over outcomes evidenced significant declines in health. Apparently, it is only when people learn to experience their environment as supporting self-determination, only when they become more autonomous (rather than merely perceiving that they have control over outcomes), that there will be long-term positive effects on their health.

All of the research thus far reported has focused on the effects of inputs from the environment,

whether specific events or interpersonal contexts. From these social psychological investigations, there is indication that when contextual factors function to support autonomy rather than to control, people tend to be more intrinsically motivated, more creative, more cognitively flexible, more trusting, more positive in emotional tone, and more healthy; they tend to have higher self-esteem, perceived competence, and preference for choice; their behaviour tends to be appropriately persistent and to be less controlling; and they project less aggression. We turn now to studies that have focused on person variables rather than contextual variables: studies that are considered more in the province of personality.

Person Factors

Two sets of studies have focused on person factors. The first is composed of laboratory experiments on intrapersonal events or states—person processes such as ego involvement—that can be characterized as being either autonomy supportive or controlling. The second is composed of individual difference studies that focus primarily on causality orientations, which are people's tendencies to orient toward events and contexts that are autonomy supportive and those that are controlling.

Intrapersonal Events: Autonomy versus Control

Many of the inputs relevant to the initiation and regulation of behaviour are intrapsychic and can be independent of external circumstances. Imagine, for example, a colleague who is lying on the beach with his or her mind idly wandering. An idea for a new experiment spontaneously occurs to the person, so with excitement he or she begins to design the experiment. The event that prompted the behaviour was an internal, cognitive–affective event that could be characterized as autonomous. But one could easily imagine the person, while on vacation, designing an experiment out of an internal obligation, with the pressured feeling that he or she has to do an experiment to prove his or her worth. This event would also be intrapersonal, but it would be controlling. We predict that the consequences of these two types of internal events, which prompted the same overt behaviours, would be quite different and would have parallels to the consequences of the two types of external events.[5]

Although this hypothesis has received less empirical attention than the hypotheses discussed earlier, several studies have supported it. Ryan (1982) argued that the state of ego involvement as described by Sherif and Cantril (1947), a condition where people's self-esteem is hinged on performance, leads the people to pressure themselves in a way similar to the way external forces can pressure them. He suggested that this type of ego involvement is controlling and will thus undermine self-determination. In his study, college students worked on hidden-figures puzzles. Half of them were told that hidden-figures performance reflects creative intelligence and as such is used in some IQ tests. These subjects, being students in a competitive university, were expected to become quite ego-involved and thus to be internally controlling. The other subjects were given a more task-involving induction, which was expected to initiate more autonomous self-regulation.

Results of this study supported the hypothesis. Those subjects who had been given the ego-involving induction displayed significantly less intrinsic motivation in a subsequent free-choice period than did those who had been given the task-involving induction. In addition, those subjects in the internally controlling (i.e., ego-involved) condition reported experiencing significantly greater pressure and tension than did those in the internally non-controlling (i.e., task-involved) condition. It appears, therefore, that people can—and presumably do—pressure themselves in much the same way that they can be pressured by external events, and the results of controlling themselves in these ways are similar to the results of being externally controlled.

. . .

Effects of Internal Events: Autonomy versus Control

The consequences of autonomous versus internally controlled initiation and regulation have been less well explored though we predict the same types of consequences as those reported for external initiation and regulation. Ryan (1982) found greater pressure and tension associated with internally controlling than with more autonomous self-regulation, and that parallels Ryan et al. (1983) finding of greater pressure and tension associated with controllingly administered rewards than with non-controlling rewards. We predict that such parallels would also appear for the other relevant dependent variables such as emotional tone and health. Indeed, it is possible that internal controlling regulation is involved in various stress-related syndromes.

Working in the area of achievement motivation, Nicholls (1984) recently suggested that there would be differences in the preferences and performance of task-involved versus ego-involved subjects. When task involved, he hypothesized, subjects will prefer moderately difficult tasks (ones that represent optimal challenges). When ego involved, however, subjects will focus on proving their competence (or not appearing incompetent), so they will select either very easy tasks that will allow them to succeed or very difficult tasks so they will have a good excuse for failing. Although Nicholls (1984) did not test these hypotheses directly, he reviewed studies that provide inferential support. For our purposes, the importance of the work is its suggestion that ego-involved subjects behave and attribute in a more defensive and self-aggrandizing way than do task-involved subjects. Being internally controlled leads subjects to focus on proving and defending themselves rather than engaging in activities for growth and challenge.

In sum, we have argued that the autonomy promoting versus controlling distinction is relevant to the categorization of intrapersonal events just as it is to the categorization of contextual events. When behaviour is prompted by thoughts such as 'I have to . . .' or 'I should . . .' (what we call internally controlling events), the behaviour is theorized to be less self-determined than when it is characterized by more autonomy-related thoughts such as 'I'd find it valuable to . . .' or 'I'd be interested in . . .' Accordingly, we predict that the qualities associated with external controlling events and with external autonomy-supportive events will also be associated with their intrapsychic counterparts.

Causality Orientations

Elsewhere, we suggested that people have general orientations regarding what they attend to and how they initiate and regulate their behaviour (Deci & Ryan, 1985a). These orientations are conceptualized with respect to the autonomy–control distinction, and they are theorized to influence the degree to which inputs are perceived as autonomy supportive or controlling. These personality characteristics are referred to as *causality orientations* and are labelled the *autonomy* orientation and the *control* orientation, respectively.[6] In validating a measure of these constructs, we provided further evidence about the concomitants of self-determined versus controlled behaviours.

The measure of general causality orientations was based on the assumption that people are to some degree oriented toward autonomy and to some degree oriented toward control, so the scale was constructed to measure each orientation independently rather than in a bipolar fashion. The separate orientations were then correlated with a variety of relevant variables. Because the method of investigation entailed correlating individual difference measures, the research in this section presents correlates of the autonomy orientation and the control orientation rather than antecedents and consequences of self-determined versus controlled regulation.

. . .

Behaviours, Attitudes, and Emotions

Causality orientations have also been correlated with a variety of behavioural and attitudinal

measures. King (1984) used the autonomy scores of 50 people who were scheduled for voluntary cardiac surgery to predict the extent to which they would view the experience as a challenge rather than a threat. She found that the higher the patients' autonomy scores, the more their preoperative attitudes involved challenge rather than threat and the more their postoperative attitudes were positive.

In a spontaneous-learning study (Ryan, Connell, Plant, Robinson, & Evans, 1985), subjects who had completed the Causality Orientations Scale read a passage and used the Differential Emotions Scale (Izard, Dougherty, Bloxom, & Kotsch, 1974) to describe their feelings while reading the passage. Results showed a correlation between autonomy orientation scores and interest in the passage.

Deci et al. (1986) used a domain-specific version of the Causality Orientations Scale with 201 employees of a large corporation. Analyses revealed that the autonomy orientation was positively correlated with workers' trust in the corporation, their satisfaction with opportunities to make inputs, and their general satisfaction. It seems that workers who are more oriented toward autonomy experience their work situation differently, perhaps actually creating a different interpersonal environment for themselves, than do workers who are less oriented toward autonomy. This finding complements the earlier mentioned finding that employees with autonomy-supportive managers have a higher level of trust and more positive attitudes.

Research has also found the control orientation to be related to various behaviours, attitudes, and emotions. For example, Deci and Ryan (1985a) reported a negative correlation between the control orientation and the test performance of undergraduates in a large personality course. This finding adds important corroboration to the findings reported earlier that controlling external events impair learning (Benware & Deci, 1984; Grolnick & Ryan, 1987). When controlled, whether by events or contexts outside themselves or by their own orientations to experience situations as controlling, people tend to learn less well, particularly on conceptual material.

. . .

To summarize, person factors, whether studied in terms of specific internal events using an experimental paradigm or in terms of general causality orientations using an individual difference paradigm, have been shown to be related to the distinction between self-determined versus controlled behaviour in ways that parallel the relation of external events and contexts to the two types of behaviour. As such, it seems that both contextual and person factors can be analyzed in corresponding ways and that the parallel findings from these analyses provide multi-method validation of the self-determined versus controlled distinction.

Persons and Contexts

Much of the research related to this issue of autonomy and control in human behaviour has focused on contextual factors. Yet the theory emphasizes that the functional significance of a contextual factor, rather than its objective characteristics, is the critical consideration in predicting the effects of that factor. Functional significance refers to the motivationally relevant psychological meaning that events or contexts are afforded or imbued with. This means that a person's perception of an event is an active construction influenced by all the kinds of factors herein discussed. And it is the person's own perception (i.e., construction) of the event to which he or she responds. The external event is an affordance (Gibson, 1979) for their constructive interpretations.

It is, of course, possible, on the basis of definitions, to predict whether events or contexts will have an autonomy-supportive or a controlling functional significance. This can be useful for purposes of prescriptive formulations. Conceptually, however, this is merely a matter of referring to the average functional significance that an event or context is likely to be given, as contextual factors

cannot be disembedded from the psychological meaning given them by the individual.

These points were illustrated in a recent investigation by Ryan and Grolnick (1986). Schoolchildren in Grades 4 through 6 used a measure developed by deCharms (1976) to describe the degree to which their classroom climate (i.e., their teacher) tends to support autonomy or to control behaviour. Consistent with the research reported earlier, the average ratings of the classroom climate correlated significantly with the children's mastery motivation, perceived competence, and self-esteem. However, when these average perceptions were partialled out of individual children's ratings, the residual predicted even more of the variance in the children's motivationally relevant variables than did the average.

. . .

Self-Determined versus Controlled Activity

The picture that emerges from this wide range of evidence is that when the functional significance of events or contexts is autonomy supportive, people initiate regulatory processes that are qualitatively different from those that are initiated when the functional significance of the events or context is controlling. Autonomy-supportive events and contexts facilitate self-determined or autonomous activity, which entails an inner endorsement of one's actions, a sense that they are emanating from oneself. Such activity is regulated more flexibly, with less tension and a more positive emotional tone, and this flexible use of information often results in greater creativity and conceptual understanding. When self-determined, people experience a greater sense of choice about their actions, and these actions are characterized by integration and an absence of conflict and pressure. Indeed, integration is the ultimate hallmark of autonomous regulation. By contrast, controlling events and contexts conduce toward compliance or defiance but not autonomy. Control, whether by external forces or by oneself, entails regulatory processes that are more rigid, involve greater pressure and tension and a more negative emotional tone, and result in learning that is more rote-oriented and less integrated.

The Intrinsic–Extrinsic Metaphor

Intrinsically motivated behaviour is by definition self-determined. It is done freely for the inherent satisfactions associated with certain activities and with undertaking optimal challenges. Many of the studies of self-determination have thus focused on intrinsic motivation. As a result, the self-determination versus control distinction has often been wrongly equated with the intrinsic versus extrinsic distinction. Even though intrinsically motivated behaviour is the paradigmatic case of self-determination, it is not the only case of self-determined activity; extrinsically motivated behaviour can also be self-determined.

Extrinsic motivation pertains to a wide variety of behaviours where the goals of action extend beyond those inherent in the activity itself. Persons can be described as extrinsically motivated whenever the goal of their behaviour is separable from the activity itself, whether that goal be the avoidance of punishment or the pursuit of a valued outcome. Extrinsically motivated behaviour is not necessarily either self-determined or controlled. One could willingly and freely pursue some extrinsic end (in which case it would be autonomous), or one could be pressured toward a goal (in which case it would be controlled).

This highlights an important definitional matter regarding intrinsic versus extrinsic motivation. What distinguishes the two is merely a teleological aspect, whether the behaviour is done for its inherent satisfaction (intrinsic) or is done in order to obtain a separable goal. Although this distinction has historical and practical importance (see Deci & Ryan, 1985b), it does not fully or adequately explicate the psychology of behavioural regulation because extrinsic or goal-oriented activity can vary considerably in terms of the degree to which it is autonomously regulated or controlled.

As an example, consider a person who derives considerable aesthetic pleasure from having a clean house but who does not enjoy the process of cleaning. If this person willingly chooses to clean the house, he or she would be self-determined in doing it. But the behaviour would be extrinsic because it is instrumental to having a clean house, and the satisfaction is in the outcome rather than in the behaviour itself. By contrast, consider another person who cleans because of a feeling that he or she has to, whether to get the approval of a business associate who will be visiting, to avoid guilt, or to satisfy a compulsion. In the case of this latter person, the extrinsically motivated behaviour would be controlled.

In recent developmental work, Ryan, Connell, and Deci (1985) have outlined the processes through which children take on and eventually integrate extrinsic regulations so that initially external regulations can be the basis of self-determined functioning. The natural development of extrinsic motivation is described as a process of progressive internalization in which there is movement away from dependence on external prompts and controls toward greater self-regulation (Connell & Ryan, 1986; Ryan, Connell, & Grolnick, 1992). This process involves identification with and integration of originally externally regulated action and results in more autonomous self-regulation. Work by Grolnick and Ryan (1986, 1987) and by Connell and Ryan (1986) indicates that the more extrinsic behaviour is characterized by autonomy, the less it is accompanied by pressure and anxiety and the more it is associated with personal valuing of the goals involved.

Deci and Ryan (1985b) have hypothesized that internalization and particularly identification are more likely to occur under autonomy-supportive than under controlling conditions. Two recent studies have provided initial support for this hypothesis. In the first, Grolnick and Ryan (1986) found that elementary school children became more self-determined at extrinsically motivated activities with autonomy-supportive teachers than with controlling teachers. Furthermore, the researchers reported that children with autonomy-supportive parents were more self-determined in doing chores and homework than were children with controlling parents. Earlier research by Hoffman (1960) on moral behaviour showed the complementary result that power-assertive (i.e., controlling) parenting styles were less effective for the internalization of moral behaviours than were styles more closely aligned to autonomy support.

In a second experimental study (Eghrari & Deci, 1986), subjects engaged in an uninteresting computer-tracking task. Two groups of subjects received a rationale for doing the task and positive feedback about their performance on it. For one group the context was autonomy supportive, and for the other it was controlling. Results indicated that the autonomy-supportive context led to greater internalization of task value and greater persistence than did the controlling context and that internalization was positively correlated with experienced self-determination.

These studies suggest that extrinsically motivated behaviours can become self-determined through the process of integration and that the integrative process itself depends on the context's having an autonomy-supportive functional significance. In such cases the behaviour is still extrinsically motivated, however, because the activity is still engaged in for reasons other than its inherent interest.

The Internal–External Metaphor

The internal–external distinction has been widely used in the past three decades in studies related to the regulation of behaviour. Therefore, we shall briefly discuss its relevance to autonomy versus control. Basically, the metaphor has been used in two broad ways: to describe who or what is believed to control outcomes, and to describe the experienced source of causality of one's behaviour. Consider these in turn.

Rotter (1966) used the internal–external distinction to refer to expectations about control over reinforcements. One has an internal *locus of control* if one expects behaviours and reinforcements to be reliably related. Bandura (1977) added that expectations of competence are also necessary for internal control. The concept of internal control is therefore different from that of self-determination in two important ways. First, as we said earlier, expectations of behaviour–outcome dependence and of competence promote intentional behaviour, but they do not provide a basis of distinguishing between self-determined and controlled behaviours. Second, because the concept of locus of control was anchored to reinforcements, it failed to consider intrinsically motivated behaviours, which require no reinforcements.

Other work on internal–external control (e.g., Connell, 1985; Lefcourt, 1976) has used the term *perceived control over outcomes* (rather than locus of control of reinforcements). That work has included intrinsically motivated as well as reinforcement-dependent behaviours, but it too does not address whether the initiation and regulation of behaviour is self-determined or controlled. Both self-determined and controlled behaviours can involve internal perceived control of outcomes.

The other way in which the internal–external metaphor has been used relates to the initiation and regulation of behaviour. DeCharms (1968), elaborating on an earlier discussion by Heider (1958), spoke of an internal or an external *locus of causality* for behaviour, pointing out that intrinsically motivated behaviour has an internal locus of causality with the concomitant feeling of free choice, whereas extrinsically motivated behaviour has an external locus of causality with the concomitant sense of dependence. We (Deci & Ryan, 1985b) have modified the use of the locus of causality distinction to convey one's experience of whether a behaviour is self-determined or controlled, namely whether one has a sense of 'choice' versus 'having to'. Thus, the distinction does not strictly parallel the intrinsic–extrinsic distinction, nor does it refer to whether the initiating and regulatory factors are inside or outside the person. In motivational terms, factors inside the person are always involved in intentional behaviour. However, all intentional behaviour can be characterized as varying in the degree of relative autonomy, at one extreme having an external perceived locus of causality and at the other having an internal perceived locus of causality. For us, an internal perceived locus of causality describes the experience of an action's being one's own and being freely undertaken, whereas an external perceived locus of causality describes the experience of having to do something, of being compelled by heteronomous forces. Contextual factors as well as person factors can have either an autonomy-supportive or a controlling functional significance and can therefore promote either an internal or an external perceived locus of causality.

Weiner (1986, p. 46) has used the concepts internal–external control and internal–external causality interchangeably to refer to whether people attribute the cause of (i.e., the control over) outcomes such as successes or failures to factors such as effort that are inside the person (internal) or to factors such as luck that are outside the person (external). Therefore, Weiner's use of the locus of causality concept relates to the attributed causes of outcomes rather than to the experienced source of initiation and regulation of behaviour, and it equates internal versus external causality with factors inside versus outside the person. Thus, his usage is consistent with the way the concept of internal–external control has traditionally been used, but it is inconsistent with our use of the concept of internal–external causality.

A straightforward and important implication of this discussion concerns what is typically referred to as the psychology of self-control (e.g., Bandura, 1977; Kanfer, 1975). A person can evidence self-control either through rigid, self-punitive methods or through more integrated, flexible methods. The former is herein categorized as internally controlling regulation and is exemplified by processes of introjection and ego involvement (Ryan, 1982; Ryan, Connell, & Deci, 1985). The latter, more

autonomous self-control can be described in terms of identification and integration of values and behavioural regulations. The clinical importance of this qualitative distinction has been treated elsewhere (Deci & Ryan, 1985b).

Concluding Comments

In this article we have considered the implications of people's capacity to be autonomous and their vulnerability to being controlled. We have suggested that intentional behaviour can be regulated in two qualitatively different ways: It can be flexibly and choicefully self-regulated or it can be controlled. Autonomous regulation is facilitated when events and contexts have an autonomy-supportive functional significance, and controlled regulation is promoted when events and contexts have a controlling functional significance.

When considered in terms of social psychology, the autonomy–control distinction is especially important in interpersonal situations involving power differentials: situations such as those of parent–child, teacher–student, manager–subordinate, or therapist–patient. Whether the basis of power (French & Raven, 1959) is rewards, force, position, expertise, or charisma, the person who is one down is particularly vulnerable to being controlled. An understanding of the autonomy–control issue can therefore clarify how authority relationships influence individuals' behaviour, development, and experience. When considered in terms of personality psychology, the autonomy–control distinction is also very important for understanding behaviour, development, and experience. It helps to clarify individual differences in selecting and responding to social situations, and it adds a qualitative dimension to the psychology of self-control.

The general framework offered herein thus highlights some ways in which the enigma of human choice and autonomy can be explored empirically to help explicate the dynamic interaction between persons and contexts.

Notes

1. Like most dichotomies in psychology, being self-determined versus controlled is intended to describe a continuum. Behaviours can thus be seen as being more or less self-determined.

2. According to cognitive evaluation theory (Deci & Ryan, 1985b), inputs can also have an amotivating functional significance. These inputs signify or promote incompetence at reliably obtaining desired outcomes. They are not relevant to this discussion, however, as they promote non-intentional responding and impersonal causation.

3. Negative feedback has also been studied and has been found to reduce intrinsic motivation; however, we interpret these decreases as resulting from the feedback being experienced as amotivating rather than controlling.

4. In cognitive evaluation theory (Deci & Ryan, 1985b), inputs that both alarm competence and promote self-determination are referred to as informational.

5. Internal events can also be amotivating, though again they are not germane to the current discussion.

6. A third orientation, the impersonal orientation, refers to the tendency to orient to amotivating inputs, in other words, the tendency to experience oneself as being incompetent to attain desired outcomes.

Discussion Questions

1. The authors present a continuum between autonomy and control. In most of their studies, 'autonomy-supportive' versus 'controlled' is operationalized as a dichotomous variable. In real life, however, it is likely that most of our actions fall into a wide grey area in which it is difficult to tell whether the action was autonomous or controlled. Give three examples of actions you have performed recently in which it is not easy to say whether it was autonomous or controlled.

2. When might people prefer to be controlled? When might being controlled improve rather than hinder performance?

3. Relate Deci & Ryan's autonomy/controlled distinction to the intrinsic/extrinsic motivation distinction. A good exercise is to first argue that the two continua reflect independent constructs that may be orthogonally manipulated. Then argue that, in fact, they are not independent, but merely slightly different versions of the same overarching distinction.

4. How does Deci & Ryan's theory speak to the classic distinction that social and personality psychologists have made between causality that comes from the 'person' and causality that comes from the 'situation'?

7. The Psychological Effects of Insufficient Rewards

Leon Festinger, Stanford University

□ ■ □

Editor's Introduction

People have theories about how motivation works. Most people think that if you offer one person a large reward for doing something and another person a small reward for doing the same task, the person getting the large reward—because he or she associates good things with the task—will come to enjoy the task more. As another example, do you think it would be easier to train your dog to give you a high-five by rewarding him with kibble or with steak? Most people will say the steak.

In 1959 Leon Festinger and Merrill Carlsmith offered undergraduates either $1 or $20 for doing a boring task. What do you think they found? Contrary to most people's intuition, participants in the $1 condition said they liked the task more than those in the $20 condition; the smaller reward led to greater liking. This counterintuitive finding has made this study one of the most well-known in all of behavioural science research. But how is it possible that people liked the task more when they were paid less?

This finding was, in fact, predicted by Festinger's cognitive dissonance theory. According to Festinger (1957, 1962), people possess a powerful motivation to maintain cognitive consistency. That is, people do not at all like to be caught in a situation of self-contradiction. When faced with a situation in which two of their cognitions are in logical conflict, people change one of the two so as to bring the two cognitions back into 'consonance'. According to Festinger, the participants in the $1 condition were put into a situation of insufficient justification. That is, the $1 reward was considered insufficient justification for doing a boring task, while $20 (over $80 in present-day dollars) made doing the boring task completely justified.

Doing a task with insufficient justification creates dissonance between two cognitions: (a) 'I am not a person who voluntarily does boring tasks' and (b) 'I just did a boring task'. Cognitive dissonance theory predicts that people will resolve this dissonance by changing one of the cognitions. Because changing the first cognition would require a relatively difficult and dramatic reappraisal of the self, most people will reconcile the dissonance by changing the second cognition. In particular, they might think, 'That task wasn't really all that bad'. Perhaps it might even be possible to see the good in the task (e.g., 'It may have seemed boring but after a while it put me into a kind of Zen-like meditative state'). In sum, it's not the absolute reward that matters but the *meaning* of the reward. People generally do not passively accept rewards at face value. Instead, they dig deeper and seek further implications of receiving the reward on the self.

The present article presents another form of insufficient justification. Rather than enduring a low reward, participants may actually endure psychological pain. For example, one study recounted in this article was conducted by Aronson and Mills (1959). Participants auditioned to join a group that conducted frank and explicit discussions about sex. To gain entry, they needed to pass a 'screening test'. For some participants, that test required answering highly embarrassing questions. For others, the test was not embarrassing. After taking the test (and 'passing'), all participants were put in a position where they overheard the group already in discussion. The discussion, though about sex, was actually boring (it was about the reproduction of spores). Yet participants who had answered the embarrassing questions rated the group members and the discussion much more attractive than those who did not have to answer the embarrassing questions. The researchers concluded that suffering can lead to increased liking through the process of dissonance reduction. ('I am willing to suffer embarrassment in order to experience something great. I just suffered embarrassment. Therefore, this group must be great.') Notice that the hazing rituals of fraternities, sororities, military forces, and other organizations that demand loyalty often take advantage of just such a process in order to strengthen group bonds.

Cognitive dissonance theory is perhaps the most storied theory in social psychology. It has spawned an enormous amount of research literature in the 50 years since its inception. Much of the work has helped to delineate the boundary conditions that need to be in place to obtain the full dissonance reduction effect. Other work, however, has suggested that Festinger got it wrong and the effect is not motivational at all (Bem, 1967). Because space limits do not permit a full review here, it is suggested that the reader pay close attention to the section on cognitive dissonance in the 1990 article by Kunda (in Unit 5).

Some fields of psychology have for many years been dominated by ideas concerning the importance of rewards in the establishment and maintenance of behaviour patterns. So dominant has this notion become, that some of our most ingenious theoretical thinking has been devoted to imagining the existence of rewards in order to explain behaviour in situations where, plausibly, no rewards exist. It has been observed, for example, that under some circumstances an organism will persist in voluntarily engaging in behaviour which is frustrating or painful. To account for such behaviour it has, on occasion, been seriously proposed that the cessation of the frustration or pain is rewarding and thus reinforces the tendency to engage in the behaviour.

I want to maintain that this type of explanation is not only unnecessary but also misleading. I certainly do *not* wish to say that rewards are unimportant, but I propose to show that the absence of reward or the existence of inadequate reward produces certain specific consequences which can account for a variety of phenomena which are difficult to deal with if we use our usual conceptions of the role of reward.

Before I proceed, I would like to say that most of the thinking and most of the experimental work which I will present are the result of collaboration between Douglas H. Lawrence and myself. Indeed, whatever you find interesting in what I say you may safely attribute primarily to him.

I will start my discussion in a rather roundabout manner with some remarks which concern themselves primarily with some aspects of the thinking processes of human beings. Human thinking is sometimes a strange mixture of 'plausible' and 'magical' processes. Let us examine more closely what I mean by this. For example, imagine that a person knows that some event is going to occur, and that the person can do something to prepare himself to cope more adequately with the impending event. Under such circumstances it is very reasonable (perhaps you might even want to use the word 'rational') for the person to do whatever is necessary in preparation for the coming event. Human thinking, however, also works in reverse. Consider a person who goes to a lot of trouble to prepare himself for a future event which might possibly occur. Such a person will subsequently tend to persuade himself that the event is rather likely to occur. There is nothing very plausible or rational about this kind of mental process—rather, it has almost a magical quality about it. Let me illustrate this briefly by describing an experiment recently conducted by Ruby Yaryan.

Under the pretext of investigating the manner in which students study for examinations, she asked subjects to study a list of arbitrary definitions of symbols in preparation for a possible test. Two conditions were experimentally created for the subjects. Half of the subjects were told that, if they actually took the test, this list of definitions of the symbols would be in their possession during the test, and so, all that was necessary in preparation was to familiarize themselves with the list. This was, essentially, an 'easy preparation' condition. That is, not much effort was required of the subjects in advance preparation for the test.

The other half of the subjects were told that, if they actually took the test, they would *not* have the list of definitions with them and so it was necessary for them to memorize the symbols and their definitions in preparation for the test. It is clear that this constitutes a much more 'effortful preparation' condition. Considerable effort was required of these subjects in advance preparation for the possible test.

It was carefully explained to each subject that not everyone would actually have to take the test. Specifically, they were told that only half of the people in the experiment *would* take the test. It was also carefully explained that the selection of who would, and who would not, have to take the test had already been made in consultation with their teachers (the subjects were all high school girls). Nothing that happened during the experiment would affect whether or not they took the test—this had already been decided in advance for each of them.

After they finished studying the list of definitions, they were asked a number of questions to preserve the fiction that the experiment was concerned with study habits. Each subject was also asked to indicate how likely she thought it was that she, personally, would have to actually take the test. The results show, quite clearly, that subjects in the effortful preparation condition, on the average, thought it was more likely that they would

have to take the test than did subjects in the easy preparation condition. In other words, those who were experimentally induced to engage in a lot of preparatory effort persuaded themselves that the thing they were preparing for would actually occur.

The relevance of this experiment to the problem of the effects of inadequate rewards will become clearer in the following example which illustrates the same psychological process. Consider some person who is strongly attracted to some goal. It is quite reasonable for this person to be willing to expend more effort, or to endure more pain, in order to reach the goal than he would be if he were less attracted. Once more, however, one finds the same process of reasoning in reverse. That is, if a person exerts a great deal of effort, or endures pain, in order to reach some ordinary objective, there is a strong tendency for him to persuade himself that the objective is especially valuable or especially desirable. An experiment conducted by Elliot Aronson and Judson Mills (1959) shows the effect quite nicely.

The subjects in the experiment by Aronson and Mills were college girls who volunteered to join small discussion groups. Each subject, when she appeared for the discussion group, was told that, instead of being put into a new group, she was being considered for inclusion in an ongoing group which had recently lost one of its members. However, the subject was told, because of the group's concern that the replacement be someone who would be able to discuss things freely and openly, the experimenter had agreed to test the replacement before admitting her to the group. Some subjects were then given a very brief and not painful test while others were given a rather extended and embarrassing test. The experimenter then, of course, told each subject that she had done well and was admitted to the group. Thus, there were some subjects who had attained membership in the group easily and some subjects who had endured a painful experience in order to be admitted to the group.

The experimenter then explained to the subject that the discussion was carried on by means of an intercommunication system, each girl being in a separate room. She was brought into her room which contained a microphone and earphones. The experimenter told her that the others had already started and perhaps it would be best for her not to participate in the discussion this time but just to listen. Next meeting, of course, she would participate fully. Speaking into the microphone the experimenter then went through the illusion of introducing her to the three other girls in the group. He then 'disconnected' the microphone and gave the subject the earphones to wear. The subject then listened for about 25 minutes to a tape recording of a rather dull and halting discussion. All subjects, of course, heard exactly the same tape recording thinking they were listening to the actual live group discussion.

When the discussion was finished, the experimenter explained to the subject that, after each meeting, each of the girls filled out a 'post-meeting reaction form'. She was then given a questionnaire to complete which asked a variety of questions concerning how interesting she had found the discussion to be, how much she liked the other members of the group, and other similar questions, The results show, as anticipated, that those subjects who had gone through a painful procedure in order to be admitted to the group thought the discussion was more interesting and liked the other group members better than did those who had gained admission to the group easily. In other words, we see the same process operating here as we noted in the previous experiment. If someone is somehow induced to endure embarrassment in order to achieve something, she then persuades herself that what she has achieved is valuable.

In both of the examples which I have discussed (and one could present many more examples of similar nature) a situation has been produced where the organism has two pieces of information (or cognitions) which do not fit together. In the first example, these two pieces of information were: (a) I have worked hard in preparation for an event, (b) the event is not too likely to occur. In the second example, the two cognitions which did not fit together were: (a) I have endured pain to attain an objective, (b) the objective is not very attractive. This kind of 'non-fitting' relationship between two pieces of information may be termed a dissonant relation (Festinger, 1957). The reason, of course, that dissonance exists between these cognitions is that, psychologically, the obverse of one follows from the other. Psychologically, if an objective is very attractive, it follows that one would be willing to endure pain to attain it; or if the objective is *not* attractive, it follows that one does *not* endure pain to attain it. This specification of why a given relation between cognitions is dissonant also provides the clues to predicting specifically how the organism will react to the existence of the dissonance. Assuming that the organism will attempt to reduce the dissonance between the cognitions, there are obviously two major classes of ways in which this can be done. He can attempt to persuade himself that the pain which he endured was not really painful or he can attempt to persuade himself that the objective is very attractive.

I will not spend any more time than this in general theoretical discussion of the theory of dissonance and the reduction of dissonance. I hope that this small amount of general theoretical discussion will be enough to give context to the specific analysis of the psychological effects of insufficient rewards.

Let us consider in more detail what is suggested by the example of the experiment by Aronson and Mills and by the theory of cognitive dissonance. In that experiment the dissonance which was created was reduced by enhancing the value of the goal. This suggests that organisms may come to like and value things for which they have worked very hard or for which they have suffered. Looking at it from another aspect, one might say that they may come to value activities for which they have been inadequately rewarded. At first glance this may seem to contradict a widely accepted notion in psychology, namely, that organisms learn to like things for which they *have* been rewarded. In a sense it is contradictory, but not in the sense that it denies the operation of this widely assumed process. It does, however, state that another process also operates which is rather of an opposite character.

Let us analyze the situation with which we are concerned somewhat more carefully and more precisely. We are concerned with the dissonance between two possible cognitions. One of these is a cognition the organism has concerning his behaviour, namely, I have voluntarily done something which, all other things being equal, I would avoid doing. The other is a cognition about the environment or about the result of his action, namely, the reward that has been obtained is inadequate. As we mentioned before, this dissonance can be reduced if the organism can persuade himself that he really likes the behaviour in which he engaged or if he enhances for himself the value of what he has obtained as a result of his actions.

There is, of course, another way to reduce the dissonance, namely, for the organism to change his behaviour. That is, having done something which resulted in an inadequate reward the organism can refuse to perform the action again. This means of reducing the dissonance is undoubtedly the one most frequently employed by organisms. If the organism obtains information which is dissonant with his behaviour, he usually modifies his behaviour so that it fits better what he knows concerning his environment. Here, however, I am going to consider only situations in which this means of reducing dissonance is not available to the organism. That is, I will consider only situations in which the organism is somehow tricked or seduced into continuing to engage in the activity in spite of the dissonance which is introduced. Under these circumstances we would expect one of the two previously mentioned dissonance reduction mechanisms to be used. If one thinks for a while about the possible behavioural consequences of such a psychological process as we have described,

an explanation suggests itself for the well-known finding that resistance to extinction is greater after partial reward than after complete reward.

. . .

Let us examine what occurs, psychologically, during a series of trials on which the behaviour of an organism is only occasionally rewarded. Imagine a hungry animal who dashes frantically down some runway and into some so-called 'goal box' only to find that there is nothing there. The cognition that he has obtained nothing is dissonant with the cognition that he has expended effort to reach the goal box. If this state of affairs were continually repeated, as we all know, the animal would reduce the dissonance by refusing to go to the goal box, that is, he would change his behaviour. But, in a partial reward situation, the animal is tricked into continuing to run to the goal box because an appreciable number of times that he goes there he does find food. But, on each non-rewarded trial dissonance is introduced when the animal finds the goal box empty. The assumed process of dissonance reduction would lead us to expect that, gradually, the animal develops some extra preference either for the activity or for the goal box itself. A comparable animal that was rewarded every time he ran to the goal box would not develop such extra preference.

Consider the situation, then, when extinction trials begin. In addition to realizing that food is no longer present, the partially rewarded animal also has to overcome his extra preference before he stops going to the goal box. We would thus expect 'extinction' to take longer for a partially rewarded animal than for an animal that was always rewarded. The magnitude of the difference should be far greater than just the slight effect which would exist if the 100 per cent animal discovers more rapidly that the situation has changed.

If this explanation is correct, then the greater resistance to extinction following partial reward is a direct consequence of the process of dissonance reduction.

. . .

Consider the question of delay of reinforcement. Once more, thinking of our hypothetical test situation, we can be reasonably certain that a rat, if faced with a choice where one alternative led to immediate reward while the other alternative involved an appreciable delay before the rat was allowed to continue to the goal box to obtain food, the rat would rather consistently choose the alternative that led to immediate reward. We should then expect that, in a non-choice situation, delay of reward should lead to greater resistance to extinction. Existing data show that this is indeed correct. Appreciable delay of reward does lead to greater resistance to extinction. I will briefly review some of the data which exist on delay of reward to give you some idea of the effect which is obtained.

The usual experiment that has been done on extinction following delay of reinforcement compares one condition in which the rats encounter no enforced delay between starting down a runway and obtaining food in the goal box with other conditions in which, on some trials, the rats are detained in a delay chamber before being allowed to proceed to the food. The usual period of delay which has been used has been about 30 seconds. Crum, Brown, and Bitterman (1951) and Scott and Wike (1956) both find that a group of rats delayed on half the trials shows much greater resistance to extinction than a group which was never delayed. In another experiment, Wike and McNemara (1957) ran three groups which differed in the percentage (and of course, number) of trials on which they were delayed. They find that the larger the percentage or number of trials on which the animal experiences delay, the greater is the resistance to extinction. The same kind of result is obtained by Fehrer (1956) who compared rats who were delayed for 20 seconds on *every* trial with ones who were never delayed. She also finds that delay results in increased resistance to extinction.

. . .

Let us go on now to examine the matter of work and effort. If we return to a consideration of our hypothetical test situation we know that, given a choice between an effortless path to food and a path requiring expenditure of effort, the hungry animal will choose the effortless path rather regularly. Hence, in accordance with our analysis concerning dissonance and dissonance reduction, we would expect the requirement of greater effort during acquisition to lead to increased resistance to extinction.

It is surprising that, in spite of the relative consistency of results among the studies which exist in the literature, the effect of effort during acquisition on resistance to extinction has not been generally noted. People have rather tended to note the finding that the greater the effort required during extinction, the faster does extinction occur. But the data are also clear with respect to the effect of effort during acquisition. They show quite clearly that, holding effort during extinction constant, the more effort required during acquisition, the more resistance there is to extinction.

. . .

Let us then briefly examine the implications of these findings and of the theory of dissonance for our traditional conception of how reward functions. It seems clear that the inclination to engage in behaviour after extrinsic rewards are removed is not so much a function of past rewards themselves. Rather, and paradoxically, such persistence in behaviour is increased by a history of non-rewards or inadequate rewards. I sometimes like to summarize all this by saying that rats and people come to love things for which they have suffered.

Discussion Questions

1. In his writings, Festinger made the analogy between the desire for cognitive consonance and basic needs like hunger and thirst. What is your view of that analogy? How, if at all, might consonance-seeking and food-seeking differ?
2. Cognitive dissonance theory is a theory about the reduction of a psychological discrepancy. What other theories covered in this book have the concept of 'discrepancy' at their core? What are the differences, if any, in the ways the different theorists operationalize their discrepancies?

Unit Three Further Reading

The literature on intrinsic motivation is vast. A number of researchers have isolated variables that help to elucidate the nature of intrinsic motivation and when it is more likely to be manifest. Two examples are

Iyengar, S.S., & Lepper, M.R. (1999). Rethinking the value of choice: A cultural perspective on intrinsic motivation. *Journal of Personality and Social Psychology, 76,* 349–66.

Elliot, A.J., & Harackiewicz, J.M. (1996). Approach and avoidance achievement goals and intrinsic motivation: A mediational analysis. *Journal of Personality and Social Psychology, 70,* 461–75.

Recent developments in social neuroscience have allowed researchers to revisit classic issues in cognitive dissonance from a fresh perspective. A good example of this is

Harmon-Jones, E., Harmon-Jones, C., Fearn, M., Sigelman, J.D., & Johnson, P. (2008). Left frontal cortical activation and spreading of alternatives: Tests of the action-based model of dissonance. *Journal of Personality and Social Psychology, 94,* 1–15.

Unit Four

Success and Failure

Why is it that when some people encounter failure they fall to pieces, while others dust themselves off and 'get back on the horse'? Who exposes himself or herself to possible failure in the name of growth, and who tends to take the safe road? These questions, with their obvious implications for such fields as education and management, have yielded a rich and varied literature in social and personality psychology.

Answers to these questions date back as far as the 1930s, when Kurt Lewin, one of the fathers of social psychology, conducted an influential program of research on 'level of aspiration'. These studies were primarily concerned with how high people set their goals after experiencing success versus failure. Lewin and his colleagues found that, after success, people's level of aspiration tended to go up, but after failure it tended to go down. Why? As Lewin persuasively writes in the 1936 article included in this Unit, absolute levels of attainment are not nearly as important as the subjective *meaning* that these levels of attainment take on, given one's past performance. In particular, the objective score is less important than whether or not that score beats expectations. Put differently, the expectation provides the context that gives *meaning* to the absolute score. It is thus not surprising that in the financial world, the stock price of a company is typically based more on whether it beats the projections than on the absolute amount of profit or loss. This means that a company with significant losses could see an increase in stock price if even bigger losses were expected.

Lewin and his colleagues (e.g., Lewin, Dembo, Festinger, & Sears, 1944) formalized these ideas in their resultant valence theory, which characterized level of aspiration as a problem that individuals solve by considering the value of success, the likelihood of success, the value of failure, and the likelihood of failure. As such, this theory was one of the first theories to enshrine the concepts of *expectancy* and *value* as principal predictors of behaviour (e.g., Feather & Newton, 1982; Heckhausen, 1977; Vroom, 1964; Weiner, 1985).

McClelland, Atkinson, and colleagues took the level of aspiration idea into new directions in the 1950s with their theory of achievement motivation. Central to the McClelland/Atkinson approach was its focus on individual differences. Using a projective test called the Thematic Apperception Test (TAT), McClelland identified those who were high in the need for achievement compared to those with a high fear of failure. McClelland and Atkinson provided evidence that people whose need for achievement was higher than their fear of failure were more attracted to tasks of moderate difficulty than tasks of extremely low or extremely high difficulty. According to McClelland and Atkinson, these people are attracted to tasks that optimize 'pride in accomplishment'; success on a trivially easy task provides little pride while extremely difficult tasks provide little chance of any success at all.

On the other side of the coin, those whose fear of failure is stronger than their need for achievement are more attracted to extremely easy or extremely difficult tasks, and *least* attracted to tasks of moderate difficulty. For these people, the shame of failure is so great that they prefer to focus on easy tasks that promise a high likelihood of success, or extremely difficult tasks with a likelihood of success so low that most people will fail and, thus, failure should not induce any shame. An influential 1957 article provided preliminary evidence for this model.

Subsequent research, however (e.g., Atkinson & Feather, 1966; Trope, 1975) found lackluster support for the McClelland/Atkinson model as it was initially proposed. This prompted researchers to propose updates to the model (e.g., Trope & Brickman, 1975; Weiner & Kukla, 1970). For example, Trope argued that people are strongly motivated by self-assessment, or the desire to reduce uncertainty about exactly how their ability compares to others. As such, people do not place as much emphasis on task *difficulty* as they do on task *diagnosticity* (Trope, 1975; Trope & Brickman, 1975). Diagnosticity refers to the difference between the proportion of people with high and low ability who succeed on a task. According to Trope, people select tasks based not on what will minimize pain and maximize pleasure, but on what will provide the most meaningful information about how *people in general* tend to perform on the task. Armed with this information, people may gain a more accurate sense of exactly where they stand. Notice that, in making this claim, Trope touches upon the social comparison processes alluded to in Unit 2.

In another influential program of research, Carol Dweck and her colleagues have addressed similar questions using a different approach. Rather than focusing on chronic personality dispositions (as McClelland and Atkinson did) or particular attributes of the task (as Trope did), Dweck and colleagues have focused on the goals that people bring to the task. As described in the 2003 article included in this Unit, Heidi Grant and Carol Dweck found that goals exert a powerful influence on behaviour. Those who approach a task with the primary goal of demonstrating or validating one's ability tend to react significantly worse following a setback than those who approach the same task with the goal of improving and cultivating one's ability. People with performance goals are more reluctant than people with learning goals to try challenging tasks and are more likely to give up after a setback. The good news, however, is that either goal can be activated in people's mind with relative ease.

Moreover, certain underlying beliefs (or implicit theories) about human traits that have been found to be strongly associated with performance and learning goals can also be activated at a moment's notice (e.g., Plaks & Stecher, 2007). The *entity theory* holds that human qualities are fixed and largely resistant to change. Its counterpart is the *incremental theory*, which holds that human qualities are malleable and cultivatable. The key to optimal motivation and performance, according to Dweck, is to approach a task with the proper mindset, (i.e., a learning goal and the assumption that your ability is malleable). A good deal of data support this hypothesis.

Andrew Elliott and his colleagues have proposed a modification to Dweck's performance/learning goal distinction by suggesting that, in fact, there are *two* types of performance goals. In several articles, including the 2006 article included in this Unit, Elliot discusses evidence that one type of goal, *performance-avoidance*, is more strongly associated with a negative, helpless response following failure than the other type (*performance-approach*). In fact, according to Elliott and colleagues, performance-approach goals actually carry a number of important benefits. As you will see when you read both the Grant/Dweck and Elliott articles, the literature on the nature and function of achievement goals has seen its share of competing claims and controversy. Notice how the Grant and Dweck article in this Unit offers a reappraisal and reconciliation of different positions in the achievement goals literature.

8. Psychology of Success and Failure

Kurt Lewin

□ ■ □

Editor's Introduction

Why is it that two people may experience the same outcome, and one considers it a failure while the other considers it a success? Clearly, a full account of the psychology of success and failure must go beyond the objective outcome and consider each individual's *subjective* understanding of the outcome. According to William James (1890), feelings of success are a function of actual success and an inverse function of 'pretensions'. This insight was empirically developed by Kurt Lewin and his colleagues in the literature on level of aspiration.

Level of aspiration is defined as the 'level of future performance in a familiar task which an individual, knowing his level of past performance in that task, explicitly undertakes to reach' (Frank, 1935, p. 119). In other words, level of aspiration involves *choice*—choice about how much difficulty to take on and how high to set one's sights. Consider how often we make some sort of level of aspiration decision on both trivial matters (e.g., 'Should I play tennis against a better or worse opponent?') and weighty matters (e.g., 'Should I choose the difficult major or the easier major?' 'Should I ask out the person who might be out of my league or should I settle for the person who represents the safe choice?').

According to Lewin and his colleagues, level of aspiration is determined primarily by the achievement or non-achievement of the previous level of aspiration, regardless of the overall, absolute level of achievement. Thus, a student striving for an A who receives a B will be disappointed, but a student striving for a C who gets a B will be satisfied. Following perceived success aspiration level typically increases, and following perceived failure

aspiration level typically goes down. However, even early researchers in the field quickly noticed that people occasionally exhibit atypical reactions and lower their level of aspiration after success or raise it after failure. What do you think might account for such a phenomenon?

Following his typical approach of attempting to quantify psychological forces into mathematical formulae, Lewin and colleagues (1944) proposed resultant valence theory. According to this theory, anticipated success has a positive valence and anticipated failure a negative valence. The valences of success and failure depend, at least in part, on the difficulty of the task. In other words, success is more delicious when the task is difficult, and failure is more painful when the task is easy.

Based on this idea alone, however, one would predict that people would always choose the most difficult task available. But we know that is not the case. Thus, another element must also be involved. According to Escalona (1940) and Festinger (1942) that other element is the subjective likelihood, or certainty, of success or failure. (The term used by those researchers was *potency*, but in contemporary language *subjective likelihood*, *probability*, or *expectancy* would be more appropriate.) For each level of difficulty there are corresponding subjective likelihoods of success or failure. Thus, taken together, to fully predict an individual's level of aspiration, one would need to measure the valence of success times the subjective likelihood of success minus the valence of failure times the subjective likelihood of failure.

Exactly these sorts of calculations were further specified and carried out by Atkinson, McClelland, and their colleagues a generation later. As noted in the introduction to this Unit, resultant valence theory was one of the first theories to formalize the concepts of expectancy and value as predictors of motivated behaviour (e.g., Feather & Newton, 1982; Heckhausen, 1977; Vroom, 1964; Weiner, 1985).

I

The great importance of success and failure is recognized by practically all psychological schools. Thorndike's law of effect,[1] as well as Adler's ideas, has close relation to this problem. Pedagogically, the importance of success is universally stressed. Indeed, success and failure influence deeply the emotional status of the person, his goals, and his social relations. From the point of view of guidance one can emphasize the fact that these problems are important throughout the whole age range, and are as basic for the very young child as for the adult.

In spite of the common recognition of these factors, our knowledge about the psychology of success and failure is meagre. The law of effect may, for instance, suggest that a person who has succeeded in a special activity will have a tendency to repeat that activity. Indeed, children of two or three years tend to repeat activities again and again. Yet, experiments show, at least for older persons, that a spontaneous repetition of a successful act is not very likely, and that in case it does occur, the activity is generally distinctly changed. As a matter of fact, the tendency to go back spontaneously to a special activity is, as Ovsiankina has shown, about 90 times as high if the activity is not completed as if it is successfully completed. This shows, at least, that the whole problem is much more complicated than one might expect.

II

The first question one should be able to answer is: Under what conditions will a person experience success or failure? The experiments of Hoppe point to some fundamental facts which one could have learned from everyday experience; namely, it is not possible to correlate the objective achievement on the one side with the feeling of success or failure on the other. The same achievement can result once in the feeling of great success, another time in the feeling of complete failure. This is true not only for different individuals, but even for the same individual. For instance, a person may throw a discus 40 yards the first time. The second time he may reach 50, and feel successful. After short practice, he may reach 65. If he then throws 50 yards again, he will experience a definite failure in spite of the fact that he got a thrill out of the same achievement but a short time before. This means that the experience of success and failure does not depend upon the achievement as such, but rather upon the relation between the achievement and the person's expectation. One can speak, in this respect, about the person's 'level of aspiration', and can say that the experience and the degree of success and failure depend upon whether the achievement is above or below the momentary level of aspiration.

One may ask whether a person always has a definite level of aspiration in respect to a certain task. The answer is no. If one, for instance, does something for the first time, one generally does not set himself a definite goal. It is interesting additional evidence of the relation between success and the level of aspiration that in such situations no strong failure is experienced. If one wishes to avoid or diminish the feeling of failure in the child, one often says to him: 'Just try.' In this way a definite level of aspiration is eliminated.

Not only is the level of aspiration fundamental for the experience of success and failure, but the level of aspiration itself is changed by success and failure. After success, a person generally sets himself a higher goal. After failure, his level of aspiration generally goes down. There are some exceptions to this general trend that one should notice. In the experiments of Hoppe, success led to a rise of the level of aspiration only in 69 per cent; in 7 per cent it remained the same; and in 24 per cent the person stopped the activity entirely. After failure, the level of aspiration was never raised, but it was lowered in only 50 per cent of the cases. In 21 per cent it remained the same, in 2 per cent the person consoled himself by the realization of previous successes; and in 27 per cent the person ceased the activity entirely. This varying behaviour is due partly to the fact that there are cases that are neither clear successes nor clear failures. On the whole, the person is more ready to raise the level of aspiration after success than to lower it after failure.

It is important to note that a person instead of lowering his level of aspiration after failure may stop entirely. There is a significant difference between individuals in this respect. Some persons are relatively easily influenced to lower their levels of aspiration, whereas others show a stiff backbone. The latter maintain their levels of aspiration in spite of failures and may prefer to leave the field entirely rather than to lower it. Lack of persistence sometimes has to be attributed to such an unwillingness to yield. On the other hand, there are cases of apparent persistence, in which a person sticks to an activity only at the price of constantly lowering his level of aspiration. This sort of persistency may be found in the hysteric type. In problems of guidance involving unusually high or low persistency, the possible reasons behind such behaviour should be carefully examined, because the advisable measures should be different in accordance with the underlying psychological facts.

Surprisingly enough, a person may leave the field of activity not only after failure, but after success too. Such abandonment of the field after success occurs generally when this success follows a series of failures. One obviously does not like to quit a task after failure. One continues, eager to find a successful termination, and uses the first occasion to stop, out of fear that further repetitions may bring new failures.

III

One has to consider quite detailed facts in order to understand the forces which govern level of aspiration.

The first point to mention is that any goal has a position within a set of goals. If a child is asked, 'How much is 3 times 4?' the answer '12' determines a definite circumscribed goal he has to reach. The answer will be either right or wrong. But if the child has to write an English composition, or to translate a passage of French, or to build a wooden boat, there is no such absolutely determined goal, but rather a variety of possible achievements which may differ greatly in quality. Most tasks are of this nature. It is generally technically possible to order the different possible achievements of a task according to their degree of difficulty. This allows one to compare the achievement and the level of aspiration of different persons, and to determine in a given case the effect of success and failure. The range of acceptable achievement has often a 'natural maximum' and a 'natural minimum'. In Hoppe's experiment, for instance, the subject had to solve one of a group of puzzles, different in difficulty. A subject who was not able to solve any one of the puzzles, but who was able to return the stones to their proper places in the box, would certainly not have reached the natural minimum of the task. On the other hand, it would be above the natural maximum to reach a solution of the most difficult puzzle within one second. Some tasks have no natural maximum. This holds, for instance, for many sports activities—there is always the possibility of jumping higher and running faster. The lack of this natural maximum within the goal structure of many sport activities has led to a biologically unsound race without end.

The individual usually is conscious of the variety of possible goals within the task. He conceives the single action in its significance for a larger field of actions. Besides the goals for the momentary act, he has some general goal in regard to this larger field. For instance, when a person in a competition throws a discus, his goal for a certain trial might be to throw at least 50 yards; his goal for the whole group of trials would be to win! There always exists besides the goal for the next act, or, as we may say, besides the immediate goal, an ideal goal. This ideal goal may be to become the best discus thrower of the college or even to become world champion.

Such a goal can possess any degree of reality or unreality. For the student who does well in the first weeks of his sporting activities, the ideal to become world champion may be only an occasional daydream without any significance. The ideal goal, to become the best player at the university, may have considerably more reality. In a vague way, a student entering college may dream about the possibility of becoming a leading surgeon, and without even confessing this goal to himself. If he progresses in college, and does well in medical school, this idea goal may become somewhat more real. According to Hoppe, success narrows the gap between the immediate goal and the ideal goal, and brings the ideal goal from the level of unreality gradually down to the level of reality. Failure has the opposite effect: a previously real goal vanishes into the world of dreams. In case the ideal goal should be reached (a case more frequent in experiments than in life) generally a new ideal goal arises.

IV

If it is true that the degree of success and failure depends upon the amount of difference between the immediate goal and the achievement, it should be possible to create a very strong feeling of success by making the task so easy that the achievement will be much better than the task demands. On the other hand, it should be possible to create a very strong feeling of failure by assigning a very difficult task. Experiments show that this is not true. If the task is above a certain degree of difficulty, no feeling of failure arises, and no feeling of

success arises if the task is below a certain degree of difficulty. In other words, if one represents the possible degree of difficulty of a task on a scale, this scale is infinite in direction, both to greater ease and to greater difficulty. But an individual reacts with success and failure only to a small region within this scale. In fact, the tasks which an individual considers as 'very easy', 'easy', 'medium', 'difficult', and 'very difficult', circumscribe only a small region in the scale. Above and below this region lie a great many tasks which the individual calls 'too easy' or 'too difficult'. The 'too difficult' tasks are considered as 'objectively impossible', entirely out of the range of the individual's ability, and no feeling of failure is attached to such a task. Similarly, in the case of a 'too easy' task, the achievement is taken so much for granted that no feeling of success is aroused. Contrary to the scale of possible difficulties, the scale of possible achievements is not infinite, but has a definite upper limit for a given individual at a given time. Both success and failure occur only if the difficulty of the task lies close to the upper limit of achievement. In other words, the feeling of failure occurs only if there is a chance for success, and a feeling of success occurs only if there is a chance for failure. Behind success and failure stands, therefore, always a conflict situation.

This conflict situation makes somewhat understandable the laws which govern the position and the change in the level of aspiration. These laws are probably among the most fundamental for all human behaviour. They are quite complicated, and we are only beginning to understand them. If it were true that life is ruled by the tendency to get as much pleasure as possible, one might expect that everybody would keep his level of aspiration as low as possible, because in this case, his performance would always be above his level of aspiration, and he would feel successful. As a matter of fact, there is a marked tendency to keep the level of aspiration down out of fear of failure. On the other hand, there is at the same time a strong tendency to raise the level of aspiration as high as possible. The experiments of J.D. Frank show that both tendencies are of different strength in different individuals, and that a third tendency may have to be distinguished, namely, the tendency to keep one's expectations about one's performance as close as possible to reality. A cautious person usually starts with a relatively low level of aspiration, and after succeeding, he raises the level only by short steps. Other persons tend to maintain their levels or aspiration well above their achievements. The rigidity of the level of aspiration, that is, the tendency to keep the level constant rather than to shift it, shows marked differences among individuals. Frank found that these differences are highly reliable and largely independent of the special nature of the task.

It is important to know whether success and failure change the level of aspiration only in the particular activity in question, or whether success and failure in one task influence the level of aspiration in another task too. This is important for problems of guidance, where the effects of achievement or failure in different fields of activity on each other are of great significance, as for instance, in the realm of school motivation and of delinquency. Frank found a marked relationship between success and failure in one task and the level of aspiration in another, if the tasks concerned had sufficient psychological relations. Mr Jucknat's experiments verified this result but showed that this influence is weak or negligible if past experience has rigidly fixed the level of aspiration within a task.

V

These studies point to a relation between the level of aspiration for a specific task and something that one may call the self-esteem, which means the feeling of the person about his own status and general standards. All experiments indicate that this relation is very fundamental. There is, for instance, a marked tendency in the case of failure to blame an inadequate tool or an accident for the lack of achievement. To experience success or failure the person has to attribute the result of an action to himself in a very specific way. In case of inadequate performance, the person often tries to get rid of the feeling of failure by cutting the tie of belongingness between him and the result, and by rejecting his responsibility for the outcome. Also, the tendency to raise the level of aspiration as high as possible seems to be closely related to the self-esteem, particularly to the feeling of the person about his status in the social group. The level of aspiration is determined on the one side by the upper limit of the person's achievements; in other words, by his ability. A second fundamental factor is the level of achievement prevailing in the social group to which a person belongs; for instance, among his business friends, his comrades, his playmates. The social group can have a strong influence in keeping the level of aspiration either too high or too low for a person's ability. This is especially true for children. The expectation of his parents or the standards of his group may keep the level of aspiration for the less able child too high and lead to continuous failure and overtension. Whereas the level of aspiration for the very able child may be kept too low. (This may be the reason for Wellman's finding that children with a relatively high IQ gain less in IQ in the nursery school than children with a relatively low IQ.)

Fajans has shown that success and failure influence greatly the degree of activeness among active and passive children. Chase found an increase in achievement following success. Fajans has further determined the degree to which praise has an effect similar to real success. The effects of being successful, and being socially recognized or being loved, resemble each other closely. This relation is important for adults, and even more so in the case of adolescents and children.

Note

1. Law of effect: One learns quickly those reactions that are accompanied or followed by a satisfying state of affairs; one does not learn quickly those which result in an annoying state of affairs or learns not to make such reactions.

Discussion Questions

1. Based on regulatory focus theory (Higgins, 1997, see Unit 5), how might an individual's promotion or prevention focus influence level of aspiration following success and following failure?
2. Based on what you know about implicit theories of personality (Dweck & Leggett, 1988; Grant and Dweck, 2003, included in this Unit), how might entity or incremental theory influence level of aspiration following success and following failure?
3. What variables might predict when people will purposely 'undershoot' or 'overshoot'?

9. Clarifying Achievement Goals and Their Impact

Heidi Grant and Carol S. Dweck

□ ■ □

Editor's Introduction

The research of Carol Dweck and her colleagues is, at its root, about the power of mental representation. Whenever people perform a self-relevant task (e.g., a student taking an exam), subtle differences in the representation of what they are doing (e.g., 'This is a demonstration of my ability' vs 'This is just one step in my continual development') can yield powerful effects on thought, emotion, and behaviour. By now, scores of studies have documented that those who approach a task aiming to demonstrate their ability consistently underperform compared to those who approach the same task with the view that it represents an opportunity for learning and growth. This is the case even when the two groups start out equal in ability and self-esteem.

As the present article notes, however, not all performance goals are created equal. Certain kinds of performance goals may not necessarily hurt performance. In several studies, Grant and Dweck distinguished between three types of performance goals: outcome goals (wanting to do well), ability-linked performance goals, and normative performance goals. Using both laboratory data and naturalistic data gathered from students in an undergraduate course, Grant and Dweck found it was the ability-linked performance goals that tended to produce the worst outcomes, while outcome goals and normative goals had less of a debilitating effect.

It appears that considering success or failure on a task as a far-reaching testament to one's ability and self-worth is all well and good when you succeed. But everyone encounters failure at some point, whether it's bombing an exam, being rejected by a potential partner, choking in the big game, or any of life's lesser insults. More often than

not, those who approach a task with a learning goal are able to recover quickly and effectively, and even thrive, after failure. Those who approach a task with an ability-linked performance goal are more likely to wallow in defeat and leave the field altogether.

What predicts whether people will adopt one type of goal or another? In several articles, Dweck and colleagues have argued that these goals are by-products of differing underlying assumptions, or implicit theories, about human ability. The assumption that abilities are fixed and largely resistant to change (the entity theory) tends to foster performance goals. After all, if your ability cannot change, you should show the world that your ability is high. On the other hand, the assumption that abilities are cultivatable (the incremental theory) fosters learning goals. After all, true learning requires the presupposition that one can experience significant growth. Indeed, those who believe in the entity theory often endorse what Dweck calls the *inverse rule* of effort and ability: People who have to try hard must not be very talented. In contrast, those who believe in the incremental theory tend to view effort and ability as going hand-in-hand: High ability is the result of practice, practice, practice. Thus, different starting points lead to entirely different ways of perceiving identical situations, with clear implications for motivation and performance.

As Dweck and Leggett (1988) noted in a previous article, theirs is 'a model in which individuals' goals set up their pattern of responding, and these goals, in turn, are fostered by individuals' self-conceptions.' For example, in a recent longitudinal study that tracked Grade 7 students over the course of the school year, those who believed in the incremental theory adopted learning goals and displayed a significant improvement while those who believed in the entity theory tended to adopt performance goals and their performance remained flat (Blackwell, Trzesniewski, & Dweck, 2007). In Study 2, an intervention teaching the incremental theory to some of the students caused significant positive change in classroom motivation and performance compared with a control group.

Fortunately, people's implicit theories are not set in stone. As much as we would like to believe otherwise, these theories are often placed into our heads via ambient cues in the environment rather than our own deeply held principles. Indeed, consider that both theories are highly intuitive to most people (entity: 'A leopard never changes its spots'; incremental: 'Turn over a new leaf'). This means that they are easy to change. Numerous studies have found that, regardless of which theory people may be endorsing when they walk into the lab, they can be coaxed into adopting either theory with relative ease. Several studies have shown that simply activating the incremental mindset can activate all the benefits associated with that view (e.g., Plaks & Stecher, 2007).

☐ ■ ☐

Considerable evidence suggests that much of achievement motivation (e.g., intrinsic interest, strategy use, and persistence) can be understood in terms of the different goals individuals bring to the achievement context (see Ames, 1992; Ames & Archer, 1988; Butler, 1987, 1993; Dweck & Elliott, 1983; Dweck & Leggett, 1988; Elliott & Dweck, 1988; Harackiewicz, Barron, Carter, Lehto, & Elliot, 1997; Kaplan & Maehr, 1999; Middleton & Midgely, 1997; Nicholls, 1984; Pintrich, 2000a; Rawsthorne & Elliot, 1999; Utman, 1997). However, there are some disagreements and some conflicting findings on the nature of these relations. Specifically, researchers disagree on how to best define and operationalize the major classes of goals, and on the precise impact of these goals on motivation and achievement.

In the original goal models, two classes of goals were identified—*performance goals*, where the purpose is to validate one's ability or avoid demonstrating a lack of ability, and *learning goals*, where the aim is to acquire new knowledge or skills (i.e., to increase one's ability; see Dweck & Elliott, 1983). Different researchers have used different labels for these two classes of goals—performance goals have also been called *ego-involved goals* (e.g., Nicholls, 1984) or *ability goals* (e.g., Ames, 1992), and learning goals have also been called *mastery goals* (e.g., Ames, 1992; Butler, 1993; Elliot & Harackiewicz, 1996; Meece & Holt, 1993) or *task goals* (e.g., Middleton & Midgely, 1997; Nicholls, 1984).

These two classes of goals were then linked to motivation and performance in achievement situations. Performance goals, with their emphasis on outcomes as measures of ability, were shown to produce a vulnerability to helplessness and debilitation after a setback or negative feedback, particularly in cases where current perceptions of ability were low (Ames & Archer, 1988; Butler, 1993; Elliott & Dweck, 1988; Jagacinski & Nicholls, 1987; Meece, Blumenfeld, & Hoyle, 1988). That is, when the goal is to validate ability and individuals do not believe they can accomplish this, motivation and performance tend to suffer. Learning goals, with their emphasis on understanding and growth, were shown to facilitate persistence and mastery-oriented behaviours in the face of obstacles, even when perceptions of current ability might be low (Ames & Archer, 1988; Butler, 1993; Elliott & Dweck, 1988; Jagacinski & Nicholls, 1987; Utman, 1997).

Performance and learning goals have also been shown to predict real-world performance, including exam grades, course grades, and achievement test scores, controlling for past performance (Dweck & Sorich, 1999; Greene & Miller, 1996;

Kaplan & Maehr, 1999; Meece & Holt, 1993; Midgely & Urdan, 1995; Roeser, Midgely, & Urdan, 1996). In addition, goal effects obtain both when the goals have been experimentally manipulated (Butler, 1987; Elliott & Dweck, 1988; Graham & Golen, 1991) and when students' naturally existing goals have been assessed (Ames & Archer, 1988; Bouffard, Boisvert, Verzeau, & Larouche, 1995; Midgely, Anderman, & Hicks, 1995; Miller, Behrens, Greene, & Newman, 1993; Pintrich & DeGroot, 1990; Pintrich & Garcia, 1991). The fact that induced goals have been found to have strong impact is important for two reasons. First, it means that goals can have a causal role in producing achievement patterns. Second, it means that learning environments can be constructed in ways that enhance achievement (Ames, 1992; Maehr & Midgley, 1991; Roeser et al., 1996).

Despite early agreement regarding the effects of performance and learning goals on motivation and performance, recent research has revealed a more complicated picture. Some researchers have questioned whether learning goals affect performance at all, suggesting that they chiefly influence intrinsic motivation (e.g., Barron & Harackiewicz, 2001; Elliot & Church, 1997; Harackiewicz et al., 1997; Harackiewicz, Barron, Tauer, Carter, & Elliot, 2000). Some have argued that performance goals predict higher, not lower, grades, and do not affect intrinsic motivation (e.g., Barron & Harackiewicz, 2001; Elliot & Church, 1997; cf. Rawsthorne & Elliot, 1999).

We propose that looking at the ways in which performance and learning goals have been defined or operationalized can help account for the discrepant findings that have been obtained by different researchers. To test this proposal, items were created to measure the different forms of goals that have been prominently represented in existing research. Five studies explore the relationships among these goals, their ability to predict intrinsic motivation and performance under highly challenging or difficult circumstances, and the mechanisms through which they may bring about

those effects. We begin by describing the important dimensions along which the operationalizations of performance and learning goals vary in current achievement goal research, and describing how each of these dimensions is represented in the following studies.

What Is a Performance Goal and What Is Its Effect?

Achievement goal researchers have already made one important distinction among performance goals—namely, the distinction between performance *approach* goals (where the focus is on attaining success) and performance *avoidance* goals (where the focus is on the avoidance of failure; Elliot, 1999; Elliot & Church, 1997; Elliot & Harackiewicz, 1996; Middleton & Midgely, 1997; Pintrich, 2000a). In general, this program of research has suggested that it is the avoidance form of performance goals that predict lower intrinsic motivation and performance, with approach goals often relating positively to performance.

However, as discussed below, the positive and negative effects of performance approach goals have typically been found when performance goals are operationalized in particular ways, and the positive and negative effects of different types of performance approach goals have not been systematically explored. Thus our purpose in this article is to distinguish among approach forms of performance goals, and we propose that they take at least three distinct forms: (a) goals that are linked to validating an aspect of self (e.g., one's ability), (b) goals that are explicitly normative in nature, and (c) goals that are simply focused on obtaining positive outcomes (i.e., doing well). It is the first form that was linked to impairment in the earlier models, but it has tended to be the second two forms that have been linked to more positive outcomes in recent work. Let us take a closer look at these different forms of approach goals.

For some researchers, the essence of a performance goal is seeking to validate one's ability (operationalized either by suggesting to participants that their performance on a task measures the extent to which they possess a valued ability, or by assessing the extent to which they generally strive to validate their ability). Debilitation occurs when outcomes indicate a lack of ability, but performance maintenance or enhancement can occur when success is expected (Ames, 1992; Elliott & Dweck, 1988; see Dweck & Leggett, 1988). It should be noted that debilitation here requires the presence of challenges, setbacks, or failure—an easy task or course is not expected to produce debilitation, even in the presence of strong performance goals. To represent this view, we developed *ability* goal items (e.g., 'It is important to me to validate that I am smart').

For others, the essence of a performance goal is a normative comparison (i.e., wanting to perform better than others), and a goal that is non-normative (e.g., using an absolute standard such as a perfect score, or tying absolute performance to self-worth) is not considered to be a performance goal (Elliot, 1999; Elliot & Church, 1997; Elliot & Harackiewicz, 1996; Maehr & Midgely, 1991; Pintrich, 2000b). Here, performance goals are often operationalized by informing participants that their performance on a task will be evaluated normatively, or by measuring their agreement with statements such as 'It is important to me to do well compared to others in this class' (Elliot & Church, 1997).

The issue of whether normative performance goals are empirically distinct from performance goals that do not contain a normative standard has not been systematically addressed in the achievement goal literature. Yet it is an important question, because to some theorists, as noted, the presence of normative comparison is the essence of a performance goal (Elliot & Harackiewicz, 1996; see Rawsthorne & Elliot, 1999), and to others, a potentially interesting but non-essential aspect of a performance goal (Elliott & Dweck, 1988). It would be interesting to find that normative and non-normative performance goals do indeed differ,

particularly if these differences could illuminate discrepancies in the reported effects of performance goals on motivation and performance. The following studies contain both normative and non-normative versions of performance goals. An example of an explicitly normative goal would be the following: 'One of my major goals in school is to feel that I am more intelligent than other students.' In contrast, the goal item, 'It is important to me to validate that I am intelligent' is not explicitly normative.

Sometimes goal items used to measure performance-goal orientation simply ask the participant about wanting to do well on a task, such as wanting to earn a high grade in a course. For people who are focused on doing well, negative outcomes do not necessarily indicate a lack of ability (i.e., holding this type of goal does imply a particular causal attribution for success or failure). We refer to the goal of wanting to do well on a particular task as an *outcome* goal, and it, too, is represented in our studies (e.g., 'It is important to me to get good grades in my classes'). A closely related construct is 'competence valuation', or the degree to which a task is perceived to be important (Elliot & McGregor, 2001), which has been found to relate positively to intrinsic motivation and performance (Barron & Harackiewicz, 2001). We find this type of goal particularly interesting, because 'wanting to do well' can also be an important part of a learning goal framework. In other words, a person with a learning goal may care very much about doing well on a task, but perhaps for different reasons (i.e., in order to maximize learning, as an indicator of successful learning, or for instrumental reasons). Later, we address the question of whether outcome goals are best understood as performance goals.

What Is a Learning Goal? When Is It Helpful?

There is generally less controversy and more agreement with respect to the nature of learning goals. As noted learning goals, task goals, and mastery goals have often been regarded as conceptually equivalent (Ames, 1992; Linnenbrink & Pintrich, 2000). Yet, potentially important differences among operationalizations do exist. For some (Ames, 1992; Elliot & Church, 1997; Elliott & Dweck, 1988; Harackiewicz et al., 1997; Middleton & Midgley, 1997), a learning goal is an active striving toward development and growth of competence and is operationalized by emphasizing the importance and benefits of learning some new knowledge or skill to the participant, or by asking participants to indicate the extent to which learning and developing new skills are major academic goals. However, the terms 'task goals' and 'mastery goals' do not put an explicit emphasis on learning; thus, we thought it important to test the extent to which the desire to learn may be similar to or different from the desire to master challenges. As a result, we included items measuring two forms of learning goals. An example of a learning goal without an explicit challenge-mastery component is 'I strive to constantly learn and improve in my courses'. An example of an explicit challenge-mastery item is 'It is very important to me to feel that my coursework offers me real challenges.'

It should be reiterated that, despite the substantial agreement among researchers with respect to the concept of a learning goal, the data with respect to the influence of learning goals on motivation and performance are not without inconsistencies. Typically, those who adopt learning goals are found to engage in deeper, more self-regulated learning strategies, have higher intrinsic motivation, and perform better, particularly in the face of challenge or setbacks (Ames, 1992; Dweck & Leggett, 1988; Kaplan & Midgley, 1997; Pintrich, 2000a; Pintrich & Garcia, 1991; Utman, 1997; see also Barron & Harackiewicz, 2000). However, recently, several studies have failed to find enhanced performance outcomes resulting from learning goals (although enhanced intrinsic motivation was found; Elliot & Church, 1997; Elliot, McGregor, & Gable, 1999).

Conditions Under which Goal Effects Are Tested

The effects of learning and performance goals on motivation and achievement have been tested under a wide variety of circumstances—with students working on interesting 'NINA' puzzles (Elliot & Harackiewicz, 1996), performing a concept-formation task (Elliott & Dweck, 1988), solving math problems (designed to be highly challenging in one condition; Barron & Harackiewicz, 2001; cf. Middleton & Midgely, 1997), or taking an intermediate-level psychology course (Elliot & Church, 1997). Importantly, these tasks may have varied with respect to the degree of difficulty or challenge encountered by the participant, and the degree to which performance on the task had importance or meaning to the participant. We feel that conditions where the degree of difficulty is substantial for a large number of participants and the outcome is highly important are more likely to reveal goal effects on motivation, coping, and achievement, and have tried to use such conditions in the studies reported here.

In summary, there have been major differences in the ways goals have been operationalized, and it is not surprising that the data are inconsistent with respect to how and when performance and learning goals affect motivation and achievement. In the following studies, we attempted to illuminate these issues. In three studies, we developed and tested a set of items to tap different forms of learning and performance goals. In the fourth study, to gain an initial sense of the patterns associated with each goal type, we presented students with scenarios depicting important academic setbacks and examined how the different goals predicted intrinsic motivation and coping. In the fifth study, the different goals were used to predict intrinsic motivation, study strategies, and performance in an important and challenging course.

. . .

Study 4

We believe that it is important to look at goal effects when individuals experience major setbacks or failure on highly valued tasks, because it is under these conditions that we would expect goal effects on motivation, coping, and achievement to be maximal. Studies 4 and 5 were designed to look at how each of the different goals we identified predicts indexes of intrinsic motivation, mastery-oriented coping, and performance, after a significant or sustained difficulty or setback, by means of hypothetical failure scenarios (Study 4), reports of habitual coping style (Study 4), and a very challenging pre-med college course (Study 5).

We also included measurements of some of the affective and cognitive variables that comprise the psychological processes that accompany goal pursuit. Much recent achievement goal work pays little attention to the psychological concomitants of goals: attributions, beliefs, and contingency of self-worth (Molden & Dweck, 2000). By including these measures, we hoped to capture a richer motivational picture of performance and learning goal processes.

In Study 4, two scenarios were generated in which the participant encounters failure in an important achievement setting (adapted from Zhao & Dweck, 1997). The use of hypothetical scenarios was used here as a first step in relating the different goals to the variety of cognitive, affective, and behavioural variables involved in coping with difficulty in achievement situations.

Participants in Study 4 also completed a measure of chronic coping style (COPE; Carver, Scheier, & Weintraub, 1989), so that we might look at the relationship between goal orientation and participants' own personal history of coping with setbacks. Thus, the first part of Study 4 asks participants to indicate how they would respond to a situation if it occurred, and the second part of Study 4 asks them to reflect on past situations that have actually occurred.

Method

Participants

A total of 92 participants (40 men, 52 women) were recruited for pay from the Columbia University community. Sixty-one per cent of participants were Caucasian, 21 per cent African American, 12 per cent Asian, and 6 per cent were 'other' or unidentified. They received $5 for their participation.

Procedure

Participants completed the goal items, and then, after a 5-minute word-completion filler task, they received one of two randomly assigned scenarios, shown in previous work to elicit motivational differences (see Zhao & Dweck, 1997). The scenario asked them to read about a failure experience in a college classroom (either getting a bad grade on an important essay in a key course or doing poorly on the Graduate Record Examination when they strongly wished to go to graduate school), and to imagine it happening to them. These two scenarios were vividly written and were selected to represent situations that they could easily personally relate to (i.e., doing poorly on an essay in a course in your major, and doing poorly on a test in science class). Here is an example:

Imagine that during your second semester at Columbia, you take an important course in your major, in which students are required to read their essays out loud to the entire class. This happens several times throughout the semester. The time comes for the first readings. By the time it's your turn, most of the students have already presented their essays. All of them did pretty well, and you know that their essays got good grades from the professor. But when you read your essay to the class, the professor and the other students don't seem to like your presentation very much, and later you find out that the grade he gave you was a C−.

Participants were then asked to indicate what they would think, how they would feel, and how they would behave after the failure by rating their degree of agreement with a series of statements. These statements include items assessing *loss of intrinsic motivation* (e.g., 'I'd probably feel less interested in the subject'), *help-seeking* (e.g., 'I would seek help from my professor or my classmates'), *planning* (e.g., 'I'd start planning how to do better on the next presentation'), and *time and energy withdrawal* (e.g., 'I would devote less time and energy to the class'), as well as *attributions* for the failure (e.g., 'I would feel like I wasn't smart enough'), *loss of self-worth* (e.g., 'I would feel like a loser'), and *rumination* (e.g., 'I would dwell on my failure'). Responses were made by circling a number on a 7-point scale ranging from 1 (*not at all true of me*) to 7 (*very true of me*).

After a second 5-minute word-completion filler task, participants were asked to complete the Ways of Coping Scale (COPE; Carver et al., 1989). This scale measures the ways in which individuals have coped with difficulties when they have arisen. Subscales include Active Coping, Planning, Positive Reinterpretation, Denial, and Behavioural Disengagement.

Results

For each of the analyses conducted, scenario version (1 or 2) was entered as a predictor, and no effect for scenario version was found. Therefore, all analyses reported were conducted collapsing across scenario version. Each of the four goal types (learning, outcome, ability, and normative) was entered as a predictor in a series of simultaneous regressions that included all two-way interactions. There were no significant two-way interactions, so these terms were dropped in subsequent analyses. Thus, the effects of each goal on the variables of interest control for any effects of the other three classes of goals. In this way, we could determine what, if any, were the unique effects of each class of goal on our achievement variables.

Intrinsic Motivation

Table 9.1 depicts the unique relationship between each type of goal and an index of loss of intrinsic motivation, created by adding together responses from the following three items ($\alpha = 0.89$): 'I'd probably feel less interested in the subject,' 'I probably wouldn't enjoy the course as much as before,' and 'I wouldn't really be excited about the course anymore.'

As can be seen, learning goals were negatively related to decreases in intrinsic motivation, whereas outcome and ability goals were significantly correlated with decreases in intrinsic motivation. Of interest, normative goals did not predict loss of intrinsic motivation. This finding is worth noting, in that the program of research that has

Table 9.1 Goals and Responses to Failure

Goal	Loss of intrinsic motivation	Withdrawal of time and effort	Help-seeking	Planning
Learning	−.39***	−.40***	.17	.57***
Outcome	.29**	.00	.36**	.03
Ability	.40***	.32**	−.02	−.02
Normative	−.11	−.02	−.16	−.16

Note: Values are standardized regression coefficients.
**p < .01. ***p < .001.

most consistently found that approach forms of performance goals do not negatively influence intrinsic motivation has used a normative definition of performance goal (e.g., Elliot & Church, 1997). Also, Epstein and Harackiewicz (1992) have found that students high in achievement motivation who were assigned competitive goals (which are inherently normative) experienced increased interest in a task when they were given a failure expectancy. This finding suggests that competitive strivings may buffer individuals when they experience difficulty or failure in ways that ability-focused strivings do not.

Behavioural Coping

Endorsement of several possible behavioural responses by goal type is also displayed in Table 9.1. Consistent with the maintenance of intrinsic motivation, learning goals predicted planning (one item: 'I'd start planning how to do better on the next presentation'), and negatively predicted withdrawal of time and energy (one item: 'I would devote less time and energy to the class'). Ability goals, in contrast, positively predicted withdrawal of time and energy.

Outcome goals were the only goals that were positively related to help-seeking (one item: 'I would seek help from my professor or my classmates'). Help-seeking may be perceived as a good way to obtain the good grades that those who endorse outcome goals clearly value.

Attributions

Turning to the psychological processes that accompany goal pursuit, learning goals ($\beta = 0.56$, $p < .001$) were predictive of effort-based attributions for failure (one item: 'I think that if I work harder, I can do better'), whereas ability goals ($\beta = 0.22$, $p < .05$) and outcome goals ($\beta = 0.36$, $p < .01$), in contrast, were predictive of ability-based attributions (one item: 'I feel like I'm just not good at this subject'). Learning goals were negatively related to making ability attributions for poor performance ($\beta = -0.37$, $p < .01$).

These results are consistent with prior research, which found attributions to low ability to be associated with drops in intrinsic motivation and helplessness, whereas attributions to effort were associated with intrinsic motivation maintenance and mastery-oriented coping (e.g., Mueller & Dweck, 1998).

Again, normative goals were not reliable predictors of negative ability attributions. Taken together with the finding that these goals do not reliably predict loss of intrinsic motivation, the data begin to suggest that normative performance goals may be a hardier form of performance goal (i.e., one that does not tend to lead to 'helpless' forms of coping and behaviour). This is again consistent with Elliot and colleagues' findings (see Elliot & Church, 1997; Elliot et al., 1999) that (normative) performance approach goals do not lead to lower motivation and performance.

Loss of Self-Worth

Loss of self-worth is akin to a negative ability attribution, but it is more global. It, too, can often accompany helpless motivational and behavioural responses to a setback (e.g., Covington, 1992; Crocker & Wolfe, 2001). A composite index of self-worth loss was created by adding together responses from the following three items: 'I would feel like a loser,' 'I would feel like a failure,' and 'I'd think less of myself as a person' ($\alpha = 0.84$). Consistent with results thus far, ability ($\beta = 0.56$, $p < .001$) goals were positively correlated with loss of self-worth.

Rumination

The tendency to ruminate on one's setbacks has been associated with helplessness. A composite index of ruminating and dwelling on the failure was created by adding together responses from the following two items: 'I would dwell on how poorly I did' and 'I would replay it all over and over again in my mind' ($\alpha = 0.92$). Rumination was fairly strongly related to ability goals ($\beta = 0.47$, $p < .001$). Thus, those goals that tend to lead to ability attributions and negative self-evaluation also predict dwelling on the negative outcome and its meaning.

The results from the hypothetical failure scenarios revealed a consistent pattern among the motivational and coping variables. Learning goals predicted active, engaged responding, whereas ability goals predicted self-denigration and withdrawal. Outcome goals were associated with a hybrid response pattern (i.e., low ability attributions and decreased intrinsic motivation as well as help-seeking). Finally, normative goals were not reliable predictors of mastery-oriented or helpless responding.

Chronic Coping Style

We now turn to the question of whether different goals predict different reported histories of coping with setbacks in past achievement situations. Different styles of chronic coping were measured by the Ways of Coping Scale (Carver et al., 1989), which asks participants to indicate the extent to which they have typically engaged in various coping strategies.

Consistent with the responses to the failure scenarios, learning goals predicted *active coping* ($\beta = 0.38$, $p < .01$) and *planning* ($\beta = 0.33$, $p < .01$). They were also predictive of *positive reinterpretation* of a setback ($\beta = 0.30$, $p < .05$) and negatively related to *denial* ($\beta = -0.36$, $p < .01$), *behavioural disengagement* ($\beta = -0.35$, $p < .01$), and *mental disengagement* ($\beta = -0.28$, $p < .05$).

Ability goals negatively predicted positive reinterpretation of a setback ($\beta = -0.30$, $p < .05$). Of interest, normative goals were significant predictors of denial after a setback ($\beta = 0.25$, $p < .05$) and behavioural disengagement ($\beta = 0.28$, $p < .01$). The finding for denial perhaps suggests that competitive striving might keep individuals from recognizing a poor performance when they produce one. This may provide some explanation for the consistent finding that normative goals did not predict negative cognitive, affective, and behavioural responding to a hypothetical setback (e.g., loss of

intrinsic motivation, low ability attributions, loss of self-worth, rumination) as strongly or consistently as non-normative ability goals.

In summary, learning goals were associated with active coping, and a wide range of positive, mastery-oriented indicators. Learning goals appear to be a powerful predictor of behaviours that will preserve intrinsic motivation and performance in the face of difficulty. In contrast, ability goals were associated with a loss of motivation and common indexes of helplessness. Outcome goals (which are related to both learning goals and ability goals) also predicted a loss of motivation and low ability attributions for failure, but predicted proactive behaviours as well (e.g., help-seeking). Taken together, these results suggest that valuing doing well is not in itself a good predictor of responses to failure—rather, the goals that accompany valuing doing well (learning or validating ability) seem responsible for much of the 'action'. Normative goals were not among the performance goals that related strongly or consistently to the variables measured, suggesting that under some circumstances, competitive performance goal items may not predict maladaptive cognitions, affect, or coping when other types of performance goals (i.e., ability goals) do.

Study 5

Study 5 differed from Study 4 in several ways. First, the goal items were used to predict motivation and performance in a 'real-world' setting, specifically for freshman and sophomore undergraduates taking an important and often career-defining course. Study 5 also differed from many past course-taking studies in the level of sustained challenge or difficulty encountered by participants (and, as explained below, in our special attention to students who encountered successive setbacks over the course of the semester). For this reason, we would expect to see more facilitative effects of learning goals on motivation and performance, as well as the debilitating effects of performance goals.

Aside from being a real-world study, Study 5 differed from Study 4 in another important way. Study 4 presented students with a *fait accompli*— a defined failure—and therefore, perhaps did not allow us to see the potentially beneficial effects of performance goals for people experiencing challenge but not failure. Study 5 allowed us to monitor students throughout the semester, by looking in on students as they began this new, important, and challenging course. Here we might find that for students who are doing well, ability goals will provide a boost over time, whereas for students who are encountering difficulty, ability goals will predict further impairment. In other words, Study 5 allowed us to see goal effects as they played out over time—both their facilitative effects and their detrimental effects.

Most potential pre-med, engineering, and science majors at Columbia University enrol in General Chemistry in the Fall of their freshman year. The permission and support of the Columbia University Provost, Deans of the College of Arts and Sciences, and General Chemistry instructors were granted to conduct an intensive study of these students throughout the semester. Surveys tracked students' intrinsic motivation and performance at several points throughout the semester, and grades were obtained from the Chemistry Department with permission of the students.

Method

Participants
Participants were 85 per cent freshmen, 50 per cent female and 50 per cent male. The number of participants in each wave of the study varied between 78 and 128, depending on class/recitation attendance. In the largest sample, participants were 59 per cent Caucasian, 7 per cent African American, 26 per cent Asian, and 8 per cent Latino. The average grade on any exam in this course was a C+, suggesting that this was a course in which many participants experienced difficulty or setbacks.

For the smaller samples, we tested to ensure that the participants were entirely representative of the larger sample and that no systematic attrition had occurred. Thus, although attendance (and hence participation in the study) varied over the waves of the study, no significant differences among samples at the different time points were found in terms of gender, ethnicity, goal endorsement, or grades.

Procedure
General Chemistry is a lecture course that is structured around three mid-terms and a final exam. Data were collected from participants at four points during the semester: twice two to three weeks before the first mid-term, once immediately after the first mid-term, and again two weeks before the final exam. Data were collected in the last 15–20 minutes of class or recitation. The measures were presented (along with other measures in a packet of questionnaires) in the following sequence:

Session 1 (2–3 weeks before first mid-term):
    goal items, demographic information
Session 2 (1 week after Session 1): intrinsic
    motivation, perception of chemistry ability
Session 3 (after first mid-term): general study
    strategies (from Elliot et al., 1999)
Session 4 (before final exam): intrinsic
    motivation

Consistent with the results of Study 4, we predicted that learning goals would be positively related to intrinsic motivation and grades (despite the lack of the influence of learning goals on performance found in previous studies in what may have been less academically strenuous or personally relevant contexts). We expected ability goals to be associated with lower performance after multiple setbacks, as suggested by Dweck and Leggett (1988), but not necessarily with lower performance overall. In fact, we expected that students who were doing well in the course might experience a 'boost' from holding strong ability goals.

Results

Perceived Ability

If different types of goals are systematically related to different levels of perceived ability, then it is possible that the effects of goals obtained in this study are simply due to this confounding factor. To rule out this explanation, perceived level of ability in chemistry was measured at the beginning of the course (one item: 'Compared to other students in this course, please rate your ability in chemistry' on a 10-point scale ranging from *top 10 per cent to lower 10 per cent*). Perception of ability in chemistry was related to overall course grade ($r = 0.27$, $p < .01$). It was also related to intrinsic motivation at the beginning ($r = 0.26$, $p < .01$) and at the end ($r = 0.31$, $p < .05$) of the course.

Correlations between perceived ability in chemistry and goal type revealed that normative goals were significantly positively related to perceived ability ($r = 0.38$, $p < .001$). In other words, people with normative goals tended to believe that their ability was high relative to others. This could help account for the resilience (or, better put, lack of negative consequences) associated with normative goals in Study 4. Outcome goals were also positively related to perceived ability ($r = 0.21$, $p < .05$), whereas learning and ability goals were unrelated to perceptions of chemistry ability.

Intrinsic Motivation

In a set of linear regressions, we looked at the relationship between goal type and intrinsic motivation, measured by enjoyment of and interest in the course (two items, $\alpha = 0.88$). These data were collected at the beginning of the course and again before the final exam. The regressions controlled for perceived ability (though an essentially identical pattern emerged when perceived ability was not included in the analysis) and for the effects of each of the other three goal indexes. We also included gender in our initial analyses, but gender did not predict intrinsic motivation and was dropped from subsequent analyses predicting intrinsic motivation.

In this highly difficult course, learning goals predicted higher intrinsic motivation at the beginning ($\beta = 0.23$), $t(128) = 2.34$, $p < .05$, and at the end ($\beta = 0.22$), $t(78) = 2.02$, $p < .05$, of the course. This is consistent with the findings of Elliot, Harackiewicz, and their colleagues (Elliot & Church, 1997; Elliot & McGregor, 1998; Harackiewicz & Elliot, 1998) that learning goals positively predict intrinsic motivation. There were no other significant predictors of intrinsic motivation.

Grades

We looked at the relationship between each goal type and students' total grades, controlling for Scholastic Aptitude Test (SAT) score, perceived ability in chemistry, number of prior courses in chemistry, and gender, as well as the effects of other goal indexes. Gender predicted total grade ($\beta = -0.19$), $t(126) = -3.03$, $p < .01$, such that men tended to have higher grades than women. In addition, we looked at the extent to which each goal type predicted improvement from Exam 1 to the final exam, controlling for performance on Exam 1 (the interaction of each goal with performance on Exam 1 was also included as a predictor).

Total Course Grade

Consistent with the pattern of effort attribution and mastery-oriented coping associated with learning goals in Study 4, learning goals positively predicted course grade ($\beta = 0.20$), $t(120) = 2.42$, $p < .05$. No other goals were significant predictors of course grade. The fact that learning goals emerged as a significant predictor of performance supplements the findings of Elliot, Harackiewicz, and their colleagues (e.g., Elliot & Church, 1997; Harackiewicz et al., 1997), who have suggested that performance goals, and not learning goals, predict course performance. This result could imply that when a course involves sustained challenge, learning goals do positively affect course performance.

Improvement in Grade from Exam 1 to Final Exam

Learning goals also significantly predicted grade improvement ($\beta = 0.25$), $t(122) = 2.94$, $p < .01$, and were the only goals to do so.

Final Exam Grade

Earlier, we had predicted that ability goals would have a negative effect on performance for those students who had experienced prolonged setbacks. To address this question, we looked at how goals predicted performance on the final exam for those students who had performed poorly throughout the semester. We simultaneously regressed each goal type, the average of students' Exam 1, 2, and 3 grades (our index of past performance), and the interaction of goal type with average exam grades, onto final exam grades. We predicted a significant interaction for ability goals, such that students who had done poorly throughout the semester (i.e., those with low average exam grades) would suffer for holding strong ability goals, whereas those who had done well throughout the semester might receive a boost on the final.

As predicted, there was a significant interaction between ability goals and average grade on Exams 1, 2, and 3 ($\beta = 0.52$), $t(71) = 2.23$, $p < .05$. Figure 9.1 illustrates this effect. We have plotted data for participants who were either one standard deviation above or below the mean endorsement of ability goals (see Jaccard, Turrisi, & Wan, 1990). Participants were further separated into high- and low-course performance groups (based on a median split of performance on exams prior to final). As shown, participants with low pre-final grades score lower on the final exam if they are high rather than low in ability goals. In contrast, participants with higher pre-final grades earn better scores on the final exam if they are high rather than low in ability goals. This finding suggests that when setbacks are repeated, ability goals predict poor performance, but may indeed provide a boost when an individual is doing well (see Elliott & Dweck, 1988).

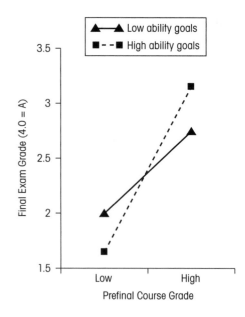

Figure 9.1 Final exam grade predicted by past performance and ability goals.

Study Strategies

To further understand the differences we found in performance, we looked at three study strategies (deep processing, surface processing, and disorganized processing) that were adapted from a scale used by Elliot et al. (1999) and were assessed immediately after students took the first exam. The tendency to engage in deep processing was significantly correlated with grade in the course ($r = 0.29$, $p < .01$). Disorganized processing was negatively related to course grade ($r = -0.36$, $p < .001$). Surface processing was unrelated to course grade ($r = 0.08$, ns).

Outcome goals predicted surface processing of course material ($r = 0.29$, $p < .01$), and learning goals predicted deeper processing of course material ($r = 0.31$, $p < .01$). In contrast, normative goals were negatively related to deep processing ($r = -0.21$, $p < .05$), suggesting that one drawback associated with a competitive goal might be the absence of deep analysis of issues or material.

Table 9.2 **Summary of Learning and Ability Goal Effects from Studies 4 and 5**

Goal	Study 4	Study 5
Learning	No decrease in intrinsic motivation	Higher intrinsic motivation at beginning *and* end
	Less time and effort withdrawal	of course
	Effort attributions	Higher grades
	Planning	Greater improvement over time
	Seeking positive reinterpretation and growth	Deeper processing
Ability	Lower intrinsic motivation	Lower grades after repeated poor performance
	Loss of self-worth	Higher grades after repeated good performance
	Low ability attributions	
	Time and effort withdrawal	
	Rumination	

Mediational Analyses for Learning Goal Effects on Course Grade

The significant correlation between learning goals and deep processing ($r = 0.31$), as well as the correlation between deep processing and course grade ($r = 0.29$), suggested processing style as a possible mediator of the effect of learning goals on course grade. Consistent with this hypothesis, the relationship between learning goals and course grade (controlling as we had earlier for SAT score, perceived ability in chemistry, past chemistry course experience, and gender), when controlling for extent of deep processing, is not significant ($\beta = -0.06$, *ns*), whereas deep processing remains a significant predictor of course grade ($\beta = 0.43$, $p < .05$; see Table 9.2 and Figure 9.2).

General Discussion

Items measuring different types of performance and learning goals were created and used in five studies to help shed light on several important, unresolved issues in current achievement goal research. Studies 1–3 yielded evidence for four types of goals: learning goals, outcome goals (wanting to do well), ability-linked performance goals, and normative performance goals. Individuals' responses in these three preliminary studies and two more comprehensive studies suggested

answers to a number of the fundamental questions posed in the literature.

First, are there different types of learning goals? What is the relationship of learning goals to intrinsic motivation and performance? We looked at two types of learning goals: striving to learn and develop versus seeking to master challenges. These two goals were highly correlated and loaded together in two principal-components analyses, so the items were combined into a single learning goal measure. Although we did not find evidence in our studies for separating these two types of learning goals, they may still differ importantly from the 'task goals' found in past research that are

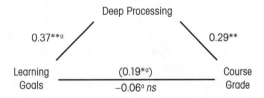

Figure 9.2 **Processing style mediates the effects of learning goals on course grade.**

Values are standardized regression coefficients.
[a]Standardized regression coefficient controlling for Scholastic Aptitude Test, perceived chemistry ability, past chemistry course experience, and gender.
*$p < 0.05$. **$p < 0.01$.

often operationalized in ways that contain neither striving to learn nor challenge-seeking.

Studies 4 and 5 provided evidence for the positive effects of learning goals on both intrinsic motivation and performance, consistent with the early research on achievement goals (e.g., Ames, 1992; Ames & Archer, 1988; Butler, 1987; Dweck & Leggett, 1988; Elliott & Dweck, 1988; Meece et al., 1988; Nicholls, 1984). Individuals who endorse learning goals should be more likely to see negative outcomes as information about ways to improve the learning process, rather than as indicators of stable low ability. As expected, in response to a major hypothetical failure (Study 4), learning goals predicted a wide range of positive, mastery-oriented indicators—including sustained intrinsic motivation, planning, and persistence. Participants with strong learning goals also reported a history of having used more mastery-oriented coping methods (e.g., active coping, planning) in response to past setbacks.

In Study 5, in an important and difficult college course, learning goals predicted better processing of course material, higher intrinsic motivation, higher grades, and greater improvement over time. Further analysis suggested that the relationship between learning goals and course grades was mediated by the tendency to engage in deeper processing of course material. The impact of learning goals on performance may be seen chiefly when a high degree of challenge is present, when a task is personally important, or when the processing of complex, difficult material is necessary. A potentially important topic for future research is the role that these factors play in the presence or absence of learning-goal effects on performance.

Turning to other questions posed earlier: Is wanting to do well different from wanting to prove your ability? When might performance goals predict vulnerability, and when might they prove beneficial to intrinsic motivation and/or performance? Individuals who endorse ability goals (i.e., seek to validate their ability) should be more likely to see negative outcomes as indicative of a lack of ability. Consistent with this prediction, ability goals were associated with common indexes of helplessness after a significant hypothetical failure in Study 4. These goals predicted attributions to low ability, loss of self-worth, rumination about the setback, and loss of intrinsic motivation. In Study 5, consistent with the results of Study 4, after multiple setbacks, ability goals predicted lower grades. Thus, ability goals tend to predict a pattern of negative affect and cognition, as well as poorer subsequent performance, after a significant setback or a series of setbacks. These findings are also consistent with the early work on achievement goals (Ames & Archer, 1988; Butler, 1993; Elliott & Dweck, 1988; Jagacinski & Nicholls, 1987; Meece et al., 1988; see also Midgley, Kaplan, & Middleton, 2001). However, ability goals do not appear to have negative effects on performance when one is still 'in the running' (i.e., when success is still possible), or when one is doing well, and may in these cases sometimes even boost performance because so much is on the line.

Why do the negative effects of ability goals occur? Dweck and Leggett (1988) suggested several potential cognitive and affective mechanisms of debilitation for individuals who hold ability goals in the face of difficulty. These include the loss of belief in the efficacy of effort (i.e., 'My ability is so low, no amount of effort could help me'), defensive withdrawal of effort (either as a form of self-handicapping or as a response to the belief that the need to put in effort confirms that one has low ability), and interference of negative affect with concentration or test performance. Another possibility is that students with ability goals may withdraw effort strategically when they are doing poorly to redirect the resources to courses where they have a better chance at getting a good grade. Although these data do not test specifically for this possibility, the pattern of negative attributions, rumination, and loss of self-worth associated with ability goals suggest that withdrawal is not a solely cool-headed strategic process.

Outcome goals had surprisingly few effects. Although correlated with many key outcomes, these effects were almost always due to the association of outcome goals with either learning goals (e.g., for active coping and effort attributions) or ability goals (e.g., for loss of self-worth and rumination). These effects did not survive simultaneous regression analyses that controlled for the influence of learning, ability, and normative goals. Taken together, these results suggest that those researchers interested in studying the unique effects of performance goals would do better not to operationalize them this way, as outcome goals (wanting to do well) can clearly be as much a part of a learning framework as a performance framework. In fact, doing well can be a means of assessing the acquisition and mastery of new skills and knowledge or of demonstrating ability.

Finally, *do* normative and non-normative performance goals produce different effects? Unlike (non-normative) ability goals, normative performance goals did not predict any of the affective, cognitive, or behavioural variables measured in Study 4, with the exception of the tendency on the COPE scale (Carver et al., 1989) to report engaging in denial and behavioural disengagement after experiencing an academic setback. In other words, wanting to outperform others might lead you to be reluctant to perceive your performance as a failure. In Study 5, normative goals, unlike ability goals, did not predict vulnerable performance, and in fact, were associated with higher levels of perceived ability. As mentioned earlier, the absence of a relationship between competitive goals and helplessness is worth noting, in that those researchers who have most consistently found that performance goals do not negatively influence intrinsic

motivation and performance have used a normative definition of performance goal (e.g., Elliot & Church, 1997). Further research is warranted to explore the roles that perceived ability and denial may play in this protective function. Moreover, it is striking that although deep processing mediates the beneficial effects of learning goals on grades, the negative relationship between normative goals and deep processing did not seem to predict poorer grades. If the lower level of deep processing was not a hindrance in this setting, it is very likely that competitive zeal could have positive effects in the many settings in which deep processing is not required (Kanfer & Ackerman, 2000). Because ability performance goals and normative performance goals appear to behave so differently, it would seem important for researchers to include both types of performance goals in future studies. In this way, we could continue to gain knowledge about when, why, and for whom each has costs and benefits.

. . .

In conclusion, we have found evidence to suggest that a careful examination of different types of performance and learning goals can indeed begin to clarify current controversies in the field. These studies have shown that learning goals do exert a positive influence on both intrinsic motivation and performance when individuals encounter prolonged challenge or setbacks. In addition, although performance goals that are focused on validating ability can have beneficial effects on performance when individuals are meeting with success, these same goals can predict impaired motivation and performance after setbacks.

Discussion Questions

1. When is a performance goal beneficial for performance and when does it hurt? How is simply wanting to do well different from wanting to prove your ability?
2. Grant and Dweck suggest different ways of distinguishing between different types of performance goals than Elliot (included in this Unit). In what ways do their conceptualizations differ?

10. The Hierarchical Model of Approach-Avoidance Motivation

Andrew J. Elliot

□ ■ □

Editor's Introduction

At first glance, the statement 'people approach pleasure and avoid pain' may seem self-evident and not particularly insightful. It is, in fact, the gateway to a complex and nuanced literature on the nature of human action. Over the past 15 years or so, Andrew Elliot and his colleagues have been reinvigorating the approach-avoidance concept in mainstream social psychological research. In particular, they have demonstrated that the same goal may be mentally represented in either an 'approach' or 'avoidance' manner, with profound implications for the individual's motivational striving.

Consider, for example, the classic distinction between 'performance' and 'learning' goals (e.g., Ames, 1984; Dweck, 1986; Maehr, 1984; Nicholls, 1984). While a good deal of evidence has accrued indicating that, in general, people with learning goals tend to set higher levels of aspiration and respond more adaptively to setbacks, Elliot and colleagues have argued that even more of the variability in the data might be accounted for by considering a 2 × 2 framework: performance-learning × approach-avoidance. This framework generates the novel hypothesis that performance-approach goals will not be the same as performance-avoidance goals; striving to demonstrate one's competence is a qualitatively different psychological experience from striving to *avoid* demonstrating one's incompetence.

Several studies have provided evidence for this idea (Elliot, 1994, 1997; Elliot & Church, 1997; Elliot & Harackiewicz, 1996). For example, Elliot and Church (1997) found that students with performance-avoidance goals tended to base their classroom efforts on a fear of failure, while those with performance-approach goals were oriented to both achievement and fear of failure equally. More importantly, performance-approach goals led to higher marks than performance-avoidance goals. (See Grant & Dweck's article in this Unit for a different take on these ideas.)

In the present 2006 article, Elliot attempts to synthesize several perennial motivational constructs into one framework. The Atkinson/ McClelland notion of 'motives' is seen as generally operating at the level of long-standing individual differences; some people's personalities are more oriented toward approaching success while others' are more oriented toward avoiding failure. At a lower level, however, these personality predispositions may activate either performance or learning goals and either approach or avoidance versions of these goals. Thus, Elliot's model has more flexibility than the Atkinson/McClelland approach and can account for the fact that most people are perfectly capable of adopting either performance-approach or performance-avoidance goals at any given moment.

Note that other researchers have developed the approach-avoidance idea in different directions. For example, Cacioppo and colleagues (e.g., Cacioppo & Berntson, 1994) have compellingly argued that approach-avoidance should not be considered a single dimension but two separate, largely independent dimensions. That is, when people evaluate something they simultaneously ask (a) 'Is this something to approach?' *and* (b) 'Is this something to avoid?' This means that certain objects may induce distinct forms of conflict;

something that is both high in approach and high in avoidance induces ambivalence as the individual is pulled in opposite directions. But something that is both low in approach and low in avoidance induces indifference. These two experiences are clearly quite different from each other. What implications might this distinction have on an individual's motivation?

□ ■ □

The approach-avoidance distinction is not new in analyses of motivation and behaviour. On the contrary, this distinction may be considered one of the oldest ideas in the history of psychological thinking about organisms. What is new is the depth and sophistication with which the approach-avoidance distinction is being used to explain and predict motivated behaviour. In the following, I provide a brief overview of this approach-avoidance distinction, as well as a brief overview of a contemporary model of motivation in which this distinction plays an integral role—the hierarchical model of approach-avoidance motivation.

The Approach-Avoidance Distinction

History

Scholars have made use of the approach-avoidance distinction for over 2000 years. It first appeared in the writing of the ancient Greek philosopher Democritus (460–370 BCE) who articulated an ethical hedonism in which the immediate pursuit of pleasure and avoidance of pain were prescribed as the guide for human action (see also the writings of Epicurus [342–270 BCE] and Socrates's pupil Aristippus [435–356 BCE]). The eighteenth century British philosopher Jeremy Bentham was the first to postulate a psychological hedonism that moved beyond a prescription of how we ought to behave to a description of how we actually do behave. This principle is directly stated in what is one of Bentham's most oft-quoted propositions: 'Nature has placed mankind under the governance of two sovereign masters, pain and pleasure. It is for them alone to point out what we ought to do, as well as to determine what we shall do' (Bentham, 1779/1879, p. 1).

Within the field of scientific psychology, the approach-avoidance distinction was utilized from the very beginning. William James (1890), in his classic *Principles of Psychology* (vol. 2), for example, considered pleasure and pain to be 'springs of action', noting that pleasure is a 'tremendous reinforcer' of behaviour and pain a 'tremendous inhibitor' of behaviour (pp. 549–559). Likewise, Freud (1915) construed the procurement of pleasure and the avoidance of pain (i.e., unpleasure) as the basic motivational impetus underlying psychodynamic activity. Indeed, many other prominent contributors to psychological theory from the time of James and Freud through the 1960s also made central use of the approach-avoidance distinction (see Elliot, 1999; Elliot & Covington, 2001; for reviews).

In the 1970s through the 1980s, cognitive and social-cognitive theorists drew a sharp distinction between cognition and motivation, and sought alternative, non-affective explanations for motivational accounts of behaviour. In this context, the approach-avoidance distinction was still utilized in theorizing to some degree, but in a much more limited way than in years past. It was with the acknowledgement in the 1990s that cognition and motivation are deeply intertwined, and need not be viewed as conceptual competitors, that motivational considerations in general, and the approach-avoidance distinction specifically, returned to prominence.

This return to prominence is noteworthy, because use of the approach-avoidance distinction in the contemporary scene would appear to differ from prior use in two important ways. First, until recently, the approach-avoidance distinction had been widely utilized and applied without taking a step back to explicitly define and articulate the nature of approach and avoidance motivation per se. Thus, philosophers, theorists, and researchers over the years have proffered approach- and avoidance-relevant ideas and constructs, and have even debated the sufficiency of hedonism as an explanatory principle, but rarely have they taken a step back to clearly explicate the conceptual space represented by approach and avoidance motivation. Recent work has directly attended to this definitional issue (see Elliot & Covington, 2001; Elliot & Mapes, 2005). Second, until recently, the approach-avoidance distinction has been applied to isolated situations and constructs without broader consideration of how this distinction might be applied as a general organizer of motivation and action. In essence, the approach-avoidance distinction has moved from the ground to the figure, such that this distinction is now being considered as fundamental and basic in many motivational analyses (see Cacioppo & Bernston, 1994; Carver & Scheier, 1998; Elliot & Church, 1997; Higgins, 1997).

Definition

Approach motivation may be defined as the energization of behaviour by, or the direction of behaviour toward, positive stimuli (objects, events, possibilities), whereas avoidance motivation may be defined as the energization of behaviour by, or the direction of behaviour away from, negative stimuli (objects, events, possibilities). Five aspects of this definition are considered further in the following.

First, being a motivational distinction, approach-avoidance encompasses both the *energization* and *direction* of behaviour. Energization refers to the initial instigation or 'spring to action' (James, 1890/1950, vol. 2, p. 555) that orients the organism in a general way (Elliot, 1997). This use of energization does not presume that the organism is passive until instigated to action; on the contrary,

the organism is viewed as perpetually active, with instigation functionally representing a shift from one form of orienting to another (Atkinson & Birch, 1970). Direction herein refers to the guiding or channelling of behaviour in a precise way.

Second, inherent in the approach-avoidance distinction is the concept of physical or psychological movement. Positively evaluated stimuli are inherently associated with an approach orientation to bring or keep the stimuli close to the organism (literally or figuratively), whereas negatively evaluated stimuli are inherently associated with an avoidance orientation to push or keep the stimuli away from the organism (literally or figuratively). Although positively and negatively evaluated stimuli produce (at minimum) a physiological and somatic preparedness for physical movement toward and away from the stimuli, respectively (Arnold, 1960; Corwin, 1921), this preparedness may or may not be translated directly into overt behaviour.

Third, implicit in the aforementioned point is the notion that movement toward a positive stimulus and movement away from a negative stimulus each have two distinguishable forms. 'Movement toward' can represent getting something positive that is currently absent or it can represent keeping something positive that is currently present (functionally, continuing toward). Likewise, 'movement away' can represent keeping away from something negative that is currently absent (functionally, continuing away from) or it can represent getting away from something negative that is currently present. In other words, the initial presence/absence of a stimulus may be crossed with its valence to discern two different types of approach and avoidance motivation (for a conceptual parallel, see Herzberg, 1966). Thus, approach motivation not only encompasses promoting new positive situations, but also maintaining and sustaining existing positive situations, and avoidance motivation not only encompasses preventing new negative situations, but also escaping from and rectifying existing negative situations.

Fourth, positive/negative valence is conceptualized as the core evaluative dimension of approach-avoidance motivation. 'Positive' and 'negative' are presumed to take on somewhat different meanings in different contexts, including beneficial/harmful, liked/disliked, and desirable/undesirable. Research indicates that these dimensions are conceptually and empirically comparable to a high degree, although some empirical work suggests that they may be separable in certain instances (Berridge, 1999). At present, given their substantial comparability, it seems best to construe beneficial/harmful, liked/disliked, and desirable/undesirable as functionally equivalent dimensions that may be subsumed under the positive/negative rubric (i.e., in essence, the three dimensions are conceptualized as indicators of a positive/negative latent variable). Nevertheless, it is possible that subsequent research will establish a need to distinguish among these dimensions in defining the approach-avoidance distinction.

Fifth, 'stimuli' as used herein may represent concrete, observable objects/events/possibilities, or they may represent abstract, internally generated representations of objects/events/possibilities. Furthermore, 'stimuli' is meant to connote an essentially limitless, idiographic array of focal endpoints (somewhat obliquely characterized as 'objects/events/possibilities').

The Hierarchical Model of Approach-Avoidance Motivation

In the following, I provide an overview of the hierarchical model of approach-avoidance motivation. This overview will be brief; those interested in further details may refer to the following articles: Elliot (1997); Elliot and Church (1997); Elliot, Gable, and Mapes (2006); Elliot and Thrash (2001); and Elliot and Thrash (2002).

A core premise of the hierarchical model is that the approach-avoidance distinction is fundamental and basic to motivation, so much so that it may be used as a conceptual lens through which to view the structure and function of self-regulation. There is much evidence to support the fundamental nature of approach-avoidance motivation. Approach-avoidance processes are present across phyla. They may be seen in single-cell organisms, crustaceans, fish, snakes, birds, dogs, monkeys, and, of course, human beings (see Elliot & Covington, 2001, for a review). Approach and avoidance processes are absolutely essential for successful adaption to the environment. Tooby and Cosmides (1990) characterize approach-avoidance behavioural decisions as the most critical adaptive judgments that organisms have had to make in the evolutionary past, and it is likely that this adaptive function is the reason that approach-avoidance process are witnessed across animate forms of life (Schneirla, 1959). Another indicator of the fundamental nature of approach-avoidance motivation is the immediacy and ubiquity of approach-avoidance evaluative judgments in human functioning. Research indicates that humans automatically evaluate most, if not all, encountered stimuli on a positive/negative dimension (Bargh, 1997; Osgood, Suci, & Tannenbaum, 1957), and that these evaluations instantaneously evoke approach and avoidance behavioural predispositions (Corwin, 1921; Lewin, 1935).

Approach-avoidance motivation is represented in many different and partially independent ways throughout the human body (Cacioppo & Bernston, 1994; Stellar & Stellar, 1985). Humanity's lengthy evolutionary history appears to have resulted in multiple levels of valence-based evaluative mechanisms, ranging from rudimentary spinal cord reflexes (Sherington, 1906) to subcortical affective computions (LeDoux, 1995; Shizgal, 1999) to our vaunted cortical processes (Davidson, 1993; Lang, 1995). These multiple approach-avoidance processes operate in tandem and in sequence, and produce the urges, affects, motor responses, cognitive representations, and commitments that comprise the contents of our daily experience and regulation.

Given the complex, multiply determined nature of approach-avoidance motivation, any theoretical framework that seeks to account for it must by necessity be selective. In the hierarchical model, the goal construct has been selected as the conceptual centrepiece. A goal is a cognitive representation of a future object that one is committed to approach or avoid (Elliot & Fryer, 2008). This construct holds a central place in the hierarchical model because goal-directedness appears to be a cardinal characteristic of human behaviour (McDougal, 1908), and it is difficult to envision a satisfactory account of motivated action that excludes this feature. Furthermore, goals occupy a unique place in self-regulation in that they commonly represent the final component of the motivational process; stated otherwise, goals are often the proximal predictors of behaviour. As such, goals have tremendous utility in not only explaining, but also predicting behaviour.

Goals are posited to serve a directional function in motivation. That is, goals focus on a specific, cognitively represented end point, and serve to guide the individual's behaviour toward or away from that end point. Goals are conscious, intentional commitments, although once in place in the cognitive system, they may be activated and may operate in automatic, non-conscious fashion (Bargh & Ferguson, 2000). Importantly, the definition of goal and the functional role imparted to goals in the hierarchical model is much narrower than in many other conceptualizations. Many theorists define the goal construct broadly in terms of any purpose or reason for action, and construe goals as serving both energizational and directional functions. Unfortunately, placing such a heavy burden on the goal construct seems to result in a lack of conceptual precision and explanatory clarity (see Elliot & Fryer, 2008, for a review). From the standpoint of the hierarchical model, a more restricted definition of and role for the goal construct is critical, in that it not only affords clarity with regard to the nature of goals, but also affords clarity with regard to how goals fit in the overall motivational process.

In the hierarchical model, goals are not sufficient to account for motivated behaviour; it is also necessary to consider the motivation underlying goals. This motivation comes from many different sources and may be represented in many different ways, but for the present purposes I will focus primarily on two important sources: motives and temperaments. A motive is an affectively based tendency that orients individuals toward domain-specific positive or negative stimuli (McClelland, 1985). Most of daily life transpires in achievement contexts and/or social contexts, and socialization histories within these contexts produce recurrent approach and avoidance tendencies with regard to achievement (i.e., the need for achievement and fear of failure) and affiliation (i.e., the need for affiliation and fear of rejection). A temperament is a general neurobiological sensitivity to positive (approach temperament) or negative (avoidance temperament) stimuli that is rooted in biological processes across the neuraxis (Elliot & Thrash, 2002). Temperaments produce immediate affective, cognitive, and behavioural inclinations in response to encountered or imagined stimuli, and operate in a rather rigid, reactive manner across domains and situations.

Although quite different constructs, motives and temperaments are similar in that they both produce broad motivational tendencies that function as energizers of approach and avoidance behaviour. Motives and temperaments orient individuals (motives to domain-specific positive or negative stimuli; temperaments to domain-general positive or negative stimuli), but they do not provide precise guidance for how general desires or concerns may be approached or avoided. Instead, goals serve this function. That is, goals are commonly recruited to serve underlying motive- or temperament-based motivation by strategically guiding it toward concrete aims that address the underlying desire or concern. Motives and temperaments can and sometimes do lead directly to behaviour, but such regulation can often appear rigid and/or unfocused (Elliot, McGregor, & Thrash, 2002). Goals provide precise direction that can lead to more effective and efficient regulation.

Motives and temperaments are discussed herein for illustrative purposes, but there are many other sources of motivation that underlie goals as well. Such sources include self-conceptions, implicit theories, attachment schemas, environmental affordances and impedances, cultural values and norms, and so on; the ultimate underlying source of much human motivation is likely the establishment and maintenance of meaning. The study of motivation entails identifying and specifying the most important antecedents of goal adoption, and examining the specific links between these underlying sources of motivation and the goals they presumably serve. In short, a full account of motivation will attend to both direction (goal) and energization (the motivation underlying the goal).

When goals are viewed as conceptually separate from, but hierarchically linked to, general sources of motivation such as temperaments and motives, the flexibility of self-regulation comes into bold relief. That is, it becomes easy to see that the same goal can be used in the service of many different underlying motivations, and the same motivation can be channelled through many different types of goals. Indeed, intriguing possibilities abound with regard to combinations of goals and underlying motivations. For example, approach goals may be adopted in the service of underlying avoidance motivation, as when performance-approach goals are adopted in the service of fear failure (Elliot & Church, 1997). This hierarchical combination of approach and avoidance (i.e., approaching in order to avoid) allows individuals with aversive dispositional tendencies to cope with them in an adaptive manner by channelling them toward appetitive possibilities. Another example is that goals in one domain can emerge from motivational desires or concerns in another domain, as when individuals who are concerned about rejection by close others adopt performance-avoidance goals in achievement contexts (Elliot & Reis, 2003; Elliot & Thrash, 2004). This dynamic commingling of the affiliation and achievement domains is undoubtedly commonplace, and can only be detected when

multiple levels of motivation are considered. These examples highlight both the flexibility afforded by goal adoption and the added insight provided by a hierarchical analysis of approach and avoidance processes.

A primary assumption of the hierarchical model is that conceptually, goals and the underlying motivations they serve must be construed as separate entities. Nevertheless, it is also posited that in the actual process of regulation, goals and underlying motivations remain closely intertwined (see also Lewin, 1935), and that these underlying motivations exert an influence throughout the process of goal pursuit. A third construct is posited to account for this intertwining of goals and their underlying motivations, specifically 'goal complex' (Elliot & Thrash, 2001; Thrash & Elliot, 2001; for conceptual parallels, see Allport, 1937; Murray, 1938). A goal complex is construed as a context-specific regulatory construct that is formed upon adoption of a goal, and is represented in memory until the goal and/or underlying motivational desire/concern is achieved, altered, or abandoned. This goal complex is presumed to include information regarding both the goal and the underlying reason that it is being pursued. Often the motivation underlying a goal is not consciously accessible and, therefore, cannot be explicated; when the motivation underlying the goal is accessible, the goal complex may be characterized in the propositional form: '[goal] IN ORDER TO [underlying reason].' Different goal complexes are posited to lead to different processes and outcomes, even when the goal is the same. Stated differently, goal pursuit feels different and has different effects when it is impelled by different underlying motivations.

Both approach and avoidance motivation are part of our evolutionary heritage, and we certainly cannot survive, either physically or psychologically, without both types of motivation. Certain tasks in negotiating the environment and our social world require avoidance motivation, and avoidance motivation is undoubtedly adaptive in some instances. For example, it is imperative that our perceptual system be perpetually vigilant for physical danger or it is likely that our lifespan would be greatly truncated; likewise, tasks and challenges such as air traffic controlling and ceasing to smoke would seem to require avoidance regulation. Nevertheless, it is important to highlight that by its very nature, avoidance motivation is aversive and is greatly overused in contemporary life (that is, used in instances where it is not necessary). As such, in the hierarchical model, it is the negative implications of avoidance motivation that are typically highlighted.

Avoidance motivation entails using a negative object as the hub of regulatory activity. As such, avoidance motivation is experienced as stressful, and even when effective, can take a toll on enjoyment and, eventually, well-being (Elliot & Sheldon, 1997; 1998). For example, even if avoidance regulation allows air traffic controllers to effectively keep airplanes from crashing into each other, the constant monitoring of negative possibilities is draining; accordingly, it is not surprising that this occupation has one of the highest turnover rates on record (Hopkin, 1995). Furthermore, avoidance motivation is limited in a structural sense, in that by its very nature it can only lead to the absence of a negative outcome (when effective) or the presence of a negative outcome (when ineffective). This may be contrasted with approach motivation, which uses a positive object as the hub of regulatory activity and, therefore, can lead to the presence of a positive outcome (when effective) or the absence of a positive outcome (when ineffective; see Mowrer, 1960, for a conceptual parallel). Thus, avoidance motivation is designed to facilitate surviving, whereas approach motivation is designed to facilitate thriving. Individuals often utilize survival mode even when danger is not imminent, thereby missing positive opportunities for development and growth. Importantly, the overutilization of avoidance motivation not only leads to missed opportunities, but it also, in self-fulfilling fashion, often produces the very negative outcomes that it is designed to avoid. For example, in achievement situations, performance-avoidance and mastery-avoidance goals produce worry and distraction that undermine performance and intrinsic motivation (Cury, Elliot, Da Fonseca, & Moller, 2006; Elliot & Harackiewicz, 1996).

Avoidance motivation is posited to be problematic at all levels of the hierarchy. In some respects, avoidance motivation would seem most pernicious at the higher, more general levels (e.g., temperament), because such levels exert a pervasive influence on behaviour. However, as discussed earlier, individuals can cope with higher-order avoidance motivation through the use of lower-order regulatory tools, such as approach goals that channel aversive energization in a positive direction. Avoidance motivation at the level of goals also seems quite inimical, given the role of goals as direct, proximal regulators of behaviour. What seems quite clear is that goal complexes comprised entirely of approach motivation would be optimal for functioning in most instances.

Closing Statement

As illustrated in the hierarchical model of approach-avoidance motivation, the approach-avoidance distinction is clearly of considerable conceptual and empirical utility in motivational analyses of behaviour. This approach-avoidance distinction may be applied to nearly any psychological construct, and doing so commonly yields a precision of knowledge that would not otherwise be attainable. That organisms are motivated in multifarious ways to approach the positive and avoid the negative may be construed as something of a psychological law, and in my experience, the deep, penetrating application of this law invariably yields much theoretical fruit. It is important to bear in mind, however, that as valuable as the approach-avoidance distinction is, other psychological distinctions are needed to fully understand motivated behaviour. In this sense, the approach-avoidance distinction may be considered a necessary, but not sufficient, component of a complete account of motivation.

Discussion Questions

1. How exactly do people make the computation of whether to approach or avoid a stimulus?
2. What are the different strategies people might use to approach pleasure and avoid pain?
    Compare Elliot's conceptualization of approach-avoidance with Higgins's notion of promotion
    prevention (see Unit 5)? What key differences do you notice?
3. Under what circumstances might people approach pain and avoid pleasure?

Unit Four Further Reading

A considerable literature has investigated the effect of people's self-esteem on their reactions to success and failure. For a good example of this, see

Brown, J.D., & Dutton, K.A. (1995). The thrill of victory, the complexity of defeat: Self-esteem and people's emotional reactions to success and failure. *Journal of Personality and Social Psychology, 68,* 712–22.

For recent research on variables that influence people's subjective calculations of expectancy and value in goal pursuit, see

Shah, J. & Higgins, E.T. (1997). Expectancy X value effects: Regulatory focus as determinant of magnitude *and* direction. *Journal of Personality and Social Psychology, 73,* 447–58.

Elliot is not the only researcher in recent years who has focused on approach and avoidance. Other related influential research has focused on the nature of approach and avoidance and their relationship to affect and evaluation. For example, see

Cacioppo, J.T., & Berntson, G.G. (1994). Relationship between attitudes and evaluative space: A critical review, with emphasis on the separability of positive and negative substrates. *Psychological Bulletin, 115,* 401–23.

Carver, C.S., & White, T.L. (1994). Behavioural inhibition, behavioural activation, and affective responses to impending reward and punishment: The BIS/BAS scales. *Journal of Personality and Social Psychology, 67,* 319–33.

Unit Five

Motivation's Effect on Cognition

The notion that our thought is systematically biased by our wishes and desires is highly intuitive. After all, it seems that for any televised political debate, supporters of both candidates overwhelmingly believe that *their* candidate clearly demolished the opposition. But do people really see what they want to see, believe what they want to believe, and remember what they want to remember? The answer, it turns out, is not so simple.

In a highly cited 1990 review article, Ziva Kunda spelled out her 'case for motivated reasoning'. The fact that there was a need for such a case to be made reveals the fraught history of the concept of motivation in social psychology. As early as in the 1940s and 1950s, Bruner and colleagues provided evidence that motivation affects basic perceptual processes (for a review, see Bruner, 1957). For example, Postman, Bruner, and McGinnies (1948) used a device called a tachistoscope to vary how long each word in a list was presented to participants. The words started out appearing for only very brief periods of time (a fraction of a second) so that they could not be consciously registered. The words were then presented for longer and longer periods until they became consciously visible. Postman et al. (1948) found that, from the list of words, participants were quicker to recognize words that related to their deeply held values (which had been assessed previously with a questionnaire) than words that did not relate to these values. Thus, participants appeared to have a lower detection threshold for stimuli that they cared for (*perceptual vigilance*). On the other side of the coin, McGinnies (1949) and others presented evidence that people exhibit *higher* detection thresholds for taboo words (*perceptual defence*).

These findings were subjected, however, to stinging attacks from those who argued that the effect of values on perception could be accounted for by non-motivational factors like frequency (Howes & Solomon, 1950; Howie, 1952). For example, a person with deeply held religious values is likely to be exposed frequently to religion-related words, and it is this increased exposure that lowers the detection threshold. Moreover, these researchers presented evidence that people are quicker in general to recognize words that appear more frequently in the English language. Partly as a consequence of these counterarguments, work on motivation's effect on cognition dwindled precipitously in the 1950s and 1960s.

In the 1970s, a version of this debate reappeared. When several researchers presented evidence that people exhibit motivated biases in the way they view themselves, other theorists again argued that although such phenomena may appear motivational in nature, they may be explained in purely non-motivational terms (e.g., Bem, 1967; Miller & M. Ross, 1975; Nisbett & L. Ross, 1980). For example, the self-serving bias—the tendency for most people to rate themselves as 'above average'—may not be due to the desire for self-enhancement as much as the fact that the undergraduates at elite institutions who typically serve as participants in such experiments *are* in many respects above average. Thus, participants' claims may not have been biased at all. The researchers who made this argument provided a valuable service to the field by exhorting researchers who claimed to uncover a motivational phenomenon to provide evidence that their phenomenon was truly motivational.

Kunda (1990) took up the challenge. Her paper articulated for the first time the ways in which particular links in the information-processing chain (e.g., memory, use of decision rules) may be systematically influenced by the desire to reach particular conclusions. In so doing, she helped to demystify the human capacity for *self-deception* by showing how similar biased processing is to non-biased processing. As you read her case for the motivated aspects of different phenomena, continually ask yourself if that result may be obtained through a non-motivated path as well.

One example of motivation's impact on basic cognitive processes can be seen in Tory Higgins's concept of regulatory focus. As Higgins describes in the 1997 article included in this Unit, people may approach tasks with a promotion focus or a prevention focus. A promotion focus refers to the motivational state of eagerness associated with self-regulation toward ideals and aspirations. In such a state, people are especially attuned to what Higgins terms 'gains versus non-gains'. In contrast, a prevention focus refers to a motivational state of vigilance associated with self-regulation toward duties and obligation. In such a state, people are especially attuned to 'losses versus non-losses'. Several studies have shown that basic cognitive processes are directly influenced by which state one is in. For example, being in a promotion focus causes people to have better memory for information related to gains or non-gains than information related to losses or non-losses (Tykocinski & Higgins, 1992). The reverse is true for prevention focus.

What are the implications of this? Consider the staggering amount of information potentially hitting our sensory system at any given time. To the extent that this barrage of stimulation is too much for the mind to handle, perception requires decisions: How does the mind decide what to 'land on' and what to 'fly over'? A variable that makes predictions about what sorts of objects in the stimulus array people will pick out is highly valuable. Higgins essentially argues that people pick out those aspects of the stimulus array that are most relevant to their pressing motivational focus.

11. The Case for Motivated Reasoning

Ziva Kunda, Princeton University

□ ■ □

Editor's Introduction

On the one hand, people are powerfully motivated to confirm what they wish to believe. But on the other hand, it is generally not feasible for people to go through life believing only what they want to believe, evidence be damned. Given these two seemingly irreconcilable forces, how is self-deception possible? How do people manage to know and not know something at the same time? These questions lie at the heart of the paradox of motivated cognition. On the one hand we seek desired conclusions, but on the other hand we have to be at least minimally open to undesired information or else risk living in delusion. How do people navigate this tension?

As Ziva Kunda notes in the present article, for a long time the very existence of motivated cognition was a matter of some controversy. Behavioural scientists from a range of theoretical perspectives argued—with considerable empirical backing—that many apparently motivated phenomena can in fact be reduced to non-motivated principles. Consider, for example, the 'Lake Woebegone Effect' whereby a majority of people claim themselves to be above average (which is, of course, impossible!). What at first may look like an obvious case of wishful thinking may actually have an alternative explanation: Most of the undergraduates who serve as participants in these types of studies tend to be talented, elite individuals who *have* historically scored above the mean on most of the tests they've ever taken. Thus, when asked, they might simply be reporting truthfully. Motivated biases need not be present at all.

To refute such claims, researchers like Kunda, Kruglanski, and Pyszczynski began in the 1980s to open up the 'black box' of motivated cognition and by documenting the steps people follow from wanting something to be true to believing it is true. By identifying and concretizing the processes involved in motivated cognition, one could begin to prove its existence.

According to Kunda, 'people motivated to arrive at a particular conclusion attempt to be rational and to construct a justification of their desired conclusion that would persuade a dispassionate observer.' In other words, rather than recklessly confirming all desired conclusions, people instead carefully build and manage their motivated cognition with an imagined audience in mind. As Kunda notes, 'They draw the desired conclusion only if they can muster up the evidence necessary to support it (cf. Darley & Gross, 1983). In other words, they maintain an 'illusion of objectivity' (Pyszczynski & Greenberg, 1987; cf. Kruglanski, 1980). That is, people engage in a subtle give-and-take with the evidence, maximizing the desired conclusions *within* the incontrovertible 'hard constraints' that may exist.

In this article, Kunda marshals a wide range of evidence from her own lab and the labs of others to suggest particular mechanisms through which motivated cognition occurs. These mechanisms include biases in memory, biases in the use of statistical knowledge, and biased accessing of conclusion-supporting beliefs. Kunda notes, however, that people deploy these mechanisms within the limits imposed by reality constraints. In so doing, people are able to maintain the illusion of objectivity.

□ ■ □

The notion that goals or motives affect reasoning has a long and controversial history in social psychology. The propositions that motives may affect perceptions (Erdelyi, 1974), attitudes (Festinger, 1957), and attributions (Heider, 1958) have been put forth by some psychologists and challenged by others. Although early researchers and theorists took it for granted that motivation may cause people to make self-serving attributions and permit them to believe what they want to believe because they want to believe it, this view, and the research used to uphold it, came under concentrated criticism in the 1970s. The major and most damaging criticism of the motivational view was that all research purported to demonstrate motivated reasoning could be reinterpreted in entirely cognitive, non-motivational terms (Miller & Ross, 1975; Nisbett & Ross, 1980). Thus, people could draw self-serving conclusions not because they wanted to but because these conclusions seemed more plausible, given their prior beliefs and expectancies. Because both cognitive and motivational accounts could be generated for any empirical study, some theorists argued that the hot versus cold cognition controversy could not be solved, at least in the attribution paradigm (Ross & Fletcher, 1985; Tetlock & Levi, 1982).

One reason for the persistence of this controversy lies in the failure of researchers to explore the mechanisms underlying motivated reasoning. Recently, several authors have attempted to rectify this neglect (Kruglanski & Freund, 1983; Kunda, 1987; Pyszczynski & Greenberg, 1987; Sorrentino & Higgins, 1986). All these authors share a view of motivation as having its effects through cognitive processes: People rely on cognitive processes and representations to arrive at their desired conclusions, but motivation plays a role in determining which of these will be used on a given occasion.

. . .

In this article I explore the possibility that motivation may affect reasoning through reliance on a biased set of cognitive processes: strategies for accessing, constructing, and evaluating beliefs. I review a large and diverse body of research that has been concerned directly or indirectly with this issue and argue that the proposed mechanisms can account for all of it. By *motivation* I mean any wish, desire, or preference that concerns the outcome of a given reasoning task, and I do not attempt to address the thorny issue of just how such motives are represented. The discussion is restricted to cases in which motivation can be construed as affecting the process of reasoning: forming impressions, determining one's beliefs and attitudes, evaluating evidence, and making decisions. Studies in which motivation was viewed as regulating behaviour and determining which people or information one would like to observe (e.g., Frey, 1986; Swann, 1983) are excluded unless the behavioural choices are viewed as indicative of biased reasoning.

The motivated reasoning phenomena under review fall into two major categories: those in which the motive is to arrive at an accurate conclusion, whatever it may be, and those in which the motive is to arrive at a particular, directional conclusion. The importance of this distinction has been stressed in the work of Kruglanski and his colleagues (Kruglanski, 1980; Kruglanski & Ajzen, 1983; Kruglanski & Klar, 1987; see also Chaiken, Liberman, & Eagly, 1989; Pyszczynski & Greenberg, 1987). The two categories are often discussed in the same breath because they are both indicative of motivated reasoning, but, as pointed out by Kruglanski and his colleagues, it is important to distinguish between them because there is no reason to believe that both involve the same kinds of mechanism. To foreshadow my conclusions, I argue that both kinds of goals affect reasoning by influencing the choice of beliefs and strategies applied to a given problem. But accuracy goals lead to the use of those beliefs and strategies that are considered most appropriate, whereas directional goals lead to the use of those that are considered most likely to yield the desired conclusion.

Reasoning Driven by Accuracy Goals

The work on accuracy-driven reasoning suggests that when people are motivated to be accurate, they expend more cognitive effort on issue-related reasoning, attend to relevant information more carefully, and process it more deeply, often using more complex rules. These ideas go back to Simon's (1957) notion of satisficing, according to which decision makers form aspirations as to how good an alternative they should find and terminate their search for alternatives as soon as they find one that meets that level. Stigler (1961) extended these ideas by pointing out that search strategies have costs that may be weighted against their utility. The implication is that people may focus not only on how good an outcome they desire but also, and sometimes predominantly, on how much cognitive effort they are willing to expend. In other words, people are aware of the effort-accuracy trade-off and select strategies by considering both their costs and their benefits (Beach & Mitchell, 1978; Payne, Bettman, & Johnson, 1988).

An experimental investigation by McAllister, Mitchell, and Beach (1979, Experiment 3) provides some support for these ideas. They manipulated subjects' motivation to be accurate by informing them that the target task was highly important or by leading them to expect to defend their judgments to their peers. Subjects motivated to be more accurate in these ways chose more complex and time-consuming decision-making strategies. But inasmuch as subjects were explicitly provided with lists of strategies to choose from and with details about the probability that each strategy would be accurate, it is not obvious that people motivated to be accurate will choose more complex strategies spontaneously, in the absence of such information. More interesting, from my perspective, are those studies in which subjects' spontaneous selection of cognitive strategies was examined. The researchers who did this also extended these ideas from decision making, construed as choosing among options, to the more general process of forming judgments and beliefs.

In these studies, accuracy goals are typically created by increasing the stakes involved in making a wrong judgment or in drawing the wrong conclusion, without increasing the attractiveness of any particular conclusion. The key strategy used to demonstrate that accuracy motives lead to more deep and careful cognitive processing involves showing that manipulations designed to increase accuracy motives lead to an elimination or reduction of cognitive biases. Thus Kruglanski and Freund (1983; Freund, Kruglanski, & Shpitzajzen, 1985) showed that subjects motivated to be accurate (because they expected to be evaluated, expected to justify their judgments, expected their judgments to be made public, or expected their evaluations to affect the evaluated person's life) showed less of a primacy effect in impression formation, less tendency to use ethnic stereotypes in their evaluations of essay quality, and less anchoring when making probability judgments. Similarly, Tetlock (1983) showed that subjects motivated to be accurate (because they expected to justify their beliefs to others) showed less of a primacy effect in their judgments of guilt in a simulated murder trial.

Although these findings may be due to deeper and more careful processing, they may also result merely from a tendency to make more conservative, less extreme judgments in the presence of accuracy goals. A study by Tetlock (1985) ruled out the latter possibility. Subjects motivated to be accurate (because they expected to justify their beliefs to others) were less susceptible to the fundamental attribution error. In comparison with other subjects, accuracy-motivated subjects made less extreme dispositional attributions about a target person when they knew that the target person had little choice in deciding whether to engage in the observed behaviour, but not when they knew that the target person had a high degree of choice.

Because the less extreme judgments occurred only in the low-choice condition, they appear to be due to careful processing rather than to undifferentiated conservatism. Other researchers (Pittman & D'Agostino, 1985) have also found that need for accuracy (resulting from control deprivation) reduced the magnitude of the fundamental attribution error. Similarly, Kassin and Hochreich (1977) found that need for accuracy (aroused by instructions indicating that the task reflected an important ability or was important to the experimenter) decreased the tendency to attribute briefly described behaviours to the person.

The underlying assumption in these studies is that many biases and errors result from hasty reasoning; therefore, elimination of these biases indicates more careful thinking. This interpretation is supported by the finding that such biases are exaggerated when subjects are required to make judgments under time pressure—that is, when they are forced to be hasty (Freund et al., 1985; Kruglanski & Freund, 1983).[1] There is some evidence that the deeper processing appears to be triggered by accuracy goals rather than by self-presentational pressures, because accuracy-promoting manipulations reduce biases only when they are delivered before subjects' exposure to information. When they are delivered after subjects view the information but before they make their judgments, such manipulations have no impact on judgment (Tetlock, 1983, 1985). Thus, the deeper processing results from accuracy motives that affect the initial encoding and processing of information.

More direct evidence that accuracy goals lead to more complex and elaborate reasoning comes from two studies in which the researchers attempted to examine thought processes directly, rather than infer them from their outcome, the judgment. Tetlock and Kim (1987) showed that subjects motivated to be accurate (because they expected to justify their beliefs to others) wrote more cognitively complex descriptions of persons whose responses to a personality test they had seen: They considered more alternatives and evaluated the

persons from more perspectives, and they drew more connections among characteristics. Partly as a result of this increased complexity of processing, subjects motivated to be accurate were in fact more accurate than others in predicting the persons' responses on additional personality measures and were less overconfident about the correctness of their predictions.[2]

. . .

In sum, the case for accuracy-motivated reasoning appears quite strong. In the above studies subjects had no reason to prefer one conclusion or outcome over another; their sole goal was to be accurate. The evidence that people process information more carefully under such circumstances is considerable and persuasive. The bulk of this evidence is indirect; the greater complexity of processing is inferred from the fact that the judgments tended to be more accurate and to reflect less reliance on biased strategies or cognitive shortcuts. Although some of these findings may be due to mere conservatism rather than to deeper processing, others may not. There also exists some more compelling, direct evidence that accuracy-motivated subjects use more complex strategies in their thinking. Taken together, the evidence is impressive in its diversity: Several different kinds of bias have been shown to be weakened in the presence of accuracy goals, and such findings have been obtained by different investigators working in diverse content areas and operationalizing the need for accuracy in a variety of different ways. It seems reasonable to conclude that people motivated to be accurate are more likely to access and use those rules and strategies for processing information that are deemed more appropriate.

One should not assume, however, that accuracy goals will always eliminate biases and improve reasoning. In several studies, incentives or admonitions to be accurate did not eliminate bias (Fischhoff, 1977; Kahneman & Tversky, 1972a; Lord, Lepper, & Preston, 1984; Tversky & Kahneman, 1973). For accuracy to reduce bias, it is crucial that subjects possess more appropriate reasoning strategies, view these as superior to other strategies, and be capable of accessing them at will. This is most probably not the case for the biases that have been resistant to accuracy manipulations: for example, biases resulting from using the availability heuristic and from the failure to use the law of large numbers in some situations, and the hindsight bias. One may even imagine that biases will sometimes be exacerbated and reasoning worsened in the presence of accuracy goals. This will occur if people erroneously believe faulty reasoning procedures to be best and are more likely to access these faulty procedures upon reflection. Indeed, it has been shown that subjects motivated to be accurate (because they expected to justify their judgments to others) were *more* susceptible than other subjects to the dilution effect—that is, were more likely to moderate their predictions about a target when given non-diagnostic information about that target—and this tendency appeared to have resulted from more complex processing of information (Tetlock & Boettger, 1989). Thus accuracy goals led to more complex processing, which in turn led to less rational judgment.

The notion that accuracy goals lead to more complex processing is compatible with and broader than Kruglanski and his colleagues' views on how accuracy goals affect reasoning (Kruglanski, 1980; Kruglanski & Ajzen, 1983). In their view, accuracy goals (or fear of invalidity, in their terminology) may delay the 'freezing' of the process of generating and evaluating hypotheses; that is, they may delay the arrival at a conclusion. This delay results from a tendency to entertain a greater number of alternative hypotheses and to consider more evidence. Such lengthier processing is consistent with my view, but my view is broader in that it allows for the possibility that, in addition to increasing the quantity of processing, accuracy goals may also affect its quality, in that they may lead directly to the use of more complex inferential procedures.

The research just reviewed did not address the issue of what impact accuracy goals will have when they are accompanied by directional goals—that is, when the person also wants to arrive at a particular conclusion. I turn next to an examination of the effects of directional goals on reasoning.

Reasoning Driven by Directional Goals

Mechanisms for Motivated Directional Biases

As will become clear from the work reviewed in this section, an explanation for how directional goals affect reasoning has to account not only for the existence of motivated biases but also for the findings suggesting that such biases are not unconstrained: People do not seem to be at liberty to conclude whatever they want to conclude merely because they want to. Rather, I propose that people motivated to arrive at a particular conclusion attempt to be rational and to construct a justification of their desired conclusion that would persuade a dispassionate observer. They draw the desired conclusion only if they can muster up the evidence necessary to support it (cf. Darley & Gross, 1983). In other words, they maintain an 'illusion of objectivity' (Pyszczynski & Greenberg, 1987; cf. Kruglanski, 1980). To this end, they search memory for those beliefs and rules that could support their desired conclusion. They may also creatively combine accessed knowledge to construct new beliefs that could logically support the desired conclusion. It is this process of memory search and belief construction that is biased by directional goals (cf. Greenwald, 1980). The objectivity of this justification construction process is illusory because people do not realize that the process is biased by their goals, that they are accessing only a subset of their relevant knowledge, that they would probably access different beliefs and rules in the presence of different directional goals, and that they might even be capable of justifying opposite conclusions on different occasions.

For example, people who want to believe that they will be academically successful may recall more of their past academic successes than of their failures. They may also use their world knowledge to construct new theories about how their particular personality traits may predispose them to academic success (Kunda, 1987). If they succeed in accessing and constructing appropriate beliefs, they may feel justified in concluding that they will be academically successful, not realizing that they also possess knowledge that could be used to support the opposite conclusion. The biasing role of goals is thus constrained by one's ability to construct a justification for the desired conclusion: People will come to believe what they want to believe only to the extent that reason permits. Often they will be forced to acknowledge and accept undesirable conclusions, as they appear to when confronted with strong arguments for undesired or counterattitudinal positions (Petty & Cacioppo, 1986).

The proposed mechanisms are based on the assumption that directional goals may influence which beliefs and rules are accessed and applied on a given occasion. This assumption seems reasonable because there is considerable evidence that people access different beliefs and rules on different occasions: They endorse different attitudes (Salancik & Conway, 1975; Snyder, 1982), express different self-concepts (Fazio, Effrein, & Falender, 1981), make different social judgments (Higgins & King, 1981), and use different statistical rules (Kunda & Nisbett, 1986; Nisbett, Krantz, Jepson, & Kunda, 1983). Although most relevant evidence shows that different knowledge structures are accessed because different external, contextual cues make them differentially salient, the work on the effects of accuracy goals on reasoning reviewed above suggests that people may also access different beliefs and strategies under the influence of different goals.

The proposed view has much in common with the models suggested by Kruglanski and his colleagues (Kruglanski, 1980; Kruglanski & Ajzen, 1983; Kruglanski & Klar, 1987) and by Pyszczynski and Greenberg (1987). In Kruglanski and his colleagues' view, as in mine, directional goals (or, in their terminology, the need for specific conclusions or structures) affect reasoning by affecting which information will be considered in the reasoning process. However, their view differs somewhat from mine in that their model implies that essentially the same sequence of reasoning will be followed in the presence of different goals but that the sequence will be arrested, or frozen, at different points in time, depending on one's goals. My view, in addition to allowing for the possibility that directional goals may lead to more or less lengthy processing under different circumstances, also allows for the possibility that different goals will lead directly to the consideration of different beliefs and rules.

Pyszczynski and Greenberg's (1987) model delineating the effects of the self-esteem motive on self-serving attributions is even closer in spirit to the current one. Pyszczynski and Greenberg likened the attribution process to a process of hypothesis generation and evaluation and proposed that motives may have an effect on any or all of the stages of the hypothesis-testing sequence—that is, on the generation and evaluation of hypotheses, of inference rules, and of evidence. My ideas are fully compatible with this view in that all the processes outlined by Pyszczynski and Greenberg may be regarded as resulting from a biased search through memory for relevant beliefs and rules. In this article I wish to extend these ideas by showing that such biased memory search is not restricted to the domain of self-serving attribution. Rather, it may take place under the influence of a broad variety of directional goals and in many reasoning tasks. Furthermore, by shifting the focus of discussion from the process of hypothesis testing to the process of justification construction, my view points to some novel implications of these ideas, particularly the notion that the biased memory search will result in the formation of additional biased beliefs and theories that are constructed so as to justify desired conclusions.

In the following section, I review evidence that directional goals bias reasoning. The studies reviewed came from diverse theoretical perspectives and focused on a variety of content areas. I argue that the biased memory search and belief construction mechanisms that I propose can account for all this research. Although few of the studies reviewed were explicitly concerned with the mechanisms underlying motivated reasoning, many provided indirect evidence for the proposed mechanisms and some provide more direct support for them. I first review evidence indicating that directional goals may bias the accessing and construction of beliefs about the self, other people, and events. Next, I review evidence that directional goals may bias use of inferential rules. Finally, I review evidence that directional goals may bias the evaluation of scientific evidence by biasing the selection of both beliefs and rules.

Biased Accessing of Beliefs

Dissonance Research

The most extensive evidence that directional goals may bias reasoning comes from work carried out in the dissonance tradition that has shown that people may bias their self-characterizations when motivated to do so. Most of the research designed to test this theory has been carried out within the induced compliance paradigm, in which people are induced to make statements or to perform behaviours that are counterattitudinal. Having done so, people typically then alter their attitudes to make them more consistent with their behaviour (for an extensive review, see Wicklund & Brehm, 1976).

Why does counterattitudinal behaviour lead to such attitude change? In its original formulation, dissonance theory proposed that holding two contradictory cognitions causes an unpleasant state of cognitive dissonance that a person strives to reduce by changing one or more of the relevant cognitions (Festinger, 1957), The cognitions 'I believe X' and 'I have stated or done not X' seem dissonant, and to reduce this dissonance, people change their beliefs so as to bring them into correspondence with their actions (Festinger & Carlsmith, 1959). Thus the

general goal was presumed to be to reduce inconsistency among beliefs, and the subgoal of changing one's beliefs and endorsing particular attitudes was constructed as one means of doing so.

More recently, examination of the hundreds of empirical investigations within the induced compliance paradigm has led to a modification and restriction of the original theory. It is now believed that dissonance is aroused only when one freely chooses to engage in behaviour that has foreseeable negative consequences (Cooper & Fazio, 1984). These conditions suggest that dissonance arousal requires a threat to the self: The cognition that one has knowingly chosen to engage in a bad or foolish behaviour is inconsistent with a self-image as a decent and intelligent person (Aronson, 1968; Greenwald & Ronis, 1978). This interpretation is strengthened by findings showing that dissonance reduction through attitude change is eliminated when one is given alternative means of boosting one's self-image (Steele & Liu, 1983). Subjects' goal in the typical dissonance experiment, then, is to disconfirm the view of themselves as bad or foolish, and the subgoal of changing one's attitudes is created to this end. Thus according to both the original and the modified versions of dissonance theory, people are motivated to believe that they hold a particular attitude. In other words, they hold directional goals.

This motivational account has been challenged by attempts to reinterpret the dissonance findings in non-motivational terms. Bem (1972) argued that the findings could also result from self-perception: The subjects, who have limited direct access to their attitudes, may infer their attitudes from their behaviours. It has been shown, however, that self-perception cannot fully account for the phenomena, because attitude change in dissonance experiments requires the presence of arousal that cannot be misattributed to other sources (Zanna & Cooper, 1974; for review, see Cooper & Fazio, 1984). The crucial role of such arousal indicates that non-cognitive processes are involved. The precise role of arousal in motivated reasoning is discussed in a later section. For now, the important point is that most theorists have accepted this as evidence that attitude change in dissonance experiments results, at least in part, from motivation.

But how does motivation lead to attitude change? The dissonance literature is, for the most part, mute on this question. The work has not been concerned with the processes leading from the arousal of dissonance motivation to attitude change, and it therefore offers little direct evidence about the nature of these processes. There is some indirect evidence, however, that attitude change results from a memory search among existing beliefs for evidence that one has the desired attitude. This evidence lies in the fact that attitude change appears to be constrained by pre-existing beliefs and attitudes, which suggests that these are accessed in the process of constructing current attitudes. Dissonance clearly would be most effectively reduced if one were able to espouse an attitude that corresponds perfectly to one's behaviour. Yet this is not always the case. In many dissonance experiments, the attitudes after performing the counterattitudinal behaviour remain in opposition to the behaviour.

For example, after endorsing a law limiting free speech, subjects were less opposed to the law than were control subjects, but they remained opposed to it (Linder, Cooper, & Jones, 1967). Similarly, after endorsing police brutality on campus, subjects were less opposed to such brutality than were control subjects but they remained opposed to it (Greenbaum & Zemach, 1972). Induced compliance studies in which subjects are led to describe boring tasks as enjoyable often do produce shifts from negative to positive task evaluations, but in these studies, initial attitudes are not very negative (e.g., −0.45 on a scale whose highest negative value was −5 in Festinger & Carlsmith's classic 1959 study), and post-dissonance attitudes still seem considerably less positive than subjects' descriptions of the task. For example, after they were induced to describe a task as 'very enjoyable . . . a lot of fun . . . very interesting . . . intriguing . . .

exciting', subjects rated the task as 1.35 on a scale whose highest positive value was 5 (Festinger & Carlsmith, 1959).

If we assume that subjects in these induced compliance studies were motivated to espouse attitudes corresponding to their dissonance-arousing behaviour, it seems likely that in their attempt to do so, they accessed their initial attitudes and were constrained by them. However, they may have accessed a biased subset of these initial attitudes, which permitted them to shift their current attitudes somewhat in the desired direction. The constraints imposed by prior beliefs on attitude change imply that prior beliefs were accessed in the process of constructing current ones, and the directional shift in attitudes implies that only a biased subset of the relevant prior beliefs were accessed. Therefore, these data lend indirect support to the view that the post-dissonance attitude is the end product of a biased search through existing knowledge structures for evidence that one holds the desired attitude. Such a biased search may yield an attitude that is somewhat more positive or somewhat more negative than the attitude that one would report in the absence of motivation, but it is unlikely to completely overturn existing attitudes. Apparently, people are not at liberty to espouse any attitude they want to; they can do so only within the limits imposed by their prior beliefs.

It is also possible that the constraints imposed by prior knowledge reflect a process of anchoring and adjustment (Tversky & Kahneman, 1974). According to this view, the extremity of the behaviour that subjects are induced to perform serves as an anchor, and the espoused attitudes are shifted toward it. However, it seems unlikely that anchoring alone can account for the obtained attitude change, because attitudes do not change when the same behaviours are performed under low-choice conditions. If one assumes that anchoring processes occur only in those conditions in which motivation is aroused, it is not clear how the anchoring account differs from the one proposed here. The mechanisms underlying anchoring phenomena are not well understood and may well involve a process of biased memory search and belief construction comparable with the one that I proposed.

The evidence that counterattitudinal behaviours will create dissonance only when they involve a threat to the self is considerable and compelling. But there is no reason to assume that such behaviours constitute the only source of dissonance or motivation to espouse particular conclusions. Indeed, it seems somewhat puzzling that, given the enormous breadth of the original theory, the research generated by it remained, for the most part, restricted to so narrow a domain. Much of the research to be reviewed in the next section was not carried out within the dissonance tradition, even though its findings could have been derived from that theory.

Additional Evidence of Biased Self-Characterizations

Several additional studies indicate that directional goals may bias people's construals of their attitudes, traits, and preferences. For the most part, these studies provide indirect evidence about the processes through which motivation affects self-characterizations, but several of them also provide more direct evidence that motivation may instigate biased memory search through relevant self-knowledge.

In a study providing indirect evidence for the biased memory search and construction model, Kunda and Sanitioso (1989) showed that subjects induced to theorize that a given trait (extraversion or introversion) was conducive to academic success came to view themselves as characterized by higher levels of that trait than did other subjects, presumably because they were motivated to view themselves as possessing success-promoting attributes. These changes in self-concepts were constrained by prior self-knowledge: The subjects, who were predominantly extraverted to begin with, viewed themselves as less extraverted when they believed introversion to be more desirable,

but they still viewed themselves as extraverted. Further evidence for such constraints was found in a study in which experimenters pre-selected subjects who were extraverts or introverts and exposed them to similar manipulations (Sanitioso, Kunda, & Fong, 1990). Both groups viewed themselves as more extraverted when induced to believe that extraversion was beneficial than when induced to believe that introversion was beneficial. But in all conditions the extraverts still viewed themselves as considerably more extraverted than the introverts viewed themselves. In other words, the effects of the manipulation on self-concepts were constrained by prior self-knowledge. These constraints imply that motivated changes in self-concepts may result from a biased search through memory for evidence that one has the desired self-concept; the resulting self-concepts are constrained by the evidence accessed in this process.

. . .

More direct evidence for biased memory search was obtained by Sanitioso et al. (1990), who used a similar paradigm. In one study, subjects were asked to generate autobiographical memories reflecting their standing on the extraversion–introversion dimension. Subjects led to view introversion as desirable were more likely to generate introverted memories first and generated more introverted memories than did subjects led to view extraversion as more desirable. In another study, subjects led to view introversion as desirable were faster to generate autobiographical memories reflecting introversion and slower to generate memories reflecting extraversion than were subjects led to view extraversion as desirable. These studies both indicate that the accessibility of autobiographical memories reflecting a desired trait was enhanced, which suggests that the search for relevant memories was biased.

. . .

Positive self-characterizations may be maintained not only by biased recall and construction of one's own traits and behaviours but also through biased construction of the traits. There is considerable evidence that people tend to view themselves as above average on many dimensions (e.g., Weinstein, 1980, 1982). Dunning, Meyerowitz, and Holzberg (1989) showed that this tendency is constrained by people's ability to construe traits in a self-serving manner. Thus people may all view themselves as above average in sensitivity only if they can each define sensitivity as consisting primarily of attributes on which they have high levels. In line with this reasoning, Dunning et al. showed that people are more likely to see themselves as above average on ambiguous traits that are open to multiple construals than they are on unambiguous traits, and even for ambiguous traits, the tendency is reduced when people are asked to use specific definitions of each trait in their judgments.

Another way of maintaining a positive view of oneself is through self-serving attribution of the causes of one's behaviour. There is now considerable evidence that people tend to take credit for their successes and, to a lesser extent, that people tend to deny responsibility for failure. Because this line of work has been reviewed extensively elsewhere, I do not discuss it at length. In the most recent review, Pyszczynski and Greenberg (1987) argued, in line with my ideas, that directional goals play a role in producing this bias and that they do so by leading to biased reliance on cognitive processes.

The studies just cited show that motivation may bias self-characterizations and provide some evidence for the biased memory search and belief construction model of motivated reasoning. The following studies showing motivationally biased self-characterizations provide no evidence for these mechanisms, but they are all consistent with them.

McGuire (1960) showed that the perceived desirability of events may be biased by motivation. Subjects who were persuaded that some events were more likely to occur came to view these events as more desirable, presumably because they were motivated to view the future as pleasant. Subjects also enhanced the desirability of logically related beliefs that had not been specifically

addressed by the manipulation, which suggests that they were attempting to construct a logically coherent pattern of beliefs.

. . .

In sum, there is considerable evidence that directional goals may bias people's self-conceptions as possessing various attitudes, traits, and histories. These motivated self-characterizations often appear to be constrained by prior self-knowledge, and these constraints provide indirect evidence that motivation biases self-conceptions by biasing the memory search for relevant information. There is also some direct evidence for this, coming from the biased content of reported memories and from the enhanced speed both of generating memories that are consistent with desired self-views and of endorsing desired self-conceptions.

Biased Beliefs about Others

Evidence for the effect of directional goals on judgments about others comes from research involving a manipulation termed *outcome dependency*: Subjects expect their own outcomes to depend in some way on a target person. Such manipulations bias the perceptions of others in ways that are consistent with the biased memory search and belief construction model, though most studies provide no direct evidence for it.

Several studies indicate that people tend to see others as more likable if they expect to interact with them. In a study by Darley and Berscheid (1967), subjects who expected to hold intimate sexual discussions with one target person but not with another read personality descriptions of both. Subjects liked their expected partner better than they liked the other person, presumably because they wanted their partner to be likable. In a later study, Berscheid, Graziano, Monson, and Dermer (1976) employed a similar but more powerful manipulation in which subjects who expected to date one of three persons observed a taped discussion among the three. Once again, subjects liked the person whom they expected to date better than they liked the other persons. Ratings of the three persons' personalities were affected as well: Subjects rated their expected dates more extremely and positively on traits and were more confident of their ratings. Subjects also awarded more attention to their prospective dates and recalled more information about them than about other target persons, but the enhanced liking and trait ratings were not due to differential attention. One may understand these data by assuming that subjects had both a directional goal and an accuracy goal: They wanted their date to be nice so that the expected interactions would be pleasant, and they wanted to get a good idea of what the date was like so that they could better control and predict the interaction. The accuracy goal led to more intense processing, and the directional goal created bias.

A slightly different paradigm employed by Neuberg and Fiske (1987) also showed that outcome dependency enhances liking. In their studies, all subjects expected to interact with the target person, but half the subjects expected the reward that they would get for their own performance to depend on the target person's performance (outcome dependency), whereas half the subjects expected their own performance to be rewarded independently. All subjects observed written or videotaped self-descriptions allegedly produced by the target person. When the information contained in these self-descriptions was not inconsistent with subjects' expectations about the target person, subjects in the outcome-dependency condition attended to this information longer and, after exposure to this information, liked the target person better than did other subjects. Thus these subjects showed the same combination of more intense processing and bias obtained in Berscheid et al.'s (1976) study, which suggests that they too may have held both accuracy and directional goals.[3]

. . .

Biased Beliefs about Events

There are several sources of evidence that directional goals may bias people's beliefs about the nature, the causes, and the likelihood of various events. Klein and Kunda's (1989) study indicated that the goal of disparaging or enhancing another's abilities at a given task may lead to changes in one's beliefs about the nature of that task. Theories about the causal determinants of events may also be influenced by goals. Kunda (1987) showed that people tend to believe that their own attributes are more conducive to marital happiness and to academic success than are other attributes. It is possible that people construct such beliefs by selectively accessing only information that is consistent with them, but there is no evidence for this. The motivational interpretation of this bias as resulting from people's wish to believe that they will experience desirable outcomes was strengthened by the finding that in the domain of academic success, the effect was not found for people for whom the outcome was not personally relevant.

Similarly, Dunning, Story, and Tan (1989) found that people view their strengths as more predictive of success than their weaknesses are. They showed that the self-ratings of management students on a variety of dimensions correlated positively with their beliefs about the importance of these dimensions for success as a business executive. They also found that undergraduates preselected because they had strong verbal and weak math skills or strong math and weak verbal skills were more positive in their evaluations of prospective students who shared their strengths and weaknesses than of those with an opposing pattern of strengths and weaknesses. In both Kunda's (1987) and Dunning, Story, and Tan's (1989) studies, however, subjects were not randomly assigned to motivational conditions, and so the findings may also be due to different prior beliefs held by people with different attributes.

. . .

There is some evidence that people's evaluations of medical conditions may be biased by goals. In two studies (Ditto, Jemmott, & Darley, 1988; Jemmott, Ditto, & Croyle, 1986), subjects were given a laboratory test said to diagnose the presence of a potentially risky (fictitious) enzyme deficiency.

In both studies, subjects diagnosed as having the deficiency rated it as less serious and health threatening and rated the diagnostic test as less accurate than did subjects diagnosed as not having it. These findings could result from a motivated attempt to minimize the likelihood that one has the disease and the danger involved in having it. However, the findings may also result from prior beliefs: College students tend to assume that they are and will be healthier than average (Weinstein, 1980). They therefore may infer that a test diagnosing deficiencies is invalid or that a deficiency that they have cannot be serious.

. . .

Research by Sanitioso and Kunda (1991) suggested that goals may affect the use of a variant of the law of large numbers. Subjects had to decide how many instances of athletic competitions they would want to observe before they predicted how the participating athletes would be ranked at the end of the season. Subjects were led to believe that the observation of each competition would require either high or low effort, and they were then asked to assess the predictability of the athletes' final scores either from a single competition or from an aggregate of competitions. Only subjects expecting evidence collection to be highly effortful accessed the aggregation principle—that is, believed that aggregates afforded greater predictability than did single instances. Because these high-effort subjects wanted to avoid collecting large samples, their goal was to conclude that they needed only small samples of competitions to arrive at reasonable levels of predictability. Their belief that predictability increased sharply with sample size could allow these subjects to arrive at that conclusion: As the increase of predictability with sample size becomes sharper, the size of the sample yielding a given level of predictability becomes smaller. Thus, it appears that motivation may affect whether the aggregation principle will be accessed. But, once again, it is not clear whether high-effort subjects' use of the heuristic resulted from a more intense but essentially objective search for heuristics or whether it resulted

from a biased search for a heuristic that would yield the desired conclusion. This is because the study did not permit assessment of the intensity of processing engaged in by low-effort subjects.

. . .

Biased Research Evaluation

The studies reviewed so far indicate that directional goals may bias the selection and construction of beliefs, as well as the selection of inferential rules. In studies concerning biased evaluation of scientific research, experimenters explore an arena for the biased selection of both types of knowledge structures. In the typical study, subjects are exposed to alleged scientific evidence whose conclusions are differentially acceptable to different subjects, and they are then asked for their reactions to this evidence. The typical finding is that subjects motivated to disbelieve the evidence are less likely to believe it, and there is some evidence that this outcome is mediated by differential processing of the information.

Wyer and Frey (1983) gave subjects success or failure feedback on an intelligence test and then exposed them to a report containing favourable and unfavourable information about intelligence tests. Afterwards, subjects receiving failure feedback judged intelligence tests to be less valid than did subjects receiving success feedback. Indirect evidence that this was mediated by failure subjects' attempts to refute the pro-test arguments is provided by the findings that they recalled more of these arguments, but there is no direct evidence for such attempts at refutation. More direct evidence that subjects are critical of research that they are motivated to disbelieve was found in a similar study by Pyszczynski, Greenberg, and Holt (1985). Subjects were given success or failure feedback on a social sensitivity test and then exposed to two studies, one concluding that the test's validity was high and another concluding that it was low. In comparison with failure subjects, success subjects judged the high-validity study to be more convincing and better conducted, and they judged the low-validity study to be less convincing and less well conducted. Pyszczynski et al. did not attempt to assess what mediated subjects' evaluation of how well the research was conducted. In both their study and Wyer and Frey's, the reluctance to believe in the validity of tests indicating failure may have resulted from a non-motivational inference: Subjects who believe themselves to have high levels of a certain ability are justified in doubting the validity of tests showing otherwise.

. . .

More direct evidence demonstrating that goals may bias the evaluation of scientific evidence comes from a study by Lord, Ross, and Lepper (1979). These authors pre-selected subjects who were for or against capital punishment and exposed them to two studies with different methodologies, one supporting and one opposing the conclusion that capital punishment deterred crime. Subjects were more critical of the research methods used in the study that disconfirmed their initial beliefs than they were of methods used in the study that confirmed their initial beliefs. The criticisms of the disconfirming study were based on reasons such as insufficient sample size, non-random sample selection, or absence of control for important variables; this suggests that subjects' differential evaluations of the two studies were based on what seemed to them a rational use of statistical heuristics but that the use of these heuristics was in fact dependent on the conclusions of the research, not on its methods. Having discounted the disconfirming study and embraced the confirming one, their attitudes, after exposure to the mixed evidence, became more polarized. Because subjects were given methodological criticisms and counterarguments, however, the study did not address whether people would spontaneously access differential heuristics. In fact, after exposure to a single study but before receiving the list of criticisms, all subjects were swayed by its conclusions, regardless of their initial attitudes. This suggests further that people attempt to be rational: They will believe undesirable evidence if they cannot refute it, but they will

refute it if they can. Also, although the differential evaluation of research obtained in this study may have been due to subjects' motivation to maintain their desired beliefs, it may also have been due to the fact that one of these studies may have seemed less plausible to them because of their prior beliefs.

B.R. Sherman and Kunda (1989) used a similar paradigm to gain insight into the process mediating differential evaluation of scientific evidence. Subjects read a detailed description of a study showing that caffeine either facilitated or hindered the progress of a serious disease. Subjects motivated to disbelieve the article (high caffeine consumers who read that caffeine facilitated disease, low caffeine consumers who read that caffeine hindered disease) were less persuaded by it. This effect seemed to be mediated by biased evaluation of the methods employed in the study because, when asked to list the methodological strengths of the research, threatened subjects spontaneously listed fewer such strengths than did non-threatened subjects. Threatened subjects also rated the various methodological aspects of the study as less sound than did non-threatened subjects. These included aspects pertaining to inferential rules such as those relating sample size to predictability, as well as to beliefs about issues such as the validity of self-reports or the prestige of research institutions.

Of importance is that all subjects were also quite responsive to the differential strength of different aspects of the method, which suggests that they were processing the evidence in depth. Threatened subjects did not deny that some aspects were strong, but they did not consider them to be as strong as did non-threatened subjects. Thus, bias was constrained by plausibility.

Taken together, these studies suggest that the evaluation of scientific evidence may be biased by whether people want to believe its conclusions. But people are not at liberty to believe anything they like; they are constrained by their prior beliefs about the acceptability of various procedures. These constraints provide indirect support for the biased memory search and belief construction model.

As a group, these studies are vulnerable to rein-terpretation in terms of non-motivational accounts. This is because the experimenters created different levels of motivation either by pre-selecting subjects presumed to have different goals, who therefore may also hold different prior beliefs, or by subject-ing subjects to success or failure experiences that may be deemed differentially likely to reflect their abilities because of prior beliefs. But such non-motivational mechanisms cannot fully account for these findings because the few researchers who attempted to rule out the role of prior beliefs obtained results similar to those of researchers who did not.

. . .

Discussion

The case for directional motivated reasoning appears quite strong. Directional goals have been shown to affect people's attitudes, beliefs, and infer-ential strategies in a variety of domains and in stud-ies conducted by numerous researchers in many paradigms. Some of these studies and paradigms are open to reinterpretation in non-motivational terms, but many are not. Even in paradigms in which individual studies may reasonably be attrib-uted to entirely cognitive processes, such as the dis-sonance paradigm, evidence indicating that arousal is crucial for motivated reasoning suggests that motivational factors are involved. The position that all self-serving biases are due to purely cognitive processes is therefore no longer tenable.

Cognitive interpretations for ambiguous phe-nomena were viewed by their proponents as preferable to motivational ones on the grounds of parsimony. The argument, which seemed per-suasive at the time, was that because all extant evidence purporting to demonstrate motiva-tional biases could be accounted for in terms of well-established cognitive processes, there was no need to infer the additional existence of moti-vational processes for which no independent evi-dence existed (Dawes, 1976; Miller & Ross, 1975;

Nisbett & Ross, 1980). The evidence reviewed in this article suggests that psychologists are now in a position to turn that argument on its head (cf. Showers & Cantor, 1985). A single motivational process for which unequivocal independent evi-dence now exists may be used to account for a wide diversity of phenomena. Many of these can-not be accounted for at all in non-motivational terms. Accounting for the others in cognitive terms would require making a multitude of auxiliary assumptions that are special for each case, many of which have no empirical support. For example, cognitive accounts may require the assumption that people with different backgrounds differ in their prior beliefs about a particular issue when no evidence or plausible grounds for such differences exist. Thus, under the current state of knowledge, the motivational account appears to be more par-simonious and coherent than the purely cognitive one (Thagard, 1989).

The Mechanisms for Motivated Reasoning

Although cognitive processes cannot fully account for the existence of self-serving biases, it appears that they play a major role in produc-ing these biases in that they provide the mecha-nisms through which motivation affects reasoning. Indeed, it is possible that motivation merely pro-vides an initial trigger for the operation of cogni-tive processes that lead to the desired conclusions.

I have proposed that when one wants to draw a particular conclusion, one feels obligated to con-struct a justification for that conclusion that would be plausible to a dispassionate observer. In doing so, one accesses only a biased subset of the rel-evant beliefs and rules. The notion that motivated reasoning is mediated by biased memory search and belief construction can account for all of the phenomena reviewed earlier, but the evidence for this process is mostly indirect. The most prevalent form of indirect evidence lies in the constraints that prior knowledge imposes on motivational biases, a pervasive finding obtained in several paradigms. In the dissonance paradigm, prior attitudes appear to

constrain motivated shifts in post-dissonance attitudes (e.g., Greenbaum & Zemach, 1972; Linder et
al., 1967). Prior self-concepts similarly appear to
constrain directional shifts toward desired selves
(Kunda & Sanitioso, 1989; Sanitioso et al., 1990).
Prior beliefs about how performance reflects ability appear to constrain motivated perceptions of
the ability of a person (Klein & Kunda, 1989) or
of a sports team (Gilovich, 1983). And prior beliefs
about the strength of scientific methods appear
to constrain motivated evaluations of scientific
research (B.R. Sherman & Kunda, 1989). The
existence of such constraints indicates that prior
knowledge is accessed in the process of arriving at
desired conclusions; the existence of bias implies
that not all relevant prior knowledge is accessed.

Such constraints, however, do not necessarily
reflect biased memory search and belief construction; they could also result from alternative processes. For example, the existence of constraints
in the dissonance paradigm may reflect a compromise between a desire to espouse new attitudes
and an opposing desire to maintain current ones
(though the process of arriving at such a compromise may still be one of biased memory search).
In the absence of measures indicating which prior
beliefs have been accessed, the existence of constraints can provide only indirect evidence for the
notion of biased memory search.

However, the interpretation of these constraints
as reflecting biased memory search processes is
strengthened by the existence of some more direct
evidence for biased memory search. Three kinds
of data are taken as evidence that directional
goals bias the accessing of relevant knowledge
structures. The first consists of cases in which
subjects spontaneously listed different memories
or beliefs under the influence of different directional goals. Thus subjects were more likely to list
those autobiographical memories that were consistent with their currently desired self-concepts
(Sanitioso et al., 1990); subjects reported performing behaviours more frequently in the past when
these behaviours reflected their currently desired

attitudes and beliefs (Ross et al., 1981; B.R. Sherman & Kunda, 1989); and subjects reported finding fewer methodological strengths in scientific
studies when they were motivated to disbelieve
the conclusions of these studies (B.R. Sherman &
Kunda, 1989).

The second type of data providing relatively
direct evidence for biased memory search processes comes from studies in which experimenters found faster reaction times for generating and
endorsing those memories and beliefs that could
be used to justify desired conclusions. Such findings suggest that these memories and beliefs had
become relatively more accessible to subjects. Thus
subjects were faster to generate those autobiographical memories that were consistent with their
currently desired self-concepts (Sanitioso et al.,
1990), and subjects were faster to endorse as self-
descriptive those traits reflecting currently desired
self-concepts (Markus & Kunda, 1986). In both
the memory-listing and the reaction-time studies,
subjects were typically asked to list, generate, or
endorse specific memories or traits before they were
asked about their current attitudes or beliefs. This
is important because it reduces the plausibility of
an alternative account for these findings: namely,
that they result from post hoc attempts at justifying
previously endorsed attitudes and beliefs.

The third type of evidence pointing to biased
memory search comes from studies showing that
people use different statistical heuristics in the presence of different goals. Thus, subjects were more
likely to use base rate information (Ginossar &
Trope, 1987) and the law of large numbers (Sanitioso
& Kunda, 1990) when the use of these heuristics
enabled them to draw desired conclusions.

These effects of directional goals on memory
listing, on reaction time, and on rule use provide
converging evidence for the notion that goals
enhance the accessibility of those knowledge
structures—memories, beliefs, and rules—that are
consistent with desired conclusions. Such selective enhanced accessibility reflects a biased search
through memory for relevant knowledge.

Even these relatively direct indications of goal-directed memory search may, however, be open to alternative interpretations because truly direct measures of cognitive processes are impossible. For example, the memory-listing findings may reflect a response bias rather than enhanced memory accessibility. Thus, the enhanced tendency to report autobiographical memories that are consistent with currently desired self-concepts may have resulted from a desire to present oneself as possessing these self-concepts. And the reaction time findings may have resulted from affective interference with speed of processing rather than from altered accessibility. However, neither of these alternative accounts provides a satisfactory explanation of the full range of findings. Thus self-presentational accounts do not provide a good explanation of reaction time findings, which are less likely to be under volitional control. And affective interference with speed of processing does not provide a good explanation for changes in overall levels of recall. Therefore, the presence of converging evidence from these different lines of work is best explained by the notion of biased memory search. Nevertheless, the evidence is as yet limited in its quantity and breadth. Thus the case for the biased accessing and construction model is by no means ironclad. But the evidence seems suggestive enough to justify concentrated efforts to strengthen the case.

If, as I propose, directional motivated reasoning results from a biased search through memory, it is still necessary to ask how the biased memory search comes about. One intriguing possibility is that the motive, or goal, merely leads people to ask themselves whether the conclusion that they desire is true; they ask themselves directional questions: 'Do I support police intervention on campus?' 'Am I extraverted?' 'Is my date nice?' Standard hypothesis-testing processes, which have little to do with motivation, then take over and lead to the accessing of hypothesis-confirming information and thereby to the arrival at conclusions that are biased toward hypothesis confirmation and, inadvertently, toward goal satisfaction.

There is substantial evidence that in testing hypotheses, people tend to rely on a positive test strategy: They seek out instances in which the hypothesized property is known or expected to be present rather than absent (for review, see Klayman & Ha, 1987). In other words, people are biased toward seeking instances that are consistent with a hypothesis that they are testing rather than instances that are inconsistent with it. Such biases have been found in the solution of logic problems (Wason & Johnson-Laird, 1965), in attempts to discover the rules governing object categorization (Klayman & Ha, 1989), in the assessment of correlations (see Nisbett & Ross, 1980), and, of greatest relevance here, in the evaluation of people (Snyder & Cantor, 1979). In many cases this strategy is useful (Klayman & Ha, 1987), and it does not preclude sensitivity to the diagnosticity of instances (e.g, Skov & Sherman, 1986; Trope & Bassok, 1983). Nevertheless, under some circumstances, this strategy will lead to the favouring of hypothesis-confirming evidence. Thus if people possess mixed evidence that includes some instances that are consistent with the hypothesis and some that are inconsistent with it, their tendency to favour consistent instances will result in a hypothesis-confirmation bias. . . .

. . .

Taken together, these findings imply that people are more likely to search spontaneously for hypothesis-consistent evidence than for inconsistent evidence. This seems to be the mechanism underlying hypothesis confirmation because hypothesis confirmation is eliminated when people are led to consider inconsistent evidence. It seems either that people are not aware of their tendency to favour hypothesis-consistent evidence or that, upon reflection, they judge this strategy to be acceptable, because accuracy goals alone do not reduce this bias.

Thus, the tendency to confirm hypotheses appears to be due to a process of biased memory search that is comparable with the process instigated by directional goals. This parallel lends support to the notion that directional goals may affect reasoning by giving rise to directional hypotheses, which are then confirmed; if the motivation to arrive at particular conclusions leads people to ask themselves whether their desired conclusions are true, normal strategies of hypothesis-testing will favour confirmation of these desired conclusions in many cases. One implication of this account is that motivation will cause bias, but cognitive factors such as the available beliefs and rules will determine the magnitude of the bias.

In its strongest form, this account removes the motivational 'engine' from the process of motivated reasoning, in that motivation is assumed to lead only to the posing of directional questions and to have no further effect on the process through which these questions are answered. If this were true, many of the distinctions between cognitive, expectancy-driven processes and motivated processes would break down. Both directional goals and 'cold' expectancies may have their effects through the same hypothesis-confirmation process. The process through which the hypotheses embedded in the questions 'Is my desired conclusion true?' and 'Is my expected conclusion true?' are confirmed may be functionally equivalent. Indeed, there are some interesting parallels between motivated reasoning and expectancy confirmation that lend support to this notion. For example, B.R. Sherman and Kunda (1989) found that implausible evidence (namely, that caffeine may be good for one's health) was subjected to elaborate and critical scrutiny that was comparable to the scrutiny triggered by threatening evidence. Similarly, Neuberg and Fiske (1987) found that evidence inconsistent with expectations received increased attention comparable in magnitude to the increase caused by outcome dependency. Finally, Bem's (1972) findings that the beliefs of observers mirrored those of actors in dissonance experiments suggest that observers' expectations and actors' motivations may lead to similar processes.[4] These parallels between motivational processes and expectancy-confirmation processes suggest that rather than attempting to distinguish

between the two, it may be more fruitful to focus attention on the mechanisms underlying both.

It is also possible, though, that the effects of motivation on reasoning may go beyond the mere posing of directional questions. For example, when motivation is involved, one may persist in asking one directional question after another (e.g., 'Is the method used in this research faulty?' 'Is the researcher incompetent?' 'Are the results weak?'), thus exploring all possible avenues that may allow one to endorse the desired conclusion. It is also possible that in addition to posing directional questions, motivation leads to more intense searches for hypothesis-confirming evidence and, perhaps, to suppression of disconfirming evidence (cf. Pyszczynski & Greenberg, 1987). If motivation does have these additional effects on reasoning, the parallels between motivated reasoning and expectancy confirmations gain new meaning. They suggest that seemingly 'cold' expectancies may in fact be imbued with motivation. The prospect of altering one's beliefs, especially those that are well established and long held, may be every bit as unpleasant as the undesired cognitions typically viewed as 'hot'. It was this intuition that led Festinger (1957) to describe the hypothetical situation of standing in the rain without getting wet as dissonance arousing.

It is difficult to tell, at this point, whether the effects of motivation on reasoning go beyond the posing of directional questions. It seems clear that the examples of motivational reasoning reviewed here could result merely from posing directional questions. Further research is necessary to determine whether motivation plays an additional role.

Implications

Although the mechanisms underlying motivated reasoning are not yet fully understood, it is now clear that directional goals do affect reasoning. People are more likely to arrive at those conclusions that they want to arrive at. Whatever the mechanisms, the implications are serious and important. Taylor and Brown (1988) implied that motivated reasoning may be beneficial because the resulting illusions promote mental health; unrealistically positive views of oneself and the world are often adaptive. This seems true for illusory beliefs that do not serve as the basis for important action. But motivated illusions can be dangerous when they are used to guide behaviour and decisions, especially in those cases in which objective reasoning could facilitate more adaptive behaviour.

For example, people who play down the seriousness of early symptoms of severe diseases such as skin cancer and people who see only weaknesses in research pointing to the dangers of drugs such as caffeine or of behaviours such as drunken driving may literally pay with their lives for their motivated reasoning. Hopefully, once the mechanisms producing such biases are fully understood, it will be possible to help people overcome them.

Notes

1. Kruglanski and Freund (1983) theorize that this occurs because time pressure leads to the arousal of a need for structure—that is, the need to arrive at a conclusion, whatever it may be.

2. A study by Sieber (1974) appears to show opposite results. Subjects motivated to be accurate were more overconfident than others in the correctness of their answers to an exam, which suggests less rather than more careful processing on their part. However, the imputation of different accuracy motives to the different groups in that study seems arbitrary. Sieber assumed that subjects who believed the exam to be their actual mid-term exam were more motivated to be accurate than were subjects who believed that if they did well enough on the exam, they would receive an A, and if not, they would receive feedback and take another exam that would determine their grade. It seems just as likely, though, that the latter subjects were more motivated to be accurate than the former, in which case the results would be consistent with Tetlock and Kim's (1987) study.

3. Neuberg and Fiske (1987) presented these findings as evidence for more accurate processing of the information about the target person, but this argument is difficult to maintain because the liking judgments made by outcome-dependent subjects were not sensitive to different levels of individuating information about the target.

4. It is known that actors' responses are not due only to expectancies, because they occur only in the presence of arousal that cannot be attributed to other sources (Cooper & Fazio, 1984).

Discussion Questions

1. Outline Bem's critique of Festinger's model of cognitive dissonance and Zanna and Cooper's reconciliation.

2. What are the key differences between Kunda's, Kruglanski's, and Pyczszynski's models of motivated cognition?

3. Work by Dweck and Leggett (1988) showed that completely opposing 'implicit theories' may become activated at different times in the same individual's head. The implicit theory idea plays a role in Kunda's research as well. According to Kunda, what variables might influence whether one of two opposing theories is activated?

12. Beyond Pleasure and Pain

E. Tory Higgins

——————— □ ■ □ ———————

Editor's Introduction

Some baseball players prefer to 'swing for the fences', accepting the risk of an embarrassing strikeout for the promise of a home run. Other players prefer to swing less hard, resulting in fewer home runs but also fewer strikeouts. Believe it or not, these two approaches to hitting a baseball just may reflect a fundamental and far-reaching motivational principle: *regulatory focus*.

As outlined by Tory Higgins in this 1997 article, it is not enough to say that people strive to approach pleasurable outcomes and avoid painful outcomes. Instead, there is great motivational importance to understanding *how* people approach good things and avoid bad things. Consider that two students may strive for the same positive outcome of 'getting an A in the class'. But the student in a 'promotion focus' will be in a state of eager enthusiasm, meaning that her approach to the class will be, for example, to speak up a lot in class discussions and do extra-credit assignments. In contrast, the student with a 'prevention focus' is in a state of vigilant caution, meaning that his approach will be to do things like making sure to avoid the temptation to watch television.

As Higgins describes, certain situations can put people into either focus. Moreover, certain people generally tend to be more promotion focused while others are more prevention focused. It is important to note that there is no implied value judgment; each focus has its costs and benefits. I certainly would prefer that the air traffic controller guiding my plane would be in a prevention-focused state, but at the same time, one would assume that most great artists are promotion focused. Most likely, the most effectively functioning people are able to toggle back and forth between the two foci as the need arises.

One of Higgins's major insights was that being in either focus sets into motion the processes of motivated cognition. For example, when you are in a promotion focus, you tend to have better memory for the presence or absence of gains, and when you are in a prevention focus you tend to have better memory for the presence of absence of losses (e.g., Tykocinski & Higgins, 1992). In this respect, each focus sets up a cognitive framework through which the complex array of stimuli bombarding our senses is filtered, much like a radar scanning the environment that picks up 'blips of meaning', to use George Kelly's (1955) classic metaphor. (For related ideas, see also Molden & Higgins, 2004.)

Another significant contribution of regulatory focus theory was to specify, for the first time, how different *types* of basic goals yield different types of emotional experiences. According to Higgins, when we experience promotion-related success, we feel joy; when we experience promotion-related failure, we feel sadness. This contrasts with the pattern under a prevention focus. Here, success leads to a qualitatively different type of positive experience (relief) and failure leads to a distinct type of negative experience (anxiety). Thus, regulatory focus theory makes explicit predictions about the *types* of positive and negative emotions people will feel when they experience different types of success and failure. This contrasts with other models such as that of Carver and White (1994) and Gray (1990) who either implicitly or explicitly equate 'reward' with 'non-punishment'.

More recently, Higgins and colleagues have developed regulatory fit theory (Higgins, 2005), which notes that the promotion/prevention distinction can be applied to both the overall orientation people are in and the *means* people use to pursue their goal. According to this theory, when there is a match between a person's overall regulatory focus and means employed, the experience 'feels right' and the person often transfers that good feeling onto whatever object is under scrutiny. For example, Higgins and colleagues (2003) manipulated fit by instructing participants to choose between a pen and a mug either by thinking about what they would gain after their choice (a fit strategy for the promotion-focused participants but a non-fit strategy for the prevention-focused participants) or what they would lose by their choice (a fit strategy for the prevention-focused participants but a non-fit strategy for the promotion-focused participants). Higgins et al. found that participants gave the mug a higher price if there had been a match between their particular choice strategy and their overall regulatory focus. Thus, this work has important implications for the economics of pricing and valuation: It turns out one of the bases upon which people value an object is whether using it 'fits' with their motivational orientation.

It seems that our entire psychical activity is bent upon *procuring pleasure* and *avoiding pain*, that it is automatically regulated by the PLEASURE-PRINCIPLE (Freud, 1920/1952, p. 365).

People are motivated to approach pleasure and avoid pain. From the ancient Greeks, through 17th- and 18th-century British philosophers, to 20th-century psychologists, this hedonic or pleasure principle has dominated scholars' understanding of people's motivation. It is the basic motivational assumption of theories across all areas of psychology, including theories of emotion in psychobiology (e.g., Gray, 1982), conditioning in animal learning (e.g., Mowrer, 1960; Thorndike, 1935), decision-making in cognitive and organizational psychology (e.g., Dutton & Jackson, 1987; Edwards, 1955; Kahneman & Tversky, 1979), consistency in social psychology (e.g., Festinger, 1957; Heider, 1958), and achievement motivation in personality (e.g., Atkinson, 1964). Even when Freud (1920/1952) talked about the ego becoming controlled by the reality principle, and in this sense developing 'beyond the pleasure principle', he made it clear that the reality principle 'at bottom also seeks pleasure—although a delayed and diminished pleasure' (p. 365). Environmental demands simply modify the pleasure principle such that avoiding pain becomes almost equal in importance to gaining pleasure. Thus, Freud's proposal to move beyond the pleasure principle did not move beyond the hedonic principle of seeking pleasure and avoiding pain.

The problem with the hedonic principle is not that it is wrong but that psychologists have relied on it too heavily as an explanation for motivation. After many centuries, it continues to be the dominant way to conceptualize approach versus avoidance. This dominance has taken attention away from other approach–avoidance principles. Is people's entire psychical activity controlled by the hedonic principle, as Freud (1920/1952) wondered, or might there be other self-regulatory principles that underlie both its operation and other psychical activities? If there are, then psychologists' understanding of the hedonic principle itself would be increased by understanding more about these other principles. Moreover, these other ways of conceptualizing approach versus avoidance could have implications beyond the hedonic principle. It's time for the study of motivation to move beyond the simple assertion of the hedonic principle that people approach pleasure and avoid pain. It's time to examine how people approach pleasure and avoid pain in substantially different strategic ways that have major consequences. It's time to move beyond the hedonic principle by studying the approach–avoidance principles that underlie it and have motivational significance in their own right.

This article begins by introducing the concept of *regulatory focus*, a principle that underlies the hedonic principle but differs radically in its motivational consequences. I describe how viewing motivation from the perspective of regulatory focus sheds light on the fundamental nature of approach–avoidance and emotional and evaluative sensitivities. I discuss how relying on the hedonic principle alone constrains and limits research and theory development, and I provide examples of the potential benefits of considering both promotion and prevention when studying phenomena that have been considered mainly in terms of either promotion (e.g., well-being) or prevention (e.g., cognitive dissonance). I briefly consider how a deeper understanding of these principles might increase psychologists' understanding of approach–avoidance motivation still further beyond the hedonic principle.

Regulatory Focus as a Motivational Principle

The notion that people are motivated to approach pleasure and avoid pain is well accepted, but what exactly does this entail? The hedonic principle is often discussed as if it were unitary. There is more than one account of this principle in the psychological literature, however. By considering these different accounts, it is possible to identify distinct principles that underlie hedonic self-regulation.

One of the earliest uses of the hedonic principle was as a lawful description of orderly event patterns. Careful observations indicated that when a situated behaviour produced pleasure it was more likely to be repeated in that situation, whereas when a behaviour produced pain it was less likely to be repeated in that situation. These observed events led to summary statements like 'pleasure stamps in' and 'pain stamps out', as Thorndike (1911) did in his law of effect. This postulated 'hedonism of the past', whether confirmed as a law or not, provided a description of events rather than an understanding of underlying processes. Thorndike (1935) later dropped the pain-stamps-out notion, leaving just the pleasure-stamps-in description of how situated behaviours

are strengthened. Around the same time, Skinner (1938) proposed the law that the occurrence of operant behaviours increases when they are followed by a reinforcer. This 'pleasure principle' also basically describes a pattern of observed events.

. . .

My discussion of regulatory focus concentrates on self-regulation toward desired end-states because this is the kind of self-regulation that has been emphasized in the literature (e.g., Carver & Scheier, 1981, 1990; Gollwitzer & Bargh, 1996; G.A. Miller, Galanter, & Pribram, 1960; Pervin, 1989; von Bertalanffy, 1968; cf. Elliot & Church, 1997; Elliot & Harackiewicz, 1996). The critical characteristic of such self-regulation is its *approach motivation*, the attempt to reduce discrepancies between current states and desired end-states. Although animal learning–biological models (e.g., Gray, 1982; Hull, 1952; Konorski, 1967; Lang, 1995; N.E. Miller, 1944; Mowrer, 1960), cybernetic-control models (e.g., Carver & Scheier, 1990; Powers, 1973), and dynamic models (e.g., Atkinson, 1964; Lewin, 1935; McClelland, Atkinson, Clark, & Lowell, 1953) all distinguish approaching desired end-states from avoiding undesired end-states, they do not distinguish between different ways of approaching desired end-states. They also do not identify different types of desired end-states that relate to different means of approach. Indeed, influential models such as that proposed by Gray explicitly treat approaching 'reward' and approaching 'non-punishment' as equivalent. In contrast, regulatory focus proposes that there are different ways of approaching different types of desired end-states.

The theory of self-regulatory focus begins by assuming that the hedonic principle should operate differently when serving fundamentally different needs, such as the distinct survival needs of nurturance (e.g., nourishment) and security (e.g., protection). Human survival requires adaptation to the surrounding environment, especially the social environment (see Buss, 1996). To obtain the nurturance and security that children need to survive, children must establish and maintain relationships with caretakers who provide them with nurturance and security by supporting, encouraging, protecting, and defending them (see Bowlby, 1969, 1973). To make these relationships work, children must learn how their appearance and behaviours influence caretakers' responses to them (see Bowlby, 1969; Cooley, 1902/1964; Mead, 1934; Sullivan, 1953). As the hedonic principle suggests, children must learn how to behave in order to approach pleasure and avoid pain. But what is learned about regulating pleasure and pain can be different for nurturance and security needs. Regulatory focus theory proposes that nurturance-related regulation and security-related regulation differ in regulatory focus. Nurturance-related regulation involves a promotion focus, whereas security-related regulation involves a prevention focus.

In earlier articles on self-discrepancy theory (e.g., Higgins, 1987, 1989a), I described how certain modes of caretaker–child interaction increase the likelihood that children will acquire strong desired end-states. These desired end-states represent either their own or significant others' hopes, wishes, and aspirations for them (strong ideals) or their own or significant others' beliefs about their duties, obligations, and responsibilities (strong oughts). Regulatory focus theory proposes that self-regulation in relation to strong ideals versus strong oughts differs in regulatory focus. Ideal self-regulation involves a promotion focus, whereas ought self-regulation involves a prevention focus. To illustrate the difference between these two types of regulatory focus, let us briefly consider how children's experiences of pleasure and pain and what they learn about self-regulation vary when their interactions with caretakers involve a promotion focus versus a prevention focus.

Consider first caretaker–child interactions that involve a promotion focus. The child experiences the pleasure of the presence of positive outcomes when caretakers, for example, hug and kiss the child for behaving in a desired manner, encourage the child to overcome difficulties, or set up opportunities for the child to engage in rewarding activities. The child experiences the pain of the absence of positive outcomes when caretakers, for example, end a meal when the child throws food, take away a toy when the child refuses to share it, stop a story when the child is not paying attention, or act disappointed when the child fails to fulfill their hopes for the child. Pleasure and pain from these interactions are experienced as the presence and the absence of positive outcomes, respectively. In both cases, the caretakers' message to the child is that what matters is attaining accomplishments or fulfilling hopes and aspirations, and it is communicated in reference to a state of the child that does or does not attain the desired end-state—either 'this is what I would ideally like you to do' or 'this is not what I would ideally like you to do'. The regulatory focus is one of promotion—a concern with advancement, growth, and accomplishment.

Consider next caretaker–child interactions that involve a prevention focus. The child experiences the pleasure of the absence of negative outcomes when caretakers, for example, childproof the house, train the child to be alert to potential dangers, or teach the child to 'mind your manners'. The child experiences the pain of the presence of negative outcomes when caretakers, for example, behave roughly with the child to get his or her attention, yell at the child when he or she doesn't listen, criticize the child for making a mistake, or punish the child for being irresponsible. Pleasure and pain from these interactions are experienced as the absence and the presence of negative outcomes, respectively. In both cases, the caretakers' message to the child is that what matters is ensuring safety, being responsible, and meeting obligations, and it is communicated in reference to a state of the child that does or does not attain the desired end-state—either 'this is what I believe you ought to do' or 'this is not what I believe you ought to do'. The regulatory focus is one of prevention—a concern with protection, safety, and responsibility.

These socialization differences illustrate how regulatory focus distinguishes between different kinds of self-regulation in relation to desired end-states. Children learn from interactions with their caretakers to regulate themselves in relation to promotion-focus ideals or in relation to prevention-focus oughts (see Higgins & Loeb, 1998). In later life phases, these significant others could be friends, spouses, co-workers, employers, or other persons rather than caretakers. More generally, regulatory focus theory distinguishes between the following two kinds of desired end-states: (a) aspirations and accomplishments (promotion focus) and (b) responsibilities and safety (prevention focus).

Momentary situations are also capable of temporarily inducing either a promotion focus or a prevention focus. Just as the responses of caretakers to their children's actions communicate to the children about how to attain desired end-states, feedback from a boss to an employee or from a teacher to a student is a situation that can communicate gain–non-gain information (promotion-related outcomes) or non-loss–loss information (prevention-related outcomes). Task instructions that present task contingency or 'if–then' rules concerning which actions produce which consequences also can communicate either gain–non-gain (promotion) or non-loss–loss (prevention) information. Thus, the concept of regulatory focus is broader than just socialization of strong promotion-focus ideals or prevention-focus oughts. Regulatory focus also can be induced temporarily in momentary situations.

People are motivated to approach desired end-states, which could be either promotion-focus aspirations and accomplishments or prevention-focus responsibilities and safety. But within this general approach toward desired end-states, regulatory focus can induce either approach or avoidance strategic inclinations. Because a promotion focus involves a sensitivity to positive outcomes (their presence and absence), an inclination to approach matches to desired end-states is the natural strategy for promotion self-regulation. In contrast, because a prevention focus involves a sensitivity to negative outcomes (their absence and presence), an inclination to avoid mismatches to desired end-states is the natural strategy for prevention self-regulation (see Higgins, Roney, Crowe, & Hymes, 1994).

Figure 12.1 summarizes the different sets of psychological variables discussed thus far that have distinct relations to promotion focus and prevention focus (as well as some variables to be discussed later). On the input side (the left side of Figure 12.1), nurturance needs, strong ideals, and situations involving gain–non-gain induce a promotion focus, whereas security needs, strong oughts, and situations involving non-loss–loss induce a prevention focus. On the output side (the right side of Figure 12.1), a promotion focus yields sensitivity to the presence or absence of positive outcomes and approach as strategic means, whereas a prevention focus yields sensitivity to the absence or presence of negative outcomes and avoidance as strategic means.

Regulatory focus is concerned with how people approach pleasure and avoid pain in different ways. It implies that differences in performance, emotions, decision making, and so on could occur as a function of regulatory focus independent of the hedonic principle per se. It even implies that some phenomena traditionally interpreted in hedonic terms might be reconceptualized in terms of regulatory focus. These implications are considered next.

When the Hedonic Principle Is Not Enough

This section reviews research on regulatory focus that examines a variety of psychological phenomena traditionally treated in hedonic terms. I begin with the phenomena of approach and avoidance that are central to the hedonic principle. Evidence is presented that promotion focus and prevention focus involve distinct approach–avoidance strategies, and these different ways of regulating pleasure and pain are shown to have important motivational consequences in their own right. Next, research on Expectancy × Value effects is

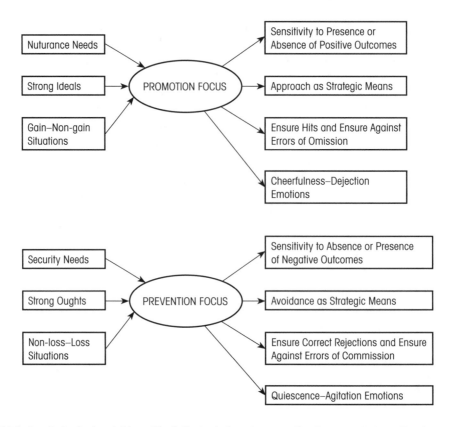

Figure 12.1 **Psychological variables with distinct relations to promotion focus and prevention focus.**

described that has found different effects for pro- motion focus and prevention focus that cannot be explained in simple hedonic terms. The role of regulatory focus in emotional and evaluative sen- sitivities is then considered. Evidence is presented that people's emotional experiences of the objects and events in their lives involve different kinds of pleasure and different kinds of pain depending on their regulatory focus, a variability not covered by the hedonic principle.

Approach and Avoidance

The hedonic principle asserts that people approach pleasure and avoid pain. It is silent, however, on how people do this. But how people approach plea- sure and avoid pain, what strategies they use, has

important motivational consequences. This section reviews some of these consequences.

Approaching Matches versus Avoiding
Mismatches as Strategic Means
Individuals can increase the likelihood that they will attain a desired end-state (i.e., reduce discrep- ancies) by either approaching matches or avoiding mismatches to that end-state. Higgins et al. (1994) tested the prediction that a strategic inclination to approach matches is more likely for promotion- focus regulation whereas a strategic inclination to avoid mismatches is more likely for prevention- focus regulation.

In one study (Higgins et al., 1994), undergrad- uate participants were asked to report on either how their hopes and goals had changed over time (priming promotion-focus ideals) or how their sense of duty and obligation had changed over time (priming prevention-focus oughts). A free-recall technique was used to reveal strategic inclinations (see also Higgins & Tykocinski, 1992). The participants read about several episodes that occurred over a few days in the life of another student. In each of the episodes, the target was trying to experience a desired end-state and used either the strategy of approaching a match or the strategy of avoiding a mismatch, as in the following examples: (a) 'Because I wanted to be at school for the beginning of my 8:30 psychology class which is usually excellent, I woke up early this morning' (approaching a match to a desired end-state), and (b) 'I wanted to take a class in photography at the community centre, so I didn't register for a class in Spanish that was scheduled at the same time' (avoiding a mismatch to a desired end-state).

It was predicted that inducing either a promotion focus or a prevention focus (operationalized by priming either ideals or oughts, respectively) would increase participants' inclinations for different regulatory strategies, which would be revealed by their recalling better those episodes that exemplified their strategic inclination. Consistent with this prediction, the participants remembered better the episodes exemplifying approaching a match to a desired end-state than those exemplifying avoiding a mismatch when a promotion focus versus a prevention focus was induced, whereas the reverse was true when a prevention focus versus a promotion focus was induced.

. . .

Approach–Avoidance and Strategic Compatibility

The literature reports inconsistent effects of incentives on performance (for a review, see Locke & Latham, 1990). One determinant of the perceived value of an incentive is its relevance to goal attainment (for a review, see Brendl & Higgins, 1996). Individuals with strong promotion goals are strategically inclined to approach matches to the goals.

An incentive that is compatible with this strategic inclination should be perceived as more goal-relevant than one that is not. For individuals with strong prevention goals, however, an incentive that is compatible with the strategic inclination to avoid mismatches to the goals should be perceived as more goal-relevant than one that is not. Shah, Higgins, and Friedman (1998) tested this hypothesis.

In Shah et al.'s (1998) study, the participants performed an anagrams task and were given the goal of identifying 90 per cent of the possible words. The promotion framed condition emphasized the strategy of approaching a match to the goal by telling participants that they would earn an extra dollar (from $4 to $5) by finding 90 per cent or more of the words. In contrast, the prevention framed condition emphasized the strategy of avoiding a mismatch to the goal by telling participants that they would avoid losing a dollar (keep their $5) by not missing more than 10 per cent of the words. Shah et al. measured participants' strength of promotion focus and strength of prevention focus (operationalized in terms of the accessibility of their ideals and oughts, respectively). Consistent with previous work on attitude accessibility (see Bassili, 1995, 1996; Fazio, 1986, 1995), the accessibility of ideals and oughts was measured through participants' response latencies when answering questions on the computer about their ideals and oughts.

The prediction was that participants with a strong regulatory focus would perform better on the anagrams task when the strategic framing of the incentive was compatible with their chronic focus. This prediction was confirmed. As individuals' strength of promotion focus increased, performance was better with the framed incentive of approaching a match than avoiding a mismatch, and as individuals' strength of prevention focus increased, performance was better with the framed incentive of avoiding a mismatch than approaching a match. These results suggest that strategic compatibility between incentives and people's goals increases motivation and performance. What about strategic compatibility between incentives, people's goals, and the strategic means by which the goals are attained? Shah et al. (1998) examined this issue in another study using the same basic paradigm.

Participants varying in promotion and prevention strength performed an anagrams task for a monetary incentive that was framed with either an approaching-a-match promotion focus or an avoiding-a-mismatch prevention focus. The anagrams were the same as those used in the first study but were divided into 'red' and 'green' subsets. The participants were told that when they found all the possible solutions for an anagram, they would gain a point if it was green and would not lose a point if it was red. Solving green anagrams (approaching a match) was compatible with a strong promotion focus, and solving red anagrams (avoiding a mismatch) was compatible with a strong prevention focus.

Shah et al. (1998) created a single variable representing the difference between participants' standardized ideal strength and standardized ought strength. They performed a median split on this difference variable, thus identifying a predominant ideal-strength group and a predominant ought-strength group. They found, as predicted, that strong promotion-focus individuals (predominant ideal strength) performed better than strong prevention-focus individuals (predominant ought strength) when working on the green anagrams in the promotion framing condition whereas strong prevention-focus individuals performed better than strong promotion-focus individuals when working on the red anagrams in the prevention framing condition.

These results suggest that motivation and performance are enhanced when the strategic nature of the means for attaining the goal is compatible with performers' regulatory focus while working on the task. Together, the results of both studies suggest that regulatory differences in strategic inclinations influence the impact of other motivational variables (i.e., incentives and means). To understand these effects, it is necessary to go beyond the hedonic principle that people approach desired end-states and recognize that they can do so by either approaching matches (promotion focus) or avoiding mismatches (prevention focus).

But this is not the end of the story. Bruner, Goodnow, and Austin (1956) noted years ago that a strategy 'refers to a pattern of decisions in the acquisition, retention, and utilization of information that serves to meet certain objectives, i.e., to insure certain forms of outcome and to insure against certain others' (p. 54). Thus, not only can people strategically approach desired end-states by either approaching matches or avoiding mismatches, but both of these different strategies include tendencies to ensure certain forms of outcome and ensure against certain others. I now consider what these tendencies might be.

Strategic Tendencies to Ensure Certain Forms of Outcome and Ensure against Certain Others

Individuals in a promotion focus, who are strategically inclined to approach matches to desired end-states, should be eager to attain advancement and gains. In contrast, individuals in a prevention focus, who are strategically inclined to avoid mismatches to desired end-states, should be vigilant to ensure safety and non-losses. One would expect this difference in self-regulatory state to be related to differences in strategic tendencies. In signal-detection terms (e.g., Tanner & Swets, 1954; see also Trope & Liberman, 1996), individuals in a state of eagerness from a promotion focus should want, especially, to accomplish hits and to avoid errors of omission or misses (i.e., a loss of accomplishment). In contrast, individuals in a state of vigilance from a prevention focus should want, especially, to attain correct rejections and to avoid errors of commission or false alarms (i.e., making a mistake). Therefore, the strategic tendencies in a promotion focus should be to ensure hits and ensure against errors of omission, whereas in a prevention focus, they should be to ensure correct rejections and ensure against errors of commission (see Figure 12.1).

It should be noted that the promotion-focus tendency to ensure against errors of omission is in the service of approaching matches and need not involve response suppression. A person in a promotion focus, for example, might persist on a difficult anagram rather than quitting to ensure against omitting a possible word. Such persistence approaches a match to the goal of finding all solutions. It also should be noted that the prevention-focus tendency to ensure correct rejections is in the service of avoiding mismatches. A person in a prevention focus, for example, might correctly reject a distractor in a recognition memory task by saying, 'No, I haven't seen that word before.' Such rejection avoids a mismatch to the goal of accuracy.

The difference between a promotion focus and a prevention focus in strategic tendencies has direct implications for the kind of decision making that has been examined in signal-detection tasks. In these tasks, a signal is either presented or not presented, and a respondent says either yes (a signal was detected) or no (no signal was detected). There are, therefore, four possible outcomes for a signal-detection trial: (a) a hit—saying yes when a signal was presented, (b) a miss—saying no when a signal was presented, (c) a false alarm—saying yes when there was no signal, and (d) a correct rejection—saying no when there was no signal. The strategic tendencies of individuals in a promotion focus are to ensure hits and ensure against errors of omission. These individuals, then, should want to ensure hits (successfully recognizing a true target) and ensure against misses (omitting a true target). They should try to recognize as many items as possible, producing an inclination to say yes (a risky bias). Individuals in a prevention focus, in contrast, have strategic tendencies to ensure correct rejections and ensure against errors of commission and thus should want to ensure correct rejections (successfully avoiding a false distractor) and ensure against false alarms (failing to avoid a false distractor). They should try not to commit mistakes, producing an inclination to say no (a conservative bias).

A study by Crowe and Higgins (1997) tested these predictions. When the participants arrived for the study, they were told that they first would perform a recognition memory task and then would be assigned a second, final task. A liked and a disliked activity had been selected earlier for each participant to serve as the final task. There were four experimental framing conditions in which participants were told that which of the alternative final tasks they would work on at the end of the session depended on their performance on the initial recognition memory task. The relation between the initial memory task and the final task was described as contingent for everyone, but the framing varied in different conditions as a function of both regulatory focus (promotion vs prevention) and valence (self-regulation working [pleasure] vs self-regulation not working [pain]). Valence was included as a variable to test whether regulatory focus influences decision making beyond any simple hedonic effects of pleasure versus pain framing.

The participants were told that first they would be given a word recognition memory task. The instructions then varied across conditions: (a) promotion working—'If you do well on the word recognition memory task, you will get to do the [liked task] instead of the other task'; (b) promotion not working—'If you don't do well on the word recognition memory task, you won't get to do the [liked task] but will have to do the other task instead'; (c) prevention working—'As long as you don't do poorly on the word recognition memory task, you won't have to do the [disliked task] and will do the other task instead'; and (d) prevention not working—'If you do poorly on the word recognition memory task, you will have to do the [disliked task] instead of the other task'. Crowe and Higgins (1997) found, as predicted, that participants in the promotion-focus condition had a risky bias of saying yes in the recognition memory task whereas participants in the prevention-focus condition had a conservative bias of saying no. Valence of framing had no effect whatsoever. Thus, regulatory focus had strategic consequences beyond the hedonic principle.

The difference in strategic tendencies between promotion and prevention focus also should produce differences in generating alternatives when problem solving. Some tasks, such as sorting, allow people to produce few or many alternatives without penalty. For example, one could use colour as the criterion to sort both fruits and vegetables, or one could use colour for vegetables and shape for fruit. The only requirement is that the sorting criterion be consistent across all members within a category. Individuals in a vigilant state from a prevention focus want to avoid errors of commission and thus should be inclined to stick to or repeat a criterion across categories, thereby simplifying the task and reducing the likelihood of making mistakes. In contrast, individuals in an eager state from a promotion focus want to ensure against omitting alternatives and thus should use alternative criteria across categories. The other prediction is that when sorting the members of a single category according to some criterion, individuals in a promotion focus should be motivated to generate many alternative subgroups to ensure hits and ensure against omissions. In contrast, individuals in a prevention focus should be motivated to generate few subgroups to simplify the task and avoid committing mistakes.

Using the same basic framing paradigm as in the recognition memory study, Crowe and Higgins (1997) examined the effects of regulatory focus on participants' sorting of fruits and vegetables. They found, as predicted, that participants in the prevention-focus framing condition were more likely to repeat their sorting criteria across both fruits and vegetables than were participants in the promotion-focus framing condition. They also found that when sorting within a category, prevention-focus participants were more likely than promotion-focus participants to use the most extreme form of simplification in which category members are sorted into just two subgroups, 'X' and 'not X', in relation to a single alternative (e.g., 'green' and

'not green' vegetables). In this study, as well, the effects of regulatory focus were independent of valence of framing (which itself had no effects).

The regulatory focus difference in strategic tendencies also should produce differences in responding to difficulties during problem solving. When a task becomes difficult, promotion-focus individuals should be eager to find hits and ensure against omitting any possible hits. In contrast, prevention-focus individuals should be vigilant against mistakes and ensure against committing the error of producing them. When a task becomes difficult, then, one would expect promotion-focus individuals to persevere and prevention-focus individuals to quit more readily. Crowe and Higgins (1997) tested these predictions with three additional tasks.

One task was to solve anagrams. In this task, success at finding a word is a correct acceptance or hit, whereas failure to find a word is an error of omission. On this task, then, the promotion-focus individuals should be eager to find words (hits) and to avoid omitting any possible words. This should yield high persistence and a strong desire to find words following a failure to find any. In contrast, the prevention-focus individuals should be vigilant against non-words and want to avoid committing the error of producing them. When individuals are experiencing difficulty, this orientation might motivate them to quit to avoid explicitly committing an error (see also Roney, Higgins, & Shah, 1995). The two other tasks were an especially difficult hidden figure in an embedded-figures task and a counting-backward task that had a difficult sequence following an easy sequence. As predicted, participants in the promotion-focus framing condition, as compared with those in the prevention-focus framing condition, solved more anagrams after experiencing difficulty on an unsolvable anagram, persisted longer on the especially difficult hidden figure, and performed better on the difficult counting-backward sequence. Once again, these effects of regulatory focus were independent of valence of framing (which itself had no effects).

The results of these studies by Crowe and Higgins (1997) highlight the need to go beyond the simple assertion of the hedonic principle that people approach pleasure and avoid pain. Not only can people generally approach desired end-states using different strategic means, but the promotion strategic inclination to approach matches involves tendencies to both ensure hits and ensure against errors of omission, and the prevention strategic inclination to avoid mismatches involves tendencies to both ensure correct rejections and ensure against errors of commission.

. . .

Emotional and Evaluative Sensitivities

The hedonic principle implies that people experience pleasure when self-regulation works and they experience pain when it does not. It is silent, however, about the different kinds of pleasure or pain that people can experience. Why is it that failure makes some people sad and other people nervous? Regulatory focus goes beyond the hedonic principle in accounting for variability in people's emotional experiences, including variability in the quality and the intensity of people's emotions, and in their emotional responses to attitude objects. This section begins by illustrating that when self-regulation does not work, people experience different kinds of painful emotions depending on their regulatory focus. Then, evidence is presented for how strength of regulatory focus moderates the intensity of different kinds of pleasant and painful emotions. Finally, studies are reviewed that demonstrate how strength of regulatory focus underlies variability in people's evaluative sensitivities to attitude objects.

Regulatory Focus Underlying Variability in Painful Emotions from Self-Discrepancies

A review of the psychological literature (see Higgins, 1987) revealed evidence that people experience dejection-related emotions, such as disappointment, dissatisfaction, or sadness, when they fail to attain their hopes or ideals whereas they experience agitation-related emotions, such as feeling uneasy, threatened, or afraid, when they fail to meet their obligations or responsibilities (e.g., Ausubel, 1955; Durkheim, 1951; Duval & Wicklund, 1972; Erikson, 1963; Freud, 1923/1961; Horney, 1950; James, 1890/1948; Kemper, 1978; Lazarus, 1968; Lewis, 1979; Piers & Singer, 1971; Rogers, 1961; Roseman, 1984; Roseman, Spindel, & Jose, 1990; Stein & Jewett, 1982; Sullivan, 1953; Wierzbicka, 1972). Such evidence suggests that discrepancies from promotion-focus ideals, which represent the absence of positive outcomes, produce different types of pain than discrepancies from prevention-focus oughts, which represent the presence of negative outcomes. This possibility was directly investigated in a series of studies testing self-discrepancy theory (Higgins, 1987). Because these studies have been reviewed elsewhere (see Higgins, 1987, 1989b, 1998), only a few illustrative studies are described here.

An early study by Strauman and Higgins (1988) used a latent-variable analysis to test the hypothesis that promotion not working, as reflected in ideal discrepancies, predicts different emotional problems than prevention not working, as reflected in ought discrepancies. One month after filling out the Selves Questionnaire measure of self-discrepancies (see Strauman & Higgins, 1988), undergraduates filled out a battery of depression and social anxiety measures. Consistent with predictions, as the magnitude of participants' actual–ideal discrepancies increased, their suffering from depression symptoms increased, and as the magnitude of their actual–ought discrepancies increased, their suffering from social anxiety symptoms increased. Actual–ideal discrepancies were not related to social anxiety, and actual–ought discrepancies were not related to depression. Subsequent studies with clinically depressed and anxious persons also have generally found that depression is related to greater actual–ideal discrepancies whereas anxiety is related to greater actual–ought discrepancies (e.g., Scott & O'Hara, 1993; Strauman, 1989).

It also should be possible to have momentary effects on dejection and agitation emotions by temporarily increasing the strength of people's promotion-focus ideals or prevention-focus oughts. This hypothesis was tested in a study by Higgins, Bond, Klein, and Strauman (1986, Study 2) that situationally primed ideals and oughts. Undergraduate participants completed the Selves Questionnaire weeks before the experiment. Individuals with either both ideal and ought discrepancies or neither type of discrepancy were recruited for the study. Half of the participants had their ideals primed when they described their own and their parents' hopes and aspirations for them. The other half of the participants had their oughts primed when they described their own and their parents' beliefs about their duties and obligations. This priming had no effect on participants with neither type of discrepancy. But the participants with both types of discrepancy experienced an increase in dejection emotions when ideals were primed and an increase in agitation-related emotions when oughts were primed.

In a replication and extension of this study, Strauman and Higgins (1987) tested whether priming just a single attribute contained in participants' ideals or oughts would produce a dejection-related or agitation-related emotional syndrome, respectively (see also Strauman, 1990). Two types of individuals were selected to study—individuals with predominant actual–ideal discrepancies (i.e., individuals with relatively high actual–ideal discrepancies and relatively low actual–ought discrepancies) and individuals with predominant actual–ought discrepancies. Self-discrepancies were primed by asking each participant to complete the phrase 'an X person _____' and selecting as 'X' whichever trait represented a self-discrepancy for that participant. For each completed sentence, a participant's total verbalization time and skin-conductance amplitude were recorded. Measures of dejection and agitation emotions also were taken. As predicted, individuals with predominant actual–ideal discrepancies experienced a dejection-related syndrome from the priming (i.e., increased dejected mood, lowered standardized skin-conductance amplitude, decreased total verbalization time), whereas individuals with predominant actual–ought discrepancies experienced an agitation-related syndrome (i.e., increased agitated mood, raised standardized skin-conductance amplitude, increased total verbalization time).

Strength of Regulatory Focus as a Moderator of Emotional Intensity

Regulatory focus clearly underlies the different kinds of pain that people experience from not attaining their goals. Other studies have shown that regulatory focus also underlies the different kinds of pleasure people experience from attaining their goals (see Higgins, Shah, & Friedman, 1997). Higgins et al. proposed that strength of regulatory focus also might moderate the intensity of people's pleasant and painful emotions. This proposal was consistent with earlier suggestions that goal strength (conceptualized as goal accessibility) might moderate the relation between goal attainment and emotional responses (see Clore, 1994; Frijda, 1996; Frijda, Ortony, Sonnemans, & Clore, 1992) and with evidence that attitude strength (operationalized as attitude accessibility) moderates the relation between attitudes and behaviour (Fazio, 1986, 1995).

In a series of correlational studies, Higgins et al. (1997) found that (a) the stronger the promotion focus (operationalized as highly accessible ideals), the stronger were the cheerfulness-related emotions experienced when promotion was working (actual–ideal congruency) and the stronger were the dejection-related emotions experienced when promotion was not working (actual–ideal discrepancy); and (b) the stronger the prevention focus (operationalized as highly accessible oughts), the stronger were the quiescence-related emotions experienced when prevention was working (actual–ought congruency) and the stronger were the agitation-related emotions experienced when prevention was not working (actual–ought discrepancy). These studies demonstrated that chronically strong promotion or prevention focus moderates the intensity of different types of pleasant and painful emotions (see Figure 12.1).

Higgins et al. (1997) hypothesized that similar effects should be obtained for situational variability in strength of regulatory focus. The task in their next study involved memorizing trigrams. As in Shah et al.'s (1998) studies, a framing paradigm was used to manipulate promotion-focus strength (i.e., emphasizing gains and non-gains) and prevention-focus strength (i.e., emphasizing non-losses and losses) while keeping constant both the criterion and consequences of success on the task. After completing the task, the participants were given false feedback that they had either succeeded or failed. It was predicted that feedback-consistent emotional change (i.e., increasing positive and decreasing negative emotions following success and decreasing positive and increasing negative emotions following failure) would be different in the two framing conditions. The study found, as predicted, that feedback-consistent change on the cheerfulness–dejection dimension was greater for participants in the promotion framing condition than the prevention framing condition whereas feedback-consistent change on the quiescence–agitation dimension was greater for participants in the prevention framing condition than the promotion framing condition (see also Roney et al., 1995).

Taken together, the results of these studies demonstrate how regulatory focus goes beyond the hedonic principle by distinguishing between types of pleasant and painful emotions with respect to both quality and intensity. Regulatory focus also goes beyond the hedonic principle by providing an explanation for the variability in people's evaluative sensitivities to objects and events in the world. This issue is considered next.

Strength of Regulatory Focus and Evaluative Sensitivity to Attitude Objects

From the perspective of the hedonic principle alone, people have pleasant or painful responses to the objects and events in their lives. This simple binary description is captured in social psychology's classic distinction between liked and disliked attitude objects. But just as success and failure can produce different types of pleasure and different types of pain, respectively, so too can attitude objects produce different types of pleasant and painful responses. A liked object, such as a painting, might make one person happy and another person relaxed. A disliked object, such as a traffic jam, might make one person discouraged and another person tense. To capture such differences in emotional evaluations of attitude objects, it is necessary to go beyond the hedonic principle. Regulatory focus strength is one variable that provides some insight into such differences.

To begin with, it should be noted that the significance of a particular emotional dimension for evaluation, such as the cheerfulness–dejection dimension, is independent of the extent to which pleasant versus painful emotions have been experienced in the past. Two persons with a strong promotion focus, for instance, might differ in their history of performance, with one experiencing primarily successes and cheerfulness and the other experiencing primarily failures and dejection. Although their specific emotional experiences differ, for both of these persons their evaluative sensitivity is to the cheerfulness–dejection significance of their personal qualities. Similarly, when evaluating other attitude objects, their sensitivity would be to the cheerfulness–dejection significance of an object (e.g., 'How happy or sad does this object make me?'). In contrast, persons with a strong prevention focus would be sensitive to the quiescence–agitation significance of their personal qualities or the qualities of other attitude objects.

If one considers a dimension like cheerfulness–dejection as a bipolar construct, then this dimension is one way to construe the world of objects and events (see Kelly, 1955). Indeed, Kelly pointed out that both similarity and contrast are inherent in the same construct. A cheerful response is similar to other cheerful responses and contrasts with dejected responses. A dejected response is similar to other dejected responses and contrasts with cheerful responses. Thus, when objects and events are evaluated in terms of their cheerfulness–dejection significance, both cheerfulness and dejection are relevant to the construal even when the emotional experience is just feeling cheerful or just feeling dejected. Because of this, the cheerfulness–dejection dimension can have special significance for two persons with a strong promotion focus despite their having different histories of feeling cheerful or dejected. Similarly, the quiescence–agitation dimension of appraisal can have special significance for two persons with a strong prevention focus despite their having different histories of feeling quiescent or agitated.

Kelly (1955) also proposed that those ways of construing that are significant for a person increase that person's sensitivity to evaluating the world in relation to the construct. Similarly, Shah and Higgins (1997a) proposed that the more a particular emotional dimension is significant for a person, the more sensitive that person will be to evaluating the world along that dimension. Such sensitivity would be revealed in faster reaction times when reporting emotional experiences along that dimension. They predicted that stronger promotion focus (operationalized as highly accessible ideals) would be related to faster emotional evaluations along the cheerfulness–dejection dimension and stronger prevention focus (operationalized as highly accessible oughts) would be related to faster emotional evaluations along the quiescence–agitation dimension.

These predictions were tested in a series of studies by Shah and Higgins (1997a). The participants in every study made emotional appraisals on cheerfulness-related scales, dejection-related scales, quiescence-related scales, and agitation-related scales. In one set of studies, the participants reported how much they experienced each emotion, either during the study or during the previous week. In another set of studies, the participants emotionally evaluated positive and negative

attitude objects that had been used in previous studies (e.g., Bargh, Chaiken, Govender, & Pratto, 1992). In each study, the analyses of reaction times statistically controlled for participants' ratings of the extent to which they experienced each emotion.

The results of these studies (Shah & Higgins, 1997a) strongly supported the predictions. In one study, for example, undergraduate participants were asked to rate how each word describing a positive object (e.g., music) or a negative object (e.g., guns) made them feel. For each participant, half of the positive object words were rated in relation to happy or satisfying and the other half in relation to relaxed; half of the negative object words were rated in relation to sad or depressing and the other half in relation to tense or agitating. Across the participants, each object word was rated on each emotional dimension an equal number of times. The study found that stronger promotion focus related to faster evaluations of the object words on the cheerfulness–dejection dimension whereas stronger prevention focus related to faster evaluations of the object words on the quiescence–agitation dimension. As in the other studies, this differential sensitivity (reflected in speed of responding) was independent of magnitude of evaluation (reflected in the extent ratings).

. . . Taken together, this research demonstrates how psychologists' understanding of important phenomena can be enhanced by moving beyond the hedonic principle to consider processes that underlie the different ways that it operates. Thus, even for classic hedonic issues like the nature of approach and avoidance, the hedonic principle is not enough. The next, more speculative section of this article considers the possibility that there also might be cases where the hedonic principle is too much. Two questions are raised in that section. First, has theory development on some classic issues, such as the motivational effects of inconsistency or low self-esteem, been handicapped by limiting psychological concepts to simple pleasure–pain distinctions? Second, might at least some phenomena classically understood in hedonic terms have little to do, in fact, with pleasure and pain at all (or at least much less than commonly assumed)? These phenomena include the psychological effects of positive versus negative emotions and the psychological nature of threat versus opportunity and optimism versus pessimism.

When the Hedonic Principle Is Too Much

A disadvantage of a principle that is intuitively appealing and simple and that promises a wide range of applicability is that it tends to be used to understand phenomena with little questioning of its hidden assumptions. This is certainly true of the hedonic principle. Not only has its application been ubiquitous in psychology and other disciplines, but this has occurred with little consideration for the alternative ways in which it might operate. This is one sense in which the influence of the hedonic principle on theory development has been too much. To illustrate this point, let us consider what it would mean for studying some classic motivational issues if promotion and prevention were treated as alternative ways in which the hedonic principle operated.

When the Hedonic Principle Hinders Theory Development

It is remarkable how much psychological applications of the hedonic principle have been dominated by a prevention focus. Freud (1920/1952) conceptualized the production of pleasure and the avoidance of pain in terms of the lowering of tension. Conceptualizing pain in terms of tension and pleasure in terms of tension reduction has also been common in classic animal learning models (e.g., Hull, 1943), social psychological models (e.g., Festinger, 1957; Heider, 1958; Lewin, 1951), and personality models (e.g., Atkinson, 1964; Murray, 1938). Even in attachment theory, where Bowlby (1969, 1973) originally recognized security and

nurturance as separate survival needs, concepts such as 'safe haven', 'secure base', and 'fear of strangers' have received the most attention, and the classic attachment styles are called 'secure', 'anxious–avoidant', and 'anxious–ambivalent'.

Undoubtedly, this pervasive emphasis on prevention has influenced psychologists' observations and understanding of phenomena. Freud (1917/1959), for example, described depression in terms of agitated-related symptoms rather than dejected-related symptoms. Such agitated symptoms would be consistent with the prevention focus of his ought-related theory of depression. Animal learning models have paid much more attention to negative reinforcement (i.e., the prevention pleasure of the absence of negative) than to positive punishment (i.e., the promotion pain of the absence of positive). Is this because negative reinforcement concerns tension reduction and involves a prevention focus, whereas positive punishment does not?

To illustrate this issue more fully, let us consider cognitive consistency models in social psychology as one example of how an emphasis on prevention focus might have constrained what was studied. Both of the most influential cognitive consistency models in social psychology, Festinger's (1957) cognitive dissonance theory and Heider's (1958) balance theory, postulated tension reduction as their underlying motivational principle. Did this prevention focus influence how these theories were developed? Might dissonance theory's prevention focus, for example, have inclined later models to emphasize individuals' feelings of responsibility for the negative consequences of their actions (e.g., Cooper & Fazio, 1984)?

It is possible that the prevention focus of dissonance and balance theory constrained which strategic resolutions to inconsistency received attention. In the classic dissonance paradigm of counterattitudinal advocacy, for example, the two resolutions that are emphasized are people rejecting responsibility for advocating the wrong position (e.g., by deciding they had no choice or derogating the experiment) and correcting what would be an error of commission by expressing a current attitude that is consistent with their advocated position. In contrast to these prevention strategies of weakening dissonant elements, a more promotion resolution would be to strengthen consonant elements, such as finding some positive consequence of one's actions, some silver lining. Similarly, Heider's (1958) resolutions for imbalance involved the prevention strategies of correcting mistaken beliefs and rejecting or denying associations, such as beginning to feel that some act is really not so bad or deciding that someone is not really responsible for his or her act. A more promotion resolution for imbalance, such as when two of one's close friends dislike each other, might be to encourage and support them to get along better.

Concentrating on the hedonic principle rather than on the different ways that it operates is a shortcoming in theory development because alternative conceptualizations are overlooked. It can lead to an overemphasis on the prevention focus to the exclusion of promotion-focus possibilities, as just noted. It also can lead to an overemphasis on the promotion focus to the exclusion of prevention-focus possibilities. As one illustration, let us briefly consider the area of self-esteem. In contrast to the prevention focus of Freud (1917/1959), Rogers (1961) had a promotion focus. His concern with actual–ideal congruencies and discrepancies inspired the next quarter century of investigating the pleasures and pains of high and low self-esteem, respectively. Once again, the field paid little attention to other principles that might underlie how self-esteem operates. In particular, psychologists remained content with conceptualizing self-esteem in terms of promotion focus with little consideration of alternatives.

An obvious alternative would be conceptualizing self-esteem in terms of prevention focus as well. If self-esteem is conceptualized as individuals' self-evaluations that they are failing to meet standards or attain goals that they or their significant others hold for them, then prevention-focus goals and standards are as relevant as promotion-focus goals and standards (see Higgins, 1996). Moreover, low self-esteem should then be predictive of agitation-related problems as well as dejection-related problems. In a similar way, psychologists study job satisfaction, marital satisfaction, life satisfaction, and so on, as if promotion working (satisfied, happy) or not working (dissatisfied, unhappy) is all that is relevant in these areas of life. Surely, prevention working (secure, relaxed) or not working (insecure, worried) is also relevant. After all, when people have problems at work, at home, and in other areas of their lives, they suffer from agitation-related distress as well as dejection-related distress.

Classic theories of cognitive consistency and well-being illustrate how psychologists' ability to address some basic issues has been handicapped by limiting psychological concepts to simple pleasure–pain distinctions. The hedonic principle is also too much when it is applied to phenomena that may have little to do with pleasure or pain at all. Illustrations of such overapplication are considered next.

When the Hedonic Principle Is Overapplied

Across all areas of psychology, there has been a fascination with the effects of positive and negative emotions. Most of the research questions have involved the simple distinction between the effects of good versus bad feelings. In social and cognitive psychology, for example, there has been an explosion of interest over the last decade in how good versus bad feelings influence cognition (for a recent review, see Schwarz & Clore, 1996). An early instance of this interest is the research on how positive versus negative moods influence memory (e.g., Bower, 1981; Isen, 1984). One especially influential conclusion from this research was that positively valenced material is more likely to be remembered in positive moods and negatively valenced material is more likely to be remembered in negative moods (see Schwarz & Clore, 1996). But are pleasure and pain really necessary for such memory effects to occur? Findings from a recent study suggest that they might not be.

Higgins and Tykocinski (1992) selected participants who had either a strong promotion focus (operationalized as predominant actual–ideal discrepancies) or a strong prevention focus (operationalized as predominant actual–ought discrepancies). All of the participants read about events in the life of another person that involved promotion working or not working (e.g., 'I've been wanting to see this movie at the 8th Street theatre for some time, so this evening I went there straight after school to find out that it's not showing anymore') and prevention working or not working (e.g., 'I was stuck in the subway for 35 minutes with at least 15 sweating passengers breathing down my neck'). The study found that events involving promotion were remembered better by promotion-focus participants than prevention-focus participants, but the reverse was true for events involving prevention. Most important, this interaction was independent of participants' pre-mood, post-mood, or change in mood. Thus, pleasure or pain experiences during the study were not necessary for memory effects to occur. What influenced memory was the compatibility between participants' chronic regulatory focus and the regulatory focus of the events.

The results of this study (Higgins & Tykocinski, 1992) raise the possibility that previous mood and memory studies might not have depended on experiences of pleasure and pain. When these studies manipulated pleasure and pain with music, movies, gifts, or recollections of past experiences, might they have manipulated more than pleasure and pain? It is likely that regulatory focus was manipulated as well, and it is possible that inducing a promotion or prevention focus is critical for the memory effects to occur. Indeed, inducing a negative prevention focus might facilitate memory for fearful events but not for equally negative sad events, or inducing a promotion focus might facilitate memory for joyful events but not for equally positive relaxing events (see Strauman, 1990).

Rather than pleasure or pain being necessary for feelings to influence memory, what might be necessary is compatibility between a person's regulatory focus and the regulatory focus represented in the to-be-remembered events.

There has been a special fascination among psychologists, especially clinicians, with how anxiety influences cognition. One major conclusion is that anxiety has negative effects on creativity. When people experience high (vs low) anxiety, for example, they produce fewer subgroups in a sorting task, which is said to reflect concrete rather than abstract thinking (e.g., Mikulincer, Kedem, & Paz, 1990). As described earlier, however, Crowe and Higgins (1997) found that individuals with a prevention focus produced fewer subgroups in a sorting task than did individuals with a promotion focus, and this effect was independent of the participants' feelings during the study. Rather than pleasure or pain being necessary for the sorting effects to occur, it was a prevention focus that produced fewer subgroupings. It should be noted in this regard that participants in the high-anxious group of previous studies (whether selected or induced) were likely to have been in a prevention focus.

The threat versus opportunity distinction in organizational psychology might be another case where the hedonic principle has been overapplied. Representing strategic issues as threats versus opportunities has been considered an important variable influencing decision makers' information processing and decisions. As Dutton and Jackson (1987) pointed out, a sense of importance and future is contained in both representations, but what differentiates them is that opportunity involves a positive situation in which gain is likely (and control is high) and threat involves a negative situation in which loss is likely (and control is low). This way of distinguishing between opportunity and threat potentially confounds the hedonic principle and regulatory focus. That is, opportunity is discussed as if it involved promotion working, and threat is discussed as if it involved prevention not working, thus confounding promotion versus prevention and pleasure versus pain.

By separating regulatory focus and the hedonic principle when studying threat versus opportunity, one might discover that there are significant independent effects of regulatory focus on decision makers' information processing and decisions. Indeed, findings of regulatory focus effects on decision making (e.g., Crowe & Higgins, 1997; Shah & Higgins, 1997b) suggest that this is the case. It is important in this area to distinguish between the opportunity for accomplishment (promotion opportunity) and the opportunity for safety or security (prevention opportunity) and between the threat of non-fulfillment (promotion threat) and the threat of committing mistakes (prevention threat). With such distinctions, it would be possible to examine threat versus opportunity effects independent of the hedonic principle.

As a final example of potential overapplication of the hedonic principle, what exactly is meant by the familiar personality distinction between optimism and pessimism? Among personality psychologists, the dimension of optimism versus pessimism refers to the extent to which a person has favourable expectancies about attaining desired end-states (e.g., Carver, Reynolds, & Scheier, 1994; Norem & Cantor, 1986b; Norem & Illingworth, 1993). From this perspective, the critical difference between optimists and pessimists is that the former experience the pleasure of favourable expectancies whereas the latter experience the pain of unfavourable expectancies. Thus, the hedonic principle is critical to this distinction. Could optimism–pessimism be conceptualized in a manner that does not depend on the hedonic principle?

One possibility is that optimism involves a promotion focus whereas pessimism involves a prevention focus. From this perspective, hedonic experiences per se would no longer be critical to understanding the motivational consequences of optimism or pessimism. Instead, regulatory focus differences in strategic inclinations would

be critical. There is some support for this position in the literature. Both defensive pessimists and depressed pessimists experience the pain of anticipated failure (see Norem & Cantor, 1986b; Norem & Illingworth, 1993). The anxious affect of defensive pessimists suggests that they have a prevention focus. If they do, they should strategically ensure against errors of commission. Indeed, the literature reports that defensive pessimists are vigilant in their efforts to avoid contemplated disaster, a strategy that reportedly works for them (see Norem & Cantor, 1986b; Norem & Illingworth, 1993). In contrast, the dejected affect of depressed pessimists suggests that they have a promotion focus. If they do, they should strategically ensure against errors of omission. In fact, the strategies of depressive pessimists include attempts to use others to obtain what they are missing, a strategy that reportedly doesn't work for them (see Coyne, Kahn, & Gotlib, 1987; Lewinsohn, 1974). Thus, the fact that defensive pessimists tend to perform well and depressive pessimists tend to perform poorly cannot be explained in terms of the hedonic principle, because both groups experience the pain of anticipating failure. It can be explained, however, in terms of differences in regulatory focus that produce different strategic inclinations that vary in effectiveness.

. . .

Concluding Comment

What do I mean by going beyond the hedonic principle? One interpretation is that psychologists should not restrict themselves to this principle's simple assertion but should examine more fully the different ways that people approach pleasure and avoid pain. I do, indeed, mean to suggest this. But I also mean to suggest something more. The subjective utility models are not just incomplete when they ignore the unpredicted negative interaction between expectancy and value for people in a prevention focus. A single emotional distress category that collapses mild depression and anxiety is not just too broad when these emotions, differing in regulatory focus, involve fundamentally different strategic motivation. Claims about biological underpinnings of emotion based on neuroimages of brain responses to pleasure and pain are not just overly general when they fail to distinguish among types of pleasure and types of pain. In such cases, the problem is not simply that psychologists overlook important distinctions by restricting themselves to the hedonic principle. The problem is that overreliance on the hedonic principle can yield misleading conclusions. To discover the true nature of approach–avoidance motivation, it is not simply desirable but essential to move beyond the hedonic principle to the principles underlying its operation.

Discussion Questions

1. How is regulatory focus theory similar to cognitive dissonance theory and how does it expand on it?
2. How is Higgins's distinction between promotion and prevention similar to and different from Elliot's conceptualization of approach and avoidance (see Unit 4)?
3. How is Higgins's distinction between promotion and prevention similar to and different from the distinction between intrinsic and extrinsic motivation?

Unit Five Further Reading

For other key readings in the area of motivated cognition, see

Bruner, J.S., & Goodman, C.C. (1947). Value and need as organizing factors in perception. *Journal of Abnormal Social Psychology, 42*, 33–44.
Ditto, P.H., & Lopez, D.F. (1992). Motivated skepticism: Use of differential decision criteria for preferred and non-preferred conclusions. *Journal of Personality and Social Psychology, 63*, 568–84.
Epley, N. & Dunning, D. (2000). Feeling 'holier than thou': Are self-serving assessments produced by errors in self or social prediction? *Journal of Personality and Social Psychology, 79*, 861–75.
Balcetis, E., & Dunning, D. (2006). See what you want to see: Motivational influences on visual perception. *Journal of Personality and Social Psychology, 91*, 612–25.

Unit Six

Cognition's Effect on Motivation

Cognitive psychologists have for some time pointed out that the same object (e.g., a car) can be mentally represented in multiple ways, ranging from a narrower, more concrete representation (e.g., a 1987 Chevrolet convertible) to a broader, more abstract representation (e.g., a mode of transportation; Rosch & Lloyd, 1978). Starting in the mid-1980s, social psychologists Robin Vallacher and Daniel Wegner began using similar ideas to understand people's representation of their own actions. According to their action identification theory, people may mentally represent the same action (e.g., voting) in a broader sense (e.g., expressing one's political views) or in a narrower sense (e.g., pulling a lever). Vallacher and Wegner's insight was to point out that how broadly versus narrowly one happens to identify an action has significant implications for motivation and self-regulation. For example, higher level identifications are better suited for 'keeping your eye on the prize', while lower level identifications are better suited for 'doing the dirty work'. Thus, Vallacher and Wegner suggest that optimal performance requires the ability to shift between levels in an appropriate manner.

In the 1987 paper included in this Unit, Vallacher and Wegner spell out specific antecedent conditions that tend to activate a high- versus low-level identification. They also describe the mechanics of when and how people shift between levels. In another work, these authors have highlighted individual differences in the general tendency to identify actions broadly versus narrowly (Vallacher & Wegner, 1989).

In a separate line of research, Peter Gollwitzer and colleagues have noted that most actions can be mentally subdivided into different stages, including the *deliberation* stage and the *implementation* stage. In the deliberation stage, the individual's focus is on weighing different outcomes to pursue based on which seems most appealing. In the implementation stage, a course of action has been selected and the focus turns to marshalling one's cognitive resources toward executing the goal. In an impressive series of demonstrations, Gollwitzer and colleagues have shown that activating the 'implementation mindset' (i.e., having people think about *how* they will reach the desired outcome) generally leads to better results than merely imagining the desired outcome. For example, among undergraduates who were asked to write a report over the Christmas holidays, 32 per cent of those who thought about the goal actually complied, in contrast with 71 per cent of those who formed implementation intentions (Gollwitzer & Brandstaetter, 1997). Thus, a subtle change in how an action is mentally represented can yield significant consequences on how (or even whether) the action is executed.

Subtle manipulations can influence more than how we represent a goal; they can also influence which goal we adopt in the first place. Chartrand and Bargh (1999), for example, demonstrated that subliminally presenting participants with words related to achievement leads to superior performance on a standardized test. Moreover, work by Shah and Kruglanski (2003) has shown that subliminally priming means (e.g., 'going to the gym') can activate corresponding goals (e.g., 'fitness'), while subliminally priming goals can activate corresponding means. Thus, particular goals and behaviours can be pushed to the forefront (i.e., made more accessible) by cues in the environment, according to the same cognitive principles that govern the accessibility of the personality traits we use to describe other people (e.g., Higgins, Rholes, & Jones, 1977). This suggests an important point about motivation: Often, the goals we pursue and the means we use to pursue them are not the result of deep-seated values or beliefs (as they often may appear to us), but are instead the result of subtle cues that happen to be in our ambient surroundings. In other words, motivation can often have more of an arbitrary quality than we may care to admit.

13. What Do People Think They're Doing? Action Identification and Human Behaviour

Robin R. Vallacher, Florida Atlantic University
Daniel M. Wegner, Trinity University

□ ■ □

Editor's Introduction

If I ask you the question, 'What are you doing?' it might seem like a trivial task to provide an answer. But upon further reflection, you will realize that how you answer that question requires you to make some critical decisions about how you want to describe your action. Are you 'following lines of print', 'reading a book on motivation', or 'furthering you knowledge'? How generally versus specifically should you describe your action? To what extent should you focus on details, the *how* of the action, and to what extent should you focus on the big picture, the *why* of the action?

Vallacher and Wegner suggest that which description you choose has profound implications on your subsequent cognition, affect, and behaviour. In many cases, focusing on lower level action identities promotes effective procedures, that is, it 'greases the wheel' and increases the likelihood that the action will accomplish its intended goal. Focusing on higher level action identities puts the action into its larger context, providing *meaning* for one's action. (After all, we do not like to feel as if we have done something for no purpose.) Thus, the most effectively operating person is able to cycle back and forth between levels, boosting attention to details when the need arises (e.g., during a surprisingly difficult patch), but boosting attention to the larger picture when the need arises (e.g., to provide a motivational reminder of why one is doing the task in the first place). In the present article you will see how these ideas about the mental representation of behaviour generate novel and interesting insights about several classic social psychological phenomena.

Vallacher and Wegner's ideas were further developed and taken in new directions in a more recent theory, construal level theory (CLT; Trope & Liberman, 2003). According to CLT, a significant predictor of what level of action identification you will select is psychological distance. For example, when thinking about hosting a party, if the date is in the distant future people will tend to focus on broader, higher level aspects (e.g., having fun with friends), but if the date is looming just around the corner, people will tend to focus on more concrete, lower level aspects (e.g., 'Did I buy enough cups?'; Liberman & Trope, 1998). (Note that Trope and colleagues have found that other forms of psychological distance, including actual distance, function similarly to temporal distance.)

A fascinating implication of this tendency involves gambles. For example, if a particular gamble involves an event in the distant future, people are disproportionately influenced by the size of the potential payoff, but if the gamble involves an event in the near future, people are more swayed by the likelihood of winning. In other words, it's 'odds now, money later' (Sagristano, Liberman, & Trope, 2002). In another motivational area—the realm of self-control—Fujita and colleagues have found that, in general, high-level construals facilitate self-control. Over a series of studies, participants who had been randomly assigned to a high- versus low-level construal exhibited better self-control in a variety of ways, including longer times gripping a resistant hand grip (Fujita et al., 2006). In a related vein, Kross and Ayduk (2008) found that people who described their emotions following a negative experience in a 'self-distanced' versus 'self-immersed' style exhibited better recovery and fewer lingering effects. It is reasonable to assume that self-distanced representations share a good deal of conceptual overlap with high-level identifications. When you read Unit 8 of this book, think back to these ideas and consider how they may affect basic self-regulatory phenomena.

□ ■ □

People always seem to be doing something. They also seem to be quite adept at identifying what they are doing. What is less clear is how these two observations relate to one another. The theory of action identification (Vallacher & Wegner, 1985; Wegner & Vallacher, 1986) is explicitly concerned with this issue. At the heart of the theory are three interacting processes that specify a causal interdependence between what people are doing and what they think they are doing. Through a delineation of these processes, we hope to reveal how action constrains one's identification of action and, in turn, how action identification exerts a selecting and guiding force in subsequent action. The proposed causal interdependence between action and action identification proves useful in understanding a host of issues in human psychology that centre on the mental control of action. These issues are thus discussed in detail, with attention given in each case to the points of contact between our analysis and prior conceptualizations. We begin by reviewing the background and principles of the theory.

Cognition and Action

That people can think about what they do is hardly a controversial idea in psychology. The suggestion, however, that specifiable causal links exist between cognitive representations of action and overt behaviour is greeted with skepticism in certain quarters. This skepticism is fuelled in part by people's capacity for seemingly unbounded constructions of behaviour. As philosophers have long noted, any segment of behaviour can be consciously identified in many different ways

(Anscombe, 1957; Austin, 1961: Danto, 1963; Goldman, 1970: Ryle, 1949; Wittgenstein, 1953). Something as simple as 'meeting someone', for instance, could be recognized by anyone with an even mildly active mental life as 'being social', 'exchanging pleasantries', 'learning about someone new', 'revealing one's personality', or even 'uttering words'. But while representations of action admit to considerable variability and seem subject to noteworthy change from moment to moment, behaviour seems to follow a more constrained path, often exhibiting a press toward completion in the face of situational forces, biological needs, and reinforcement contingencies. Thus, as interesting as cognitive representations may be in their own right, they are considered by many to operate independently of the causal mechanisms promoting overt action.

Many psychologists, of course, balk at the notion that cognitive representations of action are mere epiphenomena, with no necessary mapping onto specific overt behavioural events. Those who have addressed this issue explicitly, however, commonly advocate only a limited perspective on the link between cognitive representations and overt behaviour. Thus, some commentators have suggested that behaviour dynamics are primary, with representations of action arising after the fact, or at best, concurrently with the action. This *reflective* connection finds explicit expression in such otherwise distinct theories as self-perception theory (Bem, 1972) and psychoanalysis (Freud, 1914/1960). In self-perception theory, the true cause of behaviour is some stimulus in the action setting; if the actor does not recognize the stimulus as causal, he or she casts about for other likely

causal candidates, even inventing inner dispositions if a plausible external cause cannot be found.
In classic Freudian theory, meanwhile, the true
cause of action is some unconscious motive striving for expression in even the most mundane of
everyday settings. Cognitive representations are
said to arise after the fact in an attempt to justify
or make sense of what was done. Because the true
motive is too painful to acknowledge, moreover,
the person's post hoc cognitions are, by definition,
considered inaccurate.

Other systems stress what might be called the
intent connection. In this perspective, cognitive
representations of action function as templates for
subsequent overt behaviour. James's (1890) analysis of ideomotor action, for instance, holds that an
idea of action tends to produce the action unless
something intervenes to prevent it. This is readily
apparent in the case of simple physical movements;
to move a finger, one simply thinks about doing
so. Not surprisingly, then, the intent connection
provides a reasonable summary statement regarding contemporary work on the cognitive control of
basic movements (e.g., Adams, 1971; Norman &
Shallice, 1980; Rosenbaum, Kenny, & Derr, 1983;
Schmidt, 1975). With respect to actions of significant duration or importance in people's lives,
however, the role of cognitive representations of
action in guiding action is less established. What
little is known about the cognition-action link
in the context of meaningful behaviour has been
inferred from work in cognitive behaviour therapy
(e.g., Meichenbaum, 1977); decision making (e.g.,
Kahneman, Slovic, & Tversky, 1982); and traditional social-psychological attitude research (e.g.,
Azjen & Fishbein, 1977). A direct analysis of how
people think about their most far-reaching and
consequential actions, and how such thoughts may
affect the nature of these actions, is thus missing in
contemporary psychology.

A compelling case can be made for both the
reflective and intent connections. People do seem
to develop representations of their action after
the fact, but they also seem capable of planning

and directing their action in accord with their
cognitive representations. What is needed, then,
is a system that provides for integration of these
two prototypical cognition-action links, specifying the conditions under which one or the other
is likely to occur. This is the task of action identification theory. The theory holds that the relationship between cognitive representations and
overt behaviour is not unidirectional, but cyclical.
Through the intent connection, cognitive representations generate action, and through the reflective connection, new representations of what one
is doing can emerge to set the stage for a revised
intent connection. In this way, people sometimes
are led to maintain a course of action over an
extended period of time and on other occasions
are led to show dramatic changes in behaviour
from one moment to the next.

Action Identification Theory

The essence of the theory is that the identification
of one's action, though highly variable in principle, is ultimately constrained by reality. Through
the interplay of three processes, each framed as a
principle of the theory, people are said to gravitate toward an identification of action that proves
effective in maintaining the action. In this section,
we present these principles and show their coordinated operation in determining action identification. In the sections to follow, we develop specific
determinants of action identification that derive
from this analysis and develop the implications of
the theory for recurring issues in psychology.

Levels of Identification

Fundamental to the theory is the recognition that
the various identifications for an action do not exist
as a random assemblage of unrelated elements.
Instead, act identities bear systematic relations to
one another in an organized cognitive representation of the action—the action's *identity structure*.
An identity structure is essentially a hierarchical
arrangement of an action's various identities. Lower

level identities in this hierarchy convey the details or specifics of the action and so indicate how the action is done. Higher level identities convey a more general understanding of the action, indicating why the action is done or what its effects and implications are. Relative to low-level identities, higher level identities tend to be less movement defined and more abstract and to provide a more comprehensive understanding of the action. Identification level is a relative concept, of course, and so whether a given act identity is considered a means or an end, a detail or an implication, depends on the act identity with which it is compared.

The distinction between relatively low- and high-level identities is communicated in everyday language when people indicate that one performs one act identity *by* performing another (Goldman, 1970). Thus, one sees if someone is home *by* pushing a doorbell, and one pushes a doorbell *by* moving a finger. Although these three act identities all pertain to the same act, they exist at different levels in a cognitive hierarchy by virtue of their perceived functional asymmetry. 'Seeing if someone is home' occupies the highest level, 'pushing a doorbell' the next highest, and 'moving a finger' the lowest level. Our research has confirmed that people appreciate the notion of an asymmetric *by* relation and can use this relational property to distinguish among act identities (Vallacher, Wegner, Bordieri, & Wenzlaff, 1981).

Theoretical Principles

The differences between low- and high-level identities, when considered in conjunction with the three principles of the theory, indicate how the 'uncertain act' is resolved realistically by people in everyday life. The first principle holds that *action is maintained with respect to its prepotent identity.* This principle acknowledges the mental control of action that is reflected in a broad spectrum of theoretical traditions (e.g., Carver & Scheier, 1981; James, 1890; Luria, 1961; Miller, Galanter, & Pribram, 1960; Powers, 1973; Schank & Abelson, 1977; Vygotsky, 1962). Thus, people have in mind

a certain idea of what they are doing or want to do and use this prepotent identity as a frame of reference for implementing the action, monitoring its occurrence, and reflecting on its attainment. Because act identities exist at different levels, this principle also holds that people maintain action at different levels. A person may set out simply to 'move a finger', for instance, and monitor subsequent action to see whether this intention has been fulfilled, or the person may set out to 'dial the phone' (a higher level identity) or 'call home' (a yet higher level identity), and monitor the attainment of whichever identity is prepotent.

This principle is useful for understanding instances of action stability, the maintenance of a given action over time and across circumstances. Thus, as long as a particular act identity is prepotent, it provides direction for action in the service of identity attainment. Stability is an important and noteworthy feature of human action, of course, but so is the potential for change and apparent inconsistency. The second and third principles represent two basic processes underlying the manifestation of such change.

The second principle holds that *when both a lower and a higher level act identity are available, there is a tendency for the higher level identity to become prepotent.* The idea here is simply that people are always sensitive to the larger meanings, effects, and implications of what they are doing. This tendency is reflected, implicitly or explicitly, in a variety of psychological systems. Learning under reinforcement contingencies (e.g., Skinner, 1953), the mastery of skilled action (e.g., Bruner, 1970; Bryan & Harter, 1899; Kimble & Perlmuter, 1970), Gestalt principles of perception (e.g., Koffka, 1935), even the existentialists' focus on the 'search for meaning' (e.g., Frankl, 1963)—all of these seemingly distinct dynamics have in common the notion that act representations expand to encompass broader effects and meanings. In learning, a relatively basic act expands to incorporate the reinforcing effects of the act; in the development of mastery, discrete acts become automated and integrated into a larger action unit; in Gestalt psychology, parts become unified to produce a whole; and in existentialism, patterns discerned in distinct actions become the basis for new awareness of what one is doing and who one is.

Much of the research on action identification to date has focused on the emergence of higher level identities in accordance with the second principle (Wegner, Vallacher, Kiersted, & Dizadji, 1986; Wegner, Vallacher, Macomber, Wood, & Arps, 1984). This research confirms that any time a person has only a low-level understanding of what he or she is doing, there is a readiness to accept any higher level identity made available by the context surrounding the action and that this emergent identity can promote wholly new courses of action. In a study by Wegner et al. (1986, Experiment 1), for instance, subjects who identified the act of 'participating in an experiment' in terms of its details were found to be more susceptible to a suggestion that they were either 'behaving altruistically' (e.g., helping the experimenter) or 'behaving selfishly' (e.g., earning extra credits). These subjects, moreover, chose to participate in subsequent activities that were consistent with their emergent understanding. In another study (Wegner et al., 1986, Experiment 2), subjects were presented with bogus personality feedback indicating that they were either co-operative or competitive. In comparison with subjects who had initially described their behaviour for analysis at a comprehensive (high) level, those who described their behaviour at a detailed (low) level were more accepting of the feedback and more likely to volunteer for future activities consistent with the feedback.

If this were the only mechanism by which identifications of action showed change, people's mental life might indeed be one of fantasy, with little relation to overt behaviour. Thus, a person could come to look upon 'maintaining eye contact' as 'winning trust', 'throwing dice' as 'winning money', or even 'sitting with my legs crossed while watching TV' as 'controlling the outcome of the Super Bowl'. While these identities could well make sense at the time of their emergence, they may have a tenuous relation at best to any subsequent behaviour, no matter how much the person thought he or she was enacting them. The accumulation of high-level identities through coincidence or chance, or through more standard avenues of emergence such as environmental cues and social feedback processes, could charge even the simplest act with unconstrained significance, leaving the actor 'buried in thought' (Tolman, 1932) and allowing only occasional contact with the world of real behaviour.

Action identification is brought back to reality through a process specified in the theory's third principle: *When an action cannot be maintained in terms of its prepotent identity, there is a tendency for a lower level identity to become prepotent.* The idea here is simply that people must sometimes concern themselves with the how-to aspects of action in order to perform the action. A person may set out to 'change a light bulb', for instance, but unless that action is automated to an appreciable extent, he or she may have to consciously plan and monitor such things as 'grasping the bulb at its widest point', 'turning the bulb counterclockwise', and so forth. Even if the action has become automated through repeated experience, its details might still become prepotent if the action were to be disrupted by some means. The light bulb, for instance, may prove to be stuck in its socket, in which case the person might give conscious consideration to 'grasping' and 'turning' at the temporary expense of the higher level 'changing' identity. In the attempt to maintain action under one identity, one must often abandon that identity in favour of more performable identities. So, although a person may be inclined to adopt any of a host of higher level identities for an action, these identities dissipate in short order if they prove to be ineffective guides to subsequent action. The potential for flights of fancy that is inherent in the second principle is unlikely to represent a serious problem for most people, then, because of the reality orientation inherent in the third principle.

Research to date has documented the potential for movement to lower levels of identification in the face of high-level disruption. In a study by Wegner et al. (1984, Experiment 2), for instance, experienced coffee drinkers were asked to drink coffee from one of two rather different cups—a normal cup and an unwieldly cup weighing approximately 0.5 kg. Upon completion of this act, subjects were asked to rate how well each of 30 identities for coffee drinking described what they had done. Subjects in the normal cup condition tended to give relatively strong endorsement to identities such as 'getting energized' or 'promoting my caffeine habit'. Subjects in the unwieldly cup condition, for whom the act of drinking proved difficult to do, tended to give relatively strong endorsement to identities at a substantially lower level, such as 'drinking a liquid', 'swallowing', and 'lifting a cup to my lips'. Presumably, these subjects could not 'energize themselves' or 'promote their caffeine habit' with only these identities in mind. Instead, to accomplish the act at all, they had to think about the mechanics of coffee drinking, and this low-level orientation became prepotent, temporarily at least, in lieu of their accustomed way of thinking about the act.

A similar effect was obtained by Wegner, Connally, Shearer, and Vallacher (1983) in a study involving the act of eating. All subjects were invited to 'eat Cheetos'. But whereas some subjects were to eat the Cheetos in the usual manner (with their hands), other subjects were asked to retrieve the Cheetos with a pair of chopsticks. This latter technique proved difficult to do, and when asked subsequently what they had done, subjects in the chopsticks condition tended to eschew identities like 'eating', 'reducing hunger', and 'getting nutrition' in favour of lower level identities like 'chewing', 'swallowing', 'putting food in my mouth', and 'moving my hands'. Subjects in the non-chopsticks condition, meanwhile, gave weaker endorsement to these lower level identities and correspondingly stronger endorsement to the various higher level identities ('reducing hunger', 'getting nutrition',

etc.). As in the coffee drinking study, then, difficulty in enacting an action normally identified at high level promoted a movement to a lower level of identification.

The three principles of the theory work together in such a way that maintainable identifications of one's action ultimately develop. There is a constant press for higher level understanding and control of action, but this press is countermanded by movement to lower levels of identification when the higher level identities cannot be enacted automatically. Over time and repeated action, the oscillations reflected in this dynamic interplay begin to flatten out, and the person converges on an identity at a particular level that enables him or her to perform the action up to his or her capacity. For any given action performed by a particular person, then, the range of potential understanding is likely to be notably restricted in the service of effective action control.

Determinants of Identification Level

The principles of the theory suggest in a general way how people come to an unambiguous understanding of what they are doing. To enable predictions regarding specific instances of action identification, however, it is necessary to relate the processes outlined in the theory to factors amenable to operational definition. Three sets of such factors would seem to play especially pivotal roles in promoting unequivocal act knowledge: the context in which the action takes place, the action's difficulty, and the person's experience with the action. Each of these influences on prepotent identification is discussed in turn.

Action Context

Knowing only the physical movements involved in an action, it is difficult to know what was done. As Danto (1963) has observed, without knowledge of circumstances or events outside the action itself, one is left with only the most rudimentary of identities, or what he called a 'basic act'. It is through sensitivity to contextual cues that movement becomes represented in terms of its causal effects, conventional interpretations, and the like. What appears to be the same action can therefore be identified in vastly different ways depending on the relative salience of various cues to identification provided by the action's context. 'Solving a math puzzle', for instance, might be thought of primarily as 'keeping track of numbers' or 'making mental calculations' in one setting (e.g., the privacy of one's home) but as 'showing my math skill' or 'trying not to embarrass myself' in another (e.g., a testing situation).

Context often imparts a relatively high level of identification to action. It is difficult to look upon what one is doing as simply a set of movements when there are circumstantial and social cues as to the labels, effects, and implications of these movements. This idea, of course, is inherent in the second principle of the theory and has been confirmed in the research on action emergence alluded to earlier (Wegner et al., 1986; Wegner et al., 1984). Thus, unless one already has a clear sense of the larger meaning of what one is doing, there is a readiness to embrace new identifications of action provided by the context in which one is acting.

At the same time, certain kinds of contextual factors can move a person to relatively low levels of identification. Foremost among these factors are those that serve to disrupt action (e.g., Wegner et al., 1983; Wegner et al., 1984, Experiment 2). Thus, an awkward cup can make one think of the details associated with 'drinking', and poor transmission quality during a phone call can change the prepotent identity of one's action from 'exchanging gossip' to 'making myself heard' or 'speaking loudly and clearly'. Beyond their potential for disrupting action, some situations offer ambiguous or inconsistent cues as to the meaning or effect of what one is doing. In social situations, for instance, it is often hard to discern whether one is creating a good or bad impression, demonstrating

wit or poor taste, and so on. The only thing one knows for sure is that one is 'talking', 'gesturing', and the like. Uncertainty regarding the effects and implications of one's behaviour is especially likely in novel settings lacking familiar cues to higher level meaning. A person in such a setting may be prone to accept any higher level identities made available, but until these identities are provided the person is left with only a rudimentary sense of what he or she is doing. Finally, in some contexts a person may be asked to monitor the details of his or her behaviour as it is being enacted and in this way experience a lower level of identification than would normally be the case (e.g., Wegner et al., 1986, Experiment 2; Wegner et al., 1984, Experiment 1).

Action Difficulty

Contextual cues to identities at different levels are probably present in the majority of everyday circumstances. The novelty of a particular setting could make one sensitive to the lower level features of what one is doing, for example, while the evaluative pressures in the setting might render higher level identities (e.g., 'impress others', 'show my skill') prepotent. For this reason, context alone is rarely an unambiguous guide to a person's prepotent level of identification. Our analysis suggests a far less equivocal guide to identification level—the action's personal level of difficulty.

Some things are harder to do than others. A person may set out to 'push a doorbell', for example, and find that this identity is easily enacted. The person may then try to 'sell a set of encyclopedias' to the person answering the doorbell—a somewhat more formidable task. As the action begins to unfold, the person finds it necessary to suspend the 'selling' identity in favour of more specific identities such as 'sounding sincere', 'appearing respectful yet confident', and 'raising the issue of responsible parenthood'. Each of these identities, in turn, may prove somewhat difficult to maintain, in which case the person will probably begin to think in terms of yet lower level identities.

'Sounding sincere', for example, may require 'furrowing one's eyebrows', 'making continuous eye contact', and 'talking in a slow and deliberate tone of voice'.

This example illustrates a very basic point: The more difficult or disruption-prone an action is under a given identity, the greater the likelihood that it will be enacted under a lower level identity. Disruption potential, in turn, is traceable to more specific aspects of action. Five aspects in particular seem important and so are likely to establish identification level prepotency. We refer to these key aspects of action as *maintenance indicators,* because they indicate the level at which an action should be identified for optimal performance. Thus, an action under a particular identity can be scaled with respect to its relative *difficulty of enactment, familiarity, complexity* (variety of means or subacts), *enactment time,* and *learning time* (amount of time it takes to learn to do the action well). Compared to the act of 'selling encyclopedias', for instance, 'pushing a doorbell' is relatively easy: familiar for most people, can be enacted in only a few ways, occupies a short interval of time, and takes little time to learn. An action should be identified at a relatively high as opposed to low level to the extent that it shares these indicator values; an action with indicator values at the opposite ends of these dimensions, meanwhile, is likely to be maintained with lower level identities in mind.

To see whether such relationships exist, Wegner and Vallacher (1983) arranged for a variety of everyday actions to be rated with respect to each of the five maintenance indicators and for these actions to be reidentified at either a lower or a higher level, according to the subjects' personal preference. A sample of 274 undergraduates (155 women, 119 men) was asked to choose low- versus high-level reidentifications for each of 25 actions.[1] These actions were chosen to represent a spectrum of the things people do in daily life and included such actions as 'pushing a doorbell', 'voting', 'paying the rent', and 'reading'. Each was presented along with two alternative identities, one lower and one higher in level, and subjects were to indicate which alternative best expressed their personal understanding of the action. Because our concern centred on the level at which people would attempt to maintain a given action, we avoided high-level alternatives that were likely to be seen as unanticipated or unpleasant consequences of the action.

By tracking the proportion of high-level choices for a given action across subjects, an average identification level value was obtained for the action (possible range = 0–1). These values were normally distributed, although the mean value was fairly high level (0.66). Actions identified at a relatively low level included 'having a cavity filled', 'taking a test', and 'resisting temptation'. Actions identified at a relatively high level included 'reading', 'locking a door', and 'pushing a doorbell'.

Another sample (35 women, 15 men) was asked to rate the 25 action stems on 5-point scales for difficulty, familiarity, complexity, enactment time, and learning time. We then intercorrelated all of the ratings with identification level across the 25 actions. Results of this analysis revealed that an action's typical level of identification does indeed co-vary with each of the indicators. As predicted, an action was reidentified at a high rather than low level to the extent that it was seen as easy to do, familiar, performable in a few ways, short in duration, and requiring little time to learn well. . . .

These data should not be taken as evidence that for any action only one level of identification is likely to assume prepotence. Indeed, if that were the case, the 'uncertain act' would not have emerged as a philosophical problem in the first place, nor would people be so adept at volunteering alternative depictions of what they are doing. There does seem to be something like a central tendency across actors in an action's identification level, a tendency that reflects a concomitant central tendency in the action's maintenance indicators. This much would be predicted by a categorical judgment model (e.g., Brown, 1958; Rosch, 1973, 1978). Against this normative backdrop, though, a certain degree of variability in both identification level and indicator values is to be expected. Thus, an action may be difficult in one setting or for one person but easy in another setting or for someone else, and these differences in personal act difficulty should be reflected in the respective identities that assume prepotence.

Action Experience

To a large extent, variability in an action's difficulty is determined by the person's degree of experience with the action. Several distinct traditions in psychology have converged on the notion that with increasing action experience there is a corresponding increase in action automaticity (e.g., Fitts & Posner, 1967; Kimble & Perlmuter, 1970; Langer, 1978; Weiss, 1939). Presumably, as one gains familiarity with an action's lower level components, these components become integrated or 'chunked' into larger action units, and it is these larger units that become the basis for conscious control of the action. An accomplished pianist, for instance, does not give conscious consideration to finger movements, key selection, and pedal pushing (e.g., Sudnow, 1978). In short, with increments in action experience, there is an increment in action automaticity and personal ability, and a consequent reduction in the individual's personal difficulty in performing the action.

According to the theory, these changes should prompt corresponding changes in level of prepotent identification. Thus, when low-level identities are unfamiliar and relatively difficult to maintain, emergence to higher level identities is effectively blocked; the third principle (movement to lower level prepotence) in a sense holds sway over the second principle (movement to higher level prepotence). As the lower level identities become mastered with increasing experience, however, there is a readiness to appreciate higher level identities and attempt maintenance with respect to them; the second principle becomes ascendant over the third principle. As these high-level identities then become mastered, the person is in a position to

maintain the action with respect to yet higher level identities, and so on, in a progression that leads to both greater proficiency and more comprehensive understanding of the action. No matter how proficient one is at an action, then, there is always a way to identify what one is doing so as to rekindle the challenge of effective maintenance.

The progression from low- to high-level identity prepotence with increments in action experience is demonstrated in an investigation by Vallacher, Wegner, and Frederick (1981). We asked a group of subjects ($N = 116$) to tell us what they do when they engage in each of five distinct actions—tennis, karate, piano playing, writing, and the video game *Space Invaders*.[2] Action identification questionnaires were provided for this purpose, each consisting of 36–38 one-sentence descriptions of the action under consideration. Subjects were to rate (on 7-point scales) how well each identity statement described the action for them. Factor analyses of these ratings revealed a low-level factor for each action as well as several higher level factors. A low-level index was computed for each action that represented a subject's summed ratings of identities loading on the low-level factor relative to his or her summed ratings across all factors.

The low-level index was then correlated with a self-report measure of subjects' experience with the action. The correlations were negative for every action (rs ranged from −0.17 to −0.56), reaching statistical significance in three of the five cases. A similar pattern was observed when the low-level index was correlated with subjects' self-reported proficiency at the action (rs ranged from −0.19 to −0.45). So, for actions as diverse as video games and piano playing, there is a waning of low-level prepotence as the actor gains familiarity and proficiency with the action. In rendering actions progressively more familiar, more automatic, and otherwise easier to do, experience enables action to be understood in terms that transcend the action's mechanistic underpinnings and highlight instead its potential meanings, effects, and implications.

Identification Level and Behaviour

The principles of the theory suggest that there is always conscious mental control of action. Across diverse domains of action, and despite wide natural variation in action context, action difficulty, and personal expertise, the immediate precursor to action is a mental representation of what one is doing. The representations that guide action, however, admit to considerable variation in their level of identification, and this variability has implications for the form that action control is likely to take. In this section, we outline the basic differences in action control associated with relatively low versus high levels of identification and develop the implications of these differences for the psychology of performance impairment, personal versus situational causation, and the relationship between self-concept and behaviour.

Levels of Action Control

Variation in identification level holds two key implications for action control. The first concerns action stability. When an action is undertaken with only a relatively low-level identity in mind, there is a tendency to accept a higher level identity made available by the action's context, and this new understanding of what one is doing can serve to change dramatically the course of one's subsequent behaviour. A person who is simply 'riding a bike', for example, may come to look upon the action as 'seeing the neighbourhood', 'unwinding from a hard day', or 'getting exercise', depending on the contextual cues surrounding the act. Each of these higher level identities is associated with an array of lower level identities besides bike riding and so could transform the act entirely. 'Seeing the neighbourhood', for instance, might result in parking the bike and walking in order to get a better look; 'unwinding' might lead the person home and to the liquor cabinet.

High-level identification, meanwhile, lends itself to action stability because it effectively shields the person against the emergence of alternative identities that could substantially change the nature of subsequent action. In essence, a person with a relatively high-level understanding already knows what he or she is doing and thus is less primed to accept other understandings at the same level provided by the context surrounding the action. Such understanding allows people to maintain a course of action in the face of changing conditions and with the passage of time. The bike rider who is 'getting exercise', for instance, is likely to persist in this action regardless of new possibilities for action that might become available.

The second implication of variation in identification level concerns action flexibility. When an action is maintained at a relatively high level, its physical manifestation may appear to change markedly from one occasion to the next. The bike rider 'getting exercise', for instance, may disembark from the bike to do something that looks quite different (e.g., jogging), although phenomenologically he or she is still doing the same thing. Lower level identities, on the other hand, come closer to specifying the physical movements involved in the action and so admit to far less variability in their mode of enactment. 'Riding a bike' encompasses such lower level acts as speeding up, slowing down, and turning corners, for example, but unlike 'getting exercise', it does not encompass getting off the bike to jog. Thus, with increments in identification level, there is a corresponding increase in the range of interchangeable means available for maintaining the action, and this imparts a noteworthy degree of flexibility to action.

When an action is controlled with respect to a relatively high-level identity, then, changes in its lower level manifestations over time do not necessarily signal inconsistency. Indeed, a certain amount of flexibility is often necessary to maintain a broadly conceived action. Consistency and flexibility, however, take on different meanings when viewed in terms of low-level action control. If consistency exists at all for an action identified at a low level, it is because of stable environmental cues that keep the person mindful of the task at hand. Flexibility, meanwhile, reflects impulsive emergence to new courses of action when the environmental cues change. An action controlled at a low level, then, cannot be consistent and flexible at the same time; which orientation predominates depends on the constancy of the action context.

Performance Impairment

In view of these differences between low- and high-level identification, it is tempting to view higher level states as preferable. High-level understanding seems to come closer to capturing the essence of knowing what one is doing, and the stability and flexibility of action associated with the high-level state sound preferable to the inconsistency versus rigidity characterizing lower levels of identification. High levels of identification can prove to be a mixed blessing, however. Particularly in contexts where behaviour is highly scripted (Schank & Abelson, 1977), the inattention to detail and nuance that comes with high-level action control can appear to be 'mindless' rather than thoughtful (Langer, 1978). In terms of our account, of course, *mindless action* is a somewhat misleading term. The principles of the theory suggest that well-learned, automated acts are performed with a representation of the act in mind, just as difficult, unfamiliar acts are. If the person does not seem to know what he or she is doing—that is, if he or she appears to be acting mindlessly—it is because the observer (or psychologist, for that matter) is identifying the action at a different level.

Nonetheless, it is possible for action control to be attempted at too high a level. Our data demonstrate, of course, that people tend to gravitate toward a level of identification that is warranted by the action's difficulty (Wegner & Vallacher, 1983) and to embrace higher levels of identification only when their experience readies them for such understanding (Vallacher, Wegner, & Frederick, 1981). This tendency should not be taken to mean that people always think about what they are doing in the 'right' way, however. People choke

under pressure, suffer from evaluation apprehension, get distracted, lose concentration, revert to old habits, worry about failure, get overconfident, and in other ways manage to approach action with a dysfunctional mental set (e.g., Baumeister, 1984; Berlyne, 1963; Carver & Scheier, 1981; Norman & Shallice, 1980; Reason & Mycielska, 1982; Rosenberg, 1965; Sarason, 1972; Schwartz, 1982; Wine, 1971). The convergence on a maintainable identification level is clearly a delicate process, one that is sensitive to various forms of interference.

The potential for interference reflects the simple fact that an action's prepotent identity is shaped by the context in which the action occurs. Thus, an environmental press toward higher level identities for one's action could serve to impair performance if the action's maintenance indicators warranted relatively low-level identification. The person might move to lower levels in accord with the third principle, but the cues to higher level meanings may not be sufficiently ignored to allow appropriate attention to detail. Indeed, because the low-level state sensitizes one to higher level identities, the movement to low level in the face of high-level failure could ensure that the person would keep mindful of the disruptive higher level identities. In support of this reasoning, several lines of research have converged on the notion that social and environmental pressures to do well, engendered by such things as the promise of reward or threat of punishment, competition, audience evaluation, and the like, tend to facilitate performance on simple or well-learned tasks but to impair performance on difficult or unfamiliar tasks (e.g., Berlyne, 1963; Cofer & Appley, 1964; Fitts & Posner, 1967; Zajonc, 1965). Such factors are similar in that they emphasize the higher level meanings and effects of one's action.

At the same time, action control can be attempted at too low a level. Just as difficult or unfamiliar action can be impaired by high-level identities made available by the action's context, so too can easy or familiar action be disrupted when the context calls attention to the lower level aspects of one's action. Indeed, the idea that overlearned performance can be debilitated by explicit attention to mechanistic aspects of action represents another well-established empirical generalization regarding human performance (e.g., Bryan & Harter, 1899; Kimble & Perlmuter, 1970; Langer & Imber, 1979). Thus, for an expert typist, attention to key selection and finger movements can produce errors and disrupt rhythm, just as an experienced driver's attention to pedal pushing and steering wheel rotation can introduce awkwardness into driving. Not only are low-level identities unnecessary for easy-to-maintain action, then, but their prepotence can also serve to disintegrate an action normally integrated with respect to a higher level understanding. An action that flows smoothly when enacted at high level can become choppy when enacted at low level.

The context of action thus holds potential for impairing action performance, pulling the person away from an identification level determined by personal action difficulty. The manifestation of this potential, however, is probably tempered by people's self-selection of settings in which to act. The random assignment of people to conditions in psychological research provides valuable insight into the effects of audience pressure, competition, and the like on performance quality, of course, but it almost certainly overestimates the frequency of performance impairment in daily life. More often than not, people seek out new and more demanding contexts for action only when their experience and skill readies them for higher level challenges. Thus, whereas an inexperienced tennis player is likely to shy away from a tennis court surrounded by observers, a more proficient player might actively seek out a context that renders 'demonstrating skill' or 'impressing an audience' prepotent at the expense of more elementary act identities. More generally, when a given act identity becomes relatively easy to maintain, the person is in a pre-emergence state and thus is sensitive to new action contexts that would impart higher level understanding to the action. This sort

of self-selection could ensure that most people will undertake action with respect to an optimal level of identification much of the time.

Personal versus Situational Causation

In discussions of action control, it is common to distinguish between personal and situational causation. This purported dichotomy lies at the heart of a continuing controversy in personality and social psychology concerning the determinants of behaviour (e.g., Bowers, 1973; Epstein, 1979, 1983; Mischel, 1968; Mischel & Peake, 1982), and judging by theories of causal attribution, it is of burning interest to laypersons as well (Heider, 1958; Jones & Davis, 1965; Kelley, 1967). The basic issue seems simple enough: When a person does something, is it because of his or her personal penchant for behaving that way or because of some aspect of the action context that would elicit that behaviour from most anyone? Phrased more concretely, does behaviour reflect a manifestation of personality traits, self-conceived values, and other inner qualities, or a response to rewards, punishments, and other inducements to action in the situation?

Strictly speaking, of course, the proximate cause of behaviour is always personal, inasmuch as behaviour is initiated and guided by a mental representation of the behaviour. The issue thus becomes one of locating the source of people's prepotent act identities in their idiosyncratic identity structures versus the context surrounding the action. Conceptually, the resolution of this issue involves a straightforward extension of the argument concerning identification level and action control. When a person undertakes an action with a relatively low-level identity in mind, he or she is especially sensitive to contextual information concerning the larger meaning and significance of the act. As this information is afforded by the situation, the person's prepotent act identity—and hence, his or her subsequent behaviour—may be seen as a reflection of situational factors. On the other hand, when a person enters an action context with a relatively high-level identity for his or her action and is able to maintain this identity throughout the period of enactment, the person may be said to be acting in accordance with personal rather than situational considerations. Thus, high-level action control is likely to reflect the implementation of one's goals, values, and interests rather than reactivity to situational cues.

Though straightforward conceptually, the person-versus-situation issue can prove to be quite tricky empirically. The problem inheres in the uncertainty of action. Because an action is open to different identifications, it may be difficult for an observer (or a psychologist) to determine whether a person is acting in accordance with his or her goals, concerns, and so forth, or whether he or she instead is responding to situational cues. The criterion of cross-situational consistency is commonly invoked to make this determination. Thus, if the person behaves the same way from one context to the next, it can be assumed that he or she is acting out of personal 'causes', but if his or her behaviour co-varies with contextual factors, it can be assumed that he or she is responding to presses in the immediate situation.

Given the flexibility associated with high-level action control, this criterion of personal versus situational causation is clearly inadequate. The person might 'act sociably', for instance, by 'joking around' on one occasion and by 'discussing the world's problems' on another. To someone not privy to the high-level identity operating in both instances, these behaviours might seem independent or even inconsistent with respect to a trait dimension like humorous versus serious. By the same token, an observer might note cross-situational consistency when none exists from the person's point of view. The person might help an elderly person cross the street, for example, and sometime later assist someone of the opposite sex in retrieving a dropped armload of books. Though both actions seem like 'being helpful' to the observer, the person may have performed them under vastly different high-level identities—'show respect for the elderly' and 'strike up a friendship'.

A related criterion for determining personal versus situational causation concerns the uniqueness of a person's behaviour vis-à-vis others in a given situation. According to this criterion, which finds expression in influential models of causal attribution (e.g., Jones & Davis, 1965; Kelley, 1967), the person is said to be acting in accordance with inner determinants (traits, values, etc.) to the extent that his or her behaviour deviates from the behaviour typical of people in that situation. Conversely, if his or her behaviour matches the observer's expectancy for behaviour in that situation (e.g., if the behaviour has high consensus across actors [Kelley, 1967] or is high in social desirability [Jones & Davis, 1965]), the person is said to be responding to forces in the situation.

The problem noted for the cross-situational consistency criterion is clearly applicable here as well. Assume, for example, that the person is observed 'discussing sports', and that others in that situation are observed doing the same thing. By the within-situation variability criterion, the person is said to be responding to the situation. 'Discussing sports', however, is only one of many possible identities for the person's behaviour, any one of which may have been the prepotent identity. Thus, the person may have entered the situation with only a low-level identity like 'talking' in mind, in which case the social cues to higher level identities assumed prominence; the person begins 'discussing sports' like everyone else, thereby revealing situational causation. On the other hand, the person may have approached the setting with a higher level identity in mind, such as 'make a good impression', 'demonstrate my command of facts', or 'put others at ease'. The particular high-level identity guiding the person's behaviour may surface regularly in his or her identity structure, reflecting stable and idiosyncratic orientations toward behaviour—the hallmark of personal causation.

This reasoning helps to illuminate a purported difference between actors and observers in their respective attribution tendencies. Jones and Nisbett (1971) argued that observers are inclined toward personal causes in explaining the actor's behaviour, whereas the actor is more inclined toward invoking situational causes. The fact that this difference has been demonstrated in laboratory experiments (e.g., Storms, 1973) and in rather unusual natural settings (West, Gunn, & Chernicky, 1975) is not too surprising. Given the unfamiliarity of such contexts for action, the actor subject could well have only a rudimentary under-standing of what he or she is doing. Situational cues to higher level meaning are thus attended to, so when queried later the actor quite reasonably points to features of the setting as being causal. The observer, meanwhile, is not privy to the actor's uncertainty and may conclude that the actor is behaving in accordance with an overall plan, goal, or self-conceived personality trait. By this reason-ing, the actor–observer difference should dissipate in settings that are familiar for the actor. Because familiar settings are associated with equally famil-iar plans and anticipated effects in the actor's iden-tity structure, the actor is likely to view his or her behaviour as a manifestation of these personal high-level identities rather than as a reaction to situational forces. In support of this idea, there is evidence that actors do indeed ascribe their behav-iour to personal rather than situational causes in familiar situations (Monson & Snyder, 1977).

This analysis of actor–observer differences in attribution is speculative, of course, but it does underscore our central point concerning commonly invoked criteria of personal versus situational cau-sation. Without knowledge of a person's phenom-enal organization of action, it is difficult for an observer (lay or professional) to determine whether the person's behaviour reflects personal consider-ations that surface regularly in different contexts or responsiveness to contextual cues that provide meaning for an action undertaken at a relatively low level. In this light, it is hardly surprising that the trait approach to personality has met with only lim-ited success (e.g., Mischel, 1968). Although people differ reliably in their scores on tests designed to measure trait variation, these scores typically do

a poor job of predicting behaviour. Thus, a per-son might have a high-level identity (e.g., 'being helpful') that regularly assumes prepotence, and this identity may provide personal integration for actions that seem diverse or even inconsistent when identified at lower levels (e.g., 'giving constructive criticism to a friend', 'providing uniformly posi-tive feedback to an insecure acquaintance'). To the person, then, many different actions are seen as expressions of the same thing. But to a psycholo-gist, employing act identities derived from personal experience or past empirical evidence, these actions may be grouped in ways that depart dramatically from the person's own organization. As a result, the person is seen as acting inconsistently with his or her self-reported trait.

. . .

Self-Concept and Behaviour

To an appreciable extent, knowledge of what one is like is gleaned from knowledge of what one is doing, has done, or is inclined to do. Were it not for the self-defining potential of action, it is unlikely that people would expend so much effort justifying what they have done, rationalizing their misdeeds and failures, claiming credit for suc-cess, and attempting to discredit certain kinds of social feedback regarding their behavioural pro-pensities (Shrauger & Schoeneman, 1979; Snyder, Stephan, & Rosenfield, 1978; Swann, 1983). As we have seen, however, this simple input for self-conception—action—is inherently uncertain, open to a wide variety of prepotent identifications. The principles by which people reduce this uncer-tainty and come to an unambiguous knowledge of their action would thus seem to have natural relevance to dynamics of self-conception.

The relevance of action identification principles to self-conception begins with the recognition that act identities at high levels hold greater potential for defining one's self than do lower level act iden-tities. 'Creating a piece of art', for instance, con-veys more information about the person behind the action than does a lower level identity like 'moving a paintbrush'. 'Demonstrating one's artistic competence' or 'expressing one's world view', in turn, conveys more information about the actor than does 'creating a piece of art'. While identities at lower levels are devoid of self-defining significance, higher level identities are practically synonymous with such significance. It is not surprising, then, that assessment of people's self-conceptions typically involves self-ratings along dimensions reflective of behavioural propensities (Wylie, 1979). In this research tradition, people are said to think of themselves in terms of such high-level action dimensions as co-operative versus competitive, dominant versus submissive, and friendly versus unfriendly.

In this light, it is interesting to consider two contrasting perspectives on the relationship between self-concept and behaviour. One perspective holds that a person's self-concept admits to remarkable variability and is open to continual modification and reshaping as a result of action (e.g., Gergen, 1977; Shrauger & Schoeneman, 1979). Processes of self-perception (e.g., Bem, 1972; Freedman & Fraser, 1966) and social feedback (e.g., Mead, 1934; Miller, Brickman, & Bolen, 1975) are commonly invoked to account for this relationship between self-concept and behaviour. The other perspective holds that a person's self-concept is stable over time and across settings, providing a consistent frame of reference for action (e.g., Block, 1981; Costa & McCrae, 1980). Indeed, when a self-view is threatened by contradictory social feedback, the person is said to be especially inclined to act in accordance with his or her self-conceived values and behavioural propensities (e.g., Swann, 1983).

Action identification theory suggests that both perspectives are valid, but under different circumstances. Whether the self-concept appears to be stable or malleable depends on the level of identification that is prepotent for a person when he or she encounters a situation conducive to self-perception or social feedback. If the person's identity is at a high enough level, he or she should show stability, resisting new information afforded by the physical and social environment concerning his or her personal attributes and capacities. Under conditions that promote a relatively low-level identification, however, contextual information regarding one's self is likely to be accepted, for it provides emergent understanding in accordance with the theory's second principle (i.e., movement to higher level prepotence).

Evidence in support of this analysis is provided in a study by Wegner et al. (1986, Experiment 2), alluded to earlier. Subjects in that study were provided with bogus personality feedback indicating that they were either co-operative or competitive. The ostensible data for the personality feedback consisted of a description generated by subjects of a recent social interaction between them and someone else. Subjects were to generate five one-sentence descriptions of their behaviour in this interaction and enter each into a computer console. Half of the subjects were instructed to describe their behaviour in relatively low-level terms (e.g., particular comments, questions, and gestures). The other subjects were asked to describe their behaviour in higher-level terms (e.g., opinions expressed, values communicated, and personality traits demonstrated). Subsequent coding of their descriptions by trained raters showed this manipulation of identification level to be effective. The computer then delivered an ostensible personality analysis telling subjects that they were either very co-operative or very competitive.

After examining the feedback, subjects were asked to judge the validity of the feedback and the usefulness of the program that generated it. As predicted, subjects led to think about their behaviour at lower levels expressed greater belief in the bogus feedback and greater confidence in the program than did those who were led to conceptualize their behaviour in high-level terms. Subjects also completed a questionnaire assessing their self-image with respect to 20 personality trait dimensions, including co-operativeness and competitiveness. Results showed that subjects in the low-level condition rated themselves consistently with the ostensible feedback; those who received co-operativeness feedback rated themselves as more co-operative, whereas those who received competitiveness feedback rated themselves as more competitive. Subjects in the high-level condition, meanwhile, did not rate themselves in line with the feedback they had received. This same pattern was observed when subjects were subsequently given a chance to participate in future research projects that involved co-operative or competitive behaviour on their part. Subjects in the low-level condition opted for a co-operative task if they had received co-operative feedback but opted for a competitive task if they had received competitive feedback. Subjects in the high-level condition were not influenced by the feedback in their choice of future activities.

Beyond confirming the emergence phenomenon specified by the second principle of the theory, these results help to clarify when a self-concept is likely to be stable, serving to initiate and maintain action, and when it is likely to be malleable, undergoing transformation as a result of action. It is not surprising, for example, that self-concepts appear to be highly malleable and responsive to social feedback under laboratory conditions (Gergen, 1977). Subjects in such research are commonly called upon to do something unfamiliar (e.g., converse with a stranger over headphones) or difficult (e.g., solve anagrams) and to do so in an unusual setting (a lab). Such a state of affairs is conducive to low-level identification and thus should make subjects sensitive to contextual cues regarding the larger meaning of their action. It is inevitable, then, that subjects should appear responsive to social feedback delivered by the experimenter or an experimental confederate or that they should come to 'discover' what they are like in accordance with self-perception dynamics.

In the more routine and familiar contexts pervading everyday life, however, changes in self-concept via social feedback and self-discovery should be less frequently observed (e.g., Swann &

Hill, 1982), because people are likely to have a relatively high-level identity for what they are doing. If self-concept change is observed in daily life, it is because a crucial precondition for emergence has been established—a movement to low-level identification. People are occasionally asked to recount the details of something they have done, for example, and in this way might experience a lower level of identification than would normally be the case (as in Wegner et al., 1986, Experiment 2). Interruption of ongoing action also occurs with a certain degree of regularity in daily life, and this too can promote relatively low-level identification (e.g., Wegner et al., 1984, Experiment 2). These events, and no doubt many others that promote low-level identification, make people vulnerable to the information afforded by the contexts surrounding their action.

Summary and Conclusions

Action identification theory is not the first perspective to propose explicit links between thinking and doing. Almost a century ago, James (1890) proposed that goal-directed physical movement is preceded by a mental representation of such movement. This emphasis on mental representations of action has provided the touchstone for virtually every perspective on mind and action advanced since James's time. It is common in this theoretical tradition to posit a hierarchy—or sometimes a heterarchy—of representations to account for complex goal-directed action (e.g., Carver & Scheier, 1981; Gallistel, 1980; Lashley, 1951; Miller, Galanter, & Pribram, 1960; Newell, 1978; Norman, 1981; Powers, 1973; Schank & Abelson, 1977). The action's goal or purpose is said to occupy the highest level in such hierarchies, whereas subordinate levels serve to subdivide this goal into progressively more concrete representations, until a level is reached that specifies the actual movements to be undertaken.

Like other approaches, action identification theory emphasizes the mental representation of action and the organization of such representations in a hierarchical structure. The principles of the theory, however, tend to spawn identity structures that lack the symmetry and closure normally associated with hierarchies. Principle 1 holds that people maintain action in accord with their prepotent identity for the action, Principle 2 holds that people embrace higher level identities when these become available, and Principle 3 holds that failure to maintain action under one identity will move people to a lower level of identification. The coordinated interplay of these principles promotes action understanding that is dynamic, self-correcting, and always open to change. Every time an action is performed, there is the potential for new act identities, higher or lower in level, to be incorporated into one's identity structure. Thus, as is common in hierarchical models, a given high-level identity can come to subsume a number of different lower level identities. But by the same token, the same low-level identity can, in different contexts, generate widely divergent higher level identities. These high-level identities, meanwhile, may be related to each other only by virtue of their mutual linkages to the lower level identity and thus will operate as independent meanings for the action. As a result, a person's identity structure for a domain of action is likely to be highly complex, consisting of multiple, overlapping hierarchies.

The complexity of identity structures imparts remarkable flexibility and individuality to the mental control of action. Indeed, without knowledge of a person's phenomenal organization of action, it may be difficult for an observer to determine whether the person is maintaining a particular course of action over time or, instead, is doing different things. Among those commentators who are sensitive to this feature of mental representations, the typical response has been to challenge the alleged lawfulness of human action (e.g., Gauld & Shotter, 1977; Gergen, 1978, 1985; Harré & Secord, 1972). In this view, not only can people identify their action in many different ways and thus chart idiosyncratic and flexible courses of action, the phenomenological nature of this process renders it opaque to traditional modes of scientific inquiry. After all, if action is open to different identifications, how can a researcher be sure that he or she has hit upon the 'real' identity guiding a subject's behaviour in an experimental setting? A discipline that cannot even come to agreement on its basic unit of analysis would seem to be a discipline based on shifting sands at best and, at worst, doomed to theoretical dead ends and contradictions.

The theory we have advanced attempts to reconcile the seeming conflict between unbounded consciousness on the one hand and bounded, lawful behaviour on the other. Thus, although the identification of action appears to be open-ended, limited only by our constructive and labelling capacities, the particular identity that assumes prepotence is ultimately constrained by reality. Among the factors that restrict the range of viable identities are various contextual cues surrounding the action, the personal difficulty of the action, and the person's experience with the action. Each of these determinants of identification level, in turn, can be cast in terms of yet more specific factors. Contextual cues, for example, include such things as situational novelty versus familiarity, audience presence versus absence, and the promise of rewards versus the threat of punishment. The degree of action difficulty, meanwhile, can be specified through knowledge of the action's maintenance indicators (e.g., its unfamiliarity, complexity, and enactment time). And personal action experience can be gleaned from noting a person's history of involvement with the action. These factors operate in accordance with the three principles of the theory to dictate how a person will attempt to control action in a given circumstance.

The variation in prepotent identification level that results from the operation of these factors has extensive implications for important realms of personal functioning. Thus, a person controlling an act with relatively low-level identities in mind is prone toward inconsistent, perhaps even impulsive, behaviour and is highly sensitive to social feedback and other contextual cues to higher level meaning. The person controlling action at a relatively high level, meanwhile, can behave flexibly with respect to lower level identities while maintaining a broader goal or purpose and is effectively shielded against new high-level identities afforded by the social and physical environment. Performance impairment also can be understood in terms of variation in identification level. An action is performed effectively to the extent that the person's prepotent level of identification is in line with the action's maintenance indicators.

Finally, we wish to emphasize that the dynamic, open-ended nature of action identification processes allows for marked changes in people's identity structures throughout their lives. Every time an action is undertaken, the identities made available by the action's context, the antecedent identity that set the action in motion, and other identities that exist in the person's accumulated identity structure, compete for prepotence. Only those identities that prove to be effective guides to action win this competition—and stand ready to provide direction for action in the future. Given the multiplicity of contexts in which people act and the likelihood that such contexts are encountered with different frequencies at different points in one's life, the repeated emergence of new act identities is an ever-present possibility. When all is said and done, perhaps the only enduring characteristic of a person's identity structure is its potential for change. Yet, no matter how idiosyncratic such changes are, they are ultimately driven by desires common to everyone—to know what one is doing and to do what one can.

Notes

1. The action set was assembled initially for the construction of an instrument to assess individual differences in characteristic level of action identification (Vallacher, Wegner, & Cook, 1982).
2. The action identification tendencies of those who indicated they had never performed the action and of those who were in the initial stages of action involvement were also explored in this study. Because the perspectives of such outsiders and beginners are independent of the act maintenance considerations that influence prepotency on the part of act performers, the data relevant to these perspectives are not considered here. For a presentation and theoretical consideration of these data, see Vallacher and Wegner (1985, Chap. 7).

Discussion Questions

1. An age-old debate in psychology concerns whether cognitive representations of behaviour are prior, guiding forces on behaviour or after-the-fact epiphenomena. Where do Vallacher and Wegner stand on this issue? Where do you stand?
2. Social facilitation is the tendency for people in stressful situations (such as in front of an audience) to display better-than-usual performance on easy tasks, but worse-than-usual performance on difficult tasks (Zajonc, 1965). How does action identification theory explain social facilitation? More generally, when is thinking in terms of the big picture adaptive versus maladaptive? When is being engrossed with the details adaptive versus maladaptive?
3. How do you think the tendency to identify other people's actions in terms of higher or lower level identities will influence judgments about that person?

14. Deliberative and Implemental Mindsets: Cognitive Tuning toward Congruous Thoughts and Information

Peter M. Gollwitzer, Heinz Heckhausen, and Birgit Steller,
Max-Planck-Institut für psychologische Forschung, Munich, Federal Republic of Germany

Editor's Introduction

Have you ever noticed that some people approach a task by methodically weighing the pros and cons of all the options while others appear to jump right in and execute a course of action? What are the psychological underpinnings and consequences of these different approaches to action? For over 20 years Peter Gollwitzer and his colleagues have investigated how people's mental representation of what stage of action they are in influences their cognition, affect, and motivation as they perform the task itself.

According to Gollwitzer, all deliberate actions unfold in the following sequence: (1) pre-decisional, (2) post-decisional, (3) actional, and (4) post-actional. As a person is in each phase, a particular mode of thinking, or mindset, is set up to help facilitate the aims of that phase. In the present article, the focus is on the 'deliberative' mindset component of the pre-decisional phase and the 'implemental' mindset component of the post-decisional phase.

This article represents one of the first efforts to document how being in a particular phase institutes a particular mental framework that makes people especially sensitive to information relevant to this phase while filtering out information that is not relevant. Put differently, the action phases can be thought of as akin to 'tuning' one's mind to different frequencies. Thus, in the deliberative phase, one's mind would be particularly sensitive to information relevant to the assessment of pros and cons. But in the implemental phase, one's mind would be particularly sensitive to information relevant to actually following through on the action. The studies in this paper provide evidence that our minds are exquisitely flexible in this ability to tune in to the particular mode that best fosters our immediate concerns.

In a sense, this work draws upon classic research by Lewin and colleagues on the well-known Zeigarnik effect. In 1927, Russian psychologist Bluma Zeigarnik noticed that waiters in restaurants remembered orders only as long as the order was in the process of being served. Once the food was served, memory for who ordered what disappeared. Based on data gathered in laboratory re-creations of this scenario, Zeigarnik and colleagues argued that much of our cognition is goal-driven: While we are striving toward a goal, our thought is oriented to further the accomplishment of that goal. Once the goal has been met, however, these helpful cognitive processes (like rehearsing the relevant information) immediately cease and desist; once the food has been delivered, there is no longer any need to rehearse the order. Because the information being rehearsed has not had a chance to be encoded into long-term memory, it vanishes. Thus, Zeigarnik and colleagues found that when people are interrupted prior to completing a task, they show better memory for task-related information than immediately after completing the task.

Returning to Gollwitzer's model, several studies have found that although the deliberative phase is critical, the best predictor of actual completion of a task is the formation of concrete 'implementation intentions', That is, thinking beforehand about the 'if–then' contingencies involved in completing a complex task ('If I encounter situation X, I will perform behaviour Y') beats simply thinking about the outcome. Once formed, implementation intentions have an effect similar to an established habit. For example, in one study, recovering opiate addicts were significantly more likely to write a curriculum vitae if they had formed an implementation intention (60 per cent) than if they had not (0 per cent; Bandstatter, Lengfelder, & Gollwitzer, 2001). The benefit of mentally concretizing one's goals is consistent with several decades of research by organizational psychologists Locke and Latham (e.g., Locke & Latham, 2002). A principal finding of their research is that when employers who provide concrete (e.g., numeric) goals to their employees, these employees vastly outperform employees who are told simply to 'do your best'.

The downside, however, of implementation intentions is that they make a person more vulnerable to positive illusions (an unrealistically positive outlook for the future; Taylor & Gollwitzer, 1995). After all, in the deliberative phase, one is primarily concerned with evaluating all the options as objectively as possible before possibly launching into an erroneous course of action. In the implemental phase, however, one's critical faculties are reined in as the focus turns to getting the job done.

□ ■ □

A course of action may be conceived rather narrowly as extending from its initiation (starting point) to its termination (end point). Alternatively, one may adopt a broader perspective that embraces the motivational origins of an action as the actual starting point and the individual's evaluative thoughts about the achieved action outcome as the final end point. In the present article, we take this broader perspective and segment the course of action into four distinct, sequential phases (Heckhausen, 1986).

The first segment is the *pre-decisional* phase, where potential action goals entailed by a person's many wants and wishes are deliberated. When a decision to pursue one of these goals is made, a transition to the *post-decisional* (pre-actional) phase takes place, where the individual becomes concerned with implementing the chosen goal. However, this phase ends and the *actional* phase starts when actions geared toward achieving the chosen goal are initiated. Once these actions have resulted in a particular outcome, the *post-actional* phase is entered and the individual proceeds to evaluate the achieved outcome.

We postulate that each of these phases is accompanied by a distinct mindset (Gollwitzer, 1990). Following the lead of the Würzburg School (Külpe, 1904; Marbe, 1901; Watt, 1905; for reviews, see Boring, 1950, pp. 401–6; Gibson, 1941; and Humphrey, 1951, pp. 30–131), we assume that the characteristics of each of these mindsets are determined by the unique qualities of the different tasks to be solved within each phase. That is, the different mindsets tailor a person's cognitive apparatus to meet phase-typical task demands, thus creating a special preparedness for solving these tasks. This preparedness should extend to a person's thought production, to the encoding and retrieval of information, and to the inferences drawn on the basis of this information. In this article, we explore the issue of mindset congruous thought production as well as the encoding and retrieval of congruous information. As was done in a previous analysis of mindset effects on a person's inferences (see Gollwitzer & Kinney, 1989, on illusion of control), we limit the analysis of cognitive tuning toward mindset congruous thoughts and information to the *deliberative* mindset of the pre-decisional phase and the *implemental* mindset of the post-decisional, but pre-actional, phase.

What are the issues to which deliberative as compared with implemental mindsets are attuned? To answer this question, one must consider the specific tasks that need to be tackled in the respective action phases. In the pre-decisional phase, people's task is to choose between action goals suggested by their wants and wishes. The likelihood of a 'good' choice should be enhanced when the individual thoroughly ponders the attractiveness of the expected consequences (i.e., expected value) of these goals. Clearly, failing to think about the attractiveness of proximal and distant consequences will lead to problematic decisions associated with unexpected negative consequences. Accordingly, the deliberative mindset should gear a person's thinking toward the expected values of potential action goals.

In the post-decisional (pre-actional) phase, however, people are confronted with quite a different task: The chosen goal awaits successful implementation. Post-decisional individuals should therefore benefit from an implemental mindset that guides their thoughts toward the questions of *when, where,* and *how* to implement the chosen action goal. In this phase, thoughts about the goal's expected value should be distinctive rather than useful, because they are not immediately related to implementational issues.

The classic definition of mindset ('Einstellung') as advanced by the Würzburg School suggests that mindset effects are based on cognitive processes that promote solving the task that stimulated the rise of the mindset. With respect to deliberative and implemental mindsets, these may be conceived of as cognitive procedures relating to how one chooses between various goal alternatives or to the planning of actions one must take in order to attain a chosen goal, respectively. A deliberative mindset should, for instance, entail procedures of weighing pros and cons, whereas an implemental mindset should entail procedures of timing and sequencing of goal-oriented actions.

As Smith and Branscombe (1987) pointed out in their procedural model of social inferences, cognitive procedures may transfer from a training (priming) task to a subsequent (test) task. If these procedures are sufficiently strengthened through intensive practice in the training task, and if there is overlap in the applicability of procedures, transfer is very likely. This model suggests the following test of the postulated effects of deliberative and implemental mindsets: If we succeed in creating

strong deliberative and implemental mindsets by either having subjects intensively contemplate potential goals or plan the execution of a chosen project (training task), we should find the postulated mindset effects in an unrelated subsequent task (test task). A prerequisite would be that the subsequent task allows for those cognitive procedures that were strengthened in the training task, that is, the cognitive procedures characteristic of a deliberative or implemental mindset.

Experiment 1, testing the postulate of mindset congruous thought production, was designed along this premise. Subjects' first task (training task) was to either thoroughly contemplate an unresolved decisional problem of their own (deliberative mindset) or to make a detailed plan of how to pursue a pressing personal project (implemental mindset). Then they were confronted with a second, allegedly unrelated task (test task) that requested the spontaneous production of ideas. Because these ideas could be deliberative or implementational in nature, we expected both deliberative and implemental mindsets to guide thought production in a mindset congruous direction.

This transfer assumption allowed us to go beyond a recent experiment reported by Heckhausen and Gollwitzer (1987), where the thoughts of deliberative and implemental mindset subjects were sampled during the training task. In this study, the classification of the reported thoughts clearly evidenced cognitive tuning toward mindset congruous thoughts. This study, however, lacks an unrelated test task, and therefore the results might be based on experimenter demands.

Experiment 1: Ascribing Deliberative and Implementational Efforts to Others

Asking subjects to deliberate unresolved personal problems that are pending a change decision should create strong deliberative mindsets. Alternatively, asking subjects to plan the execution of chosen projects should evoke strong implemental mindsets. Other experiments have indicated that deliberative and implemental mindsets can reliably be produced through such a procedure (Gollwitzer, Heckhausen, & Ratajczak, 1990; Gollwitzer & Kinney, 1989). Accordingly, in the present experiment, one-third of the subjects were first asked to name an unresolved personal problem (e.g., 'Should I move from home?' or 'Should I terminate my college education?') and then asked to contemplate whether or not to make a respective change decision. Another third of the subjects were to indicate a personal goal or project they planned to execute in the near future (e.g., moving from home or terminating one's college education) and then were to plan when, where, and how they wanted to accomplish it. The final third, a control group, were asked to passively view nature slides.

We tested whether deliberative and implemental mindsets tune people's thought production in a mindset congruous direction by asking subjects to fabricate ideas on an unrelated second task. To this end, we presented subjects with the beginnings of three fairy tales in which the main character of each story faced a different decisional conflict (e.g., a king had to go to war, but had nobody to whom he could entrust his young daughter). Subjects were asked to spontaneously compose the next three sentences for each of these fairy tales.

The mindset congruency hypothesis implies that deliberative efforts (i.e., contemplating possible goals) are most frequently ascribed to the main characters of the stories in the deliberative mindset condition, less frequently in the control condition, and even less so in the implemental mindset condition. In contrast, implementational efforts (i.e., executing a chosen solution to the conflict) should be most frequently ascribed in the implemental mindset condition, less frequently in the control condition, and least frequently in the deliberative mindset condition.

Method

Subjects

The 97 participants were male students at the Ruhr-Universität Bochum. Up to four subjects were invited to each experimental session and randomly assigned to one of three conditions. Subjects were recruited on the premise that they were willing to participate in two different studies, one on people's personal problems and projects, the other a test of their creativity. Subjects were separated by partitions, such that they could easily view the experimenter but none of the other participants. They were paid DM 10 (approximately $5.50) for participating.

Design

Subjects in either a deliberative or implemental mindset were asked to continue three different, incomplete fairy tales. Subjects' stories were analyzed with respect to whether deliberative or implementational efforts were ascribed to the main characters of the fairy tales. Subjects in the control condition passively viewed photographs of various outdoor scenes before receiving the fairy tales.

Procedure

Cover story. The female experimenter explained that subjects would take part in two different experiments. In the first experiment, subjects would be requested to reflect on personal issues or on nature photographs. Subjects were told that this study was designed to answer the question of whether intense reflection on personal issues would help people act more effectively in everyday life. In the second experiment their creativity would be tested. For this purpose, three different creativity tasks would be used, all of which would request the spontaneous creation of ideas.

In order to ensure that subjects perceived the two experiments as unrelated, the format of the written materials was different in each study (e.g., typeface, colour of paper, and writing style). In addition, the materials of each alleged experiment were distributed and collected separately.

Deliberative and implemental mindset manipulation. Deliberative mindset subjects were asked to weigh the pros and cons of making or not making a personal change decision. First, they had to indicate an unresolved personal problem (e.g., 'Should I switch my major?'). Then they were to list both potential positive and negative, short-term and long-term consequences (i.e., to elaborate on the expected value). In contrast, implemental mindset subjects were asked to plan the implementation of chosen personal projects. They were instructed to first name a personal project they intended to accomplish within the following three months (e.g., to move from home). Then they had to list the five most crucial implementational steps and commit themselves to when, where, and how to execute these steps.

As a manipulation check, both groups of subjects were then asked to fill out a final questionnaire consisting of the following items:

1. 'On the line below, please indicate the point that best represents your distance from the act of change decision.' (For this purpose, a horizontal line of 13 cm was provided. The starting point was labelled 'far from having made a change decision,' the 6.5-cm mark 'act of change decision,' and the end point 'past having made a change decision.')
2. 'How determined do you feel at this moment?'
3. 'Do you feel that you have committed yourself to a certain implementational course of action?'
4. 'Do you feel that you have committed yourself to make use of a certain occasion or opportunity to act?'

Items 2–4 were accompanied by unipolar 9-point answer scales ranging from *not at all* to *very*.

Control subjects. Subjects in the control condition received a booklet containing numerous black-and-white photographs depicting various nature scenes. Subjects were instructed to passively view the pictures for about 30 minutes (i.e., the amount of time deliberative and implemental subjects needed to complete their tasks). Thereafter, the alleged second experiment was started.

Dependent variable. The experimenter began the alleged second study by distributing three different fairy tales, the order of which was counterbalanced across conditions. Subjects received the following instructions:

> All of these fairy tales end at a certain point in the plot. You are to fill in the next three sentences of each fairy tale. You should *not* write a 'novel', and the fairy tales need not have an ending. When continuing the stories, give free rein to your fantasy and don't hesitate to write down your own creative thoughts, however unusual they may be. After you have finished the three sentences, please go on to the next fairy tale.

The first fairy tale read as follows:

> Once upon a time there was a king who loved the queen dearly. When the queen died, he was left with his only daughter. The widowed king adored the little princess who grew up to be the most beautiful maiden that anyone had ever seen. When the princess turned 15, war broke out and her father had to go to battle. The king, however, did not know of anyone with whom he could entrust his daughter while he was away at war. The king . . .

The second fairy tale was about a king who had a huge forest by his castle. One day he had sent a hunter into the forest who did not return. The two hunters he sent to look for the lost hunter also failed to return. The third fairy tale described a rather hedonistic tailor who had attended a christening party out of town. Late at night and after a few drinks too many, he was on his way home and got lost in a dark forest. He suddenly found himself standing in front of a huge rock wall with a passage just large enough to permit a person to pass.

Thought production scoring.   Subjects' stories were scored by two independent blind raters. The raters proceeded as follows: First, they underlined verbs relating to the main characters of the three fairy tales. Then, they classified the episodes denoted by these verbs with respect to whether the main character tackled the pre-decisional task of choosing between action goals or the post-decisional task of implementing a chosen action goal. For this purpose, a coding scheme was developed; two mutually exclusive categories are depicted in the Appendix. Each category could be checkmarked as often as necessary, depending on how many relevant episodes the subjects' stories contained. Eighty-one per cent of the episodes could be placed into the categories provided by the coding scheme; the rest formed the category 'unassignable episodes' (19 per cent). Agreement between raters was determined by counting the number of 'hits', defined as classifications on which the two raters agreed. Interrater reliability was high, with 91 per cent of the ratings being hits.

Debriefing.   When the subjects had finished working on the third fairy tale, the experiment was terminated and the subjects were debriefed. During the debriefing session, we probed whether subjects perceived the two experiments as related or not. As it turned out, subjects were only concerned with how well they had performed on the creativity task. None of the subjects raised the issue of the two experiments being potentially related or reported suspicions after being probed.

Results

Equivalence of Groups
Deliberative and implemental mindset subjects did not differ in the domains covered by their problems

and projects, respectively. Unresolved personal problems (deliberative mindset subjects) and personal projects (implemental mindset subjects) were classified according to three different domains: career-related (42 per cent), lifestyle-related (31 per cent), and interpersonal (27 per cent), the percentages being basically identical for both unresolved personal problems and personal projects.

The three groups of subjects also did not differ significantly in the number of words they wrote when continuing the three fairy tales: $M = 110.2$ for the deliberative mindset group, $M = 112.5$ for the implemental mindset group, and $M = 119.7$ for the control group, $F(2, 84) = 0.52$, *ns*.

Manipulation Checks
Subjects had indicated their proximity (in time) to the act of making a change decision on a horizontal line. Nearly all (24 of 26) deliberative mindset subjects indicated that they had not yet made the decision. The reverse was found for implemental mindset subjects; 25 of 26 subjects indicated that they had already made the decision. In addition, deliberative mindset subjects ($M = 4.6$) felt less determined than implemental mindset subjects ($M = 8.2$), $F(1, 50) = 50.8$, $p < .001$. Implemental mindset subjects ($M = 7.6$) felt more committed to executing a certain implementational course of action than deliberative mindset subjects ($M = 5.0$), $F(1, 50) = 26.6$, $p < .001$; the same pattern held true for feelings of commitment with respect to making use of a certain occasion or opportunity to act ($M = 6.7$ vs. $M = 5.1$), $F(1, 50) = 4.6$, $p < .04$.

Dependent Variables
To analyze subjects' stories, episodes ascribing deliberative efforts to the main characters (i.e., deliberating action goals and turning to others for advice) were added together to create a deliberative efforts index; actual acting on a chosen goal and thinking about the implementation of the chosen goal were added together to form an implementational efforts index (see Appendix).

Scores on these indexes were submitted to further analyses.

To test the hypothesis that ascribing deliberative and implementational efforts varies in a mindset congruous direction, two one-way analyses of variance (ANOVAS) with linear contrast weights (see Rosenthal & Rosnow, 1985) were conducted. For ascribing deliberative efforts, these weights tested the hypothesis that the highest frequencies would be obtained among deliberative mindset subjects, followed by control subjects and then implemental subjects; for implemental efforts, the highest frequencies would be observed among implementational mindset subjects, followed by control subjects and then deliberative subjects. These analyses revealed that ascribing deliberative and implementational efforts significantly varies in a mindset congruous direction, $F(1, 84) = 4.06$, $p < .025$ (one-tailed), and $F(1, 84) = 8.48$, $p < .005$ (one-tailed), respectively. Pearson coefficients obtained by correlating ascribing deliberative and implementational efforts with the respective linear contrast coding of mindset conditions underlined these results.

When the frequencies of ascribing deliberative and implementational efforts were submitted to an ANOVA with ascribed effort (deliberative vs implementational) as a within-subjects variable and condition (deliberative, implemental, and control group) as a between-subjects variable, a significant main effect of ascribed effort emerged, $F(1, 84) = 322.5$, $p < .001$, which is qualified by the predicted interaction effect, $F(2, 84) = 4.65$, $p = .015$. We checked whether the pattern of data is different for each of the three fairy tales by computing a 3 × 2 × 3 (Fairy Tale × Ascribed Effort × Condition) ANOVA. The significant Ascribed Effort × Condition interaction effect was *not* qualified by an interaction with fairy tale; that is, the three-way interaction did not reach significance ($F < 1.0$). In addition, the order in which the fairy tales were presented also failed to affect the critical interaction ($F < 1.0$). Finally, we explored how the

episodes that could not be classified by our coding scheme were distributed across conditions. There were no significant differences among the conditions ($F < 0.25$).

Discussion

Subjects requested to ponder a personal problem in order to determine whether or not they should make a change decision fabricated fewer implementational and more deliberative ideas when writing a creative fairy tale than subjects who had been asked to plan the execution of a chosen personal goal. Deliberating and planning created distinct mindsets that persisted even after subjects had turned to the subsequent task of writing creative fairy tales. The ideas that spontaneously entered the subjects' minds when inventing their fairy tales corresponded to their deliberative or implemental mindsets.

All groups of subjects imputed more implementational than deliberative efforts to the main characters of the fairy tales. Apparently, the task of writing creative endings to unfinished fairy tales predominantly relies on cognitive procedures characteristic of the implemental mindset. As Rabkin (1979) and Rumelhart (1975, 1977) pointed out, fairy tales seem to follow a certain grammar. A 'good' fairy tale is not complete until the problem faced by the main character is solved. Because such solutions commonly require the main character to take action, ascribing implementational efforts is more in the style of a good fairy tale. Still, despite few deliberative efforts ascribed overall, we observed the predicted mindset congruency effect. However, the scarcity of ascribing deliberative efforts in the present study serves as a reminder that testing the postulated mindset congruency effects through a subsequent (test) task has its limits. If working on a subsequent task does not allow for the cognitive procedures entailed by a deliberative or implemental mindset (e.g., solving an arithmetic task), mindset congruency effects cannot be observed.

Studies conducted on category accessibility effects on social judgments seem relevant to the paradigm used here (Higgins, Rholes, & Jones, 1977; Srull & Wyer, 1979). Assuming that social constructs (e.g., kindness) are stored in memory, these constructs were first primed by confronting subjects either with trait words closely related to the target construct (Higgins et al.) or descriptions of relevant behaviours (Srull & Wyer). Then, in a presumably unrelated second experiment, subjects read descriptions of a target character who shows either ambivalent (Higgins et al.) or vague (Srull & Wyer) indications of possessing the critical personal attribute. Finally, when subjects were asked to rate the target character, distortions in the direction of the primed category were observed. Both groups of researchers suggested that priming changes some property of the critical constructs representation in memory (i.e., activation or location in a storage bin, respectively) that makes it comparatively more accessible and more likely to be used in interpreting the behaviour of the target person.

As in these priming experiments, subjects in Experiment 1 were also exposed to ambiguous information about a target character (i.e., the main character of the open-ended fairy tales) in an alleged second experiment. However, the ambiguity is about the main character's course of action and not about a potential personality attribute. We believe that subjects' ascribing of deliberative or implementational efforts was affected by cognitive procedures (or productions; Anderson, 1983) that have been strengthened through prior deliberation and planning processes. The activation of declarative knowledge (specific episodic and general semantic) through the contents touched by subjects' deliberation and planning should have played a minor role. This assumption is supported by the fact that the observed mindset effects were rather long-lived (one-quarter to half an hour), whereas conceptual priming effects were generally extremely short-lived (a matter of seconds or a few minutes). As Smith and Branscombe (1987) demonstrated, studies on category accessibility

effects only manage to produce long-lasting effects (several hours) when procedural strengthening is involved.

Experiment 2: Recalling Deliberative versus Implementational Thoughts of Others

Experiment 1 demonstrated that deliberative and implemental mindsets favour the production of congruous thoughts. This should facilitate the task of choosing between goal options and the task of implementing a chosen goal, respectively. However, both of these tasks should also be facilitated by effective processing of task-relevant information. Therefore, one would expect that people in a deliberative mindset show superior processing of information that speaks to the expected value of goal options, whereas people in an implemental mindset should show superior processing of information that speaks to the issue of when, where, and how to execute goal-oriented behaviour.

Our test of the superior processing of mindset congruent information was also based on the transfer assumption of Smith and Branscombe's (1987) model of procedural strengthening and transfer. Instead of offering deliberative and implemental mindset subjects information relevant to their decisional and implementational problem at hand, we offered information on other people's decisional and implementational problems. As this information could easily be identified as either expected value-related or implementation-related, we expected mindset congruency effects with respect to subjects' recall of this information.

This information was depicted on eight pairs of slides. The first slide of each pair showed a person said to be experiencing a personal conflict of the following kind: Should I do x or not (e.g., sell my apartment)? The second slide presented four thoughts entertained by the person depicted on the first slide. Two of these thoughts were deliberative in nature, as they referred to the expected value of making a change decision. The other two thoughts were of an implementational nature, both addressing the issue of when (timing) and how (sequencing) to execute goal-oriented actions. When constructing these sentences, we used pilot subjects to establish that both types of information (expected value vs implementation) were recalled about equally well.

A deliberative mindset was established by asking subjects to contemplate the choice between one of two available creativity tests. An implemental mindset was assumed for subjects who had just chosen between tests and were waiting to start working. A control group received and recalled the information without expecting to make a decision or to implement one already made.

Deliberative mindset subjects should show superior recall of the expected value-related information, despite its being unrelated to the decision subjects were contemplating. Implemental mindset subjects should show superior recall of the implementation-related information, despite its being unrelated to working on the chosen creativity test. Control subjects were expected to recall both expected value-related information and implementation-related information about equally well.

Method

Subjects and Equipment
The participants were 69 male students from the University of Munich. Two subjects were invited to each experimental session. They received DM 15 (approximately $8) for participation. A female experimenter ushered subjects into separate experimental cubicles where they received tape-recorded instructions through an intercom system. Each cubicle was equipped with a projection screen.

Design
Subjects were randomly assigned to one of three conditions. In the deliberative mindset condition,

information on both expected values and implementational issues was received and recalled prior to making a choice between two available creativity tests. In the implemental mindset condition, subjects received and recalled this information while waiting to begin working on their chosen creativity test. Finally, control subjects received and recalled this information without either expecting to make a choice or having made one.

Procedure
Cover story. Subjects were told that two different personality traits, that is, social sensitivity and artistic creativity, would be assessed during the course of the experiment. The experimenter further explained that for measuring each of these traits two alternative test materials had been prepared. It was stated that subjects would be allowed to choose between test materials, because only if subjects chose the test material more appropriate for them personally would test scores reflect their 'true' social or creative potential. The experimenter then distributed a short questionnaire consisting of the following items: (a) 'How creative do you think you are?' (b) 'How confident are you that you are capable of creative achievements?' and (c) 'How important is it for you to be a creative person?' Parallel questions were asked with respect to social sensitivity. (All items were accompanied by 9-point answer scales ranging from *not at all* to *very.*)

The first trait measured was *social sensitivity.* The experimenter presented subjects with short descriptions of two different interpersonal conflicts. Subjects were first asked to select the problem they personally found most engaging and then to suggest an appropriate solution to the conflict by writing a short essay. Subjects were told that they would later receive feedback concerning the usefulness of their suggested solutions.

Then the experimenter turned to the presumed second part of the experiment, that is, assessing subjects' *artistic creativity.* She explained that subjects would create collages from material cut out of different newspapers. It was the subjects' task to select various elements (e.g., people, animals, and objects) needed to depict a certain theme provided by the experimenter. Finally, subjects should place the selected elements on a white sheet of paper and arrange them so that a creative picture emerged. When they had discovered the most appealing arrangement, they should glue the collage segments onto the white sheet of paper and then hand it to the experimenter.

Most important, however, two different sets of collage materials (black-and-white vs colour elements) would be available for this task. Subjects would be given a choice because they could reach their full creative potential only if they chose that set of elements they found personally most appealing. To help subjects choose properly, she would present four black-and-white as well as four colour slides. She explained that these slides originated from a previous study on artistic creativity in which subjects had to invent the thoughts of people depicted on the slides. Subjects should view all of the slides carefully to determine which set of slides (colour or black-and-white) would bring out their full creative potential.

However, subjects were instructed to refrain from making a choice of test material while viewing the slides. Impulsive choices, as well as choices based on initial preferences only, were said to have proven problematic. Therefore, subjects should take their time, lean back, and ponder the best choice. In addition, shortly before viewing the sample pictures subjects were given false feedback with respect to the quality of their performance on the social sensitivity test. All subjects were told that if they had chosen the alternative test material, their score would have been higher than the rather modest score achieved. This feedback, as well as the instructions to refrain from impulse choices, was given for the sole purpose of stimulating intense deliberation.

Information materials.   The sample pictures were grouped into eight pairs of slides. Each pair consisted of a first slide that pictured a person said to be pondering a decisional problem (e.g., an elderly lady). On the subsequent slide, subjects read that she was reflecting on the following decisional problem: 'Should I invite my grandchildren to stay at my house during the summer—or shouldn't I?'

The slide also contained her thoughts on the expected value of a change decision: The first thought centred on possible positive consequences (i.e., *It would be good, because* they could help me keep up my garden); the second thought focused on possible negative consequences (i.e., *It would be bad, because* they might break my good china). In addition, the slide depicted two thoughts related to the implementation of a potential change decision: One focused on the timing of a necessary implementational step (i.e., *If I decide yes, then* I won't talk to the kids *before* my daughter has agreed); the other thought mapped out the sequence of two further implementational steps (i.e., *If I decide yes, then I'll first* write my daughter *and then* give her a call).

Altogether, eight different persons, each facing a specific decisional conflict, were presented (e.g., a young man who pondered the question of becoming a sculptor, a young lady who reflected on whether to quit her waitressing job, and a middle-aged man who deliberated whether or not to sell his condominium). Four slides depicting persons were in colour, and four were in black and white. The verbal information was always presented in the same format. The underlined parts of each sentence (see the example of the elderly lady above) remained analogous for each person and were written in black. The rest of the sentences were written in red.

Deliberative mindset condition.   Once subjects had viewed the eight pairs of slides, the experimenter told them that she would look for a second set of slides that might make it easier for subjects to make up their minds. While she was purportedly trying to set up this second set, subjects were to fill their time by working on a couple of tasks. Then the experimenter gave the instructions for a 5-minute distractor (subjects counted the planes of several different geometrical figures drawn on a sheet of paper) and a subsequent recall test (as described below). When subjects were finished, the experimenter explained that she had failed to set up the additional set of slides. Therefore, subjects should make their decision based solely on viewing the original set of slides.

Implemental mindset condition.   Subjects were introduced to the choice option between two sets of collage materials and were instructed to deliberate on the question of which set of collage elements they found most appealing. After subjects had indicated their decision, the experimenter explained that it would take several minutes for her to bring the chosen collage elements to the subject's cubicle. In the meantime, the subjects would view slides and solve a number of different tasks. The eight pairs of slides were then presented; the origin of these slides was described to the subjects in the same words as in the deliberative mindset condition. Following the distractor, subjects worked on the recall test.

Control condition.   Control subjects were not made to either expect a decision between collage elements or work on a set of collage elements. They were shown the slides after being told solely about their origin. Finally, subjects' recall performance was assessed following the completion of the distractor task.

Recall procedure.   Following the 5-minute distractor task, subjects were again shown the eight slides depicting the persons said to be experiencing a decisional conflict. In addition, they were given a booklet consisting of eight pages, each one entitled with the deliberation problem of one of the eight characters pictured on the slides. Subjects found those parts of the sentences printed in black on the slides that presented the depicted persons' thoughts and were instructed to complete them (i.e., fill in the parts of the sentences printed in red

on the original slides). For this recall procedure, the slides depicting the characters were shown in the order in which they were originally presented.

Post-experimental questionnaire and debriefing. Deliberative and implemental mindset subjects were asked to complete a final questionnaire that contained the following items accompanied by 9-point answer scales ranging from *not at all* to *very:* (a) 'How important is it for you to show a creative performance on the collage creativity test?' (b) 'How difficult was the choice between the two sets of collage elements?' (c) 'How important is it for you to work with the appropriate collage elements?' (d) 'How certain are you that you picked the appropriate collage elements?' (e) 'I generally prefer black-and-white pictures over colour ones!' (*don't agree–agree*), and (f) 'I generally prefer colour pictures over black-and-white ones! (*don't agree–agree*). After the subjects had completed this questionnaire, the experimenter debriefed them and paid them for their participation.

The debriefing was started by probing for suspicions. None of the subjects guessed our hypothesis. One subject (implemental mindset) guessed that we were testing whether the information associated with the chosen type of material (black-and-white vs colour) is recalled better. The rest of the subjects took the incidental recall test as a check of whether they were good subjects who collaborated in an attentive and concentrated manner. As in other studies using this paradigm (Heckhausen & Gollwitzer, 1986, 1987), subjects were primarily concerned with the upcoming creativity test, on which they wanted to give their best.

Results

Equivalence of Mindset Groups

Subjects' answers on the pre-experimental questionnaire did not differ between groups: There were no differences with respect to the belief in one's creativity (Ms = 5.65 vs. 5.66), the confidence in one's capability for creative achievements

(Ms = 5.76 vs 5.72), and the importance assigned to being a creative person (Ms = 6.94 vs 6.67), all Fs < 1.0. The relatively high means (unipolar 9-point scales) indicate that the subjects valued being creative and were quite certain of their possessing this desirable trait.

Subjects' answers on the post-experimental questionnaire also did not indicate any differences. The importance (Ms = 4.89 vs 5.17) and difficulty (Ms = 6.35 vs 6.67) of succeeding in the collage creativity test were perceived as similar in both conditions, as was also the case for the perceived importance of making the correct choice (Ms = 5.53 vs 5.17), all Fs < 1.0. These data suggest that deliberative and implemental subjects took the collage test as a valid means to demonstrate being creative, and that they felt making the correct choice would influence their performance on this test.

Although black-and-white elements were chosen more than twice as often as colour collage elements (25 vs 10), this ratio did not differ across conditions, x^2 (1, N = 35) = 0.01, p = .91; nor did their general preference for black-and-white or for colour collage elements (both Fs < 1.0).

Dependent Variables

Recall performance scores for expected value-related thoughts and implementation-related thoughts were determined by counting the respective thoughts that were recalled correctly. Deliberative mindset subjects showed the predicted superior recall for expected value-related thoughts (M = 7.29) as compared with implementation-related thoughts (M = 4.88), t(16) = 2.25, p < .02 (one-tailed). Implemental mindset subjects also evidenced mindset congruous recall, recalling implementation-related thoughts (M = 8.17) significantly better than expected value-related thoughts (M = 6.11), t(17) = 2.02, p < .03 (one-tailed). As expected, control subjects recalled expected value-related thoughts (M = 6.88) and implementation-related thoughts (M = 6.63) about equally well, t(15) = 0.24, ns (see Table 14.1).

To test the hypothesis that the recall performance for expected value-related and implementation-related information varies in a mindset congruous direction, we conducted two separate one-way ANOVAs with linear contrast weights. With respect to the implementation-related information, the weights were set to test the hypothesis that its recall is highest for implemental mindset subjects, followed by control subjects and then deliberative mindset subjects. This analysis revealed a significant F(1, 48) = 4.03, p = .025 (one-tailed); the respective correlation coefficient is r(51) = 0.28, p < .025. For expected value-related information, the weights were set to test the hypothesis that this information is recalled best by deliberative mindset subjects, followed by control subjects and then implemental mindset subjects, F(1, 48) = 1.02, ns; r(51) = 0.15, p = .15.

Although these findings indicate that for expected value-related information there is comparatively less mindset congruous recall than for implementation-related information, recall of expected value-related information and

Table 14.1   Mean Recall of Information on Expected Value and Implementation

Mindset condition	Type of information		Difference
	Thoughts about expected value	Thoughts about implementation	
Deliberative	7.29	4.88	2.41
Control	6.87	6.63	0.24
Implemental	6.11	8.17	−2.06

Note: Higher numbers indicate better recall performance.

implementation-related information combined to produce strong mindset congruous recall (as can be seen from the difference scores reported in Table 14.1). When this difference index is submitted to a one-way ANOVA with linear contrast weights, a highly significant $F(1, 48) = 9.15$, $p < .003$ (one-tailed), emerges; the respective correlation coefficient is $r(51) = 0.41$, $p < .002$. This indicates that the superior recall for expected value-related information in the deliberative mindset group was strongly reduced in the control group and reversed in the implemental mindset group.

Discussion

Deliberative mindset subjects recalled expected value-related information better than implementation-related information, whereas implemental mindset subjects showed better recall of implementation-related information than of expected value-related information. This pattern of data supports our hypothesis of superior recall of mindset congruous information.

Possible Confoundings

This conclusion rests on the assumption that the expected value-related information as well as the implementation-related information did not differ in other features (e.g., affective tone or complexity) that might be responsible for the recall performance of deliberative and implemental mindset subjects. It might be argued, however, that implementation-related information was more positive in tone and that implemental mindset subjects, because they were in a comparatively more positive mood, had an easier time recalling this information than deliberative mindset subjects. Two reasons speak against this argument. First, it is unlikely that the implementation-related information was more positive in affective valence than the expected value-related information, because both types of information entailed positive and negative aspects (i.e., pleasant and unpleasant actions vs positive and negative consequences, respectively). Second, the implemental mindset cannot generally be assumed to

produce a better mood than the deliberative mindset. Planning may be as difficult and painful as deliberating; it all depends on the issue at hand.

Also, one might argue that the implementation-related information was worded such that it was more difficult to encode and retrieve than the expected value-related information. The recall performance of control subjects speaks against this argument; they recalled both types of information about equally well. Moreover, there are no convincing reasons why implemental mindset subjects would be more effective in processing complex information as compared with deliberative mindset subjects.

Various Kinds of Congruous Information

Future studies should try to explore recall of other kinds of mindset congruous information other than that used in the present experiment. With respect to implementation-related information, for instance, one might offer information on *where* to act, thus overcoming the present study's limitation to *when* (timing) and *how* (sequencing). With respect to deliberation-related information, one might want to extend the present study's limitation to *expected values*. Choosing between potential goals demands reflection about one's chances to implement these goals; otherwise, one would choose goals that are attractive but cannot be reached. Information on the feasibility of potential goals is thus congruous to a deliberative mindset and should therefore also be processed more effectively in a deliberative as compared with an implemental mindset.

Encoding versus Retrieval

The present study is mute to the question of whether the observed mindset congruous recall was achieved more by encoding or retrieval. This question, however, can be answered by testing both mindset congruous recognition and recall in deliberative and implemental subjects. Recognition would capture the availability of the critical information (i.e., whether it was encoded or not), whereas recall would speak to the accessibility of stored information (i.e., whether it was easily retrieved or not; see Bargh & Thein, 1985; Srull, 1981, 1984).

An alternative approach may be taken by solely employing a recall procedure in a four-group design. In addition to the two groups tested in the present study, a third group would encode the critical information in a deliberative mindset and recall it in an implemental mindset. Finally, the fourth group would encode the information in an implemental mindset and recall it in a deliberative mindset. Comparisons among these four groups would allow one to determine the relative contribution of encoding and retrieval for mindset congruous recall of expected value-related and implementation-related information.

In general, one would expect mindsets to affect people's encoding of information in a mindset congruous direction. This should be particularly pronounced when subjects are confronted with informational competition, that is, when more information than they can process impinges on them. Then, subjects must allocate attention to only some of the information available. Subjects' mindsets should guide selective attention and thus favour the processing of congruous information.

But retrieval processes may also contribute to mindset congruous recall. Assuming that subjects' retrieval attempts necessitate constructing descriptions of what they are trying to retrieve (Bobrow & Norman, 1975; Norman & Bobrow, 1976, 1979), it seems plausible that mindsets provide perspectives (Bobrow & Winograd, 1977) that allow for the easy construction of specific descriptions. The deliberative mindset, for instance, should favour descriptions phrased as pros and cons, benefits and costs, or hopes and fears. As Norman and Bobrow (1979) pointed out, quick construction of specific descriptions at the time of retrieval furthers successful retrieval. It seems possible, then, that deliberative and implemental mindsets favour congruous recall by means of the prompt construction of appropriate descriptions (e.g., pros and cons vs when and how).

General Discussion

The tasks people face in the various action phases create distinct mindsets that tune people toward congruous thoughts and information. This finding is important for any theorizing on the course of action; in particular, it speaks to the question of whether the course of action should be conceptualized as homogeneous or heterogeneous, that is, compartmentalized into a number of distinct, qualitatively different phases. Lewin (Lewin, Dembo, Festinger, & Sears, 1944) suggested that the realm of goal-oriented behaviour entails at least two distinct phenomena—goal setting and goal striving. He believed that goal setting may be accounted for by expectancy × value theories, whereas different theories should be developed to account for goal striving. However, researchers interested in goal-oriented behaviour did not develop distinct theories to account for goal striving; rather, they stretched expectancy × value notions, making them account for both goal setting and goal striving (e.g., Atkinson, 1957). This has been criticized on the grounds that the extended expectancy × value theories have only been very modestly successful in predicting vital aspects of goal performance (see Klinger, 1977, pp. 22–24, 329–330).

The present experiments support Lewin's contention that goal setting and goal striving differ in nature. Individuals deliberating action goals were tuned toward thoughts and information that were different from those of individuals planning the implementation of a chosen goal. In recent experiments, further differences were observed between deliberating and planning individuals with respect to the inferences they made on the basis of available information (Gollwitzer & Kinney, 1989) and with respect to the absolute amount of available information they processed (Heckhausen & Gollwitzer, 1987, Study 2). These findings attest to differences in the natures of goal setting and goal striving; in addition, they bring to mind Lewin's claim that goal setting and goal striving deserve distinct theorizing.

Appendix

Coding Scheme for Subjects' Stories

Ascribing Deliberative Efforts to Main Character

Deliberation aimed at making a goal decision: 'The king racked his brains, wondering what to do . . .'; 'The king was thinking things over for many days and nights, weighing whether to stay at home . . .'

Turning to others for advice and listening to their suggestions: 'The king asked a monk to give him advice . . .'; 'The king listened to a fortune teller . . .'

Ascribing Implementational Efforts to Main Character

Actual acting on a chosen goal: 'The tailor forced himself through the rock passage . . .'; 'The king sent out more men to search the forest . . .'; 'The king ordered a trusted officer to stay at the castle and protect his daughter . . .'

Thinking about the implementation of the chosen goal: 'The king asked himself how could he find a trusted person who would stay home and protect his daughter . . .'; 'The tailor wondered how to climb up the steep wall . . .'

Discussion Questions

1. What similarities and differences, if any, do you think there are between deliberative versus implemental mind sets and Vallacher and Wegner's concept of high versus low action identification?
2. In Gollwitzer's formulation, the mindsets (especially implementation) are relatively 'ballistic' in the sense that once they are set into motion they are not easy to shut down. Do you agree with this idea? What variables might lead people to be more versus less flexible in their ability to toggle between deliberation and implementation?

Unit Six Further Reading

As described in the introduction to the Vallacher and Wegner article, a recent line of research conducted by Trope, Liberman, and colleagues has developed and expanded upon some of the ideas relating to action identification theory in novel and important ways. In particular, these researchers have demonstrated the importance of 'psychological distance' in many of the actions and decisions we perform in everyday life:

Liberman, N. & Trope, Y. (2008). The psychology of transcending the here and now. Science, 322, 1201–1205.

Trope, Y., & Liberman, N. (2003). Temporal construal. Psychological Review, 110, 403–21.

Unit Seven

Motivation and Emotion

In 1884, William James posed the deceptively simple question: 'What is an emotion?' Efforts to answer this question continue vigorously to this day. In this vast research literature, a host of related questions have emerged. What purpose do emotions serve? How do emotions influence our cognition and our motivational striving? How, in turn, does our motivational striving influence the emotions we experience?

Echoing Descartes's notion of mind–body dualism, cognition and emotion have traditionally been posed as distinct, often antagonistic processes. Recent research, however, has increasingly demonstrated that such a distinction is inaccurate, if not meaningless. The articles in this Unit illustrate how the phenomenologically simple and direct experience of an 'emotion' is heavily influenced by—and indeed often *requires*—a host of psychological processes traditionally labelled as cognitive.

For example, Carver and Scheier's article explicitly ties together emotion, motivation, and cognition. According to their influential 'control process' theory, people cognitively monitor their progress toward their goals. When they perceive that they are not making adequate progress, negative emotion results. When efforts to reduce this discrepancy are successful, the result is positive emotion. Thus, according to these authors, emotion serves as a signal of how well we are doing at meeting our goals. (For similar ideas, see Higgins's 1997 article in Unit 5.)

Weiner's influential 1985 paper likewise ties emotion to cognition and motivation. According to his model, human beings, in their relentless quest for understanding about themselves and their world, are constantly asking, 'Why?' (In this respect, Weiner's work fits well with the theme of Unit 2 on epistemic needs.) Weiner's major insight was that all of the myriad ways in which a person could answer a 'why' question can be boiled down to three causal dimensions: internal/external, stable/changeable, uncontrollable/controllable. More specifically, almost any explanation that people generate to explain why something occurred can be slotted into one of the eight categories implied by his framework, which applies to emotion-related events. Thus, attributing a negative event to, for example, internal, stable, and uncontrollable causes would lead to shame, while attributing the same event to internal, changeable, and controllable causes might lead to guilt. According to Weiner, the particular emotional label we affix to the somatic signals we receive from our body is the result of surprisingly sophisticated reasoning processes. Weiner's ideas follow from a tradition that has examined the fundamentally 'cognitive' aspects of emotion (e.g., Schachter & Singer, 1962).

15. Origins and Functions of Positive and Negative Affect: A Control-Process View

Charles S. Carver, University of Miami
Michael F. Scheier, Carnegie Mellon University

□■□

Editor's Introduction

Former New York City mayor Ed Koch was famous for endlessly repeating his catchphrase, 'How am I doing?' In a sense, we all do this. Any motivated action, even the most basic search for food by a primitive organism, must possess some sort of *metric* for measuring success and failure. According to Carver and Scheier, this is precisely the key function of emotions: They represent a signal of how we are doing as we attempt to reduce the discrepancy between our current state and our desired state.

Carver and Scheier's theory imports concepts from engineering to explain human emotion. According to their approach, people, much like a thermostat, compare their current state to a reference value (i.e., a goal). When they perceive that there is a discrepancy between the current state and the reference value, action is taken to reduce the discrepancy. In order for this to work, there must be a feedback loop that monitors the size of the discrepancy and 'reports back' on the state of progress. According to their model, a 'meta-monitoring' system checks the rate of discrepancy reduction over time. Interestingly, the system does not declare success or failure based on the raw amount of discrepancy still remaining. Instead, it gauges success or failure based on the *rate* of discrepancy reduction over time. In other words, it is not so much 'Am I closer to my goal?' but 'Am I moving toward my goal at a faster pace?'

How does this relate to emotion? Emotions signal the rate of one's discrepancy-reducing efforts. Thus, one may feel elated even when a long way from the goal, as long as one feels that progress is being made at a satisfactory rate. On the other hand, one may feel dispirited even when very close to the goal if one feels that progress is happening too slowly.

Beyond the concept of discrepancy reduction, Carver and Sheier's theory contains a second critical element: expectancies. People will only take action to reduce discrepancies to the extent that they feel that such actions will be successful. Thus, in many respects, this component of the model alludes to Bandura's social cognitive theory and the principle of self-efficacy in particular (see the introduction to Unit 5).

□■□

This article addresses the nature of certain aspects of emotion, as viewed from a control-theory perspective on behaviour. This perspective focuses on the feedback-based processes through which people self-regulate their actions to minimize discrepancies between actual acts and desired or intended acts. In this article we consider what such a viewpoint on behaviour may say about the nature of emotion (see also Simon, 1967). More specifically, we examine positive and negative affect, present a theory of how these feelings may arise, and consider how they function in human self-regulation.

We begin with a brief outline of a control-theory view on the organization of behaviour, to provide a context for what follows.

Self-Regulation of Behaviour

Control Processes and Self-Regulation

We construe intentional behaviour as reflecting a process of feedback control (e.g., Carver, 1979; Carver & Scheier, 1981, 1982a, 1986a, 1990; MacKay, 1963, 1966; Norman, 1981; Powers, 1973). When people move (physically or psychologically) toward goals, they manifest the functions of a negative (discrepancy reducing) feedback loop (see Figure 15.1). That is, people periodically note the qualities they are expressing in their behaviour (an input function). They compare these perceptions with salient reference values—whatever goals are temporarily being used to guide behaviour (a comparison process inherent in all feedback systems).[1] If the comparisons indicate discrepancies between reference value and present state (i.e., between intended and actual qualities of behaviour), people adjust behaviour (the output function) so that it more closely approximates the reference value.

Taken as an organized system, these component functions act to 'control' the quality that is sensed

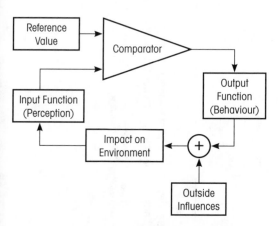

Figure 15.1 Schematic depiction of a feedback loop, the basic unit of cybernetic control.

In such a loop a sensed value is compared to a reference value or standard, and adjustments are made, if necessary, to shift the sensed value in the direction of the standard.

as input to the system. That is, when a feedback loop is functioning properly, it induces the sensed quality closer to the reference value. In terms of human behaviour, the exercise of feedback control means that the person acts to minimize any discernable discrepancy between current actions and the behavioural reference value. To put it more simply, when people pay attention to what they are doing, they usually do what they intend to do, relatively accurately and thoroughly.

This brief description obviously omits a great deal that is important, and space limitations preclude treatment of all of the issues relevant to conceptualizing behaviour. Two more sets of theoretical principles are needed, however, for us to address emotion and its role in self-regulation.

Hierarchical Organization of Behaviour

One of these principles is the notion that behaviour is organized hierarchically (e.g., Broadbent, 1977; Dawkins, 1976; Gallistel, 1980; Martin & Tesser, 1988; Ortony, Clore, & Collins, 1988; Powers, 1973; Vallacher & Wegner, 1985, 1987). In control-process terms, the output of a superordinate feedback system (the system directing behaviour at the level of present current concern—cf. Klinger, 1975; Shallice, 1978) is the resetting of reference values at the next lower level of abstraction (Figure 15.2). Powers (1973) argued that an identity between output at one level and resetting of standards at the next lower level is maintained from the level that is presently superordinate, down to the level of setting reference values for muscle tensions. Thus, the hierarchy creates the physical execution of whatever action is taking place.

We have adopted Powers's position as a conceptual heuristic, focusing on its implications at high levels of abstraction, the levels of our own interest (see Marken, 1986, and Rosenbaum, 1987, regarding the usefulness of similar notions at lower levels). The hierarchical organization in Figure 15.2 shows three high levels of control. At the highest level shown (labelled *system concepts*) are such values as the global sense of idealized self. Although

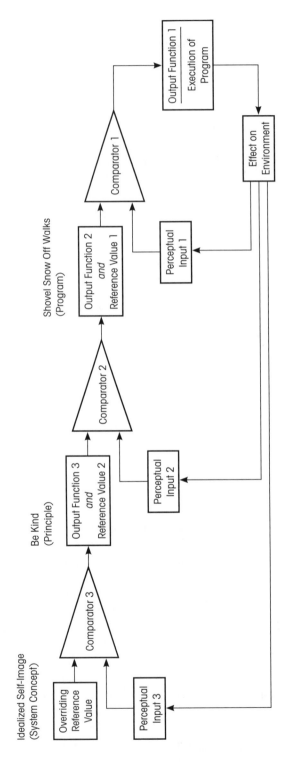

Figure 15.2 **Three-level hierarchy of feedback loops showing the top three levels of control in the model proposed by Powers (1973) and illustrating the kinds of content that reference values at these three levels can assume.**

This diagram portrays the behaviour of someone who is presently attempting to conform to his ideal self-image, by using the principle of kindness to guide his actions, a principle that presently is being manifested through the program of shovelling snow from a neighbour's sidewalk.

self is not the only reference value at this level, it provides what may be the most intuitive illustration of the type of quality that occurs here, and it may be the most frequently used value at this level. Other possibilities include the idealized sense of a relationship or of a society.

Reference values at this level are abstract and difficult to define. How do people minimize discrepancies between their behaviour and such abstract qualities? What behavioural outputs are involved? The answer suggested by Powers (1973) is that the behavioural output of this high-order system consists of providing reference values at the next lower level, which he termed the level of *principle* control. Thus, people act to 'be' who they think they want (or ought) to be by adopting any of the guiding principles that are implied by the idealized self to which they aspire. (The constituents of the idealized self to which the person aspires—and what principles are thereby implied—obviously will differ from person to person.)

Principles begin to provide some form for behaviour. Principles are probably the most abstract aspects of behaviour that have names in everyday language—for example, honesty, responsibility, and expedience. Principles are not specifications of acts but of qualities that can be manifest in many acts. People do not just go out and 'do' honesty, or responsibility, or thrift. Rather, people manifest any one (or more) of these qualities while doing more concrete activities.

The concrete activities are termed *programs* (cf. Schank & Abelson's 1977 discussion of scripts). Principles influence the program level by influencing what programs occur as potential reference values and by influencing choices made within programs. Programs of action are the sorts of activities that most people recognize more clearly as 'behaviour', although even programs are still relatively abstract. Going to the store, cooking dinner, writing a report—all these are programs.

Programs, in turn, are made up of movement *sequences*. One difference between programs and sequences is that programs involve choice points

at which decisions must be made (ranging from trivial to important), whereas the constituents of a sequence are executed all-at-a-piece. When an action becomes sufficiently well learned that its enactment (once begun) is automatic rather than effortful (e.g., Shiffrin & Schneider, 1977), it can be thought of as having become a sequence rather than a program.

An important implication of the notion of hierarchical organization is that the higher one goes into this organization, the more fundamental to the overriding sense of self are the qualities encountered. A second, related implication is that the importance of a reference value at a low level is at least partly a product of the degree to which its attainment contributes to success in the attempt to reduce discrepancies at higher levels.

A last point concerning the hierarchical model is that self-regulation does not inevitably require engaging the full hierarchy from the top downward. We tentatively assume that whatever level of the hierarchy is temporarily focal is functionally superordinate at that moment, with self-regulation at any level higher suspended until attention is redirected toward reference values at the higher level. In practice, much of human behaviour is probably self-regulated at the program level, with little or no consideration of values higher than that.

Difficulty, Disengagement, and Withdrawal

A final set of theoretical principles concerns the fact that people are not always successful in attaining their goals. Sometimes the physical setting precludes intended acts. Sometimes personal inadequacies prevent people from accomplishing what they set out to do. Regardless of the source of the impediment, and regardless of the level of abstraction at which it occurs (e.g., principle, program), there must be a way to construe the fact that people sometimes put aside their goals, aspirations, and intentions.

Assessing Expectancies

We believe that behaviour proceeds smoothly until and unless people encounter impediments

(Figure 15.3). When people encounter enough difficulty to disrupt their efforts, we assume that they step outside the behavioural stream momentarily and assess the likelihood that the desired outcome will occur, given further effort. Potential impediments to action that come to mind before action begins presumably act the same in this respect as do those confronted during the action.

This sequence of interruption and expectancy assessment can be initiated in several ways. The simplest initiator is frustration—existence of an obstacle to goal attainment, either external

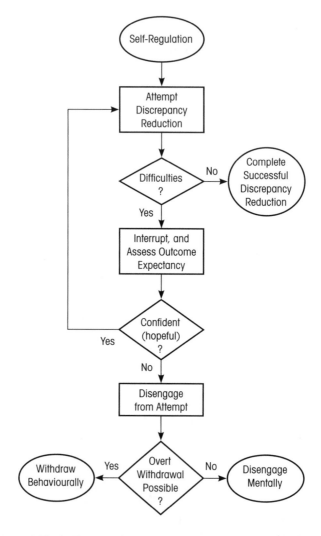

Figure 15.3 Flow diagram of the various consequences that can follow when a person attempts to match his or her behaviour to a standard of comparison.

Although self-regulation often proceeds unimpeded, discrepancy reduction efforts may be interrupted if difficulties or impediments are encountered, or anticipated. What follows this interruption is determined by the person's expectations about whether continued efforts will promote a good outcome.

(impediments or constraints) or internal (deficits of skill, knowledge, or effort). Another major class of interrupters is anxiety, which is aroused in circumstances in which a contemplated or ongoing action is in some way threatening. Although other interrupters are certainly possible, most represent conditions that hamper or interfere with goal attainment.

The process of assessing outcome expectancy (whatever the interrupter) may make use of a wide variety of information pertaining to the situation and to internal qualities such as skill, anticipated effort, and available response options (cf. Lazarus, 1966). In many cases, however, expectancy assessment relies quite heavily on memories of prior experiences. Thus, a pre-existing sense of confidence or doubt with respect to some activity can be a particularly important determinant of situational expectancies. If the expectancies that emerge from this assessment process are sufficiently favourable, the person renews his or her efforts. If the expectancies are sufficiently unfavourable, however, the person begins to disengage from the attempt at goal attainment.

Our research on this rough dichotomy among responses to adversity occurred in the context of our explorations of the effects of self-directed attention (Carver, Blaney, & Scheier, 1979a, 1979b; Carver, Peterson, Follansbee, & Scheier, 1983; Carver & Scheier, 1981; Scheier & Carver, 1982). This line of thought has also been extended to certain problems in self-management, including both test anxiety and social anxiety (Carver et al., 1983; Carver & Scheier, 1984, 1986a, 1986b; Carver, Scheier, & Klahr, 1987; see also Burgio, Merluzzi, & Pryor, 1986; Galassi, Frierson, & Sharer, 1981; Rich & Woolever, 1988; Schlenker & Leary, 1982). These discussions all emphasize the idea that expectancies about one's eventual outcome are an important determinant of whether the person responds to adversity by continuing to exert effort at goal attainment or, instead, by disengaging from the attempt. This analysis has a good deal in common with other expectancy models of behaviour

(e.g., Abramson, Seligman, & Teasdale, 1978; Bandura, 1977, 1986; Kanfer & Hagerman, 1981, 1985; Rotter, 1954; Wortman & Brehm, 1975), although there are also differences among theories (for more detail, see Scheier & Carver, 1988).

Expectancies and Affect

We have assumed for some time that the behavioural consequences of divergent outcome expectancies are paralleled by differences in affective experience (Carver, 1979), and research evidence tends to support this position (Carver & Scheier, 1982b; Andersen & Lyon, 1987; see also Weiner, 1982). When expectancies are favourable, people tend to have positive feelings, which are variously experienced as enthusiasm, hope, excitement, joy, or elation (cf. Stotland, 1969). When expectancies are unfavourable, people have negative feelings—anxiety, dysphoria, or despair. The specific tone of these feelings varies (in part) with the basis for the expectancies (Scheier & Carver, 1988). The latter is a theme that has been developed in much greater detail by Weiner (1982).

Limitation and Challenge

The preceding outline of the relations among expectancies, emotion, and behaviour seems intuitively sensible to us. Making behavioural predictions from this aspect of the model has required (and continues to require) nothing more than the ideas in the preceding section. This outline has something of an ad hoc flavour to it, however, with a number of questions being left unasked and thus unanswered.

A fundamental question that is ignored in the preceding outline is how good and bad feelings come to arise while the person is engaged in goal-directed action. We are certainly not unique in having failed to ask this question. Indeed, it is remarkable how rarely anyone ever asks where affect comes from. Even information-processing theories touching on affect (which one might expect to be particularly attuned to this question) typically discuss only what happens once affect is already present. Discussions focus on the idea that affect is information that takes up space in working memory (Hamilton, 1983), information that may serve particularly important purposes in regulating motivation (Simon, 1967), and information that is encoded in long-term memory in much the same way as other information (Bower & Cohen, 1982). But where does it come from? In the next section we examine this question. We do so by reconsidering, in somewhat different terms, the set of events we have just described. Nothing in the next section contradicts what we have already said, but our discussion takes a form that differs considerably from that of the preceding section.

A More Elaborated View: Meta-Monitoring and Emotion

We have characterized people's conscious self-regulation as a process of monitoring their present actions and comparing the qualities that they perceive therein with the reference values that presently are salient, making adjustments as necessary to render discrepancies minimal. In what follows, we will use the term *monitoring* to refer to this feedback process. As indicated earlier, we see this monitoring loop as fundamental to the control of intentional behaviour.

We suggest, however, that there is also a second feedback process that (in a sense) builds on this one, in a fashion that is orthogonal to the hierarchical organization discussed earlier. This second function operates simultaneously with the monitoring function and in parallel to it, whenever monitoring is going on. The second feedback system serves what we will term a *meta-monitoring* function.

Discrepancy Reduction and Rate of Reduction

The most intuitive way to begin in describing this meta-monitoring function is to say that the meta loop is checking on how well the action loop is doing at reducing the behavioural discrepancies

that the action loop is monitoring. More concretely, we propose that the perceptual input for the meta-monitoring loop is a representation of the *rate of discrepancy reduction in the behavioural (monitoring) system over time*. What is important to the meta loop is not merely whether discrepancies are being reduced at the level of the action loop, but how rapidly they are being reduced. If they are being reduced rapidly, the action loop's progress toward its goal (as perceived by the meta loop) is high. If they are being reduced slowly, the action loop's progress is lower. If they are not being reduced at all, the action loop's progress is zero. Any time discrepancies are enlarging at the level of action monitoring, of course, the action loop's progress is inverse.[2]

Although it may be somewhat less intuitive than the foregoing, we find an analogy useful in describing the functioning of these two systems, an analogy that may also have more literal implications. Because action implies change between states, consider behaviour to be analogous to distance (construed as a vector, because perception of one's action incorporates both the difference between successive states and also the direction of the difference). If the monitoring loop deals with distance and if (as we just asserted) the meta loop assesses the rate of progress of the monitoring loop, then the meta loop is dealing with the psychological equivalent of velocity (also directional). In mathematical terms, velocity is the first derivative of distance over time. To the extent that this physical analogy is meaningful, the perceptual input to the meta loop we are postulating presumably is the first derivative over time of the input information used by the action loop.

We propose that the meta-monitoring process functions as a feedback loop. It thus involves more than the mere sensing of the rate of discrepancy reduction in the action loop. This sensing constitutes an input function, but no more. As in any feedback system, this input is compared against a reference value (cf. Frijda, 1986, 1988). In this case, the reference value is an acceptable or desired rate of behavioural discrepancy reduction. As in other feedback systems, the comparison determines whether there is a discrepancy or deviation from the standard. If there is, an output function is engaged to reduce the discrepancy.

We suggest that the outcome of the comparison process that lies at the heart of this loop is manifest phenomenologically in two forms. The first is a hazy and non-verbal sense of outcome expectancy. The second is affect, a feeling quality, a sense of positiveness or negativeness.

When sensed progress in the action loop conforms to the desired rate of progress, the meta-monitoring system accordingly registers no discrepancy. Given an absence of discrepancy at the meta level, affect is neutral. When the action loop is making continuous, steady progress toward reducing its own discrepancy, but its rate of discrepancy reduction is slower than the meta-monitoring system's reference value, a discrepancy exists for the meta loop. The result in this case should be a degree of doubt and negative affect, proportional to the size of this meta-level discrepancy. When the rate of discrepancy reduction in the action loop is higher than the meta loop's reference value, there is a positive discrepancy at the meta loop, an overshoot of the reference value that is reflected in confidence and in positive feelings.

It is clear that the two systems under discussion (monitoring and meta-monitoring) are related to each other, but we argue that only one of them has implications for affect. In all cases, the action loop is successfully reducing discrepancies. The fact that it is doing so does not, however, determine affect. Affect may be neutral, it may be positive, or it may even be negative, depending on the adequacy of the *rate* of discrepancy reduction. Assessing the adequacy of the rate of operation of one system implies the use of a second system.

It is also important to note that the size of the discrepancy confronted by the action loop at any given point does not play an important role in the perceptual input to the meta loop. A large discrepancy—even a *very* large discrepancy—perceived

at the level of the action loop can be associated with perceptions of either abundant or insufficient progress. This same discrepancy thus can be associated with either favourable or unfavourable expectancies and with either positive or negative affect. What matters with respect to the meta-monitoring system is solely whether the perceived *rate of progress* in the action system is adequate.

The same point can also be made of cases in which the behavioural discrepancy is relatively small. If the meta-monitoring system senses that there is an abundant rate of change toward discrepancy elimination, there should be positive affect and confidence. If it senses an inadequate rate of change, there should be negative affect and doubt.

Thus, ironically, it should be possible for a person who has a large discrepancy at the action loop to feel more positively than a person who has a small discrepancy at the action loop, if the first person is perceiving a more acceptable rate of progress than the second person. In terms of the physical analogy, the first person is more distant from the goal, but is moving toward it with a higher velocity.

Just as the monitoring of action apparently can take any of several levels in a hierarchy of behavioural control as superordinate, so should the meta system be able to function at any of several levels. It seems likely, however, that discrepancies noted by the meta system have greater emotional impact when they concern a central element of self than when they bear only on a more peripheral goal (a program or a sequence of action). Sometimes a task failure has a big impact on one's feelings, sometimes not (cf. Dweck & Elliott, 1983; Dweck & Leggett, 1988; Elliott & Dweck, 1988; Hyland, 1987; Srull & Wyer, 1986). The difference between these cases would seem to be the level of abstraction at which the person is focusing. The consequences of meta-monitoring are more intense, or more impactful, at higher levels than at lower levels of the hierarchy (see also Frijda, 1988).

If the meta loop is truly a bidirectional feedback system, it follows that an overshoot of the reference value should lead to a self-corrective attempt to return to the reference value. To put it more concretely, this view argues that people who have exceeded the desired rate of progress are likely to slow their subsequent efforts. They are likely to coast for a while. The phenomenological result of this would be that the positive affect is not sustained for long.

It is important to recognize that we are not suggesting that affect is the controlled quality in this loop, but rate. Positive feelings reflect a positive discrepancy, which is good. To a system whose goal is controlling sensed rate, however, a discrepancy is a discrepancy and any sensed discrepancy should be reduced. The existence of a natural tendency that has the effect of causing positive affect to be short-lived seems, at first glance, highly improbable. A plausible basis for such a tendency can be seen, however, in the idea that human behaviour is hierarchically organized and involves multiple current concerns. That is, people typically are working toward several goals more or less simultaneously, and many lower level efforts contribute to minimizing discrepancies at high levels. To the extent that movement toward goal attainment is more rapid than expected in one domain, it permits the person to shift attention and effort toward goal strivings in another domain, at no cost. To continue the unnecessarily rapid pace in the first domain might increase positive affect with respect to that activity, but by diverting efforts from other goals, that action may create the potential for negative affect in other domains.

Changes in Rate and the Abruptness of Change

Although we have limited ourselves thus far to addressing various rates of progress toward action goals, it should be obvious that the rate of discrepancy reduction at the action loop can change. Changes in rate at the action loop are subjectively manifest, not as affect but as *change* of affect. Increases in rate are reflected in shifts toward more positive feelings, with the actual experience

depending on the initial and final rates. When the change is from a rate far below the meta standard to a rate closer to the standard but still below it, affect should change from more negative to less negative. If the change is instead to a value that exceeds the meta standard, affect should change from negative to positive.

In the same manner, downward changes in sensed rate at the action loop are also reflected in affective shifts, with the quality of the experience again depending on the initial and final rates. When the change is from a rate that exceeds the meta standard to a rate below the standard, the affective change should be from positive to negative. When the change is from just below the standard to far below the standard, the affective change should be from mildly negative to very negative.

Shifts in rate of progress at the action loop can be gradual, or they can be more abrupt. The more abrupt an increase in the action loop's progress, the more the subjective experience incorporates a rush of exhilaration, reflecting the contrast between the more negative feelings and the more positive feelings (cf. the description of 'sentimentality' by Frijda, 1988, p. 350). The more abrupt a slowing of the action loop's progress, the more the subjective experience should incorporate the well-known sinking feeling (de-exhilaration?) that reflects the contrast when feelings suddenly shift in a negative direction. Indeed, it seems reasonable to suggest that a discernible shift toward more negative feelings is often precisely the experience that causes people to interrupt ongoing action and consciously evaluate the probability of their eventual success.

We suggested earlier that the quality the meta loop senses as its input is analogous to the physical quality of velocity. Let us carry this analogy one step further. What we are addressing now is not velocity but change in velocity—acceleration. Acceleration is the second derivative of distance over time. Given that people apparently are equipped to sense these experiences, the analogy seems to suggest that some neural processor is computing a second derivative over time of the information input to the action loop. Does this imply the need to postulate a third layer of feedback control (complete with reference value and comparator)? Not necessarily. It is possible to sense a quality that is not involved in a feedback loop. In part because it is difficult for us to know what might be the implications of such a third layer of control, we are hesitant at this stage to assume its existence.

With respect to a final point, however, we are more confident. In the same way that distance and velocity are independent of each other, both are independent of acceleration. (An object moving 20 feet per second can be accelerating, decelerating, or its velocity can be constant; the same is true of an object moving 80 feet per second.) We suggest that the same independence exists on the other side of the analogy. We argued earlier that affect experienced is independent of the degree of discrepancy at the action level. In the same fashion, we argue that the rush associated with acceleration is independent of the size of the discrepancy at the action level and also independent of the rate of discrepancy reduction at the action level.

As an example, a person with a large discrepancy at the action level will have positive affect if the rate of discrepancy reduction is greater than needed. This positive affect will be free of exhilaration if the rate of discrepancy reduction is constant. If the rate has suddenly shifted upward (to the same ending value), the positive feelings will be accompanied by a sense of exhilaration.

Further Processing, and Differences between Immediate and Thought-Out Expectancies

In describing the proposed meta-monitoring function we said that one manifestation of its operation is a hazy sense of expectancy. Obviously, however, people's consciously held expectancies for an outcome do not rest entirely on their currently sensed rate of progress toward that outcome. Indeed, as noted earlier, our own research has emphasized the idea that temporary frustration or anxiety arousal is less important than are other sources of

information in producing the coping expectancies that ultimately determine subsequent behaviour (e.g., Carver et al., 1979a, 1979b; Carver et al., 1983; Carver & Scheier, 1986a). Thus, although meta-monitoring during a period of adversity does yield a sense of doubt, this transient doubt is often modified to a substantial degree by additional thought.

In more consciously judging outcome probability, people depend to a large extent on memories of their prior outcomes in similar situations. They may also consider such things as what additional resources they might bring to bear (cf. Lazarus, 1966), the possibility of taking an alternative approach, and social comparison information (e.g., Wills, 1981; Wood, Taylor, & Lichtman, 1985). Thus, the more conscious and verbalizable expectancies that people generate when they interrupt their efforts and think about the likely outcomes of those efforts can be influenced by a fairly wide range of information.[3]

In some instances the additional processing that creates this influence is very simple. It may entail nothing more than retrieving a summary memory regarding prior outcomes in this class of situations (e.g., 'I'm no good at standardized tests', 'People never like me') or engaging in self-exhortation ('You can do it—try harder'). Other instances, however, involve a wider search of diverse memories or a more extensive analysis of possibilities. This would be the case whenever the person considered such questions as whether additional information is obtainable, whether other people might provide assistance, or whether important aspects of the situation are likely to change soon enough to matter.

How do these various thoughts influence the expectancies that eventually emerge? In some cases the mechanism is probably very simple. When people retrieve relatively chronic expectancies from memory in summary form, the information already takes the form of expectancies. Presumably, these memories represent accumulations or consolidations of the products of earlier instances of meta-monitoring during behaviour. When evoked from memory, this information contributes directly to a subsequent sense of confidence or doubt. Memories of expectancies may also be linked to memories of the corresponding affective quality, thus directly influencing subsequent affective tone (cf. Mayer & Gaschke, 1988).

For cases involving more thorough processing, we suggest a more complex mechanism, which derives conceptually from the theory under discussion. When people stop and analyze the situation they are in, they typically bring to mind a series of possibilities regarding the situation. In order for these possibilities to influence subsequent expectancies, their likely consequences must be evaluated. How does this evaluation take place? One argument is that the possibilities are briefly played through mentally as behavioural scenarios. Playing through the scenarios should lead to conclusions that influence the person's sense of outcome expectancy ('If I try approaching it this way instead of that way, it should work better', 'This is the only thing I can see to do, and it will just make the situation worse').

It seems reasonable to suggest that this process engages the same mechanism that handles meta-monitoring during overt behaviour. When one's progress is temporarily stalled, playing through a scenario that is confident and optimistic will indicate a higher rate of progress than is currently being experienced, and the meta loop thus will yield a more optimistic outcome assessment than is currently being derived from overt action. If the scenario is negative and hopeless, it will indicate a further reduction in progress, and the meta loop will yield an assessment of greater doubt. Thus, expectancy-relevant rumination can either reduce or exacerbate a person's temporary hesitancy and doubt, depending on the scenario that comes to mind. We suggest, however, that the influence on subsequent expectancies (and affect, as well) may involve the same mechanism that produces more momentary effects on expectancies during the actual flow of behaviour.

. . .

Issues and Questions within the Model

The preceding portrayal of what we have termed *meta-monitoring* raises a number of issues and questions. Some of them pertain directly to the ideas that we have just outlined concerning the origins of positive and negative feelings. Others pertain more generally to the fit between this theory and other aspects of a control-process approach to behavioural self-regulation. Yet others pertain to relationships between this and other theories on emotion. These issues are addressed in the next three sections. We begin with issues that pertain directly to the emotion theory itself.

Reference Values Used in Meta-Monitoring

One important question is what reference value is being used by the meta-monitoring system. We assume that this system is capable of using widely varying definitions of adequate progress for the action loop. Sometimes the reference value is imposed from outside (as in tenure review decisions), sometimes it is self-imposed (as in someone who has a personal timetable for career development), and sometimes it derives from social comparison (as when people are in competition with each other). Sometimes the reference value is very demanding, sometimes it is less so.

As an example in which the meta standard is both stringent and externally imposed, consider the requirements of degree programs in medical or law school. In such cases, even continuous progress in an absolute sense (i.e., successful mastery of required material) is adequate only if it occurs at or above the rate required by the degree program. Thus, as the person attempts to attain the action goal of becoming a physician or a lawyer, the reference value for meta-monitoring will be a relatively stringent one.

How stringent a standard is used at the meta level has straightforward implications for the person's emotional life. If the pace of progress used as a reference point is too high, it will rarely be matched, even if (objectively) the person's rate of progress is extraordinarily high. In such a case, the person will experience negative affect often and positive affect rarely. If the pace of progress used as a reference point is low, the person's rate of behavioural discrepancy reduction will more frequently exceed it. In this case, the person will experience positive affect more often and negative affect more rarely.

What variables influence the stringency of the meta-level standard being used? One important determinant is the extent to which there is time pressure on the activity being regulated, which varies greatly from one activity to another. Some actions are clearly time dependent ('Have that report on my desk by 5 o'clock'), others are more vaguely so (it's about the time of year to fertilize the lawn), and the time dependency is even hazier for others (I want to go to China some day; I'd like to have a boat before I get too old to enjoy it). When an activity has demanding time constraints, the meta-level reference value used necessarily is stringent. When there is a relative lack of time pressure, a relatively lax standard is more likely to be used.

Although time dependence is clearest in situations that require a rapid pace, there also appears to be a second sort of time dependence. This occurs for behavioural activities that people wish to have completed but have no desire to do (a common view of chores). Such goals are highly time dependent, in the sense that people wish their attainment to be instantaneous. Given this, the meta-level reference value must necessarily be at a very high level. Because the rate of progress therefore cannot meet the standard, positive affect is nearly impossible and aversiveness is almost inevitable when the activity is being engaged in. (On the other hand, the intensity of this affect is proportional to the importance of the activity, which is often relatively low.) This set of relations would seem to define the experience of drudgery.

Changing Meta-Level Standards

As noted in the preceding section, reference values for the meta loop differ across people and across categories of behaviour. Reference values at the meta level can also shift as a result of time and experience (see also Lord & Hanges, 1987). To put it differently, as people accumulate more experience in a given domain, adjustments can occur in the pacing that they expect and demand of their efforts.

Sometimes the adjustment is downward. For example, a researcher experiencing difficulty in his attempt to be as productive as his colleagues may gradually adopt less stringent standards of pacing. One consequence of this is a more favourable balance of positive to negative affect across time (cf. Linsenmeier & Brickman, 1980). In other cases, the adjustment is upward. A person who gains work-related skills may undertake greater challenges, requiring quicker handling of each action unit. Upward adjustment has the side effect of decreasing the potential for positive affect and increasing the potential for negative affect.

This adjusting of meta-level reference values over the course of experience looks suspiciously like a self-corrective feedback process in its own right, as the person reacts to insufficient challenge by taking on a more demanding pace, and reacts to too much challenge by scaling back the criterion.[4] If a feedback process is responsible for changing standards at the meta level (or contributes to such changes), it is much slower acting than are those that are the focus of this article. Shifting the reference value downward is not the immediate response when the person has trouble keeping up with a demanding pace. First the person tries harder to keep up. Only more gradually, if the person cannot keep up, does the meta standard shift to accommodate. Similarly, an upward shift is not the immediate response when the person's rate of discrepancy reduction exceeds the standard. The more typical response is to coast for a while. Only when the overshoot is frequent does the standard shift to accommodate.

The idea that these changes are produced by a slow-acting feedback system may help to account for why it can be so difficult to shift meta standards voluntarily. That is, one can make a verbal change easily ('Stop being so demanding of yourself, and be more satisfied with what you are accomplishing'), but this sort of self-verbalization rarely takes effect immediately. If a true shift in standard relies on a slow-acting feedback loop, that would account for why subjective experience tends to lag behind the self-instruction.

It is of some interest that these patterns of shift in reference value (and the concomitant effects on affect) imply a mechanism within the organism that functions in such a way as to prevent the too-frequent occurrence of positive feeling, as well as the too-frequent occurrence of negative feeling. That is, the (bidirectional) shifting of the rate criterion over time would tend to control pacing of behaviour in such a way that affect continues to vary in both directions around neutral. We earlier suggested that the meta system does not function to maximize positive affect. In the same manner, an arrangement for changing meta-level reference values such as we are suggesting here would not work toward maximization of pleasure and minimization of pain. Rather, the affective consequence would be that the person experiences more or less

the same range of variation in his or her affective experience over extended periods of time.

Time Frames for Input to Meta-Monitoring

Another question to be raised about the model concerns the span of time over which the action loop's progress at discrepancy reduction is processed to form a perceptual input (a sensed rate) for the meta system. The time period across which information is merged may be brief or it may be quite long.[5] There seems to be nothing inherent in the meta-monitoring process per se that dictates whether it focuses on a short or a long time period. Whether input information is merged over a short or a long time period, however, can have important implications for the subjective experiences that result.

Consider the case of a person whose actions create gradual but erratic progress toward some goal (Figure 15.4). If the input function to this person's meta-monitoring loop assesses rate of discrepancy reduction over a very short time frame, the person will be intermittently happy (periods A and C) and dysphoric (periods B and D). That is, the rate of progress exceeds the standard during periods A and C (thus yielding positive affect)

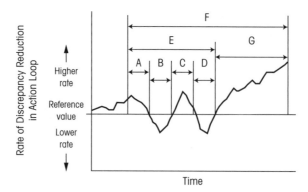

Figure 15.4 Assessing rate of discrepancy reduction across different lengths of time can produce different patterns of emotional experience.

If assessment bears on brief time spans (periods A, B, C, and D), the experience is alternately positive feelings (A and C) versus negative feelings (B and D). If assessed rate of discrepancy reduction is merged across a longer interval (E), experienced mood does not fluctuate. Assessing across too long a period, however (F), can be misleading because it can obscure meaningful changes that occur over a shorter term (G, compared with E).

but falls short of the standard during period B and most of period D (thus yielding negative affect). If the person takes a longer view on the same set of events (i.e., merges across all of period E), the frequent deviations upward and downward from the standard will be blurred (in effect, averaged) in the derivation of perceptual input for the meta system. In the general case, this will produce affect (and a concomitant sense of expectancy) that is both more stable and more moderated. In the specific case of period E, the affect experienced will be near neutral, because the upward and downward deviations cancel each other out.

This reasoning might seem to argue that it is desirable to take the broader view of events. There is, however, a potential disadvantage of deriving input through the broader view. Merging data over a very long period can result in insensitivity to what are actually meaningful changes in the rate of discrepancy reduction at the action loop. Period G reflects considerably faster progress than took place across period E, but awareness of that shift in rate will be blunted if the input is merged across period F. Thus, taking too long a view in creating input for the meta system can be as bad as taking too short a view.

This general line of reasoning suggests a possible process basis for the fact that people seem naturally to differ in how variable their moods are (e.g., Diener, Larsen, Levine, & Emmons, 1985; Larsen, 1987; Wessman & Ricks, 1966). Perhaps these differences in emotional variability reflect default differences in the time spans merged for input by people's meta-monitoring systems.

Multiple Affects from a Single Event, and the Independence of Positive and Negative Affect

Our theoretical discussion was focused on the existence of one feeling at a time. Affect associated with goal-directed effort need not be purely positive or purely negative, however. A single event may produce both of these feelings, depending on how it is viewed in meta-monitoring.

Sometimes there is more than one view on an event, even with respect to a single goal (cf. Ortony et al., 1988, pp. 51–52). For example, it may happen that the experience of a failure yields the realization of how to attain future success. The failure is displeasing, but the insight is elating. Feelings from the event thus are mixed. Focusing more on the present failure to attain the goal (inadequate progress) will yield a greater sense of negative affect. Focusing more on the insight (progress toward future success) will yield a greater sense of positive affect. Both feelings, however, are produced by different aspects of the same outcome, and both can be felt at once (or as alternating time-shared experiences).

It is perhaps more common that an action or an outcome has implications for two distinct goals. The goals making up the hierarchy of a person's self-definition are not always perfectly compatible with each other, and occasionally two conflicting goals become salient at the same time (see also Emmons, 1986; Van Hook & Higgins, 1988). For example, the goal of career advancement and the goal of spending a lot of time with one's young children may both be desirable, but the 24-hour day imposes limitations on the time available for trying to attain them. Sometimes the actions that permit progress toward one goal (working extra hours at the office) simultaneously interfere with progress toward the other goal (spending time with one's children). To the extent that both goals remain salient, the result is mixed feelings. In this case, however, the two feeling qualities stem from meta-monitoring with respect to each of two distinct goals.

This line of discussion also suggests a perspective on the assertion, made frequently in recent years, that positive and negative affective experiences are not at opposite poles of a continuum but rather are independent (e.g., Diener & Emmons, 1984; Diener & Iran-Nejad, 1986; Warr, Barter, & Brownbridge, 1983; Watson & Tellegen, 1985; Zevon & Tellegen, 1982). This argument usually focuses on the experience of moods, not on the nature of affect.[6] As a statement about mood, the argument means in part that people's moods can incorporate mixed feelings. A mood can be partly good and partly bad, though only rarely are both of these feelings intense at the same time (Diener & Iran-Nejad, 1986).

This argument also means that knowing a person is not depressed does not make it reasonable to infer that the person is happy. Knowing a person is not happy does not make it reasonable to infer that the person feels bad. Sometimes people are affectively neutral. The relative independence of these qualities thus has important methodological implications. To know about both qualities in people's overall feelings, one must assess both (cf. Wortman & Silver, 1989).

Although these two qualities of mood have been observed to vary relatively independently, there has been very little discussion of why this is so. Diener and Iran-Nejad (1986) noted that their subjects sometimes reported moderate amounts of both positive and negative affect but did not speculate why. Watson and Tellegen (1985) noted the possibility that different parts of the brain might be involved in the two affect qualities, but did not address the question of why people might ever experience mixed feelings.

The preceding discussion suggests a very simple explanation for these findings. People often have many goals at once. A person who is making rapid progress on some current concerns and poor progress on others should experience positive feelings with respect to the former and negative feelings with respect to the latter. This experience must be common, even in the course of a single day. The diversity of these 'progress reports' from the meta-monitoring system should disrupt any inverse correlation between reports of having experienced positive affect and reports of having experienced negative affect in a given time span, particularly if that span is relatively long. As the time span narrows to a given 'emotional' event, one would expect the independence of the two affects to diminish, because the person is more likely to

be dealing with only one goal (and only one perspective on it) than would otherwise be the case. This is precisely what seems to happen (Diener & Iran-Nejad, 1986).

Effects of Existing Emotion on Subsequent Experience

Our main theoretical interest is on the processes by which we think affect is created in the behaving person. We should note, however, that once an affect exists, it also influences later processing. It is now widely believed, for example, that emotional state influences the ease with which affectively toned material is brought from memory (e.g., Blaney, 1986; Bower & Cohen, 1982; Clark, Milberg, & Ross, 1983; Clark & Waddell, 1983). Positive affect makes positively valenced material more accessible; negative affect makes negatively valenced material more accessible.

It seems a reasonable inference from this that a current affective state may influence the outcomes of subsequent meta-monitoring. This is not a restatement of the point made earlier that people's consciously derived expectancies are subject to influences beyond current sensed progress. The point we are making now is that even sensed progress per se may be affected by current affect. That is, perceptions relevant to meta-monitoring (as well as monitoring) are determined partly by information drawn from the situation as it exists, and partly by information from memory (Figure 15.5). Any bias in the use of either of these sources of information will cause bias in the output of the meta process.

A current affective state may exert a bias by rendering external information consistent with current affective tone more salient for input processing, which may reflect easier access to memories consistent with that affective tone (cf. Masters & Furman, 1976; Pyszczynski, Holt, & Greenberg, 1987). More simply, being in a good mood may cause a current situation to be viewed more positively (Forgas & Moylan, 1987), because of selective encoding of favourable aspects of the situation (cf. Antes & Matthews, 1988), which may

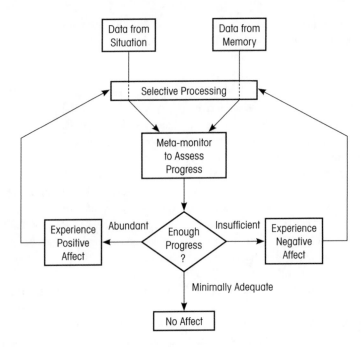

Figure 15.5 Current affect is both a consequence of, and an influence on, one's perceptions of how well one is doing at moving toward one's behavioural goals.

If meta-monitoring yields affect, that affect can cause the person to preferentialy code affect-consistent information inherent in the situation itself and to perferentially extract affect-consistent information from memory. Both of these influences can bias subsequent assessments at the meta level, perpetuating the tone of the current mood.

be facilitated by enhanced access to memories of prior successes. Being in a bad mood may cause a current situation to be viewed more negatively through selective coding of unfavourable elements of the situation, facilitated by enhanced access to memories of prior bad outcomes.

The effect of such a processing bias would be to perpetuate the original emotional tone. Being in a bad mood causes people to see things in a way that tends to keep them in a bad mood. What causes emotions ever to fade, then? An answer is provided by Solomon's (1980) argument that every emotion evokes a second, slower acting process that acts in opposition to the initial emotion. The relevant aspect of Solomon's theory in this context is that (in normal self-regulation, at least) the opponent process dampens affective tone. The opponent

process itself implies the existence of a feedback system beyond the ones on which we are focusing, in that whichever the direction of the initial emotional response (positive or negative), the opponent process acts to return the person to a neutral state.

Breadth of Intended Application

A final question to be raised about the model concerns its intended scope. Although most examples in this article come from domains of achievement and instrumental activity, this is not a theory of achievement-related affect. This analysis is intended to apply to all goal-directed behaviour, including attempts to attain goals that are amorphous and poorly specified, and goals for which the idea of assessing the rate of progress toward discrepancy reduction might at first glance seem odd.

Human goals such as developing and maintaining a sound relationship, being a good mother or father, dealing honourably and pleasantly with acquaintances, seeing someone you care for be happy and fulfilled, having a full and rich life, and even becoming immersed in the fictional lives portrayed in a novel or film are fully amenable to analysis in these terms. These are all qualities of human experience toward which people attempt to move, goals that evolve or recur across time, as do most goals underlying human action. To the extent that progress toward goals such as these is taken by the person as important, to the extent that people are invested in experiencing these qualities in their lives sooner rather than later, the meta loop produces positive and negative feelings as progress is faster or slower than the standard being used. Sometimes pacing toward such goals matters little, but sometimes it matters a lot. In the latter circumstances, we suggest, these events are capable of producing affect.

Issues Relating Emotion to Disengagement

A second set of issues and questions emerges when one considers our viewpoint on affect in relation to the model of behaviour with which we began this article. An important aspect of that model is the idea that if a person's expectancies of goal attainment are sufficiently unfavourable, the person may disengage from active pursuit of the goal (see also Klinger, 1975; Kukla, 1972; Wortman & Brehm, 1975). Thinking about disengagement, and about the emotions that often surround it, raises several issues.

Hierarchical Organization Sometimes Creates an Inability to Disengage

One issue stems from the idea that behaviour is hierarchically organized and that goals are increasingly important as one moves upward through the hierarchy. Presumably, in most cases disengagement from values low in the hierarchy of control is

easy. Indeed, the nature of programs is such that disengagement from efforts at subgoals is quite common, even while the person continues to pursue the overall goal of the program (e.g., if you go to buy something and the store is closed for inventory, you are likely to head for another store rather than give up altogether).

Sometimes, however, lower order goals are more closely linked to values at a higher level. To disengage from lower level goals in this case enlarges discrepancies at higher levels. These higher order qualities are values that are important, even central, to one's life. One cannot disengage from them, or disregard them, or tolerate large discrepancies between those values and currently sensed reality, without substantially reorganizing one's value system (Carver & Scheier, 1986c; Kelly, 1955; Millar, Tesser, & Millar, 1988). In such a case, disengagement from concrete behavioural goals is quite difficult.

Now recall the affective consequences of being in this situation. The desire to disengage was prompted in the first place by unfavourable expectancies for discrepancy reduction. These expectancies are paralleled by negative affect. In this situation, then, the person is experiencing negative feelings (because of an inability to progress toward behavioural discrepancy reduction) and is unable to do anything about the feelings (because of an inability to give up the behavioural reference value). The person simply stews in the feelings that arise from irreconcilable discrepancies (see also Martin & Tesser, 1989). In our view, this bind—being unable to let go of something that is unattainable—lies at the heart of exogenous depression (cf. Hyland, 1987; Klinger, 1975; Pyszczynski & Greenberg, 1987). It seems important to us to recognize that this bind often stems from the hierarchical nature of people's goal structures.

Disengagement Requires That There Be an Override Mechanism

The idea that people's efforts give way to disengagement from the goal as expectancies become more negative also raises a second issue. We believe that this characterization is reasonable as part of a model of motivated action. But there is a conceptual discontinuity between this idea and the feedback theories we have espoused regarding behavioural self-regulation and—now—affective experience.

Where in the model of affect is the mechanism to produce disengagement? We portrayed meta-monitoring as a feedback system in which discrepancies (inadequate progress) produce doubt and negative affect. Why should this system (and the corresponding behavioural monitoring system) not continue endlessly to attempt to reduce discrepancies, however ineffectively? Why should the negative affect not simply persist or intensify? What permits the person ever to disengage?

The answer has to be that in normal self-regulation there is an override that is capable of taking precedence over this feedback system and causing disengagement from the reference value currently being used to guide action. In the jargon of the computer field, there must be something akin to a *break* function, which permits ongoing action to be suspended or abandoned altogether. When disengagement is adaptive, it is so because it frees the system to take up other reference values and enables the person to turn to the pursuit of substitute or alternative goals. Such an override function has a critically important role in human self-regulation, inasmuch as there are any number of goals from which people simply must disengage, either temporarily or permanently (see Klinger, 1975, for a broader discussion of commitment to and disengagement from incentives).

. . .

Relations to Other Theories

Although we do not propose to examine the relationship between this theory and every other theory bearing on emotions, three comparisons that seem important are outlined in the following sections.

Interruption Can Cause Emotion

Several theorists have made statements linking the experience of emotion to the interruption of behaviour. Some have drawn the link in one causal direction, others in the opposite direction. Mandler (1984; Mandler & Watson, 1966) has proposed that interruption of an organized sequence of action causes autonomic arousal, which creates the potential for emotion (à la Schachter & Singer, 1962). The emotion most likely to occur after interruption, in Mandler's view, is anxiety. Anxiety is likely because interrupters often leave people without alternate ways to reach desired goals, and the latter circumstance is what (to Mandler) defines anxiety (cf. Millar et al., 1988).

Although Mandler (1984) views anxiety as the most likely emotional consequence of interruption, anxiety is not inevitable. Sometimes interruption leads to positive emotion. Berscheid (1983), in applying Mandler's theory to interpersonal attraction, developed this idea more completely. She argued for two circumstances in which interruptions facilitate rather than impede completion of action sequences. In the first case, the interruption is removed or shown to be less impactful than it first appeared to be. In the second case, the interruption is itself an event that produces attainment of a desired goal sooner than previously anticipated. In either of these cases, interruption can lead to positive feelings.

There are obvious similarities between this viewpoint and ours. One similarity is the idea that obstructions to goal attainment can cause emotional reactions. We agree with Mandler (1984) and Berscheid (1983) that the experience of a person who feels helpless and disorganized following an interruption will be one of negative affect. In our view, however, conditions that impede or disrupt efforts at goal attainment (i.e., the interrupting conditions) cause negative affect intrinsically, rather than merely creating a condition of affect-free arousal that then must be assigned affective meaning.

In our view, the two situations said by Berscheid (1983) to produce positive affect reduce to a single phenomenon: Each case involves a shift toward higher levels of progress toward goal attainment. When an interrupting condition is removed, a loss of progress (the initial interruption) is followed by enhanced progress. When goal attainment occurs unexpectedly quickly, the increase in progress is immediate (i.e., without an initial slowing). Both cases satisfy our condition for positive affect, in that both suggest progress at a rate likely to exceed the reference point.

We would hold, however, that the position taken by Mandler (1984) and Berscheid (1983) misses two important things. First, as regards removal of an interrupting condition, we would argue that the person experiences negative affect during the period between onset and removal of that initial interruption. Only when the removal occurs (or is anticipated) does affect shift, because only then does progress return to a high level. Second, we would argue that it is not completion of act sequences per se that is pleasing (the position taken by Mandler, 1984, and by Berscheid, 1983), but rather movement toward completion at a rate higher than needed. As it happens, Mandler and Berscheid incorporated high rates of progress into the examples they used to illustrate the emergence of positive emotion. They did not, however, build the notion of rate of completion into their theories.

One further parallel between models is noteworthy, concerning the conditions that Mandler (1984) and Berscheid (1983) believe initiate an emotional experience. The examples they used to illustrate interruption all involve abrupt changes in progress. Indeed, abruptness seems inherent in the very concept of interruption. We noted earlier that an abrupt change in progress implies an acceleration or deceleration. It would seem, then, that acceleration or deceleration is intrinsic to the events that Mandler (1984) and Berscheid (1983) term *interruptions*. This inference on our part is very consistent with our speculation earlier in the article that deceleration may be the experiential quality that causes people to interrupt their

behavioural efforts and evaluate more consciously their probable outcomes.

The notion that there is an equivalence between acceleration/deceleration and interruption suggests a basis for integrating our approach to affect with Mandler's view of emotion. Mandler (1984) has long held that the term *emotion* should be reserved for affectively toned experiences that incorporate arousal. To Mandler, without arousal there is no emotion. He views interruption as a precondition for emotion precisely because he believes that interruption creates arousal. Emotion, for Mandler, seems equivalent to what we described as an affective experience in which there also is acceleration or deceleration. Affective experiences without acceleration or deceleration have received less theoretical attention from Mandler or Berscheid (cf. Berscheid, 1983, pp. 123–124; Mandler, 1984, pp. 131–132). Thus, our analysis would appear to provide an important supplement to theirs.

Affect Can Cause Interruption and Reprioritization

Not every theorist who links interruption to emotion has placed the causal influence in the direction favoured by Mandler (1984) and Berscheid (1983). Some have suggested that affect, particularly negative affect, causes interruption of ongoing behaviour (Simon, 1967; Sloman, 1987). A potential consequence of this interruption, which suggests a function for the negative emotion, is a reconsideration and reprioritization of one's goals.

The simplest case that can be analyzed in these terms—to which we have largely restricted ourselves thus far in the article—is one in which a single reference value for behaviour is currently focal. Negative affect occurs if progress toward that focal goal is inadequate. If negative affect becomes sufficiently intense (or expectancies regarding goal attainment become sufficiently unfavourable), the person disengages from the attempt to conform to it. Once disengagement occurs, the person may turn to a new goal domain or may adopt a less exacting goal in the same domain (cf. Schönpflug,

1983, 1985). In either case, disengagement and choice of a new goal can be construed as reflecting a reprioritization, in that attaining the previous goal is now being accorded a lower priority than it was before.

In other cases, however, emotions can induce a different kind of reprioritization. It is this second type of reprioritization that Simon (1967) had in mind as a role for emotions. Simon suggested that many emotions cause people to interrupt behaviour and consider the possibility that an alternative goal (not presently focal) should be accorded a higher priority than it is presently receiving. The stronger the emotion, the stronger is the message that the less attended goal should be receiving the highest priority, in place of the goal that is presently focal.

The Need to Assume Dual Monitoring
Simon's (1967) analysis seems compatible with the ideas we are proposing, but his view on reprioritization seems to require at least one further assumption (even beyond the assumption of an override mechanism). That is, Simon's analysis seems to require that discrepancies with respect to two different reference values be monitored (and meta-monitored) simultaneously, one focally and the other less so. The emotion that serves as the call for reprioritization is being generated by what is occurring with respect to the *less* focal reference value. The call for reprioritization inevitably is a call to upgrade the priority now being accorded that second value.

The clearest illustration of this argument is what occurs when anxiety arises while the person is engaged in goal-directed effort. For example, anxiety arises when a snake phobic attempts to attain the goal of holding a snake, or when a test-anxious person attempts to attain the goal of scoring well on a test. In such cases, rate of progress toward the focal reference value—the concrete behavioural goal that the person is trying to attain—is not itself the source of the anxiety. Rather, the anxiety is produced by something that

is happening with respect to a second reference value.

This second reference value may be physical safety (in the case of the phobic), or the desire to maintain a positive self-portrayal to parents or teachers (in the case of the test-anxious person), or even such broader values as holistic personal integration (cf. Rogers, 1980). As the person attempts to do the intended behaviour, that second value (whichever it is) is being threatened. The farther the person goes in the attempted action, the greater is the perceived threat to that second goal. If a discrepancy thus is enlarging at the level of the action loop for that second goal, it should be clear that a major discrepancy has developed at the level of the meta loop for that second goal. The result is negative affect.

It is important to recognize that, in cases such as these, the threat that induces fear is occurring as a by-product of the attempt to do something else. The snake phobic is trying to hold the snake, but doing so is creating perceptions of diminishing safety. The fear thus represents a signal that the person should be devoting greater attention to the goal of safety than to the goal of holding the snake.

In most cases of this sort (perhaps all), the second, threatened value seems to be at a higher level of abstraction than the focal goal (see also Carver & Scheier, 1986a). Earlier in the article we professed no need to assume that self-regulation is always being guided by high-level reference values. Yet this view on reprioritization suggests that high-order values may often be monitored outside awareness until discrepancy enlargement is detected, at which point the value becomes more focal. Another possibility is that fear may happen only when the person is already primed in some way to be attending somewhat to this high-order value. Obviously, there are many unanswered questions here concerning how often and to what degree such parallel processing concerning multiple goal values takes place in human behaviour.

Although anxiety is the easiest emotion to address in terms of Simon's (1967) analysis of prioritization, other emotions can also be assimilated to his point of view. Guilt, for example, occurs when a discrepancy is created between the reference value of a moral standard and one's current behaviour (behaviour that may perfectly match one's action intention). Shame, or embarrassment, occurs when an action creates a discrepancy with respect to a social standard. Anger seems to result from enlarging discrepancies concerning personal control over one's experiences (cf. Averill, 1983). In each of these cases, the emotion seems not to be directly related to the reference value toward which one is trying to move. Rather, it is a by-product of that movement, occurring because the action has consequences in addition to its intended consequences. These examples thus are consistent with the idea that meta-monitoring is often occurring with respect to a second point of reference, as well as to the intention that is being enacted focally.

Types of Discrepancy and Quality of Affect

A third useful theoretical comparison is between our ideas and a theory recently proposed by Higgins (1987). One thing that makes this comparison particularly interesting is the fact that the two models both make considerable use of the concept of discrepancy. Higgins (1987) proposed that certain emotions occur as the consequence of discrepancies between pairs of psychological entities. For the sake of simplicity, we will deal here with only two kinds of discrepancies. The first is between one's perceived actual self and one's ideal self (actual–ideal discrepancies). The second is between one's perceived actual self and one's ought self (actual–ought discrepancies).[7]

An ideal self is a desired self, a self to which one aspires. This mental entity is reward based. Living up to the ideal means attaining something desired, acquiring reward. An ought self, in contrast, is a duty or obligation, a self that one feels compelled to be, rather than desires to be. This mental entity is punishment-based. Living up to

an ought means doing something so as to avoid a punishment. Each person has ideals, and each person has oughts (which may be either interrelated or distinct), and the perceived actual self may be compared to each of these reference points.

According to Higgins (1987), large discrepancies between ideal and actual yield depressed affect. Pure depression thus represents an impending failure to attain rewards (see also Finlay-Jones & Brown, 1981). In contrast, large discrepancies between ought and actual are said to yield anxiety. Pure anxiety thus represents an impending failure to avoid punishment. This separation of reference values for the self into ideal versus ought is reminiscent of Gray's (1981, 1982) discussion of stop and go systems in behaviour, which he believes are mediated by distinct physiological structures.

Three differences between Higgins's theory and ours deserve comment. First, Higgins (1987) proposed that depressed affect is a consequence of a discrepancy between an actual and an ideal representation of the self. Our position, in contrast, is that the discrepancy that matters is a discrepancy in sensed rate of progress toward ideals. If progress is inadequate—if there is a discrepancy at the meta-monitoring loop—the person experiences negative affect. Thus, from our point of view, a person who is discrepant from the ideal but is moving toward it rapidly enough should experience positive rather than negative affect.[8]

A second difference between theories is also implicit in this last statement. The model we have presented here deals with both positive affect and negative affect. The theory proposed by Higgins (1987) focuses almost exclusively on negative affect. Higgins did address positive affect, but only in passing (p. 336), and in doing so he seemed to equate positive affect with the absence of negative affect, a position we are not sure is tenable. Our analysis thus supplements his in an important way, by suggesting a basis for the existence of positive feeling qualities, as well as a basis for the existence of negative affect.

The third point of comparison between models concerns the distinction between ideals and oughts. This is the most novel aspect of the Higgins (1987) analysis, providing him a conceptual basis for differentiating anxiety from depression. Higgins framed the distinction between ideals and oughts in terms of reward and punishment contingencies. We believe this distinction can be addressed in control-process terms as well, but to do so requires distinguishing between two kinds of feedback systems.

A negative feedback loop, to which we have limited ourselves thus far, is a discrepancy *reducing,* or negating, loop (thus the term *negative*). This system has a positively valenced reference value, a desired goal. This sort of system would be construed by some people as reward based. A positive feedback loop, in contrast, is a discrepancy *amplifying* loop (see DeAngelis, Post, & Travis, 1986, for detail).[9] The reference value of this system is an undesired quality. Discrepancy amplifying loops attempt to move the currently perceived value as far away as possible from the reference value. This sort of system would be construed by some as punishment based. Deviation amplifying loops are believed to be less common in naturally occurring systems because they are unstable. Nevertheless, whenever the motive behind an act is the desire to prevent a condition from existing, the behaviour would seem to reflect a positive feedback process (see Carver & Scheier, 1981, pp. 157–165, Ogilvie, 1987, for examples).

Presumably meta-monitoring can occur with respect to both types of loops, providing (in terms of our analysis) a basis for affect in either case. To the extent the Higgins (1987) distinction is valid, then, perhaps depressed affect occurs when there is insufficient progress in a negative feedback system—that is, an approach system. Perhaps anxiety occurs when there is insufficient progress in a positive feedback system—an avoidance system (cf. Gray, 1981, 1982). The role of these latter systems in affective experience is an issue that would seem to deserve further scrutiny from a control-process perspective.

Conclusion

In the preceding pages, we have tried to indicate some of the ways in which a control-process model of the self-regulation of behaviour can incorporate assumptions about the nature and functions of certain qualities of emotion. We have attempted to specify how we think these affective qualities are created, and we have pointed to a link between them and another element that is important to self-regulation of action: expectancies. We have also tried to give a sense of how the model as a whole can provide a vehicle for conceptualizing some of the emotional difficulties that people periodically experience.

We obviously have not presented a comprehensive model of the nature of all emotional experiences (cf. Frijda, 1986; Leventhal, 1984). Nor have we catalogued the varieties of emotional experience (cf. Izard, 1977; Ortony et al., 1988; Plutchik, 1980; Tomkins, 1984). Doing so was not our intent. Our goal was less ambitious and more focused: to indicate how the nature of some emotions, as they are presently understood, seems compatible with the logic of control theory.

Our intent throughout this discussion was twofold. First, we wanted to contribute to an emerging line of argument that holds that the domain of human experience reflected in concepts such as *feeling* and *affect* is in no way inimical to information-processing or feedback models of thought and action. We believe that we have been able to address feeling states here in terms that do little or no violence either to feedback concepts or to intuitions and knowledge concerning the subjective experience of feeling states. To the extent we have done this successfully, our discussion contributes to this line of argument.

We have not, however, been entirely blind to broader concerns. To the contrary, we believe that our attempt to create a control-process account of affect has led us to conclusions that complement and supplement in useful ways other accounts of emotion. For example, we agree with Frijda (1988) that emotions arise in response to meaning structures of situations. In some sense, what we have tried to do here is to specify in generic terms what kinds of meaning structures—as inputs—may give rise to emotions. In brief, we assert that emotions intrinsically are related to goal values, and that they reflect differences between expected and experienced rates of movement toward (or away from) those goals.

They represent an organismic monitoring of 'how things are going' with respect to those values.

Clearly, others have been intuitively aware of this quality of affect (see Frijda, 1988), but the importance of this aspect of the picture has rarely been emphasized. What we have done is simply to approach the subject from a somewhat different angle, which has served to make this aspect more salient. Independent of the origins of our effort (i.e., the desire to fit affect to control theory), we hope that others will find merit in the ideas developed here.

Notes

1. A brief comment on our use of terms such as *reference value, standard,* and *goal:* We use these terms interchangeably here, despite the fact that they have slightly different connotations to many people. Reference values are qualities that are taken as guides, qualities to be approximated in one's actions. Although the word *standard* is often taken as implying social definitions of appropriateness, that is not meant here (see Carver & Scheier, 1985, for detail). The term goal often evokes an image of a 'final state', but we do not mean to imply a static, state-like quality. People have many goals of continuous action—for example, the goal of being engaged in sailing or skiing or the goal of having a successful career. Indeed, most goals underlying behaviour would seem to be of this sort. This emphasis on dynamic goals in self-regulation will become more obvious later in the article.

2. For convenience, we will treat as equivalent phrases such as *progress of the action loop* and *rate of discrepancy reduction in the action loop.*

3. Dispositional biases can have a major influence on these expectancies, even within the normal range of human experience (cf. Scheier & Carver, 1987). Stable and self-sustaining biases in expectancies are also prominent as a feature of clinical depression, representing one of the irrational beliefs that theorists such as Beck (1972) see as important in the etiology of depression.

4. A possibility that may be worth considering is that this shift of meta standard reflects the long-term consequences of the *opponent process* discussed by Solomon (1980). Solomon proposed the existence of a system that acts to dampen emotional reactions, in two senses: In the short term, the opponent process causes the affect

evoked by a given event to return to neutral. In the longer term (after repeated experiences of similar events), the event comes to elicit less of the emotional response than it did at first. This latter effect seems comparable in some ways to the idea that there has been a shift in meta standard.

5. We should distinguish between the matter under discussion here and other issues embedded in a growing literature on goal setting. One issue in goal setting concerns whether goals are close or distant in time (see Kirschenbaum, 1985, for a discussion of this and other variables). How distant a goal is in time, although important in its own right, is conceptually distinct from what we are discussing here. In general, assessment of progress toward any goal—whether close or distant—may still be made with respect to either a long or a short span of time and effort. Of course, with goals that are very close in time, one's freedom to assess over long time spans diminishes. Nor are we discussing the frequency with which a person 'samples' perceptual input. That can also vary, from sampling often to sampling rarely. What is presently under discussion is the breadth of time (or the number of discrete bits of information) over which progress is merged to *form* a perceptual input.

6. Careful examination of Watson and Tellegen's (1985) position on the structure of mood reveals, however, the involvement of another issue that is beyond the scope of this discussion. Specifically, their dimension of negative affect has heavy overtones of anxiety, rather than depression. Higgins (1987) has recently argued for the importance of a distinction between these two emotion qualities, and his argument seems to require

distinctions beyond those we are making here (as does the Watson & Tellegen position). This distinction does not, however, detract in any way from the points we are making here. We address the Higgins (1987) model in more detail in a later section of the article.

7. We will disregard another, more complex issue: the fact that ideals (as well as oughts) can be one's own or can be imposed on one by significant others. We restrict our discussion here to cases in which the ideals and oughts are one's own.

8. The degree to which this issue represents a point of active disagreement is not entirely clear. Higgins (1987) did not address this distinction, and it is likely that he had not given it serious thought.

9. There is an unfortunate opposition between the terminology of control theory (used here) and the informal terminology of learning theory. That is, behavioral psychologists often refer to reward as positive feedback and to punishment as negative feedback. That is not the meaning of these phrases in this discussion.

Discussion Questions

1. Discrepancy reduction is at the root of many classic motivational theories, including those that generally based their conclusions on experiments using non-humans (e.g., rats) as participants (e.g., Hull, 1935; Spence, 1958; Webb, 1949). In more recent social psychological research, this principle has been applied to human motivation in numerous theories including Carver and Scheier's control-processes theory and Higgins's self-discrepancy theory (see Unit 5). Compare the ways in which Carver and Scheier use the concept of discrepancy to the way Higgins uses it. What are the similarities and what are the differences? What other theories covered in this book also contain a discrepancy-reduction component?

2. Carver and Scheier's theory is 'hierarchical' in the sense that the output of one level of process sends its results to a higher, more abstract level of processing. With this in mind, compare and contrast Carver and Scheier's theory with Vallacher and Wegner's action identification theory (see Unit 6).

16. An Attributional Theory of Achievement Motivation and Emotion

Bernard Weiner, University of California

□ ■ □

Editor's Introduction

Because our emotions often feel so immediate and so intense, it may seem counterintuitive that our emotions are, in fact, the output of a highly complex cognitive process. Yet this is what the influential social psychologist Bernard Weiner advocates in this article. According to Weiner, there are at least two stages to the experience of many emotions—especially those emotions that are uniquely human such as guilt or pride. In Step 1, the mind generates a primitive, primary appraisal of the event that has just occurred, a labelling of the event in a relatively coarse manner. ('Was that good or bad?') In Step 2, the mind begins to ask, 'What kind of good?' or 'What kind of bad?' To answer that question, according to Weiner, requires a form of *causal analysis*. That is, people ask 'What was the cause of the event that brought about this feeling?'

Weiner's remarkable insight was that it is possible to boil down the myriad of possible answers to this question to only three dimensions: locus, stability, and controllability. That is, any cause that someone may name is internal or external to the person, stable or unstable, and controllable or uncontrollable (resulting in a 2 × 2 × 2 matrix). Thus, virtually any cause that a person may generate may be fit into one of the resulting eight types of explanations.

For example, consider that two people may experience the same event (e.g., failing an exam), but Alice feels shame while Betty feels guilt. What is the difference psychologically, and how do attributions play a role in this difference? Alice has attributed failing the exam to an internal/stable/uncontrollable cause (i.e., she is not smart). Betty has attributed failing the exam to an internal/unstable/controllable cause (i.e., she did not try hard enough). Thus, different cognitive explanations

for the event actually bring out different emotional experiences. More importantly, Weiner and others have shown that these different emotions then predict different motivation and different behaviour: Betty is much more likely than Alice to buckle down and study hard for the next exam.

In this article, Weiner shows how an attributional approach predicts when people will feel pride (self-esteem), anger, pity, guilt, shame, gratitude, and hopelessness. It so happens that these emotions are among the most often examined by researchers. Indeed four of these emotions—anger, pity, guilt, and gratitude—are considered to have been of particular importance for human survival over the eons (Trivers, 1971).

A different way of thinking about the attributional approach is that people not only experience positive and negative outcomes, but they also ask, 'What does this outcome mean? What does it say about me? What does it say about my circumstances?' Because people may come up with different responses to these questions, one person's failure might be another person's non-success or even potential success. As Weiner notes, the types of attributions that people generate have important implications for their expectations for the future.

Much of the literature on motivation has focused on the concept of expectancy, most notably the 'level of aspiration' literature. (See Lewin, 1936, in Unit 4.) Weiner's theory was one of the first to ask systematically 'Where do our expectancies come from?' As Weiner notes:

If conditions (the presence or absence of causes) are expected to remain the same, then the outcome(s) experienced in the past will be expected to recur. A success under these circumstances would produce relatively large increments in the anticipation of future success, and a failure would strengthen the belief that there will be subsequent failures. On the other hand, if the causal conditions are perceived as likely to change, then the present outcome may not be expected to repeat itself and there is likely to be uncertainty about subsequent outcomes or a belief that something different will result. A success therefore would yield no increments in subsequent expectancy and could give rise to decrements in the subjective probability of future success.

More recent research by Dweck and colleagues has taken the Weinerian approach one step further and asked, 'Where do our attributions come from?' For example, what predicts whether someone will generate a stable or unstable attribution? One answer appears to be the theories that people carry around with them about their abilities. Some people tend to believe that their abilities are fixed—they would presumably be more likely to generate attributions of stability. Others tend to believe that their abilities are malleable and cultivatable—these people would presumably be more likely to generate attributions of changeability. Numerous studies have, in fact, suggested as much. (For a recent example, see Plaks & Stecher, 2007.) As you read the Weiner article, think closely about how it relates to the program of research developed by Dweck and her colleagues (see Unit 4).

□ ■ □

In 1645, Miyomota Musashi was contemplating the causes of his past success as a warrior. In *A Book of Five Rings* he mused,

> When I reached 30 I looked back on my past. The previous victories were not due to my having mastered strategy. Perhaps it was natural ability, or the order of heaven, or that other schools' strategy was inferior. (1645/1974, p. 35)

About 275 years later, and approximately 11,000 miles away, the editors of *Scientific American* were wondering why America was flourishing. They reasoned, 'The wealth and general prosperity of the country are largely due to the intelligence and energy of its people, but it can hardly be disputed that it is equally due to the natural wealth of the country' (Staff, 1926, p. 228). Unfortunately, battles are lost as often as they are won, and countries undergo economic decline as well as enrichment. During our recent financial recession the *Los Angeles Times* reported,

Timber industry experts blame high interest rates, the housing slump, tough logging regulation, and expansion of the Redwood National Park for their sorry state. Tim Skaggs, the union business agent, shrugged. 'You could spend a lifetime fixing blame', he said. (Martinez, 1982, Pt. 5, p. 1)

And even the former coach of my favourite football team found it necessary to soul-search about causality following a series of losses. Again from the *Los Angeles Times*:

> Here it is Thanksgiving week, and the Los Angeles Rams are looking like the biggest turkeys in town. Coach Ray Malavasi has eliminated bad luck, biorhythms, and sunspots as the reasons why his football team has lost 9 of its last 10 games. Now he's considering the unthinkable possibilities that: (a) he has lousy players or (b) they aren't really trying. (Robert, 1982, Pt. 3, p. 3)

Why this constant pursuit of 'why'? A number of explanations come to mind (see Forsyth, 1980; Weiner, 1985). We might just want to know, that is, to understand the environment, to penetrate ourselves and our surroundings. This familiar motivational interpretation is known as the principle of mastery (White, 1959). In addition, it clearly is functional to know why an event has occurred. As Kelley (1971) stated, 'The attributor is not simply an attributor, a seeker after knowledge; his latent goal in attaining knowledge is that of effective management of himself and his environment' (p. 22). Once a cause, or causes, are assigned, effective management may be possible and a prescription or guide for future action can be suggested. If the prior outcome was a success, then there is likely to be an attempt to reinstate the prior causal network. On the other hand, if the prior outcome or event was undesired—such as exam failure, social rejection, political loss, or economic decline—then there is a strong possibility that there will be an attempt to alter the causes to produce a different (more positive) effect.

Desire for mastery and functional search, two of the generators of causal exploration, do not seem to specifically characterize one geographical area or one period of human history. The Japanese warrior in the Middle Ages and today's union representative are engaged in the same endeavour: attempting to assign causality. Indeed, one might argue that adaptation is not possible without causal analysis. The warrior needs to know why he is winning battles so he can survive the next one, just as the union representative needs to explain why the industry is doing poorly in order to urge wiser actions in the future. Because of the apparent pan-cultural, timeless aspect of causal search and exploration, and because of the evident adaptive significance of this activity, causal ascriptions are proposed to provide the building blocks for the construction of a theory of motivation and emotion.

This article advances an attributional theory of motivation and emotion, with achievement strivings as the theoretical focus. Initially, the most salient causes of success and failure in achievement-related contexts are identified. The basic properties of these causes, or the structure of causal thinking, is then determined from both a dialectic and an empirical perspective. Three causal dimensions are discovered: locus, stability, and controllability. The structure of causal thinking is next related to emotion and motivation. Thus, this article progresses from a description of causal perceptions to causal structure, and then from causal structure to an examination of the dynamics of action. It is documented that causal stability influences changes in goal anticipations, while the three causal dimensions determine the emotional experiences of anger, gratitude, guilt, hopelessness, pity, pride, and shame. Guided by Expectancy × Value theory, I presume that expectancy and affect direct motivated behaviour.

. . .

The Structure of Perceived Causality

. . . A reasonable initial question to raise is why does one want to determine causal structure? What purpose or role does this play in the goal of theory construction? In response to this query, consider that, within any particular activity, a myriad of distinct causal explanations are possible. Furthermore, for example, the causes of success and failure at achievement-related activities, such as ability and effort, may be quite unlike the perceived causes of social acceptance and rejection, such as personality or physical attractiveness. One puzzle that arises is the relation or the comparability between the various causal explanations—in what way(s) are ability and effort, or ability and physical beauty, alike and in what way(s) do they differ? A taxonomic structure enables this question to be answered, for by finding the underlying properties of causes, or their common denominators, previous incomparable qualitative distinctions can be replaced with quantitative causal comparisons. For example, rather than merely being *different*, both ability and physical beauty may be considered properties of the actor and thus are similar, whereas they both differ from a cause that is not a property of the actor, such as the objective ease or difficulty of a task. This type of analysis facilitates empirical study so that other associations may be discovered that contribute to the meaning and significance of a cause.

Logical Analysis of Causal Structure

The first systematic analysis of causal structure was proposed by Heider (1958). Rightly called the originator of the attributional approach in psychology, Fritz Heider has been in the background of much of the present theory. The most fundamental causal distinction made by Heider (1958) was stated as follows: 'In common-sense psychology (as in scientific psychology) the result of an action is felt to depend on two sets of conditions, namely, factors within the person and factors within the environment' (p. 82).

Since the early 1950s, psychologists have embraced an internal–external distinction (see Collins, Martin, Ashmore, & Ross, 1974). But the domination of internal–external comparisons in psychology arrived with the work of Rotter (1966), for his classification of individuals into internals and externals became a focus for research. Thus, the analysis of the structure of causality logically began with an internal–external (locus) dimension.

The argument was then made by Weiner et al. (1971) that a second dimension of causality was required. The reasoning was that, among the internal causes, some fluctuate, whereas others remain relatively constant. For example, ability (or, more appropriately, aptitude) is perceived as a constant capacity; in contrast, other causal factors including effort and mood are perceived as more variable, changing from moment to moment or from period to period. Among the external causes the same reasoning applies. For example, success in rowing across a lake may be perceived as due to the unchanging narrowness of the lake or because of the variable presence of wind. Weiner et al.

(1971) thus characterized the causes they thought were most dominant in achievement-related contexts, namely, ability, effort, task difficulty, and luck, within a 2 × 2 categorization scheme. Ability was classified as internal and stable, effort as internal and unstable, task difficulty was thought to be external and stable, and luck was considered external and unstable.

It is now realized that there are many shortcomings of this classification (see Weiner, 1983). Ability may be perceived as unstable if learning is possible; effort often is perceived as a stable trait, captured with the labels of lazy and industrious; tasks can be changed to be more or less difficult; and luck may be thought of as a property of a person (lucky or unlucky). Thus, the causes within the four cells did not truly represent the classification system (i.e., they did not conform to the phenomenology of the naive attributor). Less ambiguous entries might have been aptitude, temporary exertion, objective task characteristics, and chance (see Weiner, 1983). Hindsight, however, is better than foresight, and the problems so evident now were not fully recognized in 1971.

A third dimension of causality was then established with the same deductive reasoning that led to the identification of the stability dimension. Rosenbaum (1972) recognized that mood, fatigue, and temporary effort, for example, all are internal and unstable causes. Yet they are distinguishable in that effort is subject to volitional control—an individual can increase or decrease effort expenditure. This is not typically true of mood or the onset of fatigue, which under most circumstances cannot be willed to change. The same distinction is found among the internal and stable causes. Some so-called traits such as laziness, slovenliness, or tolerance often are perceived as under volitional or optional control, whereas this is not characteristic of other internal and stable causes such as math or artistic aptitude and physical coordination.

The identification of this property, now called *controllability* (Weiner, 1979), enlightened and solved some issues while creating other difficulties.

Among the illuminated topics was the distinction by Rotter (1966) between internal versus external perceptions of control of reinforcement. Within the three-dimensional taxonomy, two of the proposed causal properties are labelled *locus* and *control*. A cause therefore might be internal yet uncontrollable, such as math aptitude. If failure is ascribed to poor aptitude, then the performance is perceived as determined by skill and ability. According to Rotter, this indicates that the outcome is perceived as subject to internal control. Yet a genetically determined aptitude will not be perceived as controllable by a failing math pupil. Thus, confusion is evident in the Rotter one-dimensional taxonomy. Locus *and* control, not locus *of* control, describe causal perceptions. To avoid confusion, the locus dimension should be labelled *locus of causality*.

. . .

Motivational Dynamics of Perceived Causality: Expectancy Change

. . . I now turn from causal description and causal structure to the dynamics of behaviour. Two topics are of special importance in the understanding of action tendencies: expectancy and value.

Goal expectancies is a concern that keeps reappearing in the study of motivation. Every major cognitive motivational theorist includes the expectancy of goal attainment among the determinants of action. If one hopes to construct an attributional theory of motivation, it would therefore seem necessary to search for some connection, some linkage, between attributional thinking and goal expectancy.

Two possibilities come to mind. On the one hand, the influence of causal variables on the absolute expectancy of goal attainment could be ascertained. Heider (1958), for example, reasoned that goal expectancies in achievement-related contexts are determined by perceived ability and planned effort expenditure, relative to the perceived difficulty of the task. This is an enticing analysis to follow, inasmuch as attributional concepts already are introduced.

But other theorists have had completely different notions about the antecedents of goal expectancy. Tolman (1925), for example, stipulated that expectancy is a function of the frequency, primacy, and recency of reinforcement. According to Rotter (1966), expectancies are determined by the percentage of reinforcements of a particular response in a particular setting, the percentage of reinforcements of this response in similar situations, and individual differences in the belief that reinforcements are under personal control. And for Atkinson (1964), expectancy is influenced by the number of individuals against whom one is competing, prior reinforcement history, and communications from others concerning the likelihood of success. It therefore is evident that consensus does not exist about the antecedents of goal expectancy, although all theorists would agree that past reinforcement history does play some important role.

A second possibility is initially to find relations between attributions and changes in expectancy, and then use this information to determine the relation between causal ascriptions and absolute expectancy of success. Inasmuch as attributional search is initiated following an outcome—so that change can be examined—this seems to be a promising lead. In addition, perhaps change in goal expectancy, as opposed to absolute expectancy level, is more amenable to a general law that transcends the situational context.

Investigations of Expectancy Change

Three psychological literatures are directly related to changes in goal expectancy, and again the pertinent research has primarily been conducted in achievement-related contexts. One set of investigations is associated with level of aspiration; the second concerns the effects of outcomes at chance tasks on probabilities of future success; and the third research endeavour is linked with resistance to extinction and beliefs about locus of control.

Level of Aspiration

A number of quite replicable findings emerged from level of aspiration research. Among the most important for present purposes is that subsequent aspiration level is in part dependent on the prior outcome. In the vast majority of instances, aspiration increases after goal attainment and decreases if a prior aspiration has not been fulfilled. These so-called goal discrepancies are referred to as 'typical' aspiration shifts.

It has been assumed that aspiration level in good part reflects the subjective expectancy of success: the higher the expectancy, the higher the aspiration level. Hence, the aspiration literature can be interpreted as revealing that increments in expectancy follow success, whereas expectancy decrements follow failure. This conclusion also has been documented extensively in contexts where expectancy is directly measured, rather than inferred from statements about goal aspiration (e.g., Diggory, Riley, & Blumenfeld, 1960; Montanelli & Hill, 1969; Zajonc & Brickman, 1969).

This is not the complete story, however, for in games of skill 'atypical' reactions also are sometimes observed. In these instances, there is a decrease in aspiration level following success and an increase after failure. For example, Lewin, Dembo, Festinger, and Sears (1944) noted, in the case of non-achievement which is linked, for instance, to outside disturbances, the subject is not likely to lower his aspiration in a way that he would if he believed that the non-achievement reflected a genuine decrement in his performance ability (p. 367).

. . .

Social Learning Theory Integration

The problem is to create a conceptual framework able to incorporate the observations of typical and atypical shifts in situations of skill and chance. Social learning theorists attempted to do just that, primarily examining resistance to extinction while manipulating skill and chance task perceptions. They contended that expectancy change following success or failure is influenced by the perceived locus of control of the outcome, with internal or personal beliefs about causality (skill tasks) producing typical shifts, while external perceptions of causality (chance tasks) generate atypical shifts. In addition, given that some individuals might perceive skill tasks as determined by chance, and chance tasks as determined by personal factors, occasional reversals in the usual pattern of data would be observed. In sum, social learning theorists were the first to relate the structure of perceived causality (the locus dimension) to expectancy change (see Rotter, 1966).

Attributional Approach to Expectancy Change

In this article I have reasoned, however, that Rotter and his colleagues gave insufficient attention to the richness of causal explanation and confounded dimensions of causality. Ability (skill), in addition to being internal, also is perceived as relatively stable. On the other hand, in addition to being external, luck is perceived as relatively unstable. Hence, ability and luck differ in subjective stability and not merely on the locus dimension of causality. The observed differences in expectancy shifts given skill versus chance tasks may therefore either be attributed to the locus or to the stability dimension of causality.

The attributional position is that the stability of a cause, rather than its locus, determines expectancy shifts. If conditions (the presence or absence of causes) are expected to remain the same, then the outcome(s) experienced in the past will be expected to recur. A success under these circumstances would produce relatively large increments in the anticipation of future success, and a failure would strengthen the belief that there will be subsequent failures. On the other hand, if the causal conditions are perceived as likely to change, then the present outcome may not be expected to repeat itself and there is likely to be uncertainty about subsequent outcomes or a belief that something different will result. A success therefore would yield no increments in subsequent expectancy and could give rise to decrements in the subjective probability of future success. Similarly, a failure will not augment the belief that there will be future failures.

These principles are able to explain the data in level of aspiration research and in studies involving chance tasks. Success and failure at skill tasks most usually are ascribed to ability and effort. Ability is thought to be a relatively fixed property, and the belief that success was caused by hard work usually results in the intent to again work hard in the future (Dalai et al., 1985). Inasmuch as the causes of a prior success are perceived as relatively stable given skill-related tasks, future success should be anticipated with greater certainty and there will be increments in aspiration level and expectancy judgments. Occasionally, however, outcomes at skill tasks are ascribed to unstable factors, such as the 'disturbances' noted by Lewin et al. (1944). In addition, if failure is ascribed to low effort, then the failing person may anticipate working harder in the future. In these circumstances there would be atypical or minimal shifts in expectancy following failure.

Conversely, success at chance tasks tends to be ascribed to an unstable factor. The actor is likely to reason, 'I had good luck last time, but that probably will not happen again.' Expectancy therefore should not rise and indeed could drop following a positive outcome. But, occasionally, one might conclude that he or she is a lucky or an unlucky person or is on a winning or losing streak. In these instances, the cause of the outcome is perceived as stable, so that typical shifts will be displayed. In sum, the attributional position can account for the observed typical and atypical shifts in chance as well as in skill settings.

These ideas gave rise to a wealth of pertinent research, primarily in achievement-related contexts. Two research strategies were represented—correlational and the manipulation of causal ascriptions. In the correlational research, subjects were induced to succeed or fail at some laboratory task and their expectancies of future success as well as causal ascriptions were assessed. In the causal manipulation procedure, perceptions of task outcomes as caused by ability, effort, luck, and so forth were induced, and expectancy of success was ascertained following success or failure. . . .

. . .

Summary and Conclusions

Individuals classify their thoughts into broad categories. Hence, phenotypic dissimilarities might be connotatively, or genotypically, similar. Failure in athletics because of lack of height, failure in math because of low aptitude, failure in politics because of poor charisma, and social rejection because of unattractive features are phenotypically different events with diverse specific causes. Yet the causes are likely to be similarly categorized as enduring or stable. Hence, future hopes in these heterogeneous contexts will be minimized. On the other hand, failure in athletics because of insufficient practice, failure at math because of temporary illness, failure in politics because of a current recession, and interpersonal rejection because the desired partner is ill are diverse events that are likely to be categorized as due to unstable causes. Hopes for the future therefore are likely to be maintained.

The amount, extensity, and consistency of the empirical findings, in conjunction with the logical analysis, documents a fundamental psychological law relating perceived causal stability to expectancy change.

Expectancy Principle

Changes in expectancy of success following an outcome are influenced by the perceived stability of the cause of the event.

This principle has three corollaries:

Corollary 1.   If the outcome of an event is ascribed to a stable cause, then that outcome will be anticipated with increased certainty, or with an increased expectancy, in the future.

Corollary 2.   If the outcome of an event is ascribed to an unstable cause, then the certainty or expectancy of that outcome may be unchanged or the future may be anticipated to be different from the past.

Corollary 3.   Outcomes ascribed to stable causes will be anticipated to be repeated in the future with a greater degree of certainty than are outcomes ascribed to unstable causes.

Motivational Dynamics of Perceived Causality: Affective Reactions

The Attribution-Emotion Process

The field of emotion is vast and complex; the formulation of a complete theory of emotion is not my goal. Rather, the aims of this section of the article are to offer an attributional view of the emotion process and to propose and document laws linking attributional thinking and specific feelings (for a discussion of the assumptions guiding this approach to emotion see Weiner, 1982; Weiner & Graham, 1984).

Most emotion theorists with a cognitive persuasion conceive of emotional experience as a temporal sequence involving cognitions of increasing complexity. Arnold (1960) and Lazarus (1966), for example, contend that the perception of a distal stimulus gives rise to a primary appraisal and to a rather primitive emotional reaction. Primary appraisal is believed to be followed by a secondary appraisal that often involves ego-related or more advanced psychological mechanisms such as ego defences. The elicitation of these processes can intensify or modulate the emotional experience or alter the quality of the emotion.

Schachter and Singer (1962) proposed the most oft-cited emotion sequence. They hypothesized that the initial step in this sequence is the experience and recognition of non-differentiated internal arousal. Then the source of the arousal is determined on the basis of situational cues, and this cognitive labelling plus the arousal give rise to emotional states (although the cognition of the arousal and the cognition of the source of the arousal often take place simultaneously).

The attributional framework advanced here also assumes a sequence in which cognitions of increasing complexity enter into the emotion process to further refine and differentiate experience. It is contended that, following the outcome of an event, there is a general positive or negative reaction (a 'primitive' emotion) based on the perceived success or failure of the outcome (the 'primary appraisal'). These emotions, which include *happy* for success and *frustrated* and *sad* for failure, are labelled as *outcome dependent–attribution independent,* for they are determined by the attainment or non-attainment of a desired goal, and not by the cause of the outcome.

Following outcome appraisal and the immediate affective reaction, a causal ascription will be sought. A different set of emotions is then generated by the chosen attribution(s). For example, success perceived as due to good luck produces surprise, whereas success following a long-term period of effort expenditure results in a feeling of calmness or serenity. Emotions such as surprise and serenity are labelled *attribution dependent,* inasmuch as they are determined by the perceived cause of the prior outcome. Note that increasing cognitive involvement generates more differentiated emotional experience (for somewhat related conceptions see Abelson, 1983; Roseman, 1984; C. Smith & Ellsworth, 1985).

Additionally, causal dimensions play a key role in the emotion process. Each dimension is uniquely related to a set of feelings. For example, success and failure perceived as due to internal causes such as personality, ability, or effort respectively raises or lowers self-esteem or self-worth, whereas external attributions for positive or negative outcomes do not influence feelings about the self. Hence, self-related emotions are influenced by the causal property of locus, rather than by a specific cause per se.

. . .

The cognition-emotion process that has been proposed provides the focus and outline for the following pages. I first briefly examine outcome-related affects and then consider in detail the associations between causal dimensions and affects, ignoring here the relations between specific causes and emotional reactions (see Weiner, Russell, & Lerman, 1978, 1979). I focus on dimension-linked affects because they have had the most extensive empirical support. These associations, just as the one between causal ascription and expectancy change, form powerful and general laws.

Outcome-Generated Emotions

Two research paradigms, one simulational and reactive, the other retrospective and operant, were first used to document the associations between outcomes and emotions. Again these studies were conducted in achievement-related contexts. In the former paradigm, participants were asked to imagine that a student succeeded or failed an exam for a particular reason, such as hard work or bad luck. The subjects then reported the intensity of the affective reactions that they thought would be experienced in this situation (Weiner et al., 1978). Intensity was indicated on rating scales for a number of pre-selected affects. In the second paradigm, participants were asked to recall a time in life when they succeeded or failed for a specified reason. They also recounted the affects they experienced at that time (Weiner et al., 1979).

These studies revealed that one determinant of affect is the outcome of an action: Success at achievement-related activities was associated with the affect of *happy* regardless of the cause of that outcome, and failure seemed to be related to frustration and sadness. Thus, for example, given athletic competition, one tends to experience happiness following a victory whether that win was due to extra training, the poor play of the competitor, or good luck. Outcome-dependent affects also have been documented in quality of life research. Investigators have reported that satisfaction,

unhappiness, and frustration are related to objective life outcomes, such as income level, independent of attributions (see Bryant & Veroff, 1982; E. Smith & Kluegel, 1982). In addition, outcome-dependent affects have been postulated in the interpersonal domain. Kelley (1983) stated,

> I am pleased or displeased by the more specific and concrete things I experience [in close relationships]. So when my wife prepares a picnic lunch for the afternoon's outing, my pleasure–displeasure comes partly from the quality of the lunch itself, and also (as a partly separate matter) from the quality of love and thoughtfulness I attribute to her effort. (p. 15)

Dimension-Related Emotions

As previously indicated, the bulk of the pertinent attribution–emotion research relates causal dimensions, rather than specific causes, to affects. The emotion of pride and feelings of self-esteem are linked with the locus dimension of causality; anger, gratitude, guilt, pity, and shame all are connected with the controllability dimension; and feelings of hopelessness (hopefulness) are associated with causal stability. These relations are described here, but without detailed documentation (see Weiner, 1982, and Weiner & Graham, 1984, for fuller discussions).

Pride (Self-Esteem)

A relation between causal locus and self-esteem has been long recognized by many well-known philosophers. Hume, for example, believed that what one is proud of must belong to the person; Spinoza reasoned that pride consists of knowing one's merits; and Kant nicely captured the locus–pride union by noting that everyone at a meal might enjoy the food, but only the cook of that meal could experience pride.

It is therefore reasoned that pride and positive self-esteem are experienced as a consequence of attributing a positive outcome to the self and that negative self-esteem is experienced when a negative outcome is ascribed to the self (Stipek, 1983; Weiner et al., 1978, 1979). The relation between causal locus and feelings of self-worth also is part of naive psychology and is used by the layperson to influence the emotions of others. Thus, individuals tend to communicate ascriptions external to the requester when rejecting that person for a social engagement so that 'feelings of self-esteem are not hurt' (e.g., they indicate that they are ill rather than truthfully telling the requester that he has a poor personality; see Folkes, 1982). Children as young as five years of age have demonstrated an understanding of the relation between causal locus and hurt feelings, given a rejection (Weiner & Handel, 1985). A voluminous attributional literature also documents existence of a *hedonic bias,* or a tendency for individuals to ascribe success to internal factors and failure to external factors. As Harvey and Weary (1981) noted, 'By taking credit for good acts and denying blame for bad outcomes, the individual presumably may be able to enhance or protect his or her self-esteem' (p. 33). Pride and personal esteem therefore are self-reflective emotions, linked with the locus dimension of causality.

Anger

A large survey study by Averill (1982, 1983) illustrates the attributional antecedents of anger. Averill asked his respondents to describe a situation in which they were made angry, and then examined the characteristics of these situations. He concluded,

> The major issue for the person in the street is not the specific nature of the instigating event; it is the perceived *justification* for the instigator's behaviour. Anger, for the person in the street, is an accusation . . . More than anything else, anger is an attribution of blame. (Averill, 1983, p. 1150)

Many others have reached a similar conclusion. For example, among the very first of the pertinent investigations, Pastore (1952) demonstrated that aggression (and, by implication, anger) is not merely the result of non-attainment of a desired goal, but rather follows when a barrier imposed by others is *arbitrary* (e.g., 'Your date phones at the last minute and breaks an appointment without adequate explanation') rather than *non-arbitrary* (e.g., 'Your date phones . . . and breaks an appointment because he [she] suddenly became ill'). To summarize, the attributional antecedent for anger is an ascription of a negative, self-related outcome or event to factors controllable by others (see Weiner, 1980a, 1980b; Weiner, Graham, & Chandler, 1982).

Pity

In contrast to the linkage between controllability and anger, it is hypothesized that uncontrollable causes are associated with pity. It is said that when Helen Keller began her training, her teacher stated to Ms Keller's family: 'We do not want your pity', thus conveying that a target of pity is associated with an uncontrollable deficit. This analysis is similar to Hoffman's (1982) conception, for he stated, 'It is only when the cues indicate that . . . the victim had no control that the . . . partial transformation of empathic into sympathic distress may apply' (p. 296).

A number of research studies support this contention. Another's loss of a loved one because of an accident, or difficulties because of a physical handicap, are prototypical situations that elicit pity (see Graham, Doubleday, & Guarino, 1984; Weiner, 1980a, 1980b; Weiner, Graham, & Chandler, 1982). Note, therefore, that the perceived controllability of a cause for a negative outcome in part determines whether anger or pity is directed toward another. We feel anger toward the lazy and therefore punish lack of effort, but we feel pity toward the unable and therefore do not punish lack of ability (Weiner & Kukla, 1970).

The relations between controllability–anger and uncontrollability–pity also are part of naive psychology and are used in everyday life to control or manipulate the emotions of others. Thus, when providing an excuse (ex- = from; -cuse = cause) for failing to appear at a social engagement, uncontrollable causes tend to be communicated (e.g., 'My car had a flat tire') rather than controllable ones (e.g., 'I decided to watch TV'; see Weiner, Amirkhan, Folkes, & Wachtel, 1985). One hopes that this communication defuses anger and perhaps even alters the reaction to pity. Similar interpersonal strategies are understood and used by children as young as five years of age (Weiner & Handel, 1985).

Guilt and Shame

Philosophers and social scientists have devoted considerable attention to the experience of guilt, its antecedents, and its consequences. Reviewing the guilt literature, Wicker, Payne, and Morgan (1983) concluded, 'In general, guilt is said to follow from acts that violate ethical norms, principles of justice . . . or moral values. Guilt is accompanied by feelings of personal responsibility' (p. 26). In a similar manner, Izard (1977) concluded that 'Guilt occurs in situations in which one feels personally responsible' (p. 423), and Hoffman (1976) more precisely reasoned, 'Blaming oneself becomes possible once one has acquired the cognitive capacity to recognize the consequences of his action for others and to be aware that he has choice and control over his own behaviour' (p. 139). In support of these interpretations, my colleagues and I have found that the most prevalent guilt-eliciting situations among college students involve lying to parents, cheating on an exam, or being disloyal to a dating partner (Weiner, Graham, & Chandler, 1982), although it is evident that guilt may be evoked by either the commission or the omission of particular actions (see Hoffman, 1970).

Guilt and anger therefore are elicited by controllable causes, but guilt is directed inward, whereas anger is typically (but not necessarily) directed outward. Thus, for example, we tend to feel guilty when we have lied to others, but angry when we have discovered that someone has lied to us (see Weiner, Graham, & Chandler, 1982). In a similar manner, lack of effort toward an important goal tends to elicit anger from others (such as teachers) and also generates personal guilt.

Shame frequently is contrasted with guilt, although both involve 'negative self-evaluations that are painful, tense, agitating . . . depressing' (Wicker et al., 1983). Although there appear to be different kinds of shame, it is believed that one antecedent is an attribution for failure that is self-related and uncontrollable, such as lack of ability. In studies testing uncontrollability–shame and controllability–guilt associations, Brown and Weiner (1984), Covington and Omelich (1984), and Jagacinski and Nicholls (1984) have reported that shame-related affects (disgrace, embarrassment, humiliation, and/or shame) are linked with failure due to low ability, whereas guilt-related affects (guilt, regret, and/or remorse) are associated with failure due to lack of effort. It also has been documented that shame-related emotions give rise to withdrawal and motivational inhibition, whereas guilt-related emotions promote approach behaviour, retribution, and motivational activation (Hoffman, 1982; Wicker et al., 1983). Hence, there are linkages between low-ability–shame-inhibition and between lack-of-effort–guilt-augmentation. It also is of interest to repeat that anger tends to motivate aggression, so that three patterns of behaviour noted by Horney (going toward, going away from, going against) are related to causal controllability and the respective affects of guilt, shame, and anger.

Gratitude

There is relatively little research concerned with gratitude, but the evidence suggests that gratitude toward another is elicited if and only if the act of the benefactor was under volitional control and was intended to benefit the recipient. For example, Tesser, Gatewood, and Driver (1968) presented subjects with scenarios that involved a benefactor and asked the subjects how grateful they would feel under the various circumstances that were portrayed. They found that reported gratitude was maximized when the gift was intended to benefit only the receiver (as opposed to a situation in which the gift enhanced the reputation of the giver). In other supporting research it has been documented that reciprocity is more likely when a gift is given deliberately rather than accidentally (Greenberg & Frisch, 1972) and when help is voluntary rather than compulsory (Goranson & Berkowitz, 1966).

Hopelessness

It has been convincingly documented that causal stability in part determines expectancies regarding future success and failure. Thus, any emotion involving anticipations of goal attainment or non-attainment will likely be influenced by causal stability. One such affect has been labelled *hopelessness*. It has been found that hopelessness and resignation are elicited given an attribution for a negative outcome to stable causes (Weiner et al., 1978, 1979). That is, if the future is anticipated to remain as bad as the past, then hopelessness is experienced. In addition, affects such as pity are exacerbated when the cause of the negative state is stable rather than unstable (e.g., we tend to pity the blind more than we pity those with temporary eye problems). Similarly, we tend to be more angry at others when perceived controllable behaviour, such as lack of effort, is stable (a trait) rather than an unstable state (Weiner, Graham, & Chandler, 1982).

Summary and Conclusions

Attributions play a key role in affective life. Seven emotions were briefly examined that relate to causal structure: pride (self-esteem), anger, pity, guilt, shame, gratitude, and hopelessness. These are among the most frequently reported and written-about affective experiences (see Bottenberg, 1975; Davitz, 1969). Sociobiologists have specified that four of these emotions—anger, pity, guilt, and gratitude—are of special importance in promoting gene survival (see Trivers, 1971). These four emotions are related to the causal dimension of controllability, which is consistent

with the sociobiological position that emotions are used to aid in maintaining the social order. Finally, although the bulk of the supporting data have been generated in achievement-related contexts, the relations specified above do not seem to be confined to a particular motivational domain. As previously suggested, aptitude as a cause of achievement success, and physical attractiveness as a cause of social success, are conceptually similar in that both are internal, stable, and uncontrollable. Thus, success or positive outcomes due to these factors should enhance pride and positive self-esteem, just as negative outcomes because of their absence should lower self-esteem. But non-attainment of a goal for these reasons should provoke neither anger from others nor personal guilt. Rather, failure given both these specific ascriptions is likely to elicit pity from others and produce feelings of shame and hopelessness in the frustrated individual.

A word of caution, however, is needed about the preceding discussion. Given a causal ascription, the linked emotion does not necessarily follow. For example, one may not have put forth effort at something important, yet still be free from guilt. Or one may attribute success to help from others, yet not feel grateful. Furthermore, an emotion may be experienced in the absence of its linked antecedent. For example, one may not be responsible for an outcome, but will experience guilt (see Hoffman, 1976). Hence, the position being espoused is that the dimension-affect relations are not invariant, but are quite prevalent in our culture, and perhaps in many others as well. This position is similar to the argument that there is a linkage between frustration and aggression, although frustration elicits reactions other than aggression, and aggression has other antecedents in addition to frustration.

The Complete Theory

It is now possible to present an attributional theory of motivation and emotion based on the prior discussion of the theoretical components. The theory is presented in Figure 16.1. In contrast to other Expectancy × Value approaches, this conception is represented as a historical or temporal sequence; motivation is not conceived as an 'ahistorical problem' (Atkinson, 1964, p. 146). In addition, the theory to be proposed departs from prior Expectancy × Value conceptions by linking value to the affect elicited following goal-directed activity. Other theories of motivation have been remiss by virtually ignoring the emotions, save for an acceptance of the general pleasure–pain principle. The sequence depicted in Figure 16.1 will be used to discuss the following contrived (but surely extant) scenario: 'A Little League baseball player performs very poorly during a game. Instead of appearing for the next contest, the boy stays at home.' Other scenarios, such as the boy taking extra batting practice following failure (rather than missing the game) or taking extra batting practice after playing well (success), could have readily been used to portray how the theory shown in Figure 16.1 conceptualizes an achievement-related motivational episode. This is followed by an examination of achievement change programs, for these therapeutic attempts illustrate both how the theory has been used and document its incomplete utilization. After these analyses, I consider the generality of the theory beyond the achievement domain.

Figure 16.1 reveals that a motivational sequence is initiated by an outcome that individuals interpret as positive (goal attainment) or negative (non-attainment of the goal). Inasmuch as affects are directly linked with outcomes (the primary appraisal), Figure 16.1 includes a connection between outcome and the reactions of happy (for success) and frustrated or sad (if the outcome was interpreted as a failure). These associations are designated with a *1* in the figure. In the baseball scenario, the boy performed poorly at the game and this will elicit general negative reactions.

A causal search is then undertaken to determine why the outcome occurred (Linkage 2). Some of the conditions that particularly promote

this search, which were not discussed in the present article (see Weiner, 1985), are indicated in the figure. In our example, failure at a subjectively important act should result in the boy overtly or covertly wondering, 'Why did I perform so poorly?' A large number of antecedents influence the causal explanation(s) reached. This popular topic also was not discussed in the present article. Some of the known attributional antecedents are included in Figure 16.1, such as specific information (e.g., past personal history, performance of others; see Kelley & Michela, 1980). The blanket et cetera at the bottom of the antecedents merely conveys that there are many unlisted determinants of the selected attribution.

The causal decision is biased toward a relatively small number of causes such as ability and effort in the achievement domain. In our example, assume that the boy has played quite poorly in the past and that other children on the team are playing well. The boy also practised many hours. On the basis of the past outcome history, social comparison, and effort expenditure, the boy decides that he is low in baseball-playing ability. That is, he thinks, 'I failed because I am not any good at baseball' (Linkage 3). A unique affective reaction may be elicited by this causal decision (Linkage 4).

The cause is then located in dimensional space. This is depicted as Linkage 5 in the figure. . . . The three main properties of causes are locus, stability, and controllability, with globality and intentionality considered possible causal properties (and therefore accompanied by question marks). The Little Leaguer ascribed his performance to lack of ability, which is likely to be perceived as internal, stable, and uncontrollable (although that placement must be analyzed from the phenomenology of the perceiver). It also might be unintentional and global ('I am poor at sports').

Causal dimensions have psychological consequences, being related to both expectancy and affect (which is presumed in this conception to be the value of goal attainment). The stability of a cause influences the relative expectancy of future

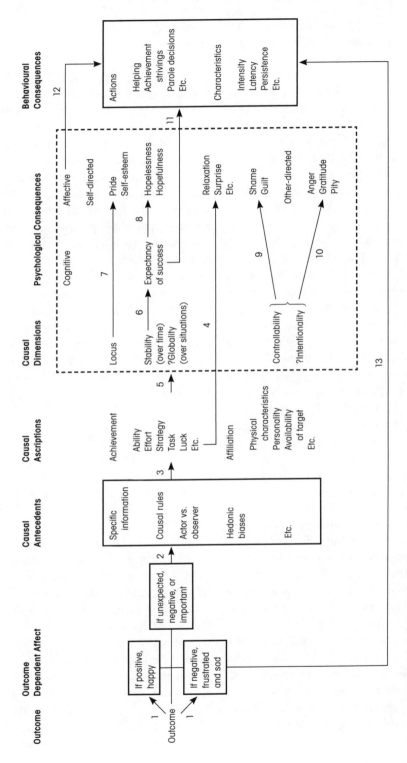

Figure 16.1 An attributional theory of motivation and emotion.

success (Linkage 6). . . . In our scenario, the boy anticipates repeated failure inasmuch as low ability is perceived as a stable cause. He also might have increased expectancy of failure in other sporting activities if the cause is perceived as global. That is, stability influences temporal aspects of expectancy, whereas globality influences cross-situational expectancies.

Turning to affective consequences, the locus of a cause exerts an influence on self-esteem and pride—internal ascriptions elicit greater self-esteem for success and lower self-esteem for failure than do external attributions (Linkage 7). The boy in our story failed because of a cause considered internal, and therefore he should be experiencing low self-esteem. The stability of the cause, by affecting expectancy, also fosters feelings of hopelessness (or hopefulness); this is indicated in Linkage 8. The Little Leaguer, with a history of failure and ascription of the current failure to low ability, should be feeling hopeless. Finally, controllability influences social emotions; controllable causes of personal failure promote feelings of guilt, whereas uncontrollable causes generate shame (Linkage 9). These are represented in the figure as self-directed affects, as are the specific attribution-linked emotions of relaxation and surprise. Among the affects directed toward others are anger (given a cause of failure controllable by others), pity (given an uncontrollable cause of failure), and gratitude (given a controllable cause; Linkage 10). The failing Little Leaguer is likely to be feeling ashamed of himself and humiliated (but not guilty), whereas his coach or his mother feels pity or feels sorry for him (but not angry).

Finally, expectancy and affect are presumed to determine action (Linkages 11, 12, and 13). The actions can be described according to their intensity, latency, and so on. In the baseball scenario, the boy has a low expectancy of future success and is feeling sad, low self-esteem, ashamed, and hopeless. These conditions promote withdrawal and behaviours that are not instrumental to the attainment of the desired goal. He then stays home from the next game.

Although Figure 16.1 appears to depict an exhaustive conceptual analysis, even greater complexity has been documented. The linkages in the figure all are unidirectional, although it is known that this is not the case. For example, expectancy of success influences attributions (see Feather & Simon, 1972). Thus, if our baseball player succeeded, his low expectancy of success would foster an attribution to an unstable cause such as good luck. In addition, affects such as pity and anger are important attributional cues (Graham, 1984; Weiner, Graham, Stern, & Lawson, 1982). For example, directing pity toward the Little Leaguer will increase his belief that personal failure was due to low ability. And feelings of happiness and sadness influence outcome perceptions (see Bower, 1981). Hence, the boy in the story might perceive an ambiguous outcome during the game as a failure because of his unhappiness and other negative affective experiences initiated prior to the outcome in question. These added intricacies are neglected here, but deserve full incorporation into the theory.

. . .

Theoretical Generality

It has been intimated throughout this article that the theory shown in Figure 16.1 is conceived as a general conceptual framework, although it has been acknowledged that the vast amount of supporting data has been generated in achievement-related contexts. Thus, although the focus of the theory concerns achievement strivings, it is tentatively believed that the conception has a wide range of applicability. This is similar to the position espoused by Atkinson (1964), who also assumed that he was developing a general theory of motivation, although achievement settings provided the site of the experimental research.

The foundation for generality in the present approach is provided by two conceptual mechanisms. First, it is proposed that a motivational episode is initiated following any outcome that can be construed as attainment or non-attainment of a goal. Achievement success and failure clearly capture this requirement, but acceptance and rejection in the affiliative domain provide a ready parallel (see Anderson, 1983a; Sobol & Earn, 1985). In addition, the conception has been used to examine a number of social and personal 'failures', including, for example, alcoholism (McHugh, Beckman, & Frieze, 1979); crime and parole decisions (Carroll, 1978); depression (Abramson et al., 1978); deprivation (Mark, 1985); loneliness (Peplau, Russell, & Helm, 1979); need for help (Betancourt, 1983; Reisenzein, 1986; Weiner, 1980a, 1980b); maladaptive reactions to rape (Janoff-Bulman, 1979); smoking (Eiser, Van der Pligt, Raw, & Sutton, 1985); and wife battering (Freize, 1979). It is especially worth noting that the popular attributional analysis of depression advanced by Abramson et al. (1978) and the oft-cited distinction between characterological versus behavioural self-blame (Janoff-Bulman, 1979) both have the present attributional approach as their source.

In these analyses, the authors first determine the perceived cause of the outcome, such as the cause of a crime or the cause of depression. Although these causes vary widely, both within and between the domains under consideration, they can be described according to their structural properties of locus, stability, and controllability. The dimensional analysis furnishes the second key mechanism for theoretical generality, for once the structure of the cause is ascertained, then its impact on expectancy, affect, and action can be tested. . . .

. . .

Concluding Comments

During the decades between 1930–50 the field of motivation was central in psychology. At present, this field is not particularly active. I suggest that one reason for the relative demise in the perceived importance of motivational thinking has been the unreliability of the 'reference experiments', that is, the basic investigations that provide the empirical foundations for the theories. For example,

regarding the unequal recall of incomplete versus completed tasks, or what is known as the *Zeigarnik effect,* Lewin (1935) stated, 'All later experimental investigations were built upon this' (p. 240). But the differential task recall observed by Lewin and Zeigarnik is not a reliable finding. In a similar manner, Atkinson (1964) contended that individuals classified as high versus low in achievement needs exhibit opposing risk preferences, given tasks differing in perceived difficulty. This central prediction from Atkinson's conception is not reliably found (see W. Meyer, Folkes, & Weiner, 1976); one suspects this is partially responsible for the lessening influence of this conception. And differences in expectancy shifts between people labelled as *internal* and *external* in perceptions of control has not been reliably demonstrated, although this is a fundamental prediction of Rotter's (1966) conception.

The empirical foundation for the theory presented here—the existence of causal search, the dominant causal perceptions, the structure of perceived causality, the relation between causal stability and expectancy change, and the associations between causal structure and the emotions of pride, anger, pity, guilt, gratitude, shame, and hopelessness, is robust. I believe that these facts and relations will survive, independent of the fate of the entire theory. In addition, the present conception has other virtues perhaps less evident in prior motivational conceptions: A full range of cognitions and emotions are incorporated and there is an explicit concern with the self. Furthermore, an attempt has been made to relate the structure of thought (in this case, causal thinking) to the dynamics of feeling and action. This is one of the basic tasks that motivational theorists must solve.

In conclusion, I believe that some attention also must be paid to the 'nothing but common sense' criticism levelled at times against attributional approaches. When critics charge that an attributional approach is 'mere' common sense, they are exclaiming that the relations pointed out or predicted by the theory represent shared knowledge (see Fletcher, 1984). I agree that the linkages between, for example, stable causes and repeated effects, internal locus and self-esteem, and causal controllability and anger, gratitude, and guilt, generally are known or at least will be positively acknowledged when presented to the lay public. What is not shared knowledge, however, is the conceptual analysis—the linking of various 'understood' empirical relations and the use of similar principles to explain a vast array of phenotypic observations. The layperson does not appreciate that expecting to be rejected for a social engagement because of prior attribution to lack of attractiveness and feeling grateful and returning a favour because of a volitionally given gift are part of the same conceptual network. It is this systemization, that is, the higher order relations between associations realized in everyday life, that represents much of this attributional contribution. That the individual parts or components are naively shared underscores their veridicality, thus further supporting the certainty of the empirical relations and thereby providing a strong foundation for theory building.

Discussion Questions

1. How does Weiner's theory expand on expectancy × value models of motivation? How does it deal with particular shortcomings in the Atkinson/McClelland model of achievement motivation?
2. How does Weiner's theory relate to moral judgment? How might different attributions of a person's outcomes produce different types of moral explanations? How might these types of attributions be systematically related to particular political attitudes (e.g., opinions regarding welfare and affirmative action)?
3. How might Weiner's theory begin to predict why people play games of complete chance (with no skill involved) like roulette and slot machines?

Unit Seven Further Reading

Much of the rich social psychological literature on emotion has centred on controversies regarding definitions and measurement. What are the core building blocks of emotion? For different perspectives on these issues, see

Barrett, L.F. (2006). Solving the emotion paradox: Categorization and the experience of emotion. *Personality and Social Psychology Review, 10*, 20–46.

Watson, D., Clark, L.A., & Tellegen, A. (1988). Development and validation of brief measures of positive and negative affect: The PANAS scale. *Journal of Personality and Social Psychology, 54*, 1063–1070.

Russell, J.A. (2003). Core affect and the psychological construction of emotion. *Psychological Review, 110*, 145–72.

Keltner, D., & Haidt, J. (1999). Social functions of emotions at multiple levels of analysis. *Cognition and Emotion, 13(5)*, 505–22.

Unit Eight
Self-Regulation

We have all faced that dreaded situation: We are at a restaurant, the meal is almost over, and there we are, face-to-face with the possibility of finishing our meal with a rich, delicious, and massively unhealthy dessert. Why is it that some people are able to muster whatever it takes to say, 'No thanks' while others cave in to temptation every time? More generally, what is will-power? Is it a character trait, an immutable deficiency of will the ancient Greeks called *akrasia*, or is it something that can be cultivated? The authors in this Unit examine willpower within the larger context of research on self-regulation. In so doing, these readings begin to demystify willpower and provide practical suggestions for avoiding short-term diversions while staying on track with one's long-term goals.

Drawing on classic psychodynamic ideas, Baumeister and colleagues proposed an influential model of self-regulation containing two central theses: (1) People are able to control their urges to some extent, but after a certain point the energy available to do so becomes depleted, and (2) all self-regulatory acts draw upon the same pool of energy. Thus, distinct self-regulatory acts that on the surface appear to have nothing in common can, in fact, have a lingering influence on one another. For example, who would have thought that people who have just eaten radishes will quit sooner on a brain teaser than people who have eaten chocolate? This is what Baumeister and colleagues found in Study 1 of the 1998 article included here. As you read these studies, ask yourself, 'Are there any alternative explanations for these findings that do not require the "limited resource" idea?'

The work of Walter Mischel and colleagues has been a continual touchstone for researchers on self-regulation. These researchers pioneered the well-known 'marshmallow test' in which child participants are put into the following conflict situation: either receive one marshmallow now or wait until the experimenter returns and receive two marshmallows. In some variations of this paradigm, the one marshmallow remains in full view during the entire waiting period (15 minutes). Thus, in order to receive the bigger payoff, the child must somehow overcome the powerful urge to consume the smaller payoff. In one longitudinal study that has tracked participants for over 40 years, the number of minutes the individual could delay gratification at age four predicted a host of consequential behaviours decades later, including standardized test scores, proclivity for delinquency, and income.

If being skilled at delay of gratification is so important for life success, how does one acquire this skill? It turns out, surprisingly easily. As described in the 1989 article included here, Mischel and colleagues have isolated particular ways of reconstruing the short-term reward so that its appetitive qualities are diminished. In other words, with some training, people can learn to mentally transform the short-term attraction into something less attractive. Raising awareness about these effective mental transformations appears to be a promising way to improve people's ability to finally resist that dessert.

17. Ego Depletion: Is the Active Self a Limited Resource?

Roy F. Baumeister, Ellen Bratslavsky, Mark Muraven, and Dianne M. Tice, Case Western Reserve University

□ ■ □

Editor's Introduction

Difficult though it may be, we are all able—at least on occasion—to draw on reserves of willpower and either do something we do not want to do (but should) or avoid doing something we really want to do (but should not). That is, we are able to exert control over our behaviour and prevent it from being slavishly driven either by primal wishes or by tantalizing stimuli in the environment. In short, *self-regulation* is, at its root, really about the exercise of free will.

It is somewhat surprising that the study of self-regulation has not fully blossomed until recent years. Part of the reason may be that advances in cognitive neuroscience have allowed researchers to understand the dynamics of 'executive function' and cognitive control better than ever before (e.g., Inzlicht & Gutsell, 2007; van Veen & Carter, 2006). A second reason is likely the lack of a language for psychologists to use as they tackled the vexing psycho-philosophical question of willpower. This latter reason was solved by the present article.

Baumeister and colleagues take the approach of understanding the *properties* of willpower to understand willpower itself. They propose that one key property is that it is finite. Whenever we deploy self-control processes, there is a cost. Baumeister and colleagues term this cost ego depletion. According to the authors, acts of self-control, even if they are phenotypically different from one another, all draw upon the same common, finite pool of energy. Thus, an act of psychological exertion in one domain (e.g., eating a bad-tasting food) can cause diminished performance in another, seemingly unrelated domain (e.g., solving a brain teaser). The analogy is made quite explicitly to

human muscular activity; exercising one muscle vigorously can lead to a general fatigue that transfers to other muscles that were not in use.

This principle of pooled resources is, in fact, a classic motivational idea that was explored in the 1940s and 1950s by such researchers as Hull, Webb, and Merryman. For example, Merryman (1952) showed that food-deprived rats showed a stronger fear response to loud noises than satiated rats. That is, hunger appeared to produce a general vulnerability that transferred to non-hunger-related areas. In a more social-psychological vein, in several papers Steele, Sherman, and colleagues have shown that 'self-affirmation' at a psychological level can prevent a range of negative effects at a physiological level. For example, Cresswell et al. (2005) showed that people who had been given the opportunity to reflect on their most cherished values subsequently showed significantly lowered symptoms of stress on a physiological stress test (e.g., lower cortisol levels) than those who reflected on less-cherished values. In other words, affirming one's values provided a psychological buffer that extended beyond values. In other work, Inzlicht and colleagues have shown that the psychological stress created by being the victim of prejudice can similarly lead to decrements on a range of seemingly unrelated cognitive and motivational tasks (Inzlicht, Mackay, & Aronson, 2006).

Thus, there does seem to be something to the notion that our capacity to surmount psychological challenges, formidable though it may be, is finite. As you read the present article, think about other everyday areas of life in which the principle of 'finite self-regulatory capacity' may come into play.

□ ■ □

Many crucial functions of the self involve volition: making choices and decisions, taking responsibility, initiating and inhibiting behaviour, and making plans of action and carrying out those plans. The self exerts control over itself and over the external world. To be sure, not all human behaviour involves planful or deliberate control by the self, and, in fact, recent work has shown that a great deal of human behaviour is influenced by automatic or non-conscious processes (see Bargh, 1994, 1997). But undoubtedly some portion involves deliberate, conscious, controlled responses by the self, and that portion may be disproportionately important to the long-term health, happiness, and success of the individual. Even if it were shown that 95 per cent of behaviour consisted of lawful, predictable responses to situational stimuli by automatic processes, psychology could not afford to ignore the remaining 5 per cent. As an analogy, cars are probably driven straight ahead at least 95 per cent of the time, but ignoring the other 5 per cent (such as by building cars without steering wheels) would seriously compromise the car's ability to reach most destinations. By the same token, the relatively few active, controlling choices by the self greatly increase the self's chances of achieving its goals. And if those few 'steering' choices by the self are important, then so is whatever internal structure of the self responsible for it.

In the present investigation we were concerned with this controlling aspect of the self. Specifically, we tested hypotheses of ego depletion, as a way of learning about the self's executive function. The core idea behind ego depletion is that the self's acts of volition draw on some limited resource, akin to strength or energy and that, therefore, one act of volition will have a detrimental impact on subsequent volition. We sought to show that a preliminary act of self-control in the form of resisting temptation (Experiment 1) or a preliminary act of choice and responsibility (Experiment 2) would undermine self-regulation in a subsequent, unrelated domain, namely persistence at a difficult and frustrating task. We then sought to verify that the effects of ego depletion are indeed maladaptive and detrimental to performance (Experiment 3). Last, we undertook to show that ego depletion resulting from acts of self-control would interfere with subsequent decision making by making people more passive (Experiment 4).

Our research strategy was to look at effects that would carry over across wide gaps of seeming irrelevance. If resisting the temptation to eat chocolate can leave a person prone to give up faster on a difficult, frustrating puzzle, that would suggest that those two very different acts of self-control draw on the same limited resource. And if making a choice about whether to make a speech contrary to one's opinions were to have the same effect, it would suggest that that very same resource is also the one used in general for deliberate, responsible decision making. That resource would presumably be one of the most important features of the self.

Executive Function

The term *agency* has been used by various writers to refer to the self's exertion of volition, but this term has misleading connotations: An agent is quintessentially someone who acts on behalf of someone else, whereas the phenomenon under discussion involves the self acting autonomously on its own behalf. The term *executive function* has been used in various contexts to refer to this aspect of self and hence may be preferable (e.g., Epstein, 1973; see Baumeister, 1998). Meanwhile, we use the term *ego depletion* to refer to a temporary reduction in the self's capacity or willingness to engage in volitional action (including controlling the environment, controlling the self, making choices, and initiating action) caused by prior exercise of volition.

The psychological theory that volition is one of the self's crucial functions can be traced back at least to Freud (1923/1961a, 1933/1961b), who described the ego as the part of the psyche that must deal with the reality of the external world by mediating between conflicting inner and outer pressures. In his scheme, for example, a Victorian gentleman standing on the street might feel urged by his id to head for the brothel and by his super-ego to go to church, but it is ultimately left up to his ego to start his feet walking in one direction or the other. Freud also seems to have believed that the ego needed to use some energy in making such a decision.

Recent research has convincingly illuminated the self's nearly relentless quest for control (Brehm, 1966; Burger, 1989; DeCharms, 1968; Deci & Ryan, 1991, 1995; Langer, 1975; Rothbaum, Weisz, & Snyder, 1982; Taylor, 1983, 1989; White, 1959). It is also known that when the self feels highly respon-sible (accountable) for its actions, its cognitive and behavioural processes change (Cooper & Scher, 1994; Linder, Cooper, & Jones, 1967; Tetlock, 1983, 1985; Tetlock & Boettger, 1989). Active responses also have more powerful effects on the self and its subsequent responses than do passive ones (Allison & Messick, 1988; Cioffi & Garner, 1996; Fazio, Sherman, & Herr, 1982). The processes by which the self monitors itself in order to approach stan-dards of desired behaviour have also been studied (Carver & Scheier, 1981; Duval & Wicklund, 1972; Wegner, 1994; Wegner & Pennebaker, 1993).

Despite these efforts, it is hard to dispute that understanding of the executive function remains far more vague and rudimentary than other aspects of self-theory. Researchers investigating cognitive representations of self have made enormous prog-ress in recent decades (for reviews, see Banaji & Prentice, 1994; Fiske & Taylor, 1991). Likewise, there has been considerable progress on interper-sonal aspects of selfhood (e.g., Leary, 1995; Leary & Kowalski, 1990; Schlenker, 1980; Tesser, 1988). In comparison, understanding of the self's execu-tive function lags behind at a fairly primitive level.

Ego Depletion

The notion that volition depends on the self's expenditure of some limited resource was antici-pated by Freud (1923/1961a, 1933/1961b). He thought the ego needed to have some form of energy to accomplish its tasks and to resist the energetic promptings of id and superego. Freud was fond of the analogy of horse and rider, because as he said the rider (analogous to the ego) is gener-ally in charge of steering but is sometimes unable to prevent the horse from going where it wants to go. Freud was rather vague and inconsistent about where the ego's energy came from, but he recog-nized the conceptual value of postulating that the ego operated on an energy model.

Several modern research findings suggest that some form of energy or strength may be involved in acts of volition. Most of these have been con-cerned with self-regulation. Indeed, Mischel (1996) has recently proposed that the colloquial notion of willpower be revived for self-regulation theory, and a literature review by Baumeister, Heatherton, and Tice (1994) concluded that much evidence about self-regulatory failure fits a model of strength depletion.

An important early study by Glass, Singer, and Friedman (1969) found that participants exposed to unpredictable noise stress subsequently showed decrements in frustration tolerance, as measured by persistence on unsolvable problems.[1] Glass et al. concluded that adapting to unpredictable stress involves a 'psychic cost', which implies an expen-diture or depletion of some valuable resource. They left the nature of this resource to future research, which has not made much further progress.

Additional evidence for a strength model was provided by Muraven, Tice, and Baumeister (1998), whose research strategy influenced the pres-ent investigation. Muraven et al. sought to show that consecutive exertions of self-regulation were characterized by deteriorating performance, even though the exertions involved seemingly unrelated spheres. In one study, they showed that trying not to think about a white bear (a thought-control task borrowed from Wegner, 1989; Wegner, Schneider, Carter, & White, 1987) caused people to give up more quickly on a subsequent anagram task. In another study, an affect-regulation exercise caused subsequent decrements in endurance at squeezing a handgrip. These findings suggest that exertions of self-control do carry a psychic cost and deplete some scarce resource.

To integrate these scattered findings and implications, we suggest the following. One important part of the self is a limited resource that is used for all acts of volition, such as controlled (as opposed to automatic) processing, active (as opposed to passive) choice, initiating behaviour, and overriding responses. Because much of self-regulation involves resisting temptation and hence overriding motivated responses, this self-resource must be able to affect behaviour in the same fashion that motivation does. Motivations can be strong or weak, and stronger impulses are presumably more difficult to restrain; therefore, the executive function of the self presumably also operates in a strong or weak fashion, which implies that it has a dimension of strength. An exertion of this strength in self-control draws on this strength and temporarily exhausts it (Muraven et al., 1998), but it also presumably recovers after a period of rest. Other acts of volition should have similar effects, and that is the hypothesis of the present investigation.

Experiment 1

Experiment 1 provided evidence for ego depletion by examining consecutive acts of self-control. The study was originally designed to test competing hypotheses about the nature of self-control, also known as self-regulation. Clearly the control over self is one of the most important and adaptive applications of the self's executive function. Research on monitoring processes and feedback loops has illuminated the cognitive structure that processes relevant information (e.g., Carver & Scheier, 1981; Wegner, 1994), but the actual process by which an organism alters its own responses or subjective states is far less well understood. At least three different models of the nature of self-regulation can be proposed. Moreover, these three models make quite different predictions about the effectiveness

of self-control immediately after an exertion of self-control in some unrelated sphere. Experiment 1 provided a test of these three competing predictions by requiring participants to engage in two seemingly unrelated acts of self-control.

One model views self-regulation as essentially a skill. In this model, people gradually develop the skill to regulate themselves over long periods of time. On any given occasion, however, skill remains roughly constant across repeated trials (except for small and gradual learning effects), so there should be little or no change in effectiveness of self-control on two successive exertions within a short time.

Another model portrays self-regulation as essentially a knowledge structure. In this view, self-control operates like a master schema that makes use of information about how to alter one's own responses or states. On the basis of this model, an initial act of self-regulation should prime the schema, thereby facilitating subsequent self-control. Another version of this view would be that the self-regulatory system is normally in a standby or depowered mode until it is pressed into action by one act of self-control. Once activated, the system would remain in operation ('on') for a time, making further acts of self-control easier.

A third model states that self-regulation resembles energy. In this view, acts of self-regulation involve some kind of exertion that expends energy and therefore depletes the supply available. Unless the supply is very large, initial acts of self-regulation should deplete it, thereby impairing subsequent self-control.

Thus, the three models respectively predict no change, an increase, or a decrease in effectiveness of self-control following an initial act of self-control. Other models are possible, such as the possibility that self-regulation involves a collection of domain-specific but unrelated knowledge structures, so that an initial act of self-control should prime and therefore facilitate self-control in the same sphere but produce no change in other, unrelated spheres. Still, these three models provide sufficiently conflicting predictions about the sequence of unrelated acts of self-control to make it worth conducting an initial test.

In the present research, we used impulse control, which to many people is the classic or paradigmatic form of self-control. More precisely, we manipulated self-control by instructing some hungry individuals to eat only radishes while they were faced with the tempting sight and aroma of chocolate. Thus, they had to resist the temptation to perform one action while making themselves perform a similar but much less desirable action. We then sought to measure self-control in an unrelated sphere, by persistence at a frustrating puzzle-solving task. A series of frustrating failures may often make people want to stop doing the task, and, so, self-control is needed to force oneself to continue working.

If resisting temptation depends on skill, then this skill would predict no change in persistence under frustration. If resisting temptation involves activating a knowledge structure or master schema, then priming this schema should facilitate self-control, and people should persist longer on the puzzles. Finally, if resisting temptation uses some kind of strength or energy, then this will be depleted afterward, and subsequent persistence should decrease.

Method

Participants

Data were collected in individual sessions from 67 introductory psychology students (31 male, 36 female) who received course credit for taking part.

Procedure

Participants signed up for a study on taste perception. Each participant was contacted to schedule an individual session, and at that time the experimenter requested the participant to skip one meal before the experiment and make sure not to have eaten anything for at least three hours.

The laboratory room was carefully set up before participants in the food conditions arrived.

Chocolate chip cookies were baked in the room in a small oven, and, as a result, the laboratory was filled with the delicious aroma of fresh chocolate and baking. Two foods were displayed on the table at which the participant was seated. One display consisted of a stack of chocolate chip cookies augmented by some chocolate candies. The other consisted of a bowl of red and white radishes.

The experimenter provided an overview of the procedures, secured an informed consent, and then elaborated the cover story. She explained that chocolates and radishes had been selected for the taste perception study because they were highly distinctive foods familiar to most people. She said that there would be a follow-up measure for sensation memory the next day, and so she asked the participant to agree not to eat any chocolates or radishes (other than in the experiment) for 24 hours after the session.

Participants in the chocolate and radish conditions were then asked to take about five minutes to taste the assigned food while the experimenter was out of the room. In the radish condition, the experimenter asked the participant to eat at least two or three radishes, and in the chocolate condition, the participant was asked to eat at least two or three cookies or a handful of the small candies. Participants were reminded to eat only the food that had been assigned to them. The experimenter left the room and surreptitiously observed the participant through a one-way mirror, recording the amount of food eaten and verifying that the participant ate only the assigned food. (To minimize self-awareness, the mirror was almost completely covered with a curtain.)

After about five minutes, the experimenter returned and asked the participant to fill out two questionnaires. One was the Brief Mood Introspection Scale (BMI; Mayer & Gaschke, 1988), and the other was the Restraint Scale (Herman & Polivy, 1975). Then the experimenter said that it was necessary to wait at least 15 minutes to allow the sensory memory of the food to fade. During that time, she said, the participant would be asked to provide some preliminary data that would help the researchers learn whether college students differed from high school students in their problem-solving ability. The experimenter said that the participant would therefore be asked to work on a test of problem solving. The problem solving was presented as if it were unrelated to the eating, but in fact it constituted the main dependent measure.

There was also a no-food control condition. Participants assigned to this condition skipped the food part of the experiment and went directly to the problem-solving part.

The problem-solving task was adapted from a task used by Glass et al. (1969), adapted from Feather (1961). The puzzle requires the person to trace a geometric figure without retracing any lines and without lifting his or her pencil from the paper. Multiple slips of paper were provided for each figure, so the person could try over and over. Each participant was initially given several practice figures to learn how the puzzles worked and how to solve them, with the experimenter present to answer any questions. After the practice period, the experimenter gave the participant the two main test figures with the instructions.

You can take as much time and as many trials as you want. You will not be judged on the number of trials or the time you will take. You will be judged on whether or not you finish tracing the figure. If you wish to stop before you finish [i.e., solve the puzzle], ring the bell on the table.

Unbeknownst to the participant, both these test figures had been prepared so as to be impossible to solve.

The experimenter then left the room and timed how long the participant worked on the task before giving up (signified by ringing the bell). Following an a priori decision, 30 minutes was set as the maximum time, and the four participants who were still working after 30 minutes were stopped by the experimenter at that point. For the rest,

when the experimenter heard the bell, she re-entered the room and administered a manipulation check questionnaire. When the participants finished, the experimenter debriefed, thanked, and dismissed them.

Results

Manipulation Check

The experimenter surreptitiously observed all participants during the eating phase to ascertain that they ate the stipulated food and avoided the other. All participants complied with the instructions. In particular, none of the participants in the radish condition violated the rule against eating chocolates. Several of them did exhibit clear interest in the chocolates, to the point of looking longingly at the chocolate display and in a few cases even picking up the cookies to sniff at them. But no participant actually bit into the wrong food.

The difficulty of the eating task was assessed on the final questionnaire. Participants in the radish condition said that they forced themselves in an effortful fashion to eat the assigned food more than participants in the chocolate condition, $F(1, 44) = 16.10, p < .001$. They also rated resisting the non-assigned food as marginally significantly more difficult, $F(1, 44) = 3.41, p < .07$. During the debriefing, many participants in the radish condition spontaneously mentioned the difficulty of resisting the temptation to eat the chocolates.

Persistence

The main dependent measure was the amount of time participants spent on the unsolvable puzzles. A one-way analysis of variance (ANOVA) indicated significant variation among the three conditions, $F(2, 64) = 26.88, p < .001$. The means are presented in Table 17.1. Pairwise comparisons among the groups indicated that participants in the radish condition quit sooner on the frustrating task than did participants in either the chocolate condition, $F(44) = 6.03, p < .001$, or the no-food (control) condition, $F(44) = 6.88, p < .001$. The chocolate

Table 17.1 Persistence on Unsolvable Puzzles (Experiment 1)

Condition	Time (min)	Attempts
Radish	8.35	19.40
Chocolate	18.90	34.29
No food control	20.86	32.81

Note: Standard deviations for Column 1, top to bottom, are 4.67, 6.86, and 7.30. For Column 2, SDs = 8.12, 20.16, and 13.38.

condition did not differ from the no-food control condition, $t < 1$, ns.

It is conceivable that the time measure was affected by something other than persistence, such as speed. That is, the interpretation would be altered if the participants in the radish condition tried just as many times as those in the chocolate condition and merely did so much faster. Hence, we also analyzed the number of attempts that participants made before giving up. A one-way ANOVA on these tallies again yielded significant variation among the three conditions, $F(2, 64) = 7.61$, $p = .001$. The pattern of results was essentially the same as with duration of persistence, as can be seen in Table 17.1. Pairwise comparisons again showed that participants in the radish condition gave up earlier than participants in the other two conditions, which did not differ from each other.[2]

Moods

The mood measure contains two subscales, and we conducted a one-way ANOVA on each, using only the radish and chocolate conditions (because this measure was not administered in the no-food control condition). The two conditions did not differ in valence (i.e., pleasant vs unpleasant) of mood, $F(1, 44) = 2.62$, ns, nor in arousal, $F < 1$, ns.

Dieting

The analyses on persistence were repeated using dieting status (from the Restraint Scale) as an independent variable. Dieting status did not show either a main effect or an interaction with condition on either the duration of persistence or the number of attempts.

Fatigue and Desire to Quit

The final questionnaire provided some additional evidence beyond the manipulation checks. One item asked the participant how tired he or she felt after the tracing task. An ANOVA yielded significant variation among the conditions, $F(2, 64) = 5.74$, $p < .01$. Participants in the radish condition were more tired ($M = 17.96$) than those in the chocolate ($M = 11.85$) or no-food ($M = 12.29$) conditions (the latter two did not differ). Participants in the radish condition also reported that their fatigue level had changed more toward increased tiredness ($M = 6.28$) than participants in either the chocolate ($M = -0.90$) or no-food ($M = 1.76$) conditions, $F(2, 64) = 5.13$, $p < .01$.

Participants in the radish condition reported that they had felt less strong a desire to stop working on the tracing task than had participants in the other two conditions, $F(2, 64) = 4.71$, $p < .01$. Yet they also reported forcing themselves to work on the tracing task more than participants in the other two conditions, $F(2, 64) = 3.20$, $p < .05$. The latter may have been an attempt to justify their relatively rapid quitting on that task. The former may indicate that they quit as soon as they felt the urge to do so, in contrast to the chocolate and no-food participants who made themselves continue for a while after they first felt like quitting.

Discussion

These results provide initial support for the hypothesis of ego depletion. Resisting temptation seems to have produced a psychic cost, in the sense that afterward participants were more inclined to give up easily in the face of frustration. It was not that eating chocolate improved performance. Rather, wanting chocolate but eating radishes instead, especially under circumstances in which it would seemingly be easy and safe to snitch some chocolates, seems to have consumed some resource and therefore left people less able to persist at the puzzles.

Earlier, we proposed three rival models of the nature of self-regulation. These results fit a strength model better than a skill or schema model. If self-regulation were essentially a knowledge structure, then an initial act of self-regulation should have primed the schema, thereby facilitating subsequent self-regulation. The present results were directly opposite to that prediction. A skill model would predict no change across consecutive acts of self-regulation, but we did find significant change. In contrast, a strength or energy model predicted that some vital resource would be depleted by an initial act of self-regulation, leading to subsequent decrements, and this corresponds to what we found.

It is noteworthy that the depletion manipulation in this study required both resisting one impulse (to eat chocolate) and making oneself perform an undesired act (eating radishes). Both may have contributed to ego depletion. Still, the two are not independent. Based on a priori assumptions and on comments made by participants during the debriefing, it seems likely that people would have found it easier to make themselves eat the radishes if they were not simultaneously struggling with resisting the more tempting chocolates.

Combined with other evidence (especially Muraven et al., 1998), therefore, it seems reasonable to infer that self-regulation draws on some limited resource akin to strength or energy and that this resource may be common for many forms of self-regulation. In Experiment 1, we found that an initial act of resisting temptation (i.e., an act of impulse control) impaired subsequent persistence at a spatial puzzle task. Muraven et al. found that an act of affect regulation (i.e., trying either to stifle or amplify one's emotional response) lowered subsequent stamina on a physical task, that an initial act of thought suppression reduced persistence at unsolvable anagrams, and that thought suppression impaired subsequent ability to hide one's emotions. These various carry-overs between thought control, emotion control, impulse control, and task performance indicate that these four main spheres of self-regulation all share the same resource. Therefore, the question for Experiment 2 was whether that same resource would also be involved in other acts of choice and volition beyond self-regulation.

Experiment 2

Experiment 2 addressed the question of whether the same resource that was depleted by not eating chocolate (in Experiment 1) would be depleted by an act of choice. For this, we used one of social psychology's classic manipulations: high choice versus low choice to engage in counterattitudinal behaviour. Festinger and Carlsmith (1959) showed that people change their attitudes to make them consistent with behaviour when they have been induced to act in ways contrary to their attitudes. Linder et al. (1967) showed that this effect occurs only when people have been led to see their own (counterattitudinal) behaviour as freely chosen, and many studies have replicated these effects.

Our interest was not in the attitudinal consequences of counterattitudinal behaviour, however. Rather, our hypothesis was that the act of making the choice to engage in counterattitudinal behaviour would involve the self and deplete its volitional resource. As an index of this ego depletion, we measured frustration tolerance using the same task that we used in Experiment 1, namely persistence at unsolvable puzzles. The puzzles, of course, had nothing to do with our independent variable (next year's tuition), and so in all direct ways the two behaviours were irrelevant.

Dissonance research has provided some evidence consistent with the view that making a choice involves an exertion by the self. The original article by Linder et al. (1967) reported that participants in the high-choice (free-decision, low-incentive) condition spent about half a minute deciding whether to engage in the counterattitudinal behaviour, even though all consented to do it, whereas low-choice participants did not spend that amount of time. This is consistent with the view that the self was engaging in some effortful activity during the choice exercise. More generally, Cooper and Scher (1994; see also Cooper & Fazio, 1984; Scher & Cooper, 1989) concluded that personal responsibility for aversive consequences is the core cause of cognitive dissonance, and their conclusion puts emphasis on the taking or accepting of personal responsibility for one's actions— thus an active response by the self.

The design of Experiment 2 thus involved having people make a counterattitudinal speech (favouring a large tuition increase, to which most students were opposed) under high- or low-choice conditions. Because our focus was on the active choice making by the self, we also included a condition in which people chose to make a pro-attitudinal speech opposing the increase. Choosing to engage in a pro-attitudinal behaviour should not cause dissonance (see Cooper & Scher, 1994; Cooper & Fazio, 1984; Festinger, 1957; Linder et al., 1967), but it should still deplete the self to some degree because it still involves an act of choice and taking responsibility. We did not have any basis for predicting whether choosing to engage in counterattitudinal behaviour would deplete the self more than choosing to engage in pro-attitudinal behaviour, but we expected that there should still be some depletion.

Method

Participants

Participants were 39 undergraduate psychology students (25 male, 14 female). They participated in individual sessions. They were randomly assigned among four experimental treatment conditions: counterattitudinal choice, counterattitudinal no choice, pro-attitudinal choice, and no speech (control). To ensure that the issue was personally relevant to all participants, we excluded eight additional potential participants who were either graduating seniors or who were on full scholarship, because preliminary testing revealed that next year's tuition did not matter to students in these categories.

Procedure

The experimenter greeted each participant and explained that the purpose of the study was to see how people respond to persuasion. They were told that they would be making stimuli that would be played to other people to alter their attitudes. In particular, they would be making an audiotape recording of a persuasive speech regarding projected tuition increases for the following academic year. The topic of tuition raises was selected on the basis of a pilot test: A survey had found that students rated the tuition increase as the most important issue to them.

The experimenter said that all participants would record speeches that had been prepared in advance. The importance of the tuition increase issue was highlighted. The experimenter also said that the university's Board of Trustees had agreed to listen to the speeches to see how much impact the messages would have on their decisions about raising tuition.

The experimenter showed the participant two folders, labelled *pro-tuition raise* and *anti-tuition raise*. Participants in the no-choice (counterattitudinal) condition were told that they had been assigned to make the pro-tuition raise speech. The experimenter said that the researchers already had enough people making the speech against the tuition raise and so it would not be possible to give the participant a choice as to which speech to make. In contrast, participants in the high-choice conditions were told that the decision of which speech to make was entirely up to them. The experimenter explained that because there were already enough participants in one of the groups, it would help the study a great deal if they chose to read one folder rather than the other. The experimenter then again stressed that the final decision would remain entirely up to the participant. All participants agreed to make the speech that they had been assigned.

Participants in the no-speech control condition did not do this part of the experiment. The issue of tuition increase was not raised with them.

At this point, all participants completed the same mood measure used in Experiment 1. The experimenter then began explaining the task for the second part of the experiment. She said there was some evidence of a link between problem-solving abilities and persuasiveness. Accordingly, the next part of the experiment would contain a measure of problem-solving ability. For participants in the speech-making conditions, the experimenter said that the problem-solving task would precede the recording of the speech.

The problem-solving task was precisely the same one used in Experiment 1, involving tracing geometric figures without retracing lines or lifting the pen from the paper. As in Experiment 1, the participant's persistence at the frustrating puzzles was the main dependent measure. After signalling the experimenter that they wished to stop working on the task, participants completed a brief questionnaire that included manipulation checks. They were then completely debriefed, thanked, and sent home.

Results

Manipulation Check

The final questionnaire asked participants (except in the control condition) how much they felt that it was up to them which speech they chose to make. A one-way ANOVA confirmed that there was significant variation among the conditions, $F(2, 31) = 15.46$, $p < .001$. Participants in the no-choice condition indicated that it was not up to them which speech to make ($M = 27.10$), whereas participants in the counterattitudinal-choice ($M = 10.21$) and pro-attitudinal-choice conditions ($M = 6.60$) both indicated high degrees of choice. Another item asked how much the participant considered reading an alternative speech to the one suggested by the experimenter, and on this too there was significant variation among the three conditions, $F(2, 31) = 11.53$, $p < .001$, indicating that high-choice

participants considered the alternative much more than participants in the no-choice condition.

Persistence

The main dependent measure was the duration of persistence on the unsolvable puzzles. The results are presented in Table 17.2. A one-way ANOVA on persistence times indicated that there was significant variation among conditions, $F(3, 35) = 8.42$, $p < .001$. Pairwise comparisons confirmed that the counterattitudinal-choice and the pro-attitudinal-choice conditions each differed significantly from both the control and the counterattitudinal-no-choice conditions. Perhaps surprisingly, the two choice conditions did not differ significantly from each other.

Similar results were found using the number of attempts (rather than time) as the dependent measure of persistence. The ANOVA indicated significant variation among the four conditions, $F(3, 35) = 3.24$, $p < .05$. The same pattern of pairwise cell differences was found: Both conditions involving high choice led to a reduction in persistence, as compared with the no-speech control condition and the no-choice counterattitudinal speech condition.[3]

Mood State

One-way ANOVAs were conducted on each of the two subscales of the BMI Scale. There was no evidence of significant variation among the four

Table 17.2 Persistence on Unsolvable Puzzles (Experiment 2)

Condition	Time (min)	Attempts
Counterattitudinal speech		
High choice	14.30	26.10
No choice	23.11	42.44
Proattitudinal speech		
High choice	13.80	24.70
No speech control	25.30	35.50

Note: Standard deviations for Column 1, top to bottom, are 6.91, 7.08, 6.49, and 5.06. For Column 2, *SDs* = 14.83, 22.26, 7.13, and 9.14.

conditions in reported valence of mood (i.e., pleasant vs unpleasant), $F(3, 35) < 1$, ns. There was also no evidence of variation in arousal, $F(3, 35) < 1$, ns. These results suggest that the differences in persistence were not due to differential moods engendered by the manipulations.

Discussion

The results supported the ego-depletion hypothesis and suggest that acts of choice draw on the same limited resource used for self-control. Participants who agreed to make a counterattitudinal speech under high choice showed a subsequent drop in their persistence on a difficult, frustrating task, as compared with participants who expected to make the same speech under low choice (and as compared with no-speech control participants). Thus, taking responsibility for a counterattitudinal behaviour seems to have consumed a resource of the self, leaving the self with less of that resource available to prolong persistence at the unsolvable puzzles.

Of particular further interest was the high-choice pro-attitudinal behaviour condition. These people should not have experienced any dissonance, yet they showed significant reductions in persistence on unsolvable problems. Dissonance is marked by an aversive arousal state (Cooper, Zanna, & Taves, 1978; Zanna & Cooper, 1974; Zanna, Higgins, & Taves, 1976), but apparently this arousal or negative affect is not what is responsible for ego depletion, because we found almost identical evidence of ego depletion among people who chose to make the non-dissonant, pro-attitudinal speech.

Thus, it is not the counterattitudinal behaviour that depletes the self. Indeed, people who expected to perform the counterattitudinal behaviour under low choice persisted just as long as no-speech control participants. Making a speech contrary to one's beliefs does not necessarily deplete the self in any way that our measure detected. Meanwhile, making a speech that supports one's beliefs did deplete the self, provided that the person made the deliberate, free decision to do so.

The implication is that it is the exercise of choice, regardless of the behaviour, that depletes the self. Whatever motivational, affective, or volitional resource is needed to force oneself to keep trying in the face of discouraging failure is apparently the same resource that is used to make responsible decisions about one's own behaviour, and apparently this resource is fairly limited.

Experiment 3

Experiments 1 and 2 suggested that self-regulation is weakened by prior exercise of volition, either in the form of resisting temptation (Experiment 1) or making a responsible choice (Experiment 2). In both studies, the dependent variable involved persistence on unsolvable problems. It is reasonable to treat such persistence as a challenge for self-regulation, because undoubtedly people would feel inclined to give up when their efforts are met with frustration and discouraging failure, and overcoming that impulse (in order to persist) would require an act of self-control.

An alternative view, however, might suggest that it is adaptive to give up early on unsolvable problems. Persistence is, after all, only adaptive and productive when it leads to eventual success. Squandering time and effort on a lost cause is thus wasteful, and optimal self-management would involve avoiding such waste (e.g., McFarlin, 1985). It is true that such an argument would require one to assume that our participants actually recognized the task as unsolvable, and there was no sign that they did. (In fact, most participants expressed surprise during the debriefing when they were told that the puzzles were in fact unsolvable.) Yet for us to contend that ego depletion has a negative effect, it seemed necessary to show some decrement in task performance. Unsolvable puzzles cannot show such a decrement, because no amount of persistence leads to success. Study 3 therefore was designed to show that ego depletion can impair performance on solvable tasks.

Because broad conclusions about ego depletion are difficult to draw from any single procedure, it seemed desirable to use very different procedures for Study 3. Accordingly, the manipulation of ego depletion involved affect regulation (i.e., controlling one's emotions). Affect regulation is one important sphere of self-regulation (e.g., Baumeister et al., 1994). In this study, some participants were asked to watch an emotionally evocative videotape and stifle any emotional reaction they might have. To ensure that the effects were due to self-regulation rather than the particular emotional response, we used both positive (humorous) and negative (sad and distressing) stimuli.

For the measure of task performance, we selected anagram solving. This is a widely used performance measure that has elements of both skill and effort. More to the point, we suspected that success at anagrams would require some degree of self-regulation. One must keep breaking and altering the tentative combinations of letters one has formed and must make oneself keep trying despite multiple initial failures. In the latter respect, anagram solving resembles the dependent measure used in the first two studies, except that persistence can actually help lead to success. The prediction was that participants who had tried to control their emotional responses to the videotape would suffer from ego depletion and, as a result, would perform more poorly at anagrams.

Method

Participants

Participants were 30 (11 male and 19 female) undergraduates who took part in connection with introductory psychology requirements. They participated in individual sessions and were randomly assigned among the conditions.

Procedure

The experimenter explained that the purpose of the study was to see which personality traits would make people more responsive to experiencing emotions. They were told that the first part of the procedure would involve watching a movie.

In the suppress-emotion condition, participants were instructed to try not to show and not to feel any emotions during the movie. The experimenter said that the participant would be videotaped while watching the film, and so it was essential to try to conceal and suppress any emotional reaction. Meanwhile, participants in the no-regulation condition were instructed to let their emotions flow while watching the movie, without any attempt to hide or deny these feelings. They were also told that their reactions would be videotaped.

Following these instructions, each participant saw a 10-minute videotape. Half of the participants in each condition saw a humorous video featuring the comedian Robin Williams. The others saw an excerpt from the film *Terms of Endearment,* portraying a young mother dying from cancer. At the end of the video clip, participants completed the BMI Scale.

Then the experimenter extended the cover story to say that they would have to wait at least 10 minutes after the film to allow their sensory memory of the movie to fade. During that time, they were asked to help the experimenter collect some preliminary data for future research by completing an anagram task. Participants received 13 sets of letters that they were to unscramble to make English words during a six-minute period. The participant was left alone to do this task. After six minutes, the experimenter returned and administered a post-experimental questionnaire. After the participant completed that, he or she was debriefed and thanked.

Results

Manipulation Check

The final questionnaire asked participants to rate how effortful it had been to comply with the instructions for watching the video clip. Participants in the suppress-emotion condition reported that they found it much more effortful ($M = 13.88$)

than participants in the no-regulation condition ($M = 5.64$), $F(28) = 2.88$, $p < .01$. Similar effects were found on an item asking people how difficult it was to follow the instructions while watching the video, $F(28) = 4.95$, $p < .001$, and on an item asking how much they had to concentrate in complying with the instructions, $F(28) = 5.42$, $p < .001$. These findings confirm that it required a greater exertion to suppress one's emotional response than to let it happen.

In addition, the films were perceived quite differently. On the item asking participants to rate the movie on a scale ranging from 1 (*sad*) to 25 (*funny*), participants rated the comedy video as much funnier ($M = 21.94$) than the sad video clip ($M = 4.54$), $t(29) = 4.62$, $p < .001$. There were no differences as a function of ego-depletion condition in how the movie was perceived.

Anagram Performance

The main dependent variable was performance on the anagram task. Participants in the suppress-emotion condition performed significantly worse than participants in the no-regulation condition in terms of number of anagrams correctly solved, $t(28) = 2.12$, $p < .05$. There was no effect for type of movie.

Mood

There was no difference in either mood valence or arousal between participants who tried to suppress their emotional reactions and those who let their emotions go. Hence, any differences in performance between these conditions should not be attributed to differential mood or arousal responses.

Discussion

The results confirm the view that ego depletion can be detrimental to subsequent performance. The alternative view, that Experiments 1 and 2 showed improved self-regulation because it is adaptive to give up early on unsolvable tasks, cannot seemingly account for the results of Experiment 3. In this study, an act of self-regulation—stifling one's emotional response to a funny or sad video

clip—was followed by poorer performance at solving anagrams. Hence, it seems appropriate to suggest that some valuable resource of the self was actually depleted by the initial act of volition, as opposed to suggesting merely that initial acts of volition alter subsequent decision making.

Experiment 4

The first three experiments provided support for the hypothesis of ego depletion. Experiment 4 was designed to provide converging evidence using quite different procedures. Also, Experiment 4 was designed to complement Experiment 2 by reversing the direction of influence: Experiment 2 showed that an initial act of responsible decision making could undermine subsequent self-regulation, and Experiment 4 was designed to show that an initial act of self-regulation could undermine subsequent decision making.

Experiment 4 used procedures that contrasted active versus passive responding. In many situations, people face a choice between one course of action that requires an active response and another course that will occur automatically if the person does nothing (also called a *default option*). In an important study, Brockner, Shaw, and Rubin (1979) measured persistence in a futile endeavour under two contrasting situations. In one, the person had to make a positive move to continue, but the procedure would stop automatically if he or she did nothing (i.e., continuing was active and quitting was passive). The other situation was the reverse, in which a positive move was required to terminate whereas continuing was automatic unless the person signalled to quit. Brockner et al. found greater persistence when persistence was passive than when it was active.

In our view, the findings of Brockner et al. (1979) may reflect a broader pattern that can be called a *passive-option effect*. The passive-option effect can be defined by saying that in any choice situation, the likelihood of any option being chosen is increased if choosing involves a passive rather than an active response. Sales organizations such as music, book, and film clubs, for example, find that their sales are higher if they can make the customer's purchasing response passive rather than active, and so they prefer to operate on the basis that each month's selection will automatically be mailed to the customer and billed unless the customer actively refuses it.

For present purposes, the passive-option effect is an important possible consequence of the limited resources that the self has for volitional response. Our assumption is that active responding requires the self to expend some of its resources, whereas passive responses do not. The notion that the self is more involved and more implicated by active responding than by passive responding helps explain evidence that active responses leave more lasting behavioural consequences. For example, Cioffi and Garner (1996) showed that people were more likely to follow through when they had actively volunteered than passively volunteered for the same act.

The passive-option effect thus provides a valuable forum for examining ego depletion. Active responses differ from passive ones in that they require the expenditure of limited resources. If the self's resources have already been exhausted (i.e., under ego depletion), the self should therefore be all the more inclined to favour the passive option.

To forestall confusion, we hasten to point out that the term *choice* can be used in two different ways, and so a passive option may or may not be understood as involving a choice, depending on which meaning is used. Passive choice is a choice in the sense that the situation presents the person with multiple options and the outcome is contingent on the person's behaviour (or non-behaviour). It is, however, not a choice in the volitional sense, because the person may not perform an intrapsychic act of volition. For example, a married couple who sleeps together on a given night may be said to have made a choice that night insofar as they could, in principle, have opted to sleep alone or with other sleeping partners. Most likely, though, they did not

go through an active-choice process that evening, but rather they simply did what they always did. The essence of passive options, in our understanding, is that the person does not engage in an inner process of choosing or deciding, even though alternative options are available. Passive choices therefore should not deplete the self's resources.

In Experiment 4, we showed participants a very boring movie and gave them a temptation to stop watching it. For some participants quitting was passive, whereas for others quitting required an active response. The dependent variable was how long people persisted at the movie. According to the passive-option effect, they should persist longer when persisting was passive than when persisting required active responses. We predicted that ego depletion would intensify this pattern.

Prior ego depletion was manipulated by altering the instructions for a task in a way that varied how much the person had to regulate his or her responses. The basic task involved crossing out all instances of the letter *e* in a text. People can learn to do this easily and quickly; and they become accustomed to scanning for every *e* and then crossing it out. To raise the self-regulatory difficulty, we told people not to cross out the letter *e* if any of several other criteria were met, such as if there was another vowel adjacent to the *e* or one letter removed. These people would presumably then scan for each *e* but would have to override the response of crossing it out whenever any of those criteria were met. Their responses thus had to be regulated according to multiple rules, unlike the others who could simply respond every time they found an *e*. Our assumption was that consulting the complex decision rules and overriding the simple response would deplete the ego, unlike the simpler version of the task.

Method

Participants

Eighty-four undergraduate students (47 males, 37 females) participated for partial fulfillment of a course requirement. Each individual testing session lasted about 30 minutes.

Procedure

The experimenter told participants that the experiment was designed to look at 'whether personality influences how people perceive movies'. After signing an informed consent form, participants completed several personality questionnaires to help maintain the cover story. (Except for an item measuring tiredness, the questionnaires are not relevant to the current study and will not be discussed further.)

Participants then completed the regulatory-depletion task. Each was given a typewritten sheet of paper with meaningless text on it (a page from an advanced statistics book with a highly technical style) and told to cross off all instances of the letter *e*. For the participants assigned to the ego-depletion condition, the task was made quite difficult, requiring them to consult multiple rules and monitor their decisions carefully. They were told that they should only cross off an *e* if it was not adjacent to another vowel or one extra letter away from another vowel (thus, one would not cross off the *e* in *vowel*). Also, the photocopy of the stimulus page had been lightened, making it relatively difficult to read and thus further requiring close attention. In contrast, participants in the no-depletion condition were given an easily legible photocopy with good contrast and resolution, and they were told to cross off every single *e* with no further rules or stipulations.

The experimenter then told participants that they were going to watch two movies and that after each movie they would answer a few simple questions about it. He explained that the videos were rather long and the participant did not have time to watch the complete movie. It would be up to the participant when to stop. The participant was, however, cautioned to 'watch the video long enough so that you can understand what happened and answer a few questions about the video'.

The experimenter next gave the participant a small box with a button attached. Participants were told to ring the buzzer when they were done watching the movie, at which point the experimenter would re-enter the room and give them a few questions to answer. Half of the participants were told to press the button down when they wanted to stop (active quit condition). The others were told to hold down the button as long as they wanted to watch more of the movie; releasing the button would cause the movie to stop (passive quit condition). The buzzer was wired to signal the experimenter when the button was pressed (active quit condition) or released (passive quit condition). In other words, half of the participants stopped the movie by pressing down on a button, whereas the other half of the participants stopped the movie by taking their hand off of a button.

Participants were then shown a film that had been deliberately made to be dull and boring. The entire film consisted of an unchanging scene of a blank white wall with a table and a computer junction box in the foreground. The movie is just a picture of a wall and nothing ever happens, although participants were unaware of this fact and were motivated to keep watching to make sure that nothing did actually occur. Participants were told that after they stopped watching this video, they would see another video of highlights from a popular, humorous television program (*Saturday Night Live*). Participants therefore believed that after they finished watching the aversive, boring picture of a wall they would get to watch a pleasant, amusing video. This was done to give participants an added incentive to stop watching the boring video and also to remove the possibility that stopping the movie would immediately allow them to leave the experiment; although, to be sure, terminating the first movie would in fact bring them closer to their presumed goal of completing the experiment and being able to leave.[4]

The experimenter left the room, surreptitiously timing how long participants watched the video. When participants rang the buzzer (either by pressing or releasing the button, depending on the condition), the experimenter noted the time and re-entered the room. At this point, participants completed a brief questionnaire about their thoughts while watching the movie and their level of tiredness. Participants were then completely debriefed, thanked, and sent home.

Results

Manipulation Check

On a 25-point scale, participants assigned to the difficult-rules condition reported having to concentrate on the task of crossing off the e's more than participants assigned to the easy-rules condition, $t(63) = 2.30$, $p < .025$. Participants in the ego-depletion condition needed to concentrate more than participants in the no-depletion condition, which should have resulted in participants in the ego-depletion condition using more ego strength than participants in the no-depletion condition.

Further evidence was supplied by having participants rate their level of tiredness at the beginning of the experiment and at the end of the experiment. Participants in the ego-depletion condition became more tired as the experiment progressed compared with participants in the no-depletion condition, $t(83) = 2.79$, $p < .01$. Changes in level of tiredness can serve as a rough index of changes in effort exerted and therefore regulatory capacity (see Johnson, Saccuzzo, & Larson, 1995), and these results suggest that participants in the ego-depletion condition indeed used more regulatory strength than participants in the no-depletion condition.

Movie Watching

The main dependent measure was how long participants watched the boring movie. The total time participants spent watching the boring movie was analyzed in a 2 (rules) × 2 (button position) ANOVA. Consistent with the hypothesis, the two-way interaction between depletion task rules (depletion vs no depletion) and what participants did to quit watching the movie (active quit vs passive quit) was significant, $F(1, 80) = 5.64$, $p < .025$.

A planned comparison confirmed that participants under ego depletion watched more of the movie when quitting required an active response than when quitting involved a passive response, $F(1, 80) = 7.21$, $p < .01$. The corresponding contrast in the no-depletion condition found no difference in movie duration as a function of which response was active versus passive, $F(1, 80) = 0.46$, ns. Thus, participants who were depleted were more likely to take the passive route compared with participants who were not as depleted.

Additionally, there was a strong trend among participants who had to make an active response in order to quit: They watched the movie longer when they were in the ego-depletion condition than in the no-depletion condition, $F(1, 80) = 3.35$, $p < .07$. In other words, when participants had to initiate an action to quit, they tended to watch the movie longer when they were depleted than when they were not depleted. Participants who had to release the button to quit tended to stop watching the movie sooner when they were depleted than when they were not depleted, although this was not statistically significant, $F(1, 80) = 2.33$, $p < .15$. Participants who had to do less work to quit tended to quit sooner when they were depleted than when they were not depleted.

Discussion

The results of Experiment 4 provide further support for the hypothesis of ego depletion, insofar as ego depletion increased subsequent passivity. We noted that previous studies have found a passive-option effect, according to which a given option is chosen more when it requires a passive response than when it requires an active response. In the present study, ego depletion mediated the passive-option effect.

Experiment 4 manipulated ego depletion by having people complete a complex task that required careful monitoring of multiple rules and frequent altering of one's responses—more specifically, they were instructed to cross out every instance of the letter e in a text except when various other conditions were met, in which case they had to override the simple response of crossing out the *e*. These people subsequently showed greater passivity in terms of how long they watched a boring movie. They watched it longer when continuing was passive (and stopping required an active response) than when continuing required active responses (and stopping would be passive). Without ego depletion, we found no evidence of the passive-option effect: People watched the movie for about the same length of time regardless of whether stopping or continuing required the active response.

Thus, Experiment 4 found the passive-option effect only under ego depletion. That is, only when people had completed an initial task requiring concentration and careful monitoring of one's own responses in relation to rules did people favour the passive option (regardless of which option was passive). These findings suggest that people are less inclined to make active responses following ego depletion. Instead, depleted people are more prone to continue doing what is easiest, as if carried along by inertia.

Earlier, we suggested that the results of Experiment 2 indicated that choice depleted the ego. It might seem contradictory to suggest that passive choice does not draw on the same resource, but in fact we think the results of the two studies are quite parallel. The procedures of Experiment 2 involved active choice, insofar as the person thought about and consented to a particular behaviour. The no-choice condition corresponded to passive choice in an important sense, because people did implicitly have the option of refusing to make the assigned counterattitudinal speech, but they were not prompted by the experimenter to go through an inner debate and decision process. The active choices in Experiment 4 required the self to abandon the path of least resistance and override any inertia that was based on how the situation was set up, and so it required the self to do something. Thus, the high- and low-choice conditions of Experiment 2 correspond to the active and passive options of Experiment 4. Only active choice draws on the self's volitional resource.

General Discussion

The present investigation began with the idea that the self expends some limited resource, akin to energy or strength, when it engages in acts of volition. To explore this possibility, we tested the hypothesis that acts of choice and self-control would cause ego depletion: Specifically, after one initial act of volition, there would be less of this resource available for subsequent ones. The four experiments reported in this article provided support for this view.

Experiment 1 examined self-regulation in two seemingly unrelated spheres. In the key condition, people resisted the impulse to eat tempting chocolates and made themselves eat radishes instead. These people subsequently gave up much faster on a difficult, frustrating puzzle task than did people who had been able to indulge the same impulse to eat chocolate. (They also gave up earlier than people who had not been tempted.) It takes self-control to resist temptation, and it takes self-control to make oneself keep trying at a frustrating task. Apparently both forms of self-control draw on the same limited resource, because doing one interferes with subsequent efforts at the other.

Experiment 2 examined whether an act of personal, responsible choice would have the same effect. It did. People who freely, deliberately consented to make a counterattitudinal speech gave up quickly on the same frustrating task used in Experiment 1. Perhaps surprisingly, people who freely and deliberately consented to make a pro-attitudinal speech likewise gave up quickly, which is consistent with the pattern of ego depletion. In contrast, people who expected to make the counterattitudinal speech under low-choice conditions showed no drop in persistence, as compared with no-speech controls.

Thus, it was the act of responsible choice, and not the particular behaviour chosen, that depleted the self and reduced subsequent persistence. Regardless of whether the speech was consistent with their beliefs (to hold tuition down) or contrary to them (to raise tuition), what mattered was whether they made a deliberate act of choice to perform the behaviour. Making either choice used up some resource and left them subsequently with less of whatever they needed to persist at a difficult, frustrating task. The effects of making a responsible choice were quite similar to the effects of resisting temptation in Experiment 1.

Experiment 3 was designed to address the alternative explanation that ego depletion actually improved subsequent self-regulation, insofar as giving up early on unsolvable problems could be considered as an adaptive response. In Experiment 3, the dependent variable was task performance on solvable puzzles. Ego depletion resulting from an exercise in affect regulation impaired performance on that task.

We had shown (in Experiment 2) that ego-depletion effects carried over from responsible decision making to have an impact on self-regulation. Experiment 4 was designed to show the effect in the opposite direction, namely that prior exertion of self-regulation would have an impact on decision making. To do this, we measured the degree of predominance of the passive option. People were presented with a choice situation in which they could respond either actively or passively. We varied the response format so that the meaning of the passive versus active response was exchanged in a counterbalanced fashion. Prior ego depletion (created by having people do a task that required monitoring their own behaviour and multiple, overriding rules) increased people's tendency to use the passive response.

The assumption underlying Experiment 4 was that active responding draws on the same resource that the self uses to make responsible decisions and exert self-control. When that resource is depleted, apparently, people have less of it available to make active responses. Therefore, they become more passive.

Taken together, these four studies point toward a broad pattern of ego depletion. In each of them, an initial act of volition was followed by a decrement in some other sphere of volition. We found that an initial act of self-control impaired subsequent self-control (Study 1), that making a responsible decision impaired subsequent self-control (Study 2), that self-control lowered performance on a task that required self-control (Study 3), and that an initial act of self-control led to increased passivity (Study 4).

The procedures used in these four studies were deliberately made to be quite different. We have no way of directly measuring the internal resource that the self uses for making decisions or regulating itself. Hence, it seemed important to demonstrate ego depletion in circumstances as diverse as possible, in order to rule out the possibility that results could be artifacts of a particular method or a particular sphere of volition. Our view is that the convergence of findings across the four studies is more persuasive evidence than any of the individual findings.

Alternative Explanations

It must be acknowledged that the present studies provided no direct measures of the limited resource and hence no direct evidence that some inner quantity is diminished by acts of volition. The view that the active self involves some limited resource is thus an inference based on behavioural observations. It is therefore especially necessary to consider possible alternative interpretations of the effects we have shown.

One alternative view is that some form of negative affect caused participants in this research to give up early on the frustrating task. The task was, after all, designed to be frustrating or discouraging, insofar as it was unsolvable. It seems plausible that depression or other negative emotions might cause people to stop working at a task.

Although negative affect can undoubtedly affect persistence, the present pattern of results does not seem susceptible to an explanation on the basis of negative affect, for several reasons. We measured negative affect repeatedly and did not find it to differ significantly among the conditions in the various experiments. Moreover, in Experiment 3, we found identical effects regardless of whether the person was trying to stifle a positive or a negative emotion. Our work converges with other evidence that mood effects cannot explain after-effects of stress (Cohen, 1980).

A second alternative explanation would be that the results were due to cognitive dissonance, especially insofar as several of the procedures required counterattitudinal behaviour such as eating radishes instead of chocolate or refusing to laugh at a funny movie. Indeed, Experiment 2 included a condition that used a dissonance procedure, namely having people consent (under high choice) to record a speech in favour of a big tuition increase, contrary to the private beliefs of nearly all participants. Still, dissonance does not seem to provide a full explanation of the present effects. There is no apparent reason that dissonance should reduce persistence on an unrelated, subsequent task. Moreover, Experiment 2 found nearly identical effects of choosing a pro-attitudinal behaviour as for choosing a counterattitudinal behaviour, whereas dissonance should only arise in the latter condition.

A variation on the first two alternate explanations is that arousal might have mediated the results. For example, cognitive dissonance has been shown to be arousing (Zanna & Cooper, 1974), and possibly some participants simply felt too aroused to sit there and keep struggling with the unsolvable problems. Given the variations and non-linearities as to how arousal affects task performance, the decrement in anagram performance in Experiment 3 might also be attributed to arousal. Our data do, however, contradict the arousal explanation in two ways. First, self-report measures of arousal repeatedly failed to show any effects. Second, high arousal should presumably produce more activity rather than passivity, but the effects of ego depletion in Experiment 4 indicated an increase in passivity. If participants were more aroused, they should not have also become more passive as a result.

As already noted, the first two experiments were susceptible to a third alternative explanation that quitting the unsolvable problems was actually an adaptive, rational act of good self-regulation instead of a sign of self-regulation failure. This interpretation assumes that participants recognized that the problems were unsolvable and so chose rationally not to waste any more time on them. This conclusion was contradicted by the evidence from the debriefing sessions, in which participants consistently expressed surprise when they learned that the problems had been unsolvable. More important, Experiment 3 countered that alternative explanation by showing that ego depletion produced decrements in performance of solvable problems.

Another explanation, based on equity considerations, would suggest that experimental participants arrive with an implicit sense of the degree of obligation they owe to the researchers and are unwilling to do more. In this view, for example, a person might feel that she has done enough by making herself eat radishes instead of chocolates and therefore feels that she does not owe the experimenter maximal exertion on subsequent tasks. Although there is no evidence for such a view, it could reasonably cover Experiments 1 and 3. It has more difficulty with Experiment 4, because someone who felt he had already done enough during the highly difficult version of the initial task would presumably be less willing to sit longer during a boring movie, which is the opposite of what happened in the active-quit condition. Experiment 2 also is difficult to reconcile with this alternative explanation, because the participants did not actually complete any initial task. (They merely agreed to one.) Moreover, in that study, the effects of agreeing to make a pro-attitudinal speech were the same as the effects of agreeing to make a counterattitudinal speech, whereas an equity calculation would almost surely assume that agreeing to make the counterattitudinal speech would be a much greater sacrifice.

Implications

The present results could potentially have implications for self-theory. The pattern of ego depletion suggests that some internal resource is used by the self to make decisions, respond actively, and exert self-control. It appears, moreover, that the same resource is used for all of these, as indicated by the carry-over patterns we found (i.e., exertion in one sphere leads to decrements in others). Given the pervasive importance of choice, responsibility, and self-control, this resource might well be an important aspect of the self. Most recent research on the self has featured cognitive representations and interpersonal roles, and the present research does not in any way question the value of that work, but it does suggest augmenting the cognitive and interpersonal aspects of self with an appreciation of this volitional resource. The operation of the volitional, agentic, controlling aspect of the self may require an energy model.

Moreover, this resource appears to be quite surprisingly limited. In Study 1, for example, a mere five minutes of resisting temptation in the form of chocolate caused a reduction by half in how long people made themselves keep trying at unsolvable puzzles. It seems surprising to suggest that a few minutes of a laboratory task, especially one that was not described as excessively noxious or strenuous, would seriously deplete some important aspect of the self. Thus, these studies suggest that whatever is involved in choice and self-control is both an important and very limited resource. The activities of the self should perhaps be understood in general as having to make the most of a scarce and precious resource.

The limited nature of this resource might conceivably help explain several surprising phenomena that have been studied in recent years. A classic article by Burger (1989) documented a broad range of exceptions to the familiar, intuitively appealing notion that people generally seek

and desire control. Under many circumstances, Burger found, people relinquish or avoid control, and moreover, even under ordinary circumstances, there is often a substantial minority of people who do not want control. The ego-depletion findings of the present investigation suggest that exerting control uses a scarce and precious resource, and the self may learn early on to conserve that resource. Avoiding control under some circumstances may be a strategy for conservation.

Bargh (1997) has recently shown that the scope of automatic responses is far wider than many theories have assumed and, indeed, that even when people seem to be consciously making controlled responses, they may in fact be responding automatically to subtle cues (see also Bargh, 1982, 1994). Assuming that the self is the controller of controlled processes, it is not surprising that controlled processes should be confined to a relatively small part of everyday functioning, because they are costly. Responding in a controlled (as opposed to automatic) fashion would cause ego depletion and leave the self potentially unable to respond to a subsequent emergency or to regulate itself. Hence, staying in the automatic realm would help conserve this resource.

It is also conceivable that ego depletion is central to various patterns of psychological difficulties that people experience, especially ones that require unusual exertions of affect regulation, choice, or other volition. Burnout, learned helplessness, and similar patterns of pathological passivity might have some element of ego depletion. Coping with trauma may be difficult precisely because the self's volitional resources were depleted by the trauma but are needed for recovery. Indeed, it is well established that social support helps people recover from trauma, and it could be that the value of social support lies partly in the way other people take over the victim's volitional tasks (ranging from affect regulation to making dinner), thus conserving the victim's resources or allowing them time to replenish. On the darker side, it may be that highly controlled people who seem to snap and abruptly perpetrate acts of violence or outrage may be suffering from some abrupt depletion that has undermined the control they have maintained, possibly for years, over these destructive impulses. These possible implications lie far beyond the present data, however.

We acknowledge that we do not have a clear understanding of the nature of this resource. We can say this much: The resource functions to connect abstract principles, standards, and intentions to overt behaviour. It has some link to physical tiredness but is not the same as it. The resource seems to have a quantitative continuum, like a strength. We find it implausible that ego depletion would have no physiological aspect or correlates at all, but we are reluctant to speculate about what physiological changes would be involved. The ease with which we have been able to produce ego depletion using small laboratory manipulations suggests that the extent of the resource is quite limited, which implies that it would be seriously inadequate for directing all of a person's behaviour, so conscious, free choice must remain at best restricted to a very small proportion of human behaviour. (By the same token, most behaviour would have to be automatic instead of controlled, assuming that controlled processes depend on this limited resource.) Still, as we noted at the outset, even a small amount of this resource would be extremely adaptive in enabling human behaviour to become flexible, varied, and able to transcend the pattern of simply responding to immediate stimuli.

Concluding Remarks

Our results suggest that a broad assortment of actions make use of the same resource. Acts of self-control, responsible decision making, and active choice seem to interfere with other such acts that follow soon after. The implication is that some vital resource of the self becomes depleted by such acts of volition. To be sure, we assume that this resource is commonly replenished, although the factors that might hasten or delay the replenishment remain unknown, along with the precise nature of this resource. If further work can answer such questions, it promises to shed considerable light on human agency and the mechanisms of control over self and world.

For now, however, two final implications of the present evidence about ego depletion patterns deserve reiterating. On the negative side, these results point to a potentially serious constraint on the human capacity for control (including self-control) and deliberate decision making. On the positive side, they point toward a valuable and powerful feature of human selfhood.

Notes

1. These researchers also showed that an illusion of controllability eliminated this effect. From our perspective, this implies that part of the stress involves the threat or anticipation of continued aversive stimulation, which the illusion of controllability dispelled. In any case, it is plausible that the psychic cost was paid in terms of affect regulation, that is, making oneself submit and accept the aversive, unpredictable stimulation.

2. As this article went to press, we were notified that this experiment had been independently replicated by Timothy J. Howe, of Cole Junior High School in East Greenwich, Rhode Island, for his science fair project. His results conformed almost exactly to ours, with the exception that mean persistence in the chocolate condition was slightly (but not significantly) higher than in the control condition. These converging results strengthen confidence in the present findings.

3. The differences between the control condition and the two high-choice conditions failed to reach significance if we used the error term from the ANOVA as the pooled variance estimate. The pro-attitudinal-choice condition did differ from the control condition in a standard t test using only the variance in those two cells, $r(18) = 2.94$, $p < .01$. The counterattitudinal-choice condition differed marginally from the no-speech control using this latter method, $t(18) = 1.71$, $p = .105$. The high

variance in the counterattitudinal-no-choice condition entailed that it also differed only marginally from the counterattitudinal-choice condition if the actual variance in those cells was used rather than the error term, $r(17) = 1.90$, $p = .07$.

4. Of course, participants were informed that they were free to leave at any time. Still, most participants preferred to complete the procedure and leave the experiment having accomplished something, as opposed to leaving in the middle of the procedure.

Discussion Questions

1. What are the three models of self-regulation that Experiment 1 attempts to test against one another?
2. What predictions might Baumeister and colleagues make regarding who will perform better than whom on Mischel, Shoda, and Rodriguez's 'marshmallow task'? (See the next reading in this Unit.)
3. Try to think of different types of self-regulatory tasks. Do you think the limited resource idea Baumeister et al. describe holds equally for each?

18. Delay of Gratification in Children

Walter Mischel, Yuichi Shoda, and Monica L. Rodriguez

□ ■ □

Editor's Introduction

Every day we are faced with countless versions of the same dilemma: We can opt for a dose of short-term pleasure now or persevere in exchange for a bigger reward in the future. For example, university students are continually faced with the opportunity to (a) watch TV now or (b) continue studying and reap the rewards associated with higher grades later. Failure to delay gratification can be disastrous both in the context of a single episode or as a chronic tendency. For example, a single failure to resist the temptation to buy an appealing but too-expensive home may lead a person into burdensome debt or bankruptcy. It is also evident that a chronic inability to delay gratification is a predictor of behavioural problems, such as criminality and addiction.

Are some people simply endowed with a superior ability to delay gratification? Walter Mischel, Yuichi Shoda, and their colleagues have devoted decades to studying why some people seem more able than others to delay gratification. The present article, published in *Science* in 1989, summarizes research (mostly with children) that had been conducted to that point on the cognitive, emotional, and motivational forces at play when people navigate the 'marshmallow' dilemma.

One of the optimistic findings from their research has been that, although there may be some genetic contribution to one's ability to delay gratification, there are also a range of cognitive manoeuvres that anyone can learn to dramatically improve performance. For example, children who were taught to imagine that pretzels were sticks of wood were able to wait significantly longer for the larger reward than those who were told to focus on the pretzels' appealing, consummatory properties. More recent research has begun to isolate particular early learning experiences that may play a key role in fostering or impairing the skills necessary to delay gratification effectively (e.g., Eigsti et al., 2006; Rodriguez et al., 2005).

Mischel and colleagues' research has shown that one reason for failure to delay has to do with people's erroneous folk beliefs about what works. For example, many people believe that keeping the forbidden fruit in sight can help individuals to delay gratification because it provides some sort of partial satisfaction, or perhaps because it reminds people to 'keep their eye on the prize'. In fact, the opposite is true: Participants who had the short-term reward in sight, but covered with a cloth, dramatically out-waited those who had the short-term reward in sight, uncovered. Thus, part of the solution to teaching people to delay gratification is simply to disabuse people of their faulty theories about how self-regulation works.

□ ■ □

For almost a century the infant has been characterized as impulse-driven, pressing for tension reduction, unable to delay gratification, oblivious to reason and reality, and ruled entirely by a pleasure principle that demands immediate satisfaction. The challenge has been to clarify how individuals, while remaining capable of great impulsivity, also become able to control actions for the sake of temporally distant consequences and goals, managing at least sometimes to forgo more immediate gratifications to take account of anticipated outcomes. The nature of this future-oriented self-control, which develops over time and then coexists with more impetuous behaviours, has intrigued students of development, who have made it central in theories of socialization and in the very definition of the 'self'. Such goal-directed self-imposed delay of gratification is widely presumed to be important in the prevention of serious developmental and mental health problems, including those directly associated with lack of resilience, conduct disorders, low social responsibility, and a variety of addictive and antisocial behaviours.

To explain how people manage to exercise self-control, concepts like 'willpower' or 'ego strength' are readily invoked, although these terms provide little more than labels for the phenomena to which they point. Some people adhere to difficult diets, or give up cigarettes after years of smoking them addictively, or continue to work and wait for distant goals even when tempted sorely to quit, whereas others fail in such attempts to better regulate themselves in spite of affirming the same initial intentions. Yet the same person who exhibits self-control in one situation may fail to do so in another, even when it appears to be highly similar. The research program reviewed here addresses the nature of these individual differences, the psychological processes that underlie them, and the conditions in which they may be predictable.

Overview

We review findings on an essential feature of self-regulation: postponing immediately available gratification in order to attain delayed but more valued outcomes. Studies in which four-year-old children attempt this type of future-oriented self-control reveal that in some laboratory situations individual differences in delay behaviour significantly predict patterns of competence and coping assessed more than a decade later. Experiments in the same laboratory situations have identified specific cognitive and attentional processes that allow the young child to sustain goal-directed delay of gratification even under difficult, frustrating conditions.

We begin with a summary of major individual differences associated with this type of self-regulation early in life, and the long-term developmental outcomes that they predict. Then we examine the specific processes that seem to underlie effective self-imposed delay of gratification in young children, as revealed by the experimental studies. These results, in turn, pointed to the types of preschool delay situations diagnostic for predicting aspects of cognitive and social competence in adolescence. Finally, we consider the development of the child's understanding of self-control and the concurrent links found among components of self-regulation in children with behavioural problems.

Measuring Self-Control: From Choice to Execution

Two complementary methods were used to investigate delay of gratification in the research program reviewed here. Initially, preferences for delayed, more valuable versus immediate but less valuable outcomes were studied as choice decisions. In this approach, individuals choose under realistic conditions among outcomes that vary in value and in the expected duration of time before they become available. Sets of such choices were given to people from a wide range of sociocultural backgrounds, family structure, and economic circumstances. As expected, these choices are affected predictably by the anticipated delay time and the subjective value of the alternatives. For example, preferences for delayed rewards decrease when the required time for their attainment increases and increase with the expectation that the delayed outcomes will occur. The choice to delay (a) increases with the values of the delayed rewards relative to the immediate ones; (b) increases with the subject's age; and (c) is susceptible to a variety of social influences, including the choice behaviour and attitudes that other people display. Choices to delay were related significantly to a number of personal characteristics assessed at about the same time. For example, children who tend to prefer delayed rewards also tend to be more intelligent, more likely to resist temptation, to have greater social responsibility, and higher achievement strivings. The obtained concurrent associations are extensive, indicating that such preferences reflect a meaningful dimension of individual differences, and point to some of the many determinants and correlates of decisions to delay.[1]

As efforts at self-reform so often attest, however, decisions to forgo immediate gratification for the sake of later consequences (e.g., by dieting) are readily forgotten or strategically revised when one experiences the frustration of actually having to execute them. Because intentions to practise self-control frequently dissolve in the face of more immediate temptations, it is also necessary to go beyond the study of initial decisions to delay gratification and to examine how young children become able to sustain delay of gratification as they actually try to wait for the outcomes they want. For this purpose, a second method was devised and used to test preschool children in the Stanford University community.

In this method, the experimenter begins by showing the child some toys, explaining they will play with them later (so that ending the delay leads to uniform positive consequences). Next, the experimenter teaches a game in which he or she has to leave the room and comes back immediately when the child summons by ringing a bell. Each child then is shown a pair of treats (such as snacks, small toys, or tokens) which differ in value, established through pretesting to be desirable and of age-appropriate interest (e.g., one marshmallow vs two; two small cookies vs five pretzels). The children are told that to attain the one they prefer they have to wait until the experimenter returns but that they are free to end the waiting period whenever they signal; if they do, however, they will get the less preferred object and forgo the other one. The items in the pair are selected to be sufficiently close in value to create a conflict situation for young children between the temptation

to stop the delay and the desire to persist for the preferred outcome when the latter requires delay. After children understand the contingency, they are left on their own during the delay period while their behaviour is observed unobtrusively, and the duration of their delay is recorded until they terminate or the experimenter returns (typically after 15 minutes). With this method, 'self-imposed delay of gratification' was investigated both as a psychological process in experiments that varied relevant features in the delay situation and as a personal characteristic in studies that examined the relation between children's delay behaviour and their social and cognitive competencies.

A recent follow-up study of a sample of these children found that those who had waited longer in this situation at four years of age were described more than 10 years later by their parents as adolescents who were more academically and socially competent than their peers and more able to cope with frustration and resist temptation. At statistically significant levels, parents saw these children as more verbally fluent and able to express ideas; they used and responded to reason, were attentive and able to concentrate, to plan, and to think ahead, and were competent and skillful. Likewise they were perceived as able to cope and deal with stress more maturely and seemed more self-assured.[2] In some variations of this laboratory situation, seconds of delay time in preschool also were significantly related to their Scholastic Aptitude Test (SAT) scores when they applied to college. The demonstration of these enduring individual differences in the course of development, as well as the significance attributed to purposeful self-imposed delay of gratification theoretically, underline the need to understand and specify the psychological processes that allow the young child to execute this type of self-regulation in the pursuit of desired outcomes.

Effects of Attention to the Rewards

Theoretical analyses of the delay process have assumed for almost a century that the individual's attention during the delay period is especially important in the development of the ability to delay gratification. William James, noting a relation between attention and self-control as early as 1890, contended that attention is the crux of self-control. Beginning with Freud, it has been proposed that attention to the delayed gratifications in thought, mental representation, or anticipation provides the mechanism that allows the young child to bridge the temporal delay required for their attainment. When children become able to represent the anticipated gratifications mentally, it was reasoned, they become able to delay for them by focusing on these thoughts or fantasies, thereby inhibiting impulsive actions. Some learning theorists also have speculated that the cognitive representation of rewards allows some sort of anticipatory or symbolic covert reinforcement that helps sustain effort and goal-directed behaviour while external reinforcement is delayed.

In spite of the fact that rewards were given paramount importance in psychological attempts to explain the determinants of behaviour, their role in the delay process had remained mostly speculative because of the difficulty of objectively studying thoughts about rewards, particularly in young children. To study how their thinking about the rewards affects self-imposed delay, preschool children in the Stanford University community were assessed in several variations of the self-imposed delay situation described earlier. If thinking about the rewards facilitates delay, then children who are exposed to the rewards or encouraged to think about them should wait longer. The first study varied systematically whether or not the rewards were available for attention while the children were waiting. For example, in one condition they waited with both the immediate (less preferred) and the delayed (more preferred) rewards facing them, exposed. In a second condition, both rewards were also present but obscured from sight (covered), and in two other conditions either the delayed reward only or the immediately available reward was exposed during the delay period. The results were

the opposite of those the investigators predicted: attention to the rewards consistently and substantially decreased delay time instead of increasing it. Preschool children waited an average of more than 11 minutes when no rewards were exposed, but they waited less than 6 minutes on average when any of the rewards were exposed during delay.

To test the effects of thinking about the rewards more directly, in a second study different types of thoughts were suggested to orient the children's attention with regard to the rewards. The results showed that when preschoolers were cued to think about the rewards when waiting, delay time was short, regardless of whether the objects were exposed or covered (Figure 18.1). When distracting ('fun') thoughts were suggested, children waited for more than 10 minutes, whether or not the rewards were exposed. On the other hand, when no thoughts were suggested, delay time was greatly reduced by reward exposure, confirming the earlier findings. Distracting thoughts counteracted the strong effects of exposure to the actual rewards, allowing children to wait about as long as they did when the rewards were covered and no thoughts were suggested. In contrast, when the rewards were covered and the children were cued to think about them, the delay time was as short as when the rewards were exposed and no distractions were suggested.[3, 4] Thus, the original prediction that attention and thought directed to the reward objects would enhance voluntary delay was consistently undermined.

Observation of children's spontaneous behaviour during the delay process also suggested that those who were most effective in sustaining delay seemed to avoid looking at the rewards deliberately, for example, covering their eyes with their hands and resting their heads on their arms. Many children generated their own diversions: they talked quietly to themselves, sang, created games with their hands and feet, and even tried to go to sleep during the waiting time. Their attempts to delay gratification seemed to be facilitated by external conditions or by self-directed efforts to

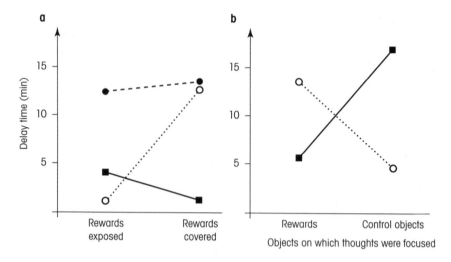

Figure 18.1

(a) Average delay time shown by 52 Stanford preschoolers when different types of thoughts were suggested (●, fun thoughts; ■, thoughts about the rewards; O, no thoughts suggested) and the rewards were exposed or covered.

(b) Delay time as a function of objects on which thoughts were focused (rewards versus comparable control objects) and type of cognitive representation in thoughts (■, arousing, vs O, abstract). All 48 Stanford preschool children were facing the exposed rewards.

reduce their frustration during the delay period by selectively directing their attention and thoughts away from the rewards. However, it also seemed unlikely that sheer suppression or distraction from the frustration caused by the situation is the only determinant of this type of self-control. Indeed, when certain types of thoughts are focused on the rewards they can facilitate self-control substantially, even more than distraction does, as the next set of experiments found.

From Distraction to Abstraction

The results so far show that exposure to the actual rewards or cues to think about them undermine delay, but the studies did not consider directly the possible effects of images or symbolic representations of rewards. Yet, it may be these latter types of representation—the images of the outcomes, rather than the rewards themselves—that mediate the young child's ability to sustain delay of gratification. To explore this possibility, the effects of exposure to realistic images of the rewards were examined by replicating the experiments on the effects of reward exposure with slide-presented images of the rewards. It was found that although exposure to the actual rewards during the delay period makes waiting difficult for young children, exposure to images of the rewards had the opposite effect, making it easier. Children who saw images of the rewards they were waiting for (shown life-size on slides) delayed twice as long as those who viewed slides of comparable control objects that were not the rewards for which they were waiting, or who saw blank slides. Thus, different modes of presenting rewards (i.e., real versus symbolic) may either hinder or enhance self-control.

To test more directly the effects of the cognitive representations of rewards on delay behaviour, preschool children were taught to transform 'in their heads' the stimuli present during delay (real rewards or pictures of them) by turning real rewards into pictures and pictures into real rewards in their imagination. How the children represented the rewards cognitively was a much more potent determinant of their delay behaviour than the actual reward stimulus that they were facing. For example, children facing pictures of the rewards delayed almost 18 minutes, but they waited less than six minutes when they pretended that the real rewards, rather than the pictures, were in front of them. Likewise, even when facing the real rewards they waited almost 18 minutes when they imagined the rewards as if they were pictures.

This pattern of results may reflect two different aspects of reinforcing (rewarding) stimuli that, in turn, may have completely different effects on self-control behaviour. Consistent with earlier work, we hypothesized that stimuli can be represented both in an arousing (consummatory) and in an abstract (non-consummatory) informative manner. In an arousing representation, the focus is on the motivating, 'hot' qualities of the stimulus that tend to elicit completion of the action sequence associated with it, such as eating a food or playing with a toy. In an abstract representation the focus is on the more informative, 'cool', symbolic aspects of the stimulus, for example, as in a cue or reminder of the contingency or reason for delaying the action sequence associated with it.

Specifically, it was suggested to one group of children that they could focus their thoughts on the arousing qualities of the rewards (such as the pretzel's crunchy, salty taste), and to another group of children that they could focus on the reward's abstract qualities and associations (by thinking about pretzel sticks, for example, as long, thin brown logs). Two other groups were given the same type of suggestions as to how they could think while waiting, but directed at comparable control objects that were not the rewards. When encouraged to focus on the abstract qualities of the rewards, children waited an average of more than 13 minutes, but they waited less than five minutes

when the same type of thoughts were directed at the comparable objects that were not the rewards, suggesting that the abstract representation of the actual reward objects provides more than just distraction.

The longest mean delay time (almost 17 minutes) occurred when the suggested thoughts were also about control objects but with regard to their arousing qualities (e.g., children waiting for marshmallows who had been cued to think about the salty, crunchy taste of pretzels). Thus, while hot ideation about the rewards made delay difficult, such ideation directed at comparable objects that are not the rewards for which one is waiting may provide very good distraction. The results support the view that attention to the rewards may have either a facilitating or an interfering effect on the duration of delay, depending on whether the focus is arousing or abstract.

The experimental results, taken collectively, help specify how young children can become able to sustain self-imposed delay gratification for substantial periods. Delay is difficult for the preschooler when the rewards are exposed, unless distractions are provided or self-generated. Suggestions to think about the rewards, or attention to them, can facilitate or interfere with delay, depending on whether the rewards are represented in ways that lead to a focus on their arousing or abstract features. An abstract focus on the rewards can help self-imposed delay even more than comparable distractions; an arousing focus makes delay exceedingly difficult. How the child represents the rewards cognitively in this regard, rather than whether they are exposed physically or as images, crucially influences the duration of delay.

Preschool Delay Conditions for Predicting Long-Term Developmental Outcomes

On the basis of the experimental research reviewed so far, it also becomes possible to specify the types of preschool delay conditions in which the child's behaviour will be more likely to predict relevant long-term developmental outcomes. The significant links noted earlier between delay of gratification at age four years and adolescent competence did not take account of the particular delay conditions. When the rewards are exposed, delay becomes highly frustrative for preschoolers, so that to sustain their goal-directed waiting they must use effective strategies, for example, by distracting themselves or by representing the rewards cognitively in an abstract, 'cool' way. When preschoolers are not given strategies for sustaining delay but the rewards are exposed, they must generate and execute such strategies on their own to delay, and therefore their behaviour should reveal most clearly individual differences in this type of competence. To the degree that this ability is stable and has enduring consequences for adaptation, we expected that preschool delay time when the rewards are exposed and no strategies are suggested would be diagnostic for predicting relevant developmental outcomes. In contrast, when the rewards are obscured, delay behaviour was not expected to reflect children's ability to generate effective self-control strategies because that situation does not require the use of such strategies.

These expectations were supported in another follow-up study of the Stanford preschool children, in which we increased the sample of respondents so that the role of conditions could be analyzed in relation to long-term outcomes. To obtain a more objective measure of cognitive academic competencies and school-related achievements in adolescence, we also included Scholastic Aptitude Test (SAT) scores. In conditions in which the rewards were exposed and no strategies were supplied, those children who delayed longer as preschoolers were rated in adolescence by their parents as significantly more attentive and able to concentrate, competent, planful, and intelligent. They also were seen as more able to pursue goals and to delay gratification, better in self-control, more able to resist temptation, to tolerate frustration, and to cope

maturely with stress. Beyond parental ratings, in the same conditions SAT scores were available for 35 children, and both their verbal and quantitative SAT scores were significantly related to seconds of preschool delay time. The linear regression slope predicting SAT verbal scores from seconds of preschool delay time was 0.10 with a standard error of 0.04; for predicting SAT quantitative scores, the slope was 0.13 with a standard error of 0.03. The correlations were 0.42 for SAT verbal scores and 0.57 for SAT quantitative scores. In contrast, individual differences in delay behaviour when the rewards were obscured did not reliably predict either parental ratings or SAT performance.

The significant correlations between preschool delay time and adolescent outcomes, spanning more than a decade, were relatively large compared to the typically low or negligible associations found when single measures of social behaviour are used to predict other behaviours, especially over a long developmental period. On the other hand, although the obtained significant associations are at a level that rivals many found between performances on intelligence tests repeated over this age span, most of the variance still remains unexplained. The small size of the SAT sample dictates special caution in these comparisons and underlines the need for replications, especially with other populations and at different ages.

As previously noted, preschool delay time in the diagnostic condition was significantly related not only to academic abilities of the sort assessed by the SAT but also to other indexes of competence. Even after statistically controlling for SAT scores, preschoolers who had delayed longer were later rated by parents as more able to cope with a number of social and personal problems, suggesting that the relation between preschool delay time and later parental judgments is not completely attributable to school-related competencies as measured by the SAT.

The causal links and mediating mechanisms underlying these long-term associations necessarily remain speculative, allowing many different interpretations. For example, an early family environment in which self-imposed delay is encouraged and modelled also may nurture other types of behaviour that facilitate the acquisition of social and cognitive skills, study habits, or attitudes which may be associated with obtaining higher scores on the SAT and more positive ratings by parents. It also seems reasonable, however, that children will have a distinct advantage beginning early in life if they use effective self-regulatory strategies to reduce frustration in situations in which self-imposed delay is required to attain desired goals. By using these strategies to make self-control less frustrating, these children can more easily persist in their efforts, becoming increasingly competent as they develop.

Of course, the self-regulatory strategies that have been described are not the only ones useful for sustaining goal-directed delay and effort. The particular strategies required depend on the type of delay situation, for example, self-imposed versus externally imposed delay. During the delay process children may use a variety of strategies, including self-instructions, rehearsal of the specific contingencies for goal attainment while avoiding an arousing focus on the rewards themselves, and self-monitoring of progress. Related research in variations of the delay of gratification situation with young children showed the value for self-control of specific, carefully rehearsed and elaborated plans for inhibiting temptations to terminate goal-directed efforts. Such plans are used spontaneously, in varying degree, even by preschool children. Similar self-regulatory strategies have been identified in research on the acquisition of cognitive skills for mastery of other tasks requiring self-control, like reading and impulse inhibition. It is also plausible that the specific competencies necessary for effective self-regulation are a component of a larger ability or set of abilities involving both cognitive and social knowledge and skills. Whereas self-regulatory competencies in the pursuit of goals are not even considered as a factor in traditional conceptions and tests of intelligence, they are directly relevant to more recent attempts to devise a theory of social intelligence that integrates findings from cognitive, social, and developmental psychology to thoroughly reconstruct the analysis of intelligent behaviour.

The Development of Knowledge about Effective Self-Regulatory Strategies

In the course of development, children show increasing understanding and awareness of the strategies that facilitate various kinds of self-control. In a sample of middle-class children in the Stanford community, from preschool through Grade 6, the children's knowledge of the strategies that might help during the delay process were assessed. The overall results indicate that four-year-olds often prefer the least effective strategies for self-imposed delay, thereby inadvertently making self-control exceedingly difficult for themselves. For example, they significantly prefer to expose the rewards during the delay period and to think about them (e.g., 'because it makes me feel good'), thus defeating their own effort to wait. Within a year, most children understand and choose more effective strategies. They soon prefer to obscure the temptations and consistently reject arousing thoughts about them as a strategy for self-control. At that age many begin to recognize the problem of increased temptation produced by thinking about the arousing attributes of the rewards and try to self-distract ('just sing a song'). They also start to see the value of self-instructions, focusing on the contingency and reiterating it ('I'll wait, so I can get the two marshmallows instead of one' or 'I'll say, "do not ring the bell" . . . If you ring the bell and the teacher comes in, I'll just get that one'). The self-control rule that does not seem to become available until some time between the third and sixth grades requires recognition of the value of abstract rather than arousing thoughts, suggesting possible links between the development of this type of understanding and the child's achieving operational thought in the Piagetian sense.

Extensions to Older Children at Risk

The research described so far specified some of the strategies that facilitate delay experimentally and summarized the development of children's growing knowledge and understanding of those strategies. However, the links between children's knowledge of effective strategies, their spontaneous use of such strategies when attempting to control themselves in the pursuit of delayed goals, and their success in sustaining delay remained unexamined. The delay process in older children with behaviour problems, such as aggressiveness, conduct disorders, or hyperactivity, has been surprisingly unstudied, although these are the very individuals for whom effective attention deployment and sustained delay of gratification are assumed to be especially difficult. So far, research on delay of gratification has concentrated on preschool children without known developmental risks. Therefore, a recent study extended the delay paradigm to a population of older children, described as having a variety of social adjustment difficulties, such as aggressiveness and withdrawal.

In this sample, ages six to 12 years, assessed in a summer residential treatment facility, children's knowledge of self-control processes was significantly correlated with duration of their self-imposed delay. For example, those who knew that an abstract rather than an arousing representation would make waiting easier also delayed longer. Similarly, the children's spontaneous attention deployment during the delay period was significantly related to their actual delay time: As the delay increased, those who were able to sustain self-control spent a higher proportion of the time distracting themselves from the frustrative situation than did those who terminated earlier. Even when controlling statistically for the effects of verbal intelligence, the relations among knowledge of self-control, spontaneous use of effective delay strategies, and duration of delay remained significant. In addition, those individuals who scored higher on these indexes of self-control in the delay situation, especially when the rewards were exposed, also were rated as significantly less aggressive throughout the summer. The overall findings obtained with older children at risk indicate that the cognitive attentional strategies that allow effective delay of gratification, as identified in the earlier experiments, also seem to be used spontaneously by individuals who delay longer.

Summary

Taken collectively, the results from the research programs we reviewed specify some of the cognitive processes that underlie this type of delay of gratification early in life. Whether or not attention to the rewards, or distraction from them, is the better strategy for sustaining self-control depends on how the rewards are represented cognitively. A focus on their arousing features makes self-control exceedingly difficult; a focus on their more abstract, informative features has the opposite effects. Moreover, the type of cognitive representation generated can overcome, and reverse, the effects of exposure to the rewards themselves.

Significant links were found between self-control behaviour as measured in this paradigm and relevant social and cognitive outcomes years later. The experimental research allowed identification of the conditions in which these long-term relations were most clearly visible. The child's spontaneous understanding of effective self-regulatory strategies also was found to develop in a clear age-related sequence. Finally, delay of gratification in the same paradigm with older children at risk showed the expected concurrent relations to knowledge of effective self-control strategies and spontaneous attention deployment while trying to exercise self-control. An unanswered question now is whether or not teaching delay of gratification skills and strategies of the sort identified to those who lack them, early in life, would in fact reduce later developmental risks such as school failure. Postponing gratification sometimes may be an unwise choice, but unless individuals have the competencies necessary to sustain delay when they want to do so, the choice itself is lost.

Notes

1. Researchers in other areas, beyond the scope of the present article, have pursue somewhat parallel problems in self-control. In one direction, a large operant conditioning literature has investigated self-control in lower organisms by using analogous situations to those in the present article. Typically, a pigeon in a Skinner box has to choose among alternatives varying in the amount and delay of the reinforcer. This research indicates that organisms sharply discount future rewards as a function of the temporal distance from the time of choice. Preference for a small, immediate reward, over a larger, more delayed one, reverts as the time between choice and delay of rewards increases. Moreover, by using analogues to the self-imposed delay of gratification situation described in this article, parallel results also were reported with pigeons. In a second direction, economists have studies how delay outcomes affect economic decisions and savings behaviour of humans, again with interesting parallels to the research reported here.

2. Studies following children's development over many years, using other measures of self-control requiring different types of delay of gratification, also found evidence of enduring psychological qualities. The particular qualities, however, depend on the specific type of delay behaviours sampled.

3. When the rewards were exposed, children cued to think about fun did not differ significantly from those who faced the covered rewards with no thoughts suggested or who were cued to think about fun. Delay time also was not significantly different for children waiting with the rewards exposed when no thoughts were suggested and those cued to think about the rewards.

4. When children waited in a similar self-imposed delay situation they also estimated the delay to be longer when the reward was present physically, supporting the interpretation that attention to the rewards in this situation increases frustration.

Discussion Questions

1. Psychological research often has a rather deterministic flavour: People are seen as reacting to stimuli more than they are seen as imposing their will on the situation. Does delaying gratification qualify as an exercise of free will? How might a strict determinist explain Mischel and colleagues' findings?

2. A common tactic that Mischel et al. suggest is cognitive reframing of the short-term reward so that the delicious, appetitive aspects are minimized and the 'cold', unappealing aspects are emphasized. But does the coward who runs away merely live to fight another day? In other words, if cognitively imagining pretzels as sticks causes you to delay longer, is it *really* self-regulation? What about those people who do the 'wrong' thing (e.g., focus on appetitive aspects) and *still* delay for a long time? Might that be a superior form of self-regulation?

3. The marshmallow test is only one kind of self-regulatory dilemma. What are some others? Do the tactics Mischel et al. suggest apply to these other examples equally well?

Unit Eight Further Reading

Research by Trope and Fishbach (2000) begins to delineate just how successful avoidance of temptation works. According to these researchers, one of the tricks people use is cognitive distortion of the type found in the articles in Unit 3 (on reward and punishment). Specifically, people increase their motivation to stick with a long-term task despite short-term pain by unwittingly raising the value of the long-term outcome. Thus, this reasoning can be considered as the mirror image of the reasoning about intrinsic motivation that Lepper and colleagues suggested people do in Unit 3. Lepper et al. (1973) argued that people reason as follows: 'The more wonderful the ultimate reward, the more awful the immediate task must be.' According to Trope and Fishbach, participants are deducing, 'The more awful the immediate task, the more wonderful the ultimate reward must be.' In both cases, basic reasoning is the platform onto which motivational bias is expressed. In the Trope and Fishbach case, however, this bias is a good thing; it's a critical tool in the toolbox that people deploy to 'keep their eye on the prize' as they navigate a challenging or distasteful task.

Trope, Y. & Fishbach, A. (2000). Counteractive self-control in overcoming temptation. *Journal of Personality and Social Psychology, 79,* 493–506.

As more and more information becomes known about the function of different systems in the brain, a good deal of research has begun to investigate brain systems implicated in self-regulation. Two good examples of this integration of mind and brain are:

Inzlicht, M. & Gutsell, J.N. (2007). Running on empty: Neural signals for self-control failure. *Psychological Science, 18,* 933–37.

Kerns, J.G., Cohen, J.D., MacDonald, A.W., III, Cho, R.Y., Stenger, V.A., & Carter, C.S. (2004). Anterior cingulate, conflict monitoring, and adjustments in control. *Science, 303,* 1023–1026.

Unit Nine

Other People as Motivational Information

The term *looking-glass self* was coined by Cooley (1902) to refer to the fact that, as inherently social creatures, our self-perceptions are highly influenced by the people around us. Even such apparently private judgments about, for example, how capable we think we are or how much effort to put into a task are expertly (though often unconsciously) calibrated against actual or imagined others. The readings in this Unit illustrate cornerstone phenomena relating to the concept of the looking-glass self.

Why is it that our judgments about ourselves depend so much on other people? Leon Festinger, in a landmark 1954 article, noted that people's self-judgments are often uncertain because they involve aspects that are difficult to measure ('Am I a kind person?' 'Am I a smart person?'). Festinger proposed that people solve this uncertainty by turning to others in their environment and engaging in a process of *social comparison*. By comparing themselves to others, people are able to see themselves in the larger context and thus gain more clarity about where exactly they stand. Since Festinger's day, generations of researchers have contributed important work to refining our understanding of the cognitive and motivational aspects of social comparison (e.g., Tesser, 1986; Lockwood & Kunda, 1997; Taylor & Lobel, 1989).

In the first article in this Unit, Baldwin and colleagues (1995) took this notion an important step further. They demonstrated that self-views can be systematically influenced by other people even outside of one's conscious awareness. When participants were exposed to subliminal images of a respected/feared authority figure, this caused them to become more self-critical. Thus, not only do people spontaneously 'check in' with others when forming judgments about themselves, they seem to do so in a highly efficient and automatic fashion. As you read the Baldwin et al. paper, keep in mind the following question: Why might such a skill be useful and adaptive?

A second context in which people use others as information is in group work. Does working on a collective task (e.g., building cars on an assembly line or playing violin in a symphony orchestra) lead to better or worse output than an equal number of people all working alone? One intuition might be that people would work harder when in a group because they are spurred on by the competition. An alternative thought might be the opposite: When working in a group, people take the opportunity to conserve their own individual energy as much as possible. Clearly, the answer to this question would have enormous implications for organizational management.

As described in the landmark article included in this Unit, Latané and colleagues have shown that groups often underperform compared to an equal number of people working alone, a phenomenon known as social loafing. Moreover, this effect appears to be due to lowered motivation rather than the possibility that groups are generally less co-ordinated and efficient than individuals. Instead, the presence of collective co-workers appears to serve as a (largely unconscious) signal to individuals that, in many cases, maximum effort is not needed.

In subsequent research, Williams and colleagues have demonstrated the other side of the coin: social compensation. In several studies, when participants expected their co-workers to be ineffective, people *increased* their effort and productivity compared to when working alone (e.g., Williams & Karau, 1991). Thus, it appears that people's mental calculations about effort expenditure are quite strategic: Rather than solely trying to 'slack off' whenever possible, people instead attempt to optimize the ratio between their input and the group's output (see Plaks & Higgins, 2000). Presumably, this is an adaptive skill; by withholding effort in some cases, one may be better positioned to intensify effort in others. This notion is consistent with expectancy-value theories of task effort, which postulate that people will exert high effort on a task only when they perceive their input to be necessary for obtaining the desired outcome (e.g., Heckhausen, 1977; Vroom, 1964). In other words, people engage in a remarkably sophisticated mental calibration process when determining how hard to try on any given group task.

19. Priming Relationship Schemas: My Adviser and the Pope Are Watching Me from the Back of My Mind

Mark W. Baldwin, Research Center for Group Dynamics
Suzanne E. Carrell, University of Waterloo
David F. Lopez, University of Waterloo

□ ■ □

Editor's Introduction

This article illustrates how human beings are continually thinking about other people. Perhaps more often than we realize, we invoke an imagined audience to guide our own behaviour. In fact, Baldwin et al. demonstrate that an imagined audience affects people's views of themselves even outside of conscious awareness.

According to Baldwin, Holmes, and others, our everyday social cognition relies heavily on 'relational schemas'. That is, when thinking about ourselves, we do not think *only* of ourselves. Instead, the mental representation of yourself is heavily intertwined with (a) a representation of important people in your life, and (b) a representation of 'self-with-other' (Baldwin, 1995). Importantly, these relational schemas are subject to the basic principles of construct accessibility (Higgins, 1996). That is, certain people—and our relationships with them—are always on our mind. Thus, thinking about yourself automatically activates thoughts about these other important people. Moreover, particular relationship schema content, even if it is not currently at the forefront of one's mind, can be brought to the forefront through subtle reminders. This is precisely what Baldwin and colleagues did in the studies presented here. They hypothesized that certain people (e.g., religious Catholics) will tend to think of themselves with respect to a respected/feared authority figure (the Pope). Thus, subliminally activating thoughts about the Pope will systematically influence the way they rate themselves. This is exactly what they found.

In more recent research, Fitzsimons and Bargh (2003) took this idea one step further. These researchers hypothesized that subliminally priming people with their relationship partner would activate the particular interpersonal goals that they typically pursue when actually in that person's presence. For example, in one study, participants were asked to think about (and answer written questions about) either a good friend or a co-worker who was not a friend. Afterwards, in an ostensibly unrelated task, participants were asked if in the future they would be willing to participate in a longer study of the same nature. The results showed that those who had been primed with thoughts about their friend expressed more willingness to help the researchers than those who had been primed with thoughts about their co-worker. According to Fitzsimons and Bargh, this is because the relational schema of one's friend contains a strong implicit aspect of helping and selflessness that the relational schema of one's co-worker does not. Thus, causing people to think about their friends automatically activates thoughts about helping.

□ ■ □

A person's sense of self at any given moment is surely influenced by a broad range of factors, including stable self-concepts, recent experiences, social roles, and various context effects. Many theorists (e.g., Mead, 1934; Sullivan, 1953), however, have held that the major determinant of how self is construed is how the person believes he or she would be regarded by significant others. Self-evaluation, for example, is assumed to involve a reflected appraisal process whereby self is assessed according to how significant others would likely respond.

The process of reflected appraisal is an ideal candidate for a social cognitive analysis, which ultimately could focus on how information about one's significant relationships is perceived, interpreted, stored, and recalled. The studies to be presented here represent a preliminary attempt at applying priming methodologies to a more modest goal, which was to examine how salient, internally represented interpersonal information can affect the experience of self.

Baldwin and Holmes (1987) used cognitive priming methodologies to assess the impact of internally represented significant others on the experience of self. In the context of a guided visualization experiment, undergraduate women subjects first visualized the faces of either two older members of their family (e.g., their parents) or two associates from campus. Ten minutes later, under the guise of a separate study, they rated the enjoyableness of some written passages. One passage described a sexual encounter, and represented a fairly permissive attitude toward sexuality. The prediction was that subjects' responses to this sexual passage would be influenced by evaluative standards associated with whichever *private audience* had been primed. As expected, those women who had been primed to experience themselves in relation to their parents rated the story as significantly less enjoyable than those who previously had visualized their (presumably more permissive) friends from campus.

An important assumption in the work just reviewed was that a visualization prime could act as a cue for cognitive structures representing one's significant others and one's relationships with them. If interpersonal information is indeed represented in cognitive structure, it should be possible to access it with minimal primes (Higgins & King, 1981). An extremely subtle cognitive priming technique involves the use of very brief stimulus exposures, and recent research has shown that it is possible to prime, below the level of subjects' conscious awareness, a wide range of phenomena. Bargh and Pietromonaco (1982), for example, used 100-ms parafoveal exposures of adjectives such as 'hostile' and 'unfriendly' to influence subjects' perceptions of a stimulus person. Robles, Smith, Carver, and Wellens (1987) exposed subjects to 17-ms exposures of frightening scenes, and observed an increase in subjects' level of anxiety. Bornstein, Leone, and Galley (1987) observed a mere exposure effect when subjects were given 4-ms exposures of emotionally neutral pictures of unfamiliar people's faces.

In an attempt to use similar methods to prime reflected appraisal information, we gave subjects brief exposures to pictures of significant authority figures' faces, and then observed effects on subjects' momentary sense of self. One of the most basic interpersonal experiences, and the one studied here, is the experience of social disapproval. Sullivan (1953) held that because of the psychological importance of maintaining secure relationships, people are motivated to learn what types of behaviour produce positive and negative responses from others. He argued that experiences of approval and disapproval from significant others form a bedrock of interpersonal contexts which guide the processing of information about self, and to which specific acceptable and unacceptable aspects of self are assimilated. Certainly the process of self-evaluation, with its implications for affect and self-esteem, is an extremely important aspect of self-conception.

Speculations about the cognitive processes involved in the priming of reflected appraisal information will be reserved for the general discussion;

first, it is necessary to establish that there is a reliable phenomenon to be discussed. In the studies to be reported here, stimuli representing disapproval by significant authority figures were presented as primes below the level of subjects' awareness. Predictions were that individuals' self-evaluations would be more negative and self-critical following disapproval primes.

Study 1

In the first study, psychology graduate students evaluated their own research ideas after 2-ms exposures to slides of either disapproving or approving faces. In preparing the stimulus slides, it seemed preferable to photograph individuals who would be truly significant evaluative others for the experimental subjects. In many situations, there are usually one or two individuals who are consensually perceived as evaluators. After chatting with some graduate students at the Research Center for Group Dynamics, it became clear that a major evaluative authority figure for them was Robert Zajonc. Zajonc is the director of the department, is a renowned and respected social psychologist, and was affectionately regarded by the students as someone who could be counted on to ask the toughest questions when one was giving a talk or presentation of some kind. He was definitely a person who might be 'in the back of their mind' when they were working on an idea or trying to decide if it was really any good or not.

Bob graciously agreed to serve as a disapproving stimulus, but suggested that given his reputation among the students as a patriarch of sorts it might be advisable to ask someone else to provide the approving expression. This seemed a wise route to go for a preliminary study, and John Ellard, then a post-doctoral fellow at Michigan who was familiar to the subjects, graciously agreed to supply a positive expression. The approving and disapproving stimuli were exposed to the students during a bogus reaction-time task, after which they evaluated the quality of their own research ideas.

There are some unresolved questions in the literature regarding the most appropriate methods and criteria for studying automatic priming effects (see Holender, 1986, for a recent review). For example, many studies include a task in which subjects are asked to discriminate one stimulus from another, on the assumption that if there is not a statistically significant degree of discrimination it can be concluded that the stimuli are below threshold. Cheesman and Merikle (1985) argue, however, that when discrimination is measured properly and thoroughly, typically using hundreds of trials, stimuli that truly cannot be discriminated also do not produce any priming results on other measures. These authors contend that subliminal primes are those that could produce discrimination results (if measured adequately), but that are at a level where subjects report not being aware of them; that is, they are below the individuals' subjective threshold for consciousness. In other words, the proper criterion for determining the threshold of conscious perception is not chance performance on a discrimination task, but rather the subjects' own self-reports of awareness. A second methodological issue is whether exposure times are best set at a single value for all subjects, or whether perception thresholds should be determined separately for each individual. Due to the unusual nature of the primes used in the present studies (pictures of familiar others' faces), it seemed undesirable to perform hundreds of discrimination trials in order to set individual thresholds prior to the experimental presentations, as this would alert subjects to the nature of the stimuli and might dilute the effects of interest. Because our interest was primarily in the interpersonal content of the primes, rather than in resolving ongoing methodological debates, we elected to employ pilot subjects' subjective reports of awareness (following Cheesman and Merikle's distinction) to set a single exposure time for each study. Experimental subjects' reports of awareness were also assessed to ensure that no subject could accurately report on the nature of the stimuli.

Method

Subjects

Sixteen (eight male, eight female) graduate students and one (female) post-doctoral fellow, affiliated with the Research Center for Group Dynamics, volunteered to participate in the study. Their mean age was 26.1 years. One subject's data were discarded due to an equipment malfunction. Subjects were randomly assigned to condition, with the restriction that there be an equal number (eight) per cell. Subjects were run individually by a male experimenter.

Apparatus

Two Kodak carousel projectors were used to present the stimulus and masking slides. Slides were projected on a wall 4.5 metres directly in front of the subject, forming an image 0.65 metres square. An IBM-XT computer recorded reaction times and controlled Lafayette and Uniblitz shutter timers, which, in turn, controlled two Uniblitz electronic shutters.

Stimulus Presentations

Previous researchers in the area have used exposures from 4 ms (e.g., Silverman, 1983) to 100 ms (e.g., Bargh & Pietromonaco, 1982) for stimulus presentations. Most of this work has involved presentation of words or phrases, however, with longer presentations typically outside the foveal visual field to ensure subliminality. Some researchers (e.g., Kunst-Wilson & Zajonc, 1980; Shevrin, Smith, & Frizler, 1971) have used exposures as short as 1 ms when stimuli were pictorial. With the centrally presented pictures of faces used in this study, it was necessary to use shutter settings of no more than 2 ms to ensure that pilot subjects could not report on the nature of the stimulus. Pilot subjects were tested under the same lighting conditions as the experimental subjects, and using multiple exposures. With a 2-ms presentation,[1] immediately followed by a 10-ms exposure of a masking slide (a collage of brightly coloured shapes), pilot subjects uniformly denied awareness of a first slide, reporting seeing only the mask. When asked to guess what the slide had been, the modal response was that the stimulus was an 'abstract painting', reflecting an awareness of only the mask. Cheesman and Merikle (1985) have argued that self-reports provide the best test of conscious awareness; thus the presentation was short enough and adequately masked to be considered out of awareness.

Stimulus presentations consisted of four exposures in succession, with 5-second intervals between exposures.

Procedure

Subjects first were asked to jot down key words to describe three of the most recent research ideas that they had been working on. They were told they would not be asked to describe the ideas in any detail, but later would need to refer back to remind them of the ideas they had chosen. The selection of ideas came at this point of the procedure so it could not be influenced by later experimental manipulations.

The procedure for the study was then explained as a series of exercises in which subjects would be evaluating their ideas and doing some reaction-time tasks. The reaction-time task would involve pressing a button as quickly as possible after seeing a flash of light on the wall they were facing. No rationale was given for the two tasks; subjects were told that the purpose of the study would be explained at the end of the session (debriefing revealed that to the extent that subjects generated hypotheses about the two tasks, they assumed that the purpose was to see if the positivity of their self-evaluations would affect their reaction times).

The experimenter left the room at this point, to avoid the possibility of biasing in some way the subjects' evaluative responses, and the remainder of the study was directed by audiotaped instructions uniform for all subjects. Also, random assignment to experimental conditions (i.e., order of slide presentation, see below) was done after the experimenter left the room, to allow the experimenter to remain blind to condition during initial phases when interaction was required.

Subjects then performed a series of reaction time trials, during which the masked priming stimuli were presented. The three stimuli included a blank slide of orange colour; the scowling, disapproving face of Robert Zajonc, the director of their program; and the smiling, approving visage of John Ellard, a post-doctoral fellow. In both pictures, the person was looking directly at the camera. The room lights were dimmed during stimulus presentations.

All subjects were exposed to the blank slide first, in order to establish that there were no pretreatment differences between groups. After four exposures of this slide, they evaluated the first of their research ideas they had indicated earlier. They marked slashes across 100-mm lines to indicate their response to the following questions: How good an idea do you feel this is, overall? (not very good/very good); How important an idea is this? (not very important/very important); How original an idea is this? (not very original/very original); How much do you like this idea? (not very much/very much). Last, subjects graded their idea out of 100 per cent.

During the next reaction-time task, half the subjects were exposed to the approval stimulus and half were shown the disapproval stimulus, after which they evaluated their second idea. Finally, they were exposed to the remaining stimulus, and they evaluated their third idea.

After the three ideas had been evaluated, the smiling slide was presented again to all subjects as part of a fourth reaction time trial in an attempt to counteract any negative effects of the disapproving slide. Prior to debriefing, subjects were asked to guess what had been flashed on the screen. Their responses mirrored those of the pilot subjects: They suggested such things as an abstract painting, a house, the letter E, and an axe, all apparently suggested by shapes in the mask. No subject was able to report on the actual nature of the experimental stimuli. Subjects then were debriefed and thanked for their participation.

Results

Each of the 100-mm line scales was converted to a score out of 100 by measuring the distance of the subject's slash, in mm, from the negative endpoint. The five rating scales (how good, important, original, and liked the idea was, plus the percentage grade) showed high intercorrelations, average pairwise $r = 0.63$, so each subject's ratings were averaged to yield one score out of 100 for each idea. High numbers indicated generally positive evaluations.

Given the lack of statistical power imposed by the necessarily limited sample size, planned comparisons were used as the most direct method of testing whether the subliminal presentations of evaluative primes had the intended effect. As predicted, the score subjects gave their ideas tended, overall, to be higher following a presentation of the approval stimulus, $M = 79.9$ out of 100, than following their chairman's scowling face, $M = 72.7$, $t(15) = 1.84$, $p < .05$ (one-tailed). As shown in Table 19.1, however, this effect is most evident after the first experimental prime. Indeed, it is not clear whether the ratings of the final idea were affected by the second face slide at all, or whether perhaps the effects of the first prime simply dissipated. Theoretically it would not be a confident prediction that a second presentation would override completely the structure accessed by the first. Focusing only on the first prime, then, there is a difference between those subjects exposed to the approving face, $M = 82.8$, and those exposed to the disapproving face, $M = 67.8$, $t(14) = 1.97$, $p < .05$ (one-tailed). This difference of 15 percentage points is sizable; in fact it is approximately equivalent to one standard deviation ($s = 15.28$).

As anticipated, there were no pre-manipulation differences between the groups, $t < 1$. There were also no significant effects on reaction times.

Table 19.1 Idea Evaluations by Stimulus and Order of Presentation

Order of stimulus presentation	Stimulus		
	Pretest	First face	Second face
Approval/disapproval	74.2	82.8	77.7
Disapproval/approval	71.3	67.8	77.0

Note: Numbers represent ratings out of 100, with higher numbers representing more positive ratings.

Discussion

The findings support the prediction that individuals' self-evaluations can be influenced by very minimal exposures to positive and negative evaluative stimuli. Graduate students' evaluative ratings of their own research ideas tended to be lower following exposure to their director's scowling face than following a post-doctoral fellow's approving face. Presumably the expressions primed cognitive structures representing evaluative interpersonal experiences, and these structures guided the self-evaluation process accordingly.

Some shortcomings of this initial study are obvious. The limited number of graduate students in this department did not allow for a sample size large enough to support a full range of statistical analyses. One question left unaddressed is the direction of effect: The design does not allow a conclusive assertion of whether it is the disapproving or the approving stimulus which is accounting for most of the variance in self-evaluations. Inspection of the means actually may suggest that the approval stimulus accounts for much of the variance, however, it is not possible to test this given the lack of an adequate control condition. The pretest measures do not provide an adequate control because being assessed at the first trial only (i.e., not randomized across trials as the experimental stimuli were), they may have been subject to a trials effect where subjects simply rated their first ideas more critically for some reason. The pretest condition did serve to establish

that there were no significant differences between groups at that point, but in our second study we instituted a more fully appropriate control condition.

Second, rather than priming different cognitive structures representing particular types of interpersonal relationships it may be that it was simply the pleasantness or unpleasantness of the expressions depicted on the slides that influenced self-evaluations, by inducing a global positive or negative mood (e.g., Isen, 1984). A second study was conducted to address some of these issues, as well as to replicate the basic phenomenon.

Study 2

In order to replicate Study 1 with a somewhat larger sample size, it was necessary to identify a new population with a recognizable authority figure. After discussions with a number of people (including the chaplain at the Roman Catholic college affiliated with the University of Waterloo), we elected to study whether Catholic students might be affected by a presentation of a moderately disapproving picture of Pope John Paul II. In an effort to create a context where the Pope's evaluations might be particularly relevant, and to build on previous research, we focused on Catholic women responding in a context of somewhat permissive sexuality (using materials previously employed by Baldwin & Holmes, 1987).

As well as replicating Study 1, we tried to address some of the issues raised there. First, rather than comparing a disapproval prime with an approval prime, which leaves the direction of effect unspecified, we decided to focus on the disapproval prime in comparison with a neutral control condition.

Second, it seemed important to rule out the possibility that the positive and negative expressions on the stimulus slides simply may have cued either globally good or globally bad moods, which then were reflected in the self-evaluations. This possibility was addressed by including a condition in which subjects were exposed to a disapproving picture of a person they did not know. As Manis (1955) and Rosenberg (1973) have pointed out, the sense of self is generally influenced more by the evaluations of certain people whose opinion one respects or whose approval one desires, than by the evaluations of less personally significant others. A familiar authority figure should therefore have a greater effect on the reflected appraisal process than an unfamiliar other. If the mood-extraction interpretation is correct, however, only the valence of expressions should make a difference, rather than the personal significance of the others. As a test of the importance of personal significance, while some subjects were exposed to the face of the Pope, some subjects were exposed instead to the photo used in Study 1 of the disapproving face of Robert Zajonc, a picture which for them would not represent a significant other and so should have less impact.

To allow an important supplementary test of the significance issue, subjects also were asked how much they practised their religion. It was expected that an exposure to the Pope's disapproving face would have a greater effect for subjects who were actively involved in their religion, and for whom the Pope truly would be a highly significant other.

Method

Subjects

Forty-six Catholic undergraduate women at the University of Waterloo volunteered to participate in the study. Most (25) were located through the psychology department's mass testing package in which students were asked to indicate their religious affiliation and to rate their degree of involvement in their religion (see the Measures section below). These subjects received course credit for their participation. As recruitment became more difficult due to an unexpectedly low number of Catholic women in the Introductory Psychology class, potential subjects were located through previous subjects, personal acquaintance, and the

Roman Catholic–affiliated campus residence. Special care was taken to ensure that all of the subjects were unaware that they were pre-selected with respect to religious affiliation.

A maximum of four subjects were tested per session, by either a male ($n = 16$) or female ($n = 30$) experimenter. Each experimenter ran approximately equal numbers of subjects in each experimental condition.

Materials and Apparatus

Stimuli were presented using a Scientific Prototype Three-field Tachistoscope. All stimuli were presented on 15 cm × 10 cm cards. Subjects were exposed to colour photographs of the face of either Pope John Paul II or Robert Zajonc (an unfamiliar other), or else a plain white card. Attempts were made to match the pictures on size, colouring, and the negativity of the disapproving expression. Both pictures were frontal shots with the head slightly tilted and the eyes directed toward the camera.

Stimulus Presentations

The forward masking procedure recently described by Bornstein et al. (1987) was adopted as a method of presenting the stimuli. These authors also used pictures of faces as stimuli, to produce a subliminal mere exposure effect, and provide discrimination and self-report tests of subjects' awareness levels following the forward masking procedure.

The illumination of both the mask and stimulus fields when measured with a white card was set at 15 fl. For each stimulus exposure, a blank energy field mask was illuminated for 3 seconds, followed by a 4 millisecond exposure of the stimulus.[2] There were five exposures, 5 seconds apart.

Procedure

Subjects first signed consent forms, and then completed a preliminary questionnaire package. This package contained some exploratory personality measures[3] and two written passages. They were instructed to read the passages carefully, as they would be given one of them to evaluate later in the session. One passage was a filler story about a local park area, and the other described a woman's sexual dream. This sexual passage was neither explicit nor erotic, but did portray a permissive attitude toward sexuality. Baldwin and Holmes (1987) found the passage to be acceptable and enjoyable to many undergraduate women. In the present study, the passage was used to establish a context of sexuality, with the expectation that this might make subjects more reactive to the disapproving Pope stimulus.

When the subjects had finished reading the sexual passage, the experimenter escorted them to a second room, which contained the tachistoscope. The experimenter explained that subjects would be exposed to five brief flashes of light, after which they were to return to the other room and complete a second questionnaire, which they would find there. Subjects were then informed that in order to control for experimenter bias, they were to complete the remainder of the study without any interaction with the experimenter. The experimenter then moved behind a partition and randomly selected each subject's stimulus condition, exposing them to either pictures of Pope John Paul II or Robert Zajonc (an unfamiliar other), or else a blank card. Note that random assignment at this point allowed the experimenter to be blind to the subject's condition throughout the first phase of the experiment when interaction was required.

After they completed the second questionnaire, which contained the dependent measures (see below), subjects were fully debriefed. Due to the personal nature of some aspects of the study, special care was taken to inform subjects that the experiment was to examine a temporary effect, a slight shift in how subjects felt about themselves which would probably not represent their most stable day-to-day feelings about themselves, their sexuality, or their religion.

Measures

As a check of whether subjects were aware of seeing the stimulus slides, they first were asked to

'please describe what you thought you saw in the *t* scope'.

As a measure of momentary self-concept, they then rated themselves on 15 nine-point bipolar adjective scales. Five adjective pairs were chosen to represent the domain of general morality (e.g., honest/dishonest, immoral/moral), five pairs were chosen to represent competency (e.g., intelligent/unintelligent, talented/untalented), and five pairs were chosen to represent anxiety (e.g., tense/at ease, calm/anxious). Each pair was randomly assigned to anchor positions, and the 15 items were randomly ordered.

After completing the self-conception inventory, subjects rated the enjoyableness and quality of the sexually permissive passage (see Baldwin & Holmes, 1987, for questions).

Finally, as an indirect measure of how significant an authority the Pope would be to them, subjects reported on a nine-point scale ranging from 'non-practising' to 'practising' the degree to which they considered themselves to be involved in their religion. This was exactly the same question that subjects who were recruited through departmental mass testing had completed at the beginning of term.

Results

Reports of what subjects felt they saw in the tachistoscope uniformly described the blank screen that was exposed prior to the experimental stimuli. No subject reported anything that indicated they may have been aware of the stimulus slide (cf. Bornstein et al., 1987).

Self-Conceptions

The major dependent measure was the index of momentary self-concept. The subject's rating of each adjective pair was assigned a score out of nine, with higher numbers representing the more positive end of the scale. Competency, anxiety, and morality subscales were computed as the mean of the five items in each category. These subscales showed a fairly high degree of intercorrelation, average pairwise $r = 59$, probably indicating a global self-evaluative response. For the first set of analyses, therefore, an overall self-conceptions score was calculated as the average across all 15 items. High scores represented generally positive self-ratings.

Preliminary analyses revealed a significant experimenter effect, $F(2, 34) = 4.75$, $p < .05$, indicating that subjects rated themselves less positively in the presence of the male as opposed to the female experimenter. This effect did not interact with either of the independent variables, however, and will not be discussed further.

A 3 (condition: control/Pope/unfamiliar other) × 2 (level of practising: high/low) analysis of variance was performed on self-conception scores. Subjects were designated as high or low practising following a median split procedure based on their post-experiment ratings of their involvement in their religion.[4] The main effect for experimental condition was significant, $F(2, 40) = 3.38$, $p < .05$ (see Table 19.2). Contrasts using the mean square error estimate from the ANOVA showed that whereas the Pope group reported significantly lower self-concept scores than control,[5] $t(40) = 2.09$, $p < .05$, the unfamiliar-other group did not differ from control, $t < 1$. As predicted, only the group exposed to the disapproving face of a personally significant other showed a lowered evaluation of self.

Table 19.2 Overall Self-Conceptions and Self-Conception Subscales by Stimulus Conditions

Measure	Stimulus condition		
	Control	Pope	Unfamiliar other
Overall self-conceptions	7.02	6.30	7.09
Subscales			
Competency	6.97	6.00	6.77
Anxiety	6.43	5.41	6.73
Morality	7.65	7.50	7.77
(n)	(15)	(16)	(15)

Note: Higher numbers represent more positive ratings.

The main effect for level of practising was not significant, $F < 1$, however the interaction between condition and practising was significant, $F(2, 40) = 3.41$, $p < .05$ (see Table 19.3). To clarify this interaction, tests were done between experimental and control groups at each level of practising. In the low practising group, neither experimental group was different from control, $ts < 1$. In the high practising group, those in the Pope condition did report lower self-concepts than those in control, $r(40) = 2.30$, $p < .05$, but those in the unfamiliar-other group did not differ from control, $t < 1$. The effect of the Pope stimulus, therefore, was limited to those subjects who considered themselves highly involved in their religion, and for whom the Pope presumably would be a highly significant evaluative authority.

Self-Conceptions Subscales
Although the three subscales of the self-conceptions measure showed patterns of means quite similar to the overall score, it is important to examine the subscales, both because they may be measuring somewhat different constructs and to ensure that the overall effect is not due entirely to one subset of measures (e.g., anxiety, cf. Robles et al., 1987). When the 3 × 2 ANOVA was conducted on the competency subscale (the average across the five competency-relevant items), there was a significant main effect for condition, $F(2, 40) = 4.21$, $p < .05$ (see Table 19.2). For the anxiety subscale, the main effect for condition was significant, $F(2, 40) = 3.61$, $p < .05$ (see Table 19.2), and the practising by condition interaction was marginally significant, $F(2, 40) = 2.64$, $p = .09$ (see Table 19.3). On the morality subscale, neither main effect was significant, but the practising by condition interaction was, $F(2, 40) = 4.27$, $p < .05$ (see Table 19.3).

Story Evaluations
There were no significant effects in analyses of the evaluations of the sexual passage. This result will be discussed below.

Table 19.3 Overall Self-Conceptions and Self-Conception Subscales by Stimulus Condition and Level of Practising

Measure	Low practising			High practising		
	Control	Pope	Unfamiliar other	Control	Pope	Unfamiliar other
Overall self-conceptions	6.93	6.70	6.64	7.11	6.00	7.77
Subscales						
Competency	6.97	6.14	6.42	6.97	5.89	7.30
Anxiety	6.45	5.89	6.11	6.40	5.04	7.67
Morality	7.37	8.06	7.40	7.97	7.07	8.33
(*n*)	(8)	(7)	(9)	(7)	(9)	(6)

Note: Higher numbers represent more positive ratings.

Discussion

The results of this study conceptually replicate those of Study 1, and address some additional issues as well. Two methods of assessing the relevance of personal significance supported the notion that exposures to truly significant others can have an effect on self-conception, when exposure to a non-significant other does not. Catholic women reported lower self-evaluations overall following exposure to the Pope's disapproving face, but not following exposure to an unfamiliar other's disapproving face. Moreover, the effect for the Pope was only evident for subjects who reported that they practised their religion on a regular basis.

The finding that personal significance of the stimulus other is a crucial factor in the phenomenon effectively rules out some simple alternative hypotheses, such as that the disapproving Zajonc stimulus was effective in Study 1 simply by virtue of portraying a negative expression. Rather, it seems that a brief exposure to the disapproving face of a recognized significant other accesses pre-existing structures representing negative evaluation by people who are personally important. The effect for personal significance is relevant to the issue of whether automatic priming effects in general reflect cognitive or affective processes (e.g., Bargh, Bond, Lombardi, & Tota, 1986; Erdley &

D'Agostino, 1988). While it may be that subjects' self-evaluative mood was fairly globally negative following exposure to the Pope stimulus, as evidenced by the similar pattern of means across subscales, there was no evidence of a parallel negative response following the strongly negative affective stimulus picture of an unfamiliar other. Recent research has suggested that face recognition is carried out separately from expression identification (Bruce, 1986; Bruce & Young, 1986; Young, McWeeny, Hay, & Ellis, 1986); the differential findings for the two experimental stimuli demonstrate that face recognition is a necessary component of the present priming effect. The effect was therefore due at least in part to the accessibility of the construct representing disapproval by the significant other, rather than simply to the unconscious extraction of the emotional content displayed in the stimulus expressions.

Indeed, one might even speculate that recognition of the stimulus person was a sufficient as well as a necessary condition for the effect, that is, that any picture of a familiar person or a significant authority figure, regardless of evaluative expression, would have produced self-criticism. This argument should hold particularly if the authority figure is typically associated with negative responses, either because of a history of negative interactions or the fact that the person is seen as holding evaluative standards that are difficult to satisfy. If one assumes that both the Pope (in this study) and Robert Zajonc (in Study 1) may have been perceived by subjects as being tough evaluators, it is not possible to disentangle the effects of the disapproving expression and a negative expectancy about the stimulus person. While it intuitively does not seem likely to us that subjects in Study 1 would have rated their ideas quite as poorly if they had seen a picture of their departmental director beaming with enthusiastic admiration, this possibility cannot be ruled out by the present data and remains an important question for further research.

A potential alternative explanation for the results might be that the Pope stimulus actually was more menacing than the Zajonc stimulus, and this could explain the greater effect on subjects' self-evaluations. In an informal sampling, however, 10 people unanimously rated the disapproving expression of the Pope stimulus as only equally or even slightly less severe than that of the Zajonc stimulus, rather than more so.

One finding of interest was that the different self-conception subscales showed slightly different effects. The presence of a main effect for stimulus condition on competency as well as anxiety ratings indicates that the stimuli probably are not simply priming anxiety, as has been shown previously with brief exposures of frightening scenes (Robles et al., 1987). Also, the evidence of an interaction between condition and degree of practising on the morality subscale implicates particular value systems rather than a global evaluative response: Only those subjects who subscribed to the value system represented by the Pope were affected by exposure to his disapproving face. Although the different patterns on the subscales are intriguing, the fairly high correlations among measures, the fact that the subscales were derived from only five items as opposed to 15 items for the overall scale, as well as the rather low n for the interaction comparisons, stand as a caution against overinterpreting these differences before they are replicated.

Although we did anticipate some effects on evaluations of the sexual passage, the null findings may not be entirely surprising. Part of this may be that the self-conceptions measure diffused some of the effects of the stimuli, or that the effect of the prime simply dissipated over time. Also, other studies (e.g., Srull & Wyer, 1980) have found that primes are not effective in changing interpretations of information that has already been processed, as the sexual story had been.

General Discussion

The results of the present studies are consistent with the hypothesis that a person's momentary sense of self can be shaped by cognitive structures representing significant interpersonal information. The studies raise many interesting questions, and suggest many important directions in which to proceed with subsequent research in this area.

There are a number of possible interpretations of the findings, each suggesting a different route for future research. One possibility is that the primes directly activated an *affective* process of some kind, rather than cognitive structures (e.g., Bower, 1981; Zajonc, 1980). Affective and motivational factors are certainly critically important in self as well as interpersonal processes, and our emphasis on cognitive factors only represents the state of development of the current information-processing paradigm, rather than any commitment to the primacy of cognition. Study 2 did address the necessity for recognition of the stimulus person, but beyond that it is not clear to what extent purely cognitive structures could be said to mediate the effects. In any event, we suspect that self-evaluative cognitions are always 'hot' cognitions, laden with affective implications which play an important role in determining subsequent processing. Until social cognitive models are integrated more fully with affective, motivational, and even motoric (e.g., Zajonc, 1988) factors, it would be wise to assume the important interdependency of all of these elements, and that experiencing oneself as being disapproved of by a significant other presumably involves *thinking that* one is disapproved of, *feeling* disapproved of, and *being motivated to* avoid disapproval and garner approval.

A second interpretation of the findings is that they may not represent a reflective appraisal process at all, but rather a social comparison process (Festinger, 1954).[6] Rather than priming disapproval by a significant authority, the stimuli may have primed a high status other, compared with whom subjects felt inferior and less worthy. Although this interpretation cannot be ruled out in the present studies, it would not apply to the related research reviewed earlier (Baldwin & Holmes, 1987), in which visualization primes produced more specific self-evaluative effects over a range of content areas. Not all questions can be addressed by any two studies, and the possibility of social comparison processes functioning outside conscious awareness must remain a question for further research.

Relationship Schemas

A third interpretation of the findings is that the primes did, in fact, activate structures representing the experience of being disapproved of by a significant other. The exact nature of the underlying structures is far from clear, as indicated in the earlier discussion of the relative importance of expectations regarding specific significant others versus the expression depicted on an experimental prime. Although the findings cannot answer unequivocally these and other questions about what structures underlie the phenomenon, perhaps some speculation is in order about what might be going on.

One might speculate that a habitual pattern of interacting, observed over time in a relationship, can become represented as procedural knowledge in the form of an interaction script that represents *a regular pattern of relating between self and other*, along with a self-schema and a schema or prototype for the significant other. Rather than trying to understand the process of self-conception by focusing on the self-schema or the other-schema in isolation, it would be wise to consider the entire relationship.

There might be advantages in examining the notion of *relationship schemas* or *interpersonal schemas*, defined as cognitive structures representing regularities in interpersonal interaction. Over one's lifetime, any experiences of negative evaluative feedback from authority figures could become organized into a relationship schema of, for example, 'being disapproved of for an incompetent performance or immoral act' (the type of schema that was assumed to be primed by the stimuli in the present studies). This learned interaction pattern might take its place beside others such as, 'being approved of for acting generously', 'being feared and avoided after expressing anger', or 'being treated with respect when one asserts one's position'. Similar concepts have been discussed elsewhere, particularly in the clinical literatures (e.g., Blatt & Lerner, 1983; Horowitz, 1979, 1988; Luborsky, 1977, 1988; Mayman & Faris, 1960; Stern, 1985; Tomkins, 1980), and it is a useful idea for social cognitive research as well.

There is a long tradition in the social psychological as well as clinical literatures that interpersonal factors play an important role in self-conception. Much past research has focused on the impact of social factors either in the environment or as represented internally in an imaginary private audience (e.g., Baldwin & Holmes, 1987). The relationship schema notion suggests that the interpersonal context for self-construal may be determined by cognitive structures based on overlearned interpersonal situations.

If so, it may be that past construals of self as competent, immoral, or whatever, as represented in stable self-schemas, have only a limited direct impact on a person's momentary sense of self. Rather, the sense of identity might always be constructed anew as an emergent product of a matrix of salient interpersonal information, from both ongoing interactions and accessible cognitive structures. And, as the present studies indicate, these structures may be primed by stimuli that are very subtle, or even outside of conscious awareness.

The present research is very compatible with another body of work also drawn from the literature on self-conception and its roots in interpersonal experience. A series of important studies by Higgins and his colleagues (see Higgins, 1987, for a review) has indicated that specific self-evaluative emotions such as depression and anxiety may be caused by cognitively accessible discrepancies between one's view of self and the evaluative standards held by self and others. Indeed, within the framework of Self-Discrepancy Theory the present studies could be seen as aimed at priming the significant other 'standpoints on the self' associated with particular evaluative standards, in contrast with other studies in which standards and discrepancies are primed more directly (e.g., Higgins, Bond, Klein, & Strauman, 1986; Strauman & Higgins, 1987). This comparison illustrates an important difference in emphasis between perspectives: While evaluative standards are obviously critical features in self-conception, we believe it would be unwise to treat standards as if, once learned, they become functionally autonomous from the interpersonal context in which they were established. As Miller (1963) points out, 'People do not internalize abstract norms, but images of themselves in concrete relationships with specific people or groups' (p. 666). Evaluative standards may be the most proximal causes of self-evaluative distress, but, as Higgins, Klein, and Strauman (1985) acknowledge, standards are only important because they have had interpersonal consequences. We would advocate concentrating more fully on the interpersonal context, which will allow the study of such evaluation-relevant issues as the degree to which a particular other is emotionally significant (e.g., Klein & Higgins, 1984, cited in Higgins, 1987), or the degree to which approval by others is experienced as conditional on successful performance (Baldwin & Holmes, 1987, Study 2). Moreover, it is important to bear in mind that evaluation is not the only consequential aspect of self-conception and interpersonal relationship: Future research into the relationship-schema notion could investigate other issues not obviously related to evaluation such as whether an internalized relationship is characterized by dependency versus autonomy (e.g., Baldwin & Shaw, 1988), or the presence versus absence of hostility (cf. psychodynamic theories of depression; e.g., Freud, 1917).

Further research is clearly required to assess more directly the relationship schema notion. As consensus grows in the literature on the best methods for studying automatic priming, additional work will also be needed to determine more clearly the effects of conscious and non-conscious primes of interpersonal information. In the future, social cognitive methodologies will be useful in experimentally investigating the extremely important question of how individuals' dysfunctional, problematic relationship schemas can be modified, and what makes them more flexible versus rigid. The first step, however, is to learn more about what type of information is stored in relationship schemas, how exactly it is represented, and how it influences the sense of self.

Notes

1. Although the shutter was set at 2 ms, it may be that the rise time for the shutter to be activated and deactivated makes the actual exposure time somewhat unreliable, and possibly longer. The onset of the masking stimulus was 2 ms after the onset of the experimental stimulus, however (as both were computer-controlled), so even if the stimulus was exposed longer it would have been degraded after that point.

2. We attempted to verify exposure times using a silicon phototransistor interfaced with a Tektronix oscilloscope (model D11). Although the peak of the presentation curve at the 4-ms setting was clearly within the 4-ms time interval, there was a fairly gradual decay such that some measurable light was present as late as 10–14 ms. It should be pointed out that the same ambiguity would likely be found in other reports that

use tachistoscopes without testing decay rates, such as Bornstein et al. (1987), who used the same model of tachistoscope at the same 4-ms setting. As work in the area of brief exposures progresses, researchers will need to verify more carefully the accuracy of exposure durations.

3. As part of the honours theses on which this article is partly based, subjects were asked to complete the Self-Consciousness Scale (Fenigstein, Scheier, & Buss, 1975) and a self-esteem scale (Rosenberg, 1965). Neither scale showed interpretable effects, and they will not be discussed further.

4. Because level of practising is to be treated as an independent variable, it ideally would have been measured before each subject participated in the study. Difficulties in recruiting an adequate number of subjects prevented this, however, and pre-measures were available for only 25 of the 46 subjects. Rather than give the measure to the remaining subjects prior to or at the beginning of the experimental session (which would alert all subjects to the relevance of religion to the study), or at a later time (after they had been debriefed), we decided to administer the measure at the very end of the session, before debriefing. Treating this type of measure as an independent variable requires some evidence that it was not affected by the experimental treatments. This post-measure was correlated with pre-scores that were available from some subjects, $r(23) = 0.79$, $p < .01$. There were no significant results for condition in either a repeated measures analysis of variance of pre- and post-test scores ($n = 25$) $Fs < 1.7$, $ns.$, or independent analyses of variance for pretest scores ($n = 25$), or post-test scores ($n = 46$), $Fs < 1.5$, $ns.$ Moreover, if analyses of the self-concept score are carried out only on data from subjects providing practising pre-measures the pattern of data is quite similar, and planned contrasts (in place of the ANOVA which obviously is weakened by the lower n) yield similar results. Finally, if post-test scores are replaced by pretest scores for those subjects for whom they were available, and the median split procedure on the whole sample then is based on this hybrid score, the self-concept ANOVA main effect and interaction remain significant.

5. All t tests reported for Study 2 are two-tailed.

6. We thank Mel Lerner and Rich Ennis for pointing out this hypothesis.

Discussion Questions

1. In the Baldwin et al. studies, does the distinction between feared versus loved authority figures matter? How do you think the results would have turned out if the experimenters had presented participants with images of a beloved, non-threatening authority figure? How do you think the results of Study 2 would have turned out if the experimenters had presented images of the Pope smiling warmly?

2. What significant other primes might induce people to rate themselves more positively?

3. What do you think would happen if the experimenters had primed role models (superiors who participants have a realistic chance of emulating some day)?

20. Many Hands Make Light the Work: The Causes and Consequences of Social Loafing

Bibb Latané, Kipling Williams, and Stephen Harkins, Ohio State University

Editor's Introduction

People have a finite amount of physical energy available at any one moment. Therefore, they must often spend their resources wisely lest exhaustion set in. The same holds true for psychological 'energy'; it is a limited resource that must be deployed judiciously. (This idea is developed in more detail in Unit 5.)

The present article introduced the concept of *social loafing* and demonstrated that people are extremely sensitive to cues indicating that 100 per cent effort may not be necessary or appropriate. One such cue is the number of other people working on the same task. Referring back to studies conducted in the early twentieth century, Latané, Williams, and Harkins (1979) find that the more people working on a task such as rope pulling or making noise, the less each individual contributes. Clearly, these findings have enormous implications for much of our everyday experiences, including in the workplace and in the classroom.

Might it be that large groups are simply clumsier than smaller groups or individuals and *this* accounts for the difference between group performance and individual performance? While this may be true in some cases, in Study 2 of the present article Latané and colleagues elegantly address the 'coordination loss' counterexplanation through the clever inclusion of 'pseudosubjects' (subjects who do not exist, although the real subjects think that they do). Using this methodology, Latané et al. are able to isolate how much of social loafing is due to a loss of motivation (most of it) and how much of it is due to loss of coordination (not much).

It is, however, too simplistic to state that people are merely 'slackers' trying to do as little work as they can get away with. Instead, studies published after the present article showed that people are *strategic* about what level of effort to deploy, sometimes loafing but sometimes intensifying their effort above the normal level. For example, Williams and Karau (1991) induced both social loafing and social compensation by manipulating participants' expectations about their teammate. In one study, the 'co-worker' (actually a confederate) said out loud either 'I don't think I'm going to work very hard' or 'I think I'm going to work very hard'. Participants with the hard-working partner showed significant social loafing, while those with the slacking partner showed an *increase* in effort and performance compared to baseline. Thus, Williams and Karau were among the first to demonstrate that social loafing/compensation is a two-sided coin. Plaks and Higgins (2000) took this idea one step further by showing that even an *implicit* expectation of an underperforming teammate (implied by stereotypes) can cause similar effects. For example, students who were told that their teammate on a math team was a woman scored higher than those who were told that their teammate was a man.

In a sense it is adaptive that humans would develop such a finely tuned sense about their effort expenditure. An organism that goes full tilt at every opportunity risks burnout, ulcers, or a range of other threats that can be caused by exhaustion, compared to an organism that paces itself. In fact, this ability may be so critical to survival that it is very easily learned and filed away as one of the tasks that can be performed automatically and unconsciously. Several studies suggest that people are not aware of when they are engaging in social loafing or social compensation. In fact, even *anticipating* an upcoming collective task has been found to yield social loafing/compensation, before the task even begins (Plaks & Higgins, 2000). Thus, our calculations of how hard to try appear to be highly automatized.

— □ ■ □ —

There is an old saying that 'many hands make light the work'. This saying is interesting for two reasons. First, it captures one of the promises of social life—that with social organization people can fulfill their individual goals more easily through collective action. When many hands are available, people often do not have to work as hard as when only a few are present. The saying is interesting in a second, less hopeful way—it seems that when many hands are available, people actually work less hard than they ought to.

Over 50 years ago a German psychologist named Ringelmann did a study that he never managed to get published. In rare proof that unpublished work does not necessarily perish, the results of that study, reported only in summary form in German by Moede (1927), have been cited by Dashiell (1935), Davis (1969), Köhler (1927), and Zajonc (1966) and extensively analyzed by Steiner (1966, 1972) and Ingham, Levinger, Graves, and Peckham (1974). Apparently Ringelmann simply asked German workers to pull as hard as they could on a rope, alone or with one, two, or seven other people, and then he used a strain gauge to measure how hard they pulled in kilograms of pressure.

Rope pulling is, in Steiner's (1972) useful classification of tasks, maximizing, unitary, and additive. In a maximizing task, success depends on how much or how rapidly something is accomplished and presumably on how much effort is expended, as opposed to an optimizing task, in which precision, accuracy, or correctness are paramount. A unitary task cannot be divided into separate subtasks—all members work together doing the same thing and no division of labour is possible. In an additive task, group success depends on the *sum* of the individual efforts, rather than

on the performance of any subset of members. From these characteristics, we should expect three people pulling together on a rope with perfect efficiency to be able to exert three times as much force as one person can, and eight people to exert eight times as much force.

Ringelmann's results, however, were strikingly different. When pulling one at a time, individuals averaged a very respectable 63 kilograms of pressure. Groups of three people were able to exert a force of 160 kilograms, only two and a half times the average individual performance, and groups of eight pulled at 248 kilograms, less than four times the solo rate. Thus the collective group performance, while increasing somewhat with group size, was substantially less than the sum of the individual efforts, with dyads pulling at 93 per cent of the sum of their individual efforts, trios at 85 per cent, and groups of eight at only 49 per cent. In a way somewhat different from how the old saw would have it, many hands apparently made light the work.

The Ringelmann effect is interesting because it seems to violate both common stereotype and social psychological theory. Common stereotype tells us that the sense of team participation leads to increased effort, that group morale and cohesiveness spur individual enthusiasm, that by pulling together groups can achieve any goal, that in unity there is strength. Social psychological theory holds that, at least for simple, well-learned tasks involving dominant responses, the presence of other people, whether as co-workers or spectators, should facilitate performance. It is thus important to find out whether Ringelmann's effect is replicable and whether it can be obtained with other tasks.

The Ringelmann effect is also interesting because it provides a different arena for testing a new theory of social impact (Latané, 1973). Social impact theory holds that when a person stands as a target of social forces coming from other persons, the amount of social pressure on the target person should increase as a multiplicative function of the strength, immediacy, and number of these other persons. However, if a person is a member of a group that is the target of social forces from outside the group, the impact of these forces on any given member should diminish in inverse proportion to the strength, immediacy, and number of group members. Impact is divided up among the group members, in much the same way that responsibility for helping seems to be divided among witnesses to an emergency (Latané & Darley, 1970). Latané further suggests that just as psychophysical reactions to external stimuli can be described in terms of a power law (Stevens, 1957), so also should reactions to social stimuli, but with an exponent having an absolute value less than 1, so that the nth person should have less effect than the $(n - 1)$th. Ringelmann's asking his workers to pull on a rope can be considered social pressure. The more people who are the target of this pressure, the less pressure should be felt by any one person. Since people are likely to work hard in proportion to the pressure they feel to do so, we should expect increased group size to result in reduced efforts on the part of individual group members. These reduced efforts can be called 'social loafing'—a decrease in individual effort due to the social presence of other persons. With respect to the Ringelmann phenomenon, social impact theory suggests that at least some of the effect should be due to reduced efforts on the part of group participants, and that this reduced effort should follow the form of an inverse power function having an exponent with an absolute value less than one.

The Ringelmann effect is interesting for a third reason: If it represents a general phenomenon and is not restricted to pulling on a rope, it poses the important practical question of when and why collective efforts are less efficient than individual ones. Since many components of our standard of life are produced through one form or another of collective action, research identifying the causes and conditions of inefficient group output and suggesting strategies to overcome these inefficiencies is clearly desirable.

For these three and other reasons, we decided to initiate a program of research into the collective performance of individuals in groups.

Experiment 1: Clap Your Hands and Shout Out Loud

One of the disadvantages of Ringelmann's rope pulling task is that the equipment and procedures are relatively cumbersome and inefficient. Therefore, we decided to keep our ears open for other tasks that would allow us to replicate the Ringelmann finding conceptually and would provide the basis for extended empirical and theoretical analysis. We chose cheering and clapping, two activities that people commonly do together in social settings and that are maximizing, unitary, and additive. As with rope pulling, output can be measured in simple physical units that make up a ratio scale.

Method

On eight separate occasions, groups of six undergraduate males were recruited from introductory psychology classes at Ohio State University; they were seated in a semicircle, 1 metre apart, in a large soundproofed laboratory and told, 'We are interested in judgments of how much noise people make in social settings, namely cheering and applause, and how loud they seem to those who hear them. Thus, we want each of you to do two things: (1) Make noises, and (2) judge noises.' They were told that on each trial 'the experimenter will tell you the trial number, who is to perform, and whether you are to cheer (Rah!) or clap. When you are to begin, the experimenter will count backwards from three and raise his hand. Continue until he lowers it. We would like you to clap or cheer for 5 seconds as loud as you can.' On each trial, both the performers and the observers were also asked to make magnitude estimates of how much noise had been produced (Stevens, 1966). Since these data are not relevant to our concerns, we will not mention them further.

After some practice at both producing and judging noise, there were 36 trials of yelling and 36 trials of clapping. Within each modality, each person performed twice alone, four times in pairs, four times in groups of four, and six times in groups of six. These frequencies were chosen as a compromise between equating the number of occasions on which we measured people making noise alone or in groups (which would have required more noisemaking in fours and sixes) and equating the number of individual performances contributing to our measurements in the various group sizes (which would have required more noisemaking by individuals and pairs). We also arranged the sequence of performances to space and counterbalance the order of conditions over each block of 36 trials, while making sure that no one had to perform more than twice in a row.

Performances were measured with a General Radio sound-level meter, Model 1565A, using the C scale and the slow time constant, which was placed exactly four metres away from each performer. The C scale was used so that sounds varying only in frequency or pitch would be recorded as equally loud. Sound level meters are read in decibel (dB) units, which are intended to approximate the human reaction to sound. For our purposes, however, the appropriate measure is the effort used in generating noise, not how loud it sounds. Therefore, our results are presented in terms of dynes/cm^2, the physical unit of work involved in producing sound pressure.

Because people shouted and clapped in full view and earshot of each other, each person's performance could affect and be affected by the others. For this reason, the group, rather than the individual, was the unit of analysis, and each score was based on the average output per person. Results were analyzed in a 4 × 2 × 2 analysis of variance, with Group Size (1, 2, 4, 6), Response Mode (clapping vs. shouting), and Replications (1, 2) as factors.

Results

Participants seemed to adapt to the task with good humour if not great enthusiasm. Nobody refused to clap or shout, even though a number seemed somewhat embarrassed or shy about making these noises in public. Despite this, they did manage to produce a good deal of noise. Individuals averaged 84 dB (C) clapping and 87 dB cheering, while groups of six clapped at 91 dB and shouted at 95 dB (an increment of 6 dB represents a doubling of sound pressure).

As might be expected, the more people clapping or cheering together, the more intense the noise and the more the sound pressure produced. However, it did not grow in proportion to the number of people: The average sound pressure generated *per person* decreased with increasing group size, $F(3, 21) = 41.5$, $p < .001$. People averaged about 3.7 dynes/cm^2 alone, 2.6 in pairs, 1.8 in foursomes, and about 1.5 in groups of six (Figure 20.1). Put another way, two-person groups performed at only 71 per cent of the sum of their individual capacity, four-person groups at 51 per cent, and six-person groups at 40 per cent. As in pulling ropes, it appears that when it comes to clapping and shouting out loud, many hands do, in fact, make light the work.

People also produced about 60 per cent more sound power when they shouted than when they clapped, $F(1, 7) = 8.79$, $p < .01$, presumably reflecting physical capacity rather than any psychological process. There was no effect due to blocks of trials, indicating that the subjects needed little or no practice and that their performance was not deleteriously affected by fatigue. In addition, there were no interactions among the variables.

Discussion

The results provide a strong replication of Ringelmann's original findings, using a completely different task and in a different historical epoch and

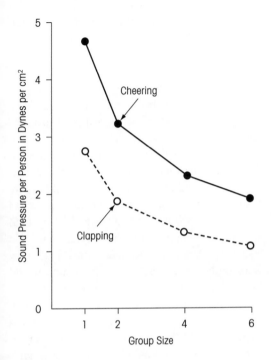

Figure 20.1 Intensity of noise as a function of group size and response mode, Experiment 1.

culture. At least when people are making noise as part of a task imposed by someone else, voices raised together do not seem to be raised as much as voices raised alone, and the sound of 12 hands clapping is not even three times as intense as the sound of two.

Zajonc's (1965) elegant theory of social facilitation suggests that people are aroused by the mere presence of others and are thus likely to work harder (though not necessarily to achieve more) when together. Although social facilitation theory might seem to predict enhanced group performance on a simple task like clapping or shouting, in the present case it would not predict any effect due to group size, since the number of people present was always eight: six participants and two experimenters. Evaluation apprehension theory (Cottrell, 1972) would also not predict any effect as long as it is assumed that co-actors and audience

members are equally effective in arousing performance anxiety. Therefore, these theories are not inconsistent with our position that an unrelated social process is involved. The results of Experiment 1 also can be taken as support for Latané's (1973) theory of social impact: The impact that the experimenters have on an individual seems to decrease as the number of co-performers increases, leading to an apparent drop in individual performance, a phenomenon we call social loafing.

However, there is an alternative explanation to these results. It may be, not that people exert less effort in groups, but that the group product suffers as a result of group inefficiency. In his invaluable theoretical analysis of group productivity, Steiner (1972) suggests that the discrepancy between a group's potential productivity (in this case n times the average individual output) and its actual productivity may be attributed to faulty social process. In the case of Ringelmann's rope pull, Steiner identifies one source of process loss as inadequate social coordination. As group size increases, the number of 'coordination links', and thus the possibility of faulty coordination (pulling in different directions at different times), also increases. Steiner shows that for Ringelmann's original data the decrement in obtained productivity is exactly proportional to the number of coordination links.

Ingham et al. (1974) designed an ingenious experiment to determine whether the process losses found in rope pulling were mainly due to problems of coordinating individual efforts and the physics of the task, or whether they resulted from reductions in personal exertion (what we have called social loafing). First, they conducted a careful replication of Ringelmann's original rope pulling study and found similar results—dyads pulled at 91 per cent of the sum of their individual capacities, trios at 82 per cent, and groups of six at only 78 per cent.

In a second experiment, Ingham et al. cleverly arranged things so that only the individual's perception of group size was varied. Individuals were blindfolded and led to believe that others were pulling with them, but in fact, they always pulled alone. Under these conditions, of course, there is no possibility of loss due to faulty synchronization. Still there was a substantial drop in output with increases in perceived group size: Individuals pulled at 90 per cent of their alone rate when they believed one other person was also pulling, and at only 85 per cent when they believed two to six others were pulling. It appears that virtually all of the performance decrement in rope pulling observed by Ingham et al. can be accounted for in terms of reduced effort or social loafing.

With respect to clapping and especially shouting, however, there are several possible sources of coordination loss that might have operated in addition to social loafing: (a) Sound cancellation will occur to the extent that sound pressure waves interfere with each other, (b) directional coordination losses will occur to the extent that voices are projected toward different locations, and (c) temporal coordination losses will occur to the extent that moment-to-moment individual variations in intensity are not in synchrony. Our second experiment was designed to assess the relative effects of coordination loss and social loafing in explaining the failure of group cheering to be as intense as the sum of individual noise outputs.

Experiment 2: Coordination Loss or Reduced Effort?

For Experiment 2 we arranged things so that people could not hear each other shout; participants were asked to wear headphones, and during each trial a constant 90-dB recording of six people shouting was played over the earphones, ostensibly to reduce auditory feedback and to signal each trial. As a consequence, individuals could be led to believe they were shouting in groups while actually shouting alone. Ingham et al. (1974) accomplished this through the use of 'pseudosubjects', confederates who pretended to be pulling with the participants but who in fact did not pull any weight at all. That is an expensive procedure—each of the

36 participants tested by Ingham et al. required the services of five pseudosubjects as well as the experimenter. We were able to devise a procedure whereby, on any given trial, one person could be led to believe that he was performing in a group, while the rest thought he was performing alone. Thus, we were able to test six real participants at one time.

Additionally, although we find the interpretation offered by Ingham et al. plausible and convincing, the results of their second experiment are susceptible to an alternative explanation. When participants were not pulling the rope, they stood and watched the pseudosubjects pull. This would lead people accurately to believe that while they were pulling the rope, idle participants would be watching.[1] Thus, as the number of performers decreased, the size of the audience increased. According to Cottrell's evaluation apprehension hypothesis (1972), the presence of an evaluative audience should enhance performance for a simple, well-learned task such as rope pulling, and, although there is little supportive evidence, it seems reasonable that the larger the audience, the greater the enhancement (Martens & Landers, 1969; Seta, Paulus, & Schkade, 1976). Thus, it is not clear whether there was a reduced effort put forth by group members because they believed other people were pulling with them, or an increase in the effort exerted by individuals because they believed other people were watching them. In Experiment 2, therefore, we arranged to hold the size of the audience constant, even while varying the number of people working together.

Method

Six groups of six male undergraduate volunteers heard the following instructions:

> In our experiment today we are interested in the effects of sensory feedback on the production of sound in social groups. We will ask you to produce sounds in groups of one, two, or six, and we will record the sound output on the

sound-level meter that you can see up here in front. Although this is not a competition and you will not learn your scores until the end of the experiment, we would like you to make your sounds as loud as possible. Since we are interested in sensory feedback, we will ask you to wear blindfolds and earphones and, as you will see, will arrange it so that you will not be able to hear yourself as you shout.

We realize it may seem strange to you to shout as loud as you can, especially since other people are around. Remember that the room is soundproofed and that people outside the room will not be able to hear you. In addition, because you will be wearing blindfolds and headsets, the other participants will not be able to hear you or to see you. Please, therefore, feel free to let loose and really shout. As I said, we are interested in how loud you can shout, and there is no reason not to do your best. Here's your chance to really give it a try. Do you have any questions?

Once participants had donned their headsets and blindfolds, they went through a series of 13 trials, in which each person shouted four times in a group of six, once in a group of two, and once by himself. Before each trial they heard the identification letters of those people who were to shout.

Interspersed with these trials were 12 trials, two for each participant, in which the individual's headset was switched to a separate track on the stereophonic instruction tape. On these trials, everybody else was told that only the focal person should shout, but that individual was led to believe either that one other person would shout with him or that all six would shout.

Thus, each person shouted by himself, in actual groups of two and six, and in pseudogroups of two and six, with trials arranged so that each person would have approximately equal rest periods between the trials on which he performed. Each trial was preceded by the specification of who was to perform. The yells were coordinated by a tape-recorded voice counting backwards from three, followed by a constant 90-dB 5-second recording of the sound of six people shouting. This background noise made it impossible for performers to determine whether or how loudly other people were shouting, or, for that matter, to hear themselves shout. Each trial was terminated by the sound of a bell. This sequence of 25 trials was repeated three times, for a total of 75 trials, in the course of which each subject shouted 24 times.

As in Experiment 1, the data were transformed into dynes/cm^2 and subjected to analyses of variance, with the group as the unit of analysis and each score based on the average output per person. Two separate 3×3 analyses of variance with group size (1, 2, 6) and trial block (1–3) were run, one on the output of trials in which groups actually shouted together, and one on the pseudogroup trials in which only one person actually shouted.

Results

Overall, participants shouted with considerably more intensity in Experiment 2 than in Experiment 1, averaging 9.22 dynes/cm^2 when shouting alone, as compared to 4.73 dynes/cm^2, $t(12) = 4.05$, $p < .01$. There are several plausible reasons for this difference. The new rationale involving the effects of reduced sensory feedback may have interested or challenged individuals to perform well. The constant 90-dB background noise may have led people to shout with more intensity, just as someone listening to music through headphones will often speak inappropriately loudly, (the Lombard reflex). The performers may have felt less embarrassed because the room was soundproofed and the others were unable to see or hear them. Finally, through eliminating the possibility of hearing each other, individuals could no longer be influenced by the output of the others, thereby lifting the pressure of social conformity.

As in Experiment 1, as the number of actual performers increased, the total sound output also increased, but at a slower rate than would be expected from the sum of the individual outputs.

Actual groups of two shouted at only 66 per cent of capacity, and groups of six at 36 per cent, $F(2, 10)$ = 226, $p < .001$. The comparable figures for Experiment 1 are 71 per cent and 40 per cent. These similarities between experiments suggest that our procedural changes, even though they made people unable to hear or see each other, did not eliminate their feeling of being in a group or reduce the amount of incoordination or social loafing.

The line connecting the solid circles in Figure 20.2 shows the decreased output per person when actually performing in groups. The dashed line along the top represents potential productivity—the output to be expected if there were no losses due to faulty coordination or to social loafing. The striped area at the bottom represents the obtained output per person in actual groups. Output is obviously lower than potential productivity,

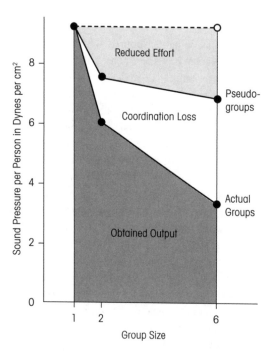

Figure 20.2 **Intensity of sound produced per person when cheering in actual or perceived groups of 1, 2, and 6, as a result of reduced effort and faulty coordination of group efforts, Experiment 2.**

and this decrease can be considered as representing the sum of the losses due to incoordination and to reduced individual effort.

In addition to shouting in actual groups, individuals also performed in pseudogroups in which they believed that others shouted with them but in which they actually shouted alone, thus preventing coordination loss from affecting output. As shown in Figure 20.2, people shouted with less intensity in pseudogroups than when alone, $F(2, 10) = 37.0$, $p < .0001$. Thus, group size made a significant difference even in pseudogroups in which coordination loss is not a factor and only social loafing can operate.

When performers believed one other person was yelling, they shouted 82 per cent as intensely as when alone, and when they believed five others to be yelling, they shouted 74 per cent as intensely. The stippled area defined at the top of Figure 20.2 by the data from the pseudogroups represents the amount of loss due to social loafing. By subtraction, we can infer that the white area of Figure 20.2 represents the amount of loss due to faulty coordination. Since the latter comprises about the same area as the former, we can conclude that, for shouting, half the performance loss decrement is due to incoordination and half is due to social loafing.

Discussion

Despite the methodological differences between Experiments 1 and 2, both experiments showed that there is a reduction in sound pressure produced per person when people make noise in groups compared to when alone. People in Experiment 1 applauded and cheered in full view of each other, with all the excitement, embarrassment, and conformity that goes along with such a situation. In Experiment 2, no one could see or hear any other person. Only the experimenters could see the people perform. And finally, the rationale changed drastically, from the experimenters' interest in 'judgments of how much noise people make in social settings' to their interest in 'the effects of sensory feedback on the production of sound in social groups'. Yet, despite differences in the task characteristics and supposed purpose, the two studies produced similar results. This points to the robust nature of both the phenomenon and the paradigm.

General Discussion

Noise Production as Group Performance

Although we do not usually think about it that way, making noise can be hard work, in both the physical and the psychological sense. In the present case, the participants were asked to produce sound pressure waves, either by rapidly vibrating their laryngeal membranes or by vigorously striking their hands together. Although superficially similar in consequence, this task should not be confused with more normal outbreaks of shouting and clapping that occur as spontaneous outbursts of exuberant expressiveness. Our participants shouted and clapped because we asked them to, not because they wanted to.

This effortful and fatiguing task resulted in sound pressure waves, which, although invisible, can be easily and accurately measured in physical units that are proportional to the amount of work performed. The making of noise is a useful task for the study of group processes from the standpoint both of production and of measurement—people are practiced and skilled at making noise and can do so without the help of expensive or cumbersome apparatus, and acoustics and audio engineering are sufficiently advanced to permit sophisticated data collection. We seem to have found a paradigm wherein people get involved enough to try hard and become somewhat enthusiastic, yet the task is still effortful enough so that they loaf when given the opportunity.

The Causes of Social Loafing

The present research shows that groups can inhibit the productivity of individuals so that people reduce their exertions when it comes to shouting and clapping with others. Why does this occur? We suggest three lines of explanation, the first having to do with attribution and equity, the second with submaximal goal setting, and the third with the lessening of the contingency between individual inputs and outcomes.

1. Attribution and Equity

It may be that participants engaged in a faulty attribution process, leading to an attempt to maintain an equitable division of labour. There are at least three aspects of the physics and psychophysics of producing sound that could have led people to believe that the other persons in their group were not working as hard or effectively as themselves. First, individuals judged their own outputs to be louder than those of the others, simply because they were closer to the sound source. Second, even if everyone worked to capacity, sound cancellation would cause group outputs to seem much less than the sum of their individual performances. Finally, the perception of the amount of sound produced in a group should be much less than the actual amount—growing only as the 0.67 power of the actual amount of sound, according to Stevens's psychophysical power law (1975).

These factors may have led individuals to believe that the other participants were less motivated or less skillful than themselves—in short, were shirkers or incompetents. Thus, differences in the perception of sound production that were essentially the result of physical and psychophysical processes may have been mistakenly attributed to a lack of either skill or motivation on the part of the others, leading individuals to produce less sound in groups because there is no reason to work hard in aid of shirkers or those who are less competent.

This process cannot explain the results of Experiment 2, since the capacity to judge the loudness of one's own output, much less that of others, was severely impaired by the 90-dB background masking noise used to signal the trials. However, rather than 'discovering' social loafing while participating in the experiment, the participants may have arrived with the pre-existing notion that people often do not pull their own weight in groups. Thus, despite being unable to hear or see one another, lack of trust and the propensity to attribute laziness or ineptitude to others could have led people to work less hard themselves.

2. Submaximal Goal Setting

It may be that despite our instructions, participants redefined the task and adopted a goal, not of making as much noise as possible, but merely of making enough noise or of matching some more or less well-defined standard. Individuals would clearly expect it to be easier to achieve this goal when others are helping, and might work less hard as a consequence. This, of course, would change the nature of noise production from what Steiner (1972) would term a *maximizing* task to an *optimizing* task. A maximizing task makes success a function of how much or how rapidly something is accomplished. For an optimizing task, however, success is a function of how closely the individual or group approximates a predetermined 'best' or correct outcome. If participants in our experiments perceived sound production as an optimizing rather than a maximizing task, they might feel the optimal level of sound output could be reached more easily in groups than alone, thereby allowing them to exert less effort.

The participants in Experiment 2 could hear neither themselves nor others and would not be able to determine whether their output was obnoxious or to develop a group standard for an optimal level. Furthermore, in both experiments, the experimenters reiterated their request to yell 'as loud as you can, every time', over and over again. Before the first trial they would ask the group how loud they were supposed to yell. In unison, the group would reply, 'As loud as we can!' We think it unlikely that participants perceived the task to be anything other than maximizing.

3. Lessened Contingency between Input and Outcome

It may be that participants felt that the contingency between their input and the outcome was lessened when performing in groups. Individuals could 'hide in the crowd' (Davis, 1969) and avoid the negative consequences of slacking off, or they may have felt 'lost in the crowd' and unable to obtain their fair share of the positive consequences for working hard. Since individual scores are unidentifiable when groups perform together, people can receive neither precise credit nor appropriate blame for their performance. Only when performing alone can individual outputs be exactly evaluated and rewarded.

Let us assume that group members expect approval or other rewards proportional to the total output of a group of n performers, but that since individual efforts are indistinguishable, the reward is psychologically divided equally among the participants, each getting $1/n$ units of reward. Under these assumptions, the average group, if it performed up to capacity and suffered no process loss, could expect to divide up n times the reward of the average individual, resulting in each member's getting $n \times 1/n$, or n/n, units of reward, the same amount as an individual.

Although the total amount of reward may be the same, the contingency on individual output is not. Any given individual under these assumptions will get back only one nth of his own contribution to the group; the rest will be shared by the others. Even though he may also receive unearned one nth of each other person's contribution, he will be tempted, to the extent that his own performance is costly or effortful, to become a 'free rider' (Olson, 1965). Thus, under these assumptions, if his own performance cannot be individually monitored, an individual's incentive to perform should be proportional to $1/n$.

Seligman (1975) has shown that animals and people become lethargic and depressed when confronted with tasks in which they have little or no control over the outcomes. Likewise, in our experiments, people may have felt a loss of control over their fair share of the rewards when they performed in groups, leading them also to become, if not lethargic and depressed, at least less enthusiastic about making lots of noise.

Since people were asked to shout both alone and in groups, they may have felt it smart to save their strength in groups and to shout as lustily as possible when scores were individually identifiable, marshalling their energy for the occasions when they could earn rewards. This line of reasoning suggests that if inputs were made identifiable and rewards contingent on them, even when in groups, it would be impossible for performers to get a free ride and they would have an incentive to work equally hard in groups of different sizes.

Social Loafing and Social Impact Theory

Each of these three lines of explanation may be described in terms of Latané's (1973) theory of social impact. If a person is the target of social forces, increasing the number of other persons also in the target group should diminish the pressures on each individual because the impact is divided among the group members. In a group performance situation in which pressures to work come from outside the group and individual outputs are not identifiable, this division of impact should lead each individual to work less hard. Thus, whether the subject is dividing up the amount of work he thinks should be performed or whether he is dividing up the amount of reward he expects to earn with his work, he should work less hard in groups.

The theory of social impact further stipulates the form that the decrease in output should follow. Just as perceptual judgments of physical stimuli follow power functions (Stevens, 1957), so also should judgments of social stimuli, and the exponent of the psychosocial power function should have an exponent of less than one, resulting in a marginally decreasing impact of additional people. Thus, social impact theory suggests that the amount of effort expended on group tasks should decrease as an inverse power function of the number of people in the group. This implication cannot be tested in Experiment 1 or with the actual groups of Experiment 2, inasmuch as coordination loss is confounded with social loafing. However, a power function with an exponent of −0.14 accounted for

93 per cent of the variance for the pseudogroups of Experiment 2. It appears that social impact theory provides a good account of both the existence and the magnitude of social loafing.

The Transsituational and Transcultural Generality of Social Loafing

The present research demonstrates that performance losses in groups occur with tasks other than rope pulling and with people other than pre-war German workers. There are, in addition, other instances of experimental research that demonstrate similar cases of social loafing. For example, Marriott (1949) and Campbell (1952) have shown that factory workers produce less per person in larger groups than in smaller ones. Latané and Darley (1970) have found that the likelihood that a bystander will intervene in a situation in which someone requires assistance is substantially reduced by the addition of other bystanders who share in the responsibility for help. Wicker (1969) has found that the proportion of members taking part in church activities is lower in large than in small churches, presumably because the responsibility for taking part is more diffuse. Similarly, Petty, Harkins, Williams, and Latané (1977) found that people perceived themselves as exerting less cognitive effort on evaluating poems and editorials when they were among groups of other unidentifiable evaluators than when they alone were responsible for the task.

These experimental findings have demonstrated that a clear potential exists in human nature for social loafing. We suspect that the effects of social loafing have far-reaching and profound consequences both in our culture and in other cultures. For example, on collective farms (*kolkhoz*) in Russia, the peasants 'move all over huge areas, working one field and one task one day, another field the next, having no sense of responsibility and no direct dependence on the results of their labor' (Smith, 1976, p. 281). Each peasant family is also allowed a private plot of up to an acre in size that may be worked after the responsibility to the collective is discharged. The produce of these plots, for which the peasants are individually responsible, may be used as they see fit. Although these plots occupy less than 1 per cent of the nation's agricultural lands (about 26 million acres), they produce 21 per cent of the total value of Soviet farm output (about $32.5 billion worth) (Yemelyanov, 1975, cited in Smith, 1976, p. 266). It is not, however, that the private sector is so highly efficient; rather, it is that the efficiency of the public sector is so low (Wädekin, 1973, p. 67).

However, before we become overly pessimistic about the potential of collective effort, we should consider the Israeli kibbutz, an example that suggests that the effects of social loafing can be circumvented. Despite the fact that kibbutzim are often located in remote and undeveloped areas on the periphery of Israel to protect the borders and develop these regions, these communes have been very successful. For example, in dairying, 1963 yields per cow on the kibbutz were 21 per cent higher than for the rest of Israel's herds, and in 1960 yields were 15 per cent higher than in England. In 1959, kibbutz chickens were producing 22 per cent of the eggs with only 16 per cent of the chickens (Leon, 1969). The kibbutz and the *kolkhoz* represent the range of possibilities for collective effort, and comparisons of these two types of collective enterprise may suggest conditions under which per person output would be greater in groups than individually.

Social Loafing as a Social Disease

Although some people still think science should be value free, we must confess that we think social loafing can be regarded as a kind of social disease. It is a 'disease' in that it has negative consequences for individuals, social institutions, and societies. Social loafing results in a reduction in human efficiency, which leads to lowered profits and lowered benefits for all. It is 'social' in that it results from the presence or actions of other people.

The 'cure', however, is not to do away with groups, because despite their inefficiency, groups make possible the achievement of many goals that individuals alone could not possibly accomplish. Collective action is a vital aspect of our lives: From time immemorial it has made possible the construction of monuments, but today it is necessary to the provision of even our food and shelter. We think the cure will come from finding ways of channelling social forces so that the group can serve as a means of intensifying individual responsibility rather than diffusing it.

Note

1. Levinger, G. Personal communication, June 1976.

Discussion Questions

1. When is social loafing more versus less likely to occur? What criteria do you think are necessary for it to occur and what variables may enhance or reduce the effect?
2. If you were a manager, how would you reduce social loafing in your workforce?
3. Do you agree with Latané et al.'s analogy of social loafing to a 'disease'? Justify your response.

Unit Nine Further Reading

One of the important directions that the social comparison literature has taken is to ask the question, 'When does comparison to someone better than you hurt versus help your own performance?' One answer to this question has been provided by Lockwood, Kunda, and others. In a series of studies, these authors showed that thinking about another person who has outperformed you can be inspiring if (a) that person's success is in a domain you care about and (b) you consider that level of performance ultimately attainable. But if these criteria are not met, thinking about superior others can be a self-deflating, emotionally difficult experience. In a related vein, Tesser and colleagues tackled the question of when people will feel pride versus envy in the accomplishments of someone they know. These researchers showed that the *closeness* of the person being compared together with the *relevance* of the domain to one's self-definition are key variables. Being outperformed by a close other in a highly self-relevant domain predicts envy, but being outperformed by a close other on a less self-relevant domain predicts pride.

Lockwood, P. & Kunda, Z. (1997). Superstars and me: Predicting the impact of role models on the self. *Journal of Personality and Social Psychology, 73,* 91–103.

Tesser, A. & Collins, J.E. (1988). Emotion in social reflection and comparison situations: Intuitive, systematic, and exploratory approaches. *Journal of Personality and Social Psychology, 55,* 695–709.

For more on the social loafing/social compensation dynamic, see

Karau, S.J. & Williams, K.D. (1993). Social loafing: A meta-analytic review and theoretical integration. *Journal of Personality and Social Psychology, 65,* 681–706.

Plaks, J.E. & Higgins, E.T. (2000). Pragmatic use of stereotyping in teamwork: Social loafing and social compensation as a function of inferred partner–situation fit. *Journal of Personality and Social Psychology, 79,* 962–974.

References

Abelson, R.P. (1968). Psychological implication. In R.P. Abelson, E. Aronson, W.J. McGuire, T.M. Newcomb, M.J. Rosenberg, & P.H. Tannenbaum (Eds.) *Theories of cognitive consistency: A sourcebook* (pp. 112–139). Chicago: Rand McNally.

———. (1983). Whatever became of consistency theory? *Personality and Social Psychology Bulletin, 9,* 37–54.

Abrams, D. (1994). Political distinctiveness: An identity optimising approach. *European Journal of Social Psychology, 24,* 357–365.

Abramson, L.Y., Seligman, M.E.P., & Teasdale, J.D. (1978). Learned helplessness in humans: Critique and reformulation. *Journal of Abnormal Psychology, 87,* 49–74.

Adams, J.A. (1971). A closed-loop theory of motor learning. *Journal of Motor Behavior,* 111–119.

Adler, A. (1964). Problems of neurosis. New York: Harper & Row. (Original work published 1929)

Adler, P. (1980). On becoming a prostitute. In E. Muga (Ed.), *Studies in prostitution* (pp. 22–26). Nairobi, Kenya: Kenya Literature Bureau.

Adorno, T.W., Frenkel-Brunswik, E., Levinson, D.J., & Sanford, R.N. (1950). *The authoritarian personality.* New York: Harper & Brothers.

Aiken, E.G. (1957). The effort variable in the acquisition, extinction, and spontaneous recovery of an instrumental response. *Journal of Experimental Pscyhology, 53,* 47–51.

Ainsworth, M.D. (1989). Attachments beyond infancy. *American Psychologist, 44,* 709–716.

Ajzen, I., & Fishbein, M. (1977). Attitude–behavior relations: A theoretical analysis and review of empirical research. *Psychological Bulletin 84,* 888–918.

———. (1980). *Understanding attitudes and predicting social behavior.* Englewood Cliffs, NJ: Prentice Hall.

Allison, S.T., & Messick, D.M. (1988). The feature-positive effect, attitude strength, and degree of perceived consensus. *Personality and Social Psychology Bulletin, 14,* 231–241.

Allport, G.W. (1937). *Personality: A psychological interpretation.* New York: Holt.

———. (1946). Effect: A secondary principle of learning. *Psychological Review, 53,* 335–347.

Amabile, T.M. (1979). Effects of external evaluations on artistic creativity. *Journal of Personality and Social Psychology, 37,* 221–233.

———. (1982). Children's artistic creativity: Detrimental effects of competition in a field setting. *Personality and Social Psychology Bulletin, 5,* 573–578.

———. (1983). *The social psychology of creativity.* New York: Springer-Verlag.

Amabile, T.M., DeJong, W., & Lepper, M.R. (1976). Effects of externally imposed deadlines on subsequent intrinsic motivation. *Journal of Personality and Social Psychology, 34,* 92–98.

Amabile, T.M., Hennessey, B.A., & Grossman, B.S. (1986). Social influence on creativity: The effects of contracted-for rewards. *Journal of Personality and Social Psychology, 50,* 14–23.

Ames, C. (1992). Classrooms: Goals, structures, and student motivation. *Journal of Educational Psychology, 84,* 261–271.

Ames, C., & Archer, J. (1988). Achievement goals in the classroom: Students' learning strategies and motivation processes. *Journal of Educational Psychology, 80,* 260–267.

Andersen, S.M., & Lyon, J.E. (1987). Anticipating desired outcomes: The role of outcome certainty in the onset of depressive affect. *Journal of Experimental Social Psychology, 23,* 428–443.

Anderson, C.A. (1983a). The causal structure of situations: The generation of plausible causal attributions as a function of type of event situation. *Journal of Experimental Social Psychology, 19,* 185–203.

———. (1983b). Motivational and performance deficits in interpersonal settings: The effects of attributional style. *Journal of Personality and Social Psychology, 45,* 1136–1147.

———. (1991). How people think about causes: Examination of the typical phenomenal organization of attributions for success and failure. *Social Cognition, 9,* 295–329.

Anderson, C.A., & Jennings, D.L. (1980). When experiences of failure promote expectations of success: The impact of attributing failure to ineffective strategies. *Journal of Personality, 48,* 393–407.

Anderson, J.R. (1983). *The architecture of cognition.* Cambridge, MA: Harvard University Press.

Anderson, N.H. (1965). Primacy effects in personality impression formation using a generalized order effect paradigm. *Journal of Personality and Social Psychology, 2,* 1–9.

Anderson, N.H., & Hubert, S. (1963). Effects of concomitant verbal recall on order effects in personality impression formation. *Journal of Verbal Learning and Verbal Behavior, 2,* 379–391.

Anderson, S.A., Russell, C.S., & Schumm, W.R. (1983). Perceived marital quality and family life-cycle categories: A further analysis. *Journal of Marriage and the Family, 45,* 127–139.

Andrews, G.R., & Debus, R.L. (1978). Persistence and causal perceptions of failure: Modifying cognitive attributions. *Journal of Educational Psychology, 70,* 154–166.

Angyal, A. (1941). *Foundations for a science of personality.* New York: Commonwealth Fund.

Ansbacher, H.L., & Ansbacher, R.R. (Eds). (1956). *The individual psychology of Alfred Adler.* New York: Basic Books.

Anscombe, G.E.M. (1957). *Intentiun.* Oxford. England: Blackwell.

Antes, J.R., & Matthews, G.R. (1988, November). *Attention and depression: Do the depressed focus on sad themes?* Paper presented at the meeting of the Psychonomic Society, Chicago.

Argyle, M. (1987). *The psychology of happiness.* London: Methuen.

Armstrong, J.G., & Roth, D.M. (1989). Attachment and separation in eating disorders: A preliminary investigation. *International Journal of Eating Disorders, 8,* 141–155.

Arnold, M.B. (1960). *Emotion and personality.* New York: Columbia University Press.

Aron, A., Aron, E.N., Tudor, M., & Nelson, G. (1991). Close relationships as including other in the self. *Journal of Personality and Social Psychology, 60,* 241–253.

Aronson, E. (1966). The psychology of insufficient justification: An analysis of some conflicting data. In S. Feldman (Ed.), *Cognitive consistency.* New York: Academic Press.

———. (1968). Dissonance theory: Progress and problems. In R.P. Abelson, E. Aronson, W.J. McGuire, T.M. Newcomb, M.J. Rosenberg, & P.H. Tannenbaum (Eds), *Theories of cognitive consistency: A sourcebook* (pp. 5–27). Chicago: Rand McNally.

Aronson, E., & Mills, J. (1959). The effect of severity of initiation on liking for a group. *Journal of Abnormal Social Psychology, 59,* 177–181.

Arrowood, A.J., & Ross, L. (1966). Anticipated effort and subjective probability. *Journal of Personality and Social Psychology, 4,* 57–64.

Asch, S.E. (1946). Forming impressions of personality. *Journal of Abnormal and Social Psychology, 41,* 258–290.

Atkinson, J.W. (1957). Motivational determinants of risk-taking behavior. *Psychological Review, 64,* 359–372.

———. (1964). *An introduction to motivation.* Princeton, NJ: Van Nostrand.

———. (1974a). The mainsprings of achievement-oriented activity. In J.W. Atkinson & J.O. Raynor (Eds), *Motivation and achievement* (pp. 13–41). New York: Wiley.

———. (1974b). Strength of motivation and efficiency of performance. In J.W. Atkinson & J.O. Raynor (Eds), *Motivation and achievement* (pp. 193–218). New York: Wiley.

Atkinson, J.W., & Birch, D. (1970). *The dynamics of action.* New York: Wiley.

Audy, J.R. (1980). Man the lonely animal: Biological roots of loneliness. In J. Hartog, J.R. Audy, & Y.A. Cohen (Eds), *The anatomy of loneliness* (pp. 111–128). New York: International Universities Press.

Austin, J.L. (1961). *Philosophical papers.* London: Oxford University Press.

Ausubel, D.P. (1955). Relationships between shame and guilt in the socializing process. *Psychological Review, 62,* 378–390.

Averill, J.A. (1982). *Anger and aggression.* New York: Springer-Verlag.

———. (1983). Studies on anger and aggression. *American Psychologist, 38,* 1145–1160.

Axelrod, R., & Hamilton, W.D. (1981). The evolution of cooperation. *Science, 211,* 1390–1396.

Baker, R.C., & Guttfreund, D.G. (1993). The effects of written autobiographical recollection induction procedures on mood. *Journal of Clinical Psychology, 49,* 563–568.

Baldwin, M.W., & Holmes. J.G. (1987). Salient private audiences and awareness of the self. *Journal of Personality and Social Psychology, 53,* 1087–1098.

Banaji, M.R., & Prentice, D.A. (1994). The self in social contexts. In L. Porter & M. Rosenzweig (Eds), *Annual review of psychology* (Vol. 45, pp. 297–332). Palo Alto, CA: Annual Reviews.

Bandura, A. (1969). *Principles of behavior modification.* New York: Holt.

———. (1977a). Self-efficacy: Toward a unifying theory of behavioral change. *Psychological Review, 84,* 191–215.

———. (1977b). Social learning theory. Englewood Cliffs, NJ: Prentice Hall.

———. (1986). *Social foundations of thought and action: A social cognitive theory.* Englewood Cliffs, NJ: Prentice Hall.

Bandura, A., & Cervone, D. (1983). Self-evaluative and self-efficacy mechanisms governing the motivational effects of goal systems. *Journal of Personality & Social Psychology, 45,* 1017–1028.

Barash, D.P. (1977). *Sociobiology and behavior.* New York: Elsevier.

Barchas, P. (1986). A sociophysiological orientation to small groups. In E. Lawler (Ed.), *Advances in group processes* (Vol. 3, pp. 209–246). Greenwich, CT: JAI Press.

Barden, R.C., Garber, J., Leiman, B., Ford, M.E., & Masters, J.C. (1985). Factors governing the effective remediation of negative affect and its cognitive and behavioral consequences. *Journal of Personality and Social Psychology, 49,* 1040–1053.

Bargh, J.A. (1982). Attention and automaticity in the processing of self-relevant information. *Journal of Personality and Social Psychology, 43,* 425–436.

———. (1994). The four horsemen of automaticity: Awareness, intention, efficiency, and control in social cognition. In R.S. Wyer, Jr, & T.K. Srull (Eds), *Handbook of social cognition* (pp. 1–40). Hillsdale, NJ: Erlbaum.

———. (1997). The automaticity of everyday life. In R.S. Wyer (Ed.), *Advances in social cognition* (Vol. 10, pp. 1–61). Mahwah, NJ: Erlbaum.

Bargh. J.A., Bond, R.N., Lombardi, W.J., & Tota, M.E. (1986). The additive nature of chronic and temporary sources of construct accessibility. *Journal of Personality and Social Psychology, 50,* 869–878.

Bargh, J.A., Chaiken, S., Govender, R., & Pratto, F. (1992). The generality of the automatic attitude activation effect. *Journal of Personality & Social Psychology, 62,* 893–912.

Bargh, J.A., & Ferguson, M.J. (2000). Beyond behaviorism: On the automaticity of higher mental processes. *Psychological Bulletin, 126,* 925–945.

Bargh, J.A., & Pietromonaco, P. (1982). Automatic information processing and social perception: The influence of trait information presented outside of conscious awareness on impression formation. *Journal of Personality and Social Psychology, 43,* 437–449.

Bargh, J.A., & Thein, R.D. (1985). Individual construct accessibility, person memory, and the recall-judgment link: The case of information overload. *Journal of Personality and Social Psychology, 49,* 1129–1146.

Bar-Hillel, M. (1973). On the subjective probability of compound events. *Organizational Behavior and Human Performance, 9,* 396–406.

Baron, R.M., & Kenny, D.A. (1986). The moderator–mediator variable distinction in social psychological research: Conceptual, strategic and statistical considerations. *Journal of Personality and Social Psychology, 51,* 173–1182.

Barocas, R., & Vance, F.L. (1974). Physical appearance and personal adjustment counseling. *Journal of Counseling Psychology, 21,* 96–100.

Barron, K.E., & Harackiewicz, J.M. (2000). Achievement goals and optimal motivation: A multiple goals approach. In C. Sansone & J. Harackiewicz (Eds), *Intrinsic and extrinsic motivation: The search for optimal motivation and performance* (pp. 229–254). San Diego, CA: Academic Press.

———, & ———. (2001). Achievement goals and optimal motivation: Testing multiple goal models. *Journal of Personality and Social Psychology, 80,* 706–722.

Bar-Tal, D., Goldberg, M., & Knaani, A. (1984). Causes of success and failure and their dimensions as a function of SES and gender: A phenomenological analysis. *British Journal of Educational Psychology, 54,* 51–61.

Barton, K., & Harackiewicz, J. (2000). Achievement goals and optimal motivation: A multiple goals approach. In C. Sansone & J. Harackiewicz (Eds), *Intrinsic and extrinsic motivation: The search for optimal motivation and performance* (pp. 229–254). San Diego, CA: Academic Press.

Bassili, J.N. (1995). Response latency and the accessibility of voting intentions: What contributes to accessibility and how it affects vote choice. *Personality & Social Psychology Bulletin, 21,* 686–695.

———. (1996). Meta-judgmental versus operative indexes of psychological attributes: The case of measures of attitude strength. *Journal of Personality & Social Psychology, 71,* 637–653.

Baumeister, R.F. (1982). A self-presentational view of social phenomena. *Psychological Bulletin, 91,* 3–26.

———. (1984). Choking under pressure: Self-consciousness and the paradoxical effects of incentives on skilled performance. *Journal of Personality and Social Psychology, 46,* 610–620.

———. (1990). Suicide as escape from self. *Psychological Review, 97,* 90–113.

———. (1991). *Meanings of life.* New York: Guilford Press.

———. (1995). The self. In D.T. Gilbert, S.T Fiske, & G. Lindzey (Eds), *Handbook of social psychology* (4th edn, pp. 680–740). New York: McGraw-Hill.

Baumeister, R.F., Heatherton, T.F., & Tice, D.M. (1994). *Losing control: How and why people fail at self-regulation.* San Diego, CA: Academic Press.

Baumeister, R.F., & Leary, M.R. (1995). The need to belong: Desire for interpersonal attachments as a fundamental human motivation. *Psychological Bulletin, 117,* 497–529.

Baumeister, R.F., Stillwell, A.M., & Heatherton, T.F. (1994). Guilt: An interpersonal approach. *Psychological Bulletin, 115,* 243–267.

———, ———, & ———. (in press). Personal narratives about guilt: Role in action control and interpersonal relationships. *Basic and Applied Social Psychology.*

Baumeister, R.F., & Tice, D.M. (1990). Anxiety and social exclusion. *Journal of Social and Clinical Psychology, 9,* 165–195.

Baumeister, R.F., & Wotman, S.R. (1992). *Breaking hearts: The two sides of unrequited love.* New York: Guilford Press.

Baumeister, R.F., Wotman, S.R., & Stillwell, A.M. (1993). Unrequited love: On heartbreak, anger, guilt, scriptlessness, and humiliation. *Journal of Personality and Social Psychology, 64,* 377–394.

Baunach, P.J. (1985). *Mothers in prison.* New Brunswick, NJ: Transaction Books.

Beach, F.A. (1942). Analysis of factors involved in the arousal, maintenance and manifestation of sexual excitement in male animals. *Psychosomatic Medicine, 4,* 173–198.

———. (1951). Instinctive behavior: Reproductive activities. In S.S. Stevens (Ed.), *Handbook of experimental psychology* (pp. 387–434). New York: Wiley.

Beach, L.R., & Mitchell, T.R. (1978). A contingency model for the selection of decision strategies. *Academy of Management Review, 3,* 439–449.

Beck, A.T. (1972). *Depression: Causes and treatment.* Philadelphia: University of Pennsylvania Press.

Beckman, K., Marsella, A.J., & Finney, R. (1979). Depression in the wives of nuclear submarine personnel. *American Journal of Psychiatry, 136,* 524–526.

Beckman. L.J. (1981). Effects of social interaction and children's relative inputs on older women's psychological well-being. *Journal of Personality and Social Psychology, 41*, 1075–1086.

Bednarski, R., & Leary, M.R. (1994). *Self-esteem and fear of death.* Unpublished manuscript, Wake Forest University, Winston-Salem, NC.

Belsky, J. (1979). The interrelation of parental and spousal behavior during infancy in traditional nuclear families: An exploratory analysis. *Journal of Marriage and the Family, 41*, 749–755.

———. (1981). Early human experience: A family perspective. *Developmental Psychology, 17*, 3–23.

Bem, D.J. (1965). An experimental analysis of self-persuasion. *Journal of Experimental Social Psychology, 1*, 199–218.

———. (1967). Self-perception: An alternative interpretation of cognitive dissonance phenomena. *Psychological Review, 74*, 183–200.

———. (1972). Self-perception theory. In L. Berkowitz (Ed.), *Advances in experimental social psychology* (Vol. 6). New York: Academic Press.

Bem, D.J., & Allen, A. (1974). On predicting some of the people some of the time: The search for cross-situational consistencies in behavior. *Psychological Review, 81*, 506–520.

Bentham, J. (1779/1879). *Introduction to the principles of morals and legislation.* Oxford: Clarendon Press.

Bentler, P.M., & Wu, E.J.C. (1995). *EQS for Windows user's guide.* Encino, CA: Multivariate Software.

Benware, C., & Deci, E.L. (1984). The quality of learning with an active versus passive motivational set. *American Educational Research Journal, 21*, 755–765.

Berkowitz, L., & Devine, P.G. (1989). Research traditions, analysis, and synthesis in social psychological theories: The case of dissonance theory. *Personality and Social Psychology Bulletin, 15*, 493–507.

Berlyne, D.E. (1950). Novelty and curiosity as determinants of exploratory behavior. *British Journal of Psychology, 41*, 68–80.

———. (1955). The arousal and satiation of perceptual curiosity in the rat. *Journal of Comparative & Physiological Pschology, 48*, 238–246.

———. (1957). Attention to change, conditioned inhibition (SXR) and stimulus satiation. *British Journal of Psychology, 48*, 138–140.

———. (1958). The present status of research on exploratory and related behavior. *Journal of Individual Pscyhology, 14*, 121–126.

———. (1960). *Conflict, arousal and curiosity.* New York: McGraw-Hill.

———. (1963). Motivational problems raised by exploratory and epistemic behavior. In S. Koch (Ed.), *Psychology: A study of a science* (Vol. 5, pp. 284–364). New York: McGraw-Hill.

Berman, W.H. (1988). The role of attachment in the post-divorce experience. *Journal of Personality and Social Psychology, 54*, 496–503.

Bernard. J. (1982). *The failure of marriage.* New Haven, CT: Yale University Press.

Berridge, K. (1999). Pleasure, pain, desire, and dread: Hidden core processes of emotion. In D. Kahneman, E. Diener, & N. Schwarz (Eds), *Wellbeing: The foundations of hedonic psychology* (pp. 525–557). New York: Russell Sage Foundation.

Berscheid, E. (1983). Emotion. In H.H. Kelley, E. Berscheid, A. Christiansen, J.H. Harvey, T.L. Huston, G. Levinger, E. McClintock, L.A. Peplau, & D.R. Peterson (Eds), *Close relationships* (pp. 110–168). San Francisco: Freeman.

Berscheid, E., Graziano, W., Monson, T., & Dermer, M. (1976). Outcome dependency: Attention, attribution, and attraction. *Journal of Personality and Social Psychology, 34*, 978–989.

Berscheid, E., & Walster, E. (1974). Physical attractiveness. In L. Berkowitz (Ed.), *Advances in experimental social psychology* (Vol. 7, pp. 158–215). New York: Academic Press.

Betancourt, H. (1983). *Causal attributions, empathy, and emotions as determinants of helping behavior: An integrative approach.* Unpublished doctoral dissertation, University of California, Los Angeles.

Bhatti, B., Derezotes, D., Kim, S., & Specht, H. (1989). The association between child maltreatment and self-esteem. In A.M. Mecca, N.J. Smelser, & J. Vasconcellos (Eds), *The social importance of self-esteem* (pp. 24–71). Berkeley: University of California Press.

Bibhing, E. (1941). The development and problems of the theories of the instincts. *International Journal of Psychoanalysis, 22*, 102–131.

Billig, M., & Tajfel, H. (1973). Social categorization and similarity in intergroup behavior. *European Journal of Social Psychology, 3*, 27– 51.

Blanck, P.D., Reis, H.T., & Jackson, L. (1984). The effects of verbal reinforcements on intrinsic motivation for sex-linked tasks. *Sex Roles, 10*, 369–387.

Blaney, P.H. (1986). Affect and memory: A review. *Psychological Bulletin, 99*, 229–246.

Blatt, S.J., & Lerner, H. (1983). Investigations in the psychoanalytic theory of object relations and object representations. In I. Masling (Ed.), *Empirical studies of psychoanalytic theories* (Vol. 1, pp. 189–249). Hillsdale, NJ: Erlbaum.

Block, J. (1981). Some enduring and consequential structures of personality. In A.I. Rabin, et al. (Eds). *Further explorations in personality* (pp. 27–43). New York: Wiley.

Bloom, B.L., White, S.W., & Asher, S.J. (1979). Marital disruption as a stressful life event. In G. Levinger & O.C. Moles (Eds), *Divorce and separation: Context, causes, and consequences* (pp. 184–200). New York: Basic Books.

Bobrow, D.G., & Norman, D.A. (1975). Some principles of memory schemata. In D.G. Bobrow & A. Collins (Eds), *Representation and understanding* (pp. 131–149). New York: Academic Press.

Bobrow, D.G., & Winograd, T. (1977). An overview of KRL, a knowledge representation language. *Cognitive Science, 1,* 3–46.

Boggiano, A.K., & Barrett, M. (1985). Performance and motivational deficits of helplessness: The role of motivational orientations. *Journal of Personality and Social Psychology, 49,* 1753–1761.

Boggiano, A.K., Klinger, C.A., & Main, D.S. (1985). Enhancing interest in peer interaction: A developmental analysis. *Child Development, 57,* 852–861.

Boggiano, A.K., & Ruble, D.N. (1979). Competence and the overjustification effect: A developmental study. *Journal of Personality and Social Psychology, 37,* 1462–1468.

Boring, E.G. (1950). *A history of experimental psychology.* New York: Appleton-Century-Crofts.

Bornstein, R.F., Leone, D.R., & Galley, D.J. (1987). The generalizability of subliminal mere exposure effects: Influences of stimuli perceived without awareness on social behavior. *Journal of Personality and Social Psychology, 53,* 1070–1079.

Bottenberg, E.H. (1975). Phenomenological and operational characteristics of factor-analytically derived dimensions of emotion. *Psychological Reports, 37,* 1253–1254.

Boudreau, L.A., Baron, R., & Oliver, P.V. (1992). Effects of expected communication target expertise and timing of set on trait use in person description. *Personality and Social Psychology Bulletin, 18,* 447–452.

Bouffard, T., Boisvert, J., Verzeau, C., & Larouche, C. (1995). The impact of goal orientation on self-regulation and performance among college students. *British Journal of Educational Psychology, 65,* 317–329.

Bower, G.H. (1981). Mood and memory. *American Psychologist, 36,* 129–148.

Bower, G.H., & Cohen, P.R. (1982). Emotional influences in memory and thinking: Data and theory. In M.S. Clark & S.T. Fiske (Eds), *Affect and cognition: The 17th Annual Carnegie Symposium on Cognition* (pp. 291–331). Hillsdale, NJ: Erlbaum.

Bowers, K.S. (1973). Situationism in psychology: An analysis and a critique. *Psychological Review, 90,* 307–336.

Bowlby, J. (1969). Attachment (*Attachment and loss,* Vol.1). New York: Basic Books.

———. (1973). Separation: Anxiety and anger (*Attachment and loss,* Vol. 2). New York: Basic Books.

Branscombe, N.R., Ellemers, N., Spears, R., & Doosje, B. (1999). The context and content of social identity threat. In N. Ellemers, R. Spears, & B. Doosje (Eds), *Social identity: Context, commitment, content* (pp. 35–58). Oxford, UK: Blackwell.

Braudy, L. (1986). *The frenzy of renown: Fame and its history.* New York: Oxford University Press.

Brehm, J. (1966). *A theory of psychological reactance.* New York: Academic Press.

Brehm, S. (1987). Social support and clinical practice. In J.E. Maddux, C.D. Stoltenberg, & R. Rosenwein (Eds), *Social processes in clinical and counseling psychology* (pp. 26–38). New York: Springer-Verlag.

Brehm, S., & Brehm, J.W. (1981). *Psychological reactance: A theory of freedom and control.* New York: Academic Press.

Breitman, R. (1991). *The architect of genocide: Himmler and the final solution.* Hanover, NH: Brandeis University Press.

Brendl, C.M., & Higgins, E.T. (1996). Principles of judging valence: What makes events positive or negative? In M.P. Zanna (Ed.), *Advances in experimental social psychology* (Vol. 28, pp. 95–160). New York: Academic Press.

Brenner, M.W. (1976). *Memory and interpersonal relations.* Unpublished doctoral dissertation, University of Michigan, Ann Arbor.

Brewer, M.B. (1979). Ingroup bias in the minimal intergroup situation: A cognitive-motivational analysis. *Psychological Bulletin, 86,* 307–324.

———. (1991). The social self: On being the same and different at the same time. *Personality and Social Psychology Bulletin, 17,* 475–482.

———. (1993a). The role of distinctiveness in social identity and group behaviour. In M.A. Hogg & D. Abrams (Eds), *Group motivation: Social psychological perspectives.* London: Harvester Wheatsheaf.

———. (1993b). Social identity, distinctiveness, and ingroup homogeneity. *Social Cognition, 11,* 150–164.

Brewer, M.B., & Harasty, A.S. (1996). Seeing groups as entities: The role of perceiver motivation. In R. Sorrentino & E.T. Higgins (Eds), *Handbook of motivation and cognition: Vol. 3. The interpersonal context* (pp. 347–370). New York: Guilford.

Brewer, M.B., Manzi, J.M., & Shaw, J.S. (1993). In-group identification as a function of depersonalization, distinctiveness, and status. *Psychological Science, 4,* 88–92.

Brewer, M.B., & Pickett, C.L. (1999). Distinctiveness motives as a source of the social self. In T. Tyler, R. Kramer, & O. John (Eds), *The psychology of the social self* (pp. 71–87). Mahwah, NJ: Lawrence Erlbaum.

Brewer, M.B., & Silver, M. (1978). Ingroup bias as a function of task characteristics. *European Journal of Social Psychology, 8,* 393–400.

Bridges, W. (1980). *Transitions: Making sense of life's changes.* Reading, MA: Addison-Wesley.

Broadbent, D.E. (1977). Lewis, hierarchies, and the locus of control. *Quarterly Journal of Experimental Psychology, 29,* 181–201.

Brockner, J., Shaw, M.C., & Rubin, J.Z. (1979). Factors affecting withdrawal from an escalating conflict: Quitting before it's too late. *Journal of Experimental Social Psychology, 15,* 492–503.

Brophy, J.E., & Rohrkemper, M.M. (1981). The influence of problem ownership on teachers' perceptions of and strategies for coping with problem students. *Journal of Educational Psychology, 73,* 295–311.

Brown, J., & Weiner, B. (1984). Affective consequences of ability versus effort ascriptions: Controversies, resolutions, and quandaries. *Journal of Educational Psychology, 76,* 146–158.

Brown, J.D. (1986). Evaluations of self and others: Self-enhancement biases in social judgments. *Social Cognition, 4,* 353–376.

Brown, R.W. (1958). How shall a thing be called? *Psychological Review, 65,* 14–21.

Browning, C.R. (1992). *Ordinary men: Reserve Police Battalion 101 and the final solution in Poland.* New York: Harper Collins.

Bruce, V. (1986). Influences of familiarity on the processing of faces. *Perception, 15,* 387–397.

Bruce, V., & Young, A. (1986). Understanding face recognition. *British Journal of Psychology, 77,* 305–327.

Bruner, J.S. (1970). The growth and structure of skill. In K. Connolly (Ed.), *Mechanisms of motor skill development* (pp. 88–103). New York: Academic Press.

Bruner, J.S., Goodnow, J.J., & Austin, G.A. (1956). *A study of thinking.* New York: Wiley.

Bruner, J.S., Matter, J., & Papanek, M.L. (1955). Breadth of learning as a function of drive level and mechanization. *Psychological Review, 62,* 1–10.

Brunswik, E. *Perception and the object world.* Leipzig: Deuticke, 1934.

Bryan, W.L., & Barter, L. (1899). Studies on the telegraphic language: The acquisition of a hierarchy of habits. *Psychological Review, 6,* 345–378.

Bryant, F.B., & Veroff, J. (1982). The structure of psychological well-being: A sociohistorical analysis. *Journal of Personality and Social Psychology, 43,* 653–673.

Buhler, C. (1954). The reality principle. *American Journal of Psychotherapy, 8,* 626–647.

Buhler, K. (1924). *Die geistige Entwicklung des Kindes* (4th edn). Jena: Gustav Fischer.

Bunker, B.B., Zubek, J.M., Vanderslice, V.J., & Rice, R.W. (1992). Quality of life in dual-career families: Commuting versus single-residence couples. *Journal of Marriage and the Family, 54,* 399–407.

Burger, J.M. (1989). Negative reactions to increases in perceived personal control. *Journal of Personality and Social Psychology, 56,* 246–256.

Burger, J.M., Cooper, H.M., & Good, T.L. (1982). Teacher attributions of student performance: Effects of outcome. *Personality and Social Psychology Bulletin, 4,* 685–690.

Burgess, E.W., & Locke, H.J. (1945). *The family: From institution to companionship.* New York: American Book.

Burgio, K.L., Merluzzi, T.V., & Pryor, J.B. (1986). The effects of performance expectancy and self-focused attention on social interaction. *Journal of Personality and Social Psychology, 50,* 1216–1221.

Burkhart, K. (1973). *Women in prison.* Garden City, NY: Doubleday.

Buss, A.H. (1983). Social rewards and personality. *Journal of Personality and Social Psychology, 44,* 553–563.

Buss, D. (1996). The evolutionary psychology of human social strategies. In E.T. Higgins & A.W. Kruglanski (Eds), *Social psychology: Handbook of basic principles* (pp. 3–38). New York: Guilford Press.

Buss, D.M. (1990). The evolution of anxiety and social exclusion. *Journal of Social and Clinical Psychology, 9,* 196–210.

———. (1991). Evolutionary personality psychology. *Annual Review of Psychology, 42,* 459–491.

Butler, R. (1987). Task-involving and ego-involving properties of evaluation: Effects of different feedback conditions on motivational perceptions, interest and performance. *Journal of Educational Psychology, 79,* 474–482.

———. (1993). Effects of task- and ego-achievement goals on information seeking during task engagement. *Journal of Personality & Social Psychology, 65,* 18–31.

Butler, R.A. (1953). Discrimination learning by rhesus monkeys to visual-exploration motivation. *Journal of Comparative & Physiological Psychology, 46,* 95–98.

———. (1958). Exploratory and related behavior: A new trend in animal research. *Journal of Individual Psychology, 14,* 111–120.

Butler, R.A., & Harlow, H.F. (1957). Discrimination learning and learning sets to visual exploration incentives. *Journal of General Psychology, 57,* 257–264.

Button, S.B., Mathieu, J.E., & Zajac, D.M. (1996). Goal orientation in organizational research: A conceptual and empirical foundation. *Organizational Behavior and Human Decision Processes, 67,* 26–48.

Cacioppo, J.T., & Bernston, G. (1994). Relationship between attitudes and evaluative space: A critical review, with emphasis on the separability of positive and negative substrates. *Psychological Bulletin, 115,* 401–422.

Cacioppo, J.T., & Petty, R.E. (1982). The need for cognition. *Journal of Personality and Social Psychology, 42,* 116–131.

Caldwell, M.A., & Peplau, L.A. (1982). Sex differences in same-sex friendship. *Sex Roles, 8,* 721–732.

Campbell, A. (1981). *The sense of well-being in America.* New York: McGraw-Hill.

Campbell, A., Converse, P.E., & Rodgers, W.L. (1976). *The quality of American life: Perceptions, evaluations, and satisfactions.* New York: Russell Sage Foundation.

Campbell, M. (1952). Group incentive payment schemes: The effects of lack of understanding and group size. *Occupational Psychology, 26,* 15–21.

Carnelley, K.B., Pietromonaco, P.R., & Jaffe, K. (1994). Depression, working models of others, and relationship functioning. *Journal of Personality and Social Psychology, 66,* 127–140.

Carroll, J.S. (1978). Causal attributions in expert parole decisions. *Journal of Personality and Social Psychology, 36,* 1501–1511.

Carroll, J.S., & Payne, J.W. (1976). The psychology of the parole decision process: A joint application of attribution theory and information processing psychology. In J.S. Carroll & J.W. Payne (Eds), *Cognition and social behavior* (pp. 13–32). Hillsdale, NJ: Erlbaum.

Carroll, J.S., & Payne, J.W. (1977). Judgements about crime and the criminal: A model and a method for investigating parole decision. In B.D. Sales (Ed.), *Prospectives in law and psychology. Vol. 1: The criminal justice system* (pp. 191–240). New York: Plenum Press.

Carver, C.S. (1979). A cybernetic model of self-attention processes. *Journal of Personality and Social Psychology, 37,* 1251–1281.

Carver, C.S., & Scheier, M, F. (1981). *Attention and self-regulation: A control-theory approach to human behavior.* New York: Springer-Verlag.

———, & ———. (1982a). Control theory: A useful conceptual framework for personality-social, clinical, and health psychology. *Psychological Bulletin, 92,* 111–135.

———, & ———. (1982b). Outcome expectancy, locus of attribution for expectancy, and self-directed attention as determinants of evaluations and performance. *Journal of Experimental Social Psychology, 18,* 184–200.

———, & ———. (1984). Self-focused attention in test anxiety: A general theory applied to a specific phenomenon. In H.M. van der Ploeg, R. Schwarzer, & C.D. Spielberger (Eds), *Advances in test anxiety research* (Vol. 3, pp. 3–20). Hillsdale, NJ: Erlbaum.

———, & ———. (1985). Aspects of self, and the control of behavior. In B.R. Schlenker (Ed.), *The self and social life* (pp. 146–174). New York: McGraw-Hill.

———, & ———. (1986a). Functional and dysfunctional responses to anxiety: The interaction between expectancies and self-focused attention. In R. Schwarzer (Ed.), *Self-related cognitions in anxiety and motivation* (pp. 111–141). Hillsdale, NJ: Erlbaum.

———, & ———. (1986b). Analyzing shyness: A specific application of broader self-regulatory principles. In W.H. Jones, J.M. Cheek, & S.R. Briggs (Eds), *Shyness: Perspectives on research and treatment* (pp. 173–185). New York: Plenum Press.

———, & ———. (1986c). Self and the control of behavior. In L.M. Hartman & K.R. Blankstein (Eds), *Perception of self in emotional disorder and psychotherapy* (pp. 5–35). New York: Plenum Press.

———, & ———. (1990). Principles of self-regulation: Action and emotion. In E.T. Higgins & R.M. Sorrentino (Eds), *Handbook of motivation and cognition: Foundations of social behavior* (Vol. 2, pp. 3–52). New York: Guilford Press.

———, & ———. (1998). *On the self-regulation of behavior.* NY: Cambridge University Press.

Carver, C.S., Blaney, P.H., & Scheier, M.F. (1979a). Focus of attention, chronic expectancy, and responses to a feared stimulus. *Journal of Personality and Social Psychology, 37,* 1186–1195.

———, ———, & ———. (1979b). Reassertion and giving up: The interactive role of self-directed attention and outcome expectancy. *Journal of Personality and Social Psychology, 37,* 1859–1870.

Carver, C.S., La Voie, L., Kuhl, J., & Ganellen, R.J. (1988). Cognitive concomitants of depression: A further examination of the roles of generalization, high standards, and self-criticism. *Journal of Social and Clinical Psychology, 7,* 350–365.

Carver, C.S., Peterson, L.M., Follansbee, D.J., & Scheier, M.F. (1983). Effects of self-directed attention on performance and persistence among persons high and low in test anxiety. *Cognitive Therapy and Research, 7,* 333–354.

Carver, C.S., Reynolds, S.L., & Scheier, M.F. (1994). The possible selves of optimists and pessimists. *Journal of Research in Personality, 28,* 133–141.

Carver, C.S., Scheier, M.F., & Klahr, D. (1987). Further explorations of a control-process model of test anxiety. In R. Schwarzer, H.M. van der Ploeg, & C.D. Spielberger (Eds), *Advances in test anxiety research* (Vol. 5, pp. 15–22). Lisse: Swets & Zeitlinger.

Carver, C.S., Scheier, M.F., & Weintraub, J.K. (1989). Assessing coping strategies: A theoretically based approach. *Journal of Personality and Social Psychology, 56,* 267–283.

Cash, T.F. (1985). Physical appearance and mental health. In J.A. Graham & A. Kligman (Eds), *The psychology of cosmetic treatments* (pp. 196–216). New York: Praeger.

Chaiken, S., Liberman, A., & Eagly, A.H. (1989). Heuristics and systematic information processing within and beyond the persuasion context. In J.S. Uleman & J.A. Bargh (Eds), *Unintended thought: Limits of awareness, intention, and control* (pp. 212–252). New York: Guilford Press.

Chapin, M., & Dyck, D.G. (1976). Persistence in children's reading behavior as a function of N length and attribution retraining. *Journal of Abnormal Psychology, 85,* 511–515.

Cheesman, J., & Merikle, P.M. (1985). Word recognition and consciousness. In D. Besner, T.G. Wailer, & G.E. MacKinnon (Eds), *Reading research: Advances in theory and practice* (Vol. 5, pp. 311–352). New York: Academic Press.

Cialdini, R.B., Darby, B., & Vincent, J. (1973). Transgression and altruism: A case for hedonism. *Journal of Experimental Social Psychology, 9,* 502–516.

Cioffi, D., & Garner, R. (1996). On doing the decision: The effects of active vs. passive choice on commitment and self-perception. *Personality and Social Psychology Bulletin, 22,* 133–147.

Clark, L.A., & Watson, D. (1988). Mood and the mundane: Relations between daily life events and self-reported mood. *Journal of Personality and Social Psychology, 54,* 296–308.

Clark, M.S. (1984). Record keeping in two types of relationships. *Journal of Personality and Social Psychology, 47,* 549–557.

Clark, M.S. (1986). Evidence for the effectiveness of manipulations of communal and exchange relationships. *Personality and Social Psychology Bulletin, 12,* 414–425.

Clark, M.S., Milberg, S., & Ross, J. (1983). Arousal cues arousal-related material in memory: Implications for understanding effects of mood on memory. *Journal of Verbal Learning and Verbal Behavior, 22,* 633–649.

Clark, M.S., & Mills, J. (1979). Interpersonal attraction in exchange and communal relationships. *Journal of Personality and Social Psychology, 37,* 12–24.

Clark, M.S., Mills, J., & Corcoran, D.M. (1989). Keeping track of needs and inputs of friends and strangers. *Personality and Social Psychology Bulletin, 15,* 533–542.

Clark, M.S., Mills, J., & Powell, M.C. (1986). Keeping track of needs in communal and exchange relationships. *Journal of Personality and Social Psychology, 51,* 333–338.

Clark, M.S., Ouellette, R., Powell, M.C., & Milberg, S. (1987). Recipient's mood, relationship type, and helping. *Journal of Personality and Social Psychology, 53,* 94–103.

Clark, M.S., & Waddell, B.A. (1983). Effects of moods on thoughts about helping, attraction, and information acquisition. *Social Psychology Quarterly, 46,* 31–35.

Clore, G.L. (1994). Why emotions vary in intensity. In P. Ekman & R.J. Davidson (Eds), *The nature of emotion: Fundamental questions* (pp. 386–393). Oxford, England: Oxford University Press.

Cofer, C.N. (1959). Motivation. *Annual Review of Psychology, 10,* 173–202.

Cofer, C.N., & Appley, M.H.(1964). *Motivation: Theory and research.* New York: Wiley.

Cohen, J., & Hansel, C.E.M. (1956). *Risk and gambling.* London: Longmans Green.

Cohen, S. (1980). After-effects of stress on human performance and social behavior: A review of research and theory. *Psychological Bulletin, 88,* 82–108.

Cohen, S., Sherrod, D.R., & Clark, M.S. (1986). Social skills and the stress-protective role of social support. *Journal of Personality and Social Psychology, 50,* 963–973.

Cohen, S., & Wills, T.A. (1985). Stress, social support, and the buffering hypothesis. *Psychological Bulletin, 98,* 310–357.

Colby, K.M. (1955). *Energy and structure in psychoanalysis.* New York: Ronald.

Collins, B.E., Martin, J.C., Ashmore, R.D., & Ross, L. (1974). Some dimensions of the internal–external

metaphor in theories of personality. *Journal of Personality and Social Psychology, 29,* 381–391.

Connell, J.P. (1985). A new multidimensional measure of children's perceptions of control. *Child Development, 6,* 281–293.

Connell, J.P., & Ryan, R.M. (1986). *Manual for the ASRQ: A theory and assessment of children's self-regulatory styles in the academic domain.* Unpublished manuscript, University of Rochester, Rochester, NY.

Conte, H.R., Weiner, M.B., & Plutchik, R. (1982). Measuring death anxiety: Conceptual, psychometric, and factor-analytic aspects. *Journal of Personality and Social Psychology, 43,* 775–785.

Cooley, C.H. (1964). *Human nature and the social order.* New York: Schocken Books. (Original work published 1902)

Coon, C.S. (1946). The universality of natural groupings in human societies. *Journal of Educational Sociology, 20,* 163–168.

Cooper, H.M., & Burger, J.M. (1980). How teachers explain students' academic performance: A categorization of free response academic attributions. *American Educational Research Journal, 17,* 95–109.

Cooper, J., & Fazio, R.H. (1984). A new look at dissonance theory. In L. Berkowitz (Ed.), *Advances in experimental social psychology* (Vol. 17, pp. 229–266). New York: Academic Press.

Cooper, J., & Scher, S.J. (1994). Actions and attitudes: The role of responsibility and aversive consequences in persuasion. In T. Brock & S. Shavitt (Eds), *The psychology of persuasion* (pp. 95–111). San Francisco: Freeman.

Cooper, J., Zanna, M.P., & Taves, P.A. (1978). Arousal as a necessary condition for attitude change following induced compliance. *Journal of Personality and Social Psychology, 36,* 1101–1106.

Corwin, G. (1921). Minor studies from the psychological laboratory of Cornell University. *American Journal of Psychology, 32,* 563–570.

Costa, P.T., & McCrae, R.R. (1980a). Influence of extraversion and neuroticism on subjective well-being: Happy and unhappy people. *Journal of Personality and Social Psychology, 38,* 668–678.

———, & ———. (1980b). Still stable after all these years: Personality as a key to some issues in adulthood and old age. In P.B. Baltes & O.G. Brim, Jr (Eds), *Life span development and behavior* (Vol. 3, pp. 66–103). New York: Academic Press.

———, & ———. (1984). Personality as a lifelong determinant of wellbeing. In C.Z. Malatesta & C.E. Izard (Eds), *Emotion in adult development* (pp. 141–157). Beverly Hills, CA: Sage.

———, & ———. (1992). *Revised NEO Personality Inventory (NEO-PI-R) and NEO Five-Factor Inventory (NEO-FFI) professional manual.* Odessa, FL: Psychological Assessment Resources.

Costa, P.T., McCrae, R.R., & Zonderman, A.B. (1987). Environmental and dispositional influences on well-being: Longitudinal followup of an American national sample. *British Journal of Psychology, 78,* 299–306.

Cottrell, N. (1972). Social facilitation. In C. McClintock (Ed.), *Experimental social psychology.* New York: Holt, Rinehart & Winston.

Covington, M.V. (1992). *Making the grade: A self-worth perspective on motivation and school reform.* New York: Cambridge University Press.

Covington, M.V., & Omelich, C.L. (1984). An empirical examination of Werner's critique of attribution research. *Journal of Educational Psychology, 76,* 1199–1213.

Coyne, J.C., & DeLongis, A. (1986). Going beyond social support: The role of social relationships in adaptation. *Journal of Consulting and Clinical Psychology, 54,* 454–460.

Coyne, J.C., Kahn, J., & Gotlib, I.H. (1987). Depression. In T. Jacobs (Ed.), *Family interaction and psychopathology: Theories, methods and findings* (pp. 509–533). New York: Plenum Press.

Craighead, W.E., Kimball, W.H., & Rehak, R.S. (1979). Mood changes, physiological responses, and self-statements during social rejection imagery. *Journal of Consulting and Clinical Psychology, 47,* 385–396.

Crittended, K.S., & Wiley, M.G. (1980). Causal attributions and behavioral response to failure. *Social Psychology Quarterly, 43,* 353–358.

Crocker, J., & Wolfe, C.T. (2001). Contingencies of self-worth. *Psychological Review, 108,* 593–623.

Crowe, E., & Higgins, E.T. (1997). Regulatory focus and strategic inclinations: Promotion and prevention in decision-making. *Organizational Behavior & Human Decision Processes, 69,* 117–132.

Crum, J., Brown, W.L., & Bitterman, M.E. (1951). The effect of partial and delayed reinforcement on resistance to extinction. *American Journal of Psychology, 64,* 228–237.

Cunningham, M.R., Steinberg, J., & Grev, R. (1980). Wanting to and having to help: Separate motivations for positive mood and guilt-induced helping. *Journal of Personality and Social Psychology, 38,* 181–192.

Cury, F., Elliot, A.J., Da Fonseca, D., & Moller, A. (in press). The social-cognitive model of achievement motivation and the 2 × 2 achievement goal framework. *Journal of Personality and Social Psychology, 90,* 666–679.

Cutrona, C.E. (1986). Behavioral manifestations of social support: A microanalytic investigation. *Journal of Personality and Social Psychology, 51,* 201–208.

———. (1989). Ratings of social support by adolescents and adult informants: Degree of correspondence and prediction of depressive symptoms. *Journal of Personality and Social Psychology, 57,* 723–730.

Dalai, A., Weiner, B., & Brown, J. (1985). *Issues in the measurement of causal stability.* Unpublished manuscript, University of California, Los Angeles.

Danheiser, P.R., & Graziano, W.G. (1982). Self-monitoring and cooperation as a self-presentational strategy. *Journal of Personality and Social Psychology, 42,* 497–505.

Danto, A. (1963). What we can do. *Journal of Philosophy, 40,* 435–445.

Darley, J.M., & Berscheid, E. (1967). Increased liking as a result of anticipation of personal contact. *Human Relations, 20,* 29–40.

Darley, J.M., & Gross, P.H. (1983). A hypothesis-confirming bias in labeling effects. *Journal of Personality and Social Psychology, 44,* 20–33.

Darley, J.M., & Latane, B. (1968). Bystander intervention in emergencies: Diffusion of responsibility. *Journal of Personality and Social Psychology, 8,* 377–383.

Dashiell, J.F. (1925). A quantitative demonstration of animal drive. *Journal of Comparative Psychology, 5,* 205–208.

———. (1935). Experimental studies of the influence of social situations on the behavior of individual human adults. In C. Murchison (Ed.), *A handbook of social psychology.* Worcester, MA: Clark University Press.

Davidson, R.J. (1993). Parsing affective space: Perspectives from neuropsychology and psychophysiology. *Neuropsychology, 7,* 464–475.

Davis, J.H. (1969). *Group performance.* Reading, MA: Addison-Wesley.

Davitz, J.R. (1969). *The language of emotion.* New York: Academic Press.

Dawes, R.M. (1976). Shallow psychology. In J. Carroll & J. Payne (Eds), *Cognition and social behavior* (pp. 3–12). Hillsdale, NJ: Erlbaum.

Dawkins, R. (1976). Hierarchical organisation: A candidate principle for ethology. In P.P.G. Bateson & R.A. Hinde (Eds), *Growing points in ethology* (pp. 7–54). Cambridge, England: Cambridge University Press.

Day, V.H. (1982). Validity of an attributional model for a specific life event. *Psychological Reports, 50,* 434.

de Rivera, J. (1984). The structure of emotional relationships. In P. Shaver (Ed.), *Review of personality and social psychology. Vol. 5: Emotions, relationships, and health* (pp. 116–145). Beverly Hills, CA: Sage.

DeAngelis, D.L., Post, W.M., & Travis, C.C. (1986). *Positive feedback in natural systems (Biomathematics, Vol. 15).* New York: Springer-Verlag.

deCharms, R. (1968). *Personal causation: The internal affective determinants of behavior.* New York: Academic Press.

———. (1976). *Enhancing motivation: Change in the classroom.* New York: Irvington.

Deci, E.L. (1971). Effects of externally mediated rewards on intrinsic motivation. *Journal of Personality and Social Psychology, 15,* 105–115.

Deci, E.L., & Cascio, W.F. (1972, April). *Changes in intrinsic motivation as a function of negative feedback and threats.* Paper presented at the meeting of the Eastern Psychological Association, Boston.

Deci, E.L., Cascio, W.E, & Krusell, J. (1975). Cognitive evaluation theory and some comments on the Calder, Staw critique. *Journal of Personality and Social Psychology, 31,* 81–85.

Deci, E.L., Connell, J.P., & Ryan, R.M. (1986). *Self-determination in a work organization.* Unpublished manuscript, University of Rochester, Rochester, NY.

Deci, E.L., Nezlek, J., & Sheinman, L. (1981). Characteristics of the rewarder and intrinsic motivation of the rewardee. *Journal of Personality and Social Psychology, 40,* 1–10.

Deci, E.L., & Ryan, R.M. (1980). The empirical exploration of intrinsically motivated processes. In L. Berkowitz (Ed.), *Advances in experimental social psychology* (Vol. 13, pp. 39–80). New York: Academic Press.

———, & ———. (1985a). The general causality orientations scale: Self-determination in personality. *Journal of Research in Personality, 19,* 109–134.

———, & ———. (1985b). *Intrinsic motivation and self-determination in human behavior.* New York: Plenum.

———, & ———. (1991). A motivational approach to self: Integration in personality. In R. Dienstbier (Ed.), *Nebraska Symposium on Motivation. Vol. 38: Perspectives on motivation* (pp. 237–288). Lincoln: University of Nebraska Press.

———, & ———. (1995). Human autonomy: The basis for true self-esteem. In M. Kernis (Ed.), *Efficacy, agency, and self-esteem* (pp. 31–49). New York: Plenum.

Deci, E.L., Schwartz, A.J., Sheinman, L., & Ryan, R.M. (1981). An instrument to assess adults' orientations toward control versus autonomy with children. *Journal of Educational Psychology, 73,* 642–650.

Deci, E.L., Spiegel, N.H., Ryan, R.M., Koestner, R., & Kauffman, M. (1982). The effects of performance standards on teaching styles: The behavior of controlling teachers. *Journal of Educational Psychology, 74,* 852–859.

DeLongis, A., Folkman, S., & Lazarus, R.S. (1988). The impact of daily stress on health and mood: Psychological and social resources as mediators. *Journal of Personality and Social Psychology, 54,* 486–495.

Devine, P.G., Sedikides, C., & Fuhrman, R.W. (1989). Goals in social information processing: The case of anticipated interaction. *Journal of Personality and Social Psychology, 56,* 680–690.

Dewey, J. (1900). *The school and society.* Chicago: University of Chicago Press, 1900.

Diamond, S. (1939). A neglected aspect of motivation. *Sociometry, 2,* 77–85.

Diener, E., & Emmons, R.A. (1984). The independence of positive and negative affect. *Journal of Personality and Social Psychology, 47,* 1105–1117.

Diener, E., & Iran-Nejad, A. (1986). The relationship in experience between various types of affect. *Journal of Personality and Social Psychology, 50,* 1031–1038.

Diener, E., Larsen, R.J., Levine, S., & Emmons, R.A. (1985). Intensity and frequency: Dimensions underlying positive and negative affect. *Journal of Personality and Social Psychology, 48,* 1253–1265.

Dienstbier, R.A., & Leak, G.K. (1976, August). *Effects of monetary reward on maintenance of weight loss: An extension of the overjustification effect.* Paper presented at the annual convention of the American Psychological Association, Washington, DC.

Diggory, J.C., Riley, E.J., & Blumenfeld, R. (1960). Estimated probability of success for a fixed goal. *American Journal of Psychology, 73,* 41–55.

DiTommaso, E., & Spinner, B. (1993). The development and initial validation of the social and emotional loneliness scale for adults. *Personality and Individual Differences, 14,* 127–134.

Ditto, P.H., Jemmott, J.B., & Darley, J.M. (1988). Appraising the threat of illness: A mental representational approach. *Health Psychology, 7,* 183–201.

Dollard, J., & Miller, N.E. (1950). *Personality and psychotherapy.* New York: McGraw-Hill.

Donne, J. (1975). *Devotions upon emergent occasions.* Montreal: McGill–Queen's University Press.

Doosje, B., & Ellemers, N. (1997). Stereotyping under threat: The role of group identification. In R. Spears, P.J. Oakes, N. Ellemers, & S.A. Haslam (Eds), *The social psychology of stereotyping and group life* (pp. 257–272). Oxford, UK: Blackwell.

Douglas, J.D. (1967). *The social meanings of suicide.* Princeton, NJ: Princeton University Press.

Drill, R.L. (1987). Young adult children of divorced parents: Depression and the perception of loss. *Journal of Divorce, 10,* 169–187.

Dunning, D., Meyerowitz, J.A., & Holzberg, A. (1989). Ambiguity and self-evaluation: The role of idiosyncratic trait definitions in self-serving assessments of ability. *Journal of Personality and Social Psychology, 57,* 1082–1090.

Dunning, D., Story, A.L., & Tan, P.L. (1989). *The self as model of excellence in social evaluation.* Unpublished manuscript, Cornell University.

Durkheim, E. (1951). *Suicide: A study in sociology.* New York: Free Press. (Original work published 1897)

———. (1963). *Suicide.* New York: Free Press. (Original work published 1897)

Dutton, J.E., & Jackson, S.E. (1987). Categorizing strategic issues: Links to organizational action. *Academy of Management Review, 12,* 76–90.

Duval, S., & Wicklund, R.A. (1972). *A theory of objective self-awareness.* New York: Academic Press.

Dweck, C.S. (1975). The role of expectations and attributions in the alleviation of learned helplessness. *Journal of Personality and Social Psychology, 31,* 674–685.

Dweck, C.S., & Elliott, E.S. (1983). Achievement motivation. In P. Mussen & E.M. Hetherington (Eds),

Handbook of child psychology (pp. 643–691). New York: Wiley.

Dweck, C.S., & Leggett, E.L. (1988). A social-cognitive approach to motivation and personality. *Psychological Review, 95,* 256–273.

Dweck, C.S., & Sorich, L. (1999). Mastery-oriented thinking. In C.R. Snyder (Ed.), *Coping* (pp. 232–251). New York: Oxford University Press.

Edwards, W. (1955). The prediction of decisions among bets. *Journal of Experimental Psychology, 51,* 201–214.

Egan, G. (1970). *Encounter: Group processes for interpersonal growth.* Monterey, CA: Brooks/Cole.

Eghrari, H., & Deci, E.L. (1986). *Facilitating internalization: The role of self-determination.* Unpublished manuscript, University of Rochester, Rochester, NY.

Eisenberger, R. (1970). Is there a deprivation–satiation function for social approval? *Psychological Bulletin, 74,* 255–275.

Eiser, J.R., & Sutton, S.R. (1977). Smoking as a subjectively rational choice. *Addictive Behaviors, 2,* 129–134.

Eiser, J.R., Van der Pligt, J., Raw, M., & Sutton, S.R. (in press). Trying to stop smoking: Effects of perceived addiction, attributions for failure and expectancy of success. *Journal of Behavioral Medicine, 8,* 321–341.

Elder, G.H., & Clipp, E.C. (1988). Wartime losses and social bonding: Influence across 40 years in men's lives. *Psychiatry, 51,* 177–198.

Elig, T.W, & Frieze, I.H. (1979). Measuring causal attributions for success and failure. *Journal of Personality and Social Psychology, 37,* 621–634.

Elliot, A.J. (1997). Integrating 'classic' and 'contemporary' approaches to achievement motivation: A hierarchical model of approach and avoidance achievement motivation. In P. Pintrich & M. Maehr (Eds), *Advances in motivation and achievement* (Vol. 10, pp. 143–179). Greenwich, CT: JAI Press.

———. (1999). Approach and avoidance motivation and achievement goals. *Educational Psychologist, 34,* 169–189.

Elliot, A.J., & Church, M.A. (1997). A hierarchical model of approach and avoidance achievement motivation. *Journal of Personality and Social Psychology, 72,* 218–232.

Elliot, A.J., & Covington, M.V. (2001). Approach and avoidance motivation. *Educational Psychology Review, 13,* 73–92.

Elliott, E.S., & Dweck, C.S. (1988). Goals: An approach to motivation and achievement. *Journal of Personality and Social Psychology, 54,* 5–12.

Elliot, A.J., & Fryer, J.W. (in press). The goal concept in psychology. In J. Shah & W. Gardner (Eds), *Handbook of motivational science.* New York: Guilford Press.

Elliot, A.J., Gable, S.L., & Mapes, R.R. (2006). Approach and avoidance motivation in the social domain. *Personality and Social Psychology Bulletin, 32,* 378–391.

Elliot, A.J., & Harackiewicz, J.M. (1996). Approach and avoidance achievement goals and intrinsic motivation: A mediational analysis. *Journal of Personality and Social Psychology, 70,* 461–475.

Elliot, A.J., & McGregor, H. (1998). Test anxiety and the hierarchical model of approach and avoidance achievement motivation. *Journal of Personality and Social Psychology, 70,* 968–980.

———, & ———. (2001). A 2 × 2 achievement goal framework. *Journal of Personality and Social Psychology, 80,* 501–519.

Elliot, A.J., McGregor, H., & Gable, S. (1999). Achievement goals, study strategies, and exam performance: A mediational analysis. *Journal of Experimental Social Psychology, 91,* 549–563.

Elliot, A.J., McGregor, H.A., & Thrash, T.M. (2002). The need for competence. In E. Deci & R. Ryan (Eds), *Handbook of Self-determination Research* (pp. 361–387). Rochester, NY: University of Rochester Press.

Elliot, A.J., & Mapes, R.R. (2005). Approach–avoidance motivation and self-concept evaluation. In A. Tesser, J. Wood, & D. Stapel (Eds), *On building, defending, and regulating the self: A psychological perspective* (pp. 171–196). Washington, DC: Psychological Press.

Elliot, A.J., & Reis, H.T. (2003). Attachment and exploration in adulthood. *Journal of Personality and Social Psychology, 85,* 317–331.

Elliot, A.J., & Sheldon, K.M. (1997). Avoidance achievement motivation: A personal goals analysis. *Journal of Personality and Social Psychology, 73,* 171–185.

———, & ———. (1998). Avoidance personal goals and the personality–illness relationship. *Journal of Personality and Social Psychology, 75,* 1282–1299.

Elliot, A.J., & Thrash, T.M. (2001). Achievement goals and the hierarchical model of achievement motivation. *Educational Psychology Review, 12,* 139–156.

———, & ———. (2002). Approach–avoidance motivation in personality: Approach and avoidance temperaments and goals. *Journal of Personality and Social Psychology, 82,* 804–818.

———, & ———. (2004). The intergenerational transmission of fear of failure. *Personality and Social Psychology Bulletin, 30,* 957–971.

Emery, R.E. (1982). Interparental conflict and the children of divorce. *Psychological Bulletin, 92,* 310–330.

Emmons, R.A. (1986). Personal strivings: An approach to personality and subjective well being. *Journal of Personality and Social Psychology, 51,* 1058–1068.

Enzle, M.E., & Ross, J.M. (1978). Increasing and decreasing intrinsic interest with contingent rewards: A test of cognitive evaluation theory. *Journal of Experimental Social Psychology, 14,* 588–597.

Epstein, J.A., & Harackiewicz, J.M. (1992). Winning is not enough: The effects of competition and achievement orientation on intrinsic interest. *Personality and Social Psychology Bulletin, 18,* 128–138.

Epstein, S. (1973). The self-concept revisited: Or a theory of a theory. *American Psychologist, 28,* 404–416.

———. (1979). The stability of behavior: I. On predicting most of the people much of the time. *Journal of Personality and Social Psychology, 37,* 1097–1126.

———. (1983). The stability of confusion: A reply to Mischel and Peake. *Psychological Review, 90,* 179–184.

———. (1992). The cognitive self, the psychoanalytic self, and the forgotten selves. *Psychological Inquiry, 3,* 34–37.

Erber, E., & Fiske, S.T. (1984). Outcome dependency and attention to inconsistent information. *Journal of Personality and Social Psychology, 47,* 709–726.

Erdelyi, M.H. (1974). A new look at the new look: Perceptual defence and vigilance. *Psychological Review, 81,* 1–25.

Erdley, C.A., & D'Agostino, P.R. (1988). Cognitive and affective components of automatic priming effects. *Journal of Personality and Social Psychology, 54,* 141–747.

Erikson, E.H. (1963). *Childhood and society* (Rev. ed.). New York: Norton.

———. (1952). *Childhood and society.* New York: Norton.

———. (1953). Growth and crises of the healthy personality. In C. Kluckhohn, H.A. Murray, & D. Schneider (Eds), *Personality in nature, society, and culture.* (2nd ed., pp. 185–225). New York: Knopf.

Estes, W.K. (1944). An experimental study of punishment. *Psychological Monographs, 57,* 263.

Eysenck, H.J. (1954). *The psychology of politics.* New York: Praeger.

Falbo, T, & Beck, R.C. (1979). Naive psychology and the attributional model of achievement. *Journal of Personality, 47,* 185–195.

Farina, A., Burns, G.L., Austad, C., Bugglin, C.S., & Fischer, E.H. (1986). The role of physical attractiveness in the readjustment of discharged psychiatric patients. *Journal of Abnormal Psychology, 86,* 510–517.

Fargo, G.A., Behrns, C., & Nolen, P. (1970). *Behavior modification in the classroom.* Belmont, CA: Wadsworth.

Fass, P. (1977). *The damned and the beautiful: American youth in the 1920s.* Oxford, England: Oxford University Press.

Fazio, R.H. (1986). How do attitudes guide behavior? In R.M. Sorrentino & E.T. Higgins (Eds), *Handbook of motivation and cognition: Foundations of social behavior* (Vol. 1, pp. 204–243). New York: Guilford Press.

———. (1995). Attitudes as object-evaluation associations: Determinants, consequences, and correlates of attitude accessibility. In R.E. Petty & J.A. Krosnick (Eds), *Attitude strength: Antecedents and consequences* (pp. 247–282). Mahwah, NJ: Erlbaum.

Fazio, R.H., Effrein, E.A., & Falender, V J. (1981). Self-perception following social interaction. *Journal of Personality and Social Psychology, 41,* 232–242.

Fazio, R.H., Sherman, S.J., & Herr, P.M. (1982). The feature-positive effect in the self-perception process: Does not doing matter as much as doing? *Journal of Personality and Social Psychology, 42,* 404–411.

Feather, N.T. (1961). The relationship of persistence at a task to expectation of success and achievement related motives. *Journal of Abnormal and Social Psychology, 63,* 552–561.

———. (1966). Effects of prior success and failure on expectations of success and subsequent performance. *Journal of Personality & Social Psychology, 3,* 287–298.

———. (1982). Actions in relation to expected consequences: An overview of a research program. In N.T. Feather (Ed.), *Expectations and actions: Expectancy-value models in psychology* (pp. 53–95). Hillsdale, NJ: Erlbaum.

Feather, N.T, & Davenport, P. (1981). Unemployment and depressive affect: A motivational and attributional analysis. *Journal of Personality and Social Psychology, 41,* 422–436.

Feather, N.T, & Simon, J.G. (1972). Causal attributions for success and failure in relation to initial confidence and success and failure of self and other. *Journal of Personality and Social Psychology, 18,* 173–188.

Fehrer, E. (1956). Effects of amount of reinforcement and of pre- and post-reinforcement delays on learning and extinction. *Journal of Experimental Psychology, 52,* 167–176.

Fenichel, O. (1945). *The psychoanalytic theory of neurosis.* New York: Norton.

Fenigstein, A., Scheier, M.F., & Buss, A.H. (1975). Public and private self-consciousness: Assessment and theory. *Journal of Consulting and Clinical Psychology, 43,* 522–527.

Festinger, L. (1950). Informal social communication. *Psychological Review, 57,* 271–282.

———. (1954). A theory of social comparison processes. *Human Relations, 7,* 117–140.

———. (1957). *A theory of cognitive dissonance.* Stanford, CA: Stanford University Press.

Festinger, L., & Carlsmith, J.M. (1959). Cognitive consequences of forced compliance. *Journal of Abnormal and Social Psychology, 58,* 203–211.

Festinger, L., Schachter, S., & Back, K. (1950). *Social pressures in informal groups: A study of a housing community.* Palo Alto, CA: Stanford University Press.

Fincham, F.D., Beach, S.R, & Baucom, D.H. (1987). Attribution processes in distressed and nondistressed couples: 4. Self-partner attribution differences. *Journal of Personality and Social Psychology, 52,* 739–748.

Fincham, F.D., & Jaspers, J.M. (1980). Attribution of responsibility: From man the scientist to man as lawyer. In L. Berkowitz (Ed.), *Advances in experimental social psychology* (Vol. 13, pp. 82–139). New York: Academic Press.

Finlay-Jones, R., & Brown, G.W. (1981). Types of stressful life event and the onset of anxiety and depressive disorders. *Psychological Medicine, 11,* 803–815.

Fischhoff, B. (1977). Perceived informativeness of facts. *Journal of Experimental Psychology: Human Perception and Performance, 3,* 349–358.

Fisher, C.D. (1978). The effects of personal control, competence, and extrinsic reward systems on intrinsic motivation. *Organizational Behavior and Human Performance, 21,* 273–288.

Fiske, S., & Taylor, S.E. (1991). *Social cognition* (2nd ed.). New York: McGraw-Hill.

Fiske, S.T., & Neuberg, S.L. (1990). A continuum of impression formation, from category-based to individuating processes: Influences of information and motivation on attention and interpretation. In M.P. Zanna (Ed.), *Advances in experimental social psychology* (Vol. 23, pp. 1–74). New York: Academic Press.

Fitts, P.M., & Posner, M.I. (1967). *Human performance.* Belmont. CA: Brooks/Cole.

Fletcher, G.O. (1984). Psychology and common sense. *American Psychologist, 39,* 203–213.

Foersterling, F. (in press). Attributional retraining: A review. *Psychological Bulletin.*

———. (1980). A multivariate analysis of perceived causes for success and failure. *Archives of Psychology, 133,* 45–52.

Folkes, V.S. (1982). Communicating the reasons for social rejection. *Journal of Experimental Social Psychology, 18,* 235–252.

———. (1984). Consumer reactions to product failure: An attributional approach. *Journal of Consumer Research, 11,* 398–409.

Fontaine, C. (1974). Social comparison and some determinants of expected personal control and expected performance in a novel task situation. *Journal of Personality and Social Psychology, 29,* 487–496.

Ford, D.H. (1987). *Humans as self-constructing living systems: A developmental perspective on behavior and personality.* Hillsdale, NJ: Erlbaum.

Ford, T.E., & Kruglanski, A.W. (1995). Effects of epistemic motivations on the use of accessible constructs in social judgment. *Personality and Social Psychology Bulletin, 21,* 950–962.

Forgas, J.P., & Moylan, S. (1987). After the movies: Transient mood and social judgments. *Personality and Social Psychology Bulletin, 13,* 467–477.

Forster, J., & Higgins, E.T. (1997). Approach and avoidance gradients from strategies in goal attainment: Regulatory focus as moderator. Unpublished manuscript, Columbia University.

Forsyth, D.R. (1991). Change in therapeutic groups. In C.R. Snyder & D.R. Forsyth (Eds), *Handbook of social and clinical psychology* (pp. 664–680). New York: Pergamon Press.

Forsyth, D.R., & Schlenker, B.R. (1977). Attributing the causes of group performance: Effects of performance quality, task importance, and future testing. *Journal of Personality, 45,* 220–236.

Forsyth, D.T. (1980). The function of attributions. *Social Psychology Quarterly, 43,* 184–189.

Frank, V.E. (1963). *Man's search for meaning.* New York: Washington Square Press.

Freedman, J. (1978). *Happy people: What happiness is, who has it, and why.* New York: Harcourt Brace Jovanovich.

Freedman, J, L., & Fraser, S.C. (1966). Compliance without pressure: The foot-in-the-door technique. *Journal of Personality and Social Psychology, 4,* 195–202.

French, J.R.P., & Raven, B. (1959). The bases of social power. In D. Cartwright (Ed.), *Studies in social power* (pp. 150–167). Ann Arbor: Institute for Social Research, University of Michigan.

French, T.M. (1952). *The integration of behavior.* Chicago: University of Chicago Press.

Frenkel-Brunswik, E. (1949). Intolerance of ambiguity as emotional and perceptual personality variable. *Journal of Personality, 18,* 108–143.

———. (1951). Personality theory and perception. In R.R. Blake & G.V. Ramsey (Eds), *Perception: An approach to personality* (pp. 226–275). New York: Ronald Press.

Freud, A. (1952). The mutual influences in the development of ego and id: Introduction to the discussion. *Psychoanalytical Studies of the Child, 7,* 42–50.

Freud, S. (1915). Repression. In J. Strachey (Ed. and Trans.), *The standard edition of the complete psychological works of Sigmund Freud* (Vol. 14). London: Hogarth.

———. (1916). *Wit and its relation to the unconscious.* New York: Moffat, Yard.

———. (1917). Mourning and melancholia. In J. Strachey (Ed. and Trans.), *The standard edition of the complete psychological works of Sigmund Freud* (Vol. 14, pp. 237–248). London: Hogarth Press.

———. (1923). The ego and the id. In J. Strachey (Ed. and Trans.), *Standard edition of the complete psychological works of Sigmund Freud* (pp. 171–225). London: Hogarth Press.

———. (1925a). Formulations regarding the two principles in mental functioning. In *Collected papers* (Vol. 4, pp. 13–21). London: Hogarth Press and Institute of Psychoanalysis.

———. (1925b). On narcissism: An introduction. In *Collected papers* (Vol. 4, pp. 30–59). London: Hogarth Press and Institute of Psychoanalysis.

———. (1925c). Instincts and their vicissitudes. In *Collected papers* (Vol. 4, pp. 60–83). London: Hogarth Press and Institute of Psychoanalysis.

———. (1927). *The ego and the id.* (Trans. J. Riviere). London: Hogarth Press.

———. (1930). *Civilization and its discontents.* (Trans. J. Riviere). London: Hogarth Press.

———. (1948). *Beyond the pleasure principle*. London: Hogarth Press.

———. (1949). *An outline of psycho-analysis*. (Trans. J. Strachey). New York: Norton.

———. (1950). *Beyond the pleasure principle*. New York: Liveright. (Original work published 1920)

———. (1952). *A general introduction to psychoanalysis*. New York: Washington Square Press. (Original work published 1920)

———. (1956). *Totem und Tabu* [Totem and taboo]. Frankfurt, Germany: Fischer Biicherei. (Original work published 1913)

———. (1959). Mourning and melancholia. In E. Jones (Ed.), *Sigmund Freud: Collected papers* (Vol. 4). New York: Basic Books. (Original work published 1917)

———. (1960). *The psychopathology of everyday life*. New York: Norton. (Original work published 1914)

———. (1961a). The ego and the id. In J. Strachey (Ed. and Trans.), *The standard edition of the complete psychological works of Sigmund Freud* (Vol. 19, pp. 3–66). London: Hogarth Press. (Original work published 1923)

———. (1961b). New introductory lectures on psychoanalysis. In J. Strachey (Ed. and Trans.), *The standard edition of the complete psychological works of Sigmund Freud* (Vol. 22, pp. 7–182). London: Hogarth Press. (Original work published 1933)

Freund, T., Kruglanski, A.W., & Schpitzajzen, A. (1985). The freezing and unfreezing of impressional primacy: Effects of the need for structure and the fear of invalidity. *Personality and Social Psychology Bulletin, 11*, 479–487.

Frey, D. (1986). Recent research on selective exposure. In L. Berkowitz (Ed.), *Advances in experimental social psychology* (Vol. 19, pp. 41–80). New York: Academic Press.

Frieze, I.H. (1976). Causal attributions and information seeking to explain success and failure. *Journal of Research in Personality, 10*, 293–305.

———. (1979). Perceptions of battered wives. In I.H. Frieze, D. Bar-Tal, & J.S. Carroll (Eds), *New approaches to social problems* (pp. 79–108). San Francisco: Jossey-Bass.

Frieze, I.H., & Snyder, H.N. (1980). Children's beliefs about the causes of success and failure in school settings. *Journal of Educational Psychology, 72*, 186–196.

Frijda, N.H. (1986). *The emotions*. Cambridge, England: Cambridge University Press.

———. (1988). The laws of emotion. *American Psychologist, 43*, 349–358.

———. (1996). Passions: Emotion and socially consequential behavior. In R.D. Kavanaugh, B. Zimmerberg, & S. Fein (Eds), *Emotion: Interdisciplinary perspectives* (pp. 1–27). Mahwah, NJ: Erlbaum.

Frijda, N.H., Ortony, A., Sonnemans, J., & Clore, G. (1992). The complexity of intensity. In M. Clark (Ed.), *Emotion:*

Review of personality and social psychology (Vol. 13, pp. 60–89). Beverly Hills, CA: Sage.

Fromm, E. (1955). *The sane society*. New York: Holt, Rinehart & Winston.

———. (1956). *The art of loving*. New York: Harper & Brothers.

Furnham, A. (1982a). Explanations for unemployment in Britain. *European Journal of Social Psychology, 12*, 335–352.

———. (1982b). Why are the poor always with us? Explanations for poverty in Britain. *British Journal of Social Psychology, 21*, 311–322.

Galassi, J.P., Frierson, H.T., Jr., & Sharer, R. (1981). Behavior of high, moderate, and low test anxious students during an actual test situation. *Journal of Consulting and Clinical Psychology, 49*, 51–62.

Gallistel, C.R. (1980). *The organization of action: A new synthesis*. Hillsdale, NJ: Erlbaum.

Garbarino, J. (1975). The impact of anticipated reward upon cross-aged tutoring. *Journal of Personality and Social Psychology, 32*, 421–428.

Gardner, R.W., Holzman, P.S., Klein, G.S., Linton, H.B., & Spence, D.P. (1959). Cognitive control: A study of individual consistencies in cognitive behavior. In G.S. Klein (Ed.), *Psychological issues* (Pt. 4, pp. 1–185). New York: International Universities Press.

Gauld, A., & Shotter, J. (1977). *Human action and its psychological investigation*. London: Routledge & Kegan Paul.

Geis, F.L., & Moon, T.H. (1981). Machiavellianism and deception. *Journal of Personality and Social Psychology, 41*, 766–775.

Gergen, K.J. (1977). The social construction of self-knowledge. In T. Mischel (Ed.) *The self: Psychological and philosophical issues* (pp. 139–169). Totowa, NJ: Rowman & Littleneld.

———. (1978). Toward generative theory. *Journal of Personality and Social Psychology, 36*, 1344–1360.

———. (1985). The social constructionist movement in modern psychology. *American Psychologist, 40*, 266–275.

Gerstel, N., & Gross, H. (1982). Commuter marriages: A review. *Marriage and Family Review, 5*, 71–93.

———, & ———. (1984). *Commuter marriage: A study of work and family*. New York: Guilford Press.

Gewirtz, J.L., & Baer, D.M. (1958). Deprivation and satiation of social reinforcers as drive conditions. *Journal of Abnormal and Social Psychology, 57*, 165–172.

Giallombardo, R. (1966). *Society of women: A study of a women's prison*. New York: Wiley.

Gibson, J.J. (1941). A critical review of the concept of set in contemporary experimental psychology. *Psychological Bulletin, 38*, 781–817.

———. (1979). *The ecological approach to visual perception*. Boston: Houghton-Mifflin.

Gilbert, D.T, Pelham, B.W., & Krull, D.S. (1988). On cognitive busyness: When person perceivers meet persons perceived. *Journal of Personality and Social Psychology,* 54, 733–740.

Gilovich, T. (1983). Biased evaluation and persistence in gambling. *Journal of Personality and Social Psychology, 44,* 1110–1126.

Ginossar, Z., & Trope, Y. (1987). Problem solving in judgment under uncertainty. *Journal of Personality and Social Psychology, 52,* 464–474.

Glass, D.C, Singer, J.E., & Friedman, L.N. (1969). Psychic cost of adaptation to an environmental stressor. *Journal of Personality and Social Psychology, 12,* 200–210.

Glenn, N.D., & McLanahan, S. (1982). Children and marital happiness: A further specification of the relationship. *Journal of Marriage and the Family, 44,* 63–72.

Goffman, E. (1971). *Relations in public.* New York: Harper Colophon.

Goldman, A.L. (1970). *A theory of human action.* Princeton, NJ: Princeton University Press.

Goldstein, K. (1939). *The organism.* New York: American Book.

———. (1940). *Human nature in the light of psychopathology.* Cambridge, MA: Harvard University Press.

Goldstein, S., Gordon, J.R., & Marlatt, C.A. (1984, August). *Attributional processes and relapse following smoking cessation.* Paper presented at the 92nd Annual Convention of the American Psychological Association, Toronto, Ontario, Canada.

Gollwitzer, P.M. (1990). Action phases and mind-sets. In E.T. Higgins & R.M. Sorrentino (Eds), *Handbook of motivation and cognition: Foundations of social behavior* (Vol. 2, pp. 53–92). New York: Guilford Press.

Gollwitzer, P.M., & Bargh, J.A. (1996). *The psychology of action: Linking cognition and motivation to behavior.* New York: Guilford Press.

Gollwitzer, P.M., & Kinney, R.F. (1989). Effects of deliberative and implemental mind-sets on illusion of control. *Journal of Personality and Social Psychology, 56,* 531–542.

Gollwitzer, P.M., Heckhausen, H., & Ratajczak, H. (1990). From weighing to willing: Approaching a change decision through pre- or postdecisional mentation. *Organizational Behavior and Human Decision Processes, 45,* 41–65.

Goode, W.J. (1956). *After divorce.* New York: Free Press.

Goodwin, J.S., Hunt, W.C., Key, C.R., & Samet, J.M. (1987). The effect of marital status on stage, treatment, and survival of cancer patients. *Journal of the American Medical Association, 258,* 3125–3130.

Goranson, R.E., & Berkowitz, L. (1966). Reciprocity and responsibility reactions to prior help. *Journal of Personality and Social Psychology, 3,* 227–232.

Gottlieb, J., & Carver, C. (1980). Anticipation of future interaction and the bystander effect. *Journal of Experimental Social Psychology, 16,* 253–260.

Gouaux, C. (1971). Induced affective states and interpersonal attraction. *Journal of Personality and Social Psychology, 20,* 37–43.

Govaerts, K., & Dixon, D.N. (1988). . . . Until careers do us part: Vocational and marital satisfaction in the dual-career commuter marriage. *International Journal for the Advancement of Counselling, 11,* 265–281.

Graham, S. (1984). Communicating sympathy and anger to black and white children: The cognitive (attributional) consequences of affective cues. *Journal of Personality and Social Psychology, 47,* 40–54.

Graham, S., & Golen, S. (1991). Motivational influences on cognition: Task involvement, ego involvement, and depth of information processing. *Journal of Educational Psychology, 83,* 187–194.

Graham, S., Doubleday, C., & Guarino, P.A. (1984). The development of relations between perceived controllability and the emotions of pity, anger and guilt. *Child Development, 55,* 561–565.

Gray, J.A. (1981). A critique of Eysenck's theory of personality. In H.J. Eysenck (Ed.), *A model for personality* (pp. 246–276). Berlin: Springer-Verlag.

———. (1982). *The neuropsychology of anxiety: An enquiry into the functions of the septo-hippocampal system.* New York: Oxford University Press.

Greenbaum, C.W, & Zemach, M. (1972). Role playing and change of attitude toward the police after a campus riot: Effects of situational demand and justification. *Human Relations, 25,* 87–99.

Greenberg, M.S., & Frisch, D.M. (1972). Effect of intentionality on willingness to reciprocate a favor. *Journal of Experimental Social Psychology, 8,* 99–111.

Greene, B.A., & Miller, R.B. (1996). Influences on achievement: Goals, perceived ability, and cognitive engagement. *Contemporary Educational Psychology, 21,* 181–192.

Greenwald, A.G. (1980). The totalitarian ego: Fabrication and revision of personal history. *American Psychologist, 35,* 603–618.

Greenwald, A.G., & Ronis, D.L. (1978). Twenty years of cognitive dissonance: Case study of the evolution of a theory. *Psychological Review, 85,* 53–57.

Grolnick, W.S., & Ryan, R.M. (1986). *Parent styles associated with children's self-regulation and competence: A social contextual perspective.* Unpublished manuscript, University of Rochester, Rochester, NY.

———, & ———. (1987). Autonomy in children's learning: An experimental and individual difference investigation. *Journal of Personality and Social Psychology, 52,* 890–898.

Groos, K. (1901). *The play of man.* (Trans. by E.L. Baldwin). New York: D. Appleton.

Groth, A.N. (1979). *Men who rape.* New York: Plenum Press.

Guisinger, S., & Blatt, S.J. (1994). Individuality and relatedness: Evolution of a fundamental dialectic. *American Psychologist, 49,* 104–111.

Haddad, Y.S. (1982). *The effect of informational versus controlling verbal feedback on self-determination and preference for challenge.* Unpublished doctoral dissertation, University of Rochester, Rochester, NY.

Hamachek, D. (1992). *Encounters with the self* (4th edn). San Diego, CA: Harcourt Brace Jovanovich.

Hamilton, V. (1983). *The cognitive structures and processes of human motivation and personality.* Chichester, England: Wiley.

Harackiewicz, J. (1979). The effects of reward contingency and performance feedback on intrinsic motivation. *Journal of Personality and Social Psychology, 37,* 1352–1363.

Harackiewicz, J., Abrahams, S., & Wageman, R. (1987). Performance evaluation and intrinsic motivation: The effects of evaluative focus, rewards, and achievement orientation. *Journal of Personality and Social Psychology, 53,* 1015–1023.

Harackiewicz, J.M., Barron, K.E., Carter, S.M., Lehto, A.T., & Elliot, A.J. (1997). Predictors and consequences of achievement goals in the college classroom: Maintaining interest and making the grade. *Journal of Personality and Social Psychology, 73,* 1284–1295.

Harackiewicz, J.M., Barron, K.E., Tauer, J.M., Carter, S.M., & Elliot, A.J. (2000). Short-term and long-term consequences of achievement goals: Predicting interest and performance over time. *Journal of Educational Psychology, 92,* 316–330.

Harackiewicz, J.M., & Elliot, A.J. (1998). The joint effects of target and purpose goals on intrinsic motivation: A mediational analysis. *Personality and Social Psychology Bulletin, 24,* 675–689.

———, ———, & ———. (in press). Competence processes and achievement motivation: Implications for intrinsic motivation. In A.K. Boggiano & T.S. Pittman (Eds), *Achievement and motivation: A social-developmental perspective.* New York: Cambridge University Press.

Harackiewicz, J.M., Manderlink, G., & Sansone, C. (1984). Rewarding pinball wizardry: Effects of evaluation and cue-valence on intrinsic interest. *Journal of Personality and Social Psychology, 47,* 287–300.

Hardy, C. J., & Crace, R.K. (1991). The effects of task structure and teammate competence on social loafing. *Journal of Sport and Exercise Psychology, 13,* 372–381.

Harkins, S.G., & Petty, R.E. (1982). Effects of task difficulty and task uniqueness on social loafing. *Journal of Personality and Social Psychology, 43,* 1214–1229.

Harkness, A.R., DeBono, K.G., & Borgida, E. (1985). Personal involvement and strategies for making contingency judgments: A stake in the dating game makes a difference. *Journal of Personality and Social Psychology, 49,* 22–32.

Harlow, H.F. (1953). Mice, monkeys, men, and motives. *Psychological Review, 60,* 23–32.

Harlow, H.F., Harlow, M.K., & Meyer, D.R. (1950). Learning motivated by a manipulation drive. *Journal of Experimental Psychology, 40,* 228–234.

Harlow, H.F., Harlow, M.K., & Suomi, S.J. (1971). From thought to therapy: Lessons from a primate laboratory. *American Scientist, 59,* 538–549.

Harre, R., & Secord, P.F. (1972). *The explanation of social behaviour.* Oxford, England: Blackwell.

Harris, M. (1974). *Cows, pigs, wars, and witches: The riddles of culture.* New York: Random House.

———. (1978). *Cannibals and kings: The origins of cultures.* New York: Random House.

———. (1979). *Cultural materialism: The struggle for a science of culture.* New York: Random House.

Harrison, A.A., & Connors, M.M. (1984). Groups in exotic environments. In L. Berkowitz (Ed.), *Advances in experimental social psychology* (Vol. 18, pp. 49–87). New York: Academic Press.

Harter, S. (1981). A new self-report scale of intrinsic versus extrinsic orientation in the classroom: Motivational and informational components. *Developmental Psychology, 17,* 300–312.

———. (1982). The perceived competence scale for children. *Child Development, 53,* 87–97.

Harter, S., & Zigler, E. (1972). *Effectance motivation in normal and retarded children.* Unpublished manuscript, Yale University.

Hartmann, H. (1950). Comments on the psychoanalytic theory of the ego. *Psychoanalytic Study of the Child, 8,* 74–95.

———. (1955). Notes on the theory of sublimation. *Psychoanalytic Study of the Child, 10,* 9–29.

———. (1956). Notes on the reality principle. *Psychoanalytic Study of the Child, 11,* 31–53.

———. (1958). *Ego psychology and the problem of adaptation.* (Trans. by D. Rapaport). New York: International University Press.

Hartmann, H., Kris, E., & Loewenstein, R. (1949). Notes on the theory of aggression. *Psychoanalytic Study of the Child, 3/4,* 9–36.

Harvey, J.H., & Weary, G. (1981). *Perspectives on attributional processes.* Dubuque, IA: Wm. C. Brown.

Hays, R.B. (1985). A longitudinal study of friendship development. *Journal of Personality and Social Psychology, 48,* 909–924.

Hazan, C., & Shaver, P.R. (1994a). Attachment as an organizational framework for research on close relationships. *Psychological Inquiry, 5,* 1–22.

———, & ———. (1994b). Deeper into attachment theory. *Psychological Inquiry, 5,* 68–79.

Heaton, A., & Kruglanski, A.W. (1991). Person perception by introverts and extraverts under time pressure: Need for closure effects. *Personality and Social Psychology Bulletin, 17,* 161–165.

Hebb, D.O. (1949). *The organisation of behavior.* New York: Wiley.

———. (1955). Drives and the C.N.S. (conceptual nervous system). *Psychological Review, 62,* 243–254.

————. (1958). The motivating effects of exteroceptive stimulation. *American Psychologist, 13,* 109–113.

Hebb, D.O., & Thompson, W.R. (1954). The social significance of animal studies. In G. Lindzey (Ed.), *Handbook of social psychology* (Vol. I., pp. 532–561). Cambridge, MA: Addison-Wesley.

Heckhausen, H. (1986). Why some time out might benefit achievement motivation research. In J.H.L. van den Bercken, T.C.M. Bergen, & E.E.J. De Bruyn (Eds), *Achievement and task motivation* (pp. 7–39). Lisse, The Netherlands: Swets & Zeitlinger.

Heckhausen, H., & Gollwitzer, P.M. (1986). Information processing before and after the formation of an intent. In F. Klix & H. Hagendorf (Eds), *In memoriam Hermann Ebbinghaus: Symposium on the structure and function of human memory* (pp. 1071–1082). Amsterdam: Elsevier/North Holland.

————, & ————. (1987). Thought contents and cognitive functioning in motivational vs. volitional states of mind. *Motivation and Emotion, 11,* 101–120.

Heider, F. (1958). *The psychology of interpersonal relations.* New York: Wiley.

————. (1960). The Gestalt theory of motivation. In M.R. Jones (Ed.), *Nebraska Symposium on Motivation* (Vol. 8, pp. 145–172). Lincoln: University of Nebraska Press.

Heilman, M.E., & Guzzo, R.A. (1978). The perceived causes of work success as a mediator of sex discrimination in organizations. *Organizational Behavior and Human Performance, 21,* 346–357.

Helson, H. (1964). *Adaptation-level theory: An experimental and systematic approach to behavior.* New York: Harper & Row.

Hendrick, I. (1942). Instinct and the ego during infancy. *Psychoanalytic Quarterly, 11,* 33–58.

————. (1943a). Work and the pleasure principle. *Psychoanalytic Quarterly, 12,* 311–329.

————. (1943b). The discussion of the 'instinct to master.' *Psychoanalytic Quarterly, 12,* 561–565.

Herman, C.P., & Polivy, J. (1975). Anxiety, restraint, and eating behavior. *Journal of Abnormal Psychology, 84,* 666–672.

Herzberg, F. (1966). *Work and the nature of man.* Cleveland, OH: Ward.

Higgins, E.T. (1987). Self-discrepancy: A theory relating self and affect. *Psychological Review, 94,* 319–340.

————. (1989). Continuities and discontinuities in self-regulatory and self-evaluative processes: A developmental theory relating self and affect. *Journal of Personality, 57,* 407–444.

————. (1989b). Self-discrepancy theory: What patterns of self-beliefs cause people to suffer? In L. Berkowitz (Ed.), *Advances in experimental social psychology* (Vol. 22, pp. 93–136). New York: Academic Press.

————. (1990). Personality, social psychology, and person-situation relations: Standards and knowledge activation as a common language. In L.A. Pervin (Ed.), *Handbook of personality* (pp. 301–338). New York: Guilford Press.

————. (1996). The 'self digest': Self-knowledge serving self-regulatory functions. *Journal of Personality & Social Psychology, 71,* 1062–1083.

————. (1997). Beyond pleasure and pain. *American Psychologist, 52,* 1280–1300.

————. (in press). Promotion and prevention: Regulatory focus as a motivational principle. In M.P. Zanna (Ed.), *Advances in experimental social psychology.* New York: Academic Press.

Higgins, E.T., Bond, R.N., Klein, R. & Strauman, T. (1986). Self-discrepancies and emotional vulnerability: How magnitude, accessibility, and type of discrepancy influence affect. *Journal of Personality & Social Psychology, 51,* 5–15.

Higgins, E.T., Grant, H., & Shah, J. (in press). Self-regulation and quality of life: Emotional and non-emotional life experiences. In D. Kahneman, E. Diener, & N. Schwartz (Eds), *Understanding quality of life: Scientific perspectives on enjoyment and suffering.* New York: Russell Sage Foundation.

Higgins, E.T., & King, G.A. (1981). Accessibility of social constructs: Information-processing consequences of individual and contextual variability. In N. Cantor & J.F. Kihlstrom (Eds), *Personality, cognition, and social interaction* (pp. 69–121). Hillsdale, NJ: Erlbaum.

Higgins, E.T., Klein. R., & Strauman, T.J. (1985). Self-concept discrepancy theory: A psychological model for distinguishing among different aspects of depression and anxiety. *Social Cognition, 3,* 51–76.

Higgins, E.T., & Loeb, I. (in press). Development of regulatory focus: Promotion and prevention as ways of living. In J. Heckhausen & C.S. Dweck (Eds), *Motivation and self-regulation across the life span.* New York: Cambridge University Press.

Higgins, E.T., Rholes, W.S., & Jones, C.R. (1977). Category accessibility and impression formation. *Journal of Experimental Social Psychology, 13,* 141–154.

Higgins, E.T., Roney, C., Crowe, E. & Hymes, C. (1994). Ideal versus ought predilections for approach and avoidance: Distinct self-regulatory systems. *Journal of Personality & Social Psychology, 66,* 276–286.

Higgins, E.T., Shah, J. & Friedman, R. (1997). Emotional responses to goal attainment: Strength of regulatory focus as moderator. *Journal of Personality & Social Psychology, 72,* 515–525.

Higgins, E.T. & Stangor, C. (1988). A 'change-of -standard' perspective on the relations among context, judgment, and memory. *Journal of Personality & Social Psychology, 54,* 181–192.

Higgins, E.T, & Trope, Y. (1990). Activity engagement theory: Implications of multiple identifiable input for intrinsic motivation. In E.T. Higgins & R.M. Sorrentino (Eds), *Handbook of motivation and cognition: Foundations of social behavior* (Vol. 2, pp. 229–264). New York: Guilford Press.

Higgins, E.T. & Tykocinski, O. (1992). Self-discrepancies and biographical memory: Personality and cognition at the level of psychological situation. *Personality & Social Psychology Bulletin, 18,* 527–535.

Hill, C.T., Rubin, Z., & Peplau, L.A. (1976). Breakups before marriage: The end of 103 affairs. *Journal of Social Issues, 32,* 147–168.

Hill, W.F. (1956). Activity as an autonomous drive. *Journal of Comparative Physiology, 49,* 15–19.

Hobfall, S.E., & London, P. (1986). The relationship of self-concept and social support to emotional distress among women during the war. *Journal of Social and Clinical Psychology, 4,* 189–203.

Hoffman, M.L. (1960). Power assertion by the parent and its impact on the child. *Child Development, 31,* 129–143.

———. (1970). Conscience, personality, and socialization techniques. *Human Development, 13,* 90–126.

———. (1976). Empathy, role-taking, guilt, and development of altruistic motives. In T. Likona (Ed.), *Morality: Theory, research and social issues* (pp. 124–143). New York: Holt, Rinehart & Winston.

———. (1982). Development of prosocial motivation: Empathy and guilt. In N. Eisenberg-Borg (Ed.), *Development of prosocial behavior* (pp. 281–313). New York: Academic Press.

Hofstede, G. (1980). *Culture's consequences: International differences in work-related values.* Beverly Hills, CA: Sage.

Hogan, R. (1983). A socioanalytic theory of personality. In M. Page & R. Dienstbier (Eds), *Nebraska Symposium on Motivation, 1982* (pp. 55–89). Lincoln: University of Nebraska Press.

Hogan, R., & Jones, W.H. (1983). A role theoretical model of criminal conduct. In W.S. Laufer & J.M. Days (Eds), *Personality theory, moral development, and criminal behavior* (pp. 3–21). Lexington, MA: Lexington Books.

Hogan, R., Jones, W.H., & Cheek, J.M. (1985). Socioanalytic theory: An alternative to armadillo psychology. In B.R. Schlenker (Ed.), *The self and social life* (pp. 175–198). New York: McGraw-Hill.

Holender, D. (1986). Semantic activation without conscious identification in dichotic listening, parafoveal vision, and visual masking: A survey and appraisal. *The Behavioral and Brain Sciences, 9,* 1–66.

Holmes, J.G., & Rempel, J.K. (1989). Trust in close relationships. In M. Clark (Ed.), *Close relationships: Review of personality and social psychology* (Vol. 10, pp. 187–220). Newbury Park, CA: Sage.

Holmes, T.H., & Rahe, R.H. (1967). The social readjustment rating scale. *Journal of Psychosomatic Research, 11,* 213–218.

Holt, J. (1964). *How children fail.* New York: Dell.

Holt, P.A., & Stone, G.L. (1988). Needs, coping strategies, and coping outcomes associated with long-distance relationships. *Journal of College Student Development, 29,* 136–141.

Hopkin, D.V. (1995). *Human factors in air traffic control.* New York: CRC Press.

Horney, K. (1945). *Our inner conflicts: A constructive theory of neurosis.* New York: Norton.

———. (1950). *Neurosis and human growth.* New York: Norton.

Hornsey, M.J., & Hogg, M.A. (1999). Subgroup differentiation as a response to an overly-inclusive group: A test of optimal distinctiveness theory. *European Journal of Social Psychology, 29,* 543–550.

Horowitz, M.J. (1979). *States of mind.* New York: Plenum.

———. (1988). Psychodynamic phenomena and their explanation. In M.J. Horowitz (Ed.), *Psychodynamics and cognition* (pp. 3–20). Chicago: University of Chicago Press.

Hotard, S.R., McFatter, R.M., McWhirter, R.M., & Stegall, M.E. (1989). Interactive effects of extraversion, neuroticism, and social relationships on subjective well-being. *Journal of Personality and Social Psychology, 57,* 321–331.

Howard, J.W, & Rothbart, M. (1980). Social categorization and memory for in-group and out-group behavior. *Journal of Personality and Social Psychology, 38,* 301–310.

Howard-Pitney, B., Borgida, E., & Omoto, A.M. (1986). Personal involvement: An examination of processing differences. *Social Cognition, 4,* 39–57.

Hoyle, R.H., & Crawford, A.M. (in press). Use of individual-level data to investigate group phenomena: Issues and strategies. *Small Group Research.*

Hoyle, R.H., Pinkley, R.L., & Insko, C.A. (1989). Perceptions of social behavior: Evidence of differing expectations for interpersonal and intergroup interaction. *Personality and Social Psychology Bulletin, 15,* 365–376.

Hull, C.L. (1943). *Principles of behavior: An introduction to behavior theory.* New York: Appleton-Century-Crofts.

———. (1952). *A behavior system: An introduction to behavior theory concerning the individual organism.* New Haven, CT: Yale University Press.

Humphrey, G. (1951). *Thinking.* London: Methuen.

Hyland, M. (1987). Control theory interpretation of psychological mechanisms of depression: Comparison and integration of several theories. *Psychological Bulletin, 102,* 109–121.

Hyman, H.H. (1942). The psychology of status. *Archives of Psychology, 269.*

Inagi, T. (1977). Causal ascription and expectancy of success. *Japanese Psychological Research, 19,* 23–30.

Ingham, A.G., Levinger, G., Graves, J., & Peckham, V. (1974). The Ringelmann effect: Studies of group size and group performance. *Journal of Experimental Social Psychology, 10,* 371–384.

Irwin, F.W. (1953). Stated expectations as functions of probability and desirability of outcomes. *Journal of Personality, 21,* 329–335.

Irwin, F.W, & Snodgrass, J.G. (1966). Effects of independent and dependent outcomes on bets. *Journal of Experimental Psychology, 71,* 282–285.

Isen, A.M. (1984). Toward understanding the role of affect in cognition. In R.S. Wyer & T.K. Srull (Eds), *Handbook of social cognition* (Vol. 3, pp. 179–236). Hillsdale, NJ: Erlbaum.

Isenberg, S. (1991). *Women who love men who kill.* New York: Simon & Schuster.

Izard, C.E. (1977). *Human emotions.* New York: Plenum.

Izard, C.E., Dougherty, F.E., Bloxom, B.M., & Kotsch, W.E. (1974). *The differential emotions scale: A method of measuring the subjective experience of discrete emotions.* Unpublished manuscript, Vanderbilt University, Nashville, TN.

Jaccard, J., Turrisi, R., & Wan, C.K. (1990). *Interaction effects in multiple regression.* Newbury Park, CA: Sage.

Jagacinski, C.M. & Nicholls, J.G. (1987). Competence and affect in task involvement and ego involvement: The impact of social comparison information. *Journal of Educational Psychology, 79,* 107–114.

Jagacinski, C.M., & Nicholls, J.G. (1984). Conception of ability and related affects in task involvement and ego involvement. *Journal of Educational Psychology, 76,* 909–919.

———, & ———. (1987). Competence and affect in task involvement and ego involvement: The impact of social comparison information. *Journal of Educational Psychology, 79,* 107–114.

James, W. (1890). *Principles of psychology.* New York: Holt.

———. (1948). *Psychology.* New York: World Publishing. (Original work published 1890)

Jamieson, D.W., & Zanna, M.P. (1989). Need for structure in attitude formation and expression. In A. Pratkanis, S. Breckler, & A.G. Greenwald. (Eds), *Attitude structure and function* (pp. 46–68). Hillsdale, NJ: Erlbaum.

Janis, I.L., & Field, P.B. (1959). The Janis and Field personality questionnaire. In C.I. Hovland & I.L. Janis, *Personality and persuasibility* (pp. 300–305). New Haven, CT: Yale University Press.

Jankowski, M.S. (1991). *Islands in the street: Gangs and American urban society.* Berkeley: University of California Press.

Janoff-Bulman, R. (1979). Characterological versus behavioral self-blame: Inquiries into depression and rape. *Journal of Personality and Social Psychology, 37,* 1798–1809.

Jemmott, J.B., Ditto, P.H., & Croyle, R.T. (1986). Judging health status: Effects of perceived prevalence and personal relevance. *Journal of Personality and Social Psychology, 50,* 899–905.

Jenkins, C.D., Rosenman, R.H., & Friedman, M. (1967). Development of an objective psychological test for the determination of the coronary prone behavior pattern in employed men. *Journal of Chronic Diseases, 20,* 371–379.

Johnson, B., & Eagly, A.H. (1989). The effects of involvement on persuasion: A meta-analysis. *Psychological Bulletin, 106,* 290–314.

Johnson, E.E. (1953). The role of motivational strength in latent learning. *Journal of Comparative Psychology, 45,* 526–530.

Johnson, N.E., Saccuzzo, D.P., & Larson, G.E. (1995). Self-report effort versus actual performance in information processing paradigms. *Journal of General Psychology, 122,* 195–210.

Jones, E.E. (1979). The rocky road from acts to dispositions. *American Psychologist, 34,* 107–117.

Jones, E.E., & Davis, K.E. (1965). From acts to dispositions: The attribution process in person perception. In L. Berkowitz (Ed.), *Advances in experimental social psychology* (Vol. 2, pp. 219–266). New York: Academic Press.

Jones, E.E., & Harris, V.A. (1967). The attribution of attitudes. *Journal of Experimental Social Psychology, 3,* 1–24.

Jones, E.E., Kanouse, D.E., Kelley, H.H., Nisbett, R.E., Valins, S., & Weiner, B. (1972). *Attribution: Perceiving the causes of behavior.* New York: General Learning Press.

Jones, E.E., & Nisbett, R.E. (1971). The actor and observer: Divergent perceptions of the causes of behavior. In E.E. Jones, D.E. Kanouse, H.H, Kelley, R.E. Nisbett, S. Valins, & B. Weiner (Eds), *Attribution: Perceiving the causes of behavior* (pp. 79–94). Morristown, NJ: General Learning Press.

Jones, W.H. (1981). Loneliness and social contact. *Journal of Social Psychology, 113,* 295–296.

Jones, W.H., & Kugler, K. (in press). Interpersonal correlates of the guilt inventory. *Journal of Personality Assessment.*

Jones, W.H., Kugler, K., & Adams, P. (1995). You always hurt the one you love: Guilt and transgressions against relationship partners. In K. Fischer & J. Tangner (Eds), *Self-conscious emotion* (pp. 301–321). New York: Guilford Press.

Kagan, J. (1955). Differential reward value of incomplete and complete sexual behavior. *Journal of Comparative Psychology, 48,* 59–64.

———. (1972). Motives and development. *Journal of Personality and Social Psychology, 22,* 51–66.

Kagan, J., & Berkun, M. (1954). The reward value of running activity. *Journal of Comparative Psychology, 47,* 108.

Kahneman, D. & Miller, D.T. (1986). Norm theory: Comparing reality to its alternatives. *Psychological Review, 93,* 136–153.

Kahneman, D., & Tversky, A. (1972a). Subjective probability: A judgment of representativeness. *Cognitive Psychology, 3,* 430–454.

———, & ———. (1972b). On prediction and judgment. *ORI Research Monograph, 12(4).*

———. & ———. (1979). Prospect theory: An analysis of decision under risk. *Econometrica, 47,* 263–291.

Kahneman, D., Slovic, P., & Tversky, A. (Eds). (1982). *Judgment under uncertainty: Heuristics and biases.* New York: Cambridge University Press.

Kanfer, F.H. (1975). Self-management methods. In F.H. Kanfer & A.P. Goldstein (Eds), *Helping people change: A textbook of methods* (pp. 309–356). New York: Pergamon Press.

Kanfer, F.H., & Hagerman, S. (1981). The role of self-regulation. In L.P. Rehm (Ed.), *Behavior therapy for depression* (pp. 143–179). New York: Academic Press.

———, & ———. (1985). Behavior therapy and the information processing paradigm. In S. Reiss & R.R. Bootsin (Eds), *Theoretical issues in behavior therapy* (pp. 3–33). New York: Academic Press.

Kanfer, F.H. & Karoly, P. (1972). Self-control: A behavioristic excursion into the lion's den. *Behavior Therapy, 3,* 398–416.

Kanfer, R., & Ackerman, P.L. (2000). Individual differences in work motivation: Further explorations of a trait framework. *Applied Psychology: An International Review, 49,* 470–482.

Kaplan, A., & Maehr, M.L. (1999). Achievement goals and student well-being. *Contemporary Educational Psychology, 24,* 330–358.

Kaplan, A., & Midgley, C. (1997). The effect of achievement goals: Does level of perceived academic competence make a difference? *Contemporary Educational Psychology, 22,* 415–435.

Kaplan, H.B., & Pokorny, A.D. (1969). Self-derogation and psychosocial adjustment. *Journal of Nervous and Mental Disease, 149,* 421–434.

Kardiner, A., & Spiegel, H. (1947). *War stress and neurotic illness.* New York: Hoeber.

Kassarjian, H.H., & Cohen, J.B. (1965). Cognitive dissonance and consumer behavior. *California Management Review, 8,* 55–64.

Kassin, S.M., & Hochreich, D.J. (1977). Instructional set: A neglected motivated reasoning 497 variable in attribution research? *Personality and Social Psychology Bulletin, 3,* 620–623.

Kast, A.D. (1983). *Sex differences in intrinsic motivation: A developmental analysis of the effects of social rewards.* Unpublished doctoral dissertation, Fordham University, New York.

Kaufman, S.R. (1986). *The ageless self: Sources of meaning in late life.* New York: Meridian.

Kelley, H.H. (1952). Two functions of reference groups. In G.E. Swanson, T.M. Newcomb, & E.L. Hartley (Eds), *Readings in social psychology* (2nd edn, pp. 410–420). New York: Holt, Rinehart & Winston.

———. (1967). Attribution theory in social psychology. In D. Levine (Ed.), *Nebraska symposium on motivation* (pp. 192–238). Lincoln: University of Nebraska Press.

———. (1971). Attribution in social interaction. In E.E. Jones, D.E. Kanause, H.H. Kelley, R.E. Nisbett, S. Valins, & B. Weiner (Eds), *Attribution: Perceiving the causes of behavior* (pp. 1–26). Morristown, NJ: General Learning Press.

———. (1983). The situational origins of human tendencies. *Personality and Social Psychology Bulletin, 9,* 8–30.

Kelley, H.H., & Michela, J.L. (1980). Attribution theory and research. In M.R. Rosenzweig & L.W. Porter (Eds), *Annual review of psychology* (Vol. 31, pp. 457–501). Palo Alto, CA: Annual Reviews.

Kelly, G.A. (1955). *The psychology of personal constructs.* New York: Norton.

Kemper, T.D. (1978). *A social interactional theory of emotions.* New York: Wiley.

Kenrick, D.T., & Cialdini, R.B. (1977). Romantic attraction: Misattribution versus reinforcement explanations. *Journal of Personality and Social Psychology, 35,* 381–391.

Kenrick, D.T., & Johnson, G.A. (1979). Interpersonal attraction in aversive environments: A problem for the classical conditioning paradigm? *Journal of Personality and Social Psychology, 37,* 572–579.

Kiecolt-Glaser, J.K., Fisher, L.D., Ogrocki, P., Stout, J.C., Speicher, C.E., & Glaser, R. (1987). Marital quality, marital disruption, and immune function. *Psychosomatic Medicine, 49,* 13–34.

Kiecolt-Glaser, J.K., Gamer, W, Speicher, C., Penn, G.M., Holliday, J., & Glaser, R. (1984). Psychosocial modifiers of immunocompetence in medical students. *Psychosomatic Medicine, 46,* 7–14.

Kiecolt-Glaser, J.K., Ricker, D., George, J., Messick, G., Speicher, C.E., Gamer, W, & Glaser, R. (1984). Urinary cortisol levels, cellular immunocompetency, and loneliness in psychiatric inpatients. *Psychosomatic Medicine, 46,* 15–23.

Kimble, G.A., & Perlmuter, L.C. (1970). The problem of volition. *Psychological Review, 77,* 361–384.

King, K.B. (1984). Coping with cardiac surgery. *Unpublished doctoral dissertation.* Rochester, NY: University of Rochester.

Kirkpatrick, L.A., & Shaver, P.R. (1992). An attachment-theoretical approach to romantic love and religious belief. *Personality and Social Psychology Bulletin, 18,* 266–275.

Kirschenbaum, D.S. (1985). Proximity and specificity of planning: A position paper. *Cognitive Therapy and Research, 9,* 489–506.

Klayman, I., & Ha, Y.W. (1987). Confirmation, disconfirmation, and information in hypothesis testing. *Psychological Review, 94,* 211–228.

——— & ———. (1989). Hypothesis testing in rule discovery: Strategy, structure, and content. *Journal of Experimental Psychology: Learning, Memory, and Cognition, 15,* 596–604.

Klein, W.M., & Kunda, Z. (1989). Motivated person perception: Justifying desired conclusions. *Paper presented at the meeting of the Eastern Psychological Association.* Boston.

Klinger, E. (1975). Consequences of commitment to and disengagement from incentives. *Psychological Review, 82,* 1–25.

———. (1977). *Meaning and void.* Minneapolis: University of Minnesota Press.

Koestner, R., Ryan, R. M., Bernieri, F., & Holt, K. (1984). Setting limits in children's behavior: The differential effects of controlling versus informational styles on intrinsic motivation and creativity. *Journal of Personality, 52,* 233–248.

Koffka, K. (1935). *The principles of gestalt psychology.* New York: Harcourt.

Kohler, O. (1927). Ueber den Gruppenwirkungsgrad der menschlichen Korperarbeit und die Bedingung optimaler Kollektivkroftreaktion. *Industrielle Psychotechnik, 4,* 209–226.

Konorski, J. (1967). *Integrative activity of the brain: An interdisciplinary approach.* Chicago: University of Chicago Press.

Koriat, A., Lichtenstein, S., & Fischhoff, B. (1980). Reasons for confidence. *Journal of Experimental Psychology: Human Learning and Memory, 6,* 107–118.

Kovenklioglu, G., & Greenhaus, J.H. (1978). Causal attributions, expectations and task performance. *Journal of Applied Psychology, 63,* 698–705.

Kramer, R.M., & Brewer, M.B. (1984). Effects of group identity on resource use in a simulated commons dilemma. *Journal of Personality and Social Psychology, 46,* 1044–1057.

Kruglanski, A.W. (1975). The endogenous-exogenous partition in attribution theory. *Psychological Review, 82,* 387–406.

———. (1980). Lay epistemo-logic-process and contents: Another look at attribution theory. *Psychological Review, 87,* 70–87.

———. (1989). *Lay epistemics and human knowledge: Cognitive and motivational bases.* New York: Plenum.

———. (1990a). Lay epistemic theory in social cognitive psychology. *Psychological Inquiry, 1,* 181–197.

———. (1990b). Motivations for judging and knowing: Implications for causal attribution. In E.X. Higgins & R.M. Sorrentino (Eds), *Handbook of motivation and cognition: Foundations of social behavior* (Vol. 2, pp. 333–368). New York: Guilford Press.

———. (in press). Motivated social cognition: Principles of the interface. In E.T. Higgins & A.W. Kruglanski (Eds), *Social psychology: A handbook of basic principles.* New York: Guilford Press.

Kruglanski, A.W., & Ajzen, I. (1983). Bias and error in human judgment. *European Journal of Social Psychology, 13,* 1–44.

Kruglanski, A.W., & Freund, T. (1983). The freezing and unfreezing of lay-inferences: Effects on impressional primacy, ethnic stereotyping, and numerical anchoring. *Journal of Experimental Social Psychology, 19,* 448–468.

Kruglanski, A.W., Friedman, I., & Zeevi, G. (1971). The effects of extrinsic incentive on some qualitative aspects of task performance. *Journal of Personality, 39,* 606–617.

Kruglanski, A.W., & Klar, Y. (1987). A view from the bridge: Synthesizing the consistency and attribution paradigms from a lay epistemic perspective. *European Journal of Social Psychology, 17,* 211–241.

Kruglanski, A.W., & Mayseless, O. (1988). Contextual effects in hypothesis testing: The role of competing alternatives and epistemic motivations. *Social Cognition, 6,* 1–21.

Kruglanski, A.W., Peri, N., & Zakai, D. (1991). Interactive effects of need for closure and initial confidence on social information seeking. *Social Cognition, 9,* 127–148,

Kruglanski, A.W., & Webster, D.M. (1991). Group members' reactions to opinion deviates and conformists at varying degrees of proximity to decision deadline and of environmental noise. *Journal of Personality and Social Psychology, 61,* 212–225.

Kruglanski, A.W., Webster, D.M., & Klem, A. (1993). Motivated resistance and openness to persuasion in the presence or absence of prior information. *Journal of Personality and Social Psychology, 65,* 861–876.

Kulpe, O. (1904). Versuche uber abstraktion [Experiments on abstraction]. *Bericht uber den 1: Kongrefl fur Experimentelle Psychologic, 1,* 56–68.

Kuhl, J. (1984). Volitional aspects of achievement motivation and learned helplessness: Toward a comprehensive theory of action control. In B.A. Maher (Ed.), *Progress in experimental personality research* (Vol. 13, pp. 99–170). New York: Academic Press.

———. (1985). Volitional mediators of cognition-behavior consistency: Self-regulatory processes and action versus state orientation. In J. Kuhl & J. Beckmann (Eds), *Action control: From cognition to behavior* (pp. 101–128). New York: Springer-Verlag.

Kuhl, J., & Helle, P. (1986). Motivational and volitional determinants of depression: The degenerated-intention hypothesis. *Journal of Abnormal Psychology, 95,* 247–251.

Kukla, A. (1972). Foundations of an attributional theory of performance. *Psychological Review, 79,* 454–470.

Kunda, Z. (1987). Motivation and inference: Self-serving generation and evaluation of evidence. *Journal of Personality and Social Psychology, 53,* 636–647.

———. (1990). The case for motivated reasoning. *Psychological Bulletin, 108,* 480–498.

Kunda, Z., & Nisbett, R.E. (1986). The psychometrics of everyday life. *Cognitive Psychology, 18,* 199–224.

Kunda, Z., & Sanitioso, R. (1989). Motivated changes in the self-concept. *Journal of Experimental Social Psychology, 25,* 272–285.

Kunst-Wilson, W.R., & Zajonc, R.B. (1980). Affective discrimination of stimuli that cannot be recognized. *Science, 207,* 557–558.

Kunz, P.R., & Woolcott, M. (1976). Season's greetings: From my status to yours. *Social Science Research, 5,* 269–278.

Lacoursiere, R.B. (1980). *The life cycles of groups: Group developmental stage theory.* New York: Human Sciences Press.

Lakey, B., & Cassady, P.B. (1990). Cognitive processes in perceived social support. *Journal of Personality and Social Psychology, 59,* 337–343.

Lang, P.J. (1995). The emotion probe: Studies of motivation and attention. *American Psychologist, 50,* 372–385.

Langer, E.J. (1975). The illusion of control. *Journal of Personality and Social Psychology, 32,* 311–328.

———. (1978). Rethinking the role of thought in social interaction. In J. Harvey, W. Ickes, & R.F. Kidd (Eds), *New directions in attribution research* (Vol. 2, pp. 35–58). Hillsdale, NJ: Erlbaum.

Langer, E.J., & Imber, L.G. (1979). When practice makes imperfect: Debilitating effects of overlearning. *Journal of Personality and Social Psychology, 37,* 2014–2024.

Langer, E.J., & Rodin, J. (1976). The effects of choice and personal responsibility for the aged: A field experiment in an institutional setting. *Journal of Personality and Social Psychology, 34,* 191–198.

Larkin, M. (1972). *Experiential groups: The uses of interpersonal encounter, psychotherapy groups, and sensitivity training.* Morristown, NJ: General Learning Press.

Larsen, R.J. (1987). The stability of mood variability: A spectral analytic approach to daily mood assessments. *Journal of Personality and Social Psychology, 52,* 1195–1204.

Lashley, K.S. (1938). Experimental analysis of instinctive behavior. *Psychological Review, 45,* 445–471.

———. (1942). The problem of cerebral organization in vision. In H. Kliiver (Ed.), *Visual mechanisms* (pp. 301–322). Lancaster, PA: Jaques Cattell.

———. (1951). The problem of serial order in behavior. In L.A. Jeffress (Ed.), *Cerebral mechanisms in behavior: the Hixon symposium* (pp. 112–136). New York: Wiley.

Latane, B. (1973). *A theory of social impact.* St. Louis, MO: Psychonomic Society.

Latane, B., & Darley, J.M. (1970). *The unresponsive bystander: Why doesn't he help?* New York: Appleton-Century-Crofts.

Latane, B., Eckman, J., & Joy, V. (1966). Shared stress and interpersonal attraction. *Journal of Experimental Social Psychology, 1* (Suppl.), 80–94.

Latane, B., & Nida, S. (1981). Ten years of research on group size and helping. *Psychological Bulletin, 89,* 308–324.

Latane, B., Williams, K., & Harkins, S.G. (1979). Many hands make light the work: The causes and consequences of social loafing. *Journal of Personality and Social Psychology, 37,* 822–832.

Lauderdale, P., Smith-Cunnien, P., Parker, J., & Inverarity, J. (1984). External threat and the definition of deviance. *Journal of Personality and Social Psychology, 46,* 1058–1068.

Lawson, A. (1988). *Adultery: An analysis of love and betrayal.* New York: Basic Books.

Lazarus, A.A. (1968). Learning theory and the treatment of depression. *Behaviour Research & Therapy, 6,* 83–89.

Lazarus, R.S. (1966). *Psychological stress and the coping process.* New York: McGraw-Hill.

Leary, M.R. (1983). *Understanding social anxiety: Social, personality, and clinical perspectives.* Beverly Hills, CA: Sage.

———. (1990). Responses to social exclusion: Social anxiety, jealousy, loneliness, depression, and low self-esteem. *Journal of Social and Clinical Psychology, 9,* 221–229.

———. (1994). *Self-presentation: Impression management and interpersonal behavior.* Dubuque, IA: Brown & Benchmark.

———. (1995). *Self-presentation: Impression management and interpersonal behavior.* Madison, WI: Brown & Benchmark.

Leary, M.R., & Downs, D.L. (in press). Interpersonal functions of the self-esteem motive: The self-esteem system as a sociometer. In M. Kernis (Ed.), *Efficacy, agency, and self-esteem.* New York: Plenum.

Leary, M.R., & Forsyth, D.R. (1987). Attributions of responsibility for collective endeavors. In C. Hendrick (Ed.), *Review of personality and social psychology. Vol. 8: Group processes* (pp. 167–188). Newbury Park, CA: Sage.

Leary, M.R., Knight, P.D., & Johnson, K.A. (1987). Social anxiety and dyadic conversation: A verbal response analysis. *Journal of Social and Clinical Psychology, 5,* 34–50.

Leary, M.R., & Kowalski, R.M. (1990). Impression management: A literature review and two-component model. *Psychological Bulletin, 107,* 34–47.

Lecky, P. (1961). *Self-consistency: A theory of personality.* New York: Shoe String Press.

LeDoux, J. (1995). Emotion: Clues from the brain. *Annual Review of Psychology, 46,* 209–235.

Lee, Y.K. (1976). *Construct validation of a new locus of control scale by multidimensional unfolding.* Paper presented at the meeting of the Western Psychological Association, Los Angeles.

Lefcourt, H. (1976). *Locus of control.* Hillsdale, NJ: Erlbaum.

Leon, D. (1969). *The kibbutz: A new way of life.* London: Pergamon Press.

Leonardelli, G.J., & Brewer, M.B. (2001). Minority and majority discrimination: When and why. *Journal of Experimental Social Psychology, 37,* 468–485.

Lepper, M.R. (1973). Dissonance, self-perception, and honesty in children. *Journal of Personality and Social Psychology, 25,* 65–74.

Lepper, M.R., & Greene, D. (1975). Turning play into work: Effects of adult surveillance and extrinsic rewards on children's intrinsic motivation. *Journal of Personality and Social Psychology, 31,* 479–486.

Lepper, M.R., Greene, D., & Nisbett, R.E. (1973). Undermining children's intrinsic interest with extrinsic rewards: A test of the 'overjustification' hypothesis. *Journal of Personality and Social Psychology, 28,* 129–137.

Lesser, A. (1988). Toward a self-evaluation maintenance model of social behavior. In L. Berkowitz (Ed.), *Advances in experimental social psychology* (Vol. 21, pp. 181–227). San Diego, CA: Academic Press.

Leuba, C. (1955). Toward some integration of learning theories: The concept of optimal stimulation. *Psychological Reports, 1,* 27–33.

Leventhal, H. (1984). A perceptual-motor theory of emotion. In L. Berkowitz (Ed.), *Advances in experimental social psychology* (Vol. 17, pp. 117–182). New York: Academic Press.

Lewin, K. (1935). *A dynamic theory of personality.* New York: McGraw-Hill.

———. (1947). Frontiers in group dynamics. *Human Relations, 1,* 5–41.

———. (1951). *Field theory in social science.* New York: Harper & Row.

———. (1951). Intention, will, and need. In D. Rapaport (Ed.), *Organization and pathology of thought* (pp. 95–153). New York: Columbia University Press.

Lewin, K., Dembo, T., Festinger, L.A., & Sears, P.S. (1944). Level of aspiration. In J.M.V. Hunt (Ed.), *Personality and the behavior disorders* (Vol. 1, pp. 333–378). New York: Ronald Press.

Lewinsohn, P.M. (1974). A behavioral approach to depression. In R.J. Friedman & M.M. Katz (Eds), *The psychology of depression: Contemporary theory and research* (pp. 157–185). Washington, DC: Winston.

Lewis, D.J. (1956). Acquisition, extinction, and spontaneous recovery as a function of percentage of reinforcement and intertrial intervals. *Journal of Experimental Psychology, 51,* 45–53.

Lewis, H.B. (1979). Shame in depression and hysteria. In C.E. Izard (Ed.), *Emotions in personality and psychopathology* (pp. 371–396). New York: Plenum.

Leyens, J. P., & Yzerbyt, V.Y. (1992). The ingroup overexclusion effect: Impact of valence and confirmation on stereotypical information search. *European Journal of Social Psychology, 22,* 549–570.

Lickel, B., Hamilton, D.L., Wieczorkowska, G., Lewis, A., Sherman, S.J., & Uhles, A.N. (2000). Varieties of groups and the perception of group entitativity. *Journal of Personality and Social Psychology, 78,* 223–245.

Lieberman, M.A., Yalom, I.D., & Miles, M.B. (1973). *Encounter groups: First facts.* New York: Basic Books.

Lilly, J. C. (1956). Mental effects of reduction of ordinary levels of physical stimuli on intact, healthy persons. *Psychiatric Research Reports, No. S.*

Linder, D.E., Cooper, J., & Jones, E.E. (1967). Decision freedom as a determinant of the role of incentive magnitude in attitude change. *Journal of Personality and Social Psychology, 6,* 245–254.

Linnenbrink, E.A., & Pintrich, P.R. (2000). Multiple pathways to learning and achievement: The role of goal orientation in fostering adaptive motivation, affect, and cognition. In C. Sansone & J.M. Harackiewicz (Eds), *Intrinsic and extrinsic motivation: The search for optimal motivation and performance* (pp. 195–227). San Diego, CA: Academic Press.

Linsenmeier, J.A.W., & Brickman, P. (1980). *Expectations, performance, and satisfaction.* Unpublished manuscript.

Linville, P.W., & Jones, E.E. (1980). Polarized appraisals of out-group members. *Journal of Personality and Social Psychology, 38,* 689–703.

Locke, E.A., & Latham, G.P. (1990). *A theory of goal setting and task performance.* Englewood Cliffs, NJ: Prentice Hall.

Locksley, A., Ortiz, V., & Hepburn, C. (1980). Social categorization and discriminatory behavior: Extinguishing the minimal intergroup discrimination effect. *Journal of Personality and Social Psychology, 39,* 773–783.

Loevinger, J. (1976). *Ego development.* San Francisco: Jossey-Bass.

Lofland, L.H. (1982). Loss and human connection: An exploration into the nature of the social bond. In W. Ickes & E.S. Knowles (Eds), *Personality, roles, and social behavior* (pp. 219–242). New York: Springer-Verlag.

Lord, C.G., Ross, L., & Lepper, M.R. (1979). Biased assimilation and attitude polarization: The effects of prior theories on subsequently considered evidence. *Journal of Personality and Social Psychology, 37,* 2098–2109.

Lord, C.O., Lepper, M.R., & Preston, E. (1984). Considering the opposite: A corrective strategy for social judgment. *Journal of Personality and Social Psychology, 47,* 1231–1243.

Lord, R.G., & Manges, P.J. (1987). A control system model of organizational motivation: Theoretical development and applied implications. *Behavioral Science, 32,* 161–178.

Lowenthal, M.E, & Haven, C. (1968). Interaction and adaptation: Intimacy as a critical variable. *American Sociological Review, 33,* 20–30.

Luborsky, L. (1977). Measuring a pervasive psychic structure in psychotherapy: The core conflictual relationship theme. In N. Freedman & S. Grand (Eds), *Communicative structures and psychic structures* (pp. 367–395). New York: Plenum.

———. (1988). Recurrent momentary forgetting: Its content and its context. In M.J. Horowitz (Ed.),

Psychodynamics and cognition (pp. 223–251). Chicago: University of Chicago Press.

Luchins, A.S. (1942). Mechanization in problem solving: The effect of Einstellung. *Psychological Monographs, 54,* Whole No. 248.

———. (1957). Primacy-recency in impression formation. In C.I. Hovland (Ed.), *The order of presentation in persuasion* (pp. 33– 61). New Haven, CT: Yale University Press.

Luria, A.R. (1961). *The role of speech in the regulation of normal and abnormal behavior* (J. Tizard, Translator). New York: Liveright.

Lynch, J.J. (1979). *The broken heart: The medical consequences of loneliness.* New York: Basic Books.

Maass, A., & Arcuri, L. (1992). The role of language in the persistence of stereotypes. In G. Semin & K. Fiedler (Eds), *Language, interaction and social cognition* (pp. 129–143). Newbury Park, CA: Sage.

———, & ———. (in press). Language and stereotyping. In N. Macrae, M. Hewstone, & C. Stangor (Eds), *The foundations of stereotypes and stereotyping.* New York: Guilford Press.

McAdams, D.P. (1985). Motivation and friendship. In S. Duck & D. Perlman (Eds), *Understanding personal relationships: An interdisciplinary approach* (pp. 85–105). Beverly Hills, CA: Sage.

McAdams, D.P., & Bryant, E.B. (1987). Intimacy motivation and subjective mental health in a nationwide sample. *Journal of Personality, 55,* 395–413.

McAllister, D.W., Mitchell, T.R., & Beach, L.R. (1979). The contingency model for the selection of decision strategies: An empirical test of the effects of significance, accountability, and reversibility. *Organizational Behavior and Human Performance, 24,* 228–244.

McCauley, C.R., & Segal, M.E. (1987). Social psychology of terrorist groups. In C. Hendrick (Ed.), *Group processes and intergroup relations: Review of personality and social psychology* (Vol. 9, pp. 231– 256). Newbury Park, CA: Sage.

McClelland, D.C. (1985). *Human Motivation.* New York: Cambridge University Press.

McClelland, D.C., Atkinson, J.W., Clark, R.A., & Lowell, E.L. (1953). *The achievement motive.* New York: Appleton-Century-Crofts.

MacCorquodale, K., & Meehl, P.E. (1948). On a distinction between hypothetical constructs and intervening variables. *Psychological Review, 55,* 95–107.

McCrae, R.R. (1993–1994). Openness to experience as a basic dimension of personality. *Imagination, Cognition and Personality, 13,* 39–55.

McCrae, R.R., & Costa, P.T. Jr. (1985). Openness to experience. In R. Hogan & W.H. Jones (Eds), *Perspectives in personality* (pp. 145–172). Greenwich, CT: JAI Press.

McDougal, W. (1908). *An introduction to social psychology.* Boston: John W. Luce and Co.

———. (1923) *Introduction to social psychology* (16th edn). Boston: John Luce.

McFarland, C., & Ross, M. (1982). Impact of causal attributions on affective reactions to success and failure. *Journal of Personality and Social Psychology, 43,* 937–946.

McFarlin, D.B. (1985). Persistence in the face of failure: The impact of self-esteem and contingency information. *Personality and Social Psychology Bulletin, 11,* 152–163.

McGraw, K.Q., & McCullers, J.C. (1979). Evidence of a detrimental effect of extrinsic incentives on breaking a mental set. *Journal of Experimental Social Psychology, 15,* 285–294.

McGuire, W.J. (1960). A syllogistic analysis of cognitive relationships. In M. J. Rosenberg, C.I. Hovland, W.J. McGuire, R.P. Abelson, & J.W. Brehm (Eds), *Attitude organization and change* (pp. 65–111). New Haven, CT: Yale University Press.

———. (1968). Theory of the structure of human thought. In R.P. Abelson, E. Aronson, W. J. McGuire, T.M. Newcomb, M.J. Rosenberg, & P.H. Tannenbaum (Eds), *Theories of cognitive consistency: A sourcebook* (pp. 140–162). Chicago: Rand McNally.

McHugh, M., Beckman, L., & Frieze, I.H. (1979). Analyzing alcoholism. In I.H. Frieze, D. Bar-Tal, & J.S. Carroll (Eds), *New approaches to social problems* (pp. 168–208). San Francisco: Jossey-Bass.

MacKay, D.M. (1963). Mindlike behavior in artefacts. In K.M. Sayre, & F.J. Crosson (Eds), *The modeling of mind: Computers and intelligence* (pp. 225–241). Notre Dame, IN: University of Notre Dame Press.

———. (1966). Cerebral organization and the conscious control of action. In J.C. Eccles (Ed.), *Brain and conscious experience* (pp. 422–445). Berlin: Springer-Verlag.

McLeod, E. (1982). *Women working: Prostitution today.* London: Croom Helm.

McMahan, I.D. (1973). Relationships between causal attributions and expectancy of success. *Journal of Personality and Social Psychology, 28,* 108–115.

McReynolds, P.A. (1956). Restricted conceptualization of human anxiety and motivation. *Psychological Reports, 2,* 293–312.

Maehr, M.L., & Midgley, C. (1991). Enhancing student motivation: A schoolwide approach. *Educational Psychologist, 26,* 399–427.

Maehr, M.L., & Stallings, W.M. (1972). Freedom from external evaluation. *Child Development, 43,* 177–185.

Mandler, G. (1975). *Mind and emotion.* New York: Wiley.

———. (1984). *Mind and body: Psychology of emotion and stress.* New York: Norton.

Mandler, G., & Watson, D.L. (1966). Anxiety and the interruption of behavior. In C.D. Spielberger (Ed.), *Anxiety and behavior* (pp. 263–288). New York: Academic Press.

Manis, M. (1955). Social interaction and the self-concept. *Journal of Abnormal and Social Psychology, 51,* 362–370.

Mann, L. (1980). Cross-cultural studies of small groups. In H. Triandis & R. Brislin (Eds), *Handbook of cross-cultural psychology: Social psychology* (Vol. 5, pp. 155–209). Boston: Allyn & Bacon.

Manucia, G.K., Baumann, D.J., & Cialdini, R.B. (1984). Mood influences on helping: Direct effects or side effects? *Journal of Personality and Social Psychology, 46,* 357–364.

Marbe, K. (1901). *Experimentell-psychologische Untersuchungen Oder das Urteil [Experimental studies on judgment].* Leipzig: W. Engelmann.

Mark, M.M. (1985). Expectation, procedural justice, and alternative reactions to being deprived of a desired outcome. *Journal of Experimental Social Psychology, 21,* 114–137.

Marken, R.S. (1986). Perceptual organization of behavior: A hierarchical control model of coordinated action. *Journal of Experimental Psychology: Human Perception and Performance, 12,* 267–276.

Marks, R.W. (1951). The effects of probability, desirability, and 'privilege' on the stated expectations of children. *Journal of Personality, 79,* 332–351.

Markus, H., & Kunda, Z. (1986). Stability and malleability of the self-concept. *Journal of Personality and Social Psychology, 51,* 858–866.

Markus, H., & Nurius, P. (1986). Possible selves. *American Psychologist, 41.* 954–969.

Marriott, R. (1949). Size of working group and output. *Occupational Psychology, 23,* 47–57.

Martens, R., & Landers, D.M. (1969). Coaction effects on a muscular endurance task. *Research Quarterly, 40,* 733–737.

Martin, L., & Tesser, A. (in press). Toward a model of ruminative thought. In J.S. Uleman & J.A. Bargh (Eds), *Unintended thought: The limits of awareness, intention, and control.* New York: Guilford.

Martinez, A. (1982). Out-of-work lumbermen not out of the woods yet. *Los Angeles Times,* Pt. 5, 1.

Maslow, A.H. (1954). *Motivation and personality.* New York: Harper.

——. (1955). Deficiency motivation and growth motivation. In M.R. Jones (Ed.), *Nebraska symposium on motivation, 1955* (pp. 1–30). Lincoln: University of Nebraska Press.

——. (1968). *Toward a psychology of being.* New York: Van Nostrand.

Masserman, J.H., Wechkin, S., & Terris, W (1964). 'Altruistic' behavior in rhesus monkeys. *American Journal of Psychiatry, 121,* 584–585.

Masters, J.C., & Furman, W. (1976). Effects of affective states on noncontingent outcome expectancies and beliefs in internal or external control. *Developmental Psychology, 12,* 481–482.

Mathes, E.W, Adams, H.E., & Davies, R.M. (1985). Jealousy: Loss of relationship rewards, loss of self-esteem, depression, anxiety, and anger. *Journal of Personality and Social Psychology, 48,* 1552–1561.

May, J.L., & Hamilton, P.A. (1980). Effects of musically evoked affect on women's interpersonal attraction and perceptual judgments of physical attractiveness of men. *Motivation and Emotion, 4,* 217–228.

Mayer, J.D., & Gaschke, Y.N. (1988). The experience and meta-experience of mood. *Journal of Personality and Social Psychology, 55,* 102–111.

Mayman, M., & Faris, M. (1960). Early memories as expressions of relationship paradigms. *American Journal of Orthopsychiatry, 30,* 507–520.

Mayseless, O., & Kruglanski, A.W. (1987). What makes you so sure? Effects of epistemic motivations on judgmental confidence. *Organizational Behavior and Human Decision Processes, 39,* 162–183.

Mead, G.H. (1934). *Mind, self, and society.* Chicago: University of Chicago Press.

Meece, J.L., Blumenfeld, P.C., & Hoyle, R.H. (1988). Students' goal orientations and cognitive engagement in classroom activities. *Journal of Educational Psychology, 80,* 514–523.

Meece, J.L., & Holt, K. (1993). A pattern analysis of students' achievement goals. *Journal of Educational Psychology, 85,* 582–590.

Meichenbaum, D. (1977). *Cognitive-behavior modification.* New York: Plenum.

Meindl, J.R., & Lerner, M.J. (1984). Exacerbation of extreme responses to an out-group. *Journal of Personality and Social Psychology, 47,* 71–84.

Merton, R.K. (1957). *Social theory and social structure.* Glencoe, IL: Free Press.

Meyer, J.P. (1980). Causal attributions for success and failure: A multivariate investigation of dimensionality, formation, and consequences. *Journal of Personality arid Social Psychology, 38,* 704–715.

Meyer, J.P., & Koelbl, S.L.M. (1982). Dimensionality of students' causal attributions for test performance. *Personality and Social Psychology Bulletin, 8,* 31–36.

Meyer, J.P., & Mulherin, A. (1980). From attribution to helping: An analysis of the mediating effects of affect and expectancy. *Journal of Personality and Social Psychology, 39,* 201–210.

Meyer, W.U. (1973). *Leistungsmotiv und Ursachenerklarung von Erfolg und Misserfolg [Achievement motivation and causal attributions for success and failure].* Stuttgart: Ernst Klett.

Meyer, W.U., Folkes, V.S., & Weiner, B. (1976). The perceived informational value and affective consequences of choice behavior and intermediate difficulty task selection. *Journal of Research in Personality, 10,* 410–423.

Miceli, M. (1992). How to make someone feel guilty: Strategies of guilt inducement and their goals. *Journal for the Theory of Social Behaviour, 22,* 81–104.

Michela, J.L., Peplau, L.A., & Weeks, D.G. (1982). Perceived dimensions of attributions for loneliness. *Journal of Personality and Social Psychology, 43,* 929–936.

Michotte, A.E. (1946). *The perception of causality.* Paris: Vrin.

Middleton, M.J., & Midgely, C. (1997). Avoiding the demonstration of lack of ability: An underexplored aspect of goal theory. *Journal of Educational Psychology, 89,* 710–718.

Midgley, C., Anderman, E., & Hicks, L. (1995). Differences between elementary and middle school teachers: A goal theory approach. *Journal of Early Adolescence, 15,* 90–113.

Midgely, C., Kaplan, A., & Middleton, M. (2001). Performance-approach goals: Good for what, for whom, under what circumstances, and at what cost? *Journal of Educational Psychology, 93,* 77–86.

Midgley, C., & Urdan, T. (1995). Predictors of middle school students' use of self-handicapping strategies. *Journal of Early Adolescence, 15,* 389–411.

Mijuskovic, B. (1980). Loneliness: An interdisciplinary approach. In J. Hartog, J.R. Audy, & Y.A. Cohen (Eds), *The anatomy of loneliness* (pp. 65–94). New York: International Universities Press.

Mikulincer, M., Kedem, P., & Paz, D. (1990). The impact of trait anxiety and situational stress on the categorization of natural objects. *Anxiety Research, 2,* 85–101.

Mikulincer, M., Yinon, A., & Kabili, D. (1991). Epistemic needs and learned helplessness. *European Journal of Personality, 5,* 249–258.

Milardo, R.M., Johnson, M.P., & Huston, T.L. (1983). Developing close relationships: Changing patterns of interaction between pair members and social networks. *Journal of Personality and Social Psychology, 44,* 964–976.

Millar, K.U., Tesser, A., & Millar, M.G. (1988). The effects of a threatening life event on behavior sequences and intrusive thought: A self-disruption explanation. *Cognitive Therapy and Research, 12,* 441–458.

Miller, D.R. (1963). The study of social relationships: Situation, identity, and social interaction. In S. Koch (Ed.), *Psychology: A study of a science* (Vol. 5, pp. 639–737). Toronto: McGraw-Hill.

Miller, D.T., & Prentice, D.A. (1996). The construction of social norms and standards. In E.T. Higgins & A.W. Kruglanski (Eds), *Social psychology: Handbook of basic principles* (pp. 799–829). New York: Guilford Press.

Miller, D.T, & Ross, M. (1975). Self-serving biases in attribution of causality: Fact or fiction? *Psychological Bulletin, 82,* 213–225.

Miller, G.A., Galanter, E., & Pribram, K.H. (1960). *Plans and the structure of behavior.* New York: Holt.

Miller, N.B., Cowan, P.A., Cowan, C.P., Hetherington, E.M., & Clingempeel, W.G. (1993). Externalizing in preschoolers and early adolescents: A cross-study replication of a family model. *Developmental Psychology, 29,* 3–18.

Miller, N.E. (1944). Experimental studies of conflict. In J.M.V. Hunt (Ed.), *Personality and the behavior disorders* (Vol. 1, pp. 431–465). New York: Ronald Press.

———. (1951). Learnable drives and rewards. In S.S. Stevens (Ed.), *Handbook of experimental psychology* (pp. 435–472). New York: Wiley.

———. (1958). Central stimulation and other new approaches to motivation and reward. *American Psychologist, 13,* 100–108.

Miller, R.B., Behrens, J.T., Greene, B.A., & Newman, D. (1993). Goals and perceived ability: Impact on student valuing, self-regulation, and persistence. *Contemporary Educational Psychology, 18,* 2–14.

Miller, R.L., Brickman, P., & Bolen, D. (1975). Attribution versus persuasion as a means of modifying behavior. *Journal of Personality and Social Psychology, 31,* 430–441.

Miller, R.S., & Leary, M.R. (1992). Social sources and interactive functions of emotion: The case of embarrassment. In M. Clark (Ed.), *Review of personality and social psychology Vol. 14: Emotion and social behavior* (pp. 202–221). Newbury Park, CA: Sage.

Mischel, W. (1968). *Personality and assessment.* New York: Wiley.

———. (1973). Toward a cognitive social learning reconceptualization of personality. *Psychological Review, 80,* 252–283.

———. (1996). From good intentions to willpower. In P. Gollwitzer & J. Bargh (Eds), *The psychology of action* (pp. 197–218). New York: Guilford Press.

Mischel, W., & Peake, P.K. (1982). Beyond deja vu in the search for cross-situational consistency. *Psychological Review, 8Q,* 730–755.

Mittlemann, B. (1954). Motility in infants, children, and adults. *Psychoanalytic Study of the Child, 9,* 142–177.

Moede, W. (1927). Die Richtlinien der Leistungs-Psychologie. *Industrielle Psychotechnik, 4,* 193–207.

Molden, D.C., & Dweck, C.S. (2000). Meaning and motivation. In C. Sansone & J.M. Harackiewicz (Eds), *Intrinsic and extrinsic motivation: The search for optimal motivation and performance* (pp. 131–159). San Diego, CA: Academic Press.

Monson, T.C., Keel, R., Stephens, D., & Genung, V. (1982). Trait attributions: Relative validity, covariation with behavior, and prospect of future interaction. *Journal of Personality and Social Psychology, 42,* 1014–1024.

Monson, T.C., & Snyder, M. (1977). Actors, observers, and the attribution process: Toward a reconceptuaiization. *Journal of Experimental Social Psychology, 13,* 89–111.

Montanelli, D.S., & Hill, K.T. (1969). Children's achievement expectations and performance as a function of two consecutive reinforcement experiences, sex of subject, and sex of experimenter. *Journal of Personality and Social Psychology, 13,* 115–128.

Montgomery, K.C. (1954). The role of the exploratory drive in learning. *Journal of Comparative & Physiological Psychology, 47,* 60–64.

Montgomery, K.C., & Monkman, J.A. (1955). The relation between fear and exploratory behavior. *Journal of Comparative & Physiological Psychology, 48,* 132–136.

Moreland, R.L. (1987). The formation of small groups. In C. Hendrick (Ed.), *Group processes: Review of personality and social psychology* (Vol. 8, pp. 80–110). Newbury Park, CA: Sage.

Moreland, R.L., & Levine, J.M. (1989). Newcomers and oldtimers in small groups. In P. Paulus (Ed.), *Psychology of group influence* (Vol. 2, pp. 143–186). Hillsdale, NJ: Eribaum.

Morgan, C.T. (1943). *Physiological psychology.* New York: McGraw-Hill.

———. (1957). Physiological mechanisms of motivation. In M.R. Jones (Ed.), *Nebraska symposium on motivation 1957* (pp. 1–35). Lincoln: University of Nebraska Press.

Morgenthau, H. (1962). Love and power. *Commentary, 33,* 247–251.

Morris, D.R. (1965). *The washing of the spears: The rise and fall of the Zulu nation.* New York: Simon & Schuster.

Mowrer, O.H. (1950). *Learning theory and personality dynamics.* New York: Ronald Press.

———. (1960). *Learning theory and behavior.* New York: Wiley.

Mueller, C.M., & Dweck, C.S. (1998). Praise for intelligence can undermine children's motivation and performance. *Journal of Personality and Social Psychology, 75,* 33–52.

Munroe, R. (1955). *Schools of psychoanalytical thought.* New York: Dryden.

Muraven, M., Tice, D.M., & Baumeistei, R.F. (1998). Self-control as limited resource: Regulatory depletion patterns. *Journal of Personality and Social Psychology, 74,* 774–789.

Murphy, G. (1947). *Personality: A biosocial approach to origins and structure.* New York: Harper.

Murray, H.A. (1938). *Explorations in personality.* New York: Oxford University Press.

Murray, H.A., & Kluckhohn, C. (1953). Outline of a conception of personality. In C. Kluckhohn, H.A. Murray, & D.M. Schneider (Eds), *Personality in nature, society, and culture* (2nd edn). New York: Knopf.

Musashi, M. (1974). *A book of five rings* (Original work written in 1645). Woodstock, NY: Overlook.

Myers, A.K., & Miller, N.E. (1954). Failure to find a learned drive based on hunger: Evidence for learning motivated by 'exploration'. *Journal of Comparative & Physiological Psychology, 47,* 428–436.

Myers, D. (1992). *The pursuit of happiness.* New York: Morrow.

Naccarato, M.F., Thompson, M.M., & Parker, K. (1986). *Update on the development of the need for structure and fear of invalidity scales.* Unpublished manuscript.

Nahemow, L., & Lawton, M.P. (1975). Similarity and propinquity in friendship formation. *Journal of Personality and Social Psychology, 32,* 205–213.

Neale, J.M., & Friend, R.M. (1972). Attributional determinants of reactions to performance in academic situations. *Perceptual and Motor Skills, 34,* 35–40.

Neuberg, S.L., & Fiske, S.T. (1987). Motivational influences on impression formation: Dependency, accuracy-driven attention, and individuating information. *Journal of Personality and Social Psychology, 53,* 431–444.

Neuberg, S.L., & Newsom, J. (1993). Individual differences in chronic motivation to simplify: Personal need for structure and social-cognitive processing. *Journal of Personality and Social Psychology, 65,* 113–131.

Newcomb, T.M. (1950). *Social psychology.* New York: Dryden Press.

Newell, K.M. (1978). Some issues on action plans. In G.E. Stelmach (Ed.), *Information processing in motor control and learning* (pp. 41–54). New York: Academic Press.

Nicholls, J.G. (1984). Achievement motivation: Conceptions of ability, subjective experience, task choice, and performance. *Psychological Review, 91,* 328–346.

Nisbett, R.E., & Ross, L. (1980). *Human inference: Strategies and shortcomings of social judgement.* Englewood Cliffs, NJ: Prentice-Hall.

Nisbett, R.E., Krantz, D.H., Jepson, C., & Kunda, Z. (1983). The use of statistical heuristics in everyday inductive reasoning. *Psychological Review, 90,* 339–363.

Nisbett, R.E., & Valins, S. (1971). *Perceiving the causes of one's own behavior.* New York: General Learning Press.

Nissen, H.W. (1930). A study of exploratory behavior in the white rat by means of the obstruction method. *Journal of Genetic Psychology, 37,* 361–376.

Norem, J.K., & Cantor, N. (1986). Anticipatory and post hoc cushioning strategies: Optimism and defensive pessimism in 'risky' situations. *Cognitive Therapy & Research, 10,* 347–362.

———, & ———. (1986). Defensive pessimism: Harnessing anxiety as motivation. *Journal of Personality & Social Psychology, 51,* 1208–1217.

Norem, J.K., & Illingworth, K.S.S. (1993). Strategy-dependent effects of reflecting on self and tasks: Some implications of optimism and defensive pessimism. *Journal of Personality & Social Psychology, 65,* 822–835.

Norman, D.A. (1981). Categorization of action slips. *Psychological Review, 88,* 1–15.

Norman, D.A., & Bobrow, D.G. (1976). On the role of active memory processes in perception and cognition. In C.N. Cofer (Ed.), *The structure of human memory* (pp. 114–132). San Francisco: Freeman and Company.

———, & ———. (1979). Descriptions: An intermediate stage in memory retrieval. *Cognitive Psychology, 11,* 107–123.

Norman, D.A., & Shallice, T. (1980). *Attention to action: Willed and automatic control of behavior* (Tech. Rep. No.

8006). San Diego: Center for Human Information Processing, University of California,

Ogilvie, D.M. (1987). The undesired self: A neglected variable in personality research. *Journal of Personality and Social Psychology, 52,* 379–385.

O'Grady, K.E. (1989). Physical attractiveness, need for approval, social self-esteem, and maladjustment. *Journal of Social and Clinical Psychology, 8,* 62–69.

Olds, J., & Milner, P. (1954). Positive reinforcement produced by electrical stimulation of septal area and other regions of rat brain. *Journal of Comparative & Physiological Psychology, 47,* 419–427.

O'Leary, K.D., & Drabman, R. (1971). Token reinforcement programs in the classroom: A review. *Psychological Bulletin, 75,* 379–398.

O'Leary, K.D., Poulos, R.W., & Devine, V.T. (1972). Tangible reinforcers: Bonuses or bribes? *Journal of Consulting and Clinical Psychology, 38,* 1–8.

Olmos, E. (Producer). (1994, April 8). *Lives in hazard.* New York: National Broadcasting Company.

Olson, J.M., Roese, N.J., & Zanna, M.P. (1996). Expectancies. In E.T. Higgins & A.W. Kruglanski (Eds), *Social psychology: Handbook of basic principles* (pp. 211–238). New York: Guilford Press.

Olson, M. (1965). *The logic of collective action: Public goods and the theory of groups.* Cambridge, MA: Harvard University Press.

Omoto, A.M., & Borgida, E. (1988). Guess who might be coming for dinner: Personal involvement and racial stereotyping. *Journal of Experimental Social Psychology, 24,* 571–593.

Orbell, J.M., van de Kragt, A., & Dawes, R.M. (1988). Explaining discussion-induced cooperation. *Journal of Personality and Social Psychology, 54,* 811–819.

Ortony, A., Clore, G.L., & Collins, A. (1988). *The cognitive structure of emotions.* Cambridge, England: Cambridge University Press.

Osgood, C., Suci, G., & Tannenbaum, P. (1957). *The measurement of meaning.* Urbana: University of Illinois Press.

Ostrom, T.M., Carpenter, S.L., Sedikides, C., & Li, E. (1993). Differential processing of in-group and out-group information. *Journal of Personality and Social Psychology, 64,* 21–34.

Paloutzian, R.E, & Janigian, A.S. (1987). Models and methods in loneliness research: Their status and direction. In M. Hoja & R. Crandall (Eds), *Loneliness: Theory, research, and applications* (pp. 31– 36). San Rafael, CA: Select Press.

Pancer, S.M. (1978). Causal attributions and anticipated future performance. *Personality and Social Psychology Bulletin, 4,* 600–603.

Pancer, S.M., & Eiser, J.R. (1977). Expectation, aspirations and evaluations as influenced by another's attribution for success and failure. *Canadian Journal of Behavioral Science, 9,* 252–264.

Panksepp, J., Siviy, S.M., & Normansell, L.A. (1985). Brain opioids and social emotions. In M. Reite & T. Field (Eds), *The psychobiology of attachment and separation* (pp. 3–49). New York: Academic Press.

Passer, M.W. (1977). *Perceiving the causes of success and failure revisited: A multidimensional scaling approach.* Unpublished doctoral dissertation, University of California, Los Angeles.

Passer, M.W., Kelley, H.H., & Michela, J.L. (1978). Multidimensional scaling of the causes for negative interpersonal behavior. *Journal of Personality and Social Psychology, 36,* 951–962.

Pastore, N. (1952). The role of arbitrariness in the frustration-aggression hypothesis. *Journal of Abnormal and Social Psychology, 47,* 728–732.

Payne, J.W., Bettman, J.R., & Johnson, E.J. (1988). Adaptive strategy selection in decision making. *Journal of Experimental Psychology: Learning, Memory, and Cognition, 14,* 534–552.

Pearce, P.L. (1980). Strangers, travelers, and Greyhound terminals: A study of small-scale helping behaviors. *Journal of Personality and Social Psychology, 38,* 935–940.

Pearlman, C.A. (1970). Separation reactions of married women. *American Journal of Psychiatry, 126,* 946–950.

Pelham, B.W., & Swann, W.B. (1989). From self-conceptions to self-worth: On the sources and structure of global self-esteem. *Journal of Personality and Social Psychology, 57,* 672–680.

Peplau, L.A., Russell, D., & Heim, M. (1979). The experience of loneliness. In I.H. Frieze, D. Bar-Tal, & J.S. Carroll (Eds) *New approaches to social problems* (pp. 53–78). San Fransisco: Jossey-Bass.

Perlman, D. (1987). Further reflections on the present state of loneliness research. In M. Hoja & R. Crandall (Eds), *Loneliness: Theory, research, and applications* (pp. 17–26). San Rafael, CA: Select Press.

Perloff, L.S., & Fetzer, B.K. (1986). Self-other judgments and perceived vulnerability to victimization. *Journal of Personality and Social Psychology, 50,* 502–510.

Pervin, L.A. (1989). *Goal concepts in personality and social psychology.* Hillsdale, NJ: Erlbaum.

Petty, R.E., & Cacioppo, J.T. (1979). Issue involvement can increase or decrease persuasion by enhancing message-relevant cognitive responses. *Journal of Personality and Social Psychology, 37,* 349–360.

———, & ———. (1986). The elaboration likelihood model of persuasion. In L. Berkowitz (Ed.), *Advances in experimental social psychology* (Vol. 19, pp. 123–205). New York: Academic Press.

Petty, R.E., Harkins, S., Williams, K., & Latane, B. (1977). The effects of group size on cognitive effort and evaluation. *Personality and Social Psychology Bulletin, 3,* 579–582.

Piaget, J. (1952). *The origins of intelligence in children* (Translated by M. Cook). New York: International University Press.

————. (1970). Piaget's theory. In P.H. Mussen (Ed.), *Carmichael's manual of child psychology* (3rd edn) (Vol. 1, pp. 703–732). New York: Wiley.

Pickett, C.L., Bonner, B.L., & Coleman, J.M. (in press). Motivated self-stereotyping: Heightened assimilation and differentiation needs result in increased levels of positive and negative self-stereotyping. *Journal of Personality and Social Psychology*.

Pickett, C.L., & Brewer, M.B. (2001). Assimilation and differentiation needs as motivational determinants of perceived ingroup and outgroup homogeneity. *Journal of Experimental Social Psychology, 37*, 341–348.

Piers, G., & Singer, M.B. (1971). *Shame and guilt*. New York: Norton.

Piliavin, I.M., Rodin, J., & Piliavin, J.A. (1969). Good samaritanism: An underground phenomenon? *Journal of Personality and Social Psychology, 13*, 289–299.

Pines, M., & Aronson, E. (1983). Antecedents, correlates, and consequences of sexual jealousy. *Journal of Personality, 51*, 108–135.

Pintrich, P.R. (2000a). An achievement goal theory perspective on issues in motivation terminology, theory, and research. *Contemporary Educational Psychology, 25*, 92–104.

————. (2000b). The role of goal orientation in self-regulated learning. In M. Boekaerts, P. Pintrich, & M. Zeidner (Eds), *Handbook of self-regulation* (pp. 451–502). San Diego, CA: Academic Press.

Pintrich, P.R., & DeGroot, E.V. (1990). Motivational and self-regulated learning components of classroom academic performance. *Journal of Educational Psychology, 82*, 33–40.

Pintrich, P.R., & Garcia, T. (1991). Student goal orientation and self-regulation in the college classroom. In M.L. Maehr & P.R. Pintrich (Eds), *Advances in motivation and achievement* (Vol. 7, pp. 371–402). Greenwich, CT: JAI Press.

Pittman, R.S., Davey, M.E., Alafat, K.A., Wetherill, K.V., & Kramer, N.A. (1980). Informational versus controlling verbal rewards. *Personality and Social Psychology Bulletin, 6*. 228–233.

Pittman, T.S. (1975). Attribution of arousal as a mediator in dissonance reduction. *Journal of Experimental Social Psychology, 11*, 53–63.

Pittman, T.S., & D'Agostino, P.R. (1985). Motivation and attribution: The effects of control deprivation on subsequent information processing. In G. Weary & J. Harvey (Eds), *Attribution: Basic issues and applications* (pp. 117–141). New York: Academic Press.

Plant, R., & Ryan, R.M. (1985). Intrinsic motivation and the effects of self-consciousness, self-awareness, and ego-involvement: An investigation of internally controlling styles. *Journal of Personality, 53*, 435–449.

Plutchik, R. (1980). *Emotion: A psychoevolutionary synthesis*. New York: Harper & Row.

Powers, W.T. (1973). *Behavior: The control of perception*. Chicago: Aldine.

Price, S.J., & McKenry, P.C. (1988). *Divorce*. Beverly Hills, CA: Sage.

Pruitt, D.G., & Hoge, R.D. (1965). Strength of the relationship between the value of an event and its subjective probability as a function of method of measurement. *Journal of Experimental Psychology, 69*, 483–489.

Pryor, J.M., & Ostrom, T.M. (1981). The cognitive organization of social life: A converging-operations approach. *Journal of Personality and Social Psychology, 41*, 628–641.

Pyszczynski, T., & Greenberg, J. (1985). Depression and preference for self-focusing stimuli after success and failure. *Journal of Personality and Social Psychology, 49*, 1066–1075.

————, & ————. (1987a). Toward an integration of cognitive and motivational perspectives on social inference: A biased hypothesis-testing model. In L. Berkowitz (Ed.), *Advances in experimental social psychology* (Vol. 20, pp. 297–340). New York: Academic Press.

————, & ————. (1987b). Self-regulatory perseveration and the depressive self-focusing style: A self-awareness theory of reactive depression. *Psychological Bulletin, 102*, 122–138.

Pyszczynski, T., Greenberg, J., & Holt, K. (1985). Maintaining consistency between self-serving beliefs and available data: A bias in information evaluation. *Personality and Social Psychology Bulletin, 11*, 179–190.

Pyszczynski, T., Holt, K., & Greenberg, J. (1987). Depression, self-focused attention, and expectancies for positive and negative future life events for self and others. *Journal of Personality and Social Psychology, 52*, 994–1001.

Quattrone, G.A. (1982). Overattribution and unit formation: When behavior engulfs the person. *Journal of Personality and Social Psychology, 42*, 593–607.

Rabbie, J.M., & Horwitz, M. (1969). Arousal of ingroup-outgroup bias by a chance win or loss. *Journal of Personality and Social Psychology, 13*, 269–277.

Rabkin, E.S. (1979). *Fantastic worlds: Myths, tales, and stories*. Oxford, England: Oxford University Press.

Rapaport, D. (1951). *Organisation and pathology of thought*. New York: Columbia University Press.

————. (1954). On the psychoanalytic theory of thinking. In R.P. Knight & C.R. Friedman (Eds), *Psychoanalytic psychiatry and psychology* (pp. 259–273). New York: International University Press.

————. (1958). The theory of ego autonomy: A generalization. *Bulletin of the Menninger Clinic, 22*, 13–35.

Rawsthorne, L.J., & Elliot, A. J. (1999). Achievement goals and intrinsic motivation: A meta-analytic review. *Personality and Social Psychology Review, 3*, 326–344.

Reason, J., & Mycielska, K. (1982). *Absent-minded? The psychology of mental lapses and everyday errors*. Englewood Cliffs, NJ: Prentice-Hall.

Reis, H.T. (1990). The role of intimacy in interpersonal relations. *Journal of Social and Clinical Psychology, 9*, 15–30.

Reis, H.T., Wheeler, L., Kernis, M.H., Spiegel, N., & Nezlek, J. (1985). On specificity in the impact of social participation on physical and psychological health. *Journal of Personality and Social Psychology, 48*, 456–471.

Reisenzein, R. (in press). A structural equation analysis of Weiner's attribution-affect model of helping behavior. *Journal of Personality and Social Psychology.*

Reiss, I.L. (1986). A sociological journey into sexuality. *Journal of Marriage and the Family, 48*, 233–242.

Rich, A.R., & Woolever, D.K. (1988). Expectancy and self-focused attention: Experimental support for the self-regulation model of test anxiety. *Journal of Social and Clinical Psychology, 7*, 246–259.

Robert, R. (1982). Malavasi questions character of some, says coaching is tough. *Los Angeles Times, Pt. 3*, 3.

Robles, R., Smith, R., Carver, C.S., & Wellens, A.R. (1987). Influence of subliminal visual images on the experience of anxiety. *Personality and Social Psychology Bulletin, 13*, 339–410.

Rodin, J., Langer, E.J. (1977). Long-term effects of a control relevant intervention with the institutionalized aged. *Journal of Personality and Social Psychology, 35*, 897–902.

Roeser, R.W., Midgely, C., & Urdan, T.C. (1996). Perceptions of the school psychological environment and early adolescents' psychological and behavioral functioning in school: The mediating role of goals and belonging. *Journal of Educational Psychology, 88*, 408–422.

Rofe, Y. (1984). Stress and affiliation: A utility theory. *Psychological Review, 91*, 235–250.

Rogers, C.R. (1959). A theory of therapy, personality, and interpersonal relationships, as developed in the client-centered framework. In S. Koch (Ed.), *Psychology: A study of a science* (Vol. 3, pp. 184–256). New York: McGraw-Hill.

———. (1961). *On becoming a person.* Boston: Houghton Mifflin.

———. (1980). *A way of being.* Boston: Houghton Mifflin.

Rokeach, M. (1960). *The open and closed mind.* New York: Basic Books.

Roney, C.J.R., Higgins, E.T., & Shah, J. (1995). Goals and framing: How outcome focus influences motivation and emotion. *Personality & Social Psychology Bulletin, 21*, 1151–1160.

Ronis, D.L., Hansen, R.D., & O'Leary, V.B. (1983). Understanding the meaning of achievement attributions: A test of derived locus and stability scores. *Journal of Personality and Social Psychology, 44*, 702–711.

Rook, K.S. (1987a). Reciprocity of social exchange and social satisfaction among older women. *Journal of Personality and Social Psychology, 52*, 145–154.

———. (1987b). Social support versus companionship: Effects on life stress, loneliness, and evaluations by others. *Journal of Personality and Social Psychology, 52*, 1132–1147.

Rosch, E.H. (1973). Natural categories. *Cognitive Psychology, 4*, 328–350.

———. (1978). Principles of categorization. In E. Rosch & B.B. Lloyd (Eds), *Cognition and categorization* (pp. 27–48). Hillsdale, NJ: Erlbaum.

Roseman, I.J. (1984). Cognitive determinants of emotion: A structural theory. *Review of Personality and Social Psychology, 5*, 11–36.

Roseman, I.J., Spindel, M.S. & Jose, P.E. (1990). Appraisals of emotion-eliciting events: Testing a theory of discrete emotions. *Journal of Personality & Social Psychology, 59*, 899–915.

Rosen, R. (1979). Some crucial issues concerning children of divorce. *Journal of Divorce, 3*, 19–25.

Rosen, S., Mickler, S.E., & Collins, J.E. (1987). Reactions of would-be helpers whose offer of help is spurned. *Journal of Personality and Social Psychology, 53*, 288–297.

Rosenbaum, D.A. (1987). Hierarchical organization of motor programs. In S.P. Wise (Ed.), *Higher brain functions: Recent explorations of the brain's emergent properties* (pp. 45–66). New York: Wiley.

Rosenbaum, D.A., Kenny, S.B., & Derr, M.A. (1983). Hierarchical control of rapid movement sequences. *Journal of Experimental Psychology: Human Perception and Performance, 9*, 86–102.

Rosenbaum, R.M. (1972). *A dimensional analysis of the perceived causes of success and failure.* Unpublished doctoral dissertation, University of California, Los Angeles.

Rosenberg, M. (1965). *Society and the adolescent self-image.* Princeton, NJ: Princeton University Press.

———. (1973). Which significant others? *American Behavioral Scientist, 16*, 829–860.

Rosenberg, M.J. (1965). When dissonance fails: On eliminating evaluation apprehension from attitude measurement. *Journal of Personality and Social Psychology, 1*, 28–42.

Rosenberg, T. (1991). *Children of Cain: Violence and the violent in Latin America.* New York: Penguin Books.

Rosenthal, R., & Jacobson, L. (1968). *Pygmalion in the classroom: Teacher expectancies and pupils' intellectual development.* New York: Holt, Rinehart & Winston.

Rosenthal, R., & Rosnow, R.L. (1985). *Contrast analysis: Focused comparisons in the analysis of variance.* New York: Cambridge University Press.

Ross, C. (1976). *The Wars of the Roses: A concise history.* New York: Thames & Hudson.

Ross, L., Greene, D., & House, P. (1977). The 'false consensus effect': An egocentric bias in social perception and attribution processes. *Journal of Experimental Social Psychology, 13*, 279–301.

Ross, L., Lepper, M.R., & Hubbard, M. (1975). Perseverance in self perception and social perception: Biased attribution processes in the debriefing paradigm. *Journal of Personality and Social Psychology, 35,* 880–892.

Ross, M. (1975). Salience of reward and intrinsic motivation. *Journal of Personality and Social Psychology, 32,* 245–254.

Ross, M., & Fletcher, G.J.O. (1985). Attribution and social perception. In G. Lindzey & E. Aronson (Eds), *Handbook of social psychology* (pp. 73–122). New York: Random House.

Ross, M., McFarland, C., & Fletcher, G.J.O. (1981). The effect of attitude on recall of past histories. *Journal of Personality and Social Psychology, 10,* 627–634.

Rosvold, H.E. (1959). Physiological psychology. *Annual Review of Psychology, 10,* 415–454.

Rothbaum, F., Weisz, J.R., & Snyder, S.S. (1982). Changing the world and changing the self: A two-process model of perceived control. *Journal of Personality and Social Psychology, 42,* 5–37.

Rothberg, J.M., & Jones, E.D. (1987). Suicide in the US Army: Epidemiological and periodic aspects. *Suicide and Life-Threatening Behavior, 17,* 119–132.

Rotter, J.B. (1954). *Social learning and clinical psychology.* New York: Prentice-Hall.

———. (1966). Generalized expectancies for internal versus external control of reinforcement. *Psychological Monograph, 80,* 1–28.

Roy, M. (Ed.). (1977). *Battered women.* New York: Van Nostrand.

Ruehlman, L.S., & Wolchik, S.A. (1988). Personal goals and interpersonal support and hindrance as factors in psychological distress and well-being. *Journal of Personality and Social Psychology, 55,* 293–301.

Rumelhart, D.E. (1975). Notes on a schema for stories. In D.G. Bobrow & A.M. Collins (Eds), *Representation and understanding* (pp. 211–236). New York: Academic Press.

———. (1977). Understanding and summarizing brief stories. In D. LaBerge & J. Samuels (Eds), *Basic processes in reading and comprehension* (pp. 265–303). Hillsdale, NJ: Erlbaum.

Rusbult, C.E. (1980). Commitment and satisfaction in romantic associations: A test of the investment model. *Journal of Experimental Social Psychology, 16,* 172–186.

Rusbult, C.E., Verette, J., & Drigotus, S.M. (1994). *Absolute commitment level, mutuality of commitment, and couple adjustment in marital relationships.* Unpublished manuscript, University of North Carolina at Chapel Hill.

Rusbult, C.E., Zembrodt, I.M., & Gunn, L.K. (1982). Exit, voice, loyalty, and neglect: Responses to dissatisfaction in romantic involvements. *Journal of Personality and Social Psychology, 43,* 1230–1242.

Russell, D., Cutrona, C., Rose, J., & Yurko, K. (1984). Social and emotional loneliness: An examination of Weiss's typology of loneliness. *Journal of Personality and Social Psychology, 46,* 1313–1321.

Rutkowski, G.K., Gruder, C.L., & Romer, D. (1983). Group cohesiveness, social norms, and bystander intervention. *Journal of Personality and Social Psychology, 44,* 545–552.

Rutter, M. (1979). Maternal deprivation, 1972–1978: New findings, new concepts, new approaches. *Child Development, 50,* 283–305.

Rutter, M., & Garmezy, N. (1983). Developmental psychopathology. In E.M. Hetherington (Ed.), *Handbook of child psychology* (Vol. 4, pp. 77 5–911). New York: Wiley.

Ryan, R.M. (1982). Control and information in the intrapersonal sphere: An extension of cognitive evaluation theory. *Journal of Personality and Social Psychology, 43,* 450–461.

———. (1991). The nature of the self in autonomy and relatedness. In J. Strauss & G.R. Goethals (Eds), *The self: Interdisciplinary approaches* (pp. 208–238). New York: Springer-Verlag.

Ryan, R.M., Connell, J.P., & Deci, E.L. (1985). A motivational analysis of self-determination and self-regulation in education. In C. Ames & R.E. Ames (Eds), *Research on motivation in education: The classroom milieu* (pp. 13–51). New York: Academic Press.

Ryan, R.M., Connell, J.P., & Grolnick, W.S. (in press). When achievement is *not* intrinsically motivated: A theory and assessment of self-regulation in school. In A.K. Boggiano & T.S. Pittman (Eds), *Achievement and motivation: A social-developmental perspective.* Cambridge: Cambridge University Press.

Ryan, R.M., Connell, J.P., Plant, R., Robinson, D., & Evans, S. (1985). *The influence of emotions on spontaneous learning.* Unpublished manuscript, University of Rochester, Rochester, NY.

Ryan, R.M., & Deci, E.L. (1986). *When free-choice behavior is not intrinsically motivated: Experiments on internally controlling regulation.* Unpublished manuscript, University of Rochester, Rochester, NY.

Ryan, R.M., & Grolnick, W.S. (1986). Origins and pawns in the classroom: Self-report and projective assessments of individual differences in children's perceptions. *Journal of Personality and Social Psychology, 50,* 550–558.

Ryan, R.M., Mims, V., & Koestner, R. (1983). Relation of reward contingency and interpersonal context to intrinsic motivation: A review and test using cognitive evaluation theory. *Journal of Personality and Social Psychology, 45,* 736–750.

Ryle, G. (1949). *The concept of mind.* London: Hutchinson.

Saklofske, D.H., & Yackulic, R.A. (1989). Personality predictors of loneliness. *Personality and Individual Differences, 10,* 467–472.

Salancik, G.R., & Conway, M. (1975). Attitude inference from salient and relevant cognitive content about behavior. *Journal of Personality and Social Psychology, 32,* 829–840.

Sampson, R.J., & Laub, J.H. (1993). *Crime in the making: Pathways and turning points through life.* Cambridge, MA: Harvard University Press.

Sanford, R.N., Adorno, E., Frenkel-Brunswik, E., & Levinson, D.J. (1950). The measurement of implicit antidemocratic trends. In E. Adorno, E. Frenkel-Brunswick, D. J. Levinson, & R.N. Sanford (Eds), *The authoritarian personality* (pp. 222–279). New York: Harper & Row.

Sanitioso, R. (1989). *Mechanisms for motivated changes in the self-concept.* Unpublished doctoral dissertation, Princeton University.

Sanitioso, R., & Kunda, Z. (in press). Ducking the collection of costly evidence: Motivated use of statistical heuristics. *Journal of Behavioral Decision Making, 4,* 161-178.

Sanitioso, R., Kunda, Z., & Fong, G.T. (1990). Motivated recruitment of autobiographical memory. *Journal of Personality and Social Psychology, 59,* 229–241.

Sansone, C. (1986). A question of competence: The effects of competence and task feedback on intrinsic interest. *Journal of Personality and Social Psychology, 57,* 918–931.

Sarason, I.G. (1972). Experimental approaches to test anxiety: Attention and the uses of information. In C.D. Spielberger (Ed.). *Anxiety: Current trends in theory and research* (Vol. 2, pp. 383–403). New York: Academic Press.

Sarbin, T. (1982). The dangerous individual: An outcome of social identity transformations. In V.L. Allen & K.E. Scheibe (Eds), *The social context of conduct* (pp. 113–118). New York: Pergamon Press.

Sarbin, T.R., Taft, R., & Bailey, D.E. (1960). Clinical inference and cognitive theory. New York: Holt, Rinehart & Winston.

Saulnier, K., & Pearlman, D. (1981). The actor-observer bias is alive and well in prison: A sequel to Wells. *Personality and Social Psychology Bulletin, 7,* 559–564.

Schachtel, E.G. (1954). The development of focal attention and the emergence of reality. *Psychiatry, 17,* 309–324.

Schachter, S. (1951). Deviance, rejection, and communication. *Journal of Abnormal and Social Psychology, 46,* 190–207.

———. (1959). *The psychology of affiliation.* Stanford, CA: Stanford University Press.

Schachter, S., & Singer, J.E. (1962). Cognitive, social and physiological determinants of emotional state. *Psychological Review, 69,* 379–399.

Schank, R.C., & Abelson, R.P. (1977). *Scripts, plans, goals, and understanding.* Hillsdale, NJ: Erlbaum.

Scheier S.J., & Cooper, J. (1989). The motivational basis of dissonance: The singular role of behavioral consequences. *Journal of Personality and Social Psychology, 56,* 899–906.

Scheier, M.F., & Carver, C.S. (1982). Cognition, affect, and self-regulation. In M.S. Clark & S.T. Fiske (Eds), *Affect and cognition: The 17th Annual Carnegie Symposium on Cognition* (pp. 157–183). Hillsdale, NJ: Erlbaum.

———, & ———. (1987). Dispositional optimism and physical well-being: The influence of generalized outcome expectancies on health. *Journal of Personality, 55,* 169–210.

———, & ———. (1988). A model of behavioral self-regulation: Translating intention into action. In L. Berkowitz (Ed.), *Advances in experimental social psychology* (Vol. 21, pp. 303–346). New York: Academic Press.

———, & ———. (1992). Effects of optimism on psychological and physical well-being: Theoretical overview and empirical update. *Cognitive Therapy & Research, 16,* 201–228.

Schlenker, B.R. (1980). *Impression management: The self-concept, social identity, and interpersonal relations.* Monterey, CA: Brooks/Cole.

Schlenker, B.R., & Leary, M.R. (1982). Social anxiety and self-presentation: A conceptualization and model. *Psychological Bulletin, 92,* 641–669.

Schmidt, R. (1975). A schema theory of discrete motor learning. *Psychological Review, 82,* 225–260.

Schneirla, T. (1959). An evolutionary and developmental theory of biphasic processes underlying approach and withdrawal. *Nebraska Symposium on Motivation* (pp. 1–42). Lincoln: University of Nebraska Press.

Schoenrade, P.A., Batson, C.D., Brandt, J.R., & Loud, R.E. (1986). Attachment, accountability, and motivation to benefit another not in distress. *Journal of Personality and Social Psychology, 51,* 557–563.

Schönpflug, W. (1983). Coping efficiency and situational demands. In G.R. Hockey (Ed.), *Stress and fatigue in human performance* (pp. 299–333). Chichester, England: Wiley.

———. (1985). Goal directed behavior as a source of stress: Psychological origins and consequences of inefficiency. In M. Frese & J. Sabine (Eds), *Goal-directed behavior: The concept of action in psychology* (pp. 172–188). Hillsdale, NJ: Erlbaum.

Schulz, R. (1976). Effects of control and predictability on the physical and psychological well-being of the institutionalized aged. *Journal of Personality and Social Psychology, 33,* 563–573.

Schulz, R., & Hanusa, B.H. (1978). Long-term effects of control and predictability-enhancing interventions: Findings and ethical issues. *Journal of Personality and Social Psychology, 36,* 1194–1201.

Schütz, A. (1967). *Collected papers I: The problem of social reality.* The Hague, Netherlands: Martinus Nijhoff.

Schwartz, B. (1982). Reinforcement-induced behavioral stereotypy: How not to teach people to discover rules. *Journal of Experimental Psychology: General, 111,* 23–59.

Schwarz, N., & Clore, G.L. (1996). Feelings and phenomenal experiences. In E.T. Higgins & A.W. Kruglanski (Eds), *Social psychology: Handbook of basic principles* (pp. 433–465). New York: Guilford Press.

Scott, E.D., & Wire, E.L. (1986). The effect of partially delayed reinforcement and trial distribution on the extinction of an instrumental response. *American Journal of Psychology, 69,* 264–268.

Scott, L., & O'Hara, M.W. (1993). Self-discrepancies in clinically anxious and depressed university students. *Journal of Abnormal Psychology, 102,* 282–287.

Scudder, K.J. (1952). *Prisoners are people.* Garden City, NY: Doubleday.

Sedikides, C., Olsen, N., & Reis, H.T. (1993). Relationships as natural categories. *Journal of Personality and Social Psychology, 64,* 71–82.

Seligman, M.E.P. (1975). *Helplessness: On depression, development, and death.* San Francisco: Freeman.

Seligman, M.E.P., Abramson, L.Y., Semmel, A., & von Baeyer, C. (1979). Depressive attributional style. *Journal of Abnormal Psychology, 88,* 242–247.

Semin, G.R., & Fiedler, K. (1988). The cognitive functions of linguistic categories in describing persons: Social cognition and language. *Journal of Personality and Social Psychology, 54,* 558–568.

Seta, J.J., Paulus, P.B., & Schkade, J.K. (1976). Effects of group size and proximity under cooperative and competitive conditions. *Journal of Personality and Social Psychology, 34,* 47–53.

Shah, J., & Higgins, E.T. (1997). Expectancy × Value effects: Regulatory focus as determinant of magnitude and direction. *Journal of Personality & Social Psychology, 73,* 447–458.

———, & ———. (1997a). *Emotional evaluations of self and other attitude objects: Distinct sensitivities from regulatory focus.* Unpublished manuscript.

Shah, J., Higgins, E.T., & Friedman, R. (in press). Performance incentives and means: How regulatory focus influences goal attainment. *Journal of Personality & Social Psychology.*

Shallice, T. (1978). The dominant action system: An information-processing approach to consciousness. In K.S. Pope & J.L. Singer (Eds), *The stream of consciousness: Scientific investigations into the flow of human experience* (pp. 117–157). New York: Wiley.

Shaver, P., & Buhrmester, D. (1983). Loneliness, sex-role orientation, and group life: A social needs perspective. In P. Paulus (Ed.), *Basic group processes* (pp. 259–288). New York: Springer-Verlag.

Shaver, P., Hazan, C., & Bradshaw, D. (1988). Love as attachment: The integration of three behavioral systems. In R.J. Sternberg & M.L. Barnes (Eds). *The psychology of love* (pp. 68–99). New Haven, CT: Yale University Press.

Sheffield, F.D., & Roby, T.B. (1950). Reward value of a nonnutritive sweet taste. *Journal of Comparative & Physiological Psychology, 43,* 471–481.

Sheffield, F.D., Roby, T.B., & Campbell, B.A. (1954). Drive reduction vs. consummatory behavior as determinants of reinforcement. *Journal of Comparative & Physiological Psychology, 47,* 349–354.

Sheffield, F.D., Wulff, J.J., & Backer, R. (1951). Reward value of copulation without sex drive reduction. *Journal of Comparative & Physiological Psychology, 44,* 3–8.

Sheffield, V.F. (1949). Extinction as a function of partial reinforcement and distribution of practice. *Journal of Experimental Social Psychology, 39,* 211–526.

Shepperd, J.A., & Arkin, R.M. (1990). Shyness and self-presentation. In W.R. Crozier (Ed.), *Shyness and embarrassment: Perspectives on social psychology* (pp. 286–314). Cambridge, England: Cambridge University Press.

Sherif, M., & Cantril, H. (1947). *The psychology of ego involvements, social attitudes and identifications.* New York: Wiley.

Sherif, M., Harvey, O.H., White, B.J., Hood, W.R., & Sherif, C.W. (1988). *The Robbers Cave experiment: Intergroup conflict and cooperation.* Middletown, CT: Wesleyan University Press. (Original work published 1961)

Sherif, M., & Hovland, C.I. (1961). *Social judgment: Assimilation and contrast effects in communication.* New Haven, CT: Yale University Press.

Sherif, M., & Sherif, C.W. (1964). *Reference groups.* New York: Harper.

Sherington, C.A. (1906). *The integrative actions of the nervous system.* New York: Scribner's.

Sherman, B.R., & Kunda, Z. (1989). *Motivated evaluation of scientific evidence.* Paper presented at the American Psychological Society convention, Arlington.

Sherman, S.J., & Gorkin, L. (1980). Attitude bolstering when behavior is inconsistent with central attitudes. *Journal of Experimental Social Psychology, 16,* 388–403.

Sherman, S.J., Hamilton, D.L., & Lewis, A.C. (1999). Perceived entitativity and the social identity value of group memberships. In D. Abrams & M.A. Hogg (Eds), *Social identity and social cognition* (pp. 80–110). Oxford, UK: Blackwell.

Shevrin, H., Smith, W.H., & Fitzler, D.E. (1971). Average evoked response and verbal correlates of unconscious mental processes. *Psychophysiology, 8,* 149–162.

Shiffrin, R.M., & Schneider, W. (1977). Controlled and automatic human information processing: II. Perceptual learning, automatic attending, and a general theory. *Psychological Review, 84,* 127–190.

Shizgal, P. (1999). On the neural computation of utility: Implications from studies of brain stimulation and reward. In D. Kahneman, E. Diener, & N. Schwarz (Eds), *Well-being: The foundations of hedonic psychology* (pp. 500–524). New York: Russell Sage Foundation.

Shostrom, E.L. (1966). *Manual for the Personal Orientation Inventory.* San Diego, CA: Educational and Industrial Testing Service.

Showers, C., & Cantor, N. (1985). Social cognition: A look at motivated strategies. *Annual Review of Psychology, 36,* 275–305.

Shrauger, J.S., & Schoeneman, T.J. (1979). Symbolic interactionist view of self-concept: Through the looking glass darkly. *Psychological Bulletin, 86,* 549–573.

Sieber, J.E. (1974). Effects of decision importance on ability to generate warranted subjective uncertainty. *Journal of Personality and Social Psychology, 30,* 688–694.

Silberman, C. (1970). *Crisis in the classroom.* New York: Random House.

Silver, M.D. (1997). *Group loyalty and group identification: The initial development and evaluation of a new measure of group loyalty.* Unpublished master's thesis, Ohio State University.

Silverman, L.H. (1983). The subliminal psychodynamic activation method: Overview and comprehensive listing of studies. In J. Masling (Ed.), *Empirical studies of psychoanalytic theories* (pp. 69–100). Hillsdale, NJ: Erlbaum.

Simon, H. (1957). *Models of man: Social and rational.* New York: Wiley.

Simon, H.A. (1967). Motivational and emotional controls of cognition. *Psychological Review, 74,* 29–39.

Simon, L., Greenberg, J., Arndt, J., Pyszczynski, T., Clement, R., & Solomon, S. (1997). Perceived consensus, uniqueness, and terror management: Compensatory responses to threats to inclusion and distinctiveness following mortality salience. *Personality and Social Psychology Bulletin, 23,* 1055–1065.

Skinner, B.F. (1938). *The behavior of organisms: An experimental analysis.* New York: Appleton-Century-Crofts.

———. (1953). *Science and human behavior.* New York: Macmillan.

Skov, R.B., & Sherman, S.J. (1986). Information gathering processes: Diagnosticity, hypothesis-confirmatory strategies, and perceived hypothesis confirmation. *Journal of Experimental Social Psychology, 22,* 93–121.

Sloman, A. (1987). Motives, mechanisms, and emotions. *Cognition and Emotion, 1,* 217–233.

Solomon, R.L. (1980). The opponent-process theory of acquired motivation: The costs of pleasure and the benefits of pain. *American Psychologist, 35,* 691–712.

Smith, C.A., & Ellsworth, P.C. (1985). Patterns of cognitive achievement motivation and emotion. *Journal of Personality and Social Psychology, 48,* 813–838.

Smith, E.R., & Branscombe, N.R. (1987). Procedurally mediated social inferences: The case of category accessibility effects. *Journal of Experimental Social Psychology, 23,* 361–382.

Smith, E.R., & Kleugel, J.R. (1982). Cognitive and social bases of emotional experience: Outcome, attribution, and affect. *Journal of Personality and Social Psychology, 43,* 1129–1141.

Smith, H. (1976). *The Russians.* New York: Ballantine Books.

Smith, W.E. (1974). *The effects of social and monetary rewards on intrinsic motivation.* Unpublished doctoral dissertation, Cornell University, Ithaca, NY.

Snyder, A.I. (1978). Periodic marital separation and physical illness. *American journal of Orthopsychiatry, 48,* 637–643.

Snyder, C.R., Higgins, R.L., & Stucky, R.J. (1983). *Excuses: Masquerades in search of grace.* New York: Wiley.

Snyder, M. (1982). When believing means doing: Creating links between attitudes and behavior. In M.P. Zanna, E.T. Higgins, & C.P. Herman (Eds), *Variability in social behavior: The Ontario Symposium* (Vol. 2, pp. 105–130). Hillsdale, NJ: Erlbaum.

———. (1984). When belief creates reality. In L. Berkowitz (Ed.), *Advances in experimental social psychology* (Vol. 18, pp. 248–306). New York: Academic Press.

Snyder, M., & Cantor, N. (1979). Testing hypotheses about other people: The use of historical knowledge. *Journal of Experimental Social Psychology, 15,* 330–342.

Snyder. M.L., Stephan, W.G., & Rosenfield, D. (1978), Attributional egotism. In J.H. Harvey, W. Ickes, & R.F. Kidd (Eds), *New direction in attribution research* (Vol. 2, pp. 91–117). Hillsdale, NJ: Erlbaum.

Sobol, M.P., & Earn, B.M. (in press). Assessment of children's attributions for social experiences: Implications for social skills training. In B.H. Schneider, J.E. Ledingham, & K.H. Rubin (Eds), *Research strategies in children's social skills training.* New York: Springer-Verlag.

Solomon, Z., Waysman, M., & Mikulincer, M. (1990). Family functioning, perceived social support, and combat-related psychopathology: The moderating role of loneliness. *Journal of Social and Clinical Psychology, 9,* 456–472.

Sorrentino, R.M., & Higgins, E.T. (1986). Motivation and cognition: Warming up to synergism. In R.M. Sorrentino & E.T. Higgins (Eds), *Handbook of motivation and cognition: foundations of social behavior* (pp. 3–19). New York: Guilford Press.

Sorrentino, R.M., & Short, J.C. (1986). Uncertainty orientation, motivation and cognition. In R.M. Sorrentino & E.T. Higgins (Eds), *Handbook of motivation and cognition: Foundations of social behavior* (pp. 379–403). New York: Guilford Press.

Sours, J.A. (1974). The anorexia nervosa syndrome. *International Journal of Psychoanalysis, 55,* 567–576.

Spanier, G.B., & Casto, R.F. (1979). Adjustment to separation and divorce: A qualitative analysis. In G. Levinger & O.C. Moles (Eds), *Divorce and separation: Context, causes, and consequences* (pp. 211–227). New York: Basic Books.

Spanier, G.B., & Lewis, R.A. (1980). Marital quality: A review of the seventies. *Journal of Marriage and the Family, 42,* 825–839.

Spivey, E. (1990). *Social exclusion as a common factor in social anxiety, loneliness, jealousy, and social depression.* Unpublished master's thesis, Wake Forest University, Winston-Salem, NC.

Srull, T.K. (1981). Person memory: Some tests of associative storage and retrieval models, *Journal of Experimental Psychology: Human Learning and Memory, 7,* 440–463.

———. (1984). Methodological techniques for the study of person memory and social cognition. In R.S. Wyer & T.K. Srull (Eds), *Handbook of social cognition* (Vol. 2, pp. 1–72). Hillsdale, NJ: Erlbaum.

Srull, T.K., & Wyer, R.S. (1979). The role of category accessibility in the interpretation of information about persons: Some determinants and implications. *Journal of Personality and Social Psychology, 37,* 1660–1672.

———, & ———. (1980). Category accessibility and social perception: Some implications for the study of person memory and interpersonal judgments. *Journal of Personality and Social Psychology, 38,* 841–856.

———, & ———. (1986). The role of chronic and temporary goals in social information processing. In R.M. Sorrentino & E.T. Higgins (Eds), *Handbook of motivation and cognition: Foundations of social behavior* (pp. 503–549). New York: Guilford.

Staff. (1926). Fifty and 100 years ago. *Scientific American,* 228.

Stark, R., & Bainbridge, W.S. (1985). *The allure of religion: Secularization, revival, and cult formation.* Berkeley: University of California Press.

Staub, E. (1989). *The roots of evil: The origins of genocide and other group violence.* Cambridge, England: Cambridge University Press.

Staw, B.M., Sandelands, D.E., & Dutton, J.E. (1981). Threat-rigidity effects in organizational behavior: A multi-level analysis. *Administrative Science Quarterly, 26,* 501–524.

Steele, C.M. (1988). The psychology of self-affirmation: Sustaining the integrity of the self. In L. Berkowitz (Ed.), *Advances in experimental social psychology* (Vol. 21, pp. 261–302). New York: Academic Press.

Steele, C.M., & Liu, T.J. (1983). Dissonance processes as self-affirmation. *Journal of Personality and Social Psychology, 45,* 5–19.

Stein, A.A. (1976). Conflict and cohesion: A review of the literature. *Journal of Conflict Resolution, 20,* 143–172.

Stein, N.L., & Jewett, J.L. (1982). A conceptual analysis of the meaning of negative emotions: Implications for a theory of development. In C.E. Izard (Ed.), *Measuring emotions in infants and children* (pp. 401–443). New York: Cambridge University Press.

Steiner, I.D. (1966) Models for inferring relationships between group size and potential group productivity. *Behavioral Science, 11,* 273–283.

———. (1972). *Group process and productivity.* New York: Academic Press.

Stellar, J.R., & Stellar, E. (1985). *The neurobiology of motivation and reward.* New York: Springer-Verlag.

Steller, E. (1954). The physiology of motivation. *Psychological Review, 61,* 5–22.

Stern, D.N. (1985). *The interpersonal world of the infant.* New York: Basic Books.

Stern, P. (1983). *A multimethod analysis of student perceptions of causal dimensions.* Unpublished doctoral dissertation, University of California, Los Angeles.

Sternberg, R.J. (1986). A triangular theory of love. *Psychological Review, 93,* 119–135.

Stevens, S.S. (1957). On the psychological law. *Psychological Review, 64,* 153–181.

———. (1966). A metric for the social consensus. *Science, 151,* 530–541.

———. (1975). *Psychophysics: Introduction to its perceptual, neural and social prospects.* New York: Wiley.

Stigler, G.J. (1961). The economics of information. *The Journal of Political Economy, 69,* 213–225.

Stipek, D.J. (1983). A developmental analysis of pride and shame. *Human Development, 26,* 42–54.

Storms, M.D. (1973). Videotape and the attribution process: Reversing actors and observers' points of view. *Journal of Personality and Social Psychology, 27,* 165–175.

Stotland, E., (1969). *The psychology of hope.* San Francisco: Jossey-Bass.

Strauss, J., & Ryan, R.M. (1987). Autonomy disturbances in subtypes of anorexia nervosa. *Journal of Abnormal Psychology, 96,* 254–258.

Strauman, T.J. (1989). Self-discrepancies in clinical depression and social phobia: Cognitive structures that underlie emotional disorders. *Journal of Abnormal Psychology, 98,* 14–22.

———. (1990). Self-guides and emotionally significant childhood memories: A study of retrieval efficiency and incidental negative emotional content. *Journal of Personality & Social Psychology, 59,* 869–880.

Strauman, T.J., & Higgins, E.T. (1987). Automatic activation of self-discrepancies and emotional syndromes: When cognitive structures influence affect. *Journal of Personality & Social Psychology, 53,* 1004–1014.

———, & ———. (1988). Self-discrepancies as predictors of vulnerability to distinct syndromes of chronic emotional distress. *Journal of Personality & Social Psychology, 56,* 685–707.

Strube, M.J. (1988). The decision to leave an abusive relationship: Empirical evidence and theoretical issues. *Psychological Bulletin, 104,* 236–250.

Sudnow, D. (1978). *Ways of the hand.* New York: Harper & Row.

Sullivan, H.S. (1953). *The collected works of Harry Stack Sullivan, Vol. 1: The interpersonal theory of psychiatry.* Ed. H.S. Perry & M.L. Gawel. New York: Norton.

Swann, W. B. (1983). Self-verification: Bringing social reality into harmony with the self. In J. Suls & A.G. Greenwald (Eds), *Social psychological perspectives on the self* (Vol. 2, pp. 33–66). Hillsdale, NJ: Erlbaum.

———. (1990). To be known or to be adored? The interplay of self enhancement and self-verification. In E.T. Higgins & R.M. Sorrentino (Eds), *Handbook of motivation and cognition: Foundations of social behavior* (Vol. 2, pp. 408–448). New York: Guilford Press.

Swann, W.B., & Hill, C.A. (1982). When our identities are mistaken: Reaffirming self-conceptions through social interaction. *Journal of Personality and Social Psychology, 43,* 59–66.

Swann, W.B., & Pittman, T.S. (1977). Initiating play activity of children: The moderating influence of verbal cues on intrinsic motivation. *Child Development, 48,* 1128–1132.

Swann, W.B., & Read, S.J. (1981). Self-verification processes: How we sustain our self-conceptions. *Journal of Experimental Social Psychology, 17,* 351–372.

Symanski, R. (1980). Prostitution in Nevada. In E. Muga (Ed.), *Studies in prostitution* (pp. 246–279). Nairobi, Kenya: Kenya Literature Bureau.

Tajfel, H. (1970). Experiments in intergroup discrimination. *Scientific American, 223,* 96–102.

Tajfel, H., & Billig, M. (1974). Familiarity and categorization in intergroup behavior. *Journal of Experimental Social Psychology, 10,* 159–170.

Tajfel, H., Flament, C., Billig, M.G., & Bundy, R.F. (1971). Social categorization and intergroup behaviour. *European Journal of Social Psychology, 1,* 149–177.

Tajfel, H., & Turner, J.C. (1986). The social identity theory of intergroup behavior. In S. Worchel & W.G. Austin (Eds), *Psychology of intergroup relations* (pp 7–24). Chicago: Nelson-Hall.

Tambor, E.S., & Leary, M.R. (1993). *Perceived exclusion as a common factor in social anxiety, loneliness, jealousy, depression, and low self-esteem.* Manuscript submitted for publication.

Tangney, J.P. (1992). Situational determinants of shame and guilt in young adulthood. *Personality and Social Psychology Bulletin, 18,* 199–206.

Tanner, W.P., & Swets, J.A. (1954). A decision-making theory of visual detection. *Psychological Review, 61,* 401–409.

Taylor, S.E. (1983). Adjustment to threatening events: A theory of cognitive adaptation. *American Psychologist, 38,* 1161–1173.

———. (1989). *Positive illusions: Creative self-deception and the healthy mind.* New York: Basic Books.

Taylor, S.E., & Brown, J.D. (1988). Illusion and well-being: A social psychological perspective on mental health. *Psychological Bulletin, 103,* 193–210.

Tesser, A. (1986). Some effects of self-evaluation maintenance on cognition and action. In R.M. Sorrentino & E.T. Higgins (Eds), *The handbook of motivation and cognition: Foundations of social behavior* (pp. 435–464). New York: Guilford Press.

———. (1991). Emotion in social comparison and reflection processes. In J. Suls & T.A. Wills (Eds), *Social comparison: Contemporary theory and research* (pp. 117–148). Hillsdale, NJ: Erlbaum.

Tesser, A., & Campbell, J. (1983). Self-definition and self-evaluation maintenance. In J. Suls & A. Greenwald (Eds), *Social psychological perspectives on the self* (Vol. 2, pp. 1–31). Hillsdale, NJ: Erlbaum.

Tesser, A., Gatewood, R., & Driver, M. (1968). Some determinants of gratitude. *Journal of Personality and Social Psychology, 3,* 233–236.

Tesser, A., Millar, M., & Moore, J. (1988). Some affective consequences of social comparison and reflection processes: The pain and pleasure of being close. *Journal of Personality and Social Psychology, 54,* 49–61.

Tetlock, P.E. (1983). Accountability and complexity of thought. *Journal of Personality and Social Psychology, 45,* 74–83.

———. (1983). Accountability and the perseverance of first impressions. *Social Psychology Quarterly, 46,* 285–292.

———. (1985). Accountability: A social check on the fundamental attribution error. *Social Psychology Quarterly, 48,* 227–236.

Tetlock, P.E., & Boettger, R. (1989). Accountability: A social magnifier of the dilution effect. *Journal of Personality and Social Psychology, 57,* 388–398.

Tetlock, P.E., & Kim, J.I. (1987). Accountability and judgment processes in a personality prediction task. *Journal of Personality and Social Psychology, 52,* 700–709.

Tetlock, P.E., & Levi, A. (1982). Attribution bias: On the inconclusiveness of the cognition-motivation debate. *Journal of Experimental Social Psychology, 18,* 68–88.

Thagard, P. (1989). Explanatory coherence. *The Behavioral and Brain Sciences, 12,* 435–467.

Thibaut, J., & Kelley, H.H. (1959). *The social psychology of groups.* New York: Wiley.

Thompson, E.P., Roman, R.J., Moscovitz, G.B., Chaiken, S., & Bargh, J.A. (1994). Accuracy motivation attenuates covert priming: The systematic reprocessing of social information. *Journal of Personality and Social Psychology, 66,* 474–489.

Thorndike, E.L. (1911). *Animal intelligence.* New York: Macmillan.

———. (1935). *The psychology of wants, interests, and attitudes.* New York: Appleton-Century-Crofts.

Thrash, T.M., & Elliot, A.J. (2001). Delimiting and integrating the goal and motive constructs in achievement motivation. In A. Efklides, J. Kuhl, & R. Sorrentino (Eds), *Trends and prospects in motivation research* (pp. 3–21). Amsterdam: Kluwer Academic Publishers.

Tice, D.M., Butler, J.L., Muraven, M.B., & Stillwell, A.M. (1994). *When modesty prevails: Differential favorability of self-presentation to friends and strangers.* Manuscript submitted for publication.

Toch, H. (1975). *Men in crisis.* Chicago: Aldine.

———. (1977). *Living in prison: The ecology of survival.* New York: Free Press.

———. (1992). *Violent men.* Washington, DC: American Psychological Association.

Toi, M., & Batson, C.D. (1982). More evidence that empathy is a source of altruistic motivation. *Journal of Personality and Social Psychology, 43,* 281–292.

Tolman, E.C. (1925). Purpose and cognition: The determinants of animal learning. *Psychological Review, 32,* 285–297.

———. (1932). *Purposive behavior in animals and men.* New York: Appleton-Century-Crofts.

———. (1948). Cognitive maps in rats and men. *Psychological Review, 55,* 189–208.

———. (1955). Principles of performance. *Psychological Review, 62,* 315–326.

———. (1959). Principles of purposive behavior. In S. Koch (Ed.), *Psychology: A study of a science* (Vol. 2, pp. 92–157). New York: McGraw-Hill.

Tomkins, S.S. (1980). Script theory: Differential magnification of affects. In H.E. Howe, Jr., & M.M. Page (Eds), *Nebraska symposium on motivation* (Vol. 27). Lincoln: University of Nebraska Press.

———. (1984). Affect theory. In K.R. Scherer & P. Ekman (Eds), *Approaches to emotion.* Hillsdale, NJ: Erlbaum.

Tooby, J., & Cosmides, L. (1990). The past explains the present: Emotional adaptions and the structure of ancestral environments. *Ethology and sociobiology, 11,* 375–424.

Triandis, H.C. (1972). *The analysis of subjective culture.* New York: Wiley.

Trivers, R.L. (1971). The evolution of reciprocal altruism. *Quarterly Review of Biology, 46,* 35–57.

Trope, Y., & Bassok, M. (1983). Information gathering strategies in hypothesis testing. *Journal of Experimental Social Psychology, 19,* 560–576.

Trope, Y., & Higgins, E.T. (1993). The 'what,' 'when' and 'how' of dispositional inference: New answers and new questions. *Personality and Social Psychology Bulletin, 19,* 493–500.

Trope, Y., & Liberman, A. (1996). Social hypothesis testing: Cognitive and motivational mechanisms. In E.T. Higgins & A.W. Kruglanski (Eds), *Social psychology: Handbook of basic principles* (pp. 239–270). New York: Guilford Press.

Trout, D.L. (1980). The role of social isolation in suicide. *Suicide and Life-Threatening Behavior, 10,* 10–23.

Turner, J.C. (1985). Social categorization and the self-concept: A social cognitive theory of group behavior. In E.J. Lawler (Ed.), *Advances in group processes: Theory and research* (Vol. 2, pp. 77–121). Greenwich, CT: JAI Press.

Turner, J.C., Hogg, M., Oakes, P., Reicher, S., & Wetherell, M. (1987). *Rediscovering the social group: A self-categorization theory.* Oxford, UK: Basil Blackwell.

Turner, J.C., Oakes, P.J., Haslam, S.A., & McGarty, C. (1994). Self and collective: Cognition and social context. *Personality and Social Psychology Bulletin, 20,* 454–463.

Tversky, A., & Kahneman, D. (1973). Availability: A heuristic for judging frequency and probability. *Cognitive Psychology, 5,* 207–232.

———, & ———. (1974). Judgment under uncertainty: Heuristics and biases. *Science, 185,* 1124–1131.

Utman, C.H. (1997). Performance effects of motivational state: A meta-analysis. *Personality and Social Psychology Review, 1,* 170–182.

Vallacher, R.R., & Nowak, A. (1994). The chaos in social psychology. In R. Vallacher & A. Nowak (Eds), *Dynamical systems in socialpsychology* (pp. 1–16). San Diego, CA: Academic Press.

———, & ———. (in press). The emergence of dynamical social psychology. *Psychological Inquiry, 8,* 73–79.

Vallacher, R.R., & Wegner, D.M. (1985). *A theory of action identification.* Hillsdale, NJ: Erlbaum.

———, & ———. (1987). What do people think they're doing? Action identification and human behavior. *Psychological Review, 94,* 3–15.

Vallacher, R.R., Wegner, D.M., Bordieri, J., & Wen-Jar, T. R. (1981). *[Models of act identity structures].* Unpublished research data.

Vallacher, R.R., Wegner, D.M., & Cook, C. (1982). *[Construction of the behavior identification form.]* Unpublished research data.

Vallacher, R.R., Wegner, D.M., & Frederick, J. (1981). *[Experience and the identification of action.]* Unpublished research data.

Valle, V.A. (1974). *Attributions of stability as a mediator in the changing of expectations.* Unpublished doctoral dissertation, University of Pittsburgh.

Vallerand, R.J., & Reid, G. (1984). On the causal effects of perceived competence on intrinsic motivation: A test of cognitive evaluation theory. *Journal of Sport Psychology, 6,* 94–102.

Van Hook, E., & Higgins, E.T. (1988). Self-related problems beyond the self-concept: Motivational consequences of discrepant self-guides. *Journal of Personality and Social Psychology, 55,* 625–633.

Vangelisti, A.L. Daly, J.A., & Rudnick, J.R. (1991). Making people feel guilty in conversations: Techniques and correlates. *Human Communication Research, 18,* 3–39.

Vaughan, D. (1986). *Uncoupling.* New York: Oxford University Press.

Vaux. A. (1988). Social and emotional loneliness: The role of social and personal characteristics. *Personality and Social Psychology Bulletin, 14,* 722–734.

Veitch, R., & Griffitt, W. (1976). Good news, bad news: Affective and interpersonal effects. *Journal of Applied Social Psychology, 6,* 69–75.

Vignoles, V.L., Chryssochoou, X., & Breakwell, G.M. (2000). The distinctiveness principle: Identity, meaning and the bounds of cultural relativity. *Personality and Social Psychology Review, 4,* 337–354.

Vinokur, A.D., & van Ryn, M. (1993). Social support and undermining in close relationships: Their independent effects on mental health of unemployed persons. *Journal of Personality and Social Psychology, 65,* 350–359.

von Bertalanffy, L. (1968). *General systems theory.* New York: Braziller.

Vroom, V.H. (1964). *Work and motivation.* New York: Wiley.

Vygotsky, L.S. (1962). *Thought and language.* Cambridge, MA: MIT Press.

Wade, W.C. (1987). *The fiery cross: The Ku Klux Klan in America.* New York: Touchstone/Simon & Schuster.

Wadekin, K. (1973). *The private sector in Soviet agriculture.* Los Angeles: University of California Press.

Warr, P., Barter, J., & Brownbridge, G. (1983). On the independence of positive and negative affect. *Journal of Personality and Social Psychology, 44,* 644–651.

Wason, P.C., & Johnson-Laird, P.N. (1965). *Psychology of reasoning: Structure and content.* London: Batsford.

Watson, D., & Tellegen, A. (1985). Toward a consensual structure of mood. *Psychological Bulletin, 98,* 219–235.

Watt, H.J. (1905). Experimentelle Beiträge zu einer Theorie des Denkens [Experiments on a theory of thinking]. *Archiv für die gesamte Psychologice, 4,* 289–436.

Wegner, D.M. (1986). Transactive memory: A contemporary analysis of the group mind. In B. Mullen & G.R. Goethals (Eds), *Theory of group behavior* (pp. 185–208), New York: Springer-Verlag.

———. (1989). *White bears and other unwanted thoughts.* New York: Vintage.

———. (1993). Motivated augmentation and reduction of the Overattribution bias. *Journal of Personality and Social Psychology, 55,* 261–271.

———. (1994). Ironic processes of mental control. *Psychological Review, 101,* 34–52.

Wegner, D.M., Connally, D., Shearer, D., & Vallacher, R.R. (1983). *[Disruption and identifications of the act of eating].* Unpublished research data.

Wegner, D.M., Erber, R., & Raymond, P. (1991). Transactive memory in close relationships. *Journal of Personality and Social Psychology, 61,* 923–929.

Webster, D.M., & Kruglanski, A.W. (1994). Individual differences in need for cognitive closure. *Journal of Personality and Social Psychology, 67,* 1049–1062.

Webster, D.M., Kruglanski, A.W, & Pattison, D.S. (1995). *Motivated language use in intergroup contexts: Need for closure effects on the linguistic intergroup bias.* Unpublished manuscript, University of Florida, Gainesville.

Wegner, D.M., & Pennebaker, J.W. (Eds). (1993). *Handbook of mental control.* Englewood Cliffs, NJ: Prentice Hall.

Webster, D.M., Richter, L., & Kruglanski, A.W. (1995). *On leaping to conclusions when feeling tired: Mental fatigue effects on impressional primacy.* Unpublished manuscript, University of Maryland, College Park.

Wegner, D.M., Schneider, D.J., Carter, S.R., & White, T.L. (1987). Paradoxical effects of thought suppression. *Journal of Personality and Social Psychology, 53,* 5–13.

Wegner, D.M., & Vallacher, R.R. (1983). *[Action identification level and maintenance indicator ratings.]* Unpublished research data.

———, & ———. (1986). Action identification. In R.M. Sorrentino & E.T. Higgins (Eds). *Handbook of motivation and cognition: Foundations of social behavior* (pp 550–582). New York: Guilford Press.

Wegner, D.M., Vallacher, R.R., Kiersted, G., & Dizadji, D. (1986). Action identification in the emergence of social behavior. *Social Cognition – Hilton, 4,* 18–38.

Wegner, D.M., Vallacher. R.R., Macomber. G., Wood, R., & Arps, K. (1984). The emergence of action. *Journal of Personality and Social Psychology, 46,* 269–279.

Weiner, B. (1979). A theory of motivation for some classroom experiences. *Journal of Educational Psychology, 71,* 3–25.

———. (1980a). A cognitive (attribution)-emotion-action model of motivated behavior: An analysis of judgements of help-giving. *Journal of Personality and Social Psychology, 39,* 186–200.

———. (1980b). May I borrow your class notes? An attributional analysis of judgements of help-giving in an achievement related context. *Journal of Educational Psychology, 72,* 676–681.

———. (1982). The emotional consequences of causal ascriptions. In M.S. Clark & S.T. Fiske (Eds), *Affect and cognition: The 17th Annual Carnegie Symposium on Cognition* (pp. 185–209). Hillsdale, NJ: Erlbaum.

———. (1983). Some methodological pitfalls in attributional research. *Journal of Educational Psychology, 75,* 530–543.

———. (1985). 'Spontaneous' causal search. *Psychological Bulletin, 97,* 74–84.

———. (1986). *An attributional theory of motivation and emotion.* New York: Spring-Verlag.

Weiner, B., Amirkhan, J., Folkes, V.S., & Wachtel, S. (1985). *An attributional analysis of excuses: Studies of a naive psychology of emotion.* Unpublished paper, University of California, Los Angeles.

Weiner, B., Frieze, I., Kukla, A., Reed, L., Rest, S., & Rosenbaum, R.M. (1971). Perceiving the causes of success and failure. In E.E. Jones, D.E. Kanouse, H.H. Kelley, R.E. Nisbett, S. Valins, & B. Weiner (Eds), *Attribution: Perceiving the causes of behavior* (pp. 95–120). Morristown, NJ: General Learning Press.

Weiner, B., & Graham, S. (1984). An attributional approach to emotional development. In C. Izard, J. Kagan, & R. Zajonc (Eds), *Emotion, cognition and behavior* (pp. 167–191). Cambridge, MA: Cambridge University Press.

Weiner, B., Graham, S., & Chandler, C. (1982). Causal antecedents of pity, anger and guilt. *Personality and Social Psychology Bulletin, 8,* 226–232.

Weiner, B., Graham, S., Stern, P., & Lawson, M.E. (1982). Using affective cues to infer causal thoughts. *Developmental Psychology, 18,* 278–286.

Weiner, B., & Handel, S. (1985). Anticipated emotional consequences of causal communications and reported communication strategy. *Developmental Psychology, 21,* 102–107.

Weiner, B., & Kukla, A. (1970). An attributional analysis of achievement motivation. *Journal of Personality and Social Psychology, 18,* 1–20.

Weiner, B., Nierenberg, R., & Goldstein, M. (1976). Social learning (locus of control) versus attributional (causal stability) interpretations of expectancy of success. *Journal of Personality, 44,* 52–68.

Weiner, B., Russell, D., & Lerman, D. (1978). Affective consequences of causal ascriptions. In J.H. Harvey, W.J. Ickes, & R.F. Kidd, (Eds), *New directions in attribution research* (Vol. 2, pp. 59–88). Hillsdale, NJ: Erlbaum.

———, ———, & ———. (1979). The cognition-emotion process in achievement-related contexts. *Journal of Personality and Social Pscyhology, 37,* 1211–1220.

Weinstein, N.D. (1980). Unrealistic optimism about future life events. *Journal of Personality and Social Psychology, 39,* 806–820.

———. (1982). Unrealistic optimism about susceptibility to health problems. *Journal of Behavioral Medicine, 5,* 441–460.

Weinstock, S. (1954). Resistance to extinction of a running response following partial reinforcement under widely spaced trials. *Journal of Comparative & Physiological Psychology, 47,* 318–322.

Weiss, P. (1939). *Principles of development.* New York: Holt.

Weiss, R.S. (1973). *Loneliness: The experience of emotional and social isolation.* Cambridge, MA: MIT Press.

———. (1979). The emotional impact of marital separation. In G. Levinger & O.C. Moles (Eds), *Divorce and separation: Context, causes, and consequences* (pp. 201–210). New York: Basic Books.

Welker, W.L. (1956). Some determinants of play and exploration in chimpanzees. *Journal of Comparative & Physiological Psychology, 49,* 84–89.

Wessman, A.E., & Ricks, D.F. (1966). *Mood and personality.* New York: Holt, Rinehart & Winston.

West, S., Newsom, J.T., & Fenaughty, A.M. (1992). Publication trends in *Journal of Personality and Social Psychology:* Stability and change in topics, methods, and theories across two decades. *Personality and Social Psychology Bulletin, 18,* 473–484.

West, S.B., Gunn, S.P., & Chernicky, P. (1975). Ubiquitous Watergate: An attributional analysis. *Journal of Personality and Social Psychology, 32,* 55–65.

Wheeler, L., & Nezlek, J. (1977). Sex differences in social participation. *Journal of Personality and Social Psychology, 35,* 742–754.

Wheeler, L., Reis, H.T., & Nezlek, J. (1983). Loneliness, social interaction, and sex roles. *Journal of Personality and Social Psychology, 45,* 943–953.

White, R.W. (1959). Motivation reconsidered: The concept of competence. *Psychological Review, 66,* 297–333.

Whitehead, A.N. (1929). *The aims of education.* New York: Mentor.

Whiting, J.W.M., & Mowrer, O.H. (1943). Habit progression and regression—a laboratory study of some factors relevant to human socialization. *Journal of Comparative Psychology, 36,* 229–253.

Wicker, A.N. (1969). Size of church membership and members support of church behavior settings. *Journal of Personality and Social Psychology, 13,* 278–288.

Wicker, F.W., Payne, G.C., & Morgan, R.D. (1983). Participant descriptions of guilt and shame. *Motivation and Emotion, 7,* 25–39.

Wicker, F.W., Wiehe, J.A., Hagen, A.S., & Brown, G. (1994). From wishing to intending: Differences in salience of positive versus negative consequences. *Journal of Personality and Social Psychology, 62,* 347–368.

Wicklund, R.A., & Brehm, J.W. (1976). *Perspectives on cognitive dissonance.* Hillsdale, NJ: Erlbaum.

Wiener, N. (1948). *Cybernetics: Control and communication in the animal and the machine.* Cambridge, MA: MIT Press.

Wierzbicka, A. (1972). *Semantic primitives.* Frankfurt, Germany: Athenaum.

Wike, E.L., & McNemara, H.J. (1957). The effects of percentage of partially delayed reinforcement on the acquisition and extinction of an instrumental response. *Journal of Comparative and Physiological Psychology, 50,* 348–351.

Wilbur, J.R., & Wilbur, M. (1988). The noncustodial parent: Dilemmas and interventions. *Journal of Counseling and Development, 66,* 434–437.

Wilder, D.A., & Thompson, J.E. (1980). Intergroup contact with independent manipulations of in-group and out-group interaction. *Journal of Personality and Social Psychology, 38,* 589–603 .

Williams, J.G., & Solano, C.H. (1983). The social reality of feeling lonely: Friendship and reciprocation. *Personality and Social Psychology Bulletin, 9,* 237–242.

Wills, T.A. (1981). Downward comparison principles in social psychology. *Psychological Bulletin, 90,* 245–271.

Willson, V.L., & Palmer, D.J. (1983). Latent partition analysis of attributions for actual achievement. *American Educational Research Journal, 20,* 581–589.

Wilson, T.D., & Linville, P.W. (1982). Improving the academic performance of college freshmen: Attribution theory revisited. *Journal of Personality and Social Psychology, 42,* 367–376.

———, & ———. (1985). Improving the performance of college freshmen with attributional techniques. *Journal of Personality and Social Psychology, 49,* 287–293.

Wilson, W., Weiss, E.J., & Amsel, A. (1955). Two tests of the Sheffield hypothesis concerning resistance to extinction, partial reinforcement, and distribution of practice. *Journal of Experimental Psychology, 50,* 51–60.

Wimer, S., & Kelley, H.H. (1982). An investigation of the dimensions of causal attribution. *Journal of Personality and Social Psychology, 43,* 1142–1162.

Wine, J.D. (1971). Test anxiety and the direction of attention. *Psychological Bulletin, 76,* 92–104.

Winer, B.J. (1962). *Statistical principles in experimental design.* New York: McGraw-Hill.

Winfield, F.E. (1985). *Commuter marriage.* New York: Columbia University Press.

Wittgenstein, L. (1953). *Philosophical infestigations.* Oxford, England: Blackwell.

Wolfe, J.B., & Kaplon, M.D. (1941). Effect of amount of reward and consummative activity on learning in chickens. *Journal of Comparative Psychology, 31,* 353–361.

Wood, J.V., Taylor, S.E., & Lichtman, R.R. (1985). Social comparison in adjustment to breast cancer. *Journal of Personality and Social Psychology, 49,* 1169–1183.

Woodworth, R.S. (1958). *Dynamics of behavior.* New York: Holt.

Wortman, C.B., & Brehm, J.W. (1975). Responses to uncontrollable outcomes: An integration of reactance theory and the learned helplessness model. In L. Berkowitz (Ed.), *Advances in experimental social psychology* (Vol. 8, pp. 277–336). New York: Academic Press.

Wortman, C.B., & Silver, R.C. (1989). The myths of coping with loss. *Journal of Consulting and Clinical Psychology, 57,* 349–357.

Wyer, R.S., & Frey, D. (1983). The effects of feedback about self and others on the recall and judgments of feedback-relevant information. *Journal of Experimental Social Psychology, 19,* 540–559.

Wylie, R.C. (1979). *The self-concept* (Vol. 2). Lincoln: University of Nebraska Press.

Yalom, I. (1985). *The theory and practice of group psychotherapy.* New York: Basic Books.

Yaryan, R.B., & Festinger, L. (1961). Preparatory action and belief in the probable occurrence of future events. *Journal of Abnormal and Social Psychology, 63,* 603–606.

Yerkes, R.M., & Dodson, J.D. (1908). The relation of strength of stimulus to rapidity of habit-formation. *Journal of Comparative Neurological Psychology, 18,* 459–482.

Young, A.W., McWeeny, K.H., Hay, D.C., & Ellis, A.W. (1986). Matching familiar and unfamiliar faces on identity and expression. *Psychological Research, 48,* 63–68.

Young, P.T. (1949). Food-seeking drive, affective process, and learning. *Psychological Review, 56,* 98–121.

———. (1955). The role of hedonic processes in motivation. In M.R, Jones (Ed.), *Nebraska symposium on motivation 1955* (pp. 193–238) . Lincoln: University of Nebraska Press.

Yzerbyt, V.Y., Castano, E., Leyens, J.P., & Paladino, M.P. (2000). The primacy of the ingroup: The interplay of entitativity and identification. In W. Stroebe & M. Hewstone (Eds), *European review of social psychology.* Chichester, UK: Wiley.

Yzerbyt, V.Y., Leyens, J.P., & Bellour, F. (1995). The ingroup overexclusion effect: Identity concerns in decisions about group membership. *European Journal of Social Psychology, 25,* 1–16.

Zajonc, R.B. (1965). Social facilitation. *Science, 149,* 269–274.

———. (1966). *Social psychology: An experimental approach.* Belmont, CA: Brooks/Cole.

———. (1980). Feeling and thinking: Preferences need no inferences. *American Psychologist, 35,* 151–175.

———. (1988). *Prolegomena for the study of access to mental events: Notes on Singer's Chapter.* In M.J. Horowitz (Ed.), *Psychodynamics and Cognition* (pp. 347–359). Chicago: University of Chicago Press.

Zajonc, R.B., & Brickman, P. (1969). Expectancy and feedback as independent factors in task performance. *Journal of Personality and Social Psychology, 11,* 148–156.

Zander, A. (1971). *Motives and goals in groups.* New York: Academic Press.

Zanna, M.P., & Cooper, J. (1974). Dissonance and the pill: An attribution approach to studying the arousal properties of dissonance. *Journal of Personality and Social Psychology, 29,* 703–709.

Zanna, M.P., Higgins, E.T., & Taves, P.A. (1976). Is dissonance phenomenologically aversive? *Journal of Experimental Social Psychology, 12,* 530–538.

Zevon, M.A., & Tellegen, A. (1982). The structure of mood change: An idiographic/nomothetic analysis. *Journal of Personality and Social Psychology, 43,* 111–122.

Zhao, W., & Dweck, C.S. (1997). *Implicit theories and vulnerability to depression-like responses.* Unpublished manuscript, Columbia University.

Zimbardo, P.G., & Miller, N.E. (1958). Facilitation of exploration by hunger in rats. *Journal of Comparative & Physiological Psychology, 51,* 43–46.

Zoeller, C., Mahoney, G., & Weiner, B. (1983). Effects of attribution training on the assembly task performance of mentally retarded adults. *American Journal of Mental Deficiency, 88,* 109–112.

Zuckerman, M., Porac, J., Lathin, D., Smith, R., & Deci, E.L. (1978). On the importance of self-determination for intrinsically motivated behavior. *Personality and Social Psychology Bulletin, 4,* 443–446.

Credits

Grateful acknowledgement is made for permission to reprint the following articles:

M.W. Baldwin, S.E. Carrell, D.F. Lopez, © 1990 Elsevier, 'Priming relationship schemas: My advisor and the Pope are watching me from the back of my mind,' *Journal of Experimental Social Psychology*, vol. 26, pp. 435–45.

R.F. Baumeister, E. Bratslavsky, M. Muraven, D.M. Tice, 'Ego depletion: Is the active self a limited resource?' *Journal of Personality and Social Psychology*, vol. 74, pp. 1252–65. Copyright © 1998 by the American Psychological Association. Reproduced with permission. The use of this information does not imply endorsement by the publisher.

R.F. Baumeister and M.R. Leary, 'The need to belong: Desire for interpersonal attachments as a fundamental human motivation,' *Psychological Bulletin*, vol. 117, pp. 497–529. Copyright © 1995 by the American Psychological Association. Reproduced with permission. The use of this information does not imply endorsement by the publisher.

C.S. Carver and M.F. Scheier, 'Origins and functions of positive and negative affect: A control-process view,' *Psychological Review*, vol. 97, pp. 19–35. Copyright © 1990 by the American Psychological Association.

E.L. Deci and R.M. Ryan, 'The support of autonomy and the control of behavior,' *Journal of Personality and Social Psychology*, vol. 53, pp. 1024–37. Copyright © 1987 by the American Psychological Association. Adapted with permission. The use of this information does not imply endorsement by the publisher.

A.J. Elliot, 'The hierarchical model of approach-avoidance motivation,' *Motivation and Emotion*, vol. 30, pp. 111–116. Copyright © 2006, Springer Netherlands. Reproduced with permission.

L. Festinger, 1961, 'The psychological effects of insufficient rewards,' *American Psychologist*, vol. 16, pp. 1–11. American Psychological Association. Content is in the Public Domain.

P.M. Gollwitzer, H. Heckhausen, and B. Stellar, 'Deliberative vs. implementational mind-sets: Cognitive tuning toward congruous thoughts and information,' *Journal of Personality and Social Psychology*, vol. 59, pp. 1119–27. Copyright © 1990 by the American Psychological Association. Reproduced with permission. The use of this information does not imply endorsement by the publisher.

H. Grant and C.S. Dweck, 'Clarifying achievement goals and their impact,' *Journal of Personality and Social Psychology*, vol. 85, pp. 541–55. Copyright © 2003 by the American Psychological Association. Adapted with permission. The use of this information does not imply endorsement by the publisher.

E.T. Higgins, 'Beyond pleasure and pain,' *American Psychologist*, vol. 52, pp. 1280–1300. Copyright © 1997 by the American Psychological Association. Adapted with permission. The use of this information does not imply endorsement by the publisher.

A.W. Kruglanski, and D.M. Webster, 'Motivated closing of the mind: "Seizing" and "freezing",' *Psychological Review*, vol. 103, pp. 263–83. Copyright © 1996 by the American Psychological Association. Adapted with permission. The use of this information does not imply endorsement by the publisher.

Z. Kunda, 'The case for motivated reasoning,' *Psychological Bulletin*, vol. 108, pp. 480–98. Copyright © 1990 by the American Psychological Association. Adapted with permission. The use of this information does not imply endorsement by the publisher.

B. Latane, K. Williams, & S. Harkins, 'Many hands make light the work: Causes and consequences of social loafing,' *Journal of Personality and Social Psychology*, vol. 37, pp. 822–32. Copyright © 1979 by the American Psychological Association. Reproduced with permission. The use of this information does not imply endorsement by the publisher.

M.R. Lepper, D. Greene, R.E. Nisbett, 'Undermining children's intrinsic interest with extrinsic reward: A test of the "overjustification" hypothesis,' *Journal of Personality and Social Psychology*, vol. 28, pp. 129–37. Copyright © 1973 by the American Psychological Association. Reproduced with permission. The use of this information does not imply endorsement by the publisher.

K. Lewin, 1936, 'Psychology of success and failure,' *Occupations*, vol. 14, pp. 926–930.

W. Mischel, Y. Shoda, and M.L. Rodriquez, © 1989 American Association for the Advancement of Science, 'Delay of gratification in children,' *Science*, vol. 244, pp. 933–8.

C.L. Pickett, M.D. Silver and M.B. Brewer, *Personality and Social Psychology Bulletin*, (vol. 28), pp. 546–58, copyright © 2002. Reprinted by Permission of SAGE Publications.

R.R. Vallacher and D.M. Wegner, 'What do people think they are doing? Action identification and human behavior,' *Psychological Review*, vol. 94, pp. 3–15. Copyright © 1997 by the American Psychological Association.

Index